MAGGIE'S HARVEST brings together over 350 of Maggie Beer's signature recipes, detailed descriptions of her favourite ingredients and inspiring accounts of memorable meals with family and friends.

The recipes highlight Maggie's philosophy of using the freshest and best seasonal produce available in the Barossa Valley, South Australia, and treating it simply, allowing the natural flavours to speak for themselves. Describing herself as a 'country cook', Maggie cooks from the heart and is passionate about instilling in others this same confidence – to use recipes as a starting point, and be guided by instinct and personal taste.

This landmark book from one of Australia's best-loved cooks is essential for anyone with an appreciation of the pleasures of sourcing, cooking and sharing food.

✦　✦　✦

MAGGIE BEER operated the Barossa Valley's famous Pheasant Farm Restaurant with her husband, Colin, for fifteen years. Since closing the restaurant in 1993, she has established an export kitchen in Tanunda to develop and make products for domestic and international markets, and now devotes much of her time to researching and developing her range.

Maggie is the author of four successful cookbooks, *Maggie's Farm*, *Maggie's Orchard*, *Cooking with Verjuice* and *Maggie's Table*, and co-author of the bestselling *Stephanie Alexander & Maggie Beer's Tuscan Cookbook*. She is also a longstanding contributor of food columns to newspapers and magazines, and is co-host of *The Cook and The Chef* on ABC TV. Her website is www.maggiebeer.com.au.

MAGGIE'S HARVEST

Maggie Beer

with photography by Mark Chew

LANTERN
an imprint of
PENGUIN BOOKS

For Colin

CONTENTS

WINTER

SPRING

INTRODUCTION

MY PASSION FOR FOOD HAS GIVEN ME SO MUCH IN LIFE – a sense of purpose, a delicious anticipation of each new day, and rewards of a much deeper kind than financial. It's inspired a joy in the simplest things, like the aroma that assails me as I watch our olives being crushed and dip a piece of wood-fired bread into that golden-green stream of fresh oil, or growing my own tomatoes using a minimum of water, for a truly intense flavour. Sharing the harvest with my family and friends and being part of a community is incredibly rewarding – I wouldn't swap my life for anything.

I can hardly remember living in the city now, as my time in the Barossa has really defined me. When I think of the 'accidents' of life that led me to where I am today, I can only reflect on how lucky I've been. My childhood was tough: I was a loner who found it hard to fit in at school, and my parents, who ran their own business, were completely engulfed by their work. I was just fourteen years old when their business failed and we lost everything, causing a massive upheaval in all our lives. So whilst it wasn't a happy childhood for many reasons, it did give me great strength. Seeing my parents rebuild their lives again taught me, at a young age, that anything was possible. From them, I inherited my mother's optimism (I was always teased for wearing rose-coloured glasses), and my father's instinct for food and great love of music.

I had absolutely no idea what I wanted to do with my life, so I spent my early twenties searching. I travelled the world, spending the biggest chunk of my time away on the west coast of Scotland – and there, for the first time in my life, I felt part of a greater expanse... it was my first real connection with the land. On returning to Australia, I met my husband Colin – a boy from Mallala, as he likes to describe himself. We married in Sydney in 1970, and spent the first few years of our married life there, before deciding to leave city life behind to pursue Colin's long-held ambition to farm pheasants. The Barossa Valley, being only 30 minutes' drive away from Colin's family at Mallala, virtually chose us, as we'd meander through this oasis each time we visited them. It's hard to say which of us was the most excited about leaving Sydney. We moved to Tanunda in April 1973, just in time for our first Vintage Festival, and within months we had bought the land the Farmshop stands on today.

Pheasants proved difficult to farm, and little information was available to help us, so Colin applied for and won a Churchill Fellowship to study game-bird breeding practices overseas. As part of our travels, we visited a turkey farm in Scotland that used every part of the bird imaginable, even the feathers, and sold the products direct to the public from the farm. This became our benchmark – although we took it one step further. Whilst we were already breeding pheasants and selling them, we weren't getting any repeat business, purely because our customers didn't know how to cook them. And so, in January 1979, the Farmshop was born, from which we sold our pheasants (along with quail and guinea fowl) prepared and cooked in different ways. As I'd never formally learnt to cook, I simply used my instincts and cooked from the heart, always adhering to the Barossa ethos of wasting nothing. I roasted pheasant, made pâté from the livers, pickled quails eggs, and stuffed quail and wrapped it in vine leaves – and we sold it all direct to the public, who would sit out on the decking and eat lunch picnic-style.

'When Colin and I began farming pheasants, we had no thoughts of opening a restaurant.'

Before the end of that first year, we had turned this humble Farmshop into a restaurant. I'm not sure where the confidence to do this came from, but I didn't hesitate – and thus began my process of discovering what I wanted to do in life. When I talk to people now about the Pheasant Farm Restaurant, I realise that many still have a soft spot for the place and what it stood for. Our basic premise was to cook simple dishes using the bounty of our seasonal harvest from the Barossa, focusing on flavour, not fashion. We really went out on a limb, as the menu was predominantly game, which divided the dining public. In all the years we ran the restaurant, Colin never made me accountable to a bottom line, and although this might seem naïve, I saw it differently. For me, the priority was making the most of that direct link between producer and restaurateur, with our vineyards and pheasants supporting the restaurant. It was a constant learning process, but it was also immensely rewarding – there is nothing quite as seductive as doing what you love, and having others love it too.

'The more everyone learns about food, the more pleasurable eating will be.'

The Pheasant Farm Restaurant, early 1980s
'The audacity of it – we were miles off the beaten track, on one of the worst roads in the state!'

Running a restaurant of this nature was pretty demanding, and as we lived right there on the farm, in the rooms adjoining the restaurant, it seemed our work was never done. My weekly escape was to go horse-riding with friends through the countryside, always taking a different path. On one of these rides I discovered a beautiful cottage, only a few kilometres away from the farm, and I fell in love with it immediately. It was surely meant to be, as a few years later, we bought the place at auction (the most traumatic 20 minutes of my life – when you really want something, the suspense can be sheer agony!).

It was, and remains, the perfect family home. The cottage, which dates from the 1860s, and its two outbuildings stand on 20 acres of land, with two dams, deep, well-drained loam soil and access to mains water (as opposed to the farm, which has clay soil and salty bore water, so limiting for a garden). A beautiful old pear tree, large as an oak and as tall as the cottage itself – and probably of similar age – still stands by the original well, planted to make the well water sweet, as tradition would have it. The well itself is made of red brick and is some 10 metres deep, with a ledge still in view where the milk was kept cool. Now safely contained, this is a favourite spot for our young grandchildren, who love the property so much that they often ask, in their brutally honest way, how long we'll live

'Home – our refuge, with the orchard in bloom.'

here, as they would love to move in. There is such a sense that this place will remain for many generations to come.

But the move was initially resisted by our two daughters, Saskia and Eliette (or Elli, as she now is), who relished the freedom and open ruggedness of the farm. A fair bit of bribery went on to make up for this, most notably the installation of a swimming pool even before we had a proper kitchen. As a result, for years I cooked in a makeshift kitchen on the back veranda, where the old louvres rattled and whistled as the chilly air blew in on winter evenings, and it was sometimes so cold that I took to cooking the family dinner in my Driza-bone!

It was here that my orchard began, soon after we moved from the farm. My dream of having my own orchard was inspired by a perfectly ripe white peach I had picked straight off a tree near our farm when we first arrived in the Valley. These are the first soft fruit of summer, and the most beautiful in their unadorned state. It takes a long time to understand a new property and so the orchard had several false starts in various locations, until it settled permanently where it is now, sentinel to the cottage. It was such a labour of love. Each tree had to have a place of importance. I chose to plant fruit that was at its best when picked warm and ripe: white peaches (of course), nectarines and apricots, in particular. I also chose fruit that was difficult to find in shops: crabapples, medlars, greengage plums, persimmons and pomegranates. I even took cuttings from friends' trees, not knowing the variety but just loving the taste of the fruit. These trees, and many others planted since, continue to provide me with a veritable bounty of fruit each season, and keep me and my treasured staff busy pickling and preserving all year round.

Ironically, the very success of the restaurant led to its closure. In 1991, the Pheasant Farm Restaurant won the Remy Martin Cognac/ *Australian Gourmet Traveller* Restaurant of the Year award, and this was the turning point. Up until then we had been just a simple country restaurant with a particularly loyal and interested clientele who kept us full almost every weekend – though, as is often the case with rural businesses, we were fairly quiet during the week. From the moment the award was announced, we suddenly had a waiting list for every meal and helicopters landing in the ram paddock, with people insisting we fit them in as they had travelled so far. I can't deny they were

'Always had a wonderful team at the restaurant – this is around the time of our 10th birthday party… what a bash!'

exciting times. But often I'm my own worst enemy – and, during 14 years at the restaurant, I found myself entirely unable to delegate, so I was tied to the stoves in my control-freakish way, with Colin farming the birds, tending the vines and waiting on tables, and our daughters somehow fitting their lives into this world we had created.

As is so often the case, it was Colin who took a step back. He saw that this was too much for me, and issued an ultimatum (only half-joking, I suspect): the restaurant or him. I knew instantly that I wanted to close the restaurant – no discussion was needed, and I left no time for reflection. It actually shocked me that I could take such a life-changing step so readily yet, in truth, I felt a great sense of relief. We set a closing date four months hence, and soon people from all over the country were clamouring to come again, or visit for the

The Pheasant Farm Restaurant closes, Nov 28th 1993 'Thanking everyone, I went from euphoria to tears in seconds.'

first time. And, with the pressure suddenly lifted, I was free to be as daring as I liked in my cooking, knowing I had the support of an amazing team of people around me and nothing to lose. Each day was a real adventure – talk about going out on a high!

We closed the restaurant on 28 November 1993. I was completely burnt out but, after taking some time to recover, I soon felt 10 years younger. I've so often been asked if I miss the restaurant, and I have to say – unequivocally – no. But there is something about the adrenaline rush you get from working with an energetic team, cooking the bounty of the harvest and serving good food to people who really enjoy it. Nothing else quite compares.

However, one door had to close for others to open, and open they did. I could never have contemplated just how full and exciting life would continue to be. Our pâté business had started in the early days of the restaurant, when our dear family friend Hilda Laurencis and I would make batch after batch in small food processors after lunch service was over

'The Farmshop – where it all began. Going there every day feels like coming home.'

for the day. We started selling pâté commercially in the early 1980s, and by the time the restaurant closed, Pheasant Farm Pâté was doing well enough to support us, even though we were really only supplying those who had heard about the product through word-of-mouth. The pâté business has now expanded considerably, and in 1996 we opened a purpose-built, state-of-the-art export kitchen. Much to everyone's amusement, I absolutely insist on calling it a kitchen, not a factory, as even though we now make pâté by the tonne, we still produce it in small batches, with no preservatives added. I am determined to uphold the same standards of quality and flavour set in those early days at the restaurant. If any of our products cannot be made to those same standards, then we simply don't make them. Whilst this has proved immensely challenging, flavour is something I just won't compromise on.

Our business provides enormous scope for me to create limited amounts of products based on the best seasonal produce available, whether it's a ute full of peaches or a trailer-load of blood oranges, free from the commercial imperative that a larger-scale operation would bring. Each of our products stems from a desire to make the most of every bit of our own harvest, in its way honouring the bird, tree or vine by wasting nothing.

When I think of how we made our first batch of verjuice in 1984 from grapes we couldn't sell that year and how, albeit gradually, we led the worldwide renaissance of this amazing ingredient and made it indispensable in so many kitchens, I have to pinch myself. We'd been vignerons since 1973, so at each vintage I'd have plenty of opportunity to experiment with using grapes in many different ways (no matter how much they were wanted for wine!). This continual experimentation, along with my voracious reading on Mediterranean culinary traditions, also led to the creation of vino cotto, Desert Pearls non-alcoholic spark-ling drink, and cabernet sauces and pastes.

So now we've come full circle. Today the Farmshop, the precursor to the much-loved restaurant, is up and running again on the same site, tucked away down a quiet country road. It's where everything began and, humble though it is, I never tire of the surprise and delight I see on people's faces as they come in. Even though we now sell our products all over the world, the Farmshop remains my direct link to the public. Every day, when I walk in the door, it's like coming home, and I know I'll never lose that feeling.

Moving to the Barossa Valley marked the start of a very personal food journey for me. All my life I'd been interested in food, yet being here has introduced me to the rhythm of the seasons. Having at my fingertips such a rich diversity of produce from this Mediterranean climate has led me to become a simple country cook, doing little more than relating to the ingredients I have at hand.

This book represents the culmination of that journey so far. The range of seasonal ingredients featured is by no means exhaustive, but instead includes those I am most passionate about. The recipes are a mixture of old favourites I've collected over the years – many of which first appeared in *Maggie's Farm* (1993) and *Maggie's Orchard* (1997), updated here to take account of the momentous changes in the Australian food scene in the intervening years – and new recipes inspired by my love of regional cooking in tune with the seasons.

'Just as I learnt so much about food in my childhood, so have my daughters, who are both incredibly hardworking young women making their own mark in the food world.'

Writing this book has shown me how far we have come since I began my food journey – to think that in the early 1980s basil was considered exotic! Australia is a young nation struggling to shed the shackles of a history that, for the most part, eschewed indigenous foods and traditions. Though we have made amazing advances, particularly in the last 30 years, there is still much to be done. I want to foster a reconnection with the seasons, and to draw on the abundance of ideas for creating innovative and exciting food that is full of flavour. If every farmer and producer were seduced by flavour, had a thirst for knowledge regarding the potential of their product, and always remained mindful of sustainable agriculture (including providing a good life and a good death for the animals we eat), then just think what a great food life we could all live.

What continues to spur me on, and leads me to think I will never retire, is my love of sharing my passion for food in every way I know how. More than anything, I want to give people the confidence to have a go, to look for quality produce, to cook together, and to share the table with family and friends. I do believe, with every fibre of my being, that such simple and time-honoured rituals can change lives.

'All our family celebrations are at home – we love a party with good food, music and friends.'

SUMMER

ANCHOVIES

 **I MUST CONFESS TO BEING PASSIONATE ABOUT THESE** salty little creatures. I suspect that those who do not share my enthusiasm tried anchovies as children, when the taste buds are more partial to sweet things, or only know the anchovy fillets that are wrapped around capers and come in little tins of awful-tasting oil. I urge all you doubters out there to give the anchovy another chance.

There is certainly nothing new about anchovies, which have been around for a few thousand years, but what is exciting is that high-quality Australian salted anchovies are once again becoming more available here, due in part to the efforts of the Mendolia family of Fremantle, Western Australia. Even though anchovies have been traditionally associated with the Mediterranean, they have always been abundant in Australian waters but until recently were not caught for anything more than bait, in the main. After some years of problems with supply, Jim Mendolia, who combines traditional European methods of processing and curing anchovies in salt with the latest machinery and equipment, is back in business.

Anchovies are only fished from September to December off the Western Australian coast. Although they are in the waters year-round, they are too small the rest of the year and best left to grow. We have had the chance to learn from the mistakes of others. The Mediterranean has been seriously over-fished and very few anchovies are caught there now; those that are sold for the fresh market come at a high price. Instead, South America supplies the European market with anchovies for salting. The Mendolias keep all theirs for salting, as demand is so high.

If ever you have the chance to buy anchovies fresh, and see anchovies and sardines displayed side by side at a fish market, you will most likely be hard-pressed to tell the difference. A closer look reveals that the anchovy's eyes sit further forward in the head and its mouth is wide open, since its large set of jaws extends past the gills. Both fish are shiny and need to be eaten super-fresh. The fresh anchovy and sardine have white flesh (the red flesh of the salted fish is a result of the curing) and are sold with their guts intact. While

the fresh fish are cooked the same way (grilled with a little extra virgin olive oil and lemon juice is about all you need), the difference is in the entrails. The sardine can be eaten whole, guts and all, but the entrails of the anchovy are very bitter. The trick is to grab the tail and press the sides – the anchovy will split in two and the flesh can be peeled away from the bones. If you wish to gut and fillet a fresh anchovy or sardine, snapping off the head will see most of the innards come away as well. The fish is then split and flattened out and the backbone is peeled away.

Salted anchovies have a firmer, meatier texture than fillets preserved in olive oil and, surprisingly, they taste more of the fish than the salt. When using salted anchovies you must remove the skeleton. I find this most easily done as I am rinsing the anchovies: I simply strip the fillets off the backbone and then pat them dry before sprinkling them with extra virgin olive oil.

Salted anchovies are stunning on their own or they can be used to perk up a dish. They add bite and saltiness, and, if used judiciously, provide an indefinable dimension without overpowering other flavours. They disappear magically into sauces, providing richness and complexity. Just remember to taste as you go along to ensure balance is maintained. If anchovies are too salty for your purpose, soak them in milk before using.

If you are buying anchovies in oil, consider the oil they are packed in as it will greatly influence the flavour. Only buy in small tins unless you are catering for a crowd as they oxidise soon after opening; whenever I need anchovies, I open a fresh 45 g tin, blotting off the oil they've been stored in before use. A good delicatessen will sell salted anchovies (the Spanish brand Ortiz is worth seeking out). This is a much easier option than trying to find anchovies in good oil.

The Sicilian marriage of pasta with anchovy fillets, sultanas, pine nuts, fennel, garlic, parsley and breadcrumbs produces a dish fit for royalty and can be pulled together at the last moment with the backup of a good store cupboard. If you don't have fennel in the garden or refrigerator, you can use fennel seeds, and you can add tomatoes too, if you wish.

Still talking of pasta, another taste sensation is rape (a variety of *Brassica*) tossed with anchovy fillets, extra virgin olive oil, freshly ground black pepper and lots of fresh Parmigiano Reggiano and served with good-quality dried orecchiette.

For a tomato sauce for pasta, chicken or lamb, sweat chopped onion in a little extra virgin olive oil, then add garlic, chopped canned or really ripe tomatoes, a good dash of verjuice or white wine, a pinch each of sugar and salt and anchovy fillets to taste. Cook until the sauce reaches the consistency you desire, then grind in lots of black pepper, stir in some pitted kalamata olives and lastly drizzle in extra virgin olive oil.

Anchovies are amazing added to eggs in any form. Take soft unsalted butter mixed with finely chopped anchovy fillets, some flat-leaf parsley, a squeeze of lemon juice and some freshly ground black pepper and chill, then top halved hard-boiled free-range eggs with it – better still, pipe it on in a small twirl. Or top the eggs with the tuna and anchovy mayonnaise used in Vitello Tonnato (see page 675).

A surprising memory of this mayonnaise came to mind when I was in Tokyo recently on one of my many trips. I went to La Playa, an extraordinary tapas bar run by Toru Kodama (fondly called Carlos), a Japanese chef who had spent seven years in Spain. Every part of the meal was amazing – including the prosciutto Toru had made and matured for five years (the pigs had been fed on acorns!). But the highlight was a tiny variety of capsicum I hadn't seen before that had been roasted and then stuffed with tuna and anchovy mayonnaise. It was simply exquisite.

If you are lucky enough to have fresh anchovies, dust them with seasoned flour and deep-fry them in extra virgin olive oil for literally seconds then serve them hot with a squeeze of lemon juice and a side dish of aïoli.

Anchoïade is a traditional spread from the south of France that is served on croutons. Blend 45 g anchovy fillets, a couple of chopped cloves of garlic, ½ cup flat-leaf parsley, 1 teaspoon red-wine vinegar and some freshly ground black pepper to a paste in a small food processor, then slowly add 80 ml extra virgin olive oil.

At one of our Symposium of Gastronomy evenings held in Adelaide, my friend, chef Cath Kerry, served hot anchovy matches to eat with a glass of champagne before we moved in to view food vignettes from films, both little-known and famous, compiled by Alan Saunders. Cath used a recipe of her mother's to produce a pastry that was as fine as a spring-roll wrapper. A strip of pastry was wound around each anchovy fillet, which was then deep-fried until golden.

Try 1 cm cubes of fresh mozzarella topped with a curled anchovy fillet brushed with extra virgin olive oil, then add a squeeze of lemon juice. Make tiny pizzettas about 4 cm wide from traditional pizza dough, then brush them with extra virgin olive oil and top with a little fresh rosemary before baking at 230°C for 10 minutes. Brush the hot pizzettas with more oil and add a slice of very ripe tomato, a piece of basil and an anchovy fillet. Or serve anchovy fillets with caramelised onion on a crouton or piece of flatbread or in a tart. My favourite is a slab of Sour-cream Pastry (see page 424), pricked and baked on a scone tray and then inhibited during cooking so it doesn't rise too much. Allow to cool for 5 minutes, then top with caramelised onions, anchovies and freshly chopped flat-leaf parsley, and cut into small squares. This is a much less fiddly way of making hors d'oeuvres. Anchovies can also be added to poached chicken, rabbit, tuna or beef.

I so eagerly await that first flush of figs that arrives in December. Once I had masses of garlic that I knew wouldn't last so I roasted the whole heads and then squeezed the garlic out. I chopped anchovies finely and processed them to a paste with the peeled figs and garlic and a squeeze of lemon juice – this was great spread on bread that had been toasted with a smear of extra virgin olive oil.

Croutons with caramelised onion, anchovies and rabbit livers splashed with vino cotto (see page 10)

Where do I begin to choose my favourite anchovy recipes to include here? I love anchovy hollandaise served with rabbit wrapped in vine leaves or with a golden shallot tarte tatin; avocado with a vinaigrette of anchovy fillets, capers and orange rind; guinea fowl in wine with capers, lemon and anchovy fillets – these were all favourites at the Pheasant Farm Restaurant and give an idea of the breadth of the anchovy's repertoire, as do the following recipes.

ANCHOVY MAYONNAISE

Makes 375 ml

Try this with poussins that have been barbecued, roasted or poached in stock. I also love it with barbecued kangaroo or pan-fried lamb's brains, but most of all, with veal or rabbit scaloppine.

2–3 anchovy fillets, chopped

2 egg yolks

2 teaspoons Dijon mustard

3 teaspoons white-wine vinegar

1 cup (250 ml) mellow extra virgin olive oil *or* half olive and half vegetable oil

sea salt flakes and freshly ground black pepper

Blend the anchovy fillets in a food processor or blender with the egg yolks, mustard and vinegar for 4–5 seconds or until incorporated. With the motor running, slowly pour in the oil in a thin and steady stream until the mayonnaise thickens and emulsifies. The trick is to do it slowly, so that the mayonnaise doesn't split. Season with salt and pepper and add a dash of hot water to thin and stabilise the mayonnaise, if necessary.

ANCHOVY AND OLIVE BUTTER

Makes 600 g

This is an intensely flavoured butter that goes beautifully with quail, rabbit or lamb chops, and keeps for months in the freezer.

1 × 45 g tin anchovy fillets, chopped

300 g black olives, pitted

300 g softened butter

dash brandy

Process the anchovy fillets and olives in a food processor. Add the butter and brandy and blend again to incorporate well. Form the butter mixture into a log, then wrap it in foil or plastic film and chill. Freeze if not using within a few days.

CROUTONS WITH CARAMELISED ONION, ANCHOVIES AND RABBIT LIVERS SPLASHED WITH VINO COTTO *Makes 12 croutons*

If you can't find rabbit livers, you can use chicken livers instead. For this recipe, you'll need 9 chicken livers, as they tend to be smaller than rabbit livers. Remove any greenish bile and cook them whole, then cut them in half once cooked and remove the connective tissue.

125 g unsalted butter

1 French stick, cut diagonally into
    12 × 1.5 cm-thick slices

1 × quantity Caramelised Onions
    (see page 461) *or* 1 × 120 g tub
    Maggie Beer Caramelised Onion

extra virgin olive oil, for drizzling

6 whole rabbit livers, cut in half

sea salt flakes

2 tablespoons vino cotto
    (see Glossary)

6 anchovy fillets, halved

24 sage leaves

freshly ground black pepper, to taste

Preheat the oven to 220°C. Melt 80 g of the butter and brush one side of each bread slice with melted butter, then bake on a baking tray until golden. Meanwhile, gently heat the caramelised onions in a small saucepan over low heat.

Heat the remaining butter in a frying pan until nut-brown, adding a little olive oil to prevent it from burning. Season the livers with salt, then add to the pan with the sage leaves and sear on both sides. Immediately deglaze the pan with the vino cotto.

Quickly assemble the warm croutons. Top each crouton with a spoonful of caramelised onion, place a liver piece on top and brush with the pan juices, then top with an anchovy half, a couple of sage leaves and a drizzle of olive oil and season with freshly ground black pepper.

SASKIA'S FILLET OF BEEF WITH ANCHOVY AND HERB STUFFING *Serves 6*

As a teenager, my daughter Saskia would cook this dish for the whole family on special occasions, and it remains a firm favourite.

2 thick slices white bread, crusts removed
    and discarded

1 large onion, finely chopped

extra virgin olive oil, for cooking

1 × 45 g tin anchovy fillets, well-drained
    and chopped

½ cup flat-leaf parsley, finely chopped

2 sprigs thyme, leaves picked

2 sprigs oregano, leaves picked and chopped

1 sprig rosemary, leaves picked and chopped

1 teaspoon fish sauce

2 teaspoons Worcestershire sauce

75 ml extra virgin olive oil

1 × 1.4 kg fillet of beef

Preheat the oven to 220°C. Toast the bread in the oven until golden brown and leave it to cool. In a food processor, reduce the toast to medium crumbs.

Sweat the onion in a frying pan in a little olive oil over gentle heat until softened. Combine the breadcrumbs, onion, anchovy fillets, herbs, fish sauce, Worcestershire sauce and the 75 ml olive oil in a bowl.

Trim the meat of all fat and sinew and 'butterfly' it open. To do this, cut down the length of the fillet, making sure you only cut halfway through it. Starting at the cut you have just made, turn your knife side on and cut through the fillet towards the edge (but not right through it). Repeat this on the other side, then open out the fillet. Place the stuffing down the middle of the opened-out fillet, then roll the meat back into shape. Tie the fillet with kitchen string, then seal it in a little hot olive oil in a roasting pan on the stove over high heat until browned on all sides. Transfer the roasting pan to the oven and roast the fillet for 12–20 minutes, depending on how well done you like your meat, then leave it to rest for 20 minutes, covered loosely with foil, before carving.

APRICOTS

IT TAKES A LONG WHILE FOR ME TO GET TIRED OF JUST EATING apricots fresh or perhaps poaching them quickly to have with yoghurt for breakfast or as a dessert with cream or ice cream. With soft fruit, the very best way to get it is picked ripe directly from the tree, but buying from a specialist greengrocer or farmers' market that doesn't refrigerate their fruit is the next best thing. Rock-hard stone fruit will soften off the tree and its flavour will develop if not refrigerated, though not to its full potential. The taste of refrigerated fruit will always be dulled.

The issue of fruit being picked before it is ripe is a vexed one. Apricots, like other soft fruits, are best when left on the tree to ripen, but the issue of transportation through our vast country and the spoilage that will so obviously occur (when it can take weeks before the fruit gets from farm to final customer) simply means that I suspect the majority of Australians will never truly know how beautiful this fruit can be. Fruit picked under-ripe still develops colour, but only a smidgeon of flavour – yet how often have I been seduced by the first apricots of the season, large and deep orange (aware of the timing of our own growers' crop, I know these aren't local and so I should resist). Recently, because I needed apricots to make a jam and it was weeks before our local growers would be ready to harvest their perfectly ripe apricots, I bought a box of the 'beautiful looking' apricots and proceeded to try and make a jam, but they were so full of water and lacking in flavour I finished up throwing the jam out. Mental note to myself: follow your nose and wait for the fruit to be perfumed, then flavour will follow.

I realise how lucky I am to live in the Barossa where I have my own trees, and neighbours like Jim and Margaret Ellis, who sell their fruit at the Barossa Farmers' Market, as well as Mark Grieger, based between Blanchetown and Swan Reach. Mark chooses our fruit and, in his packing shed, cuts it ready for our very limited supply of jam each year. For jam-making, the majority of fruit needs to be ripe yet firm, with a small percentage of green-shouldered fruit to provide the necessary pectin.

The organic movement has been a long time coming and I absolutely applaud it, but my guiding principles are flavour and sustainable agricultural practices, neither of which are exclusive to organic growers. I want to know how my food is grown and, wherever possible, who has grown it. But there has to be balance. Over the years we have had some very wet seasons, when many of our local orchardists would have lost their trees if they hadn't sprayed to combat the diseases brought on by uncharacteristic rain. Growers cannot afford to lose their crops and certainly those I know are only too concerned with doing everything they can to look after their land – this is a vital issue to all.

Here in the Barossa, they often start picking the apricot crop on Christmas Day – which always seemed the height of bad timing. One memorable summer the season was running late, much to the delight of this strong church-going community, who had the rare opportunity to relax and enjoy Christmas Day. That year it took some cajoling to convince a favourite grower to gather the first ripe apricots two days after Christmas! The whole orchard yielded just half a case of ripe fruit, but the effort was worth it. I piled all the apricots on two oval platters in my kitchen; the perfume of the fruit was so intense there was no way I was going to consign them to the refrigerator. I had special friends for lunch that day and the guest of honour walked in and said, 'Apricots, the smell of South Australia.'

Lunch under the willow tree was as simple as lunches always are at Chez Beer, but to everyone's surprise, this time it included dessert (I am not known for my sweet tooth). The apricots had to star, of course, and the dish had to be easy as I was in an unusually relaxed state. So I made an apricot and mascarpone tart. A bit of planning helped: when I was preparing for Christmas lunch I had made a double lot of Sour-cream Pastry (see page 424) and rolled half of it out to line a tart tin with a removable base, which I then lined with foil and froze. Now I had to remember to have the oven at the right temperature at

the right time (which can be a problem if you have had a glass or two of champagne beforehand) to blind bake the pastry at 200°C until golden brown. The halved and stoned apricots, with just a dash of sweet wine poured over them (or just brushed with melted butter), waited in a shallow baking dish ready for the oven to reach 230°C. I baked them for just 4 minutes, then let them cool to room temperature (alternatively, you could place them under a hot grill for 5 minutes). I stirred the juices from the cooled fruit into a cup or two of mascarpone, then spooned this into the prepared tart case. The roasted apricots were positioned rounded-side up and overlapping each other, keeping the mascarpone a secret until the cutting of the tart. A great success!

Having beaten the birds (touch wood) to our apricot harvest this year, we haven't yet beaten apricot freckle, which shows up on the fruit's skin as irregular, scaly brown spots. In *The Complete Book of Fruit Growing in Australia*, Louis Glowinski says freckle can be controlled by spraying for brown rot. Next season, I'm going to be armed with an organic spray to try to combat this. All is still not lost, however; the trick is to let the freckly apricots ripen and use them for jam.

Great apricot jam is just one tiny notch under my favourite burnt fig jam. I use 2 kg of the ripest fruit and, to avoid adding any water (which dilutes the flavour of the jam), I cover the halved fruit with 1 kg sugar and 400 ml lemon juice and leave the mixture overnight. I then cook the jam for as short a time as possible to retain the flavour, taking care that it doesn't burn. Better to have plenty of flavour and sacrifice some of the 'set'.

Apricot jam made like this is a delicacy and should be given pride of place in a more elaborate breakfast: thick pieces of wholemeal toast with lashings of unsalted butter, slathered with jam so full of fruit that you need to squash it down to make it stay on the toast. You do not have to confine it to breakfast: jam like this is worth making scones for and having afternoon tea. A neighbour brought me a flagon of apricot nectar he made from his fruit this season. Expecting it to be super-sweet, I tentatively took my first mouthful, only to find a lovely tartness on the palate. So here is another idea for those apricots that don't make the grade for eating fresh: remove the stones and purée the flesh, then serve the nectar as an aperitif on the rocks, or top with a nice, dry sparkling white wine for a new take on a Bellini.

If you are drawn to the kitchen, Upside-down Apricot Tarts (see page 17) are pretty hard to beat, and make a great summer dessert. I also love the marriage of apricots and almonds, especially in a Crumble (see page 16).

I can't talk about apricots without talking about dried apricots and how wonderful, and endangered, ours are. While I was writing this, my friend Sheri Schubert phoned to organise our annual preserving program, which always starts with apricots. Sheri, an intelligent farmer and committed volunteer in the local Country Fire Service (CFS), always has her finger on the pulse. She told me that the local apricot growers, already hardly making ends meet due to high labour costs, are being paid less again this year for their crop, competing as they are with cheaper imported dried apricots from Turkey. Some are threatening to pull their trees out as they can't afford to stay in business. I urge you to always look to see where your dried apricots come from when you buy. This is not just a matter of buying Australian as a catch-cry, it's about superior flavour and keeping communities and traditions alive.

HILDA'S APRICOT JAM
Makes about 3 litres

Hilda Laurencis was a very important person to our business and family over almost thirty years. She did everything from dishwashing and food preparation to quail-plucking in the early days of the restaurant, as well as looking after our house. It was Hilda who first made pâté with me using small domestic food processors – we burnt out many a motor together. Hilda retired three times, always deciding to come back, announcing she was bored. This happened in the early days of our export kitchen, where she would lend a hand when we went through the busiest times, and up until three years ago Hilda still helped each week with housekeeping. In all this time she would keep my store cupboard stocked with one of her jams. Just as we finished one, another would appear. Even in her late seventies, Hilda still kept her hand in helping my daughter Saskia one morning a week, and carried on the tradition of bringing the pot of jam, a bag of lemons or a bunch of flowers, that just 'appeared'. Hilda's apricot jam was an undisputed family favourite. We all owe her so much.

5 kg apricots, cut into quarters
and stoned

3 kg sugar

Cook the apricots in a large saucepan with 750 ml water on high heat for about 20 minutes or until they are 'all mashed up'. Add the sugar and cook for another 30 minutes, taking care not to burn them. Bottle in sterilised jars (see Glossary).

MUSTARD APRICOTS
Makes 1 litre

This recipe uses dried apricots; however it can also be made using very firm fresh apricots, peaches, small figs, cherries or glacé fruit. I serve these mustard fruits with pâtés, terrines, rillettes or cold meats, especially legs of sugar-cured ham or baked hands of pork.

400 g dried apricots
¾ cup (180 ml) boiling water
50 g Keen's dried mustard powder
1⅔ cups (410 ml) lemon juice
finely grated rind of 1 lemon

1 cinnamon stick
3 sprigs lemon thyme
2 cups (440 g) sugar
1 tablespoon finely grated horseradish

Sterilise two 500 ml-capacity jars (see Glossary). Put the apricots in a bowl with the boiling water and leave to soak for 1 hour. Drain the apricots and transfer to a large bowl, reserving ⅓ cup (80 ml) of the soaking liquid.

Put the mustard powder, lemon juice, lemon rind, cinnamon, lemon thyme, sugar and the reserved soaking liquid in a saucepan and bring to the boil, then simmer over low heat for 10 minutes. Stir the horseradish in to this syrup, and pour immediately over the soaked apricots, then transfer straightaway to the sterilised jars. »

Leave to mature for at least 1 week before using. Unopened jars of mustard apricots will keep for up to 12 months, although the apricots will darken a little.

APRICOT AND ALMOND CRUMBLE

Serves 4

30 large ripe apricots, halved and stoned
sugar, for sprinkling
60 g flaked almonds, lightly roasted

CRUMBLE
125 g flour
100 g sugar
100 g ground almonds
175 g butter

Preheat the oven to 200°C. Arrange the apricot halves in a shallow glass or enamelled baking dish. Sprinkle with sugar. Mix the crumble ingredients together in a bowl, rubbing in the butter with your fingers. Spread over the fruit and sprinkle with flaked almonds. Bake for about 30 minutes. Be careful not to burn the flaked almonds – cover with foil or lower the temperature if necessary. Serve warm with cream or ice cream.

DRIED APRICOT AND FRANGIPANE TARTS

Makes 4 × 22 cm tarts

This recipe is great if you are cooking for a crowd as it makes 4 large tarts or between 46 and 48 tiny cocktail tarts. If you wish to make tiny tarts, follow the same process and use smaller tins such as half-moon cake moulds, then press a dried apricot in the centre of each tart and bake for 15 minutes only.

2 × quantities Sour-cream Pastry
   (see page 424)
200 g dried apricots (about 48)
200 ml verjuice
480 g butter

480 g castor sugar
8 free-range eggs
480 g freshly ground almonds
120 g plain flour

Preheat the oven to 200°C. Make and chill the pastry as instructed. Roll out to fill four 22 cm tart tins, then cover and chill in the refrigerator for 20 minutes. Line the pastry cases with foil and weights and blind bake for 10 minutes, then remove the foil and weights and bake for a further 5 minutes.

Meanwhile, soak the dried apricots in the verjuice for 30 minutes.

Reset the oven to 180°C. To make the frangipane filling beat the butter and sugar together until lightly creamed. Beat the eggs in a separate bowl, then stir a little at a time into the butter mixture until all the egg is added, making sure the mixture doesn't curdle. In another bowl, combine the ground almonds and flour, then add this to the butter and egg mixture and mix well.

Drain the apricots, reserving the verjuice. Place the frangipane filling in the tart cases and divide the drained apricots among the tarts, pressing them gently into the filling. Brush the reserved verjuice over the apricots, then bake the tarts on baking trays for 25 minutes or until a toothpick inserted in the centre of the tarts comes out clean.

UPSIDE-DOWN APRICOT TARTS   *Serves 2*

This is a favourite dish from Jenny Ferguson's book *Cooking for You and Me*. For several years, Jenny ran a wonderful restaurant in Sydney called You and Me and when she finally closed her doors she wrote this book as a record of her time at the stoves. These tarts are extremely versatile. I use two 14 cm tart tins but they can be made smaller or larger, as you please. Plums can be substituted for the apricots, or in winter try rounds of Granny Smith apples.

Rough Puff Pastry leftovers (see page 100)	**50 g unsalted butter**
125 g castor sugar, plus extra, for sprinkling	**6 ripe apricots, halved and stoned**

Preheat the oven to 190°C. Roll out your pastry very thinly and cut out 2 circles that are just a bit wider than the tops of your tart tins. Chill the pastry rounds while you prepare the apricots.

Put the sugar and 250 ml water in a frying pan and cook to a light-golden caramel over low–medium heat. Add the butter. Let this mixture bubble for a couple of minutes without stirring, then add the apricots, cooking them for 3 minutes on each side.

Put the apricots, rounded-side down, in the bottom of the tins and cover with the caramel butter. Do not fill quite to the top. Drape a pastry circle over the top of each tin and sprinkle with some of the extra sugar. Put the tins on a baking tray to catch any spills, and bake for about 20 minutes or until the pastry is crisp.

To serve, trim off the excess pastry edges and turn upside-down (so that the pastry is now underneath) on to serving plates. Serve with thick fresh cream or crème anglaise.

BASIL

IT IS INCREDIBLE TODAY TO THINK THAT BASIL WAS ONCE considered exotic, but I remember well my first encounter with a bunch of basil: it was as large as a bouquet and amazingly intoxicating. It was presented to me by Janet Jeffs in 1980 after she'd come to work with me at the Pheasant Farm Restaurant. This was a critical and incredibly exciting period – a real coming of age for us. Janet would often walk in with trays of velvety field mushrooms, buckets of watercress and all manner of fresh goodies from our friend Susan Hackett's farm at Ngapala, just north of the Barossa. Janet later gave me the confidence to move from the *table d'hôte* menu to *à la carte* and together we cooked anything that came to hand.

Even though there are many different basils available, I tend to grow and use the well-known sweet basil and the purple-leafed variety known as red or opal-leafed basil. I find that small leaves are packed with more flavour than the huge elephant's ears you sometimes see, and continually picking the basil helps to keep the leaves small. If you have a surplus of basil you can store whole leaves layered with salt and covered with extra virgin olive oil. This keeps the flavour of the basil, but it will lose some of its colour; omitting the salt will keep the colour, but remember that olive oil is not a preservative. When adding basil to a hot dish, tear the leaves and add at the last moment, as the heat reduces the pungency of the herb.

The first time I ever served a cold pasta dish in the restaurant was when we had a wonderful party to celebrate our tenth birthday. It was mid-January 1989, so we were surrounded by ripe, ripe tomatoes, and so much basil had been planted between the roses to keep aphids at bay that we were losing the war of nipping the tops off to save the plants from going to seed. (I've since learnt that growing basil in the shade stops it from going to seed.) As the whole basis of my cooking has always been to use what is in season, basil featured in three dishes that day, and its sweet, spicy perfume pervaded the whole room.

We made Duck Egg Pasta (see page 420), our old staple, in 500 g batches, smothering each cooked and drained batch with extra virgin olive oil to stop the pasta sticking as it

Salsa agresto (see page 22)

cooled. Tomatoes were cut into chunks, neither skinned nor seeded, and left to sit a while with lots of freshly plucked basil, salt, freshly ground black pepper and fruity extra virgin olive oil to make their own highly perfumed juice. (In those days I bought my olive oil by the flagon from Angle Vale in South Australia.) At the last minute, the lot was tossed with the cooled pasta and served. This sauce is just as good with hot pasta, and can be extended in a number of ways: consider adding finely chopped red onion; or perhaps anchovy fillets and pitted olives; or even fresh ricotta or crumbled feta.

I also chopped up lots of basil to knead into gnocchi dough. After the gnocchi were poached, I pan-fried them in nut-brown butter and added lashings of Parmigiano Reggiano before taking the dish to the table.

For the final basil dish we made a pizza dough, rolled it flat and filled it with pitted black olives, roasted garlic cloves and masses of basil leaves, all anointed with extra virgin olive oil, before pulling it together like a large old-fashioned purse. The first cut after baking released a wonderful aroma as the olives came tumbling out.

It's amazing how smell can trigger evocative memories. All I need to do is brush past a basil plant and its gloriously pervasive perfume takes me straight back to that day. It was a great party and quite a milestone for us.

Jill Stone, who runs Herbivorous, a commercial herb garden in Adelaide, is a great asset to restaurateurs; we could never have grown enough of all the herbs we needed for the Pheasant Farm Restaurant. Basil is, of course, a standard for her, which means she has tremendous amounts of basil wood (the branches that form on commercially grown plants) left at the end of each season. Once Jill and I thought it would be a great idea to use this wood for grilling, but I couldn't find a chipper strong enough to take it without breaking! The basil wood sat in our shed for years; we eventually grilled quail over it and, amazingly, that wonderful perfume was still there.

If you are barbecuing a good piece of rump steak and happen to have a basil plant to hand, pluck a few leaves as you prepare to turn the meat for its final cooking. Brush the meat with extra virgin olive oil, season it with freshly ground black pepper and add a few basil leaves, then turn it over to finish cooking. Allow the cooked meat to rest before eating.

Basil and rabbit have a great affinity. I sometimes buy rabbit fillets off the bone to make a wonderfully quick meal. I arrange three or four large basil leaves, perfect-side down, along a piece of caul fat (nature's Gladwrap, says my friend Cath Kerry!) and place two fat rabbit fillets together end to end on top of the basil leaves to form an even 'log', then wrap up the meat with the caul fat. I pan-fry these tiny parcels for about 2 minutes a side, then allow them to rest before serving them with the sauce from Rabbit Saddle with Basil Cream Sauce (see page 23). I do seem fixated on rabbit, but one of my favourite ever dishes is a fresh pasta I make with black olives speckled through it, served with a rabbit 'sauce'. I pan-fry sliced rabbit fillets with rabbit kidneys and liver for just seconds in nut-brown butter and then set them aside. I add a bit of Dijon mustard to the pan and deglaze with verjuice before returning the rabbit to the pan, throwing in masses of freshly torn basil, seasoning it well and tossing it with the pasta.

I once made an exception to my rule of only adding basil to a dish at the last moment when making a pigeon terrine. I layered the mould with super-fine pieces of smoked pork fat, pigeon, livers and basil. This was then cooked in a water bath at a fairly low temperature and refrigerated to set. The perfume of the basil lingered for the whole week that the terrine stayed fresh enough to use.

PESTO

Makes 375 ml

For an explosion of flavour, float a spoonful of pesto as a raft in a vegetable soup as the French do (they call it pistou), or stir into minestrone like the Italians do. Pesto with pasta is so simple a dish it could almost be labelled convenience food, yet it is healthy and packed with flavour. Pesto can also be tossed with just-cooked green beans: drizzle a dash of extra virgin olive oil over the beans and then sprinkle on a couple of drops of your best balsamic vinegar.

Many years ago I used a mortar and pestle for pounding my basil, but I confess that time and a bad shoulder have the better of me now and I most often make pesto in the food processor. However, whenever I can convince a helper, I am reminded that making it by hand is so worth the effort; it engages you in the aroma from beginning to end, and gives a better texture and colour. Eating pesto the moment it is made is perfection.

I invariably have difficulty preventing my pesto from oxidising after a few days, finding the recommendation to cover it with a film of oil never quite sufficient (although a splash of lemon juice will help if you are planning to store it). For this reason, when basil is abundant, I often resort to making a paste with the basil, pine nuts and oil and then freezing it in tiny plastic pots with a good seal. The pots can be defrosted in hot water and then mixed with the grated cheese and garlic (garlic shouldn't be frozen as its composition will change) and perhaps a little more oil and seasoning.

100 g pine nuts	50 g freshly grated pecorino
¾ cup (180 ml) extra virgin olive oil	sea salt flakes and freshly ground
2 cloves garlic	black pepper
1 cup firmly packed basil leaves	squeeze of lemon juice (optional)
50 g freshly grated Parmigiano Reggiano	

Dry-roast the pine nuts in a frying pan over medium–high heat until golden, tossing frequently to prevent burning. Put ¼ cup olive oil and the remaining ingredients in a food processor and blend to a paste, then check the seasoning and stir in the remaining oil.

SALSA AGRESTO

Makes 700 ml

1 cup (160 g) almonds
1 cup (100 g) walnuts
2 cloves garlic
2¾ cups flat-leaf parsley leaves
½ cup firmly packed basil leaves

1½ teaspoons sea salt flakes
freshly ground black pepper
¾ cup (180 ml) extra virgin olive oil
¾ cup (180 ml) verjuice

Preheat the oven to 200°C. Roast the almonds and walnuts on separate baking trays for about 5 minutes, shaking to prevent burning. Rub walnuts in a tea towel to remove bitter skins, then leave to cool. Blend the nuts, garlic, herbs, salt and 6 grinds of black pepper in a food processor with a little of the olive oil. With the motor running, slowly add the remaining oil and verjuice. The consistency should be like pesto. (If required, thin with more verjuice.)

BASIL, ANCHOVY AND ZUCCHINI PASTA

Serves 4–6

You could use my Duck Egg Pasta for this dish (see page 420).

400 g (about 12) small zucchini, about 8 cm long
sea salt flakes
500 g fresh *or* dried pasta
extra virgin olive oil, for cooking

juice of 1 lemon
freshly ground black pepper
12 anchovy fillets, chopped
20 basil leaves
100 g freshly grated pecorino

Bring a large saucepan of water to the boil for the pasta. Bring another pan of water to the boil, then salt it and cook the whole zucchini for just a few minutes. Remove the zucchini and leave to cool for 5 minutes.

Meanwhile, add 2 tablespoons salt to the pasta pan. Slide the pasta gently into the pan as the water returns to the boil, then partially cover with a lid to bring it to a rapid boil. Cook pasta following the manufacturer's instructions (the cooking times can differ), stirring to keep it well separated (a tablespoon of olive oil in the water can help this too). If using fresh pasta, it only needs to cook for 3 minutes or so. Drain the pasta and transfer to a serving bowl. Reserve a little of the cooking water in case you want to moisten the completed dish. Do not run the pasta under water or you'll lose the precious starch that helps the oil adhere.

Slice each zucchini lengthways into 2 or 3 (depending on their thickness), drizzle with olive oil, squeeze on lemon juice and grind on black pepper, then add to the pasta. Toss the anchovies through the pasta with the basil, pecorino and another drizzle of olive oil. If the pasta needs moistening, add a little of the reserved cooking water. Serve immediately.

RABBIT SADDLE WITH BASIL CREAM SAUCE *Serves 4*

Many years ago I read somewhere a recipe of Barbara Santich's for rabbit with basil. I no longer have the notes from that recipe but this is how the dish has evolved over the years.

4 saddles of farmed rabbit (on the bone)

4 golden shallots, thinly sliced

extra virgin olive oil, for cooking

freshly ground black pepper

100 ml verjuice

100 ml Golden Chicken Stock (see page 57)

1 cup firmly packed basil leaves

⅓ cup (80 ml) cream

sea salt flakes

Preheat the oven to 200°C. Take the sinew off the top of each saddle by slipping the sharpest knife possible (a flexible boning knife, if you have it) under the skin and pulling the membrane away. (This is similar to taking the sinew off a fillet of beef.)

Sauté the shallots very gently in a frying pan in a little olive oil (taking care not to brown them), then paint the saddles with the shallots and oil and sprinkle black pepper over them. Place the saddles in a roasting pan, meat-side up, with a fair amount of space between each one. (If they are too close they will poach rather than roast.)

Heat the verjuice in a small saucepan over high heat and reduce by half. Add the chicken stock and continue to reduce. While the verjuice and stock are reducing, bake the saddles for 8–12 minutes, then transfer them to a warm serving dish and turn them over (bone-side up) to rest, loosely covered. Tear or snip the basil into thin strips. Pour the reduced stock mixture into the roasting pan, place over high heat on the stove and add the cream. Once the sauce is boiling vigorously, add the basil and adjust the seasoning. Serve the sauce over the rabbit saddles with some boiled waxy potatoes and a green salad alongside.

BEANS

THE BEGINNING OF SUMMER IS HERALDED BY THE BEST stringless beans available. Look for specimens that are round, about 10 cm long and bright green (these are not always easy to find). All you need to do is cook them in boiling salted water for a few minutes and then toss them with butter and herbs.

Butter beans are their own taste sensation – a very distinctive flavour. They are a pale, buttery colour and are best when not left to grow too long.

Damper climates may be more successful at growing snake beans than we are in South Australia. They tend to be coarser in Adelaide than in Melbourne, but are still very interesting. They can be found in good greengrocers and in Asian supermarkets. Dark green in colour, they 'snake' over the plate and I love the look of astonishment on people's faces when I serve them.

Flat beans are my beans of the moment – perfectly flat and bright green. I prefer them to any stringless beans I have bought from a greengrocer. If cooked for just a few minutes in boiling salted water and then tossed in preserved lemon butter with some freshly ground black pepper, they are crisp, juicy and delicious.

If truth be told, I wasn't a fan of beans until I fell under the spell of Tuscany, whose inhabitants are known to the rest of Italy as the 'bean eaters' or *mangiafagioli*. The catalyst was a dish of fresh cannellini beans, enjoyed at Cantinetta Antinori in Florence a couple of years ago. They had been simmered for 20 minutes with a bay leaf and garlic, before being strained, then drizzled with new-season extra virgin olive oil. I have to confess that I would never have been seduced if it hadn't been for the extra virgin olive oil. As it made contact with the hot purée, the aromas and flavours exploded; I was hooked. The beans, a creamy light-green colour, were unadorned except for the oil, some sea salt and freshly ground black pepper, and came with crusty bread – a timely reminder of how good 'simple' can be.

Flat green beans with preserved lemon butter and freshly ground black pepper (see opposite)

Broad beans engender passion in some people. There are those who hate them and those who love them. My children hate them – they must have had a deprived childhood!

Growing up, I had two very special 'maiden aunts' who shared a house. Auntie Reta did the cooking, usually a roast, and Auntie Glad was a 'school marm' in the traditional sense. Auntie Glad knew herself to be a good headmistress but a particularly bad cook, so she learnt, practised and delivered a repertoire of just two main courses, chicken casserole and a veal dish, and two desserts. (The desserts were Spanish cream and a very sherried trifle.) Neither of the main course dishes was one that I enjoyed but I did understand the love that went into their preparation, and the saving grace was that she used vegetables in season straight from their back garden. One of Auntie Glad's favourites, and mine, was the broad bean, and they were never peeled. It was a long time before I discovered that 'in the very best places' the skin was peeled from the broad beans after podding. To many, the sheer beauty of the surprising bright green of a peeled broad bean might be worth the effort, but the flavour is quite different and, as so many food memories are evocative, I'll stick to them unskinned.

At the restaurant I would often serve a very simple country dish of unpeeled broad beans. With the addition of good extra virgin olive oil and perhaps some Parmigiano Reggiano and crusty bread, I would never even consider peeling the beans as they were so sweet from being freshly picked by my neighbours.

Broad beans eaten fresh from the garden, before their sugar turns to starch and the skins toughen, are a defining flavour worth seeking out. If, when you pod them, the second skin around the bean is quite white, it is a sure sign the bean will be old and tough. If this happens, I would cook them to smithereens, purée them with some fresh herbs, salt and freshly ground black pepper, then add a good drizzle of extra virgin olive oil. In fact, this is also how I handle dried broad beans (see opposite). The purée can then be turned into a soup or the base of a meal – a grilled lamb chop on a bed of broad bean purée, made of either the beans themselves or the beans and pods, sounds pretty good to me. The pods should be bright green, crisp to the touch and without blemishes. It is best to buy them under 10 cm long. If you grow them yourself, try cooking small ones, pod and all, and tossing them with butter and fresh herbs. The smallest ones are also perfect eaten raw.

Fresh, tender broad beans team well with other spring delights such as artichokes, asparagus and fresh peas. Try braising them together in a little extra virgin olive oil and water. Start with the artichokes, then add the asparagus and broad beans. Lastly, you could add some freshly shelled peas. Adjust the flavour with a little verjuice and seasoning and serve warm as a complete dish.

In Tuscany there is a spring tradition of serving broad beans with a fresh pecorino as soon as they ripen. The pecorino is cut into thick slices and served with the beans, and the guests pod the beans as they eat them. There is a saltiness to the fresh pecorino that I imagine beautifully complements the sweetness of the young broad beans.

Broad beans are also called fava beans and are available dried (and sometimes already double-peeled); like other dried beans, they need soaking before use. If soaking dried beans, choose a bowl at least double the volume of the beans you are soaking. Fill the bowl to the top with water and soak the beans for at least 12 hours. If you have left your run too late for that, you can bring them to the boil over high heat in a saucepan of water, then cook for 2 minutes, remove from the heat and let stand for 2–3 hours, before draining and beginning your recipe.

For one of the simplest dishes, try gently sautéing some onions in olive oil with fresh herbs such as bay leaves until the onions are translucent. Season to taste with freshly ground black pepper and add a preserved lemon quarter to the pan (lemon is very much an extra, but old Florentine recipes often include this, or a dash of vinegar, to add piquancy).

Add the soaked and drained broad beans and a few whole garlic cloves and cover with water or light chicken stock and 125 ml extra virgin olive oil. Bring to a simmer and cook very slowly, covered, over low heat for 1½–2 hours or until the beans are totally soft, stirring often and adding more liquid if necessary (a simmer mat placed under the pan helps to control the heat – you want to simmer the beans, not boil them). Drain the beans, reserving a few tablespoons of the cooking liquid. Season with salt and pepper, then either serve as an accompaniment with a swirl of extra virgin olive oil and freshly chopped flat-leaf parsley, or purée with a few tablespoons of extra virgin olive oil. The amount of oil added depends on whether the purée is to accompany a grill or is to be served as an entrée with crusty bread and a salad – the latter can take a bit more. You can also use this method with haricot, borlotti or cannellini beans.

On days when I feel a bit extravagant, I simmer soaked beans for about 30 minutes, then transfer them to a pot I bought in Tuscany, adding lavish amounts of olive oil. This glazed terracotta vessel is hourglass-shaped, with handles on each side and a tight-fitting lid, and is designed especially for long, slow cooking. Traditionally this would have been used in a wood-fired oven after baking the bread, when most of the heat had dissipated (hence the need to use a simmer mat on the stove). The last time I used this pot I put simmered cannellini beans in with a little chicken stock, some ends of pancetta and a few of the whole garlic cloves that were simmered with the beans, then seasoned it and covered the lot with extra virgin olive oil. It actually did not take an amazing amount of oil (about 190 ml) and I justified using it because it was from the end of a drum. Cooked this way, the beans can take anything from 1–3 hours; and are, by the way, delicious.

This idea can be extended to make a pasta sauce by cooking fennel and pork with the beans, removing them before puréeing the beans, cutting the fennel and pork into pieces and adding them back to the purée. Or it can be turned into a soup by adding peeled roma

tomatoes, using more stock in place of the oil and adding fennel and garlic during cooking. Spoon the soup over a piece of toasted stale (but good) bread and add a swirl of extra virgin olive oil, lots of flat-leaf parsley, sea salt flakes and freshly ground black pepper – you won't need anything more to satisfy your hunger.

Fresh borlotti beans, and perhaps cannellini beans, are often only available to those who shop in autumn markets. Dried beans, however, are widely available, flavourful and inexpensive, yet I suspect are ignored by many who don't realise how wonderful they can be when cooked with care.

GREEN BEAN SALAD
Serves 4

250 g green beans
100 ml walnut oil
2 tablespoons verjuice

sea salt flakes and freshly ground
black pepper
120 g thinly sliced prosciutto
80 g walnuts, roasted and skins rubbed

Cook the beans for a few minutes in a saucepan of boiling salted water until they are cooked through but still bright green. Previously I would have said cook until al dente, but my view has changed as truly al dente is undercooked, and the bean only releases its flavour when it is just cooked (this is one vegetable I would refresh under cool water immediately to stop the cooking and keep as much colour as possible). Make a vinaigrette by whisking together the walnut oil, verjuice, salt and pepper. Drape prosciutto over a serving plate. Toss the beans and walnuts in the vinaigrette and pile onto the prosciutto.

BROAD BEANS WITH PASTA AND PROSCIUTTO
Serves 4

2 kg fresh young broad beans, shelled
½ cup (125 ml) extra virgin olive oil
sea salt flakes and freshly ground
    black pepper
250 g fresh pasta sheets (I use handmade fine
    ravioli dough cut into 6 cm × 4 cm sheets)

1 cup (70 g) toasted breadcrumbs
150 g prosciutto, cut into strips
½ cup freshly chopped mint
1 tablespoon red-wine vinegar

Bring a large saucepan of salted water to the boil in readiness for the pasta. Simmer the beans in a saucepan with just enough water to cover, a dash of the oil and a pinch of salt for 7–10 minutes or until just cooked. Meanwhile, cook the pasta sheets in the saucepan of boiling water and drain them (do not refresh, as this removes flavour). Put the sheets on to a plate or dish large enough to spread them out and drizzle with a little olive oil to stop any further cooking. »

Drain the beans immediately when they're cooked and, while still warm, transfer to a bowl and stir in the breadcrumbs, prosciutto and remaining olive oil. Add the room-temperature pasta. Balance seasoning with salt and pepper, if needed, then add the mint, and perhaps some more olive oil, along with the vinegar. Serve at room temperature.

DRIED BROAD BEAN PASTE BRUSCHETTA
WITH EXTRA VIRGIN OLIVE OIL
Serves 12

It is possible to buy dried fava or broad beans that have already been double-peeled in some Middle Eastern stores. If you can't get these, and you own a mouli, then cook them unpeeled and pass them through the mouli. Alternatively, if you purée the beans in a food processor or blender, then the skins will be part of the dish.

200 g dried broad (fava) beans
1 onion, roughly chopped
2 cloves garlic, peeled
rind of 1 lemon
extra virgin olive oil, for cooking
lemon juice, to taste

sea salt flakes and freshly ground
    black pepper
12 × 1 cm-thick slices sourdough bread
1 clove garlic, halved
½ cup freshly chopped flat-leaf parsley

Put broad beans, onion, garlic and lemon rind in a heavy-based saucepan, then cover with a generous amount of cold water. Simmer over low heat for about 1 hour or until the beans are cooked through. Drain the beans and remove the rind, then pass the beans through a mouli or purée in a food processor, adding enough extra virgin olive oil to form a thick paste. Add as much lemon juice as your taste dictates, then season with salt and pepper. Leave to cool to room temperature.

Just before serving, toast the sliced bread on both sides on a chargrill pan or barbecue over high heat. Immediately rub the cut garlic clove over the toast, then drizzle the toast with olive oil and season to taste with salt and pepper.

Spoon a generous amount of broad bean paste on top of each slice of warm bruschetta, then finish with a final flourish of extra virgin olive oil and lots of chopped flat-leaf parsley.

CAPERS

 **WHEN I WAS YOUNG I WOULD PICK CAPERS OUT OF A DISH AND** put them to one side. Considering my interest in them now, my early dislike of capers might have been an issue of acquired taste, but I think it might also have been because neither they nor the medium in which they were packed were of particularly good quality.

I first found capers to be irresistible when I came across the small ones imported from the Aeolian Islands near Sicily. These intensely flavoured, unopened flower buds of the caper bush comprise almost the entire food production of these islands, where the growers have formed co-operatives to market their capers worldwide. Caper varieties range from these exquisite tiny ones to plumper olive-green buds, and, if packed in the right medium, they can add piquancy to an amazing array of foods.

The caper bush is an attractive plant that thrives in the Mediterranean region, where it can be seen, often straggling and vine-like, growing wild out of old walls, rocks and even piles of rubbish. About a metre high, it has tough, oval-shaped leaves and exquisite pink or white flowers that carry a tassel of long purple stamens. Sadly, the flowers hardly last, but through summer the bush is green and succulent. It is a hardy plant that needs very little water to thrive. Although my six caper bushes give so little in comparison to the volume I devour, they do make a lovely addition to the garden, and bounced back coura-geously one year after having been completely decimated by caterpillars. My sort of plant! They are a great plant for terracotta pots in stone courtyards.

There is a world of difference in the quality of capers brought into Australia – the majority of which are shipped in bulk in brine and bottled here. The most exciting thing for me about capers is that they are now grown commercially in Mannum, South Australia, by Jonathon Trewartha, a mining engineer-turned-farmer. Jonathon tells me it was one of the articles I wrote on capers during my four-year stint writing a weekly column on food for *The Australian* that inspired him. I threw out a challenge, questioning why we weren't growing capers in Australia when there were many areas with a similar climate to that of the Mediterranean. At the time we imported more than 100 tonnes of capers a year so it was clear that the demand was there. Years later, I'll never forget the day in Mildura when those of us interested in slow food were gathered for the first time. We were sitting on my friend Stefano de Pieri's newly renovated riverboat to hear of his dream of the Murray becoming the 'Slow River' and to hear other speakers on slow food, one of them being Jonathon Trewartha of the Australian Caper Company. When Jonathon and his wife Samantha approached me before proceedings began, and gave me the first jar of salted capers they'd produced, I felt like I'd won the lottery. Taking them home and finding out just how good they were completed the circle. I now only hope that this can be made into a viable agricultural pursuit.

The Australian Caper Company (www.australiancapers.com.au) grow their capers organically using minimal water on the dry rocky slopes of the Murray River near Mannum, combining ancient techniques with modern research. The hardy caper bush, with a deep root system that uses very little water, is grown on land so degraded by salinity it could grow almost nothing else (except saltbush). The capers are picked at first light every day through-

out the hot summer months, and are then cured in their own juices and repackaged in salt, and sold that same season; they are therefore fresher, firmer and more flavoursome than the imported product.

Then there is Brian Noone, a nurseryman formerly of Cottage Herbs in Angle Vale, South Australia, who won a Churchill Fellowship to study caper propagation in the Mediterranean, and in this he found his calling. Since his return, he has successfully bred a caper he's called the 'Eureka', and has protected it with plant-breeder rights.

Brian already supplies the Eureka to the Australian Caper Company, and he also plans to release it to the home gardener as a variety with a long flowering cycle (from early summer through to winter), and a yield of between 5 and 7 kg of capers from each bush. Brian has fielded interest in the plant from as far afield as Morocco, Israel and Syria. Other than the high-end position occupied by the Australian Caper Company, which supplies discerning buyers with the freshest capers, Brian feels that it will be difficult for the Australian industry to compete with cheap imports of bulk capers because of our high labour costs and lack of access to the innovative and very expensive picking equipment used overseas. For more information on Brian's capers, you can visit his website, www.caperplants.com.

There's also Deirdre Baum from Laharum Grove (www.laharumgrove.com.au), near the Grampians National Park in northwest Victoria, who started growing capers in 2006 according to the same organic principles as the olive trees on her farm. The caper plants are thriving, and soon she will have planted over 300 bushes in between the rows of olive trees. Deirdre already produces salted capers and caper paste for the high-end market using both imported and local capers, and hopes to be using all her own capers in these products within two years.

Caperberries, which are also now readily available, are the result of a berry forming when the bud is not picked for capers but left to flower – just like a rosehip. The oval, olive-green caperberry varies from the size of a small fingernail to that of an olive and is sold as a pickle on quite a long stem. They're an acquired taste, combining the flavour of a caper with the crispness of a water chestnut, but they can be a great addition to an antipasto plate or a dish of rich pork rillettes. However, the limiting factor with imported caperberries is that they are only as good as the vinegar and brine mixture they're sold in.

It's only recently that I've tried the Trewarthas' caperberries and they were the best I've ever eaten. Simon Bryant and I were cooking for an episode of our ABC TV series *The Cook and The Chef*, and Simon had just been to visit the farm and returned with the first of their caperberries. While we both used some in dishes on the day, the rest of the jar was eaten in no time by both the crew and ourselves. I'm just so excited to have Australian capers and caperberries at my fingertips. However, at the moment the caperberries are only available in bulk as they can't produce enough at this stage to supply them to retail customers.

If you ever get the chance to preserve your own capers, dissolve 125 g salt in 500 ml hot water, then leave the solution to cool before immersing the capers in it for a week. Drain off the brine, then cover with a good-quality vinegar and leave for 4–5 days.

Salted capers need to be washed very gently, in order to eliminate excess salt without breaking the buds. I find using a sieve is the best way – not under running water but by immersing them in a bowl of clean water, which is changed several times between dunks.

Capers are incredibly versatile. They may be most commonly known as an accompaniment to smoked salmon with sliced onion and rye bread, but that is just the beginning. They marry well with pork, their tart saltiness cutting the richness of the meat, and they are a strong contrast to the gentle flavour of veal and rabbit. They are a natural partner to fish, and a vital ingredient in tartare sauce. Boiled vegetables can be taken to another dimension with the addition of some capers, extra virgin olive oil and flat-leaf parsley. Pasta tossed with capers, flat-leaf parsley, roasted garlic cloves, and extra virgin olive oil is a delicious dish that can be prepared in minutes.

If a meal is needed from the pantry in a hurry, just open a can of tuna in olive oil (at present, only Italian tuna in oil is of a quality I would use but perhaps the Port Lincoln fishermen will take a leaf from the caper bush . . .) and a bottle of preserved tomatoes or a can of good-quality peeled tomatoes and reduce them to a sauce with some fresh herbs and extra virgin olive oil. Toss the sauce through hot pasta with some capers: 15 minutes tops, and you're sitting at the table with a glass of red.

Extend mashed hard-boiled egg yolks with mayonnaise, a dash of lemon juice and chopped capers and serve it in the halved hard-boiled egg whites as great finger food.

Capers cut up into a good homemade mayonnaise and served with waxy potatoes or tomatoes make a wonderful luncheon dish.

It makes sense that capers combine well with most Mediterranean ingredients – olive oil, eggplants, red capsicums, anchovies and tuna, to name a few. Tapenade, originally from Provence, is a delicious paste made from capers, olives, anchovy fillets, garlic and olive oil that's perfect for spreading on crusty bread or serving with crisp raw vegetables.

Capers are often teamed with anchovies, as in Vitello Tonnato (see page 675). To make something a little less complicated to partner a simmering fowl, sweat a finely chopped onion in 1 tablespoon extra virgin olive oil and a knob of butter, then add 4 chopped

anchovy fillets, 1 tablespoon capers and 60 ml verjuice and reduce over medium heat until amalgamated. Add a squeeze of lemon juice and some freshly chopped flat-leaf parsley, then season and serve alongside the carved bird.

Many years ago at a Yalumba cooking class, chef Gay Bilson prepared a roulade of eggplant and capsicum with capers. It was such a classically simple dish that I have since made it time and time again – it's so perfect as an entrée or to take on a picnic. She roasted and peeled red capsicums, deep-fried sliced eggplant and chopped lots of flat-leaf parsley. She then laid a large rectangular piece of plastic film on a tea towel and covered it with pieces of eggplant so that they overlapped like roof tiles. Gay then covered the eggplant with the capsicum, laid flat, and sprinkled over the parsley, some salt and pepper and extra virgin olive oil, then scattered on capers and added a touch of balsamic vinegar. Using the plastic film to guide her, she rolled the lot up like a jelly roll, then chilled it before cutting. I like to serve slices of the roll with lots of tiny capers and some extra sea salt flakes alongside. You could also make this into a light meal by serving it with goat's cheese on croutons and a salad of peppery rocket.

Looking through my old menus from the Pheasant Farm Restaurant recently, I relived just some of the dishes in which capers featured: smoked kingfish with capers; tuna pot-roasted in olive oil with tomato, sorrel and capers (a dish by Janni Kyritsis I once had at Berowra Waters Inn); calf's tongue with capers; free-range chicken simmered in stock and served with a caper sauce; rabbit in many guises with capers, olives and anchovies; and, of course, one of the classics, poached brains pan-fried in nut-brown butter with capers and parsley. How could you live without them?

CAPERS AND CHICKEN LIVER CROSTINI

Serves 10

During my sojourn in Tuscany, the tradition of serving chicken liver crostini or bruschetta became part of our standard routine. It was the addition of salted capers that really made the difference – we went through packet after packet. Once again, it was their piquant flavour cutting into the dense liver that made a zesty impact. Rather than mashing the seared livers with a fork or blending in a food processor, we cut them into small pieces, as in this recipe.

1 tablespoon butter, plus extra to melt
250 g chicken livers, trimmed
3 anchovy fillets, chopped
⅓ cup (65 g) capers
¼ cup freshly chopped flat-leaf parsley
1–2 teaspoons red-wine vinegar
2 breadsticks, cut diagonally into thick slices

Preheat the oven to 200°C. In a heavy-based frying pan, heat the tablespoon of butter until it is nut-brown, then add the livers and turn the heat down to medium. Seal the first side for 1 minute, turn the livers over and cook for about 2 minutes (depending on size), then remove from the heat entirely to ensure they are still pink in the middle. When cool enough to handle, cut the livers into small pieces, then combine with the anchovies, capers, parsley and vinegar.

Brush the sliced bread with melted butter on one side only, then place on a baking tray and bake until golden. Serve the livers immediately, spread on the hot crostini.

SKATE WITH CAPERS AND OLIVES

Serves 4

I had skate for the first time in Malaysia, while holidaying on Langkawi Island. It was cooked in a simple Mediterranean style, which seemed rather out of place compared with the rest of the food on offer. On returning home I adapted the following recipe from Ann and Franco Taruschio's *Leaves from the Walnut Tree*, a favourite book. Skate, the wings of a stingray, is inexpensive; in some states it is sold untrimmed, so you may need to clean it.

4 × 225 g pieces skate
plain flour, for dusting
sea salt flakes and freshly ground
    black pepper
2 cloves garlic, finely chopped
⅓ cup (80 ml) extra virgin olive oil,
    plus extra for drizzling
handful flat-leaf parsley stalks, leaves picked
    and chopped and stems reserved
⅓ cup (65 g) capers
⅓ cup pitted and sliced black olives
⅓ cup (80 ml) verjuice
squeeze of lemon juice

Preheat the oven to 180°C and trim the skate of skin, if necessary. Season the flour with salt and pepper. Brown the garlic in the olive oil in a large, heavy-based ovenproof frying pan, being careful not to burn it. »

Dust each piece of skate with the seasoned flour and brown it in the pan with the garlic over high heat for about 2 minutes per side, depending on thickness. Add the parsley stems, capers, olives, verjuice and lemon juice to the pan, then season to taste.

Transfer the pan to the oven and bake for 4 minutes, then turn the skate over and bake for another 2 minutes. Toss the skate with the chopped parsley on a warmed serving platter, then drizzle with a little extra virgin olive oil. Reduce the sauce in the pan over high heat and pour over the fish. Serve with boiled waxy potatoes.

CAPONATA
Serves 6

The chocolate is a secret ingredient in this dish and adds a nuance that is hard to identify. Caponata is great with crusty bread or as a side dish for cold game.

extra virgin olive oil, for cooking	1½ cups pitted and sliced green olives
3 eggplants, cut into 2 cm cubes	⅓ cup (65 g) capers
2 sticks celery, cut into 1 cm pieces	1 tablespoon sugar
2 large onions, cut into 1 cm pieces	¼ cup (60 ml) red-wine vinegar
1 × 410 g can peeled chopped tomatoes *or*	½ teaspoon grated bitter chocolate
5 chopped ripe roma tomatoes and	(see Glossary)
1 tablespoon tomato paste	

Pour enough olive oil into a heavy-based frying pan to reach a depth of 3 cm and heat until very hot. Throw in a small piece of bread or eggplant to test whether the oil is hot enough – if it turns golden brown immediately, the oil is ready. Fry a quarter of the eggplant until golden brown on all sides, then remove with a slotted spoon to drain on kitchen paper. Fry the remaining eggplant in batches, then cook the celery in the same oil. Discard the oil and wipe out the pan, then add 60 ml fresh olive oil and place the pan over low heat.

Sauté the onion in the olive oil until translucent, then add the tomatoes (and the paste, if you are using fresh tomatoes) and cook for 10 minutes. Stir in the olives and capers and cook for about 10 minutes more, or until the sauce is thick. Add the sugar, vinegar, eggplant and celery, then add the chocolate and leave it to melt. Carefully stir until the melted chocolate is combined, then remove the pan from the heat and leave the caponata to cool overnight. Serve at room temperature.

CHICKEN LEGS WITH CAPERBERRIES, RAISINS, GREEN OLIVES AND ROASTED ALMONDS
Serves 6–8

I'm always presented with plenty of Barossa chicken thighs and legs by my daughter Saskia who raises chickens, as there is more demand for the breasts than the marylands, which suits me fine. I much prefer the leg to the breast, and often cook it along with lots of other good ingredients in one of my terracotta pots, and serve it straight from the oven as a complete dish.

I pulled this dish together for one of the early weeks of filming for *The Cook and The Chef* and was thrilled to have at hand some of the best raisins I've ever tasted from Tabletop Grapes in Mildura (see page 231), along with the first caperberries produced by the Australian Caper Company. Each of the core ingredients – the chook marylands, the raisins and the caperberries – was so special that the dish, as countrified as my food is, was really exceptional.

This is also a fantastic dish served cold the next day, when the juices will have become jellied.

½ cinnamon stick

3 lemons

20 free-range chicken legs (about 2.5 kg)

10 fresh bay leaves

4 sprigs rosemary

extra virgin olive oil, for cooking

80 g flaked almonds

sea salt flakes

80 g unsalted butter

½ cup (125 ml) vino cotto (see Glossary)
   or balsamic vinegar

30 green olives

1 generous cup raisins

½ cup caperberries *or* salted capers,
   rinsed and drained

finely chopped flat-leaf parsley, to serve

Finely grind the cinnamon stick using a mortar and pestle or a spice grinder. Remove the lemon rind in strips with a vegetable peeler and reserve the lemons for juicing. Marinade the chicken in a bowl with the ground cinnamon, lemon rind, bay leaves, rosemary and enough olive oil to coat the pieces, for at least 1 hour before cooking (overnight is even better).

When ready to cook, preheat the oven to 200°C. Place the flaked almonds on a baking tray and roast for 5 minutes or until golden; set aside. Season marinated chicken legs with salt, then heat the butter and a little olive oil in a flameproof roasting pan on the stove over low–medium heat. Add the chicken and gently seal until golden brown. Transfer the pan to the oven and cook for 10 minutes.

Remove the pan from the oven, then place over high heat on the stove and add a little of the vino cotto at a time to deglaze. Add the olives, raisins and caperberries, then return pan to the oven for another 5–10 minutes (depending on the size of the chook legs), or until the chicken is cooked through.

Toss with the flaked almonds and parsley, then squeeze over at least one of the lemons, adding more lemon juice if needed. Leave for 10 minutes before serving to allow the flavours to meld.

CAPSICUMS

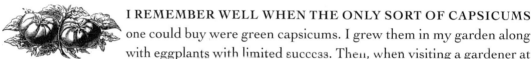 **I REMEMBER WELL WHEN THE ONLY SORT OF CAPSICUMS** one could buy were green capsicums. I grew them in my garden along with eggplants with limited success. Then, when visiting a gardener at Gawler River many years ago now to collect tomatoes too ripe for market (but perfect for sauce-making), I was shown capsicum bushes that were so lush, I was told, that they didn't allow the fruit at the centre to ripen to red. Can you believe until that moment I hadn't realised that red capsicums are merely the ripe version of the green! I felt a little foolish realising I had never planted my own capsicum bushes early enough, but always too late in the season so they didn't get the chance to become red and sweet. Green capsicums are intentionally picked before full ripeness, so can be particularly troublesome for some people to digest.

The deeper the red, the riper the capsicum is. Choose those that are smooth, shiny and heavy in the hand. If the capsicum is wrinkled, it's simply because it has been withering off the vine. For some the flesh of the capsicum, even when ripe, is indigestible unless peeled. While capsicums can be peeled with a potato peeler and eaten raw, burning off the skin gives the capsicum flesh a totally new dimension of sweetness. There are dishes where this is not essential, although they will never have the same depth of flavour. The difference in taste between a green and a red capsicum is one thing, but the leap from raw to roasted is a revelation – and the sweetness of roasted red capsicum is a taste sensation within everyone's grasp. However, it is really only in late summer and autumn, the peak of their true growing season, that capsicums reach these heights, although they are available year-round.

While the 'traditional' way to roast and peel a whole capsicum is to blister the skin over an open flame, turning it to char it evenly (some restaurant kitchens use a blow torch for this), I have to admit that charring capsicums is an outside job for me. I have never liked doing it over the open flame on the stove, mainly because of the smell that pervades the kitchen (and whose exhaust fan is ever truly efficient?). I also find that the barbecue grill

Capsicums baked with olives, goat's cheese and oregano (see page 40)

plate slows down the process a bit, as the heat is less direct, and results in a wonderfully smoky flavour. My grandchildren love watching when something is burning on the fire – and the deep-red capsicum that chars to black seems to thrill them. Another method is to roast well-oiled capsicums in a sturdy roasting pan in the oven at 230°C for about 30 minutes until blackened (turning them two or three times so that they char evenly). Before putting them in the oven, however, cut the top off each capsicum and pull out the seeds and membrane. This is much less messy than trying to do it later on, and, if you're

careful, avoids the need to run the roasted capsicums under water to clean them, which washes away some of their flavour. Whichever method you use, the blackened capsicums should be left to cool for 5 minutes, then put in a plastic bag to sweat for 10 minutes, after which time the skin will easily slip off. Wipe the flesh clean with a little olive oil, if necessary. The sweet, smoky flavour of roasted capsicum is at its height while the capsicum is still warm. The syrupy juices on the bottom of the roasting pan offer the most intense flavour of all, provided they haven't burnt – you may need to warm the pan and add a little more oil to release the juices.

If you roast a lot of red capsicums, refrigerate any leftovers steeped in extra virgin olive oil, but use them quickly as they will ferment if not totally immersed, and all that effort will be wasted. I find I never have to throw out roasted capsicums that have gone off – they never hang around in our fridge for long enough. Try roasting capsicums with extra virgin olive oil, oregano, olives and goat's cheese or ricotta. A tin of good tuna folded into a handmade mayonnaise with tiny pieces of lemon and parsley can be stuffed inside a whole roasted capsicum and served drizzled with a vinaigrette. You can also purée roasted capsicum to serve as a sauce with grilled or poached fish or chicken; or you could set it into a savoury custard with lots of roasted garlic.

If you want to go that extra step, make Rouille (see page 586). Made like a mayonnaise, but with the addition of garlic, saffron threads, tomato and the all-important purée of roasted capsicum, it is the perfect accompaniment to a fish soup or stew, and is great when served with grilled fish or squid. Try adding it to a stuffing for pot-roasted squid: cook onions in extra virgin olive oil, long and slow so they caramelise, then add rouille, lots of freshly chopped flat-leaf parsley and a chopped anchovy or two. Fill the squid, then seal with toothpicks and braise really slowly. Any leftover rouille can also be added to mashed hard-boiled egg yolks that are then returned to the whites, and piled up high; tossed into a salad of waxy potatoes with extra virgin olive oil and parsley; or added to bocconcini or goat's curd-topped croutons.

Ingredients that have a natural affinity with capsicums include anchovies, capers, eggplants, garlic, goat's cheese, olive oil, olives and tomatoes. A whole roasted red capsicum stuffed with goat's cheese, anchovies and olives – warmed in the oven to melt the cheese a little and served with a crouton of olive bread – makes a great lunch. Sliced roasted red capsicum combined with deep-fried eggplant, capers, lots of nutty flat-leaf parsley, a drizzle of extra virgin olive oil and a thimbleful of great balsamic vinegar is also wonderful.

A finger of grilled polenta about 7 × 2 × 2 cm, made with the addition of milk and cream instead of stock for a change, makes a light and tasty base on which to present other ingredients to begin a meal. Try warm polenta fingers with peeled and chopped roasted red capsicum drizzled with a little balsamic vinegar, caramelised garlic cloves, freshly grated Parmigiano Reggiano and extra virgin olive oil.

Roasted capsicum can be used to make a simple coulis, too: purée the peeled roasted capsicum and add either cream or the appropriate stock. Made with stock, red capsicum coulis is quite a counterpoint to the richness of pan-fried brains or a blue swimmer crab tartlet. If you are making a purée, note that 6 medium capsicums will yield about 500 g purée.

If you want to avoid peeling them, pan-fry sliced capsicums with garlic and thyme in extra virgin olive oil until soft and then add a little balsamic or sherry vinegar to the pan juices. Add onion and tomato to the pan, and finish off with a little chicken stock and perhaps a bit of cream, before puréeing the lot. This coulis goes well with chicken or fish.

Writing this outdoors, just metres away from trays of bright-red capsicums and sliced eggplant, my thoughts turn to drying your own vegetables at home. For those who think sun-dried tomatoes are passé and have moved on to slow-roasted baby tomatoes, I urge you to give sun-dried red capsicum or eggplant a chance; and to please re-visit sun-dried tomatoes, as the only thing that ever spoilt them was indiscriminate use, over-dried or burnt tomatoes, and poor-quality oil.

Ripe red capsicums, so sweet and luscious when grilled or roasted, can be a drag to peel. Drying them produces an incredibly intense flavour and makes peeling easier. Just cut the capsicums into quarters, then remove the seeds but leave the stems in place – they look great later – and sprinkle the cut sides with salt. Place them on wire racks in full sunshine for three days. I bring my racks in each night and return them to the drying location as soon as it is in full sun again the next day. As I look at the capsicums in front of me, after 24 hours drying out, the cut sides have curled towards the sun, so I have turned the quarters over to allow any moisture to escape. The brilliant red skins on the just-turned pieces are already delightfully crinkled and I can see they will slip off with the slightest pressure when the drying is complete – perfect.

Because mould is the enemy of dried vegetables, and comes from exposure to air, it is a good idea to store home-dried delicacies in sealed airtight containers. I prefer to steep them in extra virgin olive oil, which does not preserve the vegetables but instead keeps the oxygen out. Don't be tempted to add garlic as spores under its skin can spoil the dried product. Properly sun-dried capsicums and other vegetables such as tomatoes and eggplant do not need to be soaked before use, but they do need to be checked for mould. They will last for months if dried and stored well. Use sun-dried capsicums wherever you might use sun-dried tomatoes. If you have steeped your capsicums in oil, use this when making a vinaigrette or toss it through pasta – but please, use really good oil!

I am looking forward to enjoying these flavours of summer long after the season has drawn to a close, when I am back inside working at my desk, with only the wintry view of the willow tree to remind me of those warm days in the garden.

SWEET ROASTED RED CAPSICUM PÂTÉ — *Serves 6*

So here you have it – the basic recipe for my totally vegetarian pâté. It started as a dish for six and now we make it by the hundreds but we start every batch from scratch. We tried to see if we could make it more cost-effective by buying in the capsicums already cut, but this meant we lost control over the quality and ripeness, and the cutting by a commercial operation on the other side of Adelaide meant the capsicums had to be cut the day before they were cooked, so all those lovely juices and oils were lost. It's a lot more expensive to produce than our liver-based pâté but I wanted to be able to offer an 'off the shelf' pâté for not only the vegetable lover but also the vegetarian, who up until now has had a very limited range of top-quality commercially produced foods to choose from.

However, because I refuse to take any shortcuts, I'm not sure whether we can sustain it as one of our products, so I am sharing this recipe with you.

½ cup (125 ml) extra virgin olive oil	4 egg yolks
12 cloves garlic, peeled	120 ml thickened cream
3 sprigs thyme	sea salt flakes and freshly ground
6 red capsicums	black pepper

Preheat the oven to 230°C and use a little of the olive oil to lightly grease six 150 ml dariole moulds (ovenproof rounded coffee cups will do the job, too). Caramelise the garlic cloves very slowly in the remaining olive oil with the thyme in a saucepan over low heat, taking care not to burn them, then set the pan aside. Roast and peel the capsicums as described on page 40, coating them with the oil used to caramelise the garlic (reserve the garlic but discard the thyme). Reduce the oven temperature to 200°C.

In a food processor, purée the roasted capsicums with the juices from the roasting pan and the reserved caramelised garlic (you need 50 g purée). Blend the egg yolks and cream into the purée and season, then transfer to a bowl. Spoon the pâté into the prepared moulds, then stand them in a roasting tray of warm water (the water should come two-thirds of the way up the sides of the moulds) and bake for 45 minutes. If serving as a pâté, then cool to room temperature in the water bath and refrigerate until required. This dish can also be served hot as an entrée with hollandaise sauce, in which case it is called a mousse.

SQUAB WITH RED CAPSICUM PANCAKES *Serves 6*

These capsicum pancakes can also be served with goat's cheese warmed over them or as an adjunct to a dish of ratatouille.

sea salt flakes and freshly ground
    black pepper
6 × 450 g squabs
1 lemon
butter, for cooking
50 ml balsamic vinegar
600 ml reduced Golden Chicken Stock
    (see page 57)

PANCAKES
6 deep-red capsicums
squeeze of lemon juice
1 tablespoon extra virgin olive oil
1 free-range egg
200 ml milk
135 g self-raising flour
sea salt flakes and freshly ground
    black pepper
butter, for cooking

Preheat the oven to 230°C. To prepare the pancake batter, roast and peel the capsicums as described on page 40, then increase the oven temperature to the highest possible. Squeeze a little lemon juice over the roasted capsicums and purée them in a food processor with the olive oil (you should have 500 g purée). In a large bowl, mix the egg and milk, then add the flour. Stir in the capsicum purée, then season the batter very well and leave it to stand in the refrigerator while you prepare and cook the squab.

Season the cavity of each bird and squeeze in a little lemon juice. Heat a little butter in a frying pan until it is nut-brown and add a dash of olive oil to inhibit burning, then seal the birds on all sides over medium heat and transfer to a roasting pan. Roast for 8–10 minutes, then remove from the pan and leave to rest, breast-side down, for a good 10 minutes before serving.

While the squabs are roasting, cook the pancakes one at a time in a little melted butter in a heavy-based frying pan over low–medium heat. These pancakes need to be cooked very slowly, so that the outside is nut-brown and the inside is cooked. The batter makes 6 thick rustic pancakes. Wipe out the pan and add more butter each time before cooking the next pancake.

Drain the fat from the roasting pan, then deglaze the pan with the balsamic vinegar and reduced stock and boil vigorously until the sauce reaches your desired consistency. I prefer to serve each squab sitting on a pancake rather than carving the birds. Pour the sauce over the birds and serve any extra in a jug at the table.

Cherry clafoutis (see page 49)

CHERRIES

THE MENTION OF CHERRIES MAKES ME THINK IMMEDIATELY OF Cherry Ripe. Nowadays this has a double meaning, since one of our great food commentators and author of *Goodbye Culinary Cringe* shares that name with the childhood-favourite chocolate bar I would eat furtively from the corner shop. I always claim that I don't have a sweet tooth, but each time my children hear me saying so, they chorus derisively, 'and she only listens to the ABC too!', as they think these are my catch-cries in life. But it's exactly what my mother used to say, and yet when needing a sugar fix it was a Cherry Ripe she would reach for; it's the same for me, and it's the same for my children. All of us without a sweet tooth.

Cherries have also always meant Christmas to me. One year when I was very young and money was scarce, my mother explained in advance that there would be nothing under the Christmas tree that year, but she surprised us with huge bunches of cherries, a bottle of Coca-Cola and a small box of Old Gold chocolates each. Unbelievable treats for a child of five in 1950! Coca-Cola and chocolates aside, I have never had a Christmas since without bowls of ripe, juicy black cherries.

Cherries are graded by size, and size is related to price. A retailer will often have cherries at two or three prices, and you get what you pay for. Interestingly, retailers tell me they sell equal numbers of dear as cheap cherries, as the consumer is becoming more demanding. It's important for the industry to find a use for inferior cherries rather than selling them fresh for the table. This is more difficult now that the canning of cherries is almost non-existent in this country, but there are other possibilities, such as making liqueurs and chocolates.

The first cherries of the season always command a premium price simply based on supply and demand, and as cherries do not colour up or get any sweeter after picking, they should always be picked ripe. So getting those cherries to market is a race against the weather. Perfect hand-picked cherries will always demand a premium too, and so they should; the cherry grower has more chance of being wiped out by unseasonal storms than possibly any other fruit grower.

How I love the large juicy black ones to eat. There are many varieties to choose from and although at present only the more serious greengrocer or farmers' market will name the varieties, we the consumers can do our bit to change that by asking for more information. Some of the old-fashioned varieties of large black cherries like St Margaret or William's Favourite are still quite common. The American varieties such as Van and Stella, both of which have large blood-red fruit, and Bing, which has large bright-red fruit, have also become well established. These varieties are less acidic and their sweetness is more attractive to many, particularly the lucrative Asian export market.

As cherries have such a short season from flowering to maturity, fewer chemicals are used on them than any other fruit tree. But the risk in growing cherries commercially is

great. At the end of October the farmer assesses what their crop will be based on how each tree has 'set'; yet so many things can go wrong at the last moment that this prediction is often way off the mark. Too much rain can result in fruit splitting, and in forty-eight hours a wonderful crop can be lost; then there is the potential for hail, frost and strong winds to contend with. The early fruit is subject to bird attack and, other than netting, there is not much one can do. (Netting brings the potential for other problems: keeping predatory birds out means you also keep the helpful insect-eating birds away.)

A number of years ago I had organised to buy a small crop of morello cherries to pickle for Stephanie Alexander, who was having difficulty finding enough fruit. Everything was arranged – the ingredients, the jars, the staff – and then I had a call from the grower. The crop was lost virtually overnight in a storm. It's a very vulnerable position to be in as a farmer, particularly if the crop is your sole source of income. Having learnt from Stephanie just how good sour morello cherries are for pickling, and, even with good weather conditions, finding it very difficult to buy them commercially, I finally have quite a mature morello cherry tree whose small fruit hangs defiantly against the birds (it's obvious they don't have my palate). Sadly, our only access to morellos commercially is the imported 4.25 kg tins. The other cherry tree in my orchard is the first tree to ripen each year, but I seldom get to beat the birds.

While being parochial, I think the best cherries in Australia come from the Adelaide Hills (I know other areas would dispute that, but for me it is an issue of access to fruit with minimal transportation time). But now that chilled and cushioned transport is available, cherry-growing regions are being selected for their climate rather than their proximity to markets. In South Australia, cherries are also grown in the southeast of the state and in the Riverland, where the fruit is ready weeks ahead of Adelaide's. In Victoria, there are cherry orchards in the foothills of the Dandenongs and near Wangaratta in the northeast, while Young and Orange are the major cherry-growing areas in New South Wales.

For years I have used a dehydrator, originally bought decades ago to dry a glut of strawberries. Whilst I love morellos dried, because of their smaller size it is easier to pickle them, but any dried cherry is such a treat to add to cereal, muffins or any number of desserts – perhaps even homemade Cherry Ripes! Dried cherries are now available in some organic markets and top grocery shops.

I have to admit that I am far more likely to cook with dried cherries than fresh ones. Fresh cherries are in season for such a short time that I relish eating them with no adornment. However, I have enjoyed fresh cherries poached in red wine with sugar, cinnamon and lemon rind, much as one cooks pears. I also love using fresh cherries in a Clafoutis (see page 49). I remember well the first years of the Pheasant Farm Restaurant when it was just me and an apprentice. I had no skill or interest in making desserts, so I enlisted the help of a local cook to teach me. We tried a cherry clafoutis – and nothing sold. The next day we made another batch but called it cherry pudding. Nothing was left.

Brandied cherries are worth having in the cupboard: the cherries and their juice can be spooned over vanilla ice cream or used in a rich chocolate cake – adapt the recipe for Chocolate Cake with a Fig Centre and Ganache on page 226. Bill Bishop, who was a driving force in the early stages of Adelaide's cherry industry, recommends layering sugar, brandy and cherries, a third of a cup at a time, in a sterilised preserving jar and then screwing down the lid tightly before leaving to mature for three months. Bill says the juice is also delightful to drink!

In late 1996 I was planning a banquet to be held at the Park Hyatt in Tokyo to launch our products in Japan. The very Australian menu featured our pâté, smoked kangaroo, marron, venison, Woodside goat's cheese, Heidi Gruyère and Farmers Union matured cheddar with our quince paste, and was to end with a fresh cherry tart. Our distributor and host Toshio Yasuma had chosen Mountadam wines to accompany each course. The night before my departure I was told that the cherry crop in Tasmania had been affected by an outbreak of moth and my cherries couldn't be air-freighted to Tokyo – disaster! In a flash of inspiration I remembered the buckets of pickled morello cherries from the previous season. I had them vacuum-sealed and packed them in my suitcase (I declared them!). I made an almond tart and layered the pastry case with the cherries before adding the filling, for which I was given a 1935 brandy to use. This was served with a choice of Mountadam's ratafias: the chardonnay ratafia tasted of almonds and the pinot noir version tasted of cherries – the perfect accompaniments.

LEW KATHREPTIS'S PICKLED CHERRIES   *Makes 1 litre*

I like to pickle fresh cherries, a simple process, and prefer to use morello cherries for their sharpness and because they shrivel less during pickling. I used to follow a recipe in *Jane Grigson's Fruit Book* until I found another from former Adelaide chef Lew Kathreptis in *Stephanie's Australia*. I make jars and jars of these each year, leaving them for about six weeks to mature. Occasionally I find a jar in the back of the cupboard that is more than a year old – and the cherries are always still good! Pickled cherries are great to serve with pâté, duck or pork rillettes, terrines, hams or pickled pork. I also serve pickled morello cherries with pheasant roasted with rosemary and pancetta – the tartness of the morellos offsets the richness of the dish. If you want to use the cherries in a sweet dish, just leave out the garlic.

850 ml white-wine vinegar

700 g sugar

24 black peppercorns

12 cloves

6 bay leaves

1 clove garlic

1 kg morello cherries

Boil all ingredients except the cherries in a stainless steel saucepan for 10 minutes, then leave to cool completely.

Meanwhile, wash and dry the cherries thoroughly, discarding any that are bruised or marked. Trim the stalks to 1 cm long, then pack the fruit into a sterilised 1-litre preserving jar. Pour the cold syrup over the cherries, then seal and store for at least a month (I use mine after six weeks, but they will keep indefinitely).

CHERRY MUFFINS   *Makes 12*

135 g plain flour

2 teaspoons baking powder

pinch salt

2 heaped tablespoons brown sugar

90 g rolled oats

100 g unsalted butter, melted and cooled

1 egg

1 tablespoon walnut oil

185 ml buttermilk

300 g fresh cherries, washed, stemmed and pitted *or* 150 g dried cherries

Preheat the oven to 180°C and lightly grease a 12-hole muffin tin. Combine the flour, baking powder, salt, sugar and oats in a bowl and make a well in the centre. Mix the cooled melted butter into the flour with the egg, oil and buttermilk. Fold in the cherries, then two-thirds fill the holes of the muffin tin. Bake for about 20 minutes or until a fine skewer inserted into a muffin comes out clean, then cool the muffins on a wire rack.

CHERRY CLAFOUTIS   *Serves 6*

I prefer not to pit cherries when making a tart such as this, as the stone helps keep the shape and flavour of the fruit intact. Be sure to warn your guests, though, before they tuck in.

500 g fresh dark cherries	**¼ cup (50 g) plain flour**
1 tablespoon castor sugar	**½ cup (125 ml) crème fraîche *or* sour cream**
2 tablespoons kirsch	**½ cup (125 ml) cream**
	grated rind of 1 lemon
CUSTARD	**butter, for baking**
2 large eggs	**icing sugar, for dusting**
¼ cup (55 g) castor sugar	

Preheat the oven to 200°C. Place the cherries in a shallow baking dish and sprinkle the castor sugar and kirsch over them. Bake for 5–6 minutes or until the cherries are cooked but still firm. Set the cherries aside and reserve the cooking juices.

For the custard, beat the eggs in an electric mixer, then add the castor sugar and beat until frothy. Carefully add the flour and combine, then add 1 tablespoon of the reserved cherry cooking juices, the crème fraîche, cream and lemon rind.

Dot a gratin or small baking dish with a little butter (I use a 30 cm oval copper baking dish), then spread half the custard over the base of the dish. Spoon in the cooked cherries to cover the custard, then add the remaining custard. Bake for 25–30 minutes; the top will be golden and the cherries will appear as little mounds in the custard. Serve warm, dusted with icing sugar.

CHICKEN

THOSE OF YOU WHO ARE AROUND MY AGE WILL REMEMBER JUST how good chicken used to taste when we were children. I know it's difficult for young people to imagine, but roast chicken on Sunday was a very special treat. Added to that was the fact that the only way you had such a meal was if you had a chook pen in the backyard and were up to performing the necessary tasks to bring the bird to the table yourself. Of course, that meant that the bird was hand-plucked, which added to the flavour – something I never realised at the time.

It was in 1991 that I discovered the difference dry-plucking makes during a short stint in the Hyatt Hotel's kitchens in Adelaide, when Urs Inauen was in charge of the now-defunct Fleurieu Restaurant. Urs and I, together with fellow chefs Cheong Liew and Tom Milligan, were preparing our challenge for the Seppelt Australian Menu of the Year and all game to enter the kitchen was dry-plucked by the cooks and apprentices. The resulting guinea fowl, and the stock made from the bones, had a flavour superior to anything I had ever tasted – due, I believe, to the dry-plucking. To compound my belief, during a holiday in Umbria I was struck by the amazing flavour of the poultry. I'm sure it was the result of the birds being raised by small-scale breeders who dry-plucked them. It makes sense when you think about it: dry-plucking leaves the layer of fat under the skin intact. Fat means flavour, and, as you know, you can always take both the skin and fat off after cooking (if you are strong-willed enough).

I decided to test this new-found theory of mine at home. I roasted two well-brought-up chooks – one corn-fed and dry-plucked and the other free-ranged but wet-plucked – side by side for flavour comparison, using the basic method in Stuffed Roast Chicken on page 58 (I didn't stuff the corn-fed bird, which took about 10 minutes less to cook). Both were excellent, but the corn-fed, dry-plucked chicken was both sweeter and more intense in flavour and seemed to have a tighter, or denser, texture. The corn-fed bird certainly released a lot more fat than the other, so next time I would sit the bird on a trivet (a small

Roast tarragon chicken (see page 53)

cake rack would do the trick). The breast browned extraordinarily well; in fact I considered putting a buttered brown-paper 'hat' over the breast to protect it (much as my mother would have put a herbed and buttered piece of cheesecloth on the breast of a turkey).

Don't hold out hopes of seeing a rash of dry-plucked birds on the market, however, as the procedure is incredibly labour-intensive and it is hard to get producers to commit to it; but if you get the opportunity, it is worth paying extra for. Any farmer specialising in delivering poultry to a niche market should consider this process.

Time has marched on incredibly since my childhood, and we can now see both ends of the quality spectrum in the chicken market. Today we can conveniently buy chicken in every conceivable form and cut, yet sadly the majority is mass-produced. Whilst it's great

to be able to buy just the breast or the legs, or bones for stock as it suits, the compromise in flavour is one I will not accept. And the current fashion of selling breasts and legs skinless is deplorable. The fat from the skin of the chicken does *not* permeate the meat during cooking. In other words, cook with the skin on and, if you are worried by the fat, take the skin off afterwards. The skin provides the meat with natural protection, and cooking without it makes achieving a succulent piece of chicken almost impossible.

But thankfully there are real exceptions to this and in each state there are specialist free-range poultry producers raising birds whose flavour is so superior to the mass-produced birds they almost need another name to identify them. And of course that is what happens – these farmers 'brand' their produce. In South Australia we first had Kangaroo Island chook, a really great product, and of course my daughter Saskia's Barossa Chooks. Ian Milburn of Glenloth Game in northwest Victoria has long been providing wonderful corn-fed chickens to the restaurant industry, as well as his fabulous squab. There is a smattering of these top-class producers in every state. Your first move is to find a quality butcher and ask the right questions. Are their chickens free-range? What are they fed on? Are they grown slowly and naturally to maturity without preventative doses of antibiotics?

I have a lot to share about Barossa Chooks – funnily enough, my favourite chook of all. Eating them now is almost an everyday matter, as it would be for the families of any of the handful of great poultry producers who grow what I have long called 'well-brought-up chooks'. I certainly urge anyone who has the opportunity to purchase any of these birds to do so, as the difference between these and their battery-farmed cousins is as chalk to cheese. Even among the best of the producers there are quite specific points of difference, and certainly one that I know from my close association with Barossa Chooks – no secret here – is that they are reared on a totally vegetarian diet. The legume, wheat and corn mix the chooks feed on results in such a profound difference in flavour from that of chooks fed on protein derived from fish- and meat-meal. There is no doubt that the corn in the diet results in greater amounts of fat under the skin and a lot more marbling than other diets – but what flavour it produces.

It has been a bit of a standing joke in our family that, when the girls were growing up, I would never cook a roast dinner. Yet I had a real reminder of how easy it can be when Saskia asked Colin and I to dinner one night while her husband, Greg, was away. Despite working all day, with her youngest Rory only nine months old, Lilly five years old and Max seven, Saskia cooked a roast Barossa Chook so delicious and so evocative of my childhood, but with an absolute minimum of fuss. The 2.3 kg chicken had been stuffed under the skin with butter and lots of tarragon from the garden. Red onions, young carrots, waxy potatoes and pumpkin had all been cut into large chunks – none of them peeled – and scattered around the chook in the roasting pan, then a cup of verjuice (but it could easily have been wine) was poured into the base of the pan. The lovely thing about this meal is that it took 1 hour and 10 minutes in a hot oven without even being looked at; a truly beautiful roast chook, full of memories of the time when this was the most special meal we would ever have – those tastes, those feelings were all there and I absolutely loved it!

That perfect, simple meal reminded me of the first time I ever dined with my friend Stephanie Alexander, around twenty years ago; we had roast tarragon chicken. It was so wonderful I suspect it must have come from Ian Milburn, even in those days. To make the tarragon butter for a 2.2 kg chook, mix together 1 tablespoon freshly chopped tarragon leaves and 100 g unsalted butter, add a squeeze of lemon juice and season with sea salt and freshly ground black pepper. Spread the butter under the skin of the chook before roasting.

So here we have a call for the return of roast chook as the pièce de résistance. Stuffed Roast Chicken is such a family favourite – see the recipe on page 58. But if you don't have time to make a stuffing, tuck three squashed garlic cloves, rosemary, thyme and a good squeeze of lemon in the bird's cavity. Drizzle the skin with extra virgin olive oil and rub sea salt flakes all over, then cook it exactly as for the stuffed chook. Remember, the quality of the chook makes all the difference in the world.

My friend Damien Pignolet has been so generous with his knowledge over the years, both with the recipes he sends me on a whim (simply because he knows I would love to hear of yet another way in which he's using verjuice in his cooking), and as a sounding board for new products I have developed (he always comes back to me with an incredibly detailed and considered opinion). One very special memory was when Damien asked me to cook a course for his 50th birthday celebrations, at an intimate luncheon for around 30 people at his home. The very fact that Damien – such a perfectionist, and a chef of immense technical ability and 'feel' combined – had asked me, an absolutely haphazard cook, to contribute was a great feeling. I remember his incredibly compact kitchen, with everything you could possibly need to hand, but not that much space (especially with a couple of cooks/chefs in the kitchen, each of us presenting one course) and feeling nervous as anything. Somehow

I managed to bring it all together – a ballottine of boned Barossa Chook stuffed with livers, onions, bacon and herbs, baked slowly and already resting well before the guests arrived, so I could enjoy the party too. Simple as it was, I was inordinately proud that Damien loved the dish.

Carving at the table may be a lost art to many, but there is nothing wrong with using kitchen scissors to divide the spoils. I've yet to see a family that doesn't fight over the breast and leg meat! My mother always pinched the wings before they came to the table, just as I always commandeer the pope's nose (although if Saskia is here, there's a fight for it). My favourite bits of all are the pickings from the bones. I would actually prefer to make a meal of them, but it doesn't seem right if everyone else is being delicate. Besides, I'd probably have to share my tidbits in this family. I have often delighted in the Italian tradition where the carcass of the carved bird is brushed with olive oil and put back onto the spit for a few minutes before it is gnawed at by all and sundry. My kind of food!

It's important to cook chicken just perfectly, so that it's not pink at the bone when you are serving it. To achieve this, the bird should be removed from the oven while the meat is, in fact, still pink at the bone, then left to rest for 20–30 minutes, turned upside-down so that the juices run down over the breast (don't worry, the bird will stay warm for this length of time). It is this resting period that finishes the cooking. Overcooking means a dry and stringy bird, no matter how good its credentials are.

If you wish to have some sort of juice to serve with your roast chicken without actually making a sauce or gravy, the trick is to 'wet-roast' the bird by adding 125 ml verjuice, water, stock or wine to the roasting pan at the start of cooking, and spooning an extra 60–125 ml of it over the bird as it comes out of the oven to rest. A delicious jus forms in the bottom of the pan, especially if the bird was initially smeared with butter and had a couple of rosemary sprigs placed across its breast and the juice of half a lemon squeezed into the cavity before roasting. Another alternative is to make a warm vinaigrette. Cook 6 finely sliced shallots in 80 ml extra virgin olive oil in a small saucepan over very low heat until translucent (or I often use a nut oil such as almond). Deglaze the pan with 2 tablespoons sherry vinegar, then add a little lemon rind and thyme and whisk in 100–120 ml jus from the roasting pan after separating the fat from it.

Don't think, however, that roasting or pan-frying are the only ways to go with chicken. I love a chook (always with giblets) simmered in stock and left to cool until it becomes jellied, and even now I turn to chicken noodle soup when I'm feeling below par – and whenever my younger daughter Elli is feeling unwell she still comes home and asks for it too. It's such wonderful comfort food.

I also like to grill or barbecue chicken. To do this I 'spatchcock' the bird by cutting out the backbone with kitchen scissors or a sharp knife, then I marinate the flattened bird breast-side down. Try a marinade of extra virgin olive oil, thyme, freshly ground black pepper and strips of preserved lemon or slices of meyer lemon, or perhaps just extra virgin olive oil, sprigs of rosemary and slivers of garlic. I season the chicken just before cooking and position it about 15 cm from the heat source. The chicken is grilled skin-side up for about 5 minutes to brown it, then turned over and brushed with more marinade and grilled for about 4 minutes. The skin side is grilled again for 3 minutes, making the cooking time 12 minutes in all. Then I leave the bird to rest, breast-side down, for at least 10 minutes before serving. To cook the same bird on the barbecue, the chicken needs to be turned every minute or two after the skin has caramelised for 10 minutes, so that the skin doesn't char to oblivion.

Chicken on the barbecue is especially good, particularly poussin weighing between 400 and 500 g. 'Spatchcock' or butterfly each bird as described above then place in a marinade of extra virgin olive oil, fresh herbs (particularly rosemary or basil) and some thin slices of lemon. Shake off any excess oil before barbecuing as it tends to make the flames flare. Chicken takes a little longer to cook than most meat (this size bird should take about 20 minutes) and must be turned halfway through cooking, or earlier if it starts to burn too much on one side. Always test chicken for doneness by inserting a skewer into the thickest part – if the juices run clear, it should be cooked. It is essential to rest the cooked bird for at least 10 minutes, so keep the hungry hordes at bay.

Give barbecued chicken another dimension by using a post-cooking marinade instead of a pre-cooking one. In a flat dish, place grapes, grape or lemon juice, extra virgin olive oil and some sea salt, plus any roasted nuts you might have, or sliced fresh figs, then toss the cooked chicken with this and leave for about 15 minutes before serving. The resting chook will soak up all these flavours. The meat won't go cold and will be succulent and juicy – everyone will want to suck on the bones.

If butterflying poussins seems like too much trouble, thighs with the skin and bones intact are the easiest alternative, as each piece will be of relatively even thickness. Cook as per the poussin, but for about 10 minutes in all, and rest in the same way.

The best way I have found to cook chicken breasts is to seal them gently in nut-brown butter in an ovenproof heavy-based frying pan over low–medium heat, then to put them into a hot (230°C) oven for 4–6 minutes, depending on their thickness. Check the cooking by lifting up the little under-fillet; the flesh should be pink but not at all raw. Rest the chicken, turned over, for the same length of time it took to cook – the cooking will continue while the breast is resting and the meat will no longer be pink but lovely and moist. Degrease the browning pan and deglaze it with verjuice, then serve the chicken with these juices and a savoury jelly such as the cabernet or vino cotto jelly we make for our Farmshop, or Crabapple and Sage Jelly (see page 210).

Golden chicken stock

For a truly great sandwich, combine leftover chicken with a verjuice mayonnaise. In an electric mixer, food processor or, if you are really keen, a non-reactive bowl, mix 2 egg yolks with 60 ml verjuice and 1 teaspoon of your favourite mustard. Whisk until emulsified and then slowly drizzle in a mixture of 125 ml extra virgin olive oil and 125 ml grapeseed oil to combine and emulsify; you may need a little more oil to reach the desired consistency as the egg yolks' ability to take the oil will vary, but 250 ml should be close. Season to taste with 1 teaspoon salt, ¼ teaspoon freshly ground black pepper and ¼ teaspoon castor sugar, then stir in 1 dessertspoon freshly chopped tarragon. Fill slices of good-quality bread with diced chicken breast mixed with the mayonnaise and either watercress sprigs or shredded iceberg lettuce.

I cannot write a chapter on chicken without mentioning offal. Other than an orange cake I made for my grandmother on my eighth birthday, offal was the first meal I ever cooked. I remember clearly my dish of chicken livers: they were done in butter with herbs (most likely dried). I also remember being so thrilled with the flavour that my lifelong habit of picking as I cooked was established that day!

At the Pheasant Farm Restaurant I always kept emergency rations for when other dishes were in short supply. My secret was confit. I confited the hearts, giblets and livers of good free-range chooks separately and stored them immersed in duck fat in the cool room. If I ran out of a dish on what was always a very limited menu, I would offer a *salade gourmande*, which consisted of these delicacies offset by preserved lemons or pickled green walnuts and bitter greens. It was a beautiful dish and worth having in reserve because anyone who had it (given they loved offal) never regretted that their original choice had been unavailable.

GOLDEN CHICKEN STOCK
Makes about 2 litres

I just can't cook without a good stock, and a chook stock is the one I use most of all. While there are a few good stocks on the market, usually made by small producers, for me nothing touches the homemade. There is something incredibly rewarding about having a pot of stock simmering on the stove, especially knowing that, either reduced or frozen, it might keep you going for a month. It takes so little work and adds so much to your cooking that I urge you to do it.

The better the quality of the original chook the better your stock will be. The skin and bones (with a generous amount of meat still attached) of a mature, well-brought-up bird has not only better flavour but more gelatinous quality. It's truly important not to overcook a stock; your benchmark should be that the meat on the bones is still sweet. An overcooked stock has all the goodness cooked out of it, and the bones have a chalky flavour.

I tend to make my stock in a large batch and then freeze it in 1-litre containers. Using fresh 'bright' vegetables rather than limp leftovers, and roasting the bones and veg before simmering them, gives the stock a wonderful golden colour and a deeper flavour. You only need use enough water to cover the bones and veg by about 7 cm in your stockpot (this way in most cases your stock won't need reducing). Never allow your stock to boil, just bring it to a good simmer, and don't skim it as you'll take the fat – and the flavour – off with it (you can remove the fat easily after the cooked stock has been refrigerated.) Don't let the stock sit in the pan once it is cooked: strain it straight away, then let it cool before refrigerating.

1 large boiling chicken (about 2.2 kg), cut into pieces (if you are using bones only, you will need 3 kg)

2 large onions, unpeeled and halved

1 large carrot, roughly chopped

extra virgin olive oil, for cooking

100 ml white wine (optional)

1 large leek, trimmed, cleaned and roughly chopped

1 stick celery, roughly chopped

1 bay leaf

6 sprigs thyme

6 stalks flat-leaf parsley

1 head garlic, halved widthways

2 very ripe tomatoes, roughly chopped

Preheat the oven to 200°C. Place the chicken pieces, onion and carrot in a roasting pan and drizzle with a little olive oil. Roast for 20 minutes or until chicken and vegetables are golden brown.

Transfer the chicken and vegetables to a large stockpot, then deglaze the roasting pan with wine over high heat, if using. Add the wine with the remaining vegetables and herbs to the pot, and cover with about 2.5 litres water. Simmer, uncovered, for 3–4 hours.

Strain the stock straight away through a sieve into a bowl, then cool by immersing the bowl in a sink of cold water. Refrigerate the stock to let any fat settle on the surface, then remove the fat.

The stock will keep for up to 4 days in the refrigerator or for 3 months in the freezer. To reduce the stock, boil in a saucepan over high heat until it is reduced by three-quarters. When the reduced stock is chilled in the refrigerator, it should set as a jelly; if not, reduce again. Jellied stock will keep in the refrigerator for 2–3 days, and in the freezer for 3 months.

STUFFED ROAST CHICKEN

Serves 6

If you are roasting a supermarket chook, I'll warrant that this recipe for our family stuffing will be serious competition for the chicken itself. I really urge you, however, to seek out birds grown to maturity by small producers – then the combination of succulent, flavoursome flesh and our stuffing will return roast chicken to its place of honour on the table!

I have a variety of timers in my kitchen that I use constantly, and you might find one useful for this recipe. I'm always doing six things at once and it's all too easy to get distracted and forget to turn the chook or put the vegies on.

100 g bacon, rind removed, meat cut
    into matchsticks

1 large onion, finely chopped

¼ cup (60 ml) extra virgin olive oil

120 g chicken livers, trimmed

3 cups (210 g) coarse stale breadcrumbs

1 sprig rosemary, leaves stripped and
    finely chopped

¼ cup flat-leaf parsley leaves

2 teaspoons thyme leaves

1 × 2.4 kg free-range *or* corn-fed chicken

sea salt flakes and freshly ground
    black pepper

1 lemon

butter, for cooking

Preheat the oven to 180°C. Cook the bacon in a dry frying pan over high heat. Sauté the onion in the same pan over medium heat in half of the olive oil, then drain the excess fat from the frying pan. Sear the livers on both sides in the same pan for 2–3 minutes over medium heat, then rest them for a few minutes before slicing (the livers should still be pink in the middle).

Toast the breadcrumbs with the remaining olive oil in a roasting pan in the oven until golden, watching that they don't burn. Mix all the herbs in a bowl with the onion, bacon, livers and breadcrumbs.

Season the inside of the chicken with salt, pepper and a squeeze of lemon juice, then fill the cavity with the stuffing. Smear the outside of the chicken with butter and sprinkle with salt and pepper. Squeeze the rest of the lemon juice over the bird.

Roast the chicken on one side in a roasting pan for 20 minutes. (If the bird is browning unevenly, you may need to use a trivet or a potato to raise the unbrowned end. You may also find that a splash of water or stock needs to be added to the pan to prevent the juices burning.) Turn the bird over onto its other side and cook for another 20 minutes. Turn the chicken breast-side up and cook for another 20 minutes.

Once the chicken is cooked, remove it from the oven and turn it breast-side down to rest, covered, for at least 20 minutes before carving.

CHICKEN BREASTS WITH ROSEMARY, PINE NUTS AND VERJUICE
Serves 4

⅓ cup (55 g) raisins

¼ cup (60 ml) verjuice

2 sprigs rosemary

⅓ cup (80 ml) extra virgin olive oil,
    plus extra for drizzling

freshly ground black pepper

4 free-range chicken breasts, skin on

⅓ cup (50 g) pine nuts

1 tablespoon butter

sea salt flakes

Salsa Agresto (see page 22), to serve

Soak the raisins in the verjuice overnight. (Alternately, microwave the raisins and verjuice on the defrost setting for about 5 minutes, then leave to cool.) »

Strip the rosemary leaves and reserve for another use. Place the stalks in a bowl with 60 ml of the olive oil and a little pepper. Add the chicken breasts and marinate for at least 1 hour.

Preheat the oven to 220°C. Moisten the pine nuts with a little olive oil and roast on a baking tray for 5 minutes or until golden brown; keep an eye on them as they burn easily.

Heat the butter until golden brown in a frying pan large enough to accommodate all the chicken breasts with lots of space between them; otherwise, cook the chicken in batches. Add the remaining tablespoon of olive oil to the pan to inhibit burning, then salt the chicken breasts and pan-fry, skin-side down, over medium heat for 6–10 minutes or until well sealed and golden. Turn and cook on the other side for 3–4 minutes or until cooked through. (The total cooking time will depend on the thickness of the breasts, but as a rule, two-thirds of the cooking should be done on the skin side.) Season the chicken with salt and pepper, then rest in a warm place, skin-side down.

Discard any butter left in the pan and toss in the raisins and the verjuice, then deglaze the pan over high heat until the liquid has reduced by half. Stir in the pine nuts.

Pour the sauce over the chicken and serve with Salsa Agresto. If serving for lunch, then accompany with a salad of peppery greens. For an evening meal, serve with soft polenta (see page 62) or potatoes mashed with extra virgin olive oil.

BONED CHICKEN STUFFED WITH
GIBLETS AND PROSCIUTTO

Serves 4

½ cup (125 ml) verjuice

4 litres reduced Golden Chicken Stock
    (see page 57)

1 × 1.6 kg boned free-range chicken
    (ask your butcher to do this)

sea salt flakes

STUFFING

100 g chicken giblets, cleaned and
    sliced widthways

100 g chicken hearts

butter, for cooking

2 tablespoons freshly chopped herbs
    (preferably rosemary and marjoram)

freshly ground black pepper

1 large onion, roughly chopped

2 cups (140 g) coarse stale breadcrumbs

extra virgin olive oil, for cooking

200 g thinly sliced prosciutto, finely chopped

1 teaspoon Dijon mustard

Preheat the oven to 220°C. To make the stuffing, cook the giblets and hearts in a small frying pan over medium heat in a little butter with the herbs and a grind of black pepper, then chop them finely and set aside in a medium-sized bowl. Sweat the onion in some more butter over low heat, then add it to the giblet mixture. Toast the breadcrumbs with a little olive oil in a roasting pan in the oven until golden, watching that they don't burn. Add the prosciutto, mustard and breadcrumbs to the giblet mixture.

In a deep saucepan over high heat, reduce the verjuice by half. Add the stock to the pan and heat until warm. Flatten out the boned chicken, skin-side down, and spread it with the

stuffing, then roll up the chicken and season with salt. Wrap the chicken in a double thickness of muslin (or an old tea towel or large Chux), then secure each end with kitchen string so it is shaped like a bonbon.

Put the stuffed bird into a large saucepan with the warm stock mixture – it is important that at least three-quarters of the bird is immersed. Poach for 20 minutes over low heat at a very gentle simmer, then turn the bird over and poach it for another 20 minutes. Remove the bird and wrap it in foil to rest for 30 minutes. Reduce the poaching liquid over high heat to a sauce consistency.

Slice the stuffed chicken and serve it with the sauce and a dollop of Salsa Verde (see page 581).

BAROSSA CHOOK WITH GREEN OLIVES, FENNEL AND SOFT POLENTA

Serves 6–8

1 × 2.3 kg Barossa Chook, cut into 12 pieces
1 cup (250 ml) extra virgin olive oil,
    plus extra for drizzling
½ cup (125 ml) verjuice
2 pieces preserved lemon, flesh removed,
    rind rinsed and chopped
1 sprig rosemary
1 large fennel bulb, diced
1 large onion, diced
1 clove garlic, finely chopped
sea salt flakes and freshly ground
    black pepper
1 cup (250 ml) Golden Chicken Stock
    (see page 57)

1 × 400 g can crushed tomatoes *or*
    400 ml tomato sugo (see Glossary)
    with basil
120 g green olives

POLENTA
2 cups (500 ml) milk
1 cup (250 ml) Golden Chicken Stock
    (see page 57)
100 g butter
125 g fine polenta
sea salt flakes and freshly ground
    black pepper
¼ cup freshly grated Parmigiano Reggiano
    (optional), to serve

Marinate the chicken pieces in a large bowl with the olive oil, verjuice, preserved lemon and rosemary in the refrigerator for a few hours or overnight.

Preheat the oven to 180°C. Transfer the chicken to a roasting pan, reserving the marinade. Add the fennel, onion and garlic to the pan, drizzle with a little olive oil and season well with salt and pepper. Brown the chicken and vegetables in the oven for 10–20 minutes. Remove the pan from the oven and reset the temperature to 160°C. Deglaze the pan with a little of the reserved marinade over high heat on the stove, then add the chicken stock, tomatoes and olives. Turn the chicken pieces and roast for another 20 minutes, then turn them to the other side and roast for another 20 minutes. Remove from the oven and rest the chicken pieces, skin-side down, in the tomatoey juices.

Meanwhile, to make the polenta, bring the milk, stock and butter to scalding point in a saucepan over medium heat. Whisk in the polenta, then reduce the heat to low and season with salt and pepper. Stir the polenta for 30 minutes; there is no other way to get a creamy result, and under-cooked polenta is a pale imitation of its perfectly cooked cousin! When it is ready, stir in the Parmigiano Reggiano, if using.

Spoon the soft polenta onto a platter and top with the rested chicken and sauce. Sautéed spinach or silverbeet is a great accompaniment to this meal.

CHICKEN BREASTS STUFFED WITH APRICOTS AND GREEN PEPPERCORNS

Serves 4

8 dried apricots
verjuice, for soaking
160 g unsalted butter, at room temperature, chopped
2 teaspoons chopped green peppercorns
2 tablespoons freshly chopped flat-leaf parsley

2 teaspoons chopped thyme
4 × 250–300 g free-range chicken breast fillets, skin on
sea salt flakes and freshly ground black pepper
extra virgin olive oil, for frying

Preheat the oven to 180°C. Place the apricots and a little verjuice or water to cover in a small saucepan and simmer over low heat until apricots are plump and hydrated. Remove from the heat and leave to cool, then drain and roughly chop.

Mix the butter, apricots, peppercorns and herbs in a bowl with your hands; this stops the ingredients from breaking up too much. Divide the butter mixture into quarters. Push one quarter of the mixture gently under the skin of each breast, then run your hand over the skin to create a smooth surface.

Heat a little olive oil in a large frying pan over medium–high heat, season each breast with salt, then sear until golden on both sides. Transfer chicken to a baking tray and roast for about 9 minutes or until cooked through. Remove from the oven and leave to rest in a warm spot for 10–15 minutes, then serve with steamed broccolini and smashed waxy potatoes with extra virgin olive oil.

ROAST CHICKEN WITH FIG, GRAPE, WALNUT AND BREAD SALAD

Serves 6–8

My first trip to San Francisco in twenty years was for the 'Fancy Food' Trade Show. As trade shows are notoriously exhausting, standing for between eight and ten hours a day, talking to every potential customer and telling the same story over and over again, there had to be some treats to keep me going. I was travelling with Wayne Lyons, my General Manager at the time, who had never been to the States. He was most amused that I had a list of restaurants to visit as he expected neither of us would have the energy to do anything more than grab a bite to eat by dinnertime. However, I had my priorities, and so on our only free night we managed to get a very late booking at Zuni Café. When we arrived at about 10 p.m. and our table wasn't quite ready, I suspect we were almost past hunger. I gave Wayne no choice at all and ordered the roast chicken with bread salad for two – it was very simple and just so remarkable.

I have used the principle of the way I think they cooked it in many different forms ever since. The essentials are firstly to have a great chook, and secondly to use great bread.

1 × 2 kg free-range *or* organic chicken,
    cut into 12 pieces
sea salt flakes
½ cup (125 ml) Golden Chicken Stock
    (see page 57)
2 tablespoons verjuice

MARINADE
2 cloves garlic, thinly sliced
⅓ cup (80 ml) verjuice
⅓ cup (80 ml) extra virgin olive oil
4 sprigs tarragon
freshly ground black pepper, to taste

SALAD
6 preserved vine leaves, patted dry
2 tablespoons unsalted butter, chopped
½ cup chopped walnuts
⅓ cup (80 ml) olive oil
3 thick slices wood-fired bread, crusts
    removed, cut into chunks
8 figs, halved
1½ tablespoons red-wine vinegar
¼ preserved lemon, flesh removed,
    rind rinsed and thinly sliced
1½ cups seedless green *or* black grapes
2 tablespoons freshly chopped
    flat-leaf parsley

Mix the marinade ingredients together and place in a sealed container with the chicken pieces. Refrigerate for 2–4 hours, turning once.

Preheat the oven to 200°C. Place the drumsticks in a roasting pan, season with salt and bake for 7–10 minutes. Remove the remaining chicken pieces from the marinade, add to the pan, season and bake for another 10 minutes or until golden and cooked through. Heat the stock in a small saucepan over high heat, then add to the roasting pan along with the verjuice. Cover with foil and leave to rest while you make the salad.

Reduce the oven temperature to 180°C. Place the vine leaves on a large baking tray, dot with butter and roast for 2 minutes or until crisp. Place the walnuts on another baking tray and lightly roast in the oven. Heat 2 tablespoons of the olive oil in a frying pan over medium heat, then add the bread and fig halves and fry until golden. Mix the vinegar and remaining olive oil in a large salad bowl, tasting to check that the flavour is balanced. Toss the bread, figs, walnuts, preserved lemon and grapes in the bowl with the dressing and season to taste. Add the chook pieces, pan juices, vine leaves and flat-leaf parsley and serve.

CHICKEN PIECES ROASTED WITH OLIVES, PRESERVED LEMON AND FENNEL

Serves 6

2 kg chicken thighs, skin on, trimmed
    of excess fat
2 preserved lemons, flesh removed,
    rind rinsed and cut into long strips
1 tablespoon fennel seeds *or* 1 fennel
    bulb (when in season), cut into
    1 cm-thick slices
freshly ground black pepper

extra virgin olive oil, for cooking
24 black olives (do not pit or the flavour
    will leach out; simply warn your guests)
sea salt flakes
1–2 tablespoons verjuice
lots of freshly chopped flat-leaf parsley,
    to serve

Toss the chicken (always with the skin on, even if you are strong-willed enough to take it off after cooking – it keeps the chicken moist) in a bowl with the preserved lemon, fennel seeds or fennel, some pepper and enough extra virgin olive oil to coat the ingredients. Leave to marinate for 1 hour.

Preheat the oven to 220°C. Divide the chicken and marinade between 2 shallow roasting pans, then add the olives and season with salt. Make sure the pans are large enough so that none of the pieces overlap and there is just enough oil to coat all the chicken. Roast for about 10 minutes.

Turn the chicken over and reset the oven to 180°C, then cook for another 10 minutes or until the chicken is cooked through, keeping an eye on it to make sure the marinade ingredients are not burning.

Remove from the oven, drizzle with verjuice and a tablespoon or two of good extra virgin olive oil and leave to rest, covered, for 15 minutes. Just before serving, add the parsley and use the pan juices to moisten the chicken.

CHOKOS

 I'M SURE THAT MY AUNT'S GARDEN IN ASHFIELD WAS THE norm when I was growing up in Sydney: chokos grew rampant through the compost, and the vines rambled over the back fence and into the lane behind. The humid climate obviously suited them, and as a child it seemed to me that jungles of chokos grew wild everywhere.

I'm talking of a long time ago, in the post-war period, when there was a limited range of vegetables on offer. I don't remember chokos being for sale in shops but there was such a glut of them every summer, and no one wasted anything in those days, so they were a staple. Not only that, but as the choko readily picks up the flavour of other foods it was often used to extend jams, which were themselves part of the breakfast ritual in most families then.

Few of my contemporaries share my positive memories of chokos, with my husband Colin going so far as to say they are a waste of space – however, I love them. I find them delicate, whereas others describe them as tasteless. I suspect it is a simple matter of the offending chokos having been cooked until they became grey and watery. I was lucky in that as bad a cook as my aunt was in general, she cooked two things to perfection: chokos and broad beans. She was a passionate gardener, so these vegetables went straight from the plant to the pot. Although she always peeled chokos (under running water so the sticky milk they exuded could be washed away), we ate them so often they were always quite small when picked; at this size their skin is hardly spiky at all and their flavour is more pronounced. My aunt usually steamed the chokos in a small wire basket in her pressure cooker, which meant they didn't become waterlogged.

These days, if I ever find tiny apple-green chokos in the market I rush home and steam them whole, then cut them in half and add lashings of butter, freshly ground black pepper and lemon juice and eat the lot – skin, seeds and all. If they are slightly larger, but still unmarked and bright green, I peel them, then sauté them in extra virgin olive oil with fresh thyme and garlic. For a speedy result, cook peeled and quartered chokos for 8 minutes in barely boiling, salted water before slicing them. I have also tried baking a large choko stuffed with spicy minced meat, but it's like cooking an overgrown zucchini: the vegetable is really just a tasteless vehicle cooked only so as not to be wasted. The secret is to relish tiny chokos in season – and to compost the rest.

As the choko is seldom written about, and even less frequently honoured, I remember clearly an article written years ago by Melbourne food teacher Penny Smith. In it she revealed that it had taken an overseas trip for her to realise the potential of a vegetable in her own backyard. She had ordered a salad of crab meat and coconut in Madagascar; a shredded, pale-green crunchy vegetable was a wonderful part of the dish. It was raw choko. Since reading Penny's article, raw choko has become part of my salads – but the choko must be young.

I wrote ten years ago that, of the ten specialised vegetable books I owned, only three mentioned chokos. Jane Grigson had once again not disappointed me, as in her *Vegetable Book* she devoted a chapter to it – under the name 'Chayote', as it is more commonly known elsewhere.

Jane had written of an Australian friend of hers who picked a huge choko weighing over a kilogram (I'm sure it would have made the *Guinness Book of Records* and the front pages of the local newspapers, but only as a curiosity). The friend took it into her kitchen where, I quote, 'it soon started to wander. A long pale stem with rudimentary leaves and clinging tendrils burst through the choko from the single flat seed, and explored every cranny of the room, a triffid of a plant, until it found the door. Then she disentangled it carefully and cradled the shrunken parent to a hollow she had made by the trellis, where it could take root and rampage fruitfully.'

Much closer to home, and so important in so many ways, is Stephanie Alexander's updated edition of *The Cook's Companion*, the book I go to first these days. Stephanie has the most encyclopaedic knowledge of food, and her book has a chapter on chokos full of all the information you could want – on the varieties and season, selection and storage, preparation and cooking, as well as recipes.

I wouldn't swap my Mediterranean climate for anything, but I occasionally long for a choko vine. I cannot resist buying a choko that is going to seed and am full of optimism as I plant it, but sadly I've yet to succeed.

CRAB AND CHOKO SALAD INSPIRED BY PENNY SMITH *Serves 4*

While my copy of Penny Smith's article is long gone, I still have my notes, and the few times I've been able to get young chokos by some fluke, have made the recipe using our

South Australian blue swimmer crabs. Even though you can buy already picked crab meat, it will never be as good as crab you catch yourself. If you do find good-quality picked crab meat make sure you take it out of its vacuum packaging an hour in advance to rid it of any plastic smell – check that no bits of shell remain and moisten the crab meat with a little extra virgin olive oil.

4–6 tiny chokos	sea salt flakes and freshly ground
1 tablespoon coconut milk	black pepper
2 tablespoons lemon juice	250 g cooked crab meat, freshly picked
100 ml fruity extra virgin olive oil	1 cup coriander leaves

Peel the chokos and then slice them finely lengthways (I use a Japanese shredder), seeds and all. To make the dressing, mix the coconut milk, half the lemon juice and ¼ cup (60 ml) of the olive oil, then season with salt and pepper and adjust with more lemon juice, if necessary.

Sprinkle the crab meat with the remaining lemon juice and olive oil, then season and let stand for a minute or so. Toss the crab meat carefully with the dressing, coriander and choko and serve on a large plate.

CHOKO SALAD   *Serves 4*

6 tiny chokos	2 plump witlof
2 tablespoons lemon juice	1 × 150 g piece bacon, rind discarded,
1 teaspoon Dijon mustard	meat diced
200 ml extra virgin olive oil	1 large clove garlic, crushed
sea salt flakes and freshly ground	1 thick slice white bread, crusts removed,
black pepper	cut into small cubes
1 tablespoon freshly chopped chervil	

Peel the chokos, then slice them finely lengthways (I use a Japanese shredder), seeds and all. (If your chokos aren't tiny, boil them whole in their skins for 20 minutes and then slice them finely.)

For the vinaigrette, mix the lemon juice and mustard, then whisk in 125 ml of the olive oil and season with salt and pepper. Mix the chervil into the vinaigrette, then toss it with the choko slices and set aside.

Separate the witlof leaves without using a knife (to do so will cause discolouration), discarding any damaged outer leaves. Render the bacon in a hot, dry frying pan over high heat until cooked. Meanwhile, gently heat the remaining olive oil with the garlic in another frying pan over low heat and fry the bread cubes until golden brown, then drain on kitchen paper. Toss the croutons with the witlof, bacon and dressed chokos and serve.

CHRISTMAS

 **THERE ARE SO MANY OPTIONS FOR CHRISTMAS LUNCH BUT,** for me, the best is a lunch of simplicity and style with people I care about. I feel strongly about family traditions and somehow, in my family, all our traditions come back to food. The difficulty arises in a partnership when you suddenly find you have two differing sets of traditions.

There are two alternatives. One is to compromise to keep the extended family together; the other is for each family, at some stage, to begin their own set of traditions. When children are young, nothing is more fun than gathering together all the cousins and sharing the presents under the tree. As the children grow up, they start to want their 'special friends' to join them on Christmas Day. So, either the family gathering becomes larger (as long as each contributing family can find common ground to enjoy the day) or an alternative day is found for the extended family get-together, and new traditions develop that will probably stay in place for the next generation. Whatever path is chosen, the most important thing, as far as I am concerned, is the sharing of good food.

When I was a child in Sydney, our Christmas lunch was casual but wonderful. Both my parents were great cooks but very little work was done on Christmas Day. We shared the day with relatives and friends and the common theme was always a large table laden with food. Sometimes this would be inside, sometimes in the garden – and several times, actually on the beach.

When I was very young, the pride of the table would be a roast chook. It's hard to remember just what a luxury that was, though I do remember the kerfuffle when Dad killed it in the backyard, which my brothers delighted in – but Mum and I always had the job of plucking and cleaning it. A pretty typical household of the time!

Our food became more lavish as the years progressed, and goose became the star of the table. For me it has been so ever since – Christmas without goose just doesn't seem right. There was sometimes duck or chook as well, depending on how many people there were to feed. We often began with fresh Hawkesbury River oysters, and I do remember having wine with the meal (but never champagne, as we might today). There would be lots of salads on the table – simple things like fresh tomatoes and beetroots cooked and sliced into vinegar with onion, and lovely fresh potato salad. I think the mayonnaise was made

with condensed milk and vinegar then, but I remember it tasting wonderful. The only thing we would actually cook on the day was the potatoes – even the goose would be cooked on Christmas Eve and kept in the food safe. We would also have a ham or a hand of pork, and a wonderful brawn (see opposite), which filled the crispers of our old fridge.

Having inherited the tradition of a feast of beautifully simple food from my own parents, it is so important to me to continue that tradition for my children, and now my grandchildren. We keep it really simple so there is no stress, with much of the preparation being done the night before. The cooking of the goose, though, is always done on Christmas morning now, these days in an oven bag, while we have drinks with our friends the Schuberts who host open house.

But our favourite Christmas times are when we all sit outside, either under the pear tree at the bottom of our garden, or in the courtyard under the umbrella of what must be a one-hundred-year-old wisteria tree.

While I now make the Christmas pudding (not just one but by the thousands!) I truly can't remember ever serving it on Christmas Day. These days we're more likely to have a jelly of sparkling shiraz set with raspberries for the adults, and our vanilla bean and elderflower ice creams for the kids, and leave the pudding for the Boxing Day supper to have with the leftovers.

BRAWN

Makes enough to fill a large mixing bowl

Making brawn, as my parents did every Christmas, is not a task to be undertaken lightly. Firstly, you need a most co-operative butcher, and you may need to place your order at least a week in advance. Often the tongue is sold separately from the pig's head, so you'll need to make a separate order, or you can use 4 sheep's tongues instead. Ask for brined trotters, which give the dish that extra saltiness. Most of all, be prepared to pitch in and 'get your hands dirty' to pull all the meat away from the bone once it is cooked – not for the squeamish. For me, it's a labour of love.

1 pig's head, cut into 4 (the tongue was not present in the one I bought)

4 sheep's tongues, brined

2 brined pig's trotters (they are not salty enough if not brined)

1 veal knuckle

3 onions, chopped

2 carrots, chopped

3 leeks, white part only, chopped

5 stalks flat-leaf parsley

2 fresh bay leaves

2 sprigs thyme

10 crushed juniper berries

10 allspice berries

¼ cup (60 ml) white-wine vinegar

1 cup (250 ml) white wine

sea salt flakes and freshly ground black pepper

juice of 1 lemon

rind of 1 lemon *or* orange

½ cup freshly chopped flat-leaf parsley

Remove the brain from the pig's head, otherwise it will limit the life of the finished brawn. Wash all the meat and vegetables well. Put the meat into a large stockpot. Add the chopped vegetables, herbs and spices. Just cover with water, add the vinegar and simmer very, very slowly (over the lowest heat possible) until the meat falls off the bone. This takes about 5 hours, with a simmer pad under the pot to slow the cooking. (Brawn, like stock, can be cooked too much so that all the goodness is cooked out of it.) Skim occasionally as it cooks, and when cooked, pick through the meat whilst still warm, rejecting any skin, bone or gristle, and put the meat into a bowl. (I prefer to leave some meat whole or in large chunks, such as the tongues and cheeks. There should be a mixture of sizes and textures in the finished brawn.) Refrigerate the cooking liquid to easily remove any fat residue – it will jelly once cold.

Bring the cooking liquid to the boil and strain immediately. Take 2 cups of the strained liquid and the wine and boil it, reducing it by half. Taste and add salt, pepper and lemon juice, as required. Add the meat pieces and simmer for just a few minutes, then re-check the seasoning. Remember that the brawn will be eaten cold, so it will need to be more highly seasoned than usual. Add lemon or orange rind and freshly chopped parsley. Pour into a glass bowl and leave to set in the fridge. Serve cold with crusty bread and home-made pickles.

The following is the menu for a
simple sort of lunch for Christmas Day.

———— • ————

Yabbies with Walnut Dressing

Roast Goose with Apple, Onion and Sage Stuffing

Apple Aïoli

Aunt Reta's Christmas Pudding

YABBIES WITH WALNUT DRESSING

Serves 4

16 live yabbies (4 per person)
fresh dill (wild dill, if you can get it),
    for cooking
caraway seeds, for cooking

DRESSING
150 g walnuts

1 slice white bread, crust removed
2 tablespoons milk
2 cloves garlic
¼ cup (60 ml) lemon juice
70 ml walnut oil
sea salt flakes and freshly ground
    black pepper

First stun the yabbies by placing them in the freezer for 20 minutes. Bring a saucepan of salted water to the boil and throw in the yabbies, along with some dill and caraway seeds. Boil them rapidly for 3 minutes. Drain and leave to cool.

Preheat the oven to 200°C. For the dressing, roast the walnuts on a baking tray in the oven until they just begin to colour. While still warm, rub their skins away in a tea towel then, using a sieve or colander, shake the discarded skins away and leave the nuts to cool. Use a mortar and pestle or food processor to grind the walnuts to a fine paste. Soak the bread in the milk, squeezing out as much liquid as possible by hand. Crush the garlic cloves with a little salt under the wide blade of a chef's knife. Blend with the soaked bread and lemon juice in a food processor to make a smooth paste. Add the walnut paste and continue blending in the food processor, adding the walnut oil slowly as if making a mayonnaise, and season to taste with salt and pepper if necessary. Chill the dressing before serving.

To serve, peel the yabbies and serve with the chilled dressing.

ROAST GOOSE WITH APPLE, ONION AND SAGE STUFFING   *Serves 6*

A goose doesn't have a huge amount of meat on the breast, but what it has is incredibly rich, so a bird this size will easily feed six people. Using an oven bag to stop the meat drying out is a measure worth taking no matter the age of the goose, but an older goose requires a much longer cooking time and a very slow oven to become tender. The most important factor in achieving success is to know the age of your goose, so ask the supplier; only roast a goose without an oven bag if you are assured the goose is no older than twelve to fourteen weeks.

1 × 3.5–4 kg goose
extra virgin olive oil, for cooking
verjuice *or* lemon juice, for cooking
sea salt flakes and freshly ground
    black pepper

STUFFING
1 cup walnuts
80 g butter
250 g dried apples, minced

30 sage leaves
¼ cup (60 ml) verjuice, plus extra if needed
1 cup chopped pale-green celery leaves
100 ml extra virgin olive oil
4 small onions, finely chopped
freshly grated nutmeg, to taste
2½ cups (175 g) stale grated breadcrumbs
sea salt flakes and freshly ground
    black pepper

Preheat the oven to 200°C. For the stuffing, roast the walnuts on a baking tray in the oven until they just begin to colour. While still warm, rub their skins away in a tea towel then, using a sieve or colander, shake the discarded skins away and leave the nuts to cool. Finely chop the walnuts and set aside. Heat the butter in a frying pan, then sauté the apples and sage and, when almost cooked, deglaze the pan with verjuice, add celery leaves and transfer to a bowl. Heat the olive oil in the pan, then sauté the onions over low heat until cooked. Add a little nutmeg to taste.

While the onions are still hot, add the breadcrumbs, walnuts and apple and sage mixture, then moisten with a little extra verjuice if needed. Stuff the bird with this mixture and secure the cavity; either sew it up or plug with a whole apple to stop the stuffing escaping. When I use an apple, I find sealing the cavity with a metal skewer sufficient to keep the stuffing from falling out. Reduce the oven temperature to 160°C.

Coat the stuffed goose with a little extra virgin olive oil and verjuice or lemon juice (this will caramelise the skin as the goose cooks), season well, then place in an oven bag and transfer to a large roasting pan. For a young goose, cook for 45 minutes, then turn the bird over and cook for another 45 minutes or until the legs come away easily from the bone (with an older goose, it could take twice as long for this to occur). For an older goose, turn the oven down to 120°C after the first 45 minutes and cook for another 2 hours 15 minutes (about 3 hours in total).

When cooked, open the oven bag and increase the temperature to 210°C, then return the goose to the oven to brown the breast skin for 10 minutes.

For a casual meal, I would serve the goose with Apple Aïoli rather than a sauce (see page 74). An alternative would be a jar of quality cranberry jelly or the cabernet jelly I make at the Farmshop.

APPLE AÏOLI

Makes about 250 ml

1 Granny Smith apple
juice of 1 lemon
4 egg yolks
2 cloves garlic, crushed

2 cups (500 ml) extra virgin olive oil
sea salt flakes and freshly ground
    black pepper

Grate the apple and immediately soak in the lemon juice. Process the yolks in a food processor with the garlic, grated apple and lemon juice. While processing, add half the oil in a thin stream and then the rest more rapidly, until emulsified. Season to taste.

AUNT RETA'S CHRISTMAS PUDDING

Serves 12–16

Most families have pretty entrenched Christmas traditions surrounding food, and in ours these were definitely the province of my Aunt Reta, whose role in the household all her life was to make both the Christmas pudding and cake. The pudding was a major hit, moist and luscious, and so full of rum and threepences and sixpences that we thought it terribly daring.

Aunt Reta's Christmas pudding is a source of great nostalgia for me, so I include it here for sentimental reasons. The Christmas pudding in *Maggie's Table* is closer to the one I make commercially; the percentage of fruit is so high it needs no sugar at all.

500 g dried currants
400 g sultanas
200 g muscatels
200 g mixed peel
200 g glacé cherries
1½ cups (375 ml) overproof rum
380 g butter

380 g dark-brown sugar
8 eggs
1 tablespoon mixed ground nutmeg
    and cinnamon
675 g self-raising flour, plus extra
    for dusting
salt

Mix the fruit in a large bowl and soak overnight in the rum.

Cream the butter and sugar then mix in the eggs, one at a time. Stir in the fruit, rum and spices. Sift in the flour with a large pinch of salt and mix well. Dust a square of washed calico (approximately 45 cm square) with flour. Spoon the pudding mixture into the centre of the cloth, pull the corners and edges to the centre and tie well with kitchen string to secure.

Bring a large saucepan of water to the boil. Immerse the pudding, bring the water back to the boil and let it bubble quietly over low heat for 6 hours, keeping the pudding completely immersed. When cooked, hang in a well-ventilated place to dry until required.

Before you wish to serve, boil the pudding again in a large saucepan of water for 1 hour. Unwrap and serve.

Aunt Reta's Christmas pudding

CURRANTS

IT IS SO RARE TO SEE FRESH CURRANTS IN THE MARKETPLACE. AS a fresh fruit they are almost forgotten, yet if there's any chance at all of finding them fresh it will be between February and March. I suspect your best chance will be in organic or farmers' markets, but the flavour of the tiny, almost-black currants is so wonderfully intense that it's a shame they are not much more accessible. If you're lucky enough to find them, eat from the bottom of the cluster up, holding the stem way above your mouth – a little like the fox in *Aesop's Fables* – and just lie back and enjoy them.

There are two main varieties of currant. The zante, the one I sometimes find, is an early and very fragile variety; its thin skin and intense, sweet flavour make it perfect for eating fresh. The more commonly seen carina, the most prevalent variety planted for drying, has a tougher skin and a longer bunch than the zante, and crops twice as heavily.

Many farmers believe that currants became unfashionable as the demand for bigger and bigger grapes increased. The fresh currants I buy are about double the price of sultana grapes, but they are worth every cent. As the soft-skinned zante is so vulnerable to damage as a growing crop (rain can cause enough damage to spoil a crop two years out of three, and spoilage in transport is a real issue too), it's difficult for farmers to justify growing currants unless a real premium is paid for them. They need to target the specialty market, and even that can be too small to sustain production.

I'm often driven by romantic ideas of gardening, such as one I had of planting twenty zante currant vines to grow over a glasshouse frame. The idea was that the resulting 'tunnel' would be wide enough to hold a large refectory table, yet low enough for the hanging bunches of ripe currants to be within reach. Well, I planted them on a slope and soon realised I had them in totally the wrong position for the final part of the plan – the long table. I moved them the next year to a more appropriate place but the spark must have gone out of the idea by then and after a year of very low rainfall and with no irrigation to aid my 'folly', I lost them all.

I now have a currant cutting given to me by a reader from a one-hundred-year-old vine of hers. I planted it on a post of the chicken shed and its crop will, I hope, be ready within weeks. Planting it by the chook shed means I go past it every day, so it doesn't get forgotten.

It was actually the currant that gave me my first true taste of the Barossa. In 1973 we started to look at properties from afar, buying the South Australian papers every week while still living in Sydney. One place sounded so promising I made the journey down by bus to look at it. I have never been particularly practical, and I fell in love with a currant vine that was laden with fruit ripe for eating, which hung down through the criss-cross of a very established trellis at the back door of the kitchen. Colin, hearing my report on the telephone that night, suggested I had another, more objective look. I would have bought the property just for that old vine, but sadly the house was a bit ramshackle in the harsh light of the next day.

Of all dried fruit, the currant is my favourite because it seems to have a higher acidity, which serves savoury food well (of course, the use of dried currants in cake-making is well established). If dried currants are to be added to rich game dishes such as hare, they are particularly good if soaked in verjuice or even red-wine vinegar beforehand.

If you want to dry your own currants, the fresh bunches can be strung across the ceiling in a draught-free pantry, each bunch out of reach of the next; it will take 5–10 days, depending on the weather. Bunches of currants can also be dried in the sun: arrange them side by side on black plastic, leaving enough plastic free so that it can be folded over the currants at night to keep out any moisture. If this process is carried out between the vines, as it often is, a lot of dust accumulates and the dried currants need to be washed. Handle the bunches very gently once they're dried to keep them intact, and spray them with olive-oil cooking spray to retain their moistness.

TUNA ROLLS WITH CURRANTS, PINE NUTS AND BAY LEAVES

Serves 8

This recipe came about when I was asked to do a cooking school at Accoutrement, a cook-ware supply store in Sydney. Owner Sue Jenkins knew of my plans to holiday in Italy and thought I should hold a school inspired by the food of Tuscany, Umbria and Sicily upon my return. Then frosts and drought all but decimated our grape crop at home, so my Italian travel plans were cancelled, but I was still committed to the classes. Luckily for me, books on Italian food form the major part of my library, such is my passion for Italy, and so my research for the classes came from these: I simply looked for recipes that would work best with my local ingredients.

I based the following recipe on one in Mary Taylor Simeti's wonderful book *Pomp and Sustenance*, although my method differs, and I use tuna rather than swordfish. I choose whichever tuna is in season: bluefin if you can find it, of course, but yellowfin is also well worth it. If you cannot buy tuna trimmed of its skin and bloodline, allow an extra 150 g to ensure you end up with 1 kg trimmed weight.

1 × 1 kg piece tuna, skin removed and
    bloodline trimmed
1 large red onion, cut into quarters
32 fresh bay leaves
extra virgin olive oil, for cooking
lemon wedges, to serve

FILLING
¼ cup (35 g) dried currants
2 tablespoons verjuice

16 bamboo skewers *or* rosemary sprigs,
    leaves stripped
¼ cup (40 g) pine nuts
1–2 tablespoons extra virgin olive oil
1 cup flat-leaf parsley leaves
5 cloves garlic
sea salt flakes and freshly ground
    black pepper
120 g freshly grated pecorino

For the filling, soak the currants in the verjuice overnight or heat on the defrost setting in a microwave for 5 minutes to reconstitute. Meanwhile, soak bamboo skewers or stripped rosemary stalks for 30 minutes in water to prevent them burning during cooking.

Preheat the oven to 200°C. Moisten the pine nuts with a little of the olive oil and roast on a baking tray for about 5–8 minutes or until golden brown. Keep an eye on them as they burn easily. Chop the parsley and garlic together well, then add the pine nuts and the reconstituted currants and roughly chop. Season to taste, then thoroughly stir in the pecorino and 1 tablespoon of the olive oil.

Keep the tuna chilled until you are ready to use it. Cut the tuna into 24 thin slices about 10 cm × 7.5 cm and about 3 mm thick. Gently flatten any smaller slices by placing between two pieces of plastic film and gently tapping with a soft mallet, as you would for scaloppine.

Separate the onion into crescents. Place 1 teaspoon of the currant filling on one end of each slice of tuna and roll it up as neatly as possible, then spear it a couple of centimetres off-centre onto a skewer or rosemary stalk with a piece of onion. Follow with a bay leaf, then another roll of tuna, then onion, and so on until 8 of the skewers have been filled (3 rolls and 4 bay leaves per skewer). Run a second skewer through the rolls parallel to the first skewer, but a couple of centimetres apart, and repeat this process with the remaining skewers. Make sure the skewers aren't packed too tightly; otherwise the fish will stew rather than grill or roast.

If grilling the rolls, heat the griller as high as it can go, otherwise roast at 230°C. Cook them in batches if your grill or oven is small – it is important that the tuna parcels don't touch, again to prevent stewing. Brush the tuna rolls with olive oil and grill for 2 minutes on the first side and 1 minute on the second, or roast for 5 minutes. The tuna should be only just seared and the onion needs to be nothing more than warm. Serve with extra virgin olive oil and lemon wedges. Any leftovers are delectable the next day, when the flavours have had time to meld.

SPINACH WITH CURRANTS AND PINE NUTS

Serves 6

175 g dried currants

½ cup (125 ml) verjuice

225 g pine nuts

1 kg spinach, carefully washed

sea salt flakes

¼ cup (60 ml) extra virgin olive oil

freshly ground black pepper

Soak the currants in the verjuice overnight or heat on defrost in a microwave for 5 minutes.

Preheat the oven to 200°C. Moisten the pine nuts with a little olive oil, then roast them on a baking tray for about 5–8 minutes or until golden brown; keep an eye on them as they burn easily. Plunge the spinach into a saucepan of boiling salted water and blanch for 30 seconds. Strain the spinach in a colander, pressing down very firmly to release as much water as possible. Strain the currants.

Heat the olive oil in a large, heavy-based frying pan and toss the drained spinach until warmed through, then add the pine nuts and currants and season with salt and pepper. Serve with grilled meat or fish.

AUSTRALIAN HERRINGS (TOMMY RUFFS) WITH CURRANTS

Serves 12

The first time I made this dish I used 10 kg of tommy ruff fillets. As the 1990 Adelaide Symposium of Gastronomy coincided with Writers' Week, we planned a 'fishes and loaves' luncheon after a forum at which Stephanie Alexander, Michael Symons (author of *One Continuous Picnic*) and Don Dunstan were speaking. The luncheon was fairly loosely arranged: it was advertised very minimally as a meal to be shared by everyone, and we had no idea how many would come.

I headed off from the Barossa with my van laden with trays and trays of freshly baked bread; the tommy ruffs with currants were on the floor of the van on butcher's trays covered with plastic film. On the outskirts of Adelaide is a tricky piece of road where the speed limits change. I was deep in thought about how we'd feed the multitude if they turned up when a policeman walked out onto the road. I only just saw him in time and jumped on the brakes, which sent the bread flying off the trays, while the fish marinade spilled everywhere. I was very upset – at the policeman and my own stupidity – and said, nearly in tears, 'I'm going to a miracle with Don Dunstan, please let me go!'

Speeding fines aside, the lunch was a great success. We laid all the food out in the writers' tent in the park and people seemed to come from everywhere. It was a great example of community faith and sharing. But because I'd been so worried about not having enough food, we had far too much, so we took the leftovers around to the Salvation Army, where a gentle giant of a man called Tiny thanked us, but said he'd make soup to go with it so it wasn't too rich a feed.

Tommy ruffs are a much under-utilised small oily fish a little like a plump, sweet herring – in fact, their name was officially changed to Australian herrings in July 2006. This dish makes for great al fresco eating as the fish is three-quarters cooked beforehand (the marinade completes the cooking) and is served at room temperature with crusty bread. If tommy ruffs are not available, the flavours in this dish complement almost any oily fish.

130 g dried currants

1 cup (250 ml) verjuice

butter, for cooking

1 cup (250 ml) extra virgin olive oil

500 g tommy ruff (Australian herring) fillets

plain flour, seasoned with salt and freshly ground black pepper

3 large red onions, sliced into rings

rind and juice of 3 lemons

3 sprigs thyme

Soak the currants in verjuice overnight or heat on defrost in a microwave for 5 minutes.

Heat a knob of butter with a little of the olive oil in a heavy-based frying pan over medium heat until nut-brown. Dust each fish fillet with seasoned flour just before adding it to the pan and seal for 30 seconds on each side. Add more butter as needed before cooking the remaining fish, watching the temperature of the pan so that the butter is kept nut-brown.

Arrange the fillets in a serving dish in a single layer, topping and tailing them so that they are not on top of each other. Toss the onions in a little of the olive oil in a saucepan over medium heat for just long enough to soften, and then add the lemon juice and rind (this will change the colour of the onion from pale to deep pink or burgundy). Add as much of the remaining olive oil as required to balance the vinaigrette, then add the reconstituted currants and the thyme and warm gently over low heat. Pour the hot vinaigrette over the fish in the serving dish, where the 'cooking' will be completed. The fish can be eaten 15 minutes after the vinaigrette has been added or it can be left at room temperature (providing it isn't too hot) for eating later in the day. If refrigerating, bring back to room temperature before serving.

EGGPLANT

THERE ARE MANY MORE VARIETIES AVAILABLE THAN THE COMMON but beautiful glossy dark aubergine-coloured vegetable we call eggplant. (What came first – the colour or the vegetable?) When I bought my first really special car, I had to wait for my colour of choice to become available: the deep, lustrous purple of aubergine. The colour, shape and flavour of this fruit are all very special to me. I know most people call it eggplant, but old habits die hard, and while I still use both names, I always think 'aubergine'.

The long thin eggplants called Japanese eggplants are readily available; sometimes they are the same dark glistening aubergine colour and other times they are striped mauve and cream. There is also a variety that is similarly shaped but totally green, almost apple-green, and which makes for wonderful eating. Then there are tiny Thai eggplants I know little about. But the creamiest of all eggplants I've encountered is the Violetta di Firenze eggplant, introduced to me by Michael Voumard, a great chef and gardener now based in the Barossa. They are round, about the size of a tennis ball, and the mauve and cream of their skin is intermingled rather than striped. These are a true taste sensation, particularly if you get the chance to enjoy recently picked ones. Michael also grows a long thin apple-green variety called Thai long green or Louisiana green – also creamy and just superb.

When shopping for the dark-purple variety, choose those with the darkest, shiniest skins with no shrivelling evident. I prefer the smaller fruit, as very large eggplant have big seeds and can be bitter. Such specimens are generally only to be seen late in the season and are large simply because they are older (although bear in mind that seasons differ Australia-wide and that larger specimens may reach you from further afield earlier than those produced locally).

I have learnt that the older, larger and literally seedier ones are also paler, as if the sun has bleached their colour. In my experience, young eggplants definitely do not need salting (contrary to what is widely advised) and, in fact, can easily become soggy with salting.

While I seldom remove the skin, I have discovered that some members of the family who previously found it difficult to eat eggplant because it made their mouths sting quite badly had no trouble once it was peeled.

However, there is another reason to salt: it rids the eggplant of excess moisture and so reduces the amount of oil it soaks up as you pan-fry it. If you do salt eggplant, cut it the way you wish to use it and then sprinkle the exposed flesh with a little salt and leave it in a colander for 20 minutes to drain. The salt will leach out the juices, ridding a larger eggplant of bitterness, and revealing a mild, sweeter taste. Rinse off the salt and pat dry with kitchen paper before proceeding to cook the eggplant.

During the time of the Pheasant Farm Restaurant, I was lucky to have fantastic growers like the Fanto family on my doorstep. Like all good growers, the Fantos love to eat their own produce and Rose Fanto did not hesitate when I asked for her favourite use of their main crop. The Fantos eat a mainly vegetable-based diet and during the season eggplant fritters are a staple. Rose cuts smallish eggplants in half or sometimes quarters and then boils them briefly until they are soft right through. After leaving the eggplants to cool, she chops them with basil (she only uses basil), then adds breadcrumbs and eggs and rolls the mixture into balls, which she chills to ensure they hold their shape when deep-fried just before serving.

Recently picked ripe young eggplants have a marked sweetness about them, so char-grilling slices on the barbecue for a few minutes introduces a special flavour. Serve these as a side dish to meat or as a meal on their own, dressed with extra virgin olive oil, roughly chopped flat-leaf parsley, freshly ground black pepper, sea salt flakes and a touch of vino cotto or good balsamic vinegar.

I see no need to deep-fry eggplant, finding shallow-frying or sautéing in extra virgin olive oil best. Don't use your estate-bottled oil for this as there is no doubt it loses flavour upon heating, but extra virgin olive oil gives a crispness tinged with the fruity flavour of the olives. My next alternative would be a quality vegetable oil. A deep-sided heavy-based frying-pan works well, but handle it with care and make sure the pan is only half-filled with oil, since it will foam when you place the eggplant in. To test if the oil is hot enough, put a small piece of bread crust in the oil and if it sizzles around the crust, it is just about there. Take care that the oil is not so hot that it is smoking. Do not fry too much at a time as the temperature will drop too quickly and the eggplant will be saturated instead of crisp. Lift out when golden brown and place on crumpled kitchen paper to drain.

If you want to avoid using too much oil when cooking eggplant, you can brush slices with a little oil, sea salt and stripped rosemary and either dry-bake them until they collapse in an oven dish just big enough to fit them, or chargrill them. They can be served as an accompaniment to lamb chops, roast kid, or grilled chicken, quail or fish.

To prepare an eggplant as a meal in itself, cut a medium to large eggplant in half, spoon out the flesh and then refill each half with a mixture of breadcrumbs, beaten egg, tomato, grated cheese such as Parmigiano Reggiano, fresh herbs and the chopped eggplant flesh. This can be stewed, baked or barbecued and served with a salad or fresh tomato sauce for dinner.

Eggplant marries wonderfully with anchovies, pesto, goat's cheese, labna, garlic, tomatoes and oregano. But that's just the beginning. There are so many wonderful dishes with eggplant from so many cultures – Moroccan, Greek, Italian and French – that once you feel comfortable with this great vegetable you should search further into the dishes of these countries.

The Middle Eastern specialty baba ghanoush was probably my first-ever taste of eggplant, more years ago than I care to remember. Much later, when I was in Tasmania at a Symposium of Gastronomy, I tasted the benchmark of this classic dish at an eggplant feast prepared by Ann Ripper. Ann's former in-laws, the Haddad family, ran the Ali Akbar restaurant in Hobart, and she used dishes from their repertoire. This dinner was the most amazing statement of simplicity, with offerings arranged on platters for everyone to share. The six or seven dishes included: eggplant with red capsicum and garlic; a delicate and easy-to-handle rolled eggplant slice filled with goat's cheese and walnuts; an omelette with eggplant pasta; baba ghanoush – and oh, how I wish I could decipher the rest of my notes written on a paper serviette!

This experience took my love of eggplants to another level altogether; I couldn't wait to get home to try and replicate Ann's baba ghanoush, featuring smoked eggplant. I waited patiently for late summer, when eggplants are at their best. Success! Since then, I have had wonderful results with smoking eggplant on racks in my oven or following the method below, using a small fish smoker which can be bought from some hardware stores or the Queensland-based company Togar Ovens. Otherwise you can improvise using a barbecue with a hood.

MY TIPS FOR SMOKING EGGPLANT AND OTHER INGREDIENTS

✦ My smoker works with any sawdust that is free of contaminants. Rosemary stalks added to the sawdust give extra flavour to whatever you are smoking. Or instead of sawdust, you can use lemon tree leaves or even a mixture of brown sugar and orange pekoe tea. If using sugar, place it on a sheet of heavy-duty foil so you don't have any mess to clean up later.

✦ I find it handy to stand the smoker on a fire-resistant surface so it is high enough for me to be able to see if the flame is still burning. If the smoker is located out of the wind it will burn more slowly, which increases the intensity of the flavour.

✦ My instructions say a teacup of methylated spirits will burn for 25–30 minutes, but this depends a great deal on the conditions. Place the methylated spirits in the base of the windshield (a perforated metal ring).

✦ Make sure you use gloves or an oven mitt to lift the lid off the smoker as it gets very hot.

✦ If smoking eggplant over a naked flame, you should scrape off the charred skin before eating. Following the manufacturer's instructions, I place 2 tablespoons of sawdust and 6 rosemary stalks in the stainless steel tray, then light the methylated spirits. I then place 2 small–medium eggplants (halved lengthways), cut-side up, on the wire rack that sits above the sawdust (a second tray is used when smoking a larger quantity). With the lid on, I smoke the eggplants for 20 minutes, then turn them over, adding more methylated spirits and lighting the fire for another 10 minutes. By this time, the eggplants are perfectly cooked. I then use them to make Smoky Eggplant with Tahini (see below).

✦ Smoking food gives it a strong colour as well as flavour. You can enhance this even further by brushing the food with oil before smoking.

✦ Smoking is also suited to oily fish such as tommy ruffs (Australian herrings), while salmon fillets, particularly with the fatty belly attached, make a great and simple dish – leave the skin on to retain the moisture.

✦ The smoker is best cleaned with hot, soapy water soon after use.

SMOKY EGGPLANT WITH TAHINI

Makes about 500 ml

It is most important to use small to medium-sized eggplants that have no green tinges, as this indicates a lack of ripeness. Make sure too, that your tahini isn't past its use-by date, is of a good quality and is used at room temperature. This dish is delicious served warm or chilled on hot toast or flatbread.

2 small–medium eggplants,
　halved lengthways
1 clove garlic
¼ cup (60 ml) extra virgin olive oil
¼ cup freshly chopped flat-leaf parsley

juice of ½ lemon
150 ml tahini
sea salt flakes and freshly ground
　black pepper

Smoke the eggplants following the instructions given above. Leave the eggplants until cool enough to handle, then chop them roughly before pulsing them in a small food processor with the garlic, adding the olive oil in a thin stream. Stir in the parsley, lemon juice and tahini, then check the seasoning.

Grilled eggplant with herbs (see page 85)

ROSE'S PRESSED EGGPLANTS

Makes 2 litres

One year, my Barossa eggplant supplier, Rose Fanto, was persuaded to sell her produce at the Yalumba Harvest Picnic, held during the Barossa Vintage Festival. While Rose was sure of her own culinary traditions, she was less certain of how they might be received by the general public. Included in her selection were my favourite – pressed eggplants. Her recipe for salting, drying and pressing eggplants is worth the effort involved. Rose collects fennel from the roadside, where it grows wild, but you could use dill as an alternative.

1.5 kg eggplants, peeled and cut widthways
 into 5 mm-thick slices
2 cloves garlic, thinly sliced

1 stalk fresh wild fennel *or* dill
salt
extra virgin olive oil, for drizzling

Layer the eggplant slices with the garlic and fennel in a large rectangular glass or ceramic dish. Top with a handful of salt, put a similar-sized tray on top and weigh down with a very heavy weight, then place in the refrigerator.

Pour off the liquid which collects every 2 days, until all the moisture from the eggplant has been drained or evaporates; this may take up to 6 weeks. The only way to be sure the eggplant is ready is to taste it – take a slice and drizzle it with really good olive oil, then eat it!

If ready, pack the pressed eggplant into sterilised preserving jars (see Glossary), top with olive oil and seal. These are so more-ish that you won't keep them long, but I would store them in the refrigerator where they'll last for months.

EGGPLANT WITH VINO COTTO

Serves 4 as an accompaniment

This dish makes an excellent accompaniment for grilled meats or whitefish – or simply serve it at room temperature with slabs of grilled wood-fired bread and a small rocket salad.

¼ cup (60 ml) extra virgin olive oil
1 onion, chopped
2 eggplants, cut diagonally into
 5 mm-thick slices
sea salt flakes and freshly ground
 black pepper

¼ cup (60 ml) vino cotto (see Glossary)
1 tablespoon freshly chopped
 flat-leaf parsley

Heat the olive oil in a frying pan over medium heat, then add the onion and sauté for 5 minutes or until transparent. Season the eggplant with salt and pepper and add it to the pan to brown. Increase the heat to high and deglaze the pan with the vino cotto, cooking until the vino cotto is syrupy.

Fold through the flat-leaf parsley and serve.

VICTORIA'S STUFFED EGGPLANT WITH VERJUICE, ROCKET AND PRESERVED LEMON SAUCE

Serves 8 as an entrée or 4 as a main

Victoria Blumenstein worked for me for three years at the Farmshop after closing her own establishment, Blumenstein's, in Adelaide. Like so many of the people who have given so much to me while we've been working together over the years, Victoria has a passion for produce and cooking, coupled with a keen intelligence. I think how lucky I am that Victoria was with me at a time when I needed to devise ways of cooking with our new products, especially verjuice for the Japanese market. Never short of ideas, it was such a buzz working with her, as two minds approaching a challenge from slightly different directions are always more powerful than one. Victoria continually developed dishes for the Farmshop, using verjuice and vino cotto in ever-changing ways and recording these recipes for our customers. Here is one of her classic recipes using eggplant and verjuice.

2 eggplants, cut lengthways into
  2 cm-thick slices

STUFFING
⅓ cup (65 g) barley (to yield 1 cup
  cooked barley)
2 tablespoons chopped pitted kalamata olives
1 small red onion, finely chopped
2 tablespoons freshly chopped
  flat-leaf parsley
2 teaspoons chopped mint
finely chopped rind and juice of 1 lemon

½ cup (125 ml) extra virgin olive oil
sea salt flakes and freshly ground
  black pepper

SAUCE
3 quarters preserved lemon, flesh removed,
  rind rinsed and roughly chopped
⅓ cup (80 ml) verjuice
1 cup (250 ml) extra virgin olive oil
2 cups rocket leaves, trimmed
½ teaspoon sugar, or to taste (if needed)

For the stuffing boil the barley in water for 20 minutes. Combine the cooked barley with the remaining ingredients in a bowl and season to taste.

Meanwhile, if necessary, salt the eggplant slices, and place in a colander to drain for 20 minutes. Wash them and pat dry with kitchen paper. Heat a chargrill plate over high heat, then chargrill the eggplant slices and let cool.

Preheat the oven to 180°C. Place spoonfuls of stuffing at the widest end of the eggplant slices and roll up. Place the stuffed eggplant, seam-side down, in an oiled shallow baking dish, then bake for 12 minutes.

Meanwhile, to make the sauce, place the preserved lemon and verjuice in a blender or food processor and blend until lemon is finely chopped; the appearance should be slightly gelatinous. Add olive oil, then rocket, a little at a time, blending well before adding the next batch. The olive oil must cover the blade or the sauce will oxidise. If the sauce is a bit too sharp, adjust by adding sugar. Serve the stuffed eggplant with the sauce.

FRIED EGGPLANT WITH GARLIC, PARSLEY AND YOGHURT *Serves 4*

A dish similar to this was made for me about 20 years ago by a marvellous Frenchwoman, Kiki (who worked for me for a short period), the mother of Cath Kerry, a great cook, caterer and restaurateur for many years at the Adelaide Art Gallery. I use eggplant so much now that it seems strange to think I knew so little about it until then. Try moistening freshly cooked pasta liberally with extra virgin olive oil, then tossing this eggplant mixture through.

3 medium eggplants, peeled and cut into 1 cm × 2 cm pieces	2 tablespoons freshly chopped flat-leaf parsley
1 tablespoon salt (optional)	freshly ground black pepper
¼ cup (60 ml) extra virgin olive oil	1 cup (250 ml) yoghurt, crème frâiche
3 cloves garlic, finely chopped	*or* sour cream

If necessary, salt the eggplant slices and place in a colander to drain for 20 minutes. Wash them and pat dry with kitchen paper. Heat the oil in a frying pan over medium–high heat and fry the eggplant in small batches until golden brown. Place on kitchen paper to drain. Combine the garlic, parsley and pepper and scatter over the cooked eggplant. Toss with the yoghurt, crème frâiche or sour cream or serve the eggplant with the dressing on the side.

RABBIT SCALOPPINE WITH EGGPLANT *Serves 4*

Unless I'm using anchovies from a freshly opened tin, I always soak them in milk before use. This minimises the saltiness and counteracts a little of the oxidisation that generally occurs.

6 double rabbit fillets	VINAIGRETTE
3 medium eggplants, cut into 1 cm-thick slices, ends discarded	8 anchovy fillets
	milk, for soaking
extra virgin olive oil, for frying	¼ cup (60 ml) extra virgin olive oil
plain flour, for coating	1 clove garlic, chopped
sea salt flakes and freshly ground black pepper	2 tablespoons red-wine vinegar
	3 large green olives, pitted and sliced
butter, for frying	1 tablespoon flat-leaf parsley leaves

Place the anchovy fillets in a bowl, cover with milk and soak for 20 minutes. Drain and set aside.

Using a sharp knife, remove the sinew from the rabbit fillets as you would for a beef fillet. Wrap each fillet in plastic film and gently pound it into a scaloppine shape (flat and roughly oval).

Salt the eggplant slices if necessary; if they are in season and not too large, you shouldn't need to. In a heavy-based frying pan, heat some olive oil on high until very hot and fry the eggplant slices until brown on both sides. Drain on kitchen paper.

For the vinaigrette, heat the olive oil in a small saucepan and gently warm the garlic in the oil. Add the anchovies, red-wine vinegar, olives and parsley. Keep the mixture just warm while you cook the rabbit.

Preheat the oven to 150°C. Season the flour with salt and pepper. Heat a little butter until nut-brown in a heavy-based frying pan, then remove from the heat for a second while you toss the rabbit fillets in the seasoned flour. Put the pan back on medium heat for a moment and then seal each fillet for about 30 seconds on each side. Remove the fillets and rest them for a minute or so.

Warm the eggplant slices on a tray in the oven, then interlay the rabbit fillets with the eggplant on a serving platter, using 3 eggplant slices to 3 rabbit scaloppine. Serve immediately with the warm vinaigrette drizzled over. This is also good with Anchovy Mayonnaise (see page 9).

GOOSEBERRIES AND ELDERFLOWERS

GOOSEBERRIES ARE BECOMING MORE READILY AVAILABLE. THEY are picked whilst still green, when the sharpness of their flavour is a wonderful accompaniment to game. Their flavour softens somewhat when sugar is added to them for use in desserts. Eventually, green gooseberries will ripen to red, even if kept in the refrigerator, and will become much sweeter.

The gooseberry is a delicate-looking fruit, with its translucent, finely veined yet 'hairy' skin. It is naturally tart and, unless picked from your own garden, I doubt many would like to eat gooseberries raw; they're definitely an acquired taste. Having said that, gooseberries are wonderful added to moist puddings; or cooked and served with really rich poultry such as goose, duck or pheasant, where the sharp flavour cuts through the richness of the meat.

I've always known that gooseberries have a lyrical connection with elderflowers, but it wasn't until my first trip to Ireland in 2003 that I realised how extraordinary these flavours could be. I was there to conduct a verjuice masterclass at Ballymaloe Cooking School in County Cork, which was founded by Darina Allen. I had known of Ballymaloe for so many years before the opportunity for me to go there arose. In a magazine article I happened to read, Darina had thrown down the gauntlet from afar to see if I'd be interested in teaching there. When Darina was invited to Adelaide by Tasting Australia in October 2001, we finally met and my commitment to visiting Ballymaloe was cemented.

We arrived in that hot northern summer of June 2003, stopping first for a quick trip to Inverness, Scotland, before flying on to Ireland. In both places it was similarly warm and wild elderflowers were everywhere you looked, from country lanes to arterial roads; it was running rampant. No wonder elderflowers are such a part of the country cooking traditions of England, Ireland and Scotland.

Ballymaloe House and Ballymaloe Cooking School were more than I had dreamed of: such beautiful grounds, with seven gardeners, and a kitchen and herb garden that was

mind-blowing. Every day, baskets of fresh vegetables, herbs and fruits would be picked for me to choose for my classes.

I loved the many and varied ways that Darina used the wonderful resource of elderflowers. At dinner in her home one evening she and her husband Tim served a glass of champagne with elderflower cordial to start the meal, then a gooseberry and elderflower compote to finish. What's more, on the Ballymaloe House menu they offered elderflower cordial, elderflower sorbet with pomegranate and champagne and, naturally enough, Darina's compote.

Elderflowers so invaded my senses that I returned home to make vanilla and elderflower ice cream to serve with elderflower heads in champagne batter early that southern summer, but the magic of the combination of elderflower and gooseberry still transports me straight back to a hot summer's night in County Cork.

I've always had elderflowers growing at the farm, and, in the Pheasant Farm Restaurant, I would use them to decorate dessert plates – their lacy heads look so beautiful. I also cooked the flower heads in a light batter and dusted them with icing sugar to serve with the first of the season's raspberries and vanilla ice cream. Never seeming to have enough, I planted six bushes at home last year. They're often found in old-fashioned gardens and, when planted in the right spot, with a mixture of shade and sun, and given plenty of water, they grow enthusiastically and look beautiful.

Jane Grigson's Fruit Book inspired my version of gooseberry and elderflower jelly, which follows her procedure exactly, except I halve the amount of sugar. I'm not sure whether this is a reflection of our practice of allowing the gooseberries to ripen more, or the English palate. The elderflower gives a wonderfully fragrant note to the jelly, and when some of the tiny lacy flowers are scattered on top of the almost-set jelly, it shimmers as it quivers.

GOOSEBERRY SAUCE FOR GAME
Makes about 300 ml

The amount of sugar used here will depend on the ripeness of the gooseberries. Red gooseberries will be riper and therefore much sweeter than green gooseberries.

45 g butter

20 g sugar

250 g punnet gooseberries, washed, topped and tailed

280 ml Golden Chicken Stock (see page 57) *or* game stock

Melt the butter and sugar in a saucepan over medium–high heat and add the gooseberries. Simmer for about 3 minutes. Add stock and reduce to a sauce. The seeds are very soft and it is optional whether you strain the sauce through a sieve or not.

MACADAMIA MERINGUE WITH WHITE CHOCOLATE MOUSSE AND GOOSEBERRIES
Serves 6

Make sure when buying white chocolate that it contains cocoa butter, as some inferior brands contain vegetable fat.

¼ cup (35 g) macadamias

2 egg whites

100 g castor sugar

GOOSEBERRIES

600 g gooseberries, washed and stemmed

½ cup (110 g) sugar

1 tablespoon elderflower cordial

MOUSSE

200 g white chocolate, chopped

50 g unsalted butter

2 teaspoons finely chopped lime rind

1 cup (250 ml) 35 per cent fat cream (see Glossary)

Preheat the oven to 150°C. Roast the macadamias on a baking tray until just golden, then leave to cool. Roughly chop and set aside.

Line a baking tray with baking paper. Using an electric mixer, whisk the egg whites until soft peaks form, then slowly add the sugar, continuing to whisk until it is completely incorporated. Spread the meringue in a rectangle evenly over the baking paper on the baking tray, then bake for about 1 hour. Turn the oven off and leave the meringue inside to dry out slightly; the centre should still be a little chewy.

Meanwhile, for the mousse, melt the chocolate and butter in a small heatproof bowl over a saucepan of gently simmering water; the bowl should not touch the water. Once the chocolate melts and the butter is incorporated, add the lime rind, then remove from the heat and leave to cool. Whip the cream until stiff peaks form, then fold into the cooled chocolate mixture. Cover with plastic film and refrigerate until ready to use.

For the gooseberries, place the fruit in a small saucepan with the sugar and elderflower cordial and cook over low heat, stirring occasionally, for 10–12 minutes, or until the gooseberries are tender but still retaining their shape. Drain and leave to cool.

To assemble, trim the meringue into two pieces to fit into a deep rectangular serving dish. Place one piece of the meringue on the bottom of the dish. Spread half the mousse over the meringue, then scatter with half the gooseberries. Lay the second piece of meringue on top of the gooseberries, then repeat the layering with the remaining mousse and gooseberries. Top with chopped macadamia nuts, then chill well before serving.

GOOSEBERRY AND ELDERFLOWER COMPOTE

Serves 6

I have re-created this recipe from the wonderful and evocative memories of my trip to Ireland.

1 cup (220 g) sugar	4 elderflower heads, washed well, *or*
250 ml water	1 tablespoon elderflower cordial
	1 kg gooseberries, topped and tailed

Make a sugar syrup by combining the sugar, water and elderflower heads or cordial in a saucepan. Bring to the boil and simmer over low–medium heat until syrupy. Add the gooseberries and simmer for about 5 minutes or until tender. Remove from heat and leave to cool, then remove the elderflower heads.

Serve the compote with pouring cream.

GOOSEBERRY PAVLOVAS

Serves 10

Savour New Zealand, an annual three-day masterclass held in Christchurch for food and wine lovers, puts on some quite amazing shows for such a small committee. I've been invited to attend several times, and each visit has been a standout, but one lasting memory is of this gooseberry pavlova that Tina Duncan of White Tie Catering (and one of the prime movers behind the event) made for the Gala Dinner of the inaugural Savour New Zealand in 2001.

With such a large audience attending, Tina wanted to be prepared and so made individual pavlovas in advance. On the night she placed some stewed gooseberries in each bowl, topped with a layer of whipped cream, on top of which she served the meringue like an upside-down pavlova. This allowed the desserts to be served quickly and efficiently to such a large crowd.

This is such a fantastic combination of texture and flavour – one which Tina tells me she has fond memories of her mum serving after the Sunday roast. I can still taste this wonderful dessert as I pen this; it reminds me that gooseberries deserve so much more attention.

3 egg whites
1½ cups (330 g) castor sugar
1 teaspoon cornflour
1 teaspoon vanilla extract
¼ cup (60 ml) boiling water
2 cups (500 ml) 35 per cent fat cream
   (see Glossary)

GOOSEBERRIES
1½ cups gooseberries
⅓ cup (75 g) castor sugar, or more to taste

Preheat the oven to 150°C. Place the egg whites, sugar, cornflour and vanilla extract in the bowl of an electric mixer. Start to beat, gradually adding the boiling water, then beat for about 15 minutes or until stiff and satiny. Drop large spoonfuls onto a baking tray lined with baking paper – don't worry about the meringues being too perfect.

Bake the meringues for 20 minutes, then reduce the oven temperature to 100°C and cook for another 30 minutes. Cool on wire racks.

Meanwhile, for the stewed gooseberries, place the gooseberries and sugar in a small saucepan and simmer on low heat for 10 minutes or until cooked through. Leave to cool.

Whip the cream until soft peaks form.

If you're catering for a crowd and want to assemble dessert in advance, place a spoonful of stewed gooseberries in the bases of 10 bowls, top with whipped cream, then finish with a meringue. Otherwise, spread the cream generously on each of the meringues and top with stewed gooseberries.

NECTARINES

IF I HAD TO NOMINATE MY FAVOURITE STONE FRUIT ABOVE ALL others, hard though it is to better a perfect white peach plucked ripe from the tree, I would have to give my vote to the old-fashioned white nectarine. Forget about fancy fruit such as peacharines – give me a ripe nectarine in its perfect state and I am in heaven.

The many varieties of nectarine mean that the season is quite a long one. But, like all stone fruit, it is only when they are picked ripe that I can wax lyrical about them. If not, then I advise you to cook them rather than eat them as is. Nectarines must also be handled carefully as they bruise particularly easily. A nectarine picked green will never ripen properly and will have a bitter taste to it. Choose your greengrocer carefully: once you are familiar with ripe fruit fresh from the tree it is difficult to accept anything less.

Actually a smooth-skinned peach (not a cross between a peach and a plum, as is often erroneously thought), the nectarine has a tarter and spicier taste than the peach. As such, nectarines make great tarts or pies, whereas peaches do better simply baked or poached. Try adding ground roasted almonds to the pastry when making a nectarine tart, since almonds and nectarines are such a good duo. Or you could half-fill a pastry case with a frangipane filling of ground almonds, butter, sugar and eggs, and arrange nectarine segments on top, before baking. An old-fashioned crumble can be made in a flash with nectarines. The crumble mixture can be kept, well sealed, in the refrigerator for weeks, and dessert can then be a spur-of-the-moment idea.

The nectarine has very thin skin, which makes peeling easy. Simply pour boiling water over the fruit and leave for 15 seconds, then strip off the skin. You will find the blush that appears on the skin will also be present on the flesh. Soft-skinned fruit is wonderful poached in a verjuice or light sugar syrup, and with the nectarine you have the added bonus of that sunset-coloured blush. Blanch and peel the nectarines, then add the skin to the poaching liquid with the fruit to give it a rosy hue. A jelly can be made from the

Nectarine frangipane tart (see page 97)

poaching liquid, too, and poured over halved nectarines in a mould. Five Alba Gold gelatine leaves will be just enough to set 500 ml jelly so that it quivers when it is brought to the table, if it is made the day before and left to set. An old-fashioned jelly mould would be perfect for this: invert the jelly onto a platter and serve with dollops of Kangaroo Island or other thick cream. However, if you plan to serve this outside on a hot summer's day, then play it safe and add an extra gelatine sheet.

I often serve the wonderfully moist olive oil and sauternes cake from Alice Waters' *Chez Panisse Cooking* with poached nectarines at room temperature. I reduce the poaching liquid to a glaze and pour it over the nectarines and the cake for a great dessert.

Preserving nectarines is well worth the trouble, as long as they are ripe and not bruised. Nectarines can be pickled or spiced in the same way as peaches and served with terrines or barbecued quail. Bottled nectarines make a great difference to muesli on a winter's morning, and can be served simply with ice cream or cream for a last-minute dessert. I don't know of anyone drying nectarines commercially (apart from my neighbours, the Ellis family, who sell at the Barossa Farmers' Market every Saturday), but they have a very special flavour that teams well with a soft brie.

If you have a glut of nectarines and wish to freeze them, blanch and peel the fruit, then discard the stones and purée the pulp. Add 2 tablespoons lemon juice (this stops the fruit discolouring) and 1 cup sugar to each 2 cups purée, then freeze. One of the best ways to use the purée is to fold it, partially frozen, into a good vanilla bean ice cream just as you are serving it.

NECTARINE CRÈME PÂTISSIÈRE TART   *Serves 6–8*

1 × quantity Sour-cream Pastry (see page 424)	CRÈME PÂTISSIÈRE
8 nectarines, stoned and sliced	6 egg yolks
20 g butter	100 g castor sugar
1 tablespoon brown sugar	2½ tablespoons plain flour
	2 cups (500 ml) milk
	1 vanilla bean

Make and chill the pastry as instructed, then line a tart tin with it. Chill the pastry case for 20 minutes. Preheat the oven to 200°C. Line the pastry case with foil, then cover with pastry weights and blind bake for 15 minutes, then remove the foil and weights and bake for another 5 minutes. Set the baked pastry case aside and increase the oven temperature to 250°C.

Arrange the nectarines in a baking dish. Heat the butter with the brown sugar in a small saucepan over medium heat until melted, then brush over the nectarine slices. Bake the fruit for 15 minutes, just enough time to caramelise it, then set aside and leave to cool to room temperature. »

For the crème pâtissière, beat the egg yolks and castor sugar until creamy, then add the flour and beat to a smooth paste. Heat the milk with the vanilla bean in the top of a double boiler over low heat. (If you don't have a double boiler, use a heatproof bowl that fits snugly over a pan of boiling water.) Remove the vanilla bean (cut it in half and scrape the seeds into the hot milk, if you wish). Whisk half the milk into the egg mixture until smooth, then whisk in the remainder. Pour the mixture back into the double boiler and stir over low heat with a wooden spoon until thickened. Cook for another 2 minutes, stirring, then remove the pan from the heat and set aside to cool. Press a buttered piece of baking paper on top of the crème pâtissière to prevent a skin forming.

Fill the pastry case with the cooled crème pâtissière and top with the nectarine slices, overlapping them like roof tiles. Serve immediately.

FRENCH-STYLE NECTARINE TART *Serves 6–8*

I am a great lover of puff pastry but rarely take the time to make it. Instead, I make a rough puff pastry as described by Jacques Pepin in his *La Technique* (he calls it fast puff pastry). This method uses the same ingredients as puff pastry but puts them together differently and takes half the work. The resulting pastry isn't as refined as classic puff – which is probably why it suits my cooking style – but has almost as many applications. It is particularly good for pie tops.

The weather (more specifically, the temperature and humidity), and flour you are using affect how much liquid you need each time you make pastry, bread or pasta. Always reserve a little of the specified liquid in case not all of it is needed. I use cream rather than water when making pastry for a dessert. This recipe makes about 500 g pastry – it doesn't seem to work as well when made in small amounts. Freeze any leftover pastry: pat it into a flat 'cake', then wrap it well in plastic film the day it is made, to avoid oxidisation.

750 g ripe nectarines	ROUGH PUFF PASTRY
1 tablespoon sugar	450 g plain flour, plus extra
2 tablespoons loquat *or* apricot jam	for dusting
1 teaspoon kirsch	450 g chilled unsalted butter, cut into
	1.5–2 cm cubes
	1 teaspoon salt
	1 cup (250 ml) water *or* 300 ml cream

To make the pastry, tip the flour onto a cool bench and make a well in the centre, then add the butter and salt. Using the tips of your fingers or a pastry scraper, rub or cut the butter into the flour. Add three-quarters of the water or cream and mix into the flour mixture, but do not knead it. Add the remaining water or cream if necessary; the dough should still be lumpy with small knobs of butter.

Generously flour the bench and roll the dough out to a 1.5 cm-thick rectangle. Use your hands to even up the rectangle to make folding and rolling easier. Brush any flour from the pastry, then fold one end into the centre (brushing the flour off is important, as any extra flour will toughen the pastry). Repeat this on the other side, then fold the dough in half, creating four layers of pastry. This is your first double turn. Roll out the pastry and repeat this process twice more. If the dough becomes too difficult to manage, refrigerate it for 15–20 minutes between turns. Wrap the finished dough in plastic film and rest it in the refrigerator for 20 minutes.

Roll out the chilled pastry and use it to line a 20 cm tart tin with a removable base. Prick the base of the pastry case all over with a fork. Refrigerate the pastry case for at least 20 minutes.

Preheat the oven to 220°C. Wash and dry the nectarines, then cut them in half and remove the stones. Cut each half into 3 segments and arrange in circles over the chilled pastry case, with the slices just overlapping one another. Sprinkle the sugar over the fruit and bake for 30–35 minutes or until the fruit is cooked and the bottom of the pastry case is well browned (you may need to cover the edges of the pastry with foil during cooking to prevent burning). Carefully remove the tart from the tin and slide it onto a wire rack to cool a little. Gently warm the jam and kirsch in a small saucepan over low heat, then brush over the fruit. Serve warm with ice cream or cream.

PASSIONFRUIT

WHEN I WAS A CHILD GROWING UP IN SYDNEY, THE PASSIONFRUIT vines were as luxuriant and plentiful as the chokos that grew over most back fences, including my aunt's. We used to sit among the vines attacking the fruit with a penknife before sucking the skins dry. In the years I spent travelling through Europe and North Africa in my twenties, I never once came across passionfruit (although I'll admit I didn't go to any of the fabulous food shops of Paris). Then again, I wasn't really looking: I mistakenly thought passionfruit was a peculiarly Australian delicacy, as it seemed linked to childhood memories and Australian country cooking in a way no other fruit is.

In fact, passionfruit originated in South America. It's not hard to see how the Spanish missionaries there came to name the plant, finding that the various parts of its beautiful, complex flower reflected the sufferings of Christ. As Jane Grigson says in her *Fruit Book*, 'they believed the Creator had thoughtfully arranged the Passion Flower, the *Flos Passionis*, in this way, and had planted it in the New World ready to help in the conversion of the Indians'.

Passionfruit season can be confusing because the fruit is among the increasing number of those almost always available, particularly in hot climates, even if in reduced quantities. In warmer climes they crop lightly all year, with a flush at the end of summer and then again towards the end of winter. In cooler climates you are more likely to see a vine fruiting in late summer or early autumn. In the Barossa, passionfruit is very much a late summer fruit.

After many false starts, we had brief success with passionfruit at home by planting the vine with an ox heart at its base on the advice of a neighbour. Rumour has it that the iron from the ox heart helps the passionfruit to grow, and in this case it worked. However, the vine was close to a rainwater tank that subsided and collapsed when one of our ancient pear trees fell down, taking with it everything in its path, including the passionfruit. Refusing to give up, we've finally established one in the Pheasant Farm garden, this time using left-over livers as a source of iron. It is now bearing well against all odds, as the farm's only water comes from a bore and is higher in salt than most plants can tolerate; this makes the garden at the Pheasant Farm a continual struggle.

The fragrance and bittersweet flavour of the common, round purple passionfruit is without peer. (I once successfully planted a banana passionfruit but couldn't be bothered to eat the fruit much. I feel the same about the very large red passionfruit, which is too sweet for my taste.) No aroma can fill the senses more than a freshly opened, fully ripe passionfruit. Of all the ways to enjoy it, serving the fresh pulp with a little cream tops them all. Don't be tempted to strain the seeds away: I believe that the seeds and the pulp are not to be separated, so ignore any recipe that tells you otherwise!

When choosing passionfruit, be careful to reject those with smooth, shiny skins. Don't let their rich shades of purple seduce you: such fruit can be under-ripe and will lack the sweet counterpoint of ripe passionfruit, as well as having almost no fragrance. If the fruit is light, the pulp will have dried up. Choose instead the less vibrant, old and crinkly passionfruit that feels heavy in the hand and whose fragrance declares its readiness. Passionfruit can be stored at room temperature if the weather isn't too hot, and they keep well in the refrigerator (the pulp can be frozen, too).

The mere scent of passionfruit dolloped onto a tiny cream-filled shortcrust pastry tart sends me into orbit; that intense whiff carries its promise through to the finish. I always say I don't have a sweet tooth, but suddenly I find myself thinking about passionfruit soufflé, passionfruit butter (so rich yet tangy enough to soothe my guilt), and pavlova topped with cream, sliced ladyfinger bananas and passionfruit (a classic, whether we acknowledge it or not). The flavour of this remarkable fruit heightens the taste of anything you put it with.

Dinner parties were part of our early married life, and everyone expected dessert. I remember a time when the only piece of furniture we had was a mattress, and yet we still had dinner parties, our guests sitting uncomfortably on the floor, with plates balanced on knees. Cooking meat, fish and vegetables seemed natural to me, but desserts were another deal – so once I had perfected the pavlova it featured every time we had people to dine. I always like sneaking the leftovers the next morning, when the pavlova is moist from the fridge and the flavour of the passionfruit has really infused the cream.

It was one of my staff, Julie, who insisted on proving to me that you could make a pavlova using Muscovy duck eggs, even though I had read Harold McGee's advice in *On Food and Cooking* that duck egg whites don't beat well because they are short on the globulins that make hen egg whites foam so well. Always happy to test a theory (and knowing that Julie had a real menagerie at home and wouldn't waste anything), I was willing to try it. The resultant pavlova actually had a lighter, fluffier meringue, so these are the perfect choice for someone who prefers a marshmallow-like pavlova. We used 7 duck egg whites to 375 g castor sugar, 3 teaspoons cornflour and 1½ teaspoons white-wine vinegar (instead of lemon juice) and cooked the pavlova at 150°C for 45 minutes only.

PASSIONFRUIT BUTTER   *Makes 475 ml*

While I use a saucepan to make passionfruit butter, it can also be made in a double boiler, but it takes more time. I love passionfruit butter with biscuits warm from the oven, on toast, or to sandwich between melting moments or sponge cakes.

10 large passionfruit

3 eggs

200 g castor sugar

30 g unsalted butter

⅓ cup (80 ml) lemon juice

Cut the tops off the passionfruit with a sharp, serrated knife and extract the pulp. Beat the eggs, then tip them into a stainless steel or enamelled saucepan and add the passionfruit pulp, sugar, butter and lemon juice. Stir over low heat until the mixture comes to the boil, then keep the mixture at a simmer for 15 minutes, being careful it doesn't burn or reduce too much. By the end of the cooking time the mixture will seem quite thick, but it will only set properly when cool. While the passionfruit butter is still hot, ladle it into clean, warm sterilised jars (see Glossary) and seal. Once opened, store jars in the refrigerator.

PASSIONFRUIT AND BANANA PAVLOVA   *Serves 6*

My pavlova is of the chewy variety: the outside is crisp and the inside is still moist.

4 egg whites (at room temperature)

190 g castor sugar

1 teaspoon cornflour

juice of 1 lemon, strained

8 passionfruit

3–4 ladyfinger bananas

300 ml thickened cream, whipped

Preheat the oven to 130°C. Beat the egg whites on high speed in an electric mixer until fluffy. Still beating, slowly add the sugar until the mixture is thick and glossy, then beat in the cornflour and 1 teaspoon of the lemon juice (reserve the rest).

Line a baking tray with baking paper. Pile on the meringue, hollowing out the centre to form a 'nest'. Bake the pavlova for 1 hour 40 minutes until quite firm. Turn the oven off but leave the pavlova inside to cool completely.

Just before serving, cut the tops off the passionfruit with a sharp, serrated knife and extract the pulp. Peel and slice the bananas, then toss with the remaining lemon juice to prevent discolouration. Spread the pavlova with the whipped cream and cover generously with passionfruit and banana.

PASSIONFRUIT SPANISH CREAM   *Serves 6*

When my aunts made Spanish cream or angel's food for me as a child it always separated, with a layer of jelly on the bottom and fluff on top. But years later I read in *The Schauer Australian Cookery Book* that it 'should be a sponge right through. If the gelatine is added too hot, the jelly part will sink to the bottom and the sponge will be on top, which is not correct.' I followed this advice when making my passionfruit version, but I found that family tradition was too strong – I missed the familiar separation of the custard and jelly! In the following recipe the gelatine is not cooled and the result is as I remember – my aunts' Spanish cream.

While I usually prefer to use gelatine leaves (see Glossary), in our family this dessert would have only ever been made with gelatine powder. If you wish to use leaves, soften them in the warm water, then squeeze them well before stirring them into the custard.

6 passionfruit	3 eggs (at room temperature), separated
600 ml milk	100 ml warm water
2 tablespoons castor sugar	9 teaspoons gelatine powder

Cut the tops off the passionfruit with a sharp, serrated knife and extract the pulp. Fill the bottom half of a double boiler with water and bring it to the boil. (If you don't have a double boiler, use a heatproof bowl that fits snugly over a pan of boiling water.) Put the milk and sugar into another saucepan and bring to boiling point, stirring until the sugar dissolves.

Beat the egg yolks in the top half of the double boiler off the heat. Whisk the hot milk mixture slowly into the egg yolks, beating the whole time. Stand the egg yolk mixture over the boiling water in the double boiler for about 2 minutes, stirring with a wooden spoon to slowly thicken the custard. Remove the custard from the heat and cool a little, then add the passionfruit and leave to cool further.

Put the warm water (it should be quite warm) into a small stainless steel bowl and sprinkle the gelatine powder on top – as if you were sprinkling sugar onto the *crema* of a short black. The idea is for the warm water to absorb the gelatine without any need for stirring (this won't happen if you use cold water). Stir the gelatine mixture into the custard, then pour the custard into a glass bowl. Beat the egg whites until stiff, then fold them into the custard and leave it to set in the refrigerator – this should take less than an hour.

PEACHES

 THERE IS NOTHING TO COMPARE WITH THE PERFUME AND BLUSH of a freshly picked peach, as James de Coquet reflects in the 'Peach and Nectarine' chapter of *Jane Grigson's Fruit Book*:

Renoir used to say to young artists longing to paint – like him – the pinkish-brown tones of an opulent breast: 'First paint apples and peaches in a fruit bowl.' My greengrocer sold me worthy models for painting. Their curves were perfect and graceful. Their grooves were in exactly the right place. Their gradations of colour were an art school exercise, and as for the velvety down of their skin . . . 'It's the left cheek of my girl', as the Japanese poet has written.

Ripe peaches bring to mind that wonderful burden of having an abundance of fruit – when the whole tree ripens at once, the spoils must be shared. Each peach variety has such a short season that often you will find you have a glut with which to make jam or preserve.

Should one eat the skin or not? I once asked some fellow cooks this and they were adamant that eating peaches skin and all is the go. In contrast, my husband Colin said that the very idea made the hairs on his arms stand on end. Skin or no skin, it is difficult to eat a peach delicately. I love the juice running down my arm as I strive to savour every mouthful.

It is almost too tantalising to talk about the precious white peach, as it is so difficult to find a perfect specimen, unless you have access to a tree, a growers' market or a great greengrocer, or are prepared to order them from a mail-order company such as Snowgoose (www.snowgoose.com.au), who specialise in supplying premium-grade fruit. A perfect white peach is picked fully ripe, but such peaches bruise easily and have a limited shelf-life. The temptation to pick peaches before they are ripe is not worth it, as they will never offer the rich, sweet acidity of naturally ripened stone fruit, yet transporting these peaches correctly is the challenge. There is quite a tradition of pick-your-own berry farms – what we also need are pick-your-own stone fruit orchards.

Baked peaches with almond and ginger butter (see page 110)

If you are lucky enough to have your own tree, you will have experienced the other extreme of having too much fruit ripening all at once. I am often in this position, but enjoy the glut while it lasts. This is when I enjoy sliced white peaches over cereal, or sometimes I cut up a huge bowl of white peaches and large yellow Million Dollar peaches, then sprinkle the fruit with a little cereal, add a great dollop of yoghurt and start the day with a veritable feast.

Poaching white peaches leaves a blush on the flesh that is revealed after the skin is removed. Try them with raspberries or set them in a Sauternes jelly. Yellow peaches present more possibilities to the cook as they preserve well. While you do not need to add sugar to the bottling syrup, yellow peaches do need to be peeled as the skin dulls with cooking.

I finally made it to Harry's Bar in Venice in 2006, and even with the history attached to it and the beauty of the city, I could not hide my disappointment with their Bellinis. I much prefer the ones we make ourselves – the trick is to squeeze the white peaches by hand.

BELLINI

Here is the recipe for the Bellini from Harry's Bar. Use white peaches only, and, rather than a food mill or meat grinder, use your hands to squeeze them. Alternatively, you can buy imported white peach purée from specialty importers.

white peaches	Prosecco (Italian sparkling wine)

Squeeze the white peaches to a pulp by hand, then force through a fine sieve. If the peach purée is very tart, sweeten it with just a little sugar syrup (a syrup made from equal amounts of sugar and water). Refrigerate the purée until it is very cold, then mix with chilled Prosecco, in the proportion of 1 part peach purée to 3 parts wine or, for each drink, 30 ml peach purée and 100 ml wine. Pour the mixture into well-chilled glasses.

PEACH CHUTNEY   *Makes 750 ml*

The flavour of the peaches is paramount in this chutney – the old-fashioned, firm cling-stones have the right amount of punch.

100 g butter	100 g dried currants
1 large onion, roughly chopped	175 g dark-brown sugar
9 clingstone peaches, peeled and cut into eighths	300 ml red-wine vinegar

Heat the butter over medium heat in an enamelled or stainless steel saucepan and cook the onion until softened, then toss in the peaches. Add the remaining ingredients and stir well.

Bring the chutney to the boil, then cook just above a simmer, stirring occasionally, until it thickens. This will take between 45 minutes and 1 hour. Fill hot, sterilised jars (see Glossary) with the chutney and seal them.

GRILLED PEACH SALAD WITH PROSCIUTTO *Serves 2*

One of the great challenges of making the television show *The Cook and The Chef* on the ABC is featuring produce that will be available in the markets when the episode is screened. This is not always the easiest of logistical exercises, but I am adamant about this detail, as I am determined to highlight produce that is fresh and in season.

This is one of the dishes we cooked when wc were filming the series right in the middle of peach season.

3 yellow peaches, halved and stoned

45 g butter, chopped

1½ tablespoons brown sugar

6 slices prosciutto

¼ cup (60 ml) extra virgin olive oil

3 teaspoons balsamic vinegar *or* vino cotto
 (see Glossary)

2 handfuls witlof and rocket leaves

Preheat the grill to 240°C or high. Place the peach halves, cut-side up, on a rack lined with baking paper over a grill tray. Place a cube of butter into each peach half, sprinkle with sugar, then cook under a hot grill until they caramelise and are cooked. When cool enough to handle, slip skins off peaches.

Lay 3 slices of prosciutto on 2 plates. Combine the oil and balsamic vinegar to make a vinaigrette. Bundle half the witlof and rocket in the centre of each plate and drizzle with a little of the vinaigrette, then place 3 peach halves on top. Drizzle the remaining vinaigrette over the peaches and prosciutto and serve.

PEACH AND AMARETTO JAM *Makes 3 × 380 ml jars*

Use a mixture of really ripe peaches (for flavour) and less ripe peaches (which have higher levels of pectin). Don't keep the peaches in the fridge as this reduces their pectin levels.

1.5 kg peaches, skin on, cut into chunks
 and stones reserved

rind of 1 lemon

750 g castor sugar

juice of 2 lemons

2 tablespoons Amaretto

Put the peaches and lemon rind into a large heavy-based saucepan and simmer over very low heat for 20 minutes or until tender. Tie some of the stones in a clean Chux and add to the pan, then continue to simmer for another 20 minutes, stirring occasionally to prevent the bottom of the pan burning. When the fruit is cooked, remove the bag of stones and stir in the sugar.

Add the lemon juice and check the flavour, adjusting with more lemon juice if desired. Cook for another 20 minutes or until the jam begins to thicken and set. To test whether setting point has been reached, take out a spoonful of jam and place on a white saucer. Place the saucer in the fridge for a few minutes, then test the jam by pushing it with your finger – if it wrinkles, the jam is set. As soon as it reaches setting point, stir in the Amaretto.

Immediately fill three 380 ml clean and dry jars to the top, then seal with a lid and invert them so that the hot jam sits in the lid; all sides of the jars will be 'sterilised' by the hot jam. Leave to cool then turn right-way up. Opened jars should be stored in the refrigerator.

BAKED PEACHES WITH ALMOND AND GINGER BUTTER   *Serves 10*

120 g glacé ginger

200 g almonds

100 g sugar

200 g unsalted butter

10 peaches, stoned and cut in half

Mix the ginger, almonds and sugar together in a small bowl, then combine with the butter, and chill in the refrigerator for 20 minutes. Preheat the oven to 200°C. Hollow out the peaches slightly to make a bigger hole, and bake for 10 minutes, then allow to cool slightly before adding a large dollop of butter to each and baking for 10 more minutes.

VERJUICE-POACHED PEACHES   *Serves 6*

Peeling the peaches after poaching is optional; bear in mind that the skin of some varieties of yellow peach will be difficult to remove.

2 cups (500 ml) verjuice

2 cups (500 ml) water

700 g castor sugar

6 peaches, halved and stoned

Place the verjuice, water and sugar in a stainless steel saucepan and boil for 20 minutes to make the sugar syrup. You should have approximately 875 ml if it is the right consistency.

Place the peaches cut-side down in a saucepan or deep frying pan. Pour the sugar syrup over and poach over medium heat for 20 minutes.

Stewed blood plums with yoghurt and muesli (see opposite)

PLUMS

THE PLUM IS NOT A FASHIONABLE FRUIT – THOUGH I AM NOT sure why. There are so many varieties, each offering a different flavour fresh as opposed to cooked. Yet only a few types are available in season (January to April). As with many fruits, if you have access to some of the old-fashioned varieties found in long-established orchards you have a treat in store. Of all my summer fruiting trees, the blood plums are those least attacked by birds. Perhaps it is due to their position against a stone wall away from the other trees, or the fact that the birds have simply left the area by the time the plums ripen. Both points may be handy for any gardener frustrated by birds eating their plums, especially when it becomes obvious how much of the crop has been part-eaten as the damaged fruit continues to ripen.

Blood plums make the best crumble, as much due to their delicious flavour as the intensity of the deep-burgundy juices that seep through the streusel topping. A friend also candies these plums to great effect. Their slight tartness balances the sugar used in the candying process, and the fruit keeps quite plump through the year sealed in a glass jar.

As much as I like blood plums fresh, and particularly a little warm from the sun, I also enjoy them stewed, served on muesli with yoghurt for breakfast. Baked halved blood plums make another simple dessert: I fill them with homemade almond paste and serve them with cream or, if I'm feeling creative, an almond tuile.

The ruby blood plum is the one we use for our Maggie Beer Blood Plum Paste and Blood Plum Jam; it is intense in flavour and colour and with that edge of piquancy that makes a really vibrant jam.

The prettiest plums I have in my orchard would have to be the damsons. Hidden by the leaves, the oval fruit is small and grows in clusters like grapes. Damsons have a spicy tang when cooked and are particularly good in a sauce to cut the richness of seasonal game meat. Damsons are also very successful in a paste (see page 116), made similarly to quince paste, and make great jelly.

Every greengage I pick I'm excited about – they are such beautiful plums. Though I'd planted my greengage coincidentally near my D'Agen prune plum, which, according to Louis Glowinski in *The Complete Book of Fruit Growing in Australia*, should have helped it to pollinate, in truth it wasn't until I planted a goldengage next to it that I had any real success. The goldengage is ordinary in comparison, but helps the notoriously shy greengage to bear fruit.

Greengages make beautiful poached fruit and tarts. Topping a frangipane mix with halved greengages which have first been baked (not poached) with a little butter makes a great tart, as the flavour of the greengages marries well with almonds. However, the lovely pale green colour I had envisaged for a greengage jelly didn't quite transpire.

As plums and almonds go so beautifully together, add ground almonds to a crumble mixture; combine 100 g ground almonds, 125 g plain flour, 100 g sugar and 175 g unsalted butter. Use this mixture to top, say, 1 kg halved plums, dotted with 75 g butter and 1 tablespoon sugar then baked (add a little water or verjuice to the baking dish so they do not burn). Scatter the crumble mixture over then bake at 200°C for 25 minutes. Serve with fresh cream, mascarpone or vanilla ice cream.

The D'Agen plum, a member of the prune plum family, is a favourite of mine, fresh as well as dried. It has a very high sugar content and is relatively solid, which is why it holds its shape well during cooking and drying. The dark-purple skin and fairly insipid translucent yellow flesh of the fresh fruit transform when baked: the flesh turns a deep-golden hue and the colour of the skin intensifies tenfold, making them irresistible for open tarts.

I have only just discovered the Moya plum, a large, round prune plum. I recently started drying them in my small kitchen dehydrator. By not extracting excessive amounts of moisture, the flavour of the plum is simply intensified – the struggle then is to stop everyone pinching them. As much as I love prunes, the Moya plum handled like this adds a whole new dimension to dried prunes.

For years now I have made a plum tart using prune plums, beginning with Sour-cream Pastry (see page 424). I bake the tart shell, then fill it with thick mascarpone while it is still a little warm. I also bake the plums, first cutting them in half and dotting them with butter, in a separate dish until their flesh becomes an intense ochre-yellow; I then layer them over the mascarpone. The same method can be used for any plum. These baked plums are also great on their own with a bowl of mascarpone flavoured with a little plum brandy, or as the basis of a crumble.

While I delight in using dried prunes in many forms of cooking, the prune would have to come near the top of that list of foods people either love or hate. There is nothing like adding the word 'prune' to the menu to see the orders slow down. For months I included the thinnest, richest chocolate tart on the Pheasant Farm Restaurant menu – shiny with just-made ganache, its superfine pastry melted in the mouth – and I served it alongside alcohol-soaked prunes. It was a chocoholic's dream, yet we almost had to give it away. So we re-worded the menu, omitting any mention of the prunes, and it sold like hot-cakes (so to speak). The really interesting thing was that the prunes, which still came with the tart, were seldom left.

If you were one of those people I had to trick, at least I might have given you a new view of this much-denigrated fruit. If this has whetted your appetite, try making your own sweetmeats by soaking prunes in port overnight, then draining them. Chop the prunes with some roasted almonds or walnuts, then fold through dark couverture chocolate melted with a little cream and pour into a tin. When set, cut into tiny cubes and serve with coffee. Rich, dark chocolate and prunes are a combination that is meant to be.

I have a friend with a love of rice pudding with prunes. Knowing her mother to be a good cook, I understand this comfort food, but secretly feel that this dish, when cooked by a less-interested cook, could be one of the main offenders on the prune-hater's list.

It is perhaps in savoury dishes that I most love prunes. Not too long ago I wrote about how I was addicted to French/American food writer Madeleine Kamman's prune mustard; well, I am on another bent now. This time it is a variation on a theme from Patricia Wells' book, *At Home in Provence*. Here she gives her version of a prune and fig chutney made with red-wine vinegar and cinnamon sticks, traditional fare in southwest France, where prunes are much used. I extended the idea and poached prunes and figs in red-wine vinegar with Quatre-Épices (see page 358), then folded through a good wholegrain mustard. I keep finding uses for this prune and fig mustard, as I call it, such as in a sandwich thick with crisp local double-smoked bacon and rocket.

Talking about prunes and bacon, where have devils on horseback gone? I dare you to bring out these treats from the 1960s (or was it the '70s?). As long as you use good-quality bacon to wrap plump prunes, you will have everyone coming back for seconds.

Prunes go as well with pork as they do with bacon and they are good with lamb too. Moorish tagines combine prunes, lamb and couscous. And the Scottish cock-a-leekie is a perfect cooler-weather dish. Here, a piece of stewing beef (best with the shin attached), a boiling fowl, a bunch of leeks and another of herbs are simmered slowly, then pitted prunes are added for the last 20 minutes of cooking. This is serious comfort food, and not only for the flavours: the smells that waft through the kitchen are heartening in themselves.

If you are lucky enough to have a goose to cook, you can't go wrong if you stuff it with lots of onion, herbs, the goose liver, walnuts, bacon or pancetta, and prunes. Try making pies – for the filling, cook chicken, duck or rabbit on the bone, then cube the meat and toss it with the ingredients given for the stuffing above, adding some reduced pan juices or stock.

The sad thing is that Australian farmers are pulling plum trees out. A grower today tells me he has booked the bulldozer to pull out six varieties of choice plums, some of those only three to four years old, because not enough people relish these wonderful fruit. The prices can be rock bottom one year, okay the next and, if the growers are lucky, a good return comes one year in three.

There is, however, a property called Budgi Werri in Young, New South Wales, with a beautiful orchard of mature prune plum trees. This wonderful place is far more than just picture-postcard beautiful. The owners, Cheryl and Doug Heley, produce a variety of gourmet prune products using sustainable farming methods. The quality of this fruit is so close to that found in the southwest of France that this is a product well worth seeking out. For more details, visit their website www.budgiwerri.com.au.

DAMSON PASTE

It's not as time-consuming or dangerous making damson paste as it is quince paste, which spits furiously! I like to serve damson paste with a ripe, soft cheese or an aged cheddar. Just like quince paste, it can be cut into squares and rolled in castor sugar to be served with Turkish coffee. I'd also like to try it pressed into the centre of doughnuts and deep-fried, as I once saw demonstrated at the Croatian food stand at the Ovens Valley International Festival in Victoria's northeast.

damson plums, stalks removed and washed   **castor sugar**

Place the plums in a large, heavy-based preserving pan and cook for 30–40 minutes until soft, either in a 150°C oven, with a little water in the pan to avoid burning, or on the stove in just enough water to cover them.

Allow to cool slightly, then separate the flesh from the stones and purée the pulp in a food processor. Weigh the pulp and return it to the rinsed-out pan. For each kilogram of pulp, add 800 g sugar. Cook the paste over low heat to dissolve the sugar, stirring constantly. Increase the temperature and continue cooking, stirring frequently, until the greater part of the syrup has evaporated. By this time the pulp will have become quite stiff and require constant stirring to avoid burning. The paste is ready when it comes away from the sides of the pan. This whole process will take about 2 hours.

Coat a baking dish with a little castor sugar and add the paste, spreading it out to about a 1 cm thickness. Dry the paste in the sun on a warm afternoon or overnight in a warm place such as a gas oven with the pilot light left on. Remove from tray and wrap in baking paper, storing in the pantry, not the refrigerator, for up to several months.

PLUM SAUCE   *Makes 1 litre*

This is my interpretation of one of the many recipes for plum sauce in *The Barossa Cookery Book*, first published in 1917. This sauce is marvellous with barbecued pork sausages or grilled duck or kangaroo fillets.

3 kg blood plums

1 × 60 g piece ginger

500 g onions, roughly chopped

2 cloves garlic, sliced

extra virgin olive oil, for cooking

1.25 kg sugar

2 cups (500 ml) red-wine vinegar

2 teaspoons black peppercorns

½ teaspoon cayenne pepper

Halve the plums, leaving the stones intact. Bruise the ginger by pressing down on it with the flat blade of a knife. Sauté the onion, garlic and ginger in a little olive oil in a large pre-serving pan until softened. Add the remaining ingredients and cook for about 30 minutes or until the plum stones come away from the flesh. Strain the sauce and leave to cool. Fill hot sterilised bottles (see Glossary) with the cooled sauce and seal.

PRUNE GNOCCHI
(TO SERVE WITH POT-ROASTED MEAT)   *Serves 4 as an accompaniment*

Thoughts of slow-cooking lead me to think of a leg of mutton cooked in a heavy-based casserole with lots of rosemary, roasted garlic and just enough stock or wine to keep it all from sticking. I would use saltbush mutton for its distinctive flavour and the melt-in-the-mouth quality it develops when cooked slowly, but it is an idea that could be applied equally well to everyday lamb, a shoulder of pork or even veal. Instead of adding prunes to the pan, serve the meat with this prune gnocchi – yet another way of utilising the very delicious prune.

20 prunes, stoned

squeeze of lemon juice

400 g waxy potatoes, unpeeled

60 g butter, plus extra for cooking

125 g plain flour

sea salt flakes and freshly ground
black pepper

pinch ground cinnamon

handful sage leaves

Soak the prunes in lemon juice and water overnight. Next day, drain and set aside. Cook the potatoes in a saucepan of boiling water until tender. Drain well and press through a mouli or potato ricer back into the saucepan, then stand the pan over low heat for a minute to ensure no moisture remains. Spread the potato into a rectangular shape on your bench.

Melt the butter in a small saucepan. Meanwhile, season the flour with salt, pepper and cinnamon, then spread this over the hot potato. Drizzle over the hot melted butter and, using a pastry scraper or two knives, scrape the dough into a ball and knead for about 7 minutes. Roll the dough into a log about 2.5 cm thick and leave to rest.

Preheat the oven to 200°C. Smear a baking dish with butter and set aside. Cut off a 5 mm-thick slice of dough and flatten it out. Place a prune in the centre and roll dough around to enclose it. Repeat with remaining potato dough and prunes. »

Place half the gnocchi in a saucepan of salted boiling water, and as they come to the surface, cook them for 1 minute. Remove with a slotted spoon and put into the baking dish, then repeat the process with the second batch. Dot the gnocchi with a little extra butter, add a handful of sage leaves and bake for about 10 minutes or until butter is golden brown.

PLUM STREUSELKUCHEN   *Serves 8*

Streuselkuchen is the mainstay of Barossa bakeries, and plums make a wonderful addition. Freeze the plums whole until you need them, then cut them in half and place on top of the dough, sprinkling the streusel on top before baking – what great fruit flavour!

8 plums, halved and stoned	**STREUSEL TOPPING**
30 g unsalted butter, melted	70 g brown sugar
	½ teaspoon ground cinnamon
DOUGH	grated rind of ½ lemon
15 g fresh yeast	120 g unsalted butter, chopped
2 tablespoons sugar	150 g plain flour
140 ml milk	
250 g plain flour	
grated rind of ½ lemon	
2 eggs, beaten	
50 g melted butter *or* cream *or* beaten	
egg white, for brushing	

For the dough, mix the yeast in a cup with 1 teaspoon of the sugar, then leave in a warm place for 10 minutes or until frothy. Meanwhile, heat the milk in a small saucepan until lukewarm. Sift the flour into a warm, dry bowl, then add the remaining sugar and lemon rind. Make a well in the centre and add the yeast, then the beaten eggs and warm milk. Incorporate with a wooden spoon until mixture comes together to form a dough.

Knead dough for 20 minutes on a floured bench. Return to the bowl, cover with a tea towel and leave in a warm place until the dough doubles in size (this should take about 2 hours, depending on the weather).

Knock the dough back on a floured bench, then knead for another 1–2 minutes and form into a disc. Roll the dough to cover the base of a rectangular, shallow-sided biscuit tray. Leave to rise until it plumps up to size again. Preheat the oven to 165°C.

Meanwhile, to make the streusel topping, mix the sugar, cinnamon and lemon rind, then rub in the butter and flour, working the mixture with your fingertips, but do not incorporate the butter completely as you need some lumps for the streusel.

Brush the dough with the melted butter, cream or beaten egg white, then layer the plums over the dough, brush them with melted butter and liberally sprinkle the streusel topping over. Bake for 30 minutes. Serve warm with cream.

BAKED PRUNE PLUM AND MASCARPONE TART

Serves 6–8

1 × quantity Sour-cream Pastry
(see page 424)
1 kg fresh prune plums (about 25),
halved and stoned

60 g unsalted butter, chopped
2 cups (500 ml) mascarpone
2 teaspoons plum brandy (optional)

Make and chill the pastry as instructed, then roll it out and use to line a 20 cm tart tin with a removable base. Chill the pastry case for 20 minutes.

Preheat the oven to 200°C. Line the pastry case with foil, then cover with pastry weights and blind bake for 15 minutes, then remove the foil and weights and return the pastry case to the oven for another 5 minutes. Leave the pastry case to cool to room temperature and reset the oven to 210°C.

Arrange a layer of plums in a baking dish and dot with butter. Bake for 20 minutes or until cooked but still holding their shape, then leave to cool, reserving any juices.

Fill the pastry case with the mascarpone (if it is very thick, thin it with the brandy) and top with the plums. Transfer any reserved plum juices to a small saucepan and reduce over high heat, then drizzle over the tart. Serve immediately.

BAROSSA DRIED FRUIT COMPOTES

Serves 10

Amontillado is an aged dry sherry with a distinctively nutty flavour.

1 kg mixed dried Barossa fruits (prunes,
nectarines, apricots, peaches and apples)
3 cups (750 ml) Amontillado sherry

250 g sugar
50 ml pouring cream
double cream, to serve

Soak the fruit in the sherry for 24 hours. Line 10 individual heatproof cups or 100 ml moulds with foil. Make the caramel by boiling the sugar, pouring cream and 250 ml water together carefully over medium–high heat until very dark brown. Pour 1 tablespoon of caramel into each mould to coat the bottom. Half-fill each mould with fruit. Pour on some more caramel and then add another layer of fruit almost to the top. Finish with a final layer of caramel.

Preheat the oven to 180°C. Cover the moulds with foil, place in a roasting pan, then fill with boiling water to halfway up sides of mould. Bake in this water bath for 30 minutes or until set. Let the compotes cool a little, then turn them out on to plates and serve with the cream.

PRESERVES

THE VERY FIRST TIME I BECAME CLOSELY ASSOCIATED WITH THE Angaston Show was when I was writing my first book, *Maggie's Farm*, in 1992. Both Angaston and Tanunda in the Barossa Valley have an agriculture-based show each year, and I organised to be a fly-on-the-wall at the judging of the preserves section so as to better understand the process. What a delight it was watching the theatrical Mrs Stiller at work judging the many entries. Part of my satisfaction came from our sponsorship (with a modest sum, in business terms) of a prize for the preserves section – a feature of our local show that seemed to be dying out. Compared to the financial outlay, the joy we experienced made it the most pleasurable donation we have ever made. More small companies are following suit but not as many as are needed to keep this tradition alive. I have long wanted to see an 'unusual vegetables' category, to encourage growers of salsify, scorzorena, cavolo nero and other exotics that tend not to be grown commercially.

I have just persuaded the Tanunda Show to introduce a new category to their portfolio – 'open entry grape products' – and in sponsoring this I hope that it will be carried through to the Angaston Show too. As it happens, the Angaston Show is now held two weeks before the Tanunda Show so there is a fair bit of rivalry between the two. Everyone in the district, from restaurateurs to retail shops to families, benefits from these crafts being handed down to the younger generations, particularly here in the Barossa, where the life of self-sufficiency and barter was well established in the early days of settlement, and was still a part of daily life until sometime in the 1970s. It was such a privilege to see the final stages of setting up and the judging process, and highlighted the resourcefulness of Barossa Valley people. The source of our food is in the hands of country people, so we should encourage them and make it worth their while. I still live my life in such a rush that I seldom find the time to enjoy such occasions, but I plan to change that!

Both the Angaston Show, on the last Saturday in February, and the Tanunda Show, the second Saturday in March, make a great family day out. The local agricultural bureaus

get involved by displaying their produce – it's great to see what these small communities can achieve. As well as the agricultural emphasis, Tanunda has a very popular horse show. There are no expensive show bags, yet lots of things for children to do. Country shows such as these are held throughout the year in districts all over Australia. People like Mrs Stiller and her husband used to travel the show circuit and obviously immensely enjoyed the life they led. There are judges in every district who give so much of their time, but I've yet to meet anyone like Mrs Stiller, whose whole life seemed to revolve around 'judging time'.

One of the traditions we in the Valley hold dear is the annual making of dill pickles, so the Dill Pickle Championship is a hotly contested competition of the Tanunda Show, taken extremely seriously by both locals and judges. Having done my time many years ago as an Associate Judge, I was finally promoted one year to 'Chief Dill'. The judges of this competition have, over the years, been drawn from most of the top wine people of the Valley – the inimitable Peter Lehmann being the man who first led the charge. I can assure you that the white coats we wore and the spittoons provided were there for very practical reasons, as not every dill pickle is worthy of eating, particularly at 9 a.m. on a Sunday morning! I remember so well some of those judging mornings – there was a barricade to keep the judges and the 'dills' from the public, and those with a vested interest would hover around to see the reactions on our faces as we tested the dills. They were such good times for me.

It is so important to maintain these regional traditions, particularly in an area so steeped in food culture as the Barossa. As well as the Dill Pickle Championship, there is the German Cake Championship and the Rotegrütze Championship on the same day – all truly important traditional foods kept alive by the show society.

Getting a recipe out of any of the winners is understandably not on, given that there is many a small seasonal business on the side at stake. However, there is a wonderful book of Barossa recipes, *The Barossa Cookery Book*, put out by the Tanunda Soldiers' Memorial Hall Committee in 1917 (also the source of the Plum Sauce recipe on page 116). In its original form, this book had 500 recipes, and four or five years later it had 1000. It hasn't been altered in any way since that first publication and has sold well over 180,000 copies. There's no doubt that a lot of people here are interested in preserving, bottling and country cooking, as the recipes featured include dill pickles, grape and plum sauces, German cake and rotegrütze as well as so many others in which Silesian traditions have intermingled with the Mediterranean climate of the Barossa.

Mrs C. Kraft of Vine Vale submitted a recipe for cucumbers pickled in vine leaves to *The Barossa Cookery Book* in 1917. She gives us just a flavour of the book's tone when she writes: 'One cup salt, scalded with boiling water and cooled. Two cups water and a little dill, enough water to fill the tin. Use a benzine tin. Cover bottom of tin with vine leaves, then a layer of cucumbers and dill, another layer of leaves, and so on to the top. Last layer, vine leaves. Use young cucumbers. Cover with plate and weight for two weeks. Leave another week before using. Add more water if some should evaporate.'

PICKLED CORNICHONS
Makes 3 litres

As well as the traditional German way of preserving dill pickles, here is another method using the French cornichon, actually a baby dill about 5 cm long and best picked under-ripe with a little of the stem attached, then pickled in a straight vinegar solution. Using good-quality vinegar is important to this recipe; it must contain a minimum of 6 per cent acidity, as this affects the crispness of the pickle, which is its defining characteristic.

2 kg baby dill cucumbers

300 g coarse sea salt

8 bay leaves

1 tablespoon allspice berries

up to 2 litres quality white-wine vinegar

Rub the cucumbers with a damp cloth, then place in a bowl and toss the salt through them. Leave overnight; the salt will draw out the moisture. Next day, rinse the cucumbers, drain and dry with a clean tea towel. Place them in a sterilised jar (see Glossary) or enamel crock with the bay leaves and allspice. Pour the vinegar over until the cucumbers are immersed, with several centimetres to spare (this stage is merely to measure the vinegar needed).

Pour off the vinegar from the jar into an enamelled or stainless steel saucepan and bring to the boil. Do not reduce but immediately pour over the cucumbers and seal the jar. They take 6–8 weeks before they are ready to eat.

MRS HEIN'S QUINCE JAM
Makes 1.5–2 litres (depending on how long it is cooked)

The first year we sponsored a prize in the preserve section at the Angaston Show, we were delighted to see that lifting the prize money for the winner from $1 to $200 lifted the number of entries as well, and has done so ever since. That year, two of the prizewinners were good enough to share their favourite recipes with me, and I include them here. With all respect to Mrs Hein, I halve the quantity of sugar stated below for my taste. By leaving the quinces whole, this recipe demonstrates a wonderfully simple way to make quince jam, as they are so hard to cut and core.

1 kg under-ripe quinces

1.5 litres water

about 2 kg sugar

Rub and clean the quinces well with a rough towel. Cut the bumps off one end so they will sit flat in a large heavy-based saucepan. Place the whole quinces in the saucepan with the water and 125 g of the sugar. Boil gently, covered, for 1½–2 hours or until the quinces are light pink.

Carefully lift out the quinces on to a plate (an egg slice is good for this) and discard the cores, reserving the syrup. Chop the quinces roughly and return them to the saucepan.

Measure pulp and allow 1 cup of sugar to each cup of pulp. Re-heat slowly, stirring, until sugar is dissolved, then boil rapidly for another 20–30 minutes or until jam is set. Test this by placing a spoonful of jam on a saucer. Place saucer in the fridge for a few minutes, then test the jam by pushing it with your finger – if it wrinkles the jam is set.

MRS LOFFLER'S MUSTARD CABBAGE PICKLES *Makes 2 litres*

This recipe can be made at any time of the year and served with cold meats and cheese or used for sandwiches.

½ small cabbage (about 1 kg)

3 onions (about 500 g), sliced

2 green capsicums, seeded and
    coarsely chopped

2 red capsicums, seeded and
    coarsely chopped

¼ cup salt

2 cups (500 ml) Seppelt's white vinegar

1 cup (220 g) brown sugar, lightly packed

2 cups (440 g) white sugar

1 tablespoon Keen's mustard powder

1 teaspoon ground turmeric

1 teaspoon ground ginger

30 g flour

1 tablespoon celery seeds

1 tablespoon yellow mustard seeds

Having discarded the old outer leaves and core, shred the cabbage, then combine in a bowl with the onions and capsicums. Sprinkle salt over and let stand overnight, covered, to draw out the moisture.

The next morning, cover vegetables with water, stir well to disperse the salt and leave to drain in a colander. Meanwhile, combine the vinegar and the brown and white sugars in a large saucepan. Stir over high heat until the sugar dissolves, then bring to the boil and add vegetables. Reduce heat to low and simmer for 5 minutes. (Cooking time may be different depending on the type of cabbage; for example, it may be less if you use a soft-leaf cabbage.)

Mix the mustard, turmeric, ginger and flour to a smooth paste with 125 ml water. Stir into the vegetable mixture and continue stirring until mixture boils and thickens. Reduce the heat and simmer for 10 minutes. Add celery and mustard seeds. Pour into hot sterilised jars (see Glossary) and cool before sealing.

QUAIL

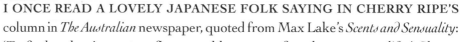

I ONCE READ A LOVELY JAPANESE FOLK SAYING IN CHERRY RIPE'S column in *The Australian* newspaper, quoted from Max Lake's *Scents and Sensuality*: 'To find and enjoy a new flavour adds seventy-five days to your life.' Cherry was discussing the fervour with which the Japanese embrace new food flavours from other countries – sadly, in this case, McDonald's and Coca-Cola in particular. But it is possible to find variety in new foods that are not 'junk' foods, and that can be prepared so easily they could almost be called 'convenience' foods. Quail is one such food.

While quail used to be fairly standard fare in restaurants and have long been bred in the backyards of Greek and Italian families, it was not until more recently that they have been widely available to the home cook. Quail is incredibly tasty, and most often eaten just using your fingers, which makes it a much more casual meal. It is healthy, relatively inexpensive and can be prepared and cooked in less than 15 minutes (if you choose not to marinate it). It can be barbecued, pan-fried, pot-roasted, stuffed and oven-baked, and is equally tasty served cold at picnics as it is warm in salads or hot for dinner – after resting, of course. What more could you want for convenience?

There is a world of difference between a perfectly cooked quail and one that has been ruined by overcooking. The best tip I can give you for quail that is to be barbecued or pan-fried, is to prepare it by cutting along the spine and squashing it flat with the palm of your hand ('butterflying') for easier cooking. Make sure to tuck the wings in so the breast cooks evenly. In readiness for cooking you can coat the quail lightly with extra virgin olive oil, some freshly ground black pepper and fresh herbs, or make a marinade. Our favourite marinade for quail at the restaurant was made of fresh ginger, sliced garlic and equal quantities of honey and soy sauce. We marinated the butterflied quail overnight, skin-side down, and brushed it with the mixture while cooking.

If you prefer something simpler, try some honey and lemon juice, or just extra virgin olive oil, lemon juice and thyme. Be careful with the lemon, though, as it will actually begin

Grilled quail in a post-cooking marinade of verjuice, lemon peel, green figs, roasted walnuts and thyme (see page 128)

'cooking' the meat before any contact with the heat – hence whenever I use lemon juice in a marinade, I only leave the meat for about 20 minutes maximum. Another option is to rest the cooked quail in a post-cooking marinade of verjuice, lemon peel, small green figs cut in half, roasted walnuts and thyme for 10 minutes, then spoon the marinade out and serve with the birds.

Another important trick of the trade when barbecuing these small birds (particularly if they have been marinaded in honey) is to turn them at 2-minute intervals. It may seem a bit of trouble but such small details make the difference between good and average cooking. If you don't turn them frequently, you will end up with a burnt offering. As they are such small birds, quail will dry out rapidly if overcooked, so, if barbecuing, allow about 8 minutes for cooking and then put aside to rest for 5 minutes before serving. The meat should still be a little pink on the breast (I don't mean raw) and will be juicy and delicious. If overcooked, they will be like cardboard.

When buying several quail, you will find at least some variation in their sizes: the plumper ones will need an extra minute or two of cooking time. This is another of those small details that make cooking more difficult, but also more rewarding when you get it right. However, you can elect to buy jumbo quail that are more consistent sizes.

If you wish to pan-fry your quail on the stove, allow closer to 12 minutes in total. The trick

here is to choose a pan large enough so that you do indeed fry gently (rather than poach) your food. For example, for two quails that have been butterflied you will need a pan measuring about 22 centimetres across. Warm 2–3 teaspoons of butter in the pan over medium–high heat, adding a dash of extra virgin olive oil so the butter doesn't burn. Make sure the butter turns golden brown before adding the quail, skin-side down. I then reduce the tempera-ture to low, season the quail with a sprinkle of sea salt and freshly ground black pepper and wait until the skin is a light golden brown all over before turning.

The important thing is to adjust the flame so the butter doesn't burn. If you can keep the butter that lovely golden brown then you know the quail is cooking gently enough. It is also important not to sear the quail as, not only will it look unattractive, it will also toughen it. This is a simple principle of cooking I often see ignored.

Because you start with quite a high temperature to get the butter golden and need to turn it down to save the quail from burning, it's difficult to move far from the stove. If you prefer, you can just brown the birds on both sides and then place the pan in a 200°C oven to finish off. Cook the quail for about 4–6 minutes in the oven and leave it to rest for another 5 minutes on a plate on top of the stove. (As everyone's oven is different, it is only practice that will teach you the right cooking time.)

If you wish to serve one quail per person for a meal, you would probably need either to stuff them or serve them with Polenta (see below) – both are fabulous options. When we first opened the Farmshop I used to serve quail stuffed with rice, lots of diced onion softened in butter, orange rind, currants, almond slices and a little thyme. People would sit outside on the decking and devour them with their fingers and then want to buy fresh quail to take home, so I'd also supply the cooking instructions. It was tasty and filling and still stands up as a dish I would cook today. I would also glaze the outside of the bird with a little orange juice and extra virgin olive oil to caramelise the skin as it baked. The stuffed birds require about 10 minutes in the oven. Test if cooked by gently prising one leg away – if it resists being pulled, it is not ready.

My favourite way of eating quail is at late summer picnics and barbecues, when I stuff them with figs, and wrap them in either bacon or a thin slice of pork fat, fastened with a toothpick. These must not be prepared in advance, however, because if the fig is left in the quail for any period before cooking it has a most unusual effect on the uncooked meat and turns it mushy.

One notable dish that stood out during a recent trip to Paris was a quail salad. The quail was carved off the bone after cooking and served with grilled figs, onions, tiny beans and radicchio, then finished with a small amount of a fabulous glaze. The flavour of the quail, which was fattier than we are used to in Australia, was intense. I presumed the bird was dry-plucked, as I had discovered is often the case with poultry in Italy and France.

POLENTA TO TEAM WITH QUAIL   *Serves 8*

I particularly like a bowl of soft polenta served in a large dish, topped with pan-fried quail and its juices, and perhaps some caramelised onions.

1.75 litres Golden Chicken Stock	**2 teaspoons salt**
(see page 57)	**100 g Parmigiano Reggiano, grated**
2 cups (340 g) polenta	**1 dessertspoon butter (optional)**

Heat half the stock in a saucepan until simmering. In another saucepan, mix the remaining stock with the polenta while it is still cold, to make a paste. Slowly add the hot stock, stirring constantly over low heat to avoid clumping. Season with salt. Continue stirring over low heat until you see the polenta coming away from the sides of the saucepan (about 20 minutes). Add the cheese and the butter, if using. Serve with barbecued or pan-fried quail.

TART OF QUAIL WITH SAGE, BACON AND GRAPES

Makes 6 tarts

This is an old Pheasant Farm Restaurant dish that often appeared in the days when we reared our own quail. We made it with quail breasts to utilise any slightly damaged birds. Even though it's a more formal dish, it's actually very simple to make once you've made the Sour-cream Pastry (which is not only foolproof but also quick; if you're in a hurry, you can even manage without resting the dough for as long – with this recipe, some pastry shrinkage doesn't matter).

½ × quantity Sour-cream Pastry
    (see page 424)
120 g butter
extra virgin olive oil, for cooking
6 quails (cut along the backbone and pressed
    down flat to butterfly)
sea salt flakes and freshly ground
    black pepper

24 sage leaves
½ cup (125 ml) verjuice
2 cups (500 ml) reduced Golden Chicken
    Stock (see page 57)
3 slices sugar-cured bacon, halved *or* 6 slices
    round pancetta
200 g seedless green *or* red grapes, stems
    removed and washed

Make and chill the pastry as instructed. Preheat the oven to 220°C. Using brioche or other small moulds, fit the pastry around the moulds, gently pressing it down on a baking tray, and cook for 10 minutes, then remove the pastry from the moulds and cook for another 5 minutes or until golden. (You can also mould the pastry around the base of an earthenware cup or heatproof glass upended on a baking tray, then bake until the pastry is golden.)

Heat 60 g butter in a frying pan over high heat until nut-brown, then add a dash of olive oil to prevent burning. Quickly season the quails with salt and pepper, then place in the pan and seal on both sides. Transfer the quail, skin-side up, to a roasting pan, drizzle with a little more olive oil, then place in the oven for 4–5 minutes. Wipe out the frying pan and heat the other 60 g butter, then add the sage leaves and gently cook until they are crisp but not burnt. Remove from pan and drain on kitchen paper. Remove the quail from the oven, transfer to a separate dish and rest them, turned skin-side down, for at least 10 minutes. When the quails are cool enough to handle, pull off the legs and, using a sharp knife, take each breast off the carcass.

Discard any excess butter from the roasting pan, then deglaze with verjuice, and reduce by half over high heat. Add the reduced stock and boil rapidly until the sauce reaches a syrupy consistency. Meanwhile grill or dry-fry the bacon or pancetta until crisp.

To assemble, place 2 legs and 2 breasts into each pastry case, followed by the bacon and sage. Place the assembled tarts in a hot oven for 2–3 minutes to warm through.

Bring the sauce back to the boil and throw in the grapes for about 30 seconds. Using a slotted spoon, place most of the grapes on top of the tarts, letting the rest cascade over. Pour the sauce around the base of the tarts and serve.

QUAIL WITH CELERIAC, APPLES AND PINE NUTS   *Serves 4*

On the last night of a recent trip to Paris I ate at Les Olivades and had the most memorable quail dish I have ever eaten. In attempting to replicate the quality of this dish, I've found jumbo quail works best.

100 g pine nuts

8 jumbo quails

hazelnut oil, for drizzling

1 tablespoon thyme leaves, finely chopped

sea salt flakes and freshly ground
    black pepper

½ cup (125 ml) reduced Golden Chicken
    Stock (see page 57), warmed

1 small celeriac

2 Granny Smith apples

juice of 1 lemon

2 heads witlof, leaves separated,
    washed and dried

2 red witlof *or* radicchio, leaves separated,
    washed and dried

1 bunch watercress, leaves picked,
    washed and dried

1 teaspoon aged balsamic vinegar

truffle oil, to serve

Preheat the oven to 200°C. Place pine nuts on a baking tray and dry-roast for 5–10 minutes or until golden brown. Place quail on their backs in a shallow heavy-based roasting pan. Drizzle them with hazelnut oil, then add thyme and season with salt and pepper. Roast quail for 10 minutes, then remove from oven, turn quail on to their breasts, pour in the warm chicken stock and leave to rest for another 10 minutes.

Meanwhile, peel and finely dice equal quantities of celeriac and apples and place in a bowl, then toss with lemon juice and hazelnut oil and season to taste.

Arrange the witlof and watercress on four plates, then spoon the celeriac and apple mixture onto the salad leaves, making a 'nest' for the quail. Place 2 cooked quail into each nest. Heat the reserved pan juices in the roasting pan over high heat, then add balsamic vinegar and the tiniest hint of truffle oil. Scatter the pine nuts over the salad greens and drizzle the pan juices over the quail and leaves. Serve immediately.

RASPBERRIES

 THE HEAVENLY FLAVOUR OF PLUMP, RIPE, VELVETY SOFT raspberries is seldom as luscious as nature intended, unless you pick the berries yourself and eat them within hours. Although the hull separates itself easily from the berry, picking raspberries is still not the easiest work in the world. So, with that in mind, I think the rise of the pick-your-own fruit farm should be encouraged. While raspberry jam is easy to make at home (as the fruit has such a high pectin content), it's an extravagant jam to make if buying raspberries by the punnet. Often the raspberry farms sell their own jams that are so thick with fruit you'll never look at commercial jam again.

The other option is to grow your own – you'll need to prepare the ground properly and use a trellis, and your bird-deterring techniques will require some forethought. A cooler climate will undoubtedly always give the best results. My local nurseryman recommends adding sulphate of potash or manure to the bed, while that learned fruit expert Louis Glowinski asserts: 'The perfect spot would be open to the east and north, but shaded by a tree on the west. Soil needs to be free-draining and high in organic matter. Planting raspberries in rows north to south, plant out 30 cm apart along the rows, leaving 1.5 m between rows.'

Actually, I have always thought raspberry growers must be made of strong stock. I tried growing plants on canes for years but became too impatient; either the heat gets the berries, the plants fail to bear due to lack of water, or I miss the flush of fruit and find dried berries all over the canes. Luckily, we have a raspberry farm in the Barossa, which sells raspberries at our Saturday market when in season. Instead of just one short burst of fruit, raspberries come and go over a few months, so you can enjoy them with the fruits of early summer – the first white peaches, for example – then with late-summer figs, not to mention other summer berries. Berries will last only a few days in the fridge and if mould is present it spreads from berry to berry in the punnet, just as with lemons, so mouldy ones must be quickly discarded.

It is difficult to tire of eating raspberries raw, picked as fresh as possible and unwashed, so the pleasure of the velvety flesh is not diminished, then simply served with cream. Raspberries served with a sponge finger or almond bread need the least amount of attention. If you want something a bit more elaborate, try a raspberry and hazelnut meringue. Grind 125 g roasted hazelnuts to a coarse powder in a food processor. Whisk 5 large egg whites until stiff, then add about 250 g castor sugar, a little at a time, and fold in the ground hazelnuts. Divide the mixture in half and spread in two discs on baking paper. Bake for about 40 minutes at 175°C, then leave to cool in the switched-off oven with the door propped open. Spread one of the cooled meringues with whipped cream or crème fraîche, then add as much of a punnet of raspberries as you can. Top with the remaining meringue and sift over icing sugar, if you like. The chewy, nutty meringue, luscious raspberries and cream make the most wonderful combination.

If you have had a real bounty and have been able to make raspberry vinegar, a tablespoon added to a glass of water makes a refreshing non-alcoholic raspberry drink. Seppelt's recently made such a drop commercially – an adult soft drink, great for the hot weather. Then there is raspberries in a trifle, or with a moist lemon cake, or with grilled figs in a tart – I love all these, but best of all, I love raspberry ice cream.

When we used to own Charlick's Feed Store, our short-lived foray into the Adelaide restaurant scene, I stopped in with a friend to trial some new dishes during one of our seemingly endless heatwaves. When we went into the kitchen we found our freezer had broken down, leaving a parfait with layers of raspberry, vanilla and chocolate at the mercy of the heat. So much work had gone into this beautiful dessert! We all ate as much as we could while it collapsed before our eyes, particularly enjoying the intensity of the raspberry layer (only a small amount of sugar was used, with lime juice added to heighten the raspberry flavour, making a great counterpoint to the richness of the chocolate and vanilla). After that, we decided to replace this dessert offering with a safer option until the freezer problem was resolved.

Summer pudding is another favourite, preferably crammed with raspberries, blackberries and redcurrants. But if summer pudding is too fiddly for you, then make a panna cotta, a simple baked custard or a crème caramel served with raspberries alongside. Better still, for freshness and lightness, make a Blancmange (see opposite) and send it quivering to the table with a huge dish of raspberries and a little cream.

When the last raspberries appear in February, as they do in my neck of the woods, try them with fresh black or green figs, picked just before they burst. Serve the figs cut open and piled high with raspberries and a good dollop of cream – a sensational way to see out the summer. I used to have twelve heart-shaped moulds for coeurs à la crème, but they have disappeared, sadly. They were made of porcelain and had little holes in the base, which allowed a soft cheese like ricotta, sweetened with a little castor sugar, to be drained. When turned out, the cheese was light and fresh – a bowl of fresh raspberries (and cream too, perhaps) was all that was needed. Losing my little hearts was a pain, but I make do by buying fresh ricotta that comes with its own perforated bowl. I line the bowl with muslin (or even a new Chux), then press in the sweetened curd and leave it to drip overnight. It is not as romantic as the traditional hearts but the results taste every bit as good.

For all their fragility, raspberries freeze particularly well and can be used to make a jam out of season or a sauce for a dessert. Process the berries to a purée with just enough icing sugar to sweeten then pass through a sieve. (Allow about a tablespoon of sugar for each cup of fruit – the rarer yellow raspberry is sweeter, so it needs less sugar.) Serve the sauce with a rich chocolate cake or over ice cream, or add it to a cold, sweeter Italian style of sparkling white wine as an aperitif.

Whichever accompaniment you choose for your raspberries, enjoy the berries while they are at their best. They come in flushes – early and late summer, and even well into autumn in some years.

BLANCMANGE WITH RASPBERRIES *Serves 4*

Recipes abound for almond blancmange. Instead of beginning by grinding your own almonds to flavour the milk, here an almond-flavoured liqueur is added to buttermilk, making this a very easy version.

vegetable oil, for greasing
2 cups (500 ml) buttermilk
40 ml Amaretto
4 × 2 g leaves gelatine
  (see Glossary)

200 ml warm water
100 g castor sugar
fresh raspberries, to serve

Lightly grease four 200 ml moulds or ramekins with a flavourless vegetable oil. Combine the buttermilk and Amaretto and set aside. Soak the gelatine leaves in a little cold water for 5 minutes to dissolve. Bring the warm water and castor sugar to the boil in a saucepan, squeeze out excess water from the gelatine leaves, then stir them in to the sugar mixture and allow to cool.

Mix the flavoured buttermilk into the gelatine mixture and chill in the refrigerator for 10 minutes. Pour the mixture into the oiled moulds and refrigerate until set. Turn out just before serving by dipping the base of each mould into hot water before inverting. Serve with fresh raspberries.

PAN-FRIED FIGS WITH FRESH RASPBERRIES AND EXTRA VIRGIN OLIVE OIL ICE CREAM *Serves 4*

One of the most luscious ice creams I ever made was with extra virgin olive oil and ver-juice – a recipe given to me by my friend Ingo Schwartz, retired Master Pâtissier. As it was difficult to make without specific equipment, I began the journey of finding another way of incorporating extra virgin olive oil into an ice cream, as the mouthfeel of it is amazing.

This is a great dessert for non-sweet-tooths like me, as the tartness of the raspberries balances the hot fig/cold ice cream combination beautifully, and if the figs are ripe from the tree, you shouldn't need to add any extra sugar.

6 large ripe figs	ICE CREAM
60 g unsalted butter	250 g sugar
dash of extra virgin olive oil	100 ml water
1 tablespoon brown sugar	pinch salt
1–2 punnets raspberries	4 eggs
icing sugar (optional, to dust	200 ml extra virgin olive oil
raspberries if too tart)	200 ml full-cream milk

For the ice cream, make a syrup by placing the sugar and water in a saucepan and reducing by half over medium heat. Add the salt and swirl in, then leave this mixture to cool. Beat the eggs in a food processor, slowly adding the extra virgin olive oil in a thin and steady stream, as you would when making mayonnaise. Once the oil is fully combined, gradually add the cooled syrup and the milk, mixing as you go. Transfer to an ice cream machine and churn (following the manufacturer's instructions).

Cut the figs in half lengthways. In a frying pan heat the butter until nut-brown, then add a dash of extra virgin olive oil to prevent burning. Add figs to pan and sprinkle with brown sugar so that they caramelise quickly, and cook them for just a minute or two.

Serve 3 fig halves on each plate, piled with a generous helping of fresh raspberries and a scoop of ice cream. Dust with icing sugar if the raspberries are not as sweet as you would like.

HAZELNUT CAKE WITH FRESH RASPBERRIES *Serves 8*

This cake is not meant to rise, but instead will be a flat, cakey meringue, and it should be lovely and moist.

250 g hazelnuts	⅓ cup plain flour
⅔ cup castor sugar	rind of 1 orange
5 egg whites	2 punnets fresh raspberries, to serve
100 g butter	double cream *or* mascarpone, to serve

Preheat the oven to 200°C. Roast the hazelnuts on a baking tray for 10 minutes or until coloured but not burnt. Whilst still hot, rub the hazelnuts in a clean tea towel to remove the skin.

Adjust the oven temperature to 150°C. Once the nuts have cooled completely, transfer them to a food processor, add 2 tablespoons of the castor sugar, and process to a fine meal.

Grease a 26 cm springform cake tin. In an electric mixer, beat the egg whites until soft peaks form, then slowly add the rest of the sugar and mix in until dissolved.

In a small pan, heat the butter to nut-brown. Meanwhile, in a large bowl, mix the plain flour with the hazelnut meal, and add the orange rind. Fold in the egg white mixture, and then pour in the warm butter, leaving any butter solids behind in the pan.

Spread the batter into the cake tin and bake for 30–35 minutes. Serve with loads of fresh raspberries and double cream or mascarpone alongside.

138 ◆ SUMMER

ROCK LOBSTERS

 I ALWAYS THOUGHT, RATHER SMUGLY, THAT RESTAURANTS offering lobster were ill-informed. Knowing that our species lack the huge claw of the European lobster, I doggedly called them 'crayfish' and thought myself much more correct. But a few years ago the Fisheries Research and Development Corporation (FRDC) decided that what was colloquially called crayfish should be known Australia-wide as the rock lobster, with the location from which each species comes providing further identification (southern, eastern, western and tropical). *Marketing Names for Fish and Seafood in Australia*, produced by the FRDC, sets the record straight on many other species as well, in a bid to encourage uniform usage of names throughout the country.

There are few people I know who would not relish a meal of freshly caught rock lobster. Yet it is a luxury food, and each year supply and demand set different price parameters (these are always in the upper range, no matter the year, as rock lobsters are never in huge supply). Surprisingly, it is not always the Christmas market that is the key to pricing, even though the seasons during which rock lobsters can be caught (different in each state) all include it.

If you find you just can't live without lobster the rest of the year then look for companies such as Ferguson Australia, based on Kangaroo Island (www.fergusonaustralia.com). They provide lobsters all year round by holding them in tanks. They have won many awards for their innovative range of products, including medallions of rock lobster, lobster mustard, lobster oil and, my favourite, lobster sashimi. When I bought a pack of this sashimi (frozen but with the end flap of the tail included), instead of serving it raw, I melted 80 g unsalted butter in a small pan until foamy and almost nut-brown, then 'waved' the lobster flesh through the butter, just long enough for it to turn opaque. I then served it piled up in the tail with Sorrel Mayonnaise (see page 142), and it was as sweet and beautiful a lobster dish as I've ever had.

One of our family traditions is that we get to choose our favourite meal on our birthday. Both our daughters were born in November and no matter whether it is Saskia or Elli

Rock lobster with sorrel mayonnaise (see page 142)

celebrating, the choice is the same every time: rock lobster. I have a sneaking suspicion that one of the reasons for this is that they feel they are getting the most mileage out of the occasion since rock lobster is so extravagant. I'm not complaining, even though we've just had our younger daughter Elli's thirtieth birthday, which coincided with the early season, so rock lobster was on the menu for thirty people. I tried in vain to suggest an alternative but only lobster would do!

The best possible way to eat a rock lobster is to take it live straight from the 'craypot', as it is still known, to the cooking pot, but this is only possible for a very few people. The best rock lobster I have ever eaten was over twenty years ago, on the only yachting holiday we've ever been on or are likely to go on. As we set sail to Kangaroo Island, my husband Colin found that he was a hopeless sailor, admittedly across one of the roughest stretches of water in the world. Things got better as we sailed in the lee of the island, but our plans of providoring by diving from the boat proved fanciful. It was with great luck that we met a fisherman on his way in after a fruitful stint at sea. We did a swap: cold beer for fresh rock lobsters. No other lobster has tasted quite so good since.

The next best thing is to buy from fishermen just after they come into port. Our family had a wonderful few days at Victor Harbor before Christmas some years ago and we called into a fish merchant there, Hinge and Ferguson. It was early in the day and they had no rock lobsters available but the boat was due in at 4.30 p.m., so we ordered two freshly cooked lobsters, to be picked up at their closing time of 5.30 p.m. We also requested that the rock lobsters not be refrigerated after they had been cooked, as refrigeration makes a remarkable difference to the flavour; we were eating them that evening so they would be fine to leave out for the short time involved.

On our return, I asked the fishmonger to cut the rock lobsters lengthways as we didn't have a knife in our lodgings; he then pushed the halves firmly together so they wouldn't dry out on the way home. My version of seafood sauce was the girls' choice, so cream, tomato sauce, Worcestershire sauce and Tabasco were duly purchased. For Colin and me it was just lemon juice, extra virgin olive oil and freshly ground black pepper. If I had had a kitchen I would have made a mayonnaise, to which I would have added the 'mustard', or digestive tract, from the rock lobster. Many reject the strong piquant mustard, washing it out, whereas I regard it as essential and use the lot.

If South Australia's Coonawarra and Limestone Coast regions are on your holiday wish list and you have a passion for rock lobster as well as for wine, then now is the time to get in on one of the area's best-kept secrets. For those in the know, almost all the vignerons and farmers in the area have holiday places at Robe and Beachport (from rudimentary beach shacks to more grand abodes) and you can bet if they have a shack then they also have a licence for a craypot.

South Australian licensing regulations have unwittingly created enmity between some families and neighbours, as the sharp-eyed ones heeded the call to apply for their recreational licences without reminding anyone else of the closing date. Only a limited number of licences are granted each year, so to lose one's licence can be pretty devastating to your foraging life. The allowed catch from these pots is four small lobsters a day, whether you have one or two licences; each licence allows one pot but the total for two licences for the one person is still four per day. Believe me, these licences are treasured, because although there is the sport of diving for them yourself, this might still seem a bit too adventurous for many. We are talking here of expensive creatures of the sea and ones that punters get tremendously excited by, almost without exception.

Don't despair if you have no personal connections to those in the know as you can still go to the local pubs and restaurants. More often than not, they have local lobsters on the menu, served with absolutely no fuss – rock lobster with little adornment, which is just as it should be. The real treat is experiencing a freshly caught and cooked rock lobster, eaten as soon as it cools down. Their sweet firm flesh is at its absolute best this way, and because it is very rich you need little of it to satisfy you.

If you decide to try diving for lobsters, then my insider tip is that the locals use fish or sheep heads for bait. When the sea is really calm at Robe you can access a reef that makes diving seem like child's play. Then, if you manage to catch some lobsters, why not try a local vigneron's cooking tip: 'take very fresh uncooked green tails, diced up into bite-sized pieces, battered and deep-fried, really rich and sweet'. The batter would just be there to protect the flesh of the lobster.

The rock lobster you buy live to cook yourself will be better than any you buy already cooked; unless you tee up the fisherman to cook it for you and collect it immediately when it is ready.

It is simple to cook rock lobster: stun it first in the freezer for 30 minutes, then immerse it in a deep, large saucepan of furiously boiling water for 12–18 minutes (depending on whether the lobster weighs around 500 g or nearer 1 kg). Add bay leaves, thickly sliced lemon, dill and a few black peppercorns if you like. Fishermen always use sea water, so if that is not to hand it makes sense to salt the water generously as it comes to the boil.

I am the last one to heap scorn on a potentially great product, but I do feel the need to warn you that a little investigation is required before you buy rock lobster. So if buying a cooked rock lobster in the city, far from the coast, is your only option, look for a specimen that is tightly curled and that flips back into position after being straightened out. This 'snap' indicates a green lobster, which will have been snap-frozen straight away after being caught – an unfurled tail is a sure sign that the lobster was left to die before being cooked, which means that the digestive tract will have started to break down, releasing enzymes that spoil the flesh. Never, but never, buy a rock lobster (or any other crustacean) that has a musty or pungent smell of ammonia – it will be off.

There is a premium trade in first-grade green tails that are snap-frozen for the fastidious Japanese market. These same tails can be bought fresh on the local market but usually only if ordered in advance. Their price – often twice as much per kilo as a whole rock lobster – may seem totally out of reach, but a calculation based on the amount of meat per dollar spent actually equates to less than the retail price for a whole rock lobster.

If rock lobster doesn't suit your budget but you love eating with your hands, look for what we call 'spiders' in South Australia – the heads of rock lobsters. Tossed in a wok with oil, onion and aromatics, these make a good feed – and don't forget the 'mustard'. A good number of spiders can also be chopped into tiny pieces to make a well-flavoured stock for soup.

Rock lobster will never be cheap, but it takes little effort to present, which can be an advantage in itself. However, it can also be extended wonderfully by the addition of really good pasta (see opposite) and a few carefully chosen ingredients: diced ripe tomatoes, artichokes preserved in good olive oil, roasted garlic cloves or caramelised fennel and a sprinkle of basil, dill, flat-leaf parsley or chervil will all give you a very special dish.

You can prepare a live rock lobster for the barbecue by stunning it in the freezer for 30 minutes and then blanching it for 2 minutes in boiling water to kill it. My favourite way is to take the tail, cut it in half lengthways and barbecue it with lots of extra virgin olive oil and lemon juice for about 4 minutes each side. Or you can cut the tail meat out of the shell, then steam or poach it and serve with the rind and juice of a lime, kaffir lime leaves, a little extra virgin olive oil and a dash of coconut milk.

If you have a cooked rock lobster, make a salad by removing the tail and cutting it into medallions. Moisten the meat with fruity extra virgin olive oil and lemon juice and toss in a little fresh dill. Boil small yellow waxy potatoes in their skins, then halve them and add warm to the rock lobster, with wedges of ripe tomato and sorrel leaves. Make a vinaigrette with more of the olive oil, a little wholegrain mustard, lemon juice and dill, then season and toss through the salad.

SORREL MAYONNAISE
Makes 375 ml

I still prefer the simplest of all accompaniments with rock lobster and nothing beats home-made mayonnaise. The piquancy of the sorrel in this version cuts the richness of the lobster beautifully. For perfection, I would serve half a rock lobster, cut as close to eating as possible to prevent it drying out, with a good dollop of this mayonnaise, boiled waxy potatoes and a salad of bitter greens.

2 egg yolks

1 cup trimmed sorrel

pinch salt

juice of ½ lemon

½ cup (125 ml) mellow extra virgin olive oil

½ cup (125 ml) grapeseed oil

freshly ground black pepper

There is no need to chop the sorrel if you are using a blender, though you may need to if using a mortar and pestle. Blend the egg yolks with the sorrel and salt, then add a squeeze of lemon juice. When amalgamated, pour in the combined oils very slowly with the motor running until the mixture becomes very thick. Add a little more lemon juice, if required, and grind in some pepper, then continue pouring in the oil (it can go in a little faster at this stage). When the mayonnaise has emulsified, check whether any extra lemon juice or seasoning is required.

PASTA WITH ROCK LOBSTER

Serves 4

1 × 1 kg live rock lobster
1 fennel bulb
salt
350 g fresh pasta sheets
extra virgin olive oil, for cooking
2 cloves garlic, finely chopped

5 peeled ripe tomatoes, chopped
pinch sugar
sea salt flakes and freshly ground
   black pepper
2 teaspoons freshly chopped basil

Chill the rock lobster in the freezer for 30 minutes to stun it. Remove any damaged outer leaves from the fennel and cut away the core, then slice the fennel finely. Reserve the fennel off-cuts. Fill a large saucepan with water, add the off-cuts, and bring to the boil. Salt the water once it is boiling.

Immerse the stunned rock lobster in the boiling water, then cover and cook for 4 minutes only. Drain the lobster and allow it to cool (do not plunge it into cold water, otherwise the meat will become soggy). When cool enough to handle, cut the lobster in half lengthways and extract the meat and the mustard. Cut the meat into medallions, then crack the legs and remove the meat.

Bring another large saucepan of water to the boil, then salt it and cook the pasta sheets for 3 minutes. Strain the pasta and drizzle olive oil over it to prevent it sticking, shaking it constantly to help stop the cooking process.

Fry the garlic gently with the sliced fennel in a little olive oil in a heavy-based saucepan over low heat until softened. Add the tomatoes, sugar and a little salt to the fennel mixture and reduce to the desired consistency. Add the rock lobster meat and 2 tablespoons olive oil and season with pepper. Remove the pan from the heat once the lobster has just warmed through. Warm the pasta by steaming it over boiling water for 2 minutes or cover it with plastic film and reheat it in a microwave oven on high for 1 minute. Toss the pasta and sauce together with the basil and serve immediately.

SALAD GREENS AND HERBS

 OVER THE PAST FEW YEARS, THERE HAS BEEN A QUIET revolution in the salad market that has taken us so far from the humble iceberg lettuce we all know that it is hard to keep up. Many still love the iceberg though, and, particularly when just picked from an organic garden, it is still worth its place on any table.

We can now choose from mignonettes, butterhead lettuce, oak leaf lettuce, curly endive, cos lettuce or baby cos (or gem) lettuce, and the list goes on. Added to that, we have rocket (whose peppery leaves are an essential part of my salad bowl), mizuna, tatsoi, rad-icchio, witlof, sorrel, lamb's lettuce (or mâche), baby spinach leaves and watercress, land cress, curled cress and mustard cress. And that's not an exhaustive list. We also have herbs of every imaginable variety available to us in almost any greengrocer (not always in the best condition maybe, but in most cases easily revived in a water bath before use), and many more people plant herbs in their own garden as a matter of course. So not only can you have herbs in perfect condition easily to hand, but in the spring you also have that profusion of mauve or purple flowers of thyme and sage to add to your cooking, whether it be a herb pasta dish, or pan-fried brains in nut-brown sage butter, using both the flowers and leaves.

Many of the lettuces mentioned above are soft and don't form a heart in the same way as an iceberg does (although cos does have an inner heart and it is the brilliant 'apple-green' inner leaves that I use; these days you can buy just the cos heart with all the outer leaves plucked off). These soft lettuces, so often grown hydroponically, are fragile and need to be transported home with care.

My big challenge is planting the right number of lettuces (indeed the right number of any vegetable). I tend to get carried away and plant three rows of the same lettuce instead of three different varieties, so they end up going to seed before I can use them, even though we eat salad every day. I obviously need more discipline!

Nurseries now have mixed punnets of lettuces where you can pick just the outside leaves for use as they grow. And rocket grows well from seeds, so well it could almost be a weed. I like to pick it very young; its peppery flavour can stand alone in a simple dish of freshly shaved Parmigiano Reggiano with slices of fresh pear, just on its own with a really good vinaigrette, or of course with ripe tomatoes or olives. You need to do so little when you have good ingredients. Even though I often grow rocket myself we have a grower in the Valley who delivers to us three days a week and the rocket is both peppery and sweet for being so fresh.

Salad burnet has a fresh cucumbery taste and makes a great addition to salads. One plant will produce all summer, with the long outside stems yielding larger and larger petals.

Sorrel is one of my favourite herbs (or is it a salad leaf?). It has such a strong piquant flavour that goes so well in sauces or savoury tarts. The baby leaves in a salad mix

shine through when teamed with something rich like smoked mackerel. I'll warn you, though: sorrel attracts snails like no other plant in my garden and I now grow it in pots off the ground.

Witlof is so versatile as a salad leaf and vegetable. Braise witlof in butter with some sugar – it will caramelise and become bittersweet, and is then great teamed with game. Just as radicchio, either grilled on the barbecue or braised in some butter and deglazed with vino cotto, is yet another flavour dimension I enjoy. Though more in season in autumn and winter, it is now available year-round.

Mesclun mix is widely available, but before buying make sure there are no brown marks at the base of the leaves, a sure sign that the mix isn't fresh.

As well as herbs, there are many sprouts to give extra texture and flavour to salads. Snow pea sprouts, sweet with a crunch, or snow pea shoots, could both be tossed through a warm salad of quail with pancetta, garlic croutons and other bitter greens.

In a salad, I would mix watercress with other, less strong leaves but, when abundant, watercress puréed with a little cream makes a really peppery sauce to serve with grills.

The vinaigrette most often used in our house, proudly my husband Colin's creation, is a mixture of 4 parts extra virgin olive oil with 1 part acidulant (a mix of ⅓ vino cotto and ⅔ red-wine vinegar), some sea salt flakes and freshly ground black pepper.

If I need a delicate vinaigrette I'll use verjuice mixed with perhaps walnut oil tempered with some grapeseed oil. While I use vino cotto rather than balsamic vinegar, this is simply because we make it ourselves. Quality red-wine or sherry vinegar, lemon or lime juices all make a great vinaigrette. Mustard is a variable, but often used. My great friend Peter Wall always uses mustard, adding a little cream and even a touch of sugar to his vinaigrettes, and for years, I always left making the vinaigrette to him whenever we ate together.

It is vital when serving salads to use quality ingredients, particularly the extra virgin olive oil. You must also wash, refresh and spin all lettuces dry; salad spinners are one of the essential kitchen tools. Other tricks are to rub a clove of garlic around the salad bowl for just that hint of flavour, as chef Damien Pignolet taught me to do; to choose the right-shaped bowl and salad servers; and to have the salad prepared but only dress it when ready to serve. The right salad servers are those that can be crossed over each other halfway up the bowl. They act as a raft for the salad vegetables to sit on until ready to serve – that one's a Stephanie Alexander trick, and used by us every day. Another idea is to toss the leaves with your fingers, making sure there is just enough vinaigrette to loosely grab onto the leaves. Drain any excess as you don't want your salad limp with vinaigrette.

A salad should have colour, flavour and crunch. A wonderfully fresh salad will make a difference to practically any meal.

WATERCRESS, WITLOF, BOCCONCINI, WALNUT AND GRAPE SALAD

Serves 4

100 g walnuts

2 teaspoons finely chopped shallots

2 red witlof, bases trimmed and
  leaves separated

handful picked watercress, washed
  and dried

handful salad burnet, washed and dried

¾ cup each red and green grapes, halved

1 lemon, thinly sliced and cut into
  small pieces

extra virgin olive oil, for drizzling

4 bocconcini balls

1 tablespoon roughly chopped
  lemon thyme leaves

VINAIGRETTE

⅓ cup (80 ml) walnut oil

2 tablespoons verjuice

freshly ground black pepper

Preheat the oven to 220°C. Roast the walnuts on a baking tray for about 5 minutes or until just starting to brown, shaking the tray to prevent the nuts from burning. Rub the walnuts in a clean tea towel to remove the bitter skins, then place in a sieve and shake away the skins. Leave to cool.

Lightly fry the shallots in a little olive oil, and reserve. Toss the salad leaves together in a bowl, then divide them among 4 plates. Mix the walnuts, grapes and lemon slices and scatter over the leaves. Pour a little olive oil over the bocconcini, then roll them in the lemon thyme. Slice thinly and add to the salad leaves, along with the shallots.

To make the vinaigrette, whisk the walnut oil and verjuice until amalgamated, then add the pepper. Dress the salads just before serving.

PRESERVED LEMON, ROCKET AND GREEN BEAN SALAD

Serves 6

4 quarters preserved lemon, flesh removed, rind rinsed and thinly sliced

½ cup (125 ml) verjuice

500 g green beans *or* flat (Roman) beans, topped and tailed

4 ripe roma tomatoes, sliced

½ cup (125 ml) extra virgin olive oil

sea salt flakes and freshly ground black pepper

½ red onion, finely sliced

½ cup basil leaves

1 cup rocket leaves, washed and dried

Soak the preserved lemon rind slices in verjuice for 30 minutes. Bring a saucepan of salted water to the boil, then blanch the beans until tender. Refresh in a bowl of iced water and set aside.

Put the tomatoes in a large bowl, drizzle with a little of the olive oil and season with salt and pepper. Drain the preserved lemon rind, reserving the verjuice, and add to the tomatoes, along with the drained beans and red onion. Whisk the verjuice and remaining olive oil together and season with pepper to taste. Pour the dressing over and toss to combine, then leave for 10 minutes. Add basil and rocket leaves and serve immediately.

PURSLANE AND BREAD SALAD

Serves 4

This rustic salad teams perfectly with fish or chicken. Or you could add goat's cheese for a substantial luncheon dish for two.

3 thick slices wood-fired white bread, crusts removed

½ cup (125 ml) extra virgin olive oil

1 clove garlic, halved

2 tablespoons verjuice

4 handfuls purslane, washed, dried and snipped into 3 cm lengths

2 quarters preserved lemon, flesh removed, rind rinsed and thinly sliced

4 large anchovy fillets, torn into small pieces

sea salt flakes and freshly ground black pepper

Preheat the oven to 220°C. Brush both sides of the bread with half the olive oil. Toast on a baking tray in the oven until golden brown, turning after the first side has coloured. Rub the toast with cut garlic, then rip into bite-sized pieces and transfer to a bowl. Sprinkle with 1 tablespoon verjuice to moisten for just a few minutes; it is important that the bread is not soggy.

In a large bowl, toss the toast with the purslane, preserved lemon rind and anchovies. Whisk the remaining olive oil and verjuice and season with salt and pepper. Toss the salad with the dressing and serve immediately.

SKYE GYNGELL'S TORN BREAD SALAD WITH ROCKET, SOUR CHERRIES, CAPERS AND VERJUICE

Serves 6

Hearing that I was to be in London in January 2006, the local Slow Food chapter asked me to present a masterclass on verjuice at Petersham Nurseries Cafe in Surrey, one of the city's absolute hotspots, with their chef Skye Gyngell, a very talented Australian. I was thrilled to accept, and even though it was to be held the day after a big Australia Day affair for 300 at Australia House (which I developed and oversaw the menu for), I knew I couldn't miss the opportunity.

The day was separated into two parts. First, a class for forty or so people, which was held in one of the greenhouses. I remember it being freezing cold and rugging up with scarves and an overcoat of some sort, but nothing could diminish my enthusiasm for sharing all I knew about verjuice, demonstrating its diverse uses, tasting and talking about it until I had no voice left. The second part was an even greater thrill. Months before, Skye had sent me copies of her menus, and they evoked in me such a sense of déjà vu: here was a produce-driven cook, surrounded by amazing bounty and working with the philosophy that only the best would do. Skye created a menu for lunch, and one dish after the other all included verjuice. It was a truly exceptional lunch; in fact, one of the great days of my food life, where the sum was even greater than its parts. Skye's dishes – so simple yet creative – simply sparkled. What generosity there was at that table! Here's one of my favourite dishes from that day.

¼ cup dried sour cherries

¼ cup (60 ml) verjuice

2 red onions, thickly sliced

2 tablespoons sugar

2 tablespoons red-wine vinegar

⅓ cup (80 ml) extra virgin olive oil

6 slices slightly stale sourdough bread,
    torn into bite-sized pieces

handful rocket leaves

small bunch chervil, sprigs picked

small bunch marjoram, leaves picked
    and chopped

2 tablespoons chopped preserved lemon rind

2 tablespoons salted capers, washed
    and dried

finely chopped rind of 1 unwaxed lemon

VINAIGRETTE

1 tablespoon Dijon mustard

¼ cup (60 ml) verjuice

sea salt flakes and freshly ground
    black pepper

¼ cup (60 ml) extra virgin olive oil

Place cherries in a bowl with ¼ cup verjuice and leave overnight to reconstitute. Drain before use.

Preheat the oven to 200°C. Combine the sliced onions, sugar, red-wine vinegar and 2 tablespoons olive oil, then arrange in one layer on a baking tray. Roast until soft and slightly caramelised.

Heat remaining 2 tablespoons oil in a frying pan and shallow-fry bread until golden and crisp. »

For the verjuice vinaigrette, place the mustard and verjuice in a small bowl and whisk to combine. Season with a little salt and pepper, then slowly whisk in the olive oil until emulsified.

Place all the ingredients, except the dressing, in a bowl, then lightly toss together with your hands. Pour over the dressing and toss thoroughly together. Taste for seasoning, adjusting the flavour with a little more salt and pepper if necessary.

HERB PASTA WITH SORREL BUTTER AND THYME

Serves 4

100 g flat-leaf parsley leaves

5 duck egg yolks

dash extra virgin olive oil

pinch salt

300 g strong flour (see Glossary)

10 sprigs thyme, to serve

SORREL BUTTER

½ cup flat-leaf parsley leaves

1 cup sorrel leaves

250 g unsalted butter, slightly softened

juice of 1 lemon

freshly ground black pepper

First, make the pasta. Blanch the parsley quickly – straight in and out of a saucepan of boiling water – and drain well but don't refresh. Purée the parsley in a food processor and add egg yolks immediately, so they take up the maximum colour from the parsley, then add the dash of oil and the salt. Add the flour to the food processor and pulse until the dough starts to combine. Take out and knead by hand until shiny. Rest the dough for 20 minutes, then roll through the pasta machine to angel-hair size.

Now make the sorrel butter. Process the parsley and sorrel leaves together and then add the butter and lemon juice. Add pepper if required. Roll into a cylinder, wrap in plastic film and place in the refrigerator. Strip thyme leaves from the sprigs.

Cook the pasta in salted boiling water. Drain, transfer to a serving bowl, and moisten with slices of sorrel butter. Toss with thyme leaves, dot with a few thyme flowers if available, and serve.

CHIVE FLOWER FRITTERS

Serves 6 as a main course

20 g butter

⅓ cup (80 ml) milk

¼ teaspoon white-wine vinegar

pinch salt

125 g plain flour

extra virgin olive oil, for frying

1 large egg white

24 chive flowers

Heat the butter, milk and ⅔ cup water in a small saucepan over medium heat, until just bubbling. Add the vinegar and allow to cool. In a bowl, mix the salt and the flour, then add the liquid slowly to avoid lumps. Leave the batter to rest for at least 20 minutes.

Heat about 2 cm of olive oil in a heavy-based saucepan until it is hot enough for a piece of stale bread to turn golden brown in a few seconds. Beat the egg white until stiff and fold into the batter. Dip a few chive flowers at a time into the batter then drop them into the hot oil and fry for a minute or two, or until golden brown. Transfer to kitchen paper to drain, then repeat with remaining batter and flowers. Serve immediately.

LEMON VERBENA ICE CREAM
Makes 600 ml

This recipe is based on the cheat's method of making anglaise (the custard that forms the basis of the ice cream) in a microwave. As each microwave will cook differently, the times may need to be adjusted.

8 unsprayed sprigs lemon verbena in flower	1 cup (250 ml) cream
	½ cup (110 g) sugar
1 cup (250 ml) milk	4 egg yolks

Finely chop the leaves and stalks of the lemon verbena, reserving the flowers. Place the milk and cream in a saucepan over medium–high heat, stirring in the sugar, then add the leaves and stalks and bring almost to the boil. Whisk in egg yolks, then transfer to a microwave-proof container and cook in the microwave on medium power for 8 minutes. Remove and whisk, then return to the microwave on medium–high power for another 4 minutes or until the mixture begins to thicken. Whisk again and leave to cool. Churn in an ice cream machine (following the manufacturer's instructions) and then add the lemon verbena flowers.

TOMATOES

 FOR THE GARDENER, THE SCENT A TOMATO BUSH RELEASES on a summer's day, and the tingle on the skin as you brush past it, is worth any amount of time spent watering. Although it has a thousand culinary possibilities, picked ripe from the garden the tomato needs no more attention than a drizzle of good extra virgin olive oil, a turn of freshly ground black pepper and a sprig of its companion in life, basil. This is the tomato as I know it, the tomato I eat as if it were an apple – not fussed by the juice running down my arm!

Unfortunately, in the 1980s, the European trend of growing a nondescript tomato acceptable to a wide range of tastes became a worldwide practice, and the rise of the supermarket ensured its survival. Supermarkets have become huge buyers of vegetables, and as their interest is in products that last a long time 'looking good' on the shelf, this trend suited them perfectly.

This led to a rise in the practice of gassing tomatoes, already common in Queensland, and these tomatoes have infiltrated most parts of Australia in a big way. Harmless ethylene gas, the natural ripening substance fruit produces, is used to change the colour of tomatoes. By gassing their tomatoes Queensland farmers give themselves a price advantage, as it means they can pick their crops at varying stages of maturity. The CSIRO tells me that there is no difference in taste between a tomato that has been gassed and one that has not. The problem is that tomatoes picked before natural ripening has begun will not have the flavour that vine-ripening ensures. Because Queensland farmers rely on gassing they may well be picking their tomatoes before they have reached a sufficiently mature stage to guarantee flavour. The enzymes that cause fruit to soften are also those that produce flavour so, picked too early, the hard-skinned variety so loved by supermarkets (and designed to be handled as roughly as a tin of tomatoes) will never be able to produce the goods. If the farmers took the CSIRO's advice, they would let the tomatoes sit in a ripening room before gassing them and would reject any that didn't start to colour up naturally.

A rising consumer backlash is evident, with more discerning, flavour-driven people moving towards specialised greengrocers, organic grocers and farmers' markets – but even then it's a real search to find naturally ripened tomatoes. Semi-commercial growers who don't have to transport their crop far from their doorstep can fill these markets with the older varieties in the natural season but I suspect it will be a long while before any solution filters through to the supermarkets.

A great surprise to me is that really good glasshouse tomatoes are grown in Murray Bridge near Adelaide during the winter. These are golf ball-sized with a thick skin like most commercially grown tomatoes, but this is one time when the skin doesn't detract from the flavour – even in winter, it's incredibly intense. The same variety is field-grown during the summer and is better still. Though these come from a large commercial grower, I've never seen them in supermarkets; instead I seek them out at our Central

Market in Adelaide. Here is a commercial tomato grown out of season that is amazingly full of flavour – so there is hope yet for better supermarket tomatoes, if the public demands it.

It is not just the ripeness of the tomato that affects its quality; flavour is closely tied to variety. Though season also has such a bearing (in that nothing is better than late summer tomatoes), I'm taken aback at how good these golf ball tomatoes are in winter. Am I going against my own philosophy of eating what's in season? I guess I am if the flavour is there.

While many people grow their own tomatoes in an effort to regain that flavour of old, my experience with buying plants from nurseries is that the varieties on offer are in the main disappointing. Happily there are other avenues. Heirloom varieties are available by seed only from The Digger's Club at Dromana, Victoria (see www.diggers.com.au). You can buy open-pollinated varieties from their mail-order catalogue so you can save your own seeds for future years. Their Tommy Toe, bearing fruit the size of an apricot, is a good bearer and stands out in the flavour stakes. If you're able to find oxheart, black oxheart (Russian) or Rouge de Marmande, they make great eating.

I belong to the Rare Fruit Society in South Australia but am sadly always too busy to go to their meetings. However, I read their newsletters religiously and, as I'm sure is the case in other states, there is a lot of seed saving and swapping going on. This year another member gave me a dozen tomato plants of a variety he has been propagating from American stock brought in legally thirty years ago. In taking them I had to accept responsibility to keep them separate from any other tomato plants and to agree to keep a quantity of seeds to share. The plants are tall and vigorous and the fruit makes very good eating. Even more exciting is a member who is growing eighty different varieties of heirloom tomatoes, and turning it into a semi-commercial enterprise – so it can be done. An important point of contact for seed saving is the Australian Seed Savers Network, run by Michael and Jude Fanton. View their website at www.seedsavers.net or email them on info@seedsavers.net for more information. Another contact I have come across, for those interested in sourcing less commonly available seeds for produce such as heirloom tomatoes, is The Italian Gardener. Their website is www.theitaliangardener.com.au and they can also be emailed at info@theitaliangardener.com.au.

I used to think that tomatoes had to be left on the vine until totally ripe, but having been challenged on that theory, I now realise that green-shouldered tomatoes, grown in full sun and coloured pinkish-red, will ripen to a really good tomato as long as they're not refrigerated (and may even rival those picked totally ripe). The only exception to this rule of not refrigerating tomatoes is when you've bought a large quantity of tomatoes for making sauce that are already riper than ripe and you need time to get organised to make the sauce – but only do it if it's essential.

I seldom plant less than twenty tomato plants at a time as there are good and bad years and I want to be assured of my own crop. This means some years I'll have more tomatoes than I could possibly use for home, but it never fazes me. Nor does it faze American cookery writer Joanne Weir, whose book *You Say Tomato* runs to almost 300 pages on this one subject alone. As well as containing recipes, it is also full of tips for preserving, slow-roasting and drying; these tips come from cooks from all around the world, including our own Phillip Searle, who as a chef makes more of a tomato than anyone I've known, and he's shared all of this knowledge with Joanne.

More years ago than I prefer to remember, I was lucky enough to see Phillip in action when he ran Oasis Seros restaurant in Sydney. Not only does he never waste a tomato, he uses every part of it in a series of processes. Firstly he cores them, then blends them until coarsely chopped, then cooks them in a stainless steel pot for 20 minutes. Once strained, he reduces the juice to one-tenth of the original volume over a low flame to give an essence that can then be used to add intensity to sauces. Then Phillip puts the leftover pulp through a mouli on its finest blade, adds a good olive oil, and cooks the pulp with a touch of sugar until very thick, resulting in a really concentrated purée. But there's still another process – no need to throw out the pulp left behind in the mouli. It is baked on a baking sheet at a low temperature until it's completely dry, then cooled and processed in the spice grinder. Now that's taking advantage of your crop!

I first learnt of *'strattu*, an intense and pure tomato concentrate, from Mary Taylor Simeti's book *Pomp and Sustenance*. For this, tomatoes are puréed and salted and then dried in the sun, where they are stirred frequently until all moisture has evaporated. Mary talked of it becoming a rare practice in Italy and I had always meant to try it, but never quite got around to it. Then at the Yalumba Harvest Picnic during the 1995 Barossa Vintage Festival I found that the parents of a valued staff member (the Fantos) were not only making

Pasta with tomatoes, basil and extra virgin olive oil (see page 158)

'strattu for themselves but had been persuaded by the organisers to sell small amounts. I couldn't believe my luck – I might not have learnt about it if the Picnic, designed to encourage small growers to value-add and show off their produce, hadn't taken place. The day opened my eyes to the wealth of tradition in this family, who had for years supplied me with the best asparagus and eggplants imaginable – and yet I had been too busy to delve any further; a salient lesson. I've since experienced bread from their backyard brick oven, have taken part in the pig-killing and sausage-making rituals, and, because of them, finally managed to hang the last of my cherry tomato crop in our shed for later use in winter dishes, to which they add an amazing intensity.

If you preserve your own tomatoes from the end-of-year crop you'll never have to use tinned tomatoes again. (Not that tinned tomatoes can't be ripe and flavoursome if you buy well, but they can have a taint that disagrees with me.) My first serious tomato-bottling took place in late summer 1996. So excited was I by the outcome that first year, when I rationed them to the dishes in which they would really make a difference, that now I preserve many more, always at the very end of the season. It is such a simple process, although it's worth checking the thermometer annually on your preserving 'outfit'. One year, while preserving with a friend, we had two kettles on the go the whole time; my thermometer wasn't registering properly and after all that work exactly half of the tomatoes fermented and bubbled over. Not only was it a dreadful waste of effort and tomatoes, it was a terrible, terrible mess to clean up.

To preserve, cut away the entire stem area from very ripe but firm tomatoes, then halve the tomatoes and pack them tightly, with the skins on, into no. 31 preserving jars (1-litre capacity); no water is added, as the tomatoes make their own juice (this is the vital part). Seal the bottles with lids and clips and then place in a preserving pan for 1 hour 15 minutes at 92°C (between settings 4 and 5 on older units). When they're done, I stand the bottles on a wad of newspaper for a minimum of 24 hours before storing them, or up to 48 hours if you can. I don't bother sterilising jars when making sauces, condiments or jams if I'm able to bottle the product in a preserving 'outfit' at near to boiling temperature, and then I invert the jar immediately – in this case an unsterilised lid presents no problem, as the heat from the contents also sterilises the lid. Don't worry that the tomatoes are not peeled when you come to use them: the skins will fall away as you remove them from the jar. And don't hide these beautiful tomatoes away in a cupboard if you have space to display them on a kitchen shelf. They glow like jewels!

Rather than waste over-ripe tomatoes too squashed for bottling, cut them into quarters and put them in a large baking dish with a drizzle of good olive oil (make sure you reject any mouldy or 'off' tomatoes in the process). Leave them overnight in an oven set on its lowest temperature or with the pilot light on so that they caramelise without burning. These tomatoes can be stored in a jar of olive oil for up to a week and added straight to any dish without puréeing.

Sun-dried tomatoes were thrown into every conceivable dish during the early 1990s, but, used in moderation, they are still a force to be reckoned with. I still find them essential in my duck egg pasta with smoked kangaroo, extra virgin olive oil and pine nuts (see page 420), or pasta with eggplant and pine nuts. Sun-dried tomatoes are also wonderful with fresh goat's cheese on bruschetta. More to my taste are tomatoes semi-dried in the oven: brush them with extra virgin olive oil infused with garlic and thyme, then season and roast them at 110°C for about 2 hours. These have a shorter shelf-life, but when covered with extra virgin olive oil and refrigerated they last for weeks. And if the tomatoes were really good to start with, these tomatoes become almost like sweetmeats that can be pinched from the fridge as a snack.

Probably my favourite way of serving tomatoes is to slice them thickly, drizzle them with extra virgin olive oil, sprinkle them with sea salt flakes and freshly ground black pepper and leave for an hour before using them. Then take some good crusty bread and perhaps some more extra virgin olive oil and, loading it up with the sliced tomatoes, dip the bread back into the juices. Not far behind this favourite is a breakfast consisting of a good piece of toasted sourdough bread with lots of unsalted butter, really ripe tomato sliced thickly, sea salt flakes and freshly ground black pepper. Or a cold pasta dish, with tomatoes cut into chunks and marinated for a while in plenty of basil, sea salt flakes, freshly ground black pepper and lots of fruity extra virgin olive oil, then served with cooled, oiled penne. You need to do so little with tomatoes in their prime.

TOMATO SAUCE
Makes 1 litre

I prefer to make my tomato sauce with these extra ingredients, so that when I reach for a bottle from my pantry, it needs no further preparation for use in pasta sauces (though being the indulgent person I am, I often gild the lily with an extra flourish of olive oil).

1.5 kg very ripe tomatoes	½ teaspoon–2 tablespoons sugar (depending
1 large onion, chopped	on the ripeness of the tomatoes)
1 carrot, chopped	¼ cup (60 ml) verjuice *or* white wine
1 stick celery, chopped	freshly ground black pepper
½ cup (125 ml) extra virgin olive oil	2 large basil leaves
sea salt flakes	

Wash the tomatoes, then cut them into quarters, discarding the calyx, or base of the green stem, from each and cutting away any blemishes, and put them into a large preserving pan. Add the onion, carrot, celery and olive oil to the tomato, tossing to coat well. Add salt and sugar and stand the pan over a fierce heat. Stir the mixture constantly, watching that it does not catch and burn, until it starts to caramelise and the liquid has evaporated, about 20 minutes. Deglaze the pan with the verjuice or white wine, then check for seasoning, adjusting with salt and sugar as necessary. Grind in black pepper, then add the torn basil. Fill sterilised, hot jars or bottles (see Glossary) with the sauce and seal. The sauce keeps for months.

TOMATO SOUP FOR VINTAGE

Serves 4

This soup was inspired by Richard Olney's Grape Harvester's Soup from his book *Simple French Food*. I first made it to feed my restaurant staff when we closed up shop to hand-pick the semillon grapes in our vineyard. I wanted something tasty and easy to transport, a meal in itself. I used about double the tomatoes and a lot less water than the original recipe and I loved it so much that it always went back on the menu at the Pheasant Farm Restaurant during vintage.

6 medium tomatoes, very ripe yet firm
1 kg onions, thinly sliced
   (I use brown onions)
⅓ cup (80 ml) extra virgin olive oil,
   plus extra to serve
4 cloves garlic, finely chopped

sea salt flakes
½ teaspoon sugar (optional), or to taste
½ cup (125 ml) verjuice *or* dry white wine
1 litre boiling water
4 slices stale wood-fired bread

Cut out the core of the tomatoes – for this rustic soup I do not peel or seed them. Cut each tomato in half and then into quarters or eighths. Using a large, heavy-based saucepan, cook the onions gently in the oil, stirring over low heat with a wooden spoon for about 10 minutes or until they are uniformly light golden and very soft. Add the garlic and salt to the pan and cook for 5 minutes. Add the tomatoes, and sugar to sweeten if you wish; the sugar merely enhances the flavour of the tomatoes and gives a boost if they are not in perfect condition.

Cook for 10 minutes and then add the verjuice or wine and water. (For an over-the-top soup you could leave out the water altogether; this is also wonderful as a topping for a hot or cold pasta dish.) Simmer, covered, for 45 minutes before serving. Drizzle a little olive oil over each slice of bread and place a slice in each serving bowl. Ladle the soup over the bread.

AVOCADO AND TOMATO JELLY   *Serves 6*

Unless you have good tomatoes to work with, it is better to add extra avocado to this dish rather than diminish it by using lesser tomatoes. If making the jelly in advance (say the day before), use 2½ × 2 g gelatine leaves, but if using straight away use 3 × 2 g leaves.

3 ripe tomatoes

1½ cups (375 ml) verjuice

1 teaspoon castor sugar

2 sprigs tarragon

3 × 2 g leaves gelatine (see Glossary)

1 large ripe reed avocado *or* 2 medium hass avocados, peeled and cut into cubes

sea salt flakes and freshly ground black pepper

extra virgin olive oil and delicate greens such as snow pea tendrils or mâche, to serve

Wash the tomatoes, remove stalks and make an incision in the top of each tomato. Blanch very briefly in boiling water until the skin starts to pull away. Peel and dice the tomatoes, removing the seeds.

Heat the verjuice, castor sugar and one sprig of tarragon in a saucepan over low heat until it starts to simmer; do not boil, or the verjuice will become cloudy. Remove from heat and set aside to infuse. Meanwhile, soak the gelatine leaves in cold water for 5 minutes. Remove the sprig of tarragon from the warm verjuice, then squeeze out the excess liquid from the gelatine and add to the verjuice.

Once verjuice has cooled, layer tomatoes and avocado in six 135 ml-capacity dariole moulds or tea cups, adding a leaf of tarragon to each mould. Season to taste. Gently pour some of the verjuice mixture to the top of each mould. Refrigerate overnight or until set.

Either dip each mould quickly in a bowl of hot water or use a knife to separate the jelly from the edge of the moulds. Gently turn out onto plates and drizzle with a little extra virgin olive oil, then season with some sea salt and serve with some delicate greens to garnish.

LITTLE BLANCHE'S RIPE TOMATO CHUTNEY *Makes 7 litres*

A close friend from Tasmania kindly passed on her family recipe for tomato chutney. I have played with the quantities, added onions and changed the vinegar.

1.5 kg Granny Smith apples, peeled,
    cored and roughly chopped
2 kg onions, finely chopped
4.5 kg vine-ripened tomatoes,
    cut into eighths
750 g raisins

125 g salt
1 kg sugar
3 cups (750 ml) red-wine vinegar
6 cloves garlic
80 g grated ginger

Cook the apples, onions and tomatoes in a large heavy-based saucepan over medium heat for 10 minutes. Add the remaining ingredients and simmer gently over low heat for 2–3 hours. Reduce any excess liquid at a high temperature. Transfer to sterilised jars (see Glossary) and seal. Unopened jars of this tomato chutney will keep for years.

RUSTIC TOMATO AND BREAD SALAD *Serves 4*

4 thick slices sourdough bread,
    crusts removed
½ cup (125 ml) very good-quality extra
    virgin olive oil
sea salt flakes
6 ripe tomatoes, cut into chunks

2 small red onions, thinly sliced
1 Lebanese cucumber, peeled and chopped
½ cup basil leaves, torn
½ cup loosely packed marjoram leaves
2½ tablespoons red-wine vinegar
freshly ground black pepper

Tear bread into small chunks and toss in a frying pan over high heat with 75 ml of the olive oil until golden and crisp. Place the bread in a large salad bowl (preferably wooden), season with salt to taste, then add the vegetables and herbs. Toss with remaining olive oil and red-wine vinegar, season to taste and mix well.

TUNA

THE BLUEFIN TUNA IS A COLD-WATER FISH AND IS CAUGHT in the waters off southern Western Australia through to Tasmania. The local bluefin is available from January until some time in March. The season's end date depends entirely on quotas: once they are filled, the season ends. Most of the fish available in Adelaide comes from Port Lincoln and is caught by pole boats, although there are some lobster fishermen who line-fish in their off-season. The sashimi market in Japan demands long-line fishing, but most of the top-quality pole-caught tuna from Port Lincoln also goes to Japan. It is hard to believe that in the 1990s it was often difficult to get local tuna in South Australia. Although yellowfin is certainly more widely available now, bluefin is much harder to find as the best always gets exported.

The process of tuna fishing is fascinating. First, the fishermen go out two to three nights in advance to catch sardines, which are kept alive in tanks on the boats. (The sardines out of Port Lincoln are apparently very sweet, but there is still no local commercial fishery for them.) Spotter planes are then sent out to locate schools of tuna. The planes radio the boats, directing them to the schools, which are marked by 'fast boats' for the following pole boats. The schools are then encircled with nets and the tuna excited by the live sardines. A line is run with large, bare hooks which shine through the water like the sardines, and the tuna take the unbaited hooks. These days the boats are big business and carry automatic poling machines.

The main requirement for quality fish is that they are killed immediately and humanely. The treatment of the fish after catching is what dictates the price, and this processing depends on the boat's facilities. Some boats are sophisticated enough to have a freeze-chill operation on board; tuna caught by these boats is shipped straight to Japan. The yellowfin fished off Cairns is killed and gutted on board and put in a brine to chill so as to avoid deterioration.

Prime-quality tuna farmed for the Japanese sashimi market take three to four months to reach the required size. Once they reach 30 kg they are harvested, killed quickly and efficiently, and placed in an ice-brine mixture to bring down their body temperature, which conserves their prime quality; they are flown to Japan daily.

Of Australia's tuna harvest exported to the Japanese market, 75 per cent is sent by sea, frozen at super-low temperatures (–60°C), and 25 per cent is sent fresh by air. The fish are held in the ice-brine from the harvest pontoon to the processing plant to preserve them, while the air-freighted fish are generally sent with two average-sized (40 kg and above) tuna in one box.

When thinking about tuna, I find it difficult deciding which particular way I like it best: raw, cured, just seared or, surprisingly, slow-cooked. If pressed, I would have to say my most outstanding tuna experience took place in Tokyo – ironically, we were eating bluefin tuna from South Australia. This was tuna at its least adorned; not just plain old raw tuna, but *toro*, or fatty tuna belly, the most amazing delicacy. For this, tuna needs to be top quality; since it is the fat that makes the *toro* so exceptional, the bluefin is preferred over the yellowfin, which is not as fatty.

The purity of this fish was extraordinary and it made me realise that I had eaten a lot of less-than-perfect raw fish in my life. The answer lies in how the fish is handled from the minute it is caught to the moment it is served. I have since learnt from Australian chefs Neil Perry and Tetsuya Wakuda that, as fish don't have kidneys, they are particularly fragile and subject to stress. If a fish is stressed, it produces lactic acid, which means it virtually self-combusts, or 'cooks' from the inside out; so there goes any chance of perfection.

Tuna is such a versatile fish, so easy to prepare and cook. Grilling or barbecuing tuna are the easiest options of all. Rather than marinating before cooking I simply brush with extra virgin olive oil, have the barbecue really hot and salt the fish just before it goes on the fire. The vital cooking tip is that the tuna should be seared quickly on both sides and left to rest, then served rare, ranging from pink to almost totally raw, depending on your personal taste and the quality of the fish. Never cook it until it's 'done' right through. Slip the resting fish into a dish with whatever fresh herbs you have to hand, some slices of lemon and extra virgin olive oil, so it is 'relubricated' as it rests in the post-cooking marinade. Tuna is also sensational served as a thick steak, seared on each side, rested and accompanied by a sophisticated reduced red-wine sauce.

Serve a really fresh piece of tuna raw, chopped into little cubes and tossed with diced cucumber, tomato, avocado and extra virgin olive oil, then add a touch of chervil and a final squeeze of lemon juice or verjuice.

SALADE NIÇOISE

Serves 4

500 g piece raw tuna

200 ml extra virgin olive oil

sea salt flakes

2 handfuls fresh herbs (chives, basil,
flat-leaf parsley), chopped

4 small waxy potatoes

12 quail eggs

16 baby green beans

12 cherry tomatoes, halved

12 yellow plum tomatoes

8 baby artichokes, preserved in vinegar

½ teaspoon Dijon mustard

2 tablespoons lemon juice

freshly ground black pepper

1 baby cos

2 tablespoons top-quality capers
(preferably Australian)

12 small Niçoise olives

Cut the tuna into steaks of approximately 2½ cm thickness. Drizzle with a little olive oil, sprinkle with salt and sear on a hot grill or barbecue plate for about 1 minute on each side. Transfer to a plate to rest, drizzle with 2 tablespoons of the olive oil and add half the fresh herbs.

Boil the potatoes and set aside. As soon as they are cool enough to handle, cut in half lengthways and drizzle the cut side with a little olive oil. Boil the quail eggs for 2 minutes until just soft. Drain, then put into cold water and peel.

Plunge the beans in boiling water for about 2 minutes or until cooked but still bright green. Drain and refresh. Add the potatoes to a bowl with the tomatoes and drizzle with more olive oil. Remove any excess vinegar from the artichokes by patting dry with kitchen paper, and cut in half. Cut the quail eggs in half.

Make the vinaigrette by combining the balance of the oil, mustard and lemon juice with the remaining herbs. Season.

Distribute the lettuce between the serving plates. Cut the tuna into chunks and pile in the centre of the lettuce. Arrange the potatoes, tomatoes, quail eggs, beans, artichokes, capers and olives evenly over the plate, then pour over the vinaigrette and serve.

TUNA PASTA

Serves 4

Many people are nervous about serving anything rare. The following recipe is delicious, and because the tuna is thinly sliced, the warmth of the pasta cooks it enough.

1 red onion, thinly sliced

100 ml extra virgin olive oil

juice of 1 lemon

2 tablespoons top-quality capers
(preferably Australian)

sea salt flakes and freshly ground
black pepper

200 g piece raw tuna, thinly sliced

2 tablespoons finely chopped flat-leaf parsley

300 g dried angel hair pasta

Sweat the red onion in a small saucepan over medium heat in olive oil until translucent, then add lemon juice (it will turn very pink), capers, salt and pepper. Check the vinaigrette for balance and toss through the raw tuna and parsley. Cook the pasta in a saucepan of boiling salted water. Drain and moisten with olive oil. Pour the vinaigrette over the hot pasta and toss through, then serve immediately. To achieve the dish's full effect it needs to be served once everyone is seated and ready, as the pasta has to be hot enough to cook, or 'set', the tuna.

CURED TUNA   *Serves 8*

The next step up from raw tuna is cured; a simple but satisfying way to serve this fish, as it is with salmon too. The difference between these two fish is that, depending on what cut of tuna you are curing, you will often be managing a much thicker piece of flesh than for salmon, meaning that the curing time will be longer. Even though tuna fillet seems expensive, you don't need to buy a large quantity of it and there is no waste.

500 g sugar

500 g sea salt

dried dill *or* coriander seeds, to taste

1 kg fillet of tuna (of uniform thickness)

Mix the sugar and salt together and flavour with the dill or coriander seeds. Line the base of a large rectangular ceramic or plastic dish with half this mixture. Lay the fish on top and cover with the remaining sugar and salt, ensuring the fish is covered in a thick, even layer. Cover with plastic film and put a tray or plate on top to weigh it down (or you could use cans as weights). Transfer to the refrigerator for 12 hours (if you like it lightly cured like I do), or 24 hours for a drier result. The timing will depend greatly on the thickness of your fillet.

Wipe the curing mixture from the fish, then slice it thinly. Toss these slices with equally thin slices of ripe avocado, a minced golden shallot, a little extra virgin olive oil, lemon juice and flat-leaf parsley. If you have meyer lemons that are beginning to ripen, thinly slice, then cut each slice into eighths and toss these through too. Alternatively, you could omit the olive oil and make a very thin mayonnaise instead. Covered well, the cured tuna keeps for up to 1 week in the fridge.

YABBIES AND MARRON

 FORAGING FOR FOOD IS A TIME-HONOURED BAROSSA TRADITION, and the poaching of yabbies (freshwater crayfish) from dams has long been a popular pastime for country people, especially kids! Yet these days poaching is becoming less tolerated. We're in the lucky position of having our own yabby dam at the farm so I have had years of experience of cooking the yabbies caught by my family.

The smellier the bait used to catch your yabby, the better. However, I well remember the way my children, when quite small and bored by my preoccupation with the restaurant, would tie pieces of soap or bread on a line to dangle over the balcony of the house, which jutted out over a pond. In a year of plenty they had no trouble catching yabbies. I could always tell when they had success by the squeals of delight intermingled with fear as they tried to haul the yabby up and grab it before it fell through the cracks of the verandah timbers. There is quite an art to picking up a yabby by the back of the head, and it is an art worth learning.

When we left this tiny house at the farm – which was really just two small bedrooms, a bathroom and an open living room, as our kitchen was the restaurant kitchen next door – we weren't prepared for our girls' reluctance to move to our present home. Although not huge, it is at least double the space, and has great character; even though it initially lacked some basic mod cons, we soon rectified that. We made a deal with the girls, that, as they were losing the dam at the farm to swim in, we would build a swimming pool between the new house and the dam at the bottom of the garden. While that was a bit of a coup for them, more important to their settling in was that the dam happened to be full of yabbies. Each night for those first few summers, the girls would lay nets for the yabbies, pulling up such great feeds that we would eat outside almost every night, starting the meal with a great pile of yabbies to share.

City friends love yabbying expeditions. One treasured day, with a refrigerator full of Christmas leftovers and a promise of yabbying, the only 'bait' was a plate of fresh quail.

Given the full net of yabbies we feasted on later, the quail was a sacrifice well worth making. There's no need to be quite so extravagant though, as the feeding response of the yabby is induced by odour. So, as I said, the smellier the bait the better.

Sadly, the home dam, either through us eating it dry, the local tradition of poaching or years of drought in the 1990s, is now empty of yabbies, so our yabby feeds are now few and far between.

It is best to yabby at night when yabbies move about to feed. If your pond is really turbid, however, you'll be able to trap them during the day too. The best net of all is an 'opera' net. They are illegal in rivers but can be left baited the night before in a dam, so you can be sure of a catch.

Not all traditional farmers are keen on the yabby (*Cherax destructor* by name and nature). Yabbies burrow into the sides of dams when the water is low, digging down to the water table, and then return to the surface when the dam refills. This digging can cause leakage through the dam walls. Legend has it that yabbies can be found 7 metres down; when farming them, it is imperative that the water level be kept constant to stop burrowing.

There is a real demand for yabbies in Europe, although this is, in large part, being satisfied by American crawfish farmed commercially in Louisiana, and also now in big numbers in China. Also, European freshwater crays were decimated after the American crawfish was introduced there some fifty or sixty years ago, carrying with it the crayfish plague. Our yabby is larger and much fuller in flavour than the crawfish, so there is hope that it can be pushed as a quality product to the discerning customer, given that it's expensive to produce and export.

There are four producers in Western Australia who already export to Europe, and indeed that state's yabby industry is a much larger concern than South Australia's. By law, every paddock in Western Australia must have a turkey-nest dam in it (this is a dam where the dam walls are above ground level). Farmers harvest their own yabbies and these are collected live for export, and then held in dams, waiting for orders from all over Australia, or to be shipped to Europe (mostly Germany). They are graded and purged before being shipped.

It is the introduced South Australian yabby that Western Australian farmers are harvesting, although two indigenous species, the gilgie and koonac, are also sometimes available. It is something of an irony that the South Australian yabby is providing such an export opportunity to Western Australia, while the introduced Western Australian marron is thriving on Kangaroo Island. The red claw is also part of the yabby family; this variety has been very successful in parts of Queensland, where the farming of it is quite an industry. While very similar to look at, its harder shell makes it more difficult to peel.

Farmers purge their yabbies by holding them in fresh water so that the customer is presented with a yabby with a clean intestinal tract (it's actually still there but it's free of grit and rubbish so doesn't need to be removed). This is done to extend their shelf-life as they are transported live, stunned on ice; given the choice, I find an unpurged dam-caught yabby has much more flavour. I err towards a 110 g yabby, as it has such a presence on the plate. However, the best weight-to-tail ratio actually comes from a smaller 80 g yabby.

Yabbies should be cooked live, having first been stunned on ice or in the freezer for 20 minutes. On no account should they be left to die by the side of the dam. The dead yabby, cooked by mistake, will have an off smell and a peculiar mushy texture.

Yabbies are usually only available cooked at fish markets. During summer you will often find live yabbies in the Barossa markets, and probably at other farmers' markets in yabby territories, which will be much better eating than those caught commercially in the wild, as in many cases these will not have been handled well and are likely to be overcooked. However, even these will never taste as good as those you have caught and cooked yourself.

If you have caught your own yabbies, there are two ways of dealing with them after stunning them in the freezer: cooking them entirely, or par-cooking them in preparation for pan-frying or barbecuing. For the first (and simplest) method, bring a stockpot of salted water to the boil with dill seeds and a lemon wedge or two in it. Toss in 6–10 stunned yabbies at a time, then allow the water to come back to the boil (this usually takes a couple of minutes – if it seems to be taking longer, cover the pan with a lid to encourage boiling, as the yabbies will overcook otherwise) and cook the yabbies for 2–3 minutes, depending on size. I use a wire 'cage' I have had made especially that is very similar to one for boiling pasta. This way I can pull the yabbies out easily. Spread the cooked yabbies out on a bench to cool. Wait until the water comes back to the boil before cooking the next batch.

For preparing yabbies you want to pan-fry or barbecue, follow the same instructions but only immerse the yabbies in the boiling water for 1 minute. At this stage you can lift the flap of the tail up and carefully pull the intestinal tract out in one piece, if you like. The yabbies are still not more than just 'set' so can cope with the balance of cooking; overcooked yabby flesh becomes stringy and unpalatable.

The claw of the yabby is delicious. Rather than bash it with a mallet and risk splintered shell spoiling the delicate flesh, take the small part of the claw and pull it until it is loose. If the yabby is fully cooked, it will release the sweet claw whole.

Brush tiny par-cooked yabbies in their shells with extra virgin olive oil and barbecue them for about 1 minute per side. If the yabbies are large, halve them lengthways and toss in a frying pan with extra virgin olive oil and a splash of Pernod for a minute or two. The flavour of the Pernod and oil on your fingers as you peel and eat the yabbies is incredibly more-ish. For a change, try using walnut oil, and then deglaze the pan with verjuice. Or cook the yabbies in nut-brown butter with a good squeeze of lemon juice and lots of freshly ground black pepper.

A traditional lemon mayonnaise or a verjuice beurre blanc is pretty special served with a large platter of freshly boiled yabbies and lots of crusty bread. To be honest, though, you need nothing more than extra virgin olive oil, lemon wedges, freshly ground black pepper and a dish of sea salt flakes to make a memorable meal from yabbies.

Eating yabbies outside has a special cachet. At home we spread a table with lots of newspaper, position an old-fashioned washstand alongside and fill it with warm water as a communal finger bowl, then offer a pile of serviettes. A bottle of extra virgin olive oil, wedges of lemon, sea salt, freshly ground black pepper and crusty bread complete the picture – along with plates stacked ready for people to make their own dipping sauce. So if you have cooked a huge tub of yabbies, let people shell their own. You'll find those driven by flavour sucking the juicy 'mustard' from the heads after devouring the tails. (My husband Colin sets the tails aside until he has enough to make a great sandwich, but I'm never patient enough to do this.)

If you tire of yabbies served à la naturel (though who would?), then they can be thrown together in so many ways. Think summer, think yabbies cooked, peeled and set in jelly in the bottom of coffee cups used as moulds, using either verjuice or a stock made from yabby shells or a mixture of both, then topped with peeled, seeded and diced ripe tomatoes and some basil. Turn them out on a bed of baby lettuce leaves and make an unctuous mayonnaise to serve alongside.

While yabbies have a great affinity with tomatoes and basil, the most ambrosial yabby dish I've ever cooked involved pan-frying yabbies with wild boletus mushrooms from a nearby pine forest. I cooked the young, dense mushrooms and the halved yabbies in the same pan in nut-brown butter and a little walnut oil with lots of freshly ground black pepper and some basil. Given the earthiness of the wild mushroom, I suspect yabbies would also be amazing pan-fried with fresh truffles, if one had the chance. Teaming globe artichokes with the first yabbies of the season, a mayonnaise flavoured with Pernod and a salad of peppery rocket would also make the most of these earthy flavours.

Don't waste the shells; find a recipe for lobster bisque and make a yabby version, although expect a more delicate flavour. Consider a yabby consommé made in the same manner as a crab consommé – even better, jelly it.

JANET'S SEA URCHIN ROE DRESSING
TO SERVE WITH YABBIES
Makes 500 ml

We prepared this dish for a very special wedding for Bronny Jones at the Pheasant Farm Restaurant in the early 1980s. Janet Jeffs, now a lauded restaurateur in Canberra, was so important in the restaurant's early days; she opened my eyes to so much and gave me confidence in my own ability. This dish was very much Janet's, and eating it was the first time I had experienced sea urchin, although it is now one of my favourite foods ever.

Bronny, a regular performer at the musical evenings we used to hold in the restaurant, had been studying and playing clarinet in New York and Paris and was to marry an American astronomer. Her memories of the Pheasant Farm Restaurant were as special to her as her playing had been to us. (The musical evenings had featured Susan Hackett, the instigator, on flute, Stephen Walter on piano, Suzannah Foulds singing and Peter Jenkin and Bronny on clarinet – each of them serious professionals with a love of food and wine. They were such special occasions, and just done for the love of it all.)

The wedding was a great feast, with Janet, Bronny's close friend, designing the menu and cooking the meal with some help from me. I remember Janet organising a friend to gather the sea urchins – they certainly weren't on the general market in those days. I was bowled over by the flavour.

½ lemon	2 teaspoons mirin
2 egg yolks	2 teaspoons light soy sauce
2 tablespoons white-wine vinegar	sea salt flakes and freshly ground
400 ml peanut oil	white pepper
roe from 2 sea urchins	

Juice the lemon and blend it with the egg yolks and white-wine vinegar in a food processor, then add the peanut oil in a slow, steady stream with the motor running to make a thick mayonnaise. Mash the roe and stir it into the mayonnaise with the mirin and soy sauce. Check the flavourings and season. Serve immediately.

YABBY SAUCE *Makes 500 ml*

If your guests are too polite to suck the heads when eating freshly boiled yabbies, put the discarded shells aside to make the following sauce as soon as possible after shelling. The sauce is great with freshly boiled yabbies, but it also makes a wonderful base for a soup, and can be tossed through pasta with boiled and peeled yabbies and fresh basil.

40 yabby heads, well crushed	⅓ cup (80 ml) Cognac
6 cloves garlic, finely chopped	150 ml tomato paste
2 carrots, finely chopped	1 cup (250 ml) white wine
2 leeks, white part only, finely chopped	2 cups (500 ml) verjuice (optional)
1 large onion, finely chopped	sea salt flakes and freshly ground
½ fennel bulb, finely chopped	black pepper
100 ml extra virgin olive oil	60 g unsalted butter (optional)

Sweat the crushed yabby heads and all the vegetables in the olive oil in a large saucepan over high heat for about 15 minutes or until the vegetables are cooked. Pour the Cognac into the pan and allow it to evaporate, then mix in the tomato paste. Add the wine and 250 ml water (or just the verjuice instead) and simmer gently for 1 hour.

Strain the sauce into a clean saucepan through a conical sieve or similar, pushing on the contents as you do so to extract as much flavour as possible. Reduce the sauce to the desired consistency, then season and add the butter to make it more velvety, if desired. This sauce should be used as soon as possible but can be kept refrigerated for a couple of days.

YABBY RICE PAPER ROLLS WITH ROASTED TOMATOES, ROAST GARLIC AÏOLI AND SNOW PEA SPROUTS

Makes 24

Yabbies were well and truly on the menu for my Paris jaunt in June 2001, where my brief was to devise a cocktail party menu for 500 (though on the night 700 people turned up). My first thought was to do yabby tails wrapped in vine leaves, then pan-fried in nut-brown butter and verjuice, but the logistics of organising 1000 perfect tender vine leaves from afar were nightmarish. Next we thought of herby risotto-encased yabby dolmades using preserved vine leaves, but the leaves retained too much of their briny flavour no matter how many times I soaked them. Little brioche balls filled with lemon myrtle-scented yabby bisque were next, but these too were rejected as we worried about the delicious yabby juices oozing all over the well-dressed guests.

In the end, the yabby tails in rice paper wrappers we prepared were far simpler than any of the above, and the dish was a great success! I got a huge kick out of serving one of my favourite ingredients so simply and so far from home. Being able to go with the flow topped off the event – that is, after all, what good cooking is all about.

24 raw yabby tails

butter, for cooking

sea salt flakes and freshly ground
    black pepper

½ cup (125 ml) verjuice

½ cup (125 ml) extra virgin olive oil

12 sunrise limes (a type of native lime)
    or 3 meyer lemons

24 large square rice paper wrappers
    (available from Asian grocers)

2 punnets snow pea sprouts

AÏOLI

1 head garlic

sea salt flakes and freshly ground
    black pepper

30 ml lemon juice

30 ml verjuice

2 large egg yolks

1 cup (250 ml) extra virgin olive oil

ROASTED TOMATOES

24 cherry *or* truss tomatoes

sea salt flakes and freshly ground
    black pepper

1 sprig thyme

extra virgin olive oil, for drizzling

To make the aïoli, preheat the oven to 180°C. Wrap the garlic in foil and bake until soft (depending on the size, it could take between 30 minutes and 1 hour). Leave to cool, then squeeze out the garlic into a food processor. Add 2 pinches salt, a little pepper, the lemon juice and verjuice. Amalgamate in the food processor, then add the egg yolks and process until well combined. Begin to add the oil in a very slow stream, then move to a steady stream as the aïoli begins to accept more oil and emulsifies.

Reduce the oven temperature to 120°C. For the roasted tomatoes, cut the base of the tomatoes with a cross, then drop them into a saucepan of boiling water for a few seconds to loosen the skins, then dip them in iced water. Remove skins and cut tomatoes in half. Place in a baking dish, season and add the thyme. Drizzle generously with olive oil and bake for 1 hour or until tomatoes collapse. Remove from the oven and add a little more olive oil to moisten, then set aside.

Peel the yabby tails, leaving the shell on the end intact. The simplest way is to place your thumb under the end of the tail and, using the thumb of your other hand, remove as for a prawn. Insert a skewer through from the tail to the end of the flesh to keep the tails straight.

Heat a little butter in a frying pan over medium–high until nut-brown and quickly pan-fry the yabby tails, then season to taste and deglaze the pan with a splash of verjuice. Rest the tails in a marinade of olive oil, half the finely sliced sunrise limes (or half the meyer lemons cut into thin slices widthways, then cut into tiny triangles) and salt and pepper, for at least 30 minutes.

Soak the rice paper wrappers in cold tap water until the edges are pliable; you can do this a couple at a time. Lay them out flat on a tea towel, then pat dry and place on a chopping board. To assemble the rolls, place a line of snow pea sprouts down the centre of each wrapper, then add a little thinly sliced lime or lemon and some roasted tomato halves. Add one yabby tail and 1 teaspoon roasted garlic aïoli. Fold one end in and roll so that the yabby tail and snow pea sprouts are exposed at one end.

MARRON

Marron may originate from Western Australia, but Kangaroo Island in South Australia has become their second home. There are now so many marron naturalised in its streams that farming them is becoming big business.

Commercial production on the island ranges from catching wild marron in streams and dams to farming them in an amazingly sophisticated way, as John Melbourne, from near Vivonne Bay, does. Originally from Adelaide, John spent most of his working life in London. He tells the story of having dinner in England with Australian friends who talked about marron, and it was as if a light bulb switched on in his head. He had just sold his business in London, the water connection made sense (he had been working in water treatment and water quality instrumentation), and he was looking for a new project.

John's initial research took him to Western Australia, but he ended up on Kangaroo Island. He made a huge investment in a mammoth turkey-nest dam, breeding ponds and growing-out dams, all wire-netted to keep the birds out and with an expansive underground network of pipes and valves to control water flow. It is a meticulously managed property and John has now opened a stylish café on the site, serving marron in many

different guises each day of the week – a must for any visitor to beautiful Kangaroo Island.

A decent-sized marron can constitute a main course, but size is dictated by age. Marron are a lot slower growing than their yabby cousins, so a perfect main-course marron may be three years old – and a lot harder to find.

The simplest way of preparing marron is to stun them in the freezer first for 20 minutes, then blanch them in a large saucepan of rapidly boiling water for up to 1 minute (depending on size) after the water returns to the boil. Plunge the marron briefly into iced water and then cut them in half, remove their intestinal tract and reserve the 'mustard' in the head for adding to a sauce or mayonnaise. Toss the marron in a saucepan with whatever flavouring or herbs you wish to use.

Marron accept highly perfumed oils such as truffle and walnut particularly well and make a great warm salad with heads of frisée, witlof, baby rocket, basil, salad burnet, flat-leaf parsley and some fresh asparagus. Make a vinaigrette of truffle or walnut oil and verjuice, and toss through the salad.

Mushrooms and marron are a surprisingly successful combination (see below). Try packing the head cavity of halved marron with sautéed diced mushroom and spring onions, then drizzle the lot with just a little real truffle oil. It is a delicious way to present marron, whether you are serving several small specimens or a large one per person.

One memorable meal at our old restaurant Charlick's was a marron poached in an aromatic fish stock with star anise, kaffir lime leaf, crushed lemongrass, coriander stems and white peppercorns. The meat was taken from the shell and tossed with cucumber, green papaya, coriander, mint and a touch of ground-up dried shrimp, all in a little extra virgin olive oil. Then a dressing was made from black rice vinegar, lemon juice with sugar to balance, peanut oil and a touch of grapeseed oil, so as not to overpower the peanut oil. What a dish!

MARRON WITH MUSHROOMS AND VERJUICE   *Serves 4*

I cooked this recipe in Tokyo a few years ago, at the Shinjuku Park Hyatt. I had the luxury of taking really large marron with me, and having the fresh markets of Paris at my disposal (via the airways, of course) to order fresh cèpes to accompany the dish. While I use pine or boletus mushrooms here, dried cèpes or porcinis reconstituted in verjuice make a very satisfactory alternative.

4 × 240 g live marron

4 golden shallots, finely chopped

150 ml walnut oil, plus extra for brushing

1 sprig thyme, leaves picked

195 ml verjuice, plus extra for brushing

sea salt flakes and freshly ground
    black pepper

4 fresh pine *or* boletus mushrooms,
    stems trimmed and caps quartered

butter, for cooking

4 large fresh vine leaves

Prepare the marron as described above. Preheat the oven to 180°C. Combine the shallots, walnut oil, thyme leaves and 70 ml of the verjuice to make a vinaigrette, then season with salt and pepper to taste.

Brush quartered mushrooms with walnut oil and verjuice, then dot with a little butter and season well. Bake mushrooms, turning once, for 10 minutes or until golden on all sides. Set aside. Reset oven to 220°C.

Poach vine leaves in a saucepan in the remaining 125 ml verjuice until cooked through (about 2 minutes for mature leaves); dry well. Heat a shallow, heavy-based roasting pan in the oven.

Brush cut surface of marron with vinaigrette and bake for 5–6 minutes. As the marron rests, pour remaining vinaigrette into the pan and stir in the mushrooms and their juices. Dot the vine leaves with butter (top-side up) and crisp in the oven for 2 minutes. Place a crisped vine leaf on each plate, top with 2 marron, then spoon over the vinaigrette. Serve immediately.

ZUCCHINI

 THE ZUCCHINI IS THE MOST ABUSED OF ALL VEGETABLES.
Sadly, many are grown thick and long. Large zucchini means old zucchini: the water content is higher, the flesh is less dense, the flavour diminishes and shelf-life is impaired. These zucchini wither and become unattractive very quickly, and are often bitter to eat.

This is one vegetable I like to eat when it's really small, so for me the best zucchini is about the size of a small cigar. Specialty farmers are now selling them at this size with the flowers attached – it's a great step forward.

Zucchini is probably the easiest of all vegetables to grow yourself, and anyone who does so will know that they grow while your back is turned. If you've missed one hidden under the umbrella of leaves, before you know it you can have a giant on your hands. I've grown four zucchini plants this year from seeds I got from my supplier The Italian Gardener (I chose the paler, ridged variety, my favourite). I've never ever had plants this large (they look more like elephant ears), and whilst at the beginning of the season I thought I should have planted at least four more, now I've decided to plant only two next year, as I'm absolutely swimming in zucchini, even when picking every second day. I can afford to be fussy, so anything longer than 12 cm goes to the chooks!

I remember clearly the days when zucchini, also referred to as baby marrows or courgettes, particularly in English and French books, were considered exotic. My mother had come to live with us in 1975 when my second daughter Elli was born. A city person, she took to gardening with a vengeance. As money was scarce, Mum would present us joyfully with baskets of vegetables she'd grown herself. Zucchini were enough of a novelty that size didn't seem to matter then, although Mum seldom picked them smaller than 18 cm. They were usually consumed the day they were picked and as such made great eating. When larger ones that had been missed were finally picked we were not allowed to waste them; instead, Mum stuffed and baked them, usually with minced meat. These days it is easy to be seduced by 'new' vegetables. But don't lose sight of the everyday ones – instead, enjoy them at their best by growing and picking (or buying) them at their optimum size and age.

The most common types of zucchini you are likely to come across are the dark-green zucchini, a paler-green striped one and a yellow zucchini. Essentially all variations on a theme, they have slightly different flavours. I find the pale-green zucchini sweeter than the dark-green, while the yellow tastes a little of tea leaves to me, like yellow squash.

The zucchini gives us the first triumph of the season, with its deliciously delicate flowers. Growing zucchini, even if it is in containers in a courtyard, is a cinch – it also means you don't have to worry about how you transport the fragile blooms home from the markets. In my garden, the long, golden blossoms are so beautiful to gaze upon, and stuffed zucchini flowers have become a firm favourite.

Now for some anatomy: the zucchini bears both male and female flowers. The male flower is much larger and particularly suited to stuffing. The female flower can also be stuffed but, as it becomes the zucchini itself in due course, it is a shame not to let it develop.

The fresher the flower, the easier it is to stuff (before the petals close up), so pick or buy them just before you plan to use them. Beware: earwigs, ants and millipedes tend to love the moist interior of these blossoms, but are highly undesirable guests to have at the table, to say the least. Make sure you check each flower very carefully before you begin cooking.

The filling for zucchini flowers depends on what you have at hand. Cheeses, from bocconcini to goat's cheese, Gruyère or Parmigiano Reggiano, cut into tiny dice so they melt in the very short cooking time and mixed with chopped anchovy and flat-leaf parsley, are delicious. Tiny cubes of peeled ripe tomato with minced garlic and flat-leaf parsley made into a paste with some olive oil is another idea. A simple dob of Pesto (see page 21) or Salsa Agresto (see page 22), with or without cheese, makes a fresh and more-ish filling.

The important points to remember are to prepare your ingredients ahead of time and to work very quickly. You can make a light batter or dip the blossoms into a dish of beaten egg, then dust them in flour or polenta before frying. Once each flower is battered, you need to cook it immediately. I tend to shallow-fry the zucchini flowers using a bulk extra virgin olive oil. This way I achieve the desired crispness while the flavour imparted by the oil is a positive one, rather than just leaving a 'fatty' aftertaste.

Young zucchini specimens, by the way, are perfect to eat raw – just make sure you do so as soon as they have been picked. Wash and slice them very thinly for the best flavour. You will be surprised by just how sweet the zucchini is – raw, washed zucchini make a great salad when sliced as thinly as possible lengthways, then dressed with a vinaigrette of extra virgin olive oil, lemon juice, garlic and basil or marjoram, and seasoned. Leave the salad for a good half an hour before eating, tossing it every now and then. Alternatively, toss thinly sliced zucchini in a little melted butter and extra virgin olive oil in a hot frying pan for just a minute, then season and add freshly chopped flat-leaf parsley.

When you take young zucchini from the garden and treat them this simply, it's a specialty all of its own. Slice 1 small zucchini into slices as thin as possible. Heat some butter with a dash of olive oil until nut-brown, toss in the zucchini with a good pinch of sea salt,

a couple of grinds of black pepper, a pinch of nutmeg and some freshly torn basil and serve immediately. The zucchini should still have a small amount of crunch and, fresh from the garden, is as sweet as sweet can be.

Small zucchini can be boiled whole for just a few minutes, then drained and left to cool a little. Sliced lengthways and served with good extra virgin olive oil, a generous squeeze of lemon juice or verjuice and freshly ground black pepper, they are delicious. If you grow zucchini, try cooking the tiny ones with their flowers still attached. I use a frying pan with a little boiling water, salt and a knob of butter added to effectively braise the zucchini, turning them over carefully with a slotted spoon.

Try pan-frying equal quantities of zucchini and eggplant cut into 1 cm pieces. Sauté the eggplant first in extra virgin olive oil, then set it aside on a warm plate and quickly cook the zucchini in fresh oil. Toss the warm vegetables together with more extra virgin olive oil and some lemon juice and fresh basil leaves, then grind on black pepper.

Chargrilling zucchini on a barbecue adds another dimension. Slice the zucchini lengthways into three or four strips, then brush with extra virgin olive oil and season with fresh thyme and freshly ground black pepper. Sear each side until coloured, then squeeze on a little lemon juice, add a drizzle of olive oil and season with salt and pepper.

Zucchini also pickle well but have to be exceptionally crisp specimens to start with. Bring 500 ml water and 500 ml white-wine vinegar to the boil and cook sliced zucchini for just a couple of minutes. Drain and dry the zucchini and transfer to a clean jar with freshly chopped herbs and garlic. Pour in enough extra virgin olive oil to cover the zucchini – you will need to top up the oil for the first few days. I store this pickle in the refrigerator for a few weeks before using it. The olive oil does not preserve the zucchini – you need an acidic component to do that – but, along with the cold of the refrigerator, it delays spoiling for a few weeks once opened.

ZUCCHINI IN AGRODOLCE   *Serves 4*

I found this recipe in Elizabeth David's *Italian Food*, but I use verjuice rather than white-wine vinegar and sugar. Look for small zucchini for this dish.

⅓ cup (80 ml) fruity extra virgin olive oil	pinch ground cinnamon
450 g small zucchini, cut into thick rounds	sea salt flakes
freshly ground black pepper	¼ cup (60 ml) verjuice

Heat the olive oil in a large frying pan with a lid and gently cook the zucchini, covered, for about 5 minutes over low heat, then remove the lid and season with pepper and cinnamon, and salt if needed. Turn up the heat to high and add the verjuice, then cook for a few minutes more until the sauce is syrupy. Serve immediately with grilled fish or pan-fried chicken breasts.

COCKTAIL ZUCCHINI FRITTERS

Makes 16 cocktail-sized fritters

I have four Italian zucchini plants in my garden this year (the pale-green, ridged variety). I've never grown these before and they are the best I've ever eaten. However, they yield so much once they're truly established that I have to be more and more inventive in coming up with ways to use them.

Getting my grandchildren to eat greens hasn't been the easiest thing, but one evening my daughter Saskia made zucchini fritters to serve with drinks, and it was touch and go as to who ate the most – the adults or the kids.

My version of these are cocktail-sized and feature labna, a staple in our household. The acidity in this works well for my palate.

160 g grated zucchini

1 teaspoon sea salt flakes

2 teaspoons chopped basil

2 teaspoons chopped mint

70 g labna (see Glossary)

½ egg (I know it seems a waste, but it's all you need for this recipe, so whisk the egg and halve it, or double the recipe depending on how many you want to serve)

2 tablespoons plain flour

squeeze of lemon juice

freshly ground black pepper

3 tablespoons extra virgin olive oil

Spread the grated zucchini out on a perforated dish, and sprinkle with the salt. Leave for a minimum of half an hour to allow the moisture to be drawn out.

Wring out the grated zucchini with your hands to extract as much liquid as possible. Transfer to a bowl and add the chopped herbs, labna, egg, flour, lemon juice and a grind of pepper, and mix through. Spoon out portions of the mixture to make fritters ½ cm thick and 2 cm round.

Choose a frying pan large enough to hold eight fritters at a time. Add half the olive oil to the pan, and when the oil is hot, add the first batch of fritters to the pan. Quickly seal the fritters on one side and when golden, flip over and cook on the other side. Remove them from the pan and set aside to rest on kitchen paper before quickly cooking the next batch in the remaining oil. Serve hot – they are absolutely scrumptious.

GILL'S ZUCCHINI AND APPLE SALAD

Serves 2 as a side dish

Gill Radford, a chef and caterer from the Barossa, helps keep me sane during the long filming seasons for the ABC TV series *The Cook and The Chef*. Together we discuss ingredients, mull over recipe ideas and taste dishes, and so often Gill's ideas add another dimension that I hadn't thought of. This dish, using local gruth cheese from Ballycroft at Greenock, is the perfect example – the fresh green apple giving that little something extra.

1 small green apple

verjuice *or* lemon juice, to dress

160 g baby zucchini

100 ml extra virgin olive oil

¼ cup firmly packed fresh herb leaves
(marjoram, thyme, flat-leaf parsley, etc),
washed and well-dried

juice of ½ lemon

½ teaspoon sea salt flakes

1 teaspoon sugar

2 tablespoons Ballycroft gruth *or* other
fresh curd cheese

freshly ground black pepper

Slice the apple into very thin strips, then toss in a small bowl with a touch of verjuice or a squeeze of lemon juice.

Bring a large pan of salted water to the boil, add the zucchini and blanch for 2–3 minutes, then remove from the water and set aside. Heat the extra virgin olive oil in a small pan until hot (but not smoking), then toss in the herbs and fry until crisp. Remove the herbs and drain on kitchen paper, retaining the oil.

Mix 60 ml of herb oil from the pan with the lemon juice, then add the salt and sugar and adjust seasoning if necessary.

Once cool enough to handle, slice the zucchini in half lengthways and drizzle the cut sides with any leftover herb oil. Toss these with the apple, then mix through the vinaigrette until well coated. Serve immediately, topped with crumbled gruth and season to taste.

ZUCCHINI FLOWERS IN BATTER WITH GRUYÈRE AND ANCHOVIES

Serves 4

You can batter just the flowers, as in this recipe, or you can batter whole baby zucchinis with the flower still attached. Just slice the zucchini with two parallel cuts, almost to the top, leaving the flower attached. This allows the zucchini to cook at the same rate as the flower. Then stuff the flower and batter the whole lot.

Even though using extra virgin olive oil for deep-frying seems extravagant, you can use the same oil many times over.

200 g Gruyère (I use Heidi Farm
Gruyère), grated

18 anchovy fillets, finely chopped

18 zucchini flowers

extra virgin olive oil, for deep-frying

sea salt flakes and freshly ground
black pepper

BATTER

200 g self-raising flour

pinch salt

1½ cups (375 ml) chilled water

Mix the Gruyère and anchovy fillets in a bowl. Check each zucchini flower for insects and remove the stamen. Distribute the cheese stuffing evenly between the flowers and gently squeeze the petals together at the top to seal.

Heat a good quantity of olive oil in a deep-fryer to 180°C, if you have one, or in a deep saucepan (about 20 cm across) until hot; the pan must be large enough to contain the hot oil as it bubbles up when the flowers are dropped into it. Test the temperature of the oil by frying a small chunk of bread in it: if the bread turns golden brown immediately, the oil is hot enough.

Make the batter just before you start cooking the stuffed flowers. Sift the flour with the salt into a bowl, then quickly stir in the cold water until just mixed (the batter will look a little lumpy). Dip the flowers into the batter, then carefully lower 3 flowers at a time into the hot oil until golden, turning them with a spoon to ensure even cooking. They will take about 5 minutes. Remove the cooked flowers and allow them to drain on kitchen paper, while cooking the remaining ones. Season to taste and serve immediately.

AUTUMN

ALMONDS

ALMONDS HAVE A SPECIAL PLACE IN MY BAROSSA LANDSCAPE.
The first trees to blossom when the weather is still bitterly cold, they are a
sign of the coming spring. The sight of these trees in flower lifts my heart
immediately, and I always sacrifice some of the promised fruit by picking
blossom for my kitchen table so I can drink in its exquisite perfume.

Did you know that an almond is actually a peach in disguise? I didn't until I opened
Louis Glowinski's *Complete Book of Fruit Growing in Australia*. He calls it a dry-fleshed close
relative: the similarity lies in the peach seeds, which Glowinski says can be sweet like an
almond. I have not eaten many peach seeds, so I can't give an opinion, but can tell you that
both trees grow very well here in South Australia.

All almond growers face the same problem each year: how to pick the crop before the
birds decimate it. In South Australia's Riverland, where there are vast almond groves,
light aircraft are used to move the birds on to another area; here in the Valley shiny pieces
of foil are tied to the trees and hawk-shaped kites are flown. It is an ever-increasing problem
and one I've almost given up trying to solve, so I usually buy my almonds fully mature
from more organised neighbours.

It was in *Stephanie's Australia* that I first read about green almonds (almonds picked
early, before the birds can strike). Stephanie Alexander stayed with us for a week while
she was writing this book, and I remember well her being on the almond trail, but at that
stage I had no trees and so wasn't quite ready to digest the information. We subsequently
planted fifteen trees, and it wasn't until cockatoos had attacked and half-eaten every
almond for several years in a row that I was reminded by sheer frustration of the culinary
benefits of green almonds.

I am so disorganised that even with a note in my diary to pick our almonds in November
while they are still green, it is always such a busy time that I only ever get the chance to
pinch a basketful for a particular dish before the birds get them. However, there is always

next year. As our almond trees surround the property, following the fence line, there is not the same impetus to do something about them as there is with the orchard, which I walk through every day – lucky birds, I say.

It was also Stephanie who, many years ago, introduced me to the books of American food writer Paula Wolfert. So, on Paula's first trip to South Australia to talk about olives and olive oil, I jumped at the chance to look after her for a day. It is difficult to explain how many ideas can be seeded in just one day in the company of women like Paula and Stephanie. It was such a shame I had to drive when I wanted so much to stop and take notes about the many possibilities of our Mediterranean climate, but I made mental notes. In response to my cries of despair about always losing my almond crop, Paula talked a lot more about green almonds, and suggested I look up various Italian references and her book *The Cooking of the Eastern Mediterranean*.

I later found mention of green almonds in *The Fruit, Herbs and Vegetables of Italy* by Giacomo Castelvetro: 'green almonds are not in season long; they are much healthier than hazelnuts and considered to be the noblest nut of all. Many people in Italy, especially in Tuscany, eat them green when the shell is still soft, or cook them like truffles.' With this in mind, I'll now commit myself, in writing, to start picking much earlier, so I'll have more green almonds than I could ever use.

Try pan-frying green almonds in nut-brown butter as an hors d'oeuvre with sea salt flakes, or to serve with pan-fried trout. Toss pan-fried sliced green almonds through pasta with a fruity extra virgin olive oil and lots of Parmigiano Reggiano.

I have often written about the difference between buying new-season almonds and those of anonymous parentage and unknown age. However, I was recently given a bag of almonds from McLaren Vale that were nine months old, yet they were still fresh, crisp and almondy (it may sound crazy but almonds don't always taste so). I was blooded on fresh Barossa almonds twenty-plus years ago, and I have to say that if my palate memory serves me right, wonderful as they were then, these almonds tasted even better.

It seems to me that, at least in South Australia, the almonds of McLaren Vale are an example of terroir – the growing environment. I have never tasted better. At a meeting in Mildura a few years ago, I remember sitting next to a former McLaren Vale almond grower who told me that their operation was moved to the Riverland because it better suited the economies of scale to grow large plots of almonds. The grower said, sadly, that there was nothing to equal the flavour of the almonds from the original grove – the unique combination of soil quality, prevailing weather conditions and position at McLaren Vale had helped to produce such wonderful almonds, and these conditions just couldn't be replicated at the new site. Unfortunately, this has resulted in a compromise in flavour: it's sometimes difficult to get the balance right.

There are two types of almond: the more commonly found sweet almond, and the hard-to-find bitter almond (most of which are imported into Australia from Spain). In Australia most almonds are grown from grafted rootstock, while in Europe the norm is to grow seedling trees. Usually 1–2 per cent of these will turn out to be bitter almonds. The nuts from these trees are not kept separate from the crop in most cases, so almond oil from France, for example, will have a tiny percentage of bitter almonds in it. Bitter almonds are also grown specifically

to make confectionery, particularly marzipan, and as the base for the Italian liqueur Amaretto di Saronno.

Bitter almonds add an edge that the sweet almond alone cannot – even two or three bitter almonds ground with 250 g sweet almonds make a startling difference to desserts. A few of these nuts give a quivering blancmange a flavour like no other, as they do ice cream. However, straight from the tree, bitter almonds are high in prussic acid, a poison which is later removed from the oil. Experts at the Botanic Gardens in Adelaide advise me that sixty untreated bitter almonds can kill a human. After eating several untreated nuts while once making marzipan, I doubt that anyone could eat more than two or three in one sitting, but I leave in the warning just in case.

It is possible to buy bitter almonds here, but not without difficulty. The best solution is to find an almond grower, who will usually have a tree or two of the bitter variety. The nuts are often kept aside since bitter almonds have very hard shells and cannot be cracked easily by the equipment designed for the softer sweet almonds.

It was during the autumn of my first year in the Barossa that I realised what a taste sensation fresh almonds are. Ed Auricht, a neighbour then well into his seventies, would crack them at night to sell to the initiated the next day. As much as an almond can tempt me at any time, when the new crop comes in my passion for them is renewed. There is a world of difference in the flavour.

Australian almonds are at times sold in the shell and, as such, keep better than shelled nuts. Happily, the paper-shell almond, which is easier to shell, is now the preference of most growers. Nuts in the shell should feel heavy for their size and have no visible cracks and certainly no mould. If you're buying almonds in the shell, allow twice the weight called for in a recipe using shelled nuts. Because the almond, like the walnut and hazelnut, contains a substantial amount of oil, it turns rancid easily once shelled. For this reason, almonds should be stored away from light, moisture and heat. While it is often suggested that shelled almonds be kept in the refrigerator to control deterioration, as oil-makers do, bitter almonds are actually best kept in the freezer as they tend to be used so sparingly.

I never blanch almonds (I might feel differently if I were a dessert cook, but I doubt it), and I never buy ground almonds as they are invariably stale. If I require ground almonds (also called almond meal), I dry-roast the nuts in a 220°C oven for 6–8 minutes until their aroma is released, then allow them to cool before grinding them in a food processor (a little rosewater or orange-flower water will prevent the nuts from 'oiling'). Better still is to use elbow grease and pound them using a mortar and pestle. The flavour from pre-ground almonds is just not the same. I use freshly ground almonds to make an Almond and Cumquat Tart (see page 568). Whenever I was lucky enough to have the dried cumquats that my friend Noëlle Tolley made, I would reconstitute them in verjuice and scatter them in the base of the tart – fantastic!

Elizabeth David's writings convinced me that blancmange made with almond milk is eons away from the blancmange I ate in hospital after having my tonsils out as a young child. I also find almond milk a refreshing drink on those autumn days that are surprisingly hot. Somewhere in my reading on early English cooking I came across an unexpected reference to almond milk being mixed with verjuice made from crabapples and used to poach salmon and eel. I have tried this with riverfish with great success. Making almond milk is a simple process: heat 500 ml milk (I sometimes use 1 part buttermilk to 3 parts milk) and then stir in 1 tablespoon castor sugar and pour the mixture over 140 g ground almonds flavoured with a few drops of orange-flower water. Allow the mixture to infuse for 4 hours, then strain the milk into a bowl through muslin (or even a new Chux), squeezing out the last drops, and refrigerate it until required.

I hated marzipan (which has bitter almonds in it) until I made a fresh almond paste myself. Rather than use it as a cake topping, I love to sandwich it between layers of butter cake to make it really moist.

Almonds are a great snack food and are often partnered with dried fruit. If you buy shelled almonds, always take the time to roast them before eating – it makes a huge difference. Put them on a tray in the oven at 220°C for a few minutes or until they pop their skins just a little. To make an adult treat, put a roasted almond inside a pitted prune, then dip in melted dark couverture chocolate. Don't skip the roasting step – the result just won't be the same.

If you like peanut butter, try a different style using almonds. Roast the almonds as above and leave to cool before pulsing in a food processor. Add a drop of cold water or rosewater after two or three pulses, so the oil in the almonds doesn't split, then add room temperature unsalted butter in the same proportion as the nuts. Pulse again until the nuts and butter are incorporated, then roll into a log and wrap in baking paper (it will oxidise if not totally covered) and refrigerate for a few days – don't keep it too long as nuts in any form are subject to rancidity. Spread wholemeal toast with almond butter for breakfast, or smother whole trout with it before cooking, adding a squeeze of lemon juice and freshly ground black pepper.

Figs and almonds are another great combination – especially to serve with coffee. Stuff good dried figs with freshly roasted almonds, skins on.

Almonds are just as good in savoury dishes. Spaghettini with flaked almonds, extra virgin olive oil, flat-leaf parsley and lots of freshly ground black pepper is a meal in a moment; a nutty ripe avocado can be sliced into this dish, too. A friend's clever twist on traditional trout with almonds is to make a flavoured butter using chopped roasted almonds. She greases baking paper or foil heavily with the softened almond butter and then places sliced lemon and dill inside the trout, which is then salted well and wrapped in the foil. The trout parcel is baked in the oven for about 15 minutes at 220°C and is turned halfway through cooking. Each person opens their parcel at the table, so that the wonderful aromas can be savoured.

Almond soup, very much a part of Mediterranean cuisines, is just as good cold as hot. Grind the almonds as for the almond butter on page 191, then stir in a mix of light chicken stock and buttermilk. A good dash of sherry provides the finishing touch. Served chilled with a garnish of fresh sultana grapes (as the version on page 234 is), this soup is perfect for warmer weather. Used as a thickening agent, ground almonds can also be added to a stock-based soup as a winter treat.

AVOCADO, GINGER AND ROASTED ALMONDS WITH PASTA AND FRESH CORIANDER

Serves 6 as an entrée or 3 as a main course

This incredibly refreshing pasta is one where it is essential that the pasta and roasted almonds are piping hot. This dish is also terrific with good-quality dried pasta (use a 500 g packet).

juice of 1 lemon

2 large reed *or* 4 medium hass avocados,
   peeled and cut into pieces

2 teaspoons finely chopped ginger
   (or extra to taste in winter)

100 ml extra virgin olive oil

½ cup (40 g) flaked almonds

500 g fresh tagliatelle

1 cup coriander leaves

sea salt flakes and freshly ground
   black pepper

Bring a large saucepan of water to the boil. Preheat the oven to 200°C.

Squeeze the lemon juice over the cut avocado. Mix the ginger with 1 tablespoon of the olive oil.

Roast the flaked almonds on a baking tray for 5 minutes or until golden brown. Meanwhile, cook the pasta in the boiling water for 3–4 minutes, then drain. Immediately toss the hot pasta with the ginger and olive oil mixture, allowing it to spread amongst the pasta. Quickly add the hot almonds, remaining olive oil, avocado and coriander.

Squeeze over a little more lemon juice to taste, then season with salt and pepper and serve.

PHEASANT WITH ALMONDS AND SHERRY   *Serves 4*

Ground almonds are often used to thicken sauces in Mediterranean cooking, particularly in Spain. A good friend of mine, whose family has a great food tradition, sent my first book, *Maggie's Farm*, to his sister in Spain. She responded by sending me a recipe she thought I would find interesting as it combined pheasant, almonds and sherry, all of which I have at my fingertips in the Barossa. I changed it to suit my method of cooking pheasant and took from the original Spanish recipe the important mix of ground almonds, sherry and garlic, which I whisked into a stock-based sauce. The result was a wonderful marriage of the nuttiness of the almonds and the sherry with the sweetness of the pheasant.

50 g almonds

juice of 1 lemon

1 × 900 g pheasant

sea salt flakes and freshly ground
    black pepper

1 onion, finely chopped

3 tomatoes, halved

2 sprigs thyme

1 fresh bay leaf

extra virgin olive oil, for cooking

150 ml dry sherry

1 cup (250 ml) jellied pheasant stock *or*
    reduced Golden Chicken Stock
    (see page 57)

1 clove garlic

Preheat the oven to 220°C. Dry-roast the almonds for 6–8 minutes, then set them aside. Squeeze the lemon juice into the cavity of the pheasant, then season it with salt and pepper. Sweat the onion and tomatoes with the thyme and bay leaf in a little olive oil in an enamelled casserole over low heat for 20 minutes.

Add the pheasant to the casserole and brown very gently on all sides. Deglaze the casserole with half the sherry, then add 100 ml of the stock and cook, covered, over very low heat at just a simmer, with the pheasant on its side, for 10 minutes. Turn the bird onto its other side and simmer for another 5 minutes, adding a little more stock if necessary. Turn the pheasant breast-side down and cook for another 5 minutes, then transfer it to a plate to rest. Using a mortar and pestle, grind the almonds with the garlic and remaining sherry to make a *picada* (paste). Add the remaining stock to the casserole and stir in the almond *picada* to thicken the sauce – turn up the heat to reduce the sauce if necessary.

Season to taste and serve. My favourite accompaniments for this dish are crisp roasted parsnips and braised cavolo nero.

ORCHARD CAKE

Serves 10–12

I first cooked this cake in 1996 for my pâté-making girls, who all had a sweet tooth and were forever trying to foist delicacies on me. I had been given a basic recipe for a Jewish cake, but instead I adapted it with different types and ratios of fruit. What made it so special was that nearly all the ingredients I used – everything except the butter, sugar and spices – came from my own orchard or from theirs. The first time I made it we were so excited that we ate the cake a little warm and it was wonderful. What a joy it is to be able to use your own produce.

This cake can be made with other dried fruit; just ensure it is of top-notch quality. Remember – bitter almonds are poisonous if eaten to excess.

90 g dried figs
90 g dried nectarines
90 g dried apricots
90 g dried peaches
310 ml verjuice
180 g dried currants
60 g almonds
120 g dark-brown sugar
180 g unsalted butter, chopped
4 eggs
180 g self-raising flour

½ teaspoon ground cinnamon
½ teaspoon ground nutmeg
120 g candied lemon peel
  or mixed peel
finely grated rind of 1 lemon

ALMOND PASTE
1¼ cups (120 g) almonds
2 bitter almonds
100 g icing sugar
1 egg yolk

Place the figs, nectarines, apricots and peaches in a bowl with 250 ml of the verjuice and soak for at least 1 hour. Strain the fruit, reserving the verjuice, then cut into pieces. Soak the currants in the reserved verjuice for 30 minutes or more, then drain, again reserving the verjuice.

Preheat the oven to 220°C and grease and line a 20 cm round cake tin with baking paper. Dry-roast the 60 g almonds on a baking tray, as well as the 120 g almonds and 2 bitter almonds for the almond paste on a separate baking tray, for 6–8 minutes, then set aside to cool separately. Reset the oven to 180°C.

To make the almond paste, blend the almonds and bitter almonds in a food processor, then add the icing sugar and egg yolk to the processor and pulse to form a stiff paste. Set aside.

Using hand-held electric beaters, cream the brown sugar and butter until pale and fluffy. Beat in the eggs one at a time, adding a spoonful of flour if the mixture curdles. Fold in the flour, spices, drained fruit, almonds and candied peel. Stir the grated lemon rind into the mixture, along with the remaining verjuice, to give a soft batter.

Spoon half the batter into the prepared tin, then spread the almond paste over the mixture and top it with the remaining batter.

Bake for 2½ hours or until a fine skewer inserted into the cake comes out clean. Leave the cake to cool a little in the tin before turning it out.

Orchard cake

ALMOND MACAROONS

Macaroons are a great way of using leftover egg whites.

350 g almonds	2 teaspoons lemon juice
few drops of rosewater	325 g icing sugar
4 egg whites	

Preheat the oven to 220°C. Dry-roast the almonds on a baking tray for 6–8 minutes, but don't let the skins blister. Reduce the oven temperature to 170°C. Once cooled, grind the almonds using a mortar and pestle or food processor until fairly fine, adding a drop or two of rosewater.

Beat the egg whites with the lemon juice in a large bowl until soft peaks form, then add the icing sugar bit by bit, beating all the time, until the meringue is stiff. Fold in the ground almonds, then spoon teaspoonfuls of the mixture 5 cm apart onto a baking tray lined with baking paper. Bake for 35 minutes or until lightly coloured, then turn off the oven and allow the macaroons to cool for 20 minutes before removing them to a wire rack. Store the cooled macaroons in an airtight container, where they will keep for a few days.

BEEF

BEEF WAS THE CENTRE OF MY FAMILY'S MEALS WHEN I GREW up, as it was in many Australian households. As much as I love really good beef, I eat far less of it now, given the widening choice of grains and our improved access to really good poultry and fish.

No matter how often we ate beef as a family, we never took it for granted. My mother would only accept her favourite cut and the butcher always knew which pieces to keep aside for us. As a family of five, with my parents running their own business, the closest thing to convenience food was steak, which we often had during the week. We developed quite a rapport with our butcher (a lesson well learnt!).

It wasn't just a steak, though; it was always the dense and juicy 'back cut' of rump from an older animal (that small piece at the end of the rump), often bought as one piece and sliced ourselves. We always preferred our steak thick and juicy. I am sure it was then, too, that I learnt the importance of resting meat. I doubt we ever had fillet steak, even when making carpetbag steak (see page 206), our family's favourite special-occasion dish, as flavour rather than tenderness was our criterion.

It is not always easy to find really good beef, as Australia hasn't succeeded in implementing a quality system across the board to assure us that every piece of beef we buy will be tender. With beef, there are so many potential variations – between breeds, and whether the animal is grass or grain fed – but more influential than anything else is how well the animal has been looked after, the age it is reared to and how it is killed, hung and aged. (I've found dry-aged beef to be the best of all.) And the best beef will inevitably have cost a lot more to rear and will therefore be more expensive. Before I had access to beef producers I trusted, I used to describe my favourite beef as 'station beef', which was always from the more mature animal. I have never liked the young, bright-red meat from yearling beef, though the more I learn the more I realise colour isn't the only guide. You simply get what you pay for, and now I always choose a branded beef I know and trust, so I buy

Richard Gunner's Coorong Angus Beef. Richard set out from the beginning to follow the path of excellence. Driven by flavour, he's learnt every bit of the trade, from the growing to the selling, and he's always striving to continually improve his product. He and my daughter Saskia share similar philosophies and know each other well. His beef is hung to tender stretch, which is a way of hanging the animal in its natural conformation. This takes a lot more room to do, so only those dedicated to maximising quality commit to this practice. I've cooked his beef rump, hung to tender stretch, and it is like butter in the mouth – better than any other beef I've eaten and full of flavour.

I have to admit I had always cooked my roast beef at a high temperature and well salted to caramelise the skin before reading Neil Perry's book *The Food I Love*. I followed his advice to cook a Coorong Angus dry-aged rib roast, taking it out of the refrigerator several hours before cooking. I rubbed the fat with lots of sea salt and finely chopped rosemary all held together with a little extra virgin olive oil. I cooked it for 3 hours at 70°C (hastily

borrowing a meat thermometer from the export kitchen before deciding that I must have one at home). After 3 hours the meat had reached 53°C and while resting (just as Neil suggested), it went to 55°C. I left it resting for 30 minutes, then slipped out the bones and seared the outer skin of the beef until caramelised. It was the juiciest, pinkest, tastiest beef I have ever had, and gave me a totally different perspective on my roast meats.

The importance of buying top-quality beef was instilled in me at a very early age. When my parents' manufacturing business failed in the 1960s they turned to cooking, first in an RSL club, then leagues clubs and later golf clubs. They never did more than keep their heads above water financially, but in their way they provided amazing food. My father was ahead of his time: even in those days he ordered aged beef (fillet for his customers, if not his family, as it was so much easier to portion than rump). If my memory serves me correctly it came in an early form of vacuum-packaging. He cooked by instinct, not giving a choice of rare, medium or well-done, and I remember that the meat melted in the mouth. Yet it was continually rejected by many of his patrons, who wanted their steaks well-done and not so 'strong'.

Considering we cooked so much offal in our house, it is surprising we rarely used the lesser cuts of beef for slow-cooking. Not so long ago at a family dinner in Sydney, a much-loved aged aunt reminded me of my mother's inability to economise and how she would make a curry with the best rump. Knowing that my mother's enemy was time and that she cooked by 'feel' rather than following recipes, I suspect she would have known that the lesser cuts such as chuck steak are better for long, slow cooking, but with so little time she knew she could cheat by sautéing onion, curry powder and other ingredients and then tossing cubed rump in this mixture for a minute or so with apple and sultanas and a little flour before adding stock, chutney and, if she was very daring, a little coconut; they were always sweet curries! As good a cook as my mother was, she never cooked anything that took loads of time, except tripe and, in summer, brawn. Her quick curry using rump wouldn't stand up to the spicy curries of today, but it seemed pretty exotic then and was always delicious.

I've never had lots of time either, but when the weather gets cooler there is nothing better than long, slow cooking. One favourite dish is chuck steak cooked as a whole piece very, very slowly for 2½ hours or more. I use a heavy-based casserole just large enough to fit the meat and lots of baby onions. I first sear the seasoned meat gently on all sides, then add a dash of stock, some oregano first warmed in a little extra virgin olive oil, and the onions. I cover the casserole tightly and put it into a slow oven (about 160°C), checking that there is enough liquid every 30 minutes or so. I then carve it into chunks to serve.

Brisket, a fatty piece of meat from the lower part of the shoulder, is often boned and rolled, and can be boiled, pot-roasted or corned. The shin (or shank) is usually sold sawn across the bone into slices; if cooked long and slow as in osso buco, the sinews become wonderfully gelatinous and tasty. The shin bones also contain marrow; a specially shaped spoon helps marrow lovers like me locate the prized pieces. And, of course, there is oxtail – slow-cooking meat at its best. I have included a recipe for Oxtail with Orange, Olives and Walnuts (see page 204), a dish that is made for enjoying with people who aren't scared to use their fingers as they suck the sweet meat from the bones.

In the middle years of the Pheasant Farm Restaurant, before the tradition of the five o'clock staff 'lunch' began, our friends the Walls would rescue us every Sunday night and cook for us. Their daughters Eloise and Cressida are very close in age to Saskia and Elli, so it worked remarkably well. Judith or Peter would cook: Judith's favourite cold-weather dish was Elizabeth David's beef and wine stew with black olives from *French Provincial Cooking*. On these nights I would be pretty boisterous for an hour or so, then, after we'd eaten and drunk and listened to great music, the whole week's exhaustion would catch up with me and I would often fall asleep on the couch fairly early in the evening.

Many restaurateurs will tell you that the simple steak (often cooked well-done) is one of their most popular dishes, which I always find a little surprising since it is so easily produced at home. Those restaurants that feature classic French dishes such as *boeuf à la ficelle* (beef on a string – a poached sirloin or fillet served with boiled vegetables and accompanied by sea salt, mustard, horseradish and cornichons or pickles) often have difficulty selling them. Do people only order what they feel comfortable with? What a shame, if that's true! I would hope that going to a restaurant might be seen as a chance to try new things and expand horizons. Huge amounts of time and skill go into creating such complex dishes, and these skills need to be used if we are not to lose them completely – this is a big issue facing the restaurant industry at the moment.

We mustn't become complacent or lazy when it comes to buying beef to cook at home either. Although we all lead busy lives, we owe it to ourselves to seek out a butcher who cares about quality. Word of mouth is a good place to start, and if you can find a butcher really interested in his or her craft, they will have a wealth of knowledge to share with you.

COORONG ANGUS BEEF PIE WITH RED WINE, FENNEL AND GREEN OLIVES

Serves 8

Although I usually make this pie with my Sour-cream Pastry (see page 424), when given the challenge of making it with a luscious gluten-free pastry I couldn't believe just how wonderful it was. As part of the TV series *The Cook and The Chef*, the ABC suggested I test out the pies at Colin's squash club, as they always have supper at the end of competition nights. I might add that as it's the Barossa squash club, the supper is usually quite a different kettle of fish from that served at most other sporting clubs. Many local wine-makers are members, and on the table that night there were at least eighteen bottles of really top-quality red; it was winter, after all, and they had been told I was coming with a beef and shiraz pie.

I made 32 individual pies, half with Choux Pastry-style Gluten-free Pastry (see page 425) and the other half with a cream cheese-based gluten-free pastry. The fascinating thing was the overwhelming support for the choux pastry-style, which absolutely flummoxed me as my own preference was for the crisper, more shortcrust style of the cream cheese version. The players were so enthusiastic that I think they would each have eaten a second one if I'd made enough. It was obvious that the combination of hard exercise, a cold winter's night and the seductive smell of freshly baked pies had great appeal – I think they'll ask me back.

While I slowly braise the meat in a crockpot on its lowest setting, it could easily be cooked in a heavy-based cast-iron casserole over low heat with a simmer mat or in a 120°C oven for a few hours.

plain flour, for dusting
sea salt flakes and freshly ground
   black pepper
1 kg Coorong Angus Beef chuck, or other
   quality beef chuck, cut into 3 cm cubes
extra virgin olive oil, for cooking
400 ml shiraz
1 medium–large fennel bulb, trimmed
   and finely chopped
400 g golden shallots, peeled
4 cloves garlic, chopped

2 cups (500 ml) veal *or* Golden
   Chicken Stock (see page 57)
1 sprig rosemary
6 sprigs thyme
2 fresh bay leaves
finely chopped rind of 1 orange
16 green olives, pitted
1 × quantity Sour-cream Pastry
   (see page 424)
1 egg, beaten

Coorong Angus beef pie with red wine, fennel and green olives

Season the flour with salt and pepper, then toss the meat in the seasoned flour, shaking off any excess. In a large deep frying pan, seal the meat in olive oil over high heat in small batches until all the meat is browned.

Heat a crockpot to its highest setting, then transfer the sealed meat to it. Deglaze the frying pan with the wine, reducing it by three-quarters over high heat, then add the wine to the crockpot. Return the frying pan to the stove, then add more olive oil and sauté the fennel and shallots over medium heat for 6–8 minutes or until soft. Add the garlic and continue to sauté for another 5 minutes.

Transfer the vegetables to the crockpot, then add stock to the frying pan, bring to a rapid boil over high heat then add it to the crockpot with the herbs. Cook on the highest setting for 30 minutes, then turn to the lowest setting and cook at this low temperature for about 6 hours (or even overnight), until the meat is melt-in-the-mouth tender, adding the orange rind and olives in the last 20 minutes. Let the beef mixture cool.

Meanwhile, make and chill the pastry as instructed.

To assemble the pies, roll pastry to a 5 mm thickness and cut to fit the bases of 8 individual pie tins (you can buy standard-sized disposable foil pie tins from the supermarket). Make sure the pastry bases overhang the lips of the pie tins, and brush the bases with beaten egg, to help seal in the juices. Cut out the pastry tops.

Divide the beef mixture among the pie tins and cover with the pastry tops. Fold the edges of the pastry to seal, then brush the tops of the pies with beaten egg. Return the pies to the refrigerator for the pastry to really set; they can be prepared and refrigerated up to 1 day in advance, but if you're short of time, you can pop them in the freezer for 10 minutes.

Preheat the oven to 220°C. Place the pie tins on a baking tray and bake for 20 minutes or until golden brown.

SLOW-BRAISED BEEF CHEEKS IN BAROSSA SHIRAZ   *Serves 12*

The late Maurice de Rohan, the Agent General in London for many years, persuaded me to present a cocktail party in Paris in 2001 to celebrate Baudin's expedition to Australia. He went on to become a good friend and asked me to cook the Australia Day Dinner in London in January 2006 for 300 guests. Maurice and I had talked of the possibility several times over the years, and as it was to be his last year as chairman of that event, I jumped at the opportunity, on the understanding that I'd have a team to work with. A lot of planning was involved in choosing the dishes that would represent a truly Australian meal, sourcing the finest quality ingredients, and ensuring each dish would be simple enough to prepare in advance, particularly given the limitation of not having access to a kitchen at Australia House.

A preliminary trip to London set my mind at rest when I was introduced to Jackson Gilmour, the catering company who would be cooking my recipes. We sat around a table, tasted my recipes and dissected the menu, then talked logistics. I'm happy to say it turned out to be a wonderful occasion and one I was proud to be involved with.

I felt the main course for this meal had to be beef, and it had to be luscious and slow-cooked so we could prepare it in advance. My choice was wagyu beef cheeks braised in Barossa shiraz. It was beautifully unctuous and tender, and in writing my menu I simply called it 'Australian Wagyu braised in Barossa Shiraz', leaving out the fact that we used the cheeks.

2 kg beef cheeks

½ cup (125 ml) extra virgin olive oil,
    plus extra for drizzling

6 cloves garlic, roughly chopped

2 tablespoons juniper berries, crushed

2 star anise

3 sprigs rosemary

10 small fresh bay leaves

sea salt flakes and freshly ground
    black pepper

½ cup (125 ml) vino cotto (see Glossary)

2 cups (500 ml) good red wine,
    such as a Barossa shiraz

2 large onions, roughly chopped

2 stalks celery, roughly chopped

2 cups (500 ml) reduced veal stock

rind of 1 orange, peeled in strips

The day before cooking, toss the beef cheeks in a little olive oil and marinade with garlic cloves and all the spices and herbs.

Preheat the oven to 120°C. Drizzle the beef cheeks with 60 ml olive oil and season with salt and pepper. Heat a frying pan over medium heat, then brown the cheeks on each side and place in a heavy-based casserole. Deglaze the frying pan with vino cotto and red wine then reduce by half and add to the casserole. Wipe out the frying pan and add the remaining olive oil, then add the onions and celery and brown. Season with salt and pepper and transfer to the casserole.

Add the veal stock and place the covered casserole in the oven. Turn the beef cheeks frequently. Check after 3 hours – depending on their size and the breed of cattle, they may take up to 6 hours to become tender. Remove the lid for the final 2 hours of cooking.

FILLET OF BEEF IN BALSAMIC VINEGAR OR VINO COTTO   *Serves 4*

While I give instructions for roasting in this recipe, the marinated fillet can also be grilled in one piece on a barbecue for 8 minutes per side. After grilling, put the hood down, turn the barbecue off and allow the meat to rest.

For a simpler dish, pan-fry seasoned thick slices of a beef cut of your choice in a heavy-based frying pan. Begin at a high temperature to seal the meat on one side, then turn it down until you're ready to flip the steak onto the other side. Seal that side at a high temperature, then turn it down again. Deglaze the pan with vino cotto, remove from the heat and leave to rest, then serve with the pan juices.

1 × 650 g fillet of beef

1 lemon (meyer, if available)

3 sprigs rosemary

1 sprig oregano

100 ml extra virgin olive oil

¼ cup (60 ml) balsamic vinegar *or* vino cotto
    (see Glossary)

sea salt flakes and freshly ground
    black pepper

Trim the meat of all sinew, then tie the thin end back on itself with kitchen string (this ensures even cooking). Dry the fillet well with kitchen paper. Remove the rind from the lemon with a potato peeler, in one piece if possible. Make a marinade of the remaining ingredients, except the salt, then add the lemon rind and the meat and marinate for several hours, turning the meat to flavour all sides.

Preheat the oven to 250°C. Season the meat, then brush with the marinade and roast in a shallow roasting pan for 10 minutes. Turn the meat over and cook for another 10 minutes. Meanwhile, warm the marinade in a pan over medium heat. Remove the meat from the oven, then pour the warmed marinade over it and leave to rest for 20 minutes before serving.

OXTAIL WITH ORANGE, OLIVES AND WALNUTS   *Serves 12*

3 large onions, roughly chopped

2 sticks celery, roughly chopped

½ cup (125 ml) extra virgin olive oil

115 g shelled walnuts

4 kg oxtail, trimmed and cut into 5 cm pieces

plain flour, for dusting

sea salt flakes and freshly ground
    black pepper

100 g butter, chopped

2 cups (500 ml) red wine

4 cloves garlic, finely chopped

10 stalks flat-leaf parsley

2 sprigs thyme

2 fresh bay leaves

500 g fresh *or* canned tomatoes,
    peeled and seeded

2 litres veal stock

4 strips orange rind

40 black olives

½ cup (125 ml) red-wine vinegar

⅓ cup (75 g) sugar

Preheat the oven to 220°C. Toss the onion and celery with a little of the olive oil in a roasting pan, then roast for 20 minutes or until caramelised. Dry-roast the walnuts on a baking tray in the oven for 6 minutes, then rub their skins off with a clean tea towel and set aside.

Toss the meat in flour seasoned with salt and pepper, shaking off the excess. In a heavy-based frying pan, brown the oxtail in batches in the remaining olive oil and the butter over high heat. Transfer each batch to a large heavy-based casserole. Deglaze the frying pan with the wine, scraping to release all the caramelised bits from the browning. Add the garlic, onions, celery, herbs and tomatoes to the frying pan and reduce the wine a little over high heat, then tip the lot into the casserole. Add the veal stock, making sure that everything is immersed, and simmer over low heat, covered, until tender – this could take 3–4 hours. Add the orange rind and olives in the last 20 minutes of cooking.

Strain the cooking juices from the meat and skim as much fat as possible from the top. Set the meat aside in a warm place. In a stainless steel or enamelled saucepan, combine the red-wine vinegar and sugar and boil until the vinegar has evaporated and the sugar has caramelised. Reduce the cooking juices to a syrupy consistency, then add the caramel mixture to taste. Toss the cooked oxtail with the walnuts and pour the sauce back over the oxtail. Serve with mashed potato, creamy polenta or pasta.

SLOW-ROASTED OYSTER BLADE WITH ONION CREAM AND BRAISED CAVOLO NERO

Serves 10–12

1 × 2 kg piece oyster blade, for roasting
½ cup (125 ml) verjuice
½ cup (125 ml) extra virgin olive oil
1 sprig rosemary
2 fresh bay leaves
finely chopped rind of 1 lemon
finely chopped rind of 1 orange
sea salt flakes and freshly ground
    black pepper
Braised Cavolo Nero (see page 367),
    to serve

ONION CREAM
2 large onions, roughly chopped
¼ cup (60 ml) extra virgin olive oil
2 cloves garlic, chopped
¼ cup (60 ml) verjuice
½ cup (125 ml) cream
sea salt flakes and freshly ground
    black pepper

Marinate the beef overnight in the verjuice, olive oil, rosemary, bay leaves and citrus rinds.

Preheat the oven to 100°C. Season the meat with salt and pepper, then transfer it to a roasting pan with the marinade and cook for approximately 4½ hours. Remove from the oven and take the meat out of the pan, reserving the pan juices.

In a large frying pan, seal the beef on each side to caramelise, then rest for 30 minutes. Meanwhile, skim any fat from the surface of the pan juices and reduce over high heat to a sauce consistency.

For the onion cream, sauté the onions in a saucepan over low heat with the olive oil until soft, adding the garlic after the first 5 minutes; do not let the onions brown. When the onions are soft, deglaze the pan with the verjuice. Cook for another 5 minutes and then add the cream. Cook until the cream evaporates – about 10 minutes over low heat – stirring often so that no colour develops. Remove from the heat and season to taste. Pass the onion mixture through a mouli or pulse in a food processor just enough to combine the ingredients. Set aside.

Place a bed of the onion cream on a serving platter. Slice the roast beef and place it on top of the onion cream, drizzling it with the pan juices, then serve with the braised cavolo nero.

CARPETBAG STEAK

Serves 6

The oysters my father used when making carpetbag steak in the 1960s were not sold on the shell as we would buy them today; instead they were Hawkesbury River oysters bottled daily in large glass jars. As our wonderful South Australian oysters are at their prime between May and September (particularly those from Smoky Bay) and this dish is both simple and spectacularly special, I commend it to you for every even slightly celebratory occasion at that time of the year.

1 × 1 kg fillet of beef *or* piece of rump, trimmed of all sinew	2 tablespoons extra virgin olive oil
freshly ground black pepper	sea salt flakes
18 fresh oysters	50 g butter
	2 sprigs rosemary

Preheat the oven to 230°C. With a sharp knife, cut a pocket down the length of the meat deep enough to hold all the oysters (do not cut right through the meat!). Grind pepper over the oysters and use them to fill the pocket, making sure the oysters aren't too near the edge. Using kitchen string, tie up the beef like a parcel. (If using a fillet, determine the thickness of the final slices by using string to define where you will cut each serving.) Rub the outside of the beef with the olive oil and season with salt and pepper.

Heat the butter to nut-brown with the rosemary in a heavy-based roasting pan. Brown the beef on all sides, then transfer the pan to the oven for 15 minutes. Remove the beef from the oven, then turn it over and leave it to rest for 15 minutes. Slice the beef thickly and serve with salt, pepper and the juices from the roasting pan.

CRABAPPLES

CRABAPPLES ARE NOT SOMETHING YOU SEE FOR SALE IN THE greengrocer as a rule. My first introduction to them was in 1983 on a visit to the beautiful garden of my friend, Lady Mary Downer, near Williamstown. Our main purpose for the visit was to collect some pheasant breeders, having lost all our birds that year in the Nuriootpa flood. (These breeders were the progeny of birds we had sold years earlier; this and other kind offers from all over Australia helped us re-establish our pheasant line and continue farming.) While the pheasants were our main focus, I couldn't help but be distracted by a crabapple tree in the garden.

I had never seen such a luxuriant tree so laden with fruit, and didn't need a second offer to take up the bounty. We picked the tree clean and, once home, I proceeded to look for as many uses as possible for the crabapples. The search was not particularly rewarding, and I had visions of these wonderfully decorative – and potentially productive – trees all around the countryside with their fruit left to drop and rot for lack of advice.

I am now a passionate advocate of the crabapple, and in my home orchard of some thirty trees I have three different varieties – the Wandin Pride, John Downie and Maypole. I have been told that crabapples can tolerate almost any neglect. I've proved that to be true – when I planted our first at the Pheasant Farm the ground was fairly inhospitable and we only had bore water, which tended to be very salty in the summer when the garden required extra attention. Only the hardiest plants survived, so the crabapples were a joy.

When buying fruit and nut trees I prefer to deal directly with experts as the amount of information on nursery tags is minimal by nature. Experts can give advice on especially interesting trees and will find varieties you might have read about in obscure magazines. Here in South Australia I deal with Perry's Nursery of McLaren Flat, which specialises in fruit and nut trees and deals interstate.

Crabapples are a great addition to any garden, even if you are not initially interested in harvesting the fruit (although I hope you won't be able to resist trying some of the ideas

here). If they're of the weeping kind, the trees tend to be sparse and willowy, each branch hanging heavy with beautiful blossom in the spring. Of the varieties that are easily available, the weeping Wandin Pride has a large apple that is sweeter than others. It is actually like a medium-sized Jonathan, mostly green with a red blush. A particular favourite in my orchard is the Downie. It has fairly large reddish-orange fruit that can be eaten off the tree, but the flavour is sharper than that of the Wandin Pride. Echtermeyer, another weeping crabapple, has smaller, sour purple fruit suitable for jelly. The productive Maypole has a sharp, deep-purple small apple that also makes a great jelly. A variety I don't have but that is the most readily seen in South Australia is the heavy-cropping Gorgeous – its long, slim bright-crimson fruit hang on the tree until late autumn.

The larger crabapples are more likely to be eaten straight from the tree – they are tart but a good accompaniment to a rich and creamy cheese. The smaller ones, which are very high in pectin, are best made into a jelly, pickle or syrup. If you are looking for a breakfast treat, I can thoroughly recommend a really nutty piece of wholemeal toast spread with lashings of unsalted butter and crabapple jelly.

Roast pheasant served with Spiced Crabapples (see opposite) was a favourite dish of the day in our restaurant. I took some of the crabapple preserving syrup and added it to the reduced pheasant jus to give a wonderfully sharp lift to the dish; the crabapples them-selves were added to the sauce in the last few minutes of cooking. I tended to use fresh rosemary in the roasting – rosemary and crabapples seem to be a natural pairing. This combination also teams well with rare roasted kangaroo or grilled quail.

Verjuice and crabapples work in harmony, too. Remove the cores from 500 g large crab-apples and cut them into eighths. Heat 60 g unsalted butter until nut-brown, sauté the crabapples until cooked through and just beginning to caramelise then deglaze the pan with 80 ml verjuice. Add a little freshly crushed cinnamon and some honey, if you like, and serve over hot pancakes with crème fraîche.

I've heard that when visiting people in Iran one is offered a sweet drink or sherbet made from sour fruit. A homemade fruit syrup based on crabapples, quinces, lemons, sour cher-ries or pomegranates is diluted with water and ice is added. I make this with less sugar than is traditional and pour it over ice cream. A vanilla bean in the syrup makes a wonder-ful addition, especially if you make your own vanilla ice cream to accompany it.

SPICED CRABAPPLES

Makes 3 cups

2 kg crabapples (preferably with stems on to enhance presentation)	3 cloves
	10 allspice berries
1 lemon	10 coriander seeds
brown sugar	½ cinnamon stick
white-wine vinegar	

Discard any bruised crabapples and wash the remainder. Put the crabapples into a large preserving pan and just cover with water. Remove the rind from the lemon in one piece using a potato peeler and add to the pan, then simmer over low heat for 15–20 minutes or until the crabapples are just tender. Using a slotted spoon, take out the crabapples and set them aside in a bowl.

Strain and measure the cooking water. For each 500 ml add 300 g brown sugar and 150 ml white-wine vinegar, then add the spices. Boil this spice syrup in the rinsed-out pan over high heat for about 10 minutes or until reduced to a light caramel consistency, then return the crabapples to the pan and cook for another 20 minutes or until the apples are almost transparent but still holding their shape. Transfer the crabapples and their syrup to a sterilised (see Glossary) wide-necked jar and seal. Leave the crabapples for 10 days before use – they keep indefinitely.

KATHY HOWARD'S WILD CRABAPPLE
AND SAGE JELLY
Makes about 3 litres

Kathy Howard, the mother of my friend Jacqui Howard, no longer produces her wonderful crabapple and sage jelly commercially, sadly, but through her generosity in sharing this recipe we can all make it now. She has told me how her family used to collect masses of wild crabapples along the roads in Victoria's Kiewa Valley on their way back from Falls Creek each year. They gathered these little 'cannonballs' in January when they were inedible raw but full of pectin – perfect for jelly. A swim in the Bright waterhole was 'payment' for the kids, including Jacqui.

Kathy smears a chicken with this jelly before roasting it with a spoonful or two of water in the pan to stop the juices burning, then deglazes the roasting pan with verjuice to create a delicious sauce. I love the jelly on barbecued short-loin lamb chops or a fillet of pork, where it melts deliciously. Wonderful with game, this jelly is also good spread over a leg of lamb ready for the oven with slivers of garlic tucked into the meat.

This jelly can be made without the sage (resulting in a straightforward crabapple jelly), or rosemary can be added instead. Pan-fry fresh rosemary leaves in a little nut-brown butter, then leave them to drain on kitchen paper before adding them to the jelly as you would the sage.

½ cup fresh *or* 3–4 tablespoons home-dried
    sage leaves
4 kg crabapples, washed and roughly
    chopped (including stems, peel and cores)

white-wine vinegar
sugar

To dry the sage leaves, spread them out on a tray and place in the direct sun for 3–4 hours, then finely chop them. Put the chopped crabapples into a large preserving pan. Barely cover with water and simmer gently over low heat for about 45 minutes or until crabapples are soft, then leave them to sit in the cooking liquid for a few hours. Put the crabapples and the liquid into a jelly bag or a muslin-lined sieve (even a clean Chux will do) and allow to drain over a bowl or bucket overnight.

Next day, measure the collected juice (do not press down on the crabapples or the jelly will be cloudy rather than sparkling clear) and discard the solids. For every 1 litre of juice, add 250 ml white-wine vinegar and 800 g sugar, then gradually bring the mixture to the boil, stirring to dissolve the sugar. Maintain a rolling boil for 10 minutes or until setting point is reached. (Test by placing a spoonful of jelly on a saucer in the fridge for a few minutes. If it wrinkles when you push it with your finger, it is set.) As the mixture boils, skim the froth from the surface very carefully. When setting point is reached, remove the pan from the heat, pour the jelly into sterilised jars (see Glossary) and leave to cool. When the jelly has started to firm up, add the sage so it sits on top. Seal once completely cool.

CRABAPPLE JELLY

Makes about 950 g

Jellies are made with the juice of the fruit rather than the pulp. When we make quince paste we drain the pulp overnight first to acquire juice to make jelly. You can do the same with any fruit – try damson plums or apples, for example. Try adding flavourings or herbs as well, as in the recipe opposite.

2.5 kg crabapples, roughly chopped
castor sugar

4 tablespoons lemon juice

Boil the crabapples in just enough water to cover for about 30 minutes or until very soft, then strain the pulp overnight through a jelly bag or a muslin-lined sieve (even a clean Chux will do) into a bucket or large bowl. Don't press down on the fruit to extract more juice the next morning as you'll lose the clarity of the jelly.

Measure the collected juice into a large, heavy-based preserving pan, and for every 500 ml of juice add 500 g castor sugar. Add the lemon juice to the pan and stir over medium heat until the sugar has dissolved, then boil rapidly over high heat for about 20 minutes or until the jelly sets. Test this by placing a spoonful of jelly on a saucer in the fridge for a few minutes. If it wrinkles when you push it with your finger, it is set. Pour the jelly into warm, sterilised jars (see Glossary) and seal.

FENNEL

FENNEL IS AN ANCIENT VEGETABLE WELL WORTH BECOMING acquainted with. A member of the parsley family, this aniseedy bulb, also called Florence fennel, grows wild in the Mediterranean. I'm so partial to bulb fennel I become impatient waiting until autumn for it; although these days baby fennel bulbs are available throughout summer, the large plump bulb in all its glory is worth the wait.

We in the Barossa would be lost without fennel seeds, which come from the bulbless common fennel plant. They are added to cooking pots of yabbies, bread dough and dill pickles, among countless other preparations. Try making a caramel of verjuice and sugar and mix in fennel seeds, sliced dried figs, roasted almonds and fresh bay leaves – serve it sliced with coffee. Rustic bread flavoured with fennel seeds teams well with cheese and dried figs. And if you've developed a love of these seeds, look out for Italian pork sausages flavoured with them (Steve Flamsteed, a very special former employee who is still very much a part of our lives, uses fennel-seed sausages in a wonderful dish in which he incorporates grape must – see page 486).

If you've enjoyed the seed you must try the bulb. For those of you who have seen the whitish-green fennel bulb in the greengrocer's, with its feathery fronds of vivid green, and not known what to do with it, try peeling back the outer layer of skin to reveal the edible part. If the bulb is fresh from your garden, you don't need to do this – in transit the outer skin is handled and becomes marked, and it can be tough if it is an old specimen. When choosing your bulb, the tighter it is the fresher and sweeter it will be. If it is round and bulbous, it will be female; if longer and thinner, it will be male. Taste and see if you think there is a difference. It is usually so with birds and animals (the female is usually sweeter!), so why not plants? And if you buy fennel, chop off the fronds (but don't discard them) to minimise deterioration.

Fennel marries well with fish, chicken, anchovies, pancetta, garlic, olives, Parmigiano Reggiano, flat-leaf parsley and oranges. It can be eaten raw, cut thinly or grated into autumn and winter salads, or just quartered and placed on the table at the end of the meal as a *digestif*. Steamed, boiled, deep-fried or poached in extra virgin olive oil or chicken stock, fennel is transformed into a wonderful cooked vegetable – it is sweet, yet its distinctive mild aniseed flavour refreshes.

To serve fennel fresh from the garden in a salad, cut off the fronds only if they look tired and dull, and discard the stalks only if fibrous (even then they can be used to add a delicate flavour and fragrance to chicken or fish stock). Trim the root end and outside skin, if necessary, then, with a very sharp knife and a steady hand, cut the fennel into paper-thin vertical slices. Arrange half the slices on a large flat dish, then season them with a little sea salt and add a layer of shaved best-quality Parmigiano Reggiano (use a potato peeler for this – I prefer the black wide-handled peeler I use for quinces). Generously sprinkle the dish with roughly chopped flat-leaf parsley, drizzle it with a fruity extra virgin olive oil, then add another layer of fennel, and so on. Grind black pepper over the lot, add the smallest amount of red-wine vinegar or lemon juice, and serve immediately. Just wonderful for an autumn lunch, sitting behind our huge stone wall, with one end of the table in the shade of the old willow for my husband Colin and the rest of us lapping up the last of the sun.

One of my favourite ways to cook fennel is to gently poach it in extra virgin olive oil and verjuice at a simmer. First toss a couple of trimmed bulbs, cut in half lengthways or quartered if large, in verjuice to stop oxidisation, then place in a stainless steel pan just large enough to hold them snugly in one layer. Add enough of equal quantities of extra virgin olive oil and verjuice to half cover the fennel. Lay on top a piece of baking paper cut to a similar size as the pan to act as a cartouche (see Glossary) during cooking. Simmer gently for about 20 minutes on low–medium heat, then turn the fennel over and cook for another 10–15 minutes until cooked through but not falling apart. I like to serve the fennel warm with such accompaniments as a roasted head of garlic, olive bread croutons crisped in the oven just before serving, or chunks of just-melted goat's cheese.

Whether cooked like this or sliced and grilled on the barbecue, fennel has a great affinity with seafood, from shellfish to almost any fish from the sea, but particularly fish with a high oil content such as tommy ruffs or sardines. It is also a great balance for the sweetness of riverfish. The late Catherine Brandel, a delightful American who was with Alice Waters' Chez Panisse restaurant for many years, made a salsa at a conference I attended once in Hawaii. It was a great combination of flavours: finely chopped fennel, diced green olives and tiny segments of thinly sliced meyer lemon all held together with extra virgin olive oil

Fennel with goat's curd

and lots of flat-leaf parsley. I can't remember what it was served with then, but I can highly recommend it with quickly seared tuna or swordfish.

Fennel oil is useful to have on hand, particularly if you cook fish regularly. Simply chop up a few trimmed bulbs and cover them generously with a good extra virgin olive oil in a stainless steel saucepan. (If the oil you start with is not good, the oil you finish with will not be either.) You can add some fennel seeds, too, but this shouldn't be necessary if the fennel you are using is truly fresh. Bring the pan to a simmer very, very slowly and leave it to cook long and slowly (for about an hour or so) at a low temperature until the fennel has almost melted into the oil. Allow the fennel to cool in the oil, so that the flavours are well infused. Strain the oil into a sterilised jar and seal. Fennel oil can also be tossed through pasta and brushed onto pizzas and bruschetta.

Caramelised fennel can become a bed for grilled fresh sardines with a squeeze of lemon juice, a little extra virgin olive oil, tiny capers and flat-leaf parsley. Halve the fennel lengthways, then cut each piece into quarters and liberally brush with extra virgin olive oil. Roast the fennel with sprigs of fresh thyme in a shallow roasting pan at 250°C for about 10 minutes or until the underside is caramelised. Turn the fennel over and cook for another 10 minutes until it has cooked through and the second side has caramelised.

FENNEL WITH GOAT'S CURD

Serves 4 as an accompaniment or 2 as a light meal

⅓ cup (80 ml) extra virgin olive oil

1 large, plump fennel bulb, trimmed and
    quartered, fronds reserved

4 fresh bay leaves

1 meyer lemon (optional), cut into 6 wedges

sea salt flakes and freshly ground
    black pepper

¼ cup (60 ml) verjuice *or* fruity white wine

100 g goat's curd

baby purple basil *or* freshly chopped flat-leaf
    parsley, to serve

Heat a little of the olive oil over low heat in a heavy-based frying pan, then gently seal the fennel quarters on both sides. Add fennel fronds, bay leaves and lemon, if using, then season with salt and pepper.

Add the verjuice or white wine and remaining olive oil, then cover and simmer for about 20 minutes or until cooked through. Remove the lid, then increase the heat to high and cook for another 5 minutes, or until fennel is coloured and pan juices are reduced to a syrup.

Remove the fennel, season to taste and serve as a warm salad, topped with spoonfuls of goat's curd and baby purple basil or chopped parsley.

PASTA WITH CARAMELISED FENNEL, PRESERVED LEMON AND GARLIC

Serves 6

You could use my Duck Egg Pasta (see page 420) for this dish.

3 fennel bulbs, fronds and stalks trimmed, then sliced

18 cloves garlic, peeled

extra virgin olive oil, for cooking

3 quarters preserved lemon, flesh removed, rind rinsed and thinly sliced

sea salt flakes

500 g good-quality dried *or* fresh pappardelle

½ cup flat-leaf parsley, roughly chopped

freshly ground black pepper

freshly shaved Parmigiano Reggiano, to serve

Steam the fennel for 3–5 minutes until almost cooked, then set aside.

Place the garlic cloves into a small heavy-based saucepan and cover them with olive oil. Cook very gently over low heat for about 20 minutes or until the garlic is golden, then remove the garlic from the oil and set it aside, reserving the oil.

Preheat the oven to 250°C. Brush the fennel with the reserved olive oil and roast in a shallow roasting pan with the preserved lemon for about 10 minutes or until caramelised (this can also be done over high heat on the stove).

To cook the pasta, bring 4 litres water to the boil in a large saucepan, then add 2 tablespoons salt. Slide the pasta gently into the pot as the water returns to the boil, then partially cover with a lid to bring it to a rapid boil. Cook the pasta according to the manufacturer's instructions, stirring to keep it well separated (a tablespoon of olive oil in the water can help this too). If using fresh pasta, it only needs to cook for 3 or so minutes. Drain the pasta – this is easiest if you have a colander for this purpose that fits inside your pot – and reserve a little of the cooking water in case you want to moisten the completed dish. Do not run the pasta under water as you'll lose the precious starch that helps the sauce or oil adhere.

Toss the hot pasta with the caramelised fennel, garlic cloves and preserved lemon, then add a drizzle of extra virgin olive oil, the parsley and a grind of pepper. You may not need salt, depending on the saltiness of the preserved lemons. Serve immediately with lots of freshly shaved Parmigiano Reggiano. Anchovies would be a great addition to this dish too.

TEA-SMOKED OCEAN TROUT WITH FENNEL

Serves 6

You need a barbecue with a hood or lid for this dish. The cooking time depends on how close the fish is to the heat source. Slower (further away from the heat source) is actually better – the slower the cooking, the smokier the flavour. You only need to cook the fish until the flesh has just set.

Ask your fishmonger to take the spine out of the fish, leaving it whole – it is much easier to serve like this.

125 g green tea *or* orange pekoe tea

250 g brown sugar

250 g castor sugar

2 small fennel bulbs, very thinly sliced
    (including the fronds)

extra virgin olive oil, for cooking

1 × 1.75 kg ocean trout *or* Atlantic salmon,
    cleaned and scaled

1 orange, sliced

1 lemon, sliced

sea salt flakes and freshly ground
    black pepper

capers and lemon slices, to serve

Make 3 rectangular 'boxes' for the smoking mixture using several layers of foil (I make the packages 15 × 12 cm to fit under the griller of my barbecue). Combine the tea and sugars and divide the mixture between the foil containers, then set them aside. Heat the barbecue to medium–high.

Sauté the fennel with a little olive oil in a frying pan over medium heat for about 5 minutes, then stuff it into the cavity of the fish with the orange and lemon. Season the fish generously and moisten it with olive oil. Skewer the opening shut with small metal or bamboo skewers to keep the stuffing in. If using bamboo skewers, soak them in water first so they won't burn.

Oil the racks of the barbecue and make sure they are absolutely clean. Put the foil containers on the coals and wait for the aroma – there will be a strong smell from the sugar caramelising but it will dissipate quickly. Turn the barbecue down to low. Put the fish onto the grill, shut the lid of the barbecue and cook for 4 minutes. Heat builds up quickly in these barbecues and the thermometer may climb as high as 150°C. If this happens, turn the fish over and turn the heat off. Cook the fish for another 4 minutes. If it is not cooked enough for your taste, or your barbecue hasn't reached 150°C, leave the fish for another 4 minutes with the heat off.

Serve the fish immediately, cut into thick slices, with capers, lemon slices, sea salt flakes and a drizzle of extra virgin olive oil.

FIGS

FIGS HAVE LONG BEEN USED IN GREEK, ITALIAN, TURKISH and Moroccan food, and in South Australia, with its Mediterranean climate, it is not unusual to find wonderful old fig trees in back gardens. If you have a tree you will know how fleeting figs are. As with so many other fruits, it is a race to see who gets them first, you or the birds! Particularly vulnerable are the large black figs I know as Black Genoa, which I prefer for eating fresh, particularly those left on the tree until they are really ripe and turn such a deep, deep red. This variety, and the large green fig, the Smyrna, are the two most commonly available at your greengrocer, packed in trays of moulded plastic to protect the fragile fruit as much as possible. The Brown Turkey or sugar fig used to be more widely available and is wonderful for jam. Sadly, most newer fig plantings are of the varieties that are better eaten fresh, so now I can never find enough Brown Turkey figs for my burnt fig jam and burnt fig ice cream.

Fig farmers or orchardists deserve every cent of the price they receive, as figs must be picked ripe to reach their potential (even though that is true of most fruits, it is particularly so for the fig). Yet when they are so beautifully ripe and luscious, they are also incredibly fragile and last only days at their peak; so much so that the farmer has to go through each tree on his orchard at least every second day, picking the next batch of fruit to ripen. There is none of this picking the whole tree at a time, as there is with other fruits – and all of this presuming that the farmer has found a way to keep the birds away from the fruit.

The only way I have found to keep birds at bay is to hang silver-painted plastic snakes (from a toy shop) on the trees. They even frighten me if I am walking through the orchard distracted by other things, so I can see quite clearly how they affect the birds. Not that I am suggesting a commercial orchardist would resort to such child's play, but I am passing the tip on to those frustrated backyard fig growers, if they have anywhere near the same problems I've had with birds.

If buying figs, go to a really top-class greengrocer and select your figs with the utmost care. If you are fortunate enough to have your own source, you will find they are the most obliging of fruit, as the trees have two flushes if the season is good, the first of which comes before Christmas. Their next flush then kicks in from late January through to April. Within each year they will deliver, day by day, just enough to keep you going on your own fig-fest.

Even though we have two wild fig trees on our farm, in the creek bed of our original vineyard, that bear like crazy, the fig trees I planted over ten years ago at home are still scraps of trees really, even though they bear a few beautiful figs. There is obviously something missing

in our soil, or perhaps because it is such deep sandy loam the water the trees need isn't retained.

Of all the old wild fig trees I've seen, nothing can touch the one my friend Belinda Hannaford has on Kangaroo Island – her fig tree is the size of a house block. The tree is so old and gnarled that she has been able to make steps in the branches so you can actually walk through the tree and sit under the canopy for lunch on a summer's day. There is space for at least twenty people. One just reaches for a fresh fig to accompany the cheese platter.

A plate of figs, deep purple or vivid green and bulging with ripeness, is a feast for the eye. Cut them in half and that inner rosy glow, so shiny and jewel-like, is like opening a chest in Aladdin's cave. Bite into them and their soft ripeness yields. When sucking the flesh away from the skin, it almost melts in the mouth – truly, the most sensuous fruit!

It is only from the best growers that you will get the chance to have figs similar to those I have experienced when I've been lucky enough to be in Italy in autumn. Figs so richly red and ripe they are almost molten – with no need to do anything but eat them, absolutely unadorned.

Perhaps I haven't revered enough the small, greeny-brown fig, duller inside but sweeter for eating fresh. When I take the time to make jam, I follow my mother's tradition of burning it (or at least, 'catching' it), which stops it being super-sweet – something that happened without her intending it, she said. The result, burnt fig jam, is always a sensation. Ironically, our fig growers, with whom we necessarily share a very close relationship, dislike my burnt fig jam and wish I would make a normal one, but the caramelisation that happens when catching the pan on the bottom is the only way for me; it is certainly my point of difference and an absolute sentimental favourite.

So often you'll buy figs that will look great but, because of the problems of transporting them, they will have been picked before they are fully ripe. If you find this, I'd halve the figs, brush them with some extra virgin olive oil and grill them to get the maximum flavour out of them. Or they could be quickly baked with some firm ricotta or goat's curd and tossed into a salad.

When you have the perfect ripe fig, either from your own tree or a farmers' market, try the classic of fresh figs with prosciutto: the sweetness of the fig and the saltiness of the prosciutto are a perfect match. This time-honoured combination had a delightful twist when Janni Kyritsis served figs as an entrée at his former restaurant, MG Garage, in Sydney; they came with very ripe, diced rockmelon and crème fraîche and were divine. I then ordered figs again for dessert, and this time they arrived in a tart, latticed with fine pastry and accompanied by more fresh, hot grilled figs and a walnut cream.

For a simple, complete meal, set out a really chewy piece of ciabatta with fresh, ripe figs, the prosciutto again and some goat's curd; all it needs is a little green extra virgin olive oil. Or, for dessert, cut fresh figs in half and drizzle with chestnut honey. If the figs aren't as ripe as you'd hoped, halve and bake them drizzled with chestnut honey and serve with crème fraîche when cooled. Fresh figs can also be served with a plate of ripe creamy Gippsland blue cheese instead of dessert.

For another simple dessert, take whole figs that are very ripe and wash carefully. While the figs are still damp, dip them into dark brown sugar and pack tightly in a baking dish. Bake for about 10 minutes in a very hot (240°C) oven, being careful they don't burn. When they are cooked, the sugar turns into caramel in the bottom of the dish. Cool and serve with a big pot of mascarpone moistened with the pan juices.

If you prefer to peel the figs, try marinating them in a little almond or walnut liqueur for about an hour after you've peeled them. Take a roasted walnut, squeeze it into the centre of each fig and coat with a batter of self-raising flour and water, then deep-fry in extra virgin olive oil in the smallest saucepan you can find so it is not too extravagant. Dusted with icing sugar and served hot, these are incredibly more-ish.

To make fig ice cream, simply purée some ripe figs and add a little lemon juice or even some finely sliced glacé ginger. Stir into some homemade vanilla ice cream and freeze. Serve with almond biscuits.

Don't forget the leaves of the fig: they can be used in so many ways to serve food. I found this wonderfully evocative quote in *Honey from a Weed* by Patience Gray: 'I recall only the "fig bread" served as a dessert in the shape of a little domed loaf unwrapped from its fig leaves, made of pressed dried figs flavoured with aniseed and bay leaves.'

Dried figs are an important part of culinary life and can be called upon in many a cooking emergency. Try stuffing them with roasted almonds and baking them in the oven for a sweetmeat to finish dinner. Then there are those wonderful dried figs of chef Cheong Liew's, poached in port and chocolate (see page 228) – a great finish to a meal.

Because figs have a natural affinity with lamb, try roasting a shoulder of lamb, boned and stuffed with fresh figs, garlic and chopped lemon rind. The same stuffing would go well with kid and quail. Don't prepare any of these in advance though, as figs have an enzymatic reaction with meat or poultry that starts to break them down. Pot-roast the lamb very slowly in some extra virgin olive oil, add seasoning and moisten with stock if it begins to dry out or the figs are causing it to burn. The meat will give off a syrupy glaze that should be served with the lamb.

Figs can also be added to pizza. First 'cure' the pizza base in the oven, by cooking it three-quarters through. Then take it out, drizzle with extra virgin olive oil, top with thick slices of fresh fig and goat's curd, return to the oven and finish cooking. Alternatively, use a combination of fresh figs and caramelised onions as a pizza topping. Add dobs of goat's cheese or ricotta and a final flourish of extra virgin olive oil and chopped flat-leaf parsley.

Who needs a recipe for figs when the best way to eat them is as they are? Here, however, are a few ideas for those times when you have a glut on your hands.

✦ Wrap figs with prosciutto and stand them in a shallow terracotta dish or a roasting pan. Drizzle with extra virgin olive oil and add a sprig or two of thyme. Bake at 240°C for 10 minutes and serve immediately. You could also either stuff the figs with blue cheese or dot goat's cheese or blue cheese over the figs for a fabulous lunch.

✦ Grill halved ripe figs topped with a tiny knob of butter under a preheated, really hot grill until caramelised, then serve hot with cream or mascarpone.

✦ Drizzle honey and squeeze lemon juice over peeled figs, then bake them at 240°C for 10 minutes.

✦ Semi-dry halved figs in a home dehydrator. Toss roasted almonds and toasted fennel seeds with a little extra virgin olive oil and the grated rind of a lemon. While they are still warm from the dehydrator, make a sandwich of the figs with the almond mixture inside. Or serve cooled figs with a ripe soft cheese.

FRESH FIG AND PROSCIUTTO SALAD   *Serves 4*

8 ripe figs (the figs will be at their best if not refrigerated)	squeeze of lemon juice
1 bunch rocket, trimmed, washed and dried	8 slices prosciutto
extra virgin olive oil, to taste	freshly shaved Parmigiano Reggiano, to serve
balsamic vinegar *or* vino cotto (see Glossary), to taste	

Cut the figs in half, then toss with the rocket in a bowl. Dress with a vinaigrette of 3–4 parts olive oil to 1 part balsamic vinegar or vino cotto (the specific quantities depend on the quality of the ingredients). Add lemon juice to taste. Divide evenly among 4 plates, then drape over two slices of prosciutto. Top with shaved Parmigiano Reggiano and serve immediately.

FIG AND PRESERVED LEMON SALAD WITH
WALNUTS AND GOAT'S CURD

Serves 6

3 quarters preserved lemon, flesh removed,
    rind rinsed and thinly sliced
verjuice, for soaking
1 cup walnuts
12–18 ripe figs, depending on size, halved
¼ cup (60 ml) vino cotto (see Glossary)

½ cup (125 ml) extra virgin olive oil
sea salt flakes and freshly ground
    black pepper
lemon juice, to taste (optional)
1 bunch rocket, washed and dried
½ cup goat's curd

Soak the preserved lemons in enough verjuice to cover for 1 hour. Preheat the oven to 200°C, then place the walnuts on a baking tray and lightly roast for 10 minutes or until golden. Rub skins off with a clean tea towel, then leave to cool.

Brush the figs with a little vino cotto, then grill under a hot griller until lightly caramelised. Place in a bowl, then drizzle with the remaining vino cotto and leave for 30 minutes.

Drain the preserved lemons, discarding the verjuice, then gently strain the vino cotto from the figs, reserving the vino cotto. Combine the vino cotto with the olive oil, whisk to emulsify, then season to taste with salt and pepper. Balance the dressing with lemon juice if required. Combine all the ingredients, except the goat's curd, then gently toss together with the dressing. Dollop the goat's curd onto the salad immediately before serving.

DRIED FIG TAPENADE

Makes 2 cups

This fig tapenade keeps well, covered with olive oil in the refrigerator, and can be pulled out to turn barbecued lamb chops or quail into something a little more special.

3 sprigs rosemary
1 cup (250 ml) extra virgin olive oil
¾ cup reconstituted dried figs, topped and
    tailed, then finely chopped
1 cup (150 g) kalamata olives, pitted

2 tablespoons capers
10 anchovy fillets
80–100 ml lemon juice
sea salt flakes and freshly ground
    black pepper

Pan-fry the rosemary sprigs in a little of the oil, then remove the rosemary and set it aside, reserving the oil. Cool the rosemary-infused oil and then add it to the balance of the oil. Process the figs, olives, fried rosemary, capers and anchovies to a purée in a food processor. Season with lemon juice, salt and pepper. With the motor running, pour in the olive oil slowly as if making a mayonnaise.

PICKLED FIGS, FARM FOLLIES STYLE

Makes 10 medium-sized jars

A bottle of pickled figs in the pantry can be used to complement poultry for a last-minute meal, and is especially good with duck or quail. Roast or pan-fry the poultry with fresh rosemary and deglaze the pan with a little of the pickling liquid. Add a little chicken stock to the sauce and then toss in some sliced pickled figs, rosemary and slices of lemon.

225 g salt
3 kg figs

PICKLING MIXTURE
1 tablespoon mixed spice
2 cloves per fig
1 litre white-wine vinegar
2 kg sugar

Add the salt to 2 litres of water to make a brine. Soak the figs in the brine for 12 hours.

To make the pickling mixture, boil the mixed spice, cloves, vinegar and 1.5 kg of the sugar for 15 minutes. Cook the fruit slowly in this syrup for 1 hour. Leave to stand overnight.

The next day, bring the figs and syrup to the boil, then drain them, reserving the syrup, and place in sterilised jars (see Glossary). Add the remaining sugar to the syrup and boil for 30 minutes. Cover the figs with the syrup and seal the jars.

FIG AND GORGONZOLA TART

Serves 8

If the figs aren't as sweet as they could be, then roast some walnuts, rub off their skins, toss them in your best honey and dot them on top of the tart.

1 × quantity Sour-cream Pastry
  (see page 424)
250 g gorgonzola piccante (see Glossary)
  or other sharp blue cheese, crumbled
250 g mascarpone

4 free-range eggs, beaten
sea salt flakes and freshly ground
  black pepper
12 ripe figs
1 tablespoon unsalted butter

Make and chill pastry following instructions. Roll out the pastry and use it to line a deep 16 cm tart tin with a removable base, then chill for 20 minutes. Preheat the oven to 200°C. Line the pastry case with foil and pastry weights, and blind bake for 10 minutes, then remove foil and weights and bake for another 6–8 minutes or until the pastry is cooked. Reset the oven to 180°C.

Mix the blue cheese with the mascarpone. Beat the eggs into the cheeses by hand, and season to taste; don't be tempted to leave out salt thinking that the blue cheese is salty enough.

Pour mixture into the hot tart shells, then bake for 12–20 minutes (depending on the depth of the tart mould) or until filling is almost set.

Meanwhile, cut the figs in half, place on a grill tray and dot with a little butter, then grill under a hot griller for approximately 10 minutes, or until the figs are caramelised.

Just as the tart is setting, lay the figs on top of the gorgonzola custard and return it to the oven for a few minutes. Leave to cool for 20 minutes before serving with a salad of rocket, witlof (both red and white) and roasted walnuts.

FIGS IN PUFF PASTRY WITH CRÈME ANGLAISE *Serves 8*

This dessert can be made as one large pastry, or 8 individual ones, cut to whatever shape you wish.

1 × quantity **Rough Puff Pastry** (see page 100)	**CRÈME ANGLAISE**
1 egg, lightly beaten	2 cups (500 ml) milk
16 figs	2 cups (500 ml) rich double cream
butter, for frying	1 vanilla bean, halved lengthways
lemon juice *or* verjuice, to taste	8 egg yolks
pure icing sugar (optional), to serve	120 g sugar

Make and chill pastry as instructed. Preheat the oven to 220°C. Roll out the pastry and rest it in the refrigerator for 30 minutes before cutting it to your desired shape (I like to cut 8 rectangles) and brushing it with beaten egg – make sure you don't brush the egg right to the edges as this will inhibit the rising of the pastry layers. Cook for about 10–15 minutes or until golden brown and cooked through. Cut each piece in half and pull out any uncooked bits of pastry if necessary.

For the crème anglaise, bring the milk and cream to the boil in a heavy-based saucepan, then remove from the heat. Scrape the vanilla seeds into this mixture, then add the vanilla bean and leave to infuse. Whisk the egg yolks and sugar until thick and pale. Carefully stir the heated milk mixture into the egg mixture. Return the crème to the pan and heat over low heat, stirring gently and constantly with a wooden spoon until the mixture begins to thicken. Take the mixture off the heat from time to time if it looks like getting too hot. Have a large bowl of iced water standing by in case you take the crème too far and need to place the saucepan in iced water to cool it down quickly. The crème should be thick enough to coat a wooden spoon and leave a trail when you draw your finger across it. Remove the vanilla bean.

Cut the figs into thick slices and fry them quickly in a little butter in a large frying pan over high heat. Don't put too many in the pan at a time – this may cause them to sweat instead of caramelise. Add a squeeze of lemon juice or verjuice.

Assemble by placing one piece of pastry on a serving plate, piling it up with figs and topping with another piece of pastry, sprinkling with a little icing sugar if you wish. Pour the crème anglaise around the pastry and serve. (If you pour crème anglaise on the plate first and then place pastry on top, your pastry will get soggy.)

CHOCOLATE CAKE WITH A FIG CENTRE AND GANACHE   *Serves 8–10*

This is an amazingly luscious cake that is best made with figs picked ripe from the tree. The base recipe is in fact Simone Beck's Very Rich Chocolate Cake with Cherries from *Simca's Cuisine*, an old favourite; the page in my copy is very fingered and chocolate-splattered! This cake is rich rather than sweet, so is perfect for my taste.

450 g bitter chocolate, chopped

1 tablespoon best-quality instant
   coffee granules

½ cup (125 ml) brandy *or* fruit liqueur

4 free-range eggs, separated

150 g unsalted butter, chopped

⅓ cup (50 g) plain flour

pinch salt

⅓ cup (75 g) castor sugar

8 plump, ripe figs, peeled and chopped

GANACHE

225 g bitter chocolate, chopped

150 ml cream

2 teaspoons best-quality instant
   coffee granules

Preheat the oven to 190°C. Grease and line a 26 cm springform cake tin. Melt the chocolate with the instant coffee granules and brandy in a heavy-based enamelled or stainless steel saucepan over low heat until smooth, then remove from the heat. Mix one egg yolk at a time into the chocolate mixture. Return the pan to the heat just to warm the yolks and thicken the mixture. Remove from the heat again and add the butter, a knob at a time, stirring until it is all incorporated. Sift the flour and stir it into the chocolate mixture.

Beat the egg whites with the salt until they form soft peaks, then add the castor sugar and beat until stiff. Fold the warm chocolate mixture carefully into the egg whites and turn the batter into the prepared tin. Bake for 20–25 minutes and remove from the oven (it is important not to overcook the cake). It will puff like a soufflé in the centre and must be left to cool in the tin for 45 minutes before it is turned out onto a wire rack. The cake will shrink and crack as it cools.

Cut a 12 cm-wide circle in the middle of the cooled cake and scrape out the cake with a dessertspoon, leaving a 2.5 cm border and the base intact. The cake you extract will be so moist and rich you could roll it into balls like truffles – instead, mix it with the figs and pile it back into the hollowed-out cake.

For the ganache, melt the chocolate with the cream and instant coffee granules in a heavy-based enamelled or stainless steel saucepan over low heat until smooth and shiny. Cool the ganache, then cover the cake generously with it. Put the cake in a cool place until required – don't refrigerate it or the ganache will lose its sheen.

FIG AND WALNUT TART

Serves 8

One of my most requested desserts, which is almost embarrassingly simple, is a fig and walnut tart. It is really just a meringue made with dark-brown sugar. This tart is meant to be sticky, soft and rustic-looking. As it is so rich, I prefer it cut in thin slices to have with coffee.

180 g walnuts

330 g plump dried figs, stems removed
  and fruit finely chopped

6 free-range egg whites

250 g soft dark-brown sugar

crème fraîche *or* sour cream, to serve

slices of candied *or* fresh lime (optional),
  to serve

Preheat the oven to 220°C. Roast the walnuts on a baking tray for about 5 minutes, shaking the tray to stop the nuts burning. Rub them in a clean tea towel to remove their bitter skins, then sieve away the skins. Allow to cool. Reduce the oven temperature to 180°C.

Line and grease a 24 cm springform cake tin with baking paper. Toss the walnuts and figs together in a bowl.

In the bowl of an electric mixer, whisk the egg whites until soft peaks form, then slowly add the sugar in heaped tablespoons until incorporated, and the resultant meringue is thick and stiff. Take a spoonful of the meringue and mix it through the figs and walnuts, then tip this mixture into the meringue and fold through. Spoon the meringue mixture into the prepared cake tin and bake in the oven for 45–50 minutes or until the meringue pulls away from the sides of the pan and the top feels 'set'. Leave to cool.

I serve this with crème fraîche or sour cream spread over the top. Candied or even fresh lime is a wonderful accompaniment to this tart – decorate the edge with a ring of very thin lime slices.

CHEONG'S FIGS

Makes 12 figs

My friend Cheong Liew, one of Australia's most important chefs and an amazingly generous and knowledgeable man, used to serve a wonderful sweetmeat in the days when he ran Adelaide's famous Neddy's restaurant. It was a Portuguese speciality based on figs stuffed with a mixture of ground almonds and grated chocolate. Cheong then poached the figs in chocolate and port. He says he used to have them sitting in a glass jar of port ready to serve after coffee. They make a stunning dessert served with crème fraîche.

¾ cup (120 g) almonds, roasted and ground
120 g dark chocolate, grated, plus 120 g
   for poaching
250 g (about 12) dried figs

1½ cups (375 ml) port (I often use
   white port *or* 12-year-old St Hallett's
   Pedro Ximenez)

Mix the almonds and grated chocolate together. Loosen each fig at the bottom and create a hole, then stuff with the almond and chocolate mixture. Place the figs in a heavy-based saucepan with the port. Simmer, but do not boil, over low–medium heat for 10 minutes. Add extra grated chocolate to taste and simmer for another 5 minutes. Take the figs out and put them in a jar. Reduce the poaching liquid until it forms a glaze and pour into the jar.

BURNT FIG JAM SLICE

Serves 8

½ × quantity Sour-cream Pastry
   (see page 424)
300 g jar Maggie Beer Burnt Fig Jam

½ cup (125 ml) crème fraîche, mascarpone
   or sour cream

Preheat the oven to 220°C. Prepare and chill the pastry as instructed. Roll out the pastry to 5 mm thick, then place it on a flat scone tray and bake until golden (about 15 minutes). While the pastry is still warm from the oven, spread generously with the jam. Cut into 4 pieces and serve with crème fraîche, mascarpone or sour cream.

GRAPES

BY FEBRUARY EACH YEAR THE BAROSSA VALLEY VINTAGE IS IN full swing. In the 33 years I have now lived here, there has been a gradual eroding of the harvesting traditions and there are now fewer hand-picking gangs. For economic reasons machine picking has become a fact of life, and with it some of the colour of the Valley has gone. The women of the Barossa were the core of the picking gangs, helped by hundreds of itinerant workers who would descend on the Valley looking for work. They were often young people on working holidays, and so over the years we had lawyers, teachers, nurses and chefs picking for us. The traditional grape pickers' party in late April at the end of the vintage was often a very spirited affair. After all the hard work of picking there was an atmosphere of camaraderie and satisfaction in the air at seeing the crop in. Nowadays, we only pick the grapes that are to go into our Home Block Shiraz and Beer Bros Old Vine Shiraz. These are seriously good wines and so the extra care and attention is well warranted, no matter the cost.

The biennial Barossa Vintage Festival, the celebration to mark the end of vintage, is a very special time in the Valley and picnics have always been a highlight. Several festivals ago, our then Farmshop manager, Jane Renner, made the setting picture perfect. Under the gum trees by the side of the dam at the Pheasant Farm Restaurant, trestle tables were covered in bright cloths and laden with bowls of grapes, figs and pomegranates. Seating consisted of a mixture of wooden folding chairs, hay bales or blankets. A big box of timber, piles of vine stumps and cuttings for fuel, and two drum spits for cooking completed the scene.

My idea was to celebrate the grape in every course, and I had planned the picnic months in advance so that it could be included in the festival program. But plans made so long beforehand easily go awry. The yabbies that were to feature in the first dish of the day were suddenly unavailable due to the long Easter break, so the menu required a late change. A few phone calls to Kangaroo Island and marron was ordered – in the end much more than a mere replacement.

Each picnicker received a plate with a marron, a terrine and a jelly as a starter; all including grapes or their by-products in one way or another. The blanched and halved marron were painted with extra virgin olive oil and verjuice before being finished in the oven. Each individual Barossa Chook terrine had been lined with both a vine leaf cooked in verjuice and the skin of the chicken, and the leg meat was simply diced and tossed with basil, roasted garlic, salt and freshly ground black pepper before the terrines were cooked in a bain-marie – the little round terrines looked beautiful turned out, vine leaf uppermost. Finally, alongside sat a scoop of grape and verjuice jelly – bearing in mind that jellies always melt at picnics, I had added some extra virgin olive oil, along with some fresh chervil, so that as it melted the jelly made its own vinaigrette.

The main course was boned, milk-fed lamb that had been stuffed with sautéed figs, walnuts, pancetta, onion, breadcrumbs and lots of rosemary and thyme. I made two bundles of lamb wrapped in caul fat with fresh bay leaves and cooked them gently over the open fire fuelled by vine cuttings. When I found myself faced with the slowly sautéed golden shallots I had meant to serve with the marron, I tossed these with boiled kipfler potatoes (cut in half and sprinkled with sea salt and freshly ground black pepper) and chopped flat-leaf parsley, to serve with the lamb bundles. Fennel pot-roasted in olive oil and deglazed with verjuice completed the dish.

My friend Sheri Schubert had cooked a huge amount of her very ripe shiraz grapes a few weeks previously and put them through a food mill before freezing the pulpy juice. The day before the picnic, Sheri used these to make two huge pots of her Rotegrütze (see page 236), the traditional Barossa dessert of grape and sago. I was keen to serve it in two large bowls from my own kitchen from which we could spoon out portions, so the sago was measured out extra carefully to get the 'set' just right. We made almond and lemon friands to serve with the rotegrütze, and thick-as-thick churned cream collected that morning from the Kernich dairy at Greenock really finished it off.

Continuing the grape theme, the bread we served with lunch was made by Tanunda's Apex Bakery using the ferment from Orlando shiraz grapes. And to finish off the picnic, we had my grape Schiacciata (see page 234), made with some very ripe grenache grapes picked at Grant Burge's vineyard the day before, which we served with Laurie Jensen's Shadows of Blue cheese from Tarago River, Victoria. The juxtaposition of the sweetness of the bread and the saltiness of the creamy blue cheese was a pretty good way to end the day, and for me a true celebration of vintage.

Only having grown wine grapes, I hadn't realised that table grapes were trellised and grown quite differently until my friend Stefano de Pieri asked me to help out at a Slow Food Dinner, to be held under the vines at the Garreffa family's property near Mildura in Victoria. I was asked to make verjuice custards for the 120 guests. A dinner in a vineyard for that number of people isn't the easiest logistical exercise, but the Garreffas had a large shed which Stefano had set up as a camp kitchen. A visiting chef from the United States had volunteered to help and the Garreffa family and friends were all happy to be involved in the food preparation.

We arrived at the vineyard in the early evening, when there was still some fierceness in the sun. We mingled with the crowd, having a glass of local wine and eating the deep-fried pastries that were being cooked over an open fire. The difference in grape growing was remarkable – the table grapes are grown on a trellis system that seems almost like hedge-rows; the vigorous vines are then canopied over 2 metres high. A long table had been placed down the row between the vines, and covered in generously draped white table-cloths – a beautiful sight. The roof of vines between the rows was hung with lanterns, giving a magical feel to the evening. On my return I looked for the right position to create something similar at home. Several years have passed now and nothing has yet transpired, but I promise myself – one day!

The Garreffas are not only very serious table grape growers, they also produce sultanas, currants, raisins and muscatels under their brand Tabletop Grapes, which are of such a high quality they bring a whole new dimension to dried grapes.

While wine grapes aren't the norm for eating, they are wonderful to cook with at the end of the season, when they're sweet and intense in colour. Not everyone has access to wine grapes, as I do, however just about every fruit shop stocks sultana grapes, that versatile and seedless grape first planted for drying and then used for bulk wine-making in years of excess. Nowadays, mint-green sultanas for the table are more to my taste than those left to ripen until golden and sweet. Today the fruit is protected by the vine canopy, making it less sweet, which suits my palate.

I can't bear to waste the grapes not captured by the mechanical pickers at the end of each season, so if we're having a party in the autumn and lighting up our wood-fired oven I pick buckets of these leftovers. We cook either really good pork sausages, beef shin or lamb shanks in huge but relatively shallow terracotta dishes. The meat, first gently sealed in nut-brown butter with a dash of oil, sits on a bed of soffrito (sweated onion and garlic) with chopped rosemary, some bay leaves and citrus rind. This mixture is then topped with the grapes and cooked until they reduce and become a thick syrupy mass. Remember that wine grapes have pips, and more sensitive souls may find this a problem. (Do we? Of course not!)

When you tire of eating bunches of fresh grapes, there are many other ways to use them. I love grapes tossed through a green salad, with a dressing of walnut oil and a little red-wine vinegar (keeping it in the grape family). I enjoy the explosion of grape juice when I come across whole grapes among the salad leaves, particularly if they are icy cold.

I've never gone as far as peeling grapes for a dish. I do, however, halve large red globe grapes and at times remove the pips before tossing them in a salad or marinade. It's not that the pips trouble me; rather, it's that the cut surface takes up the vinaigrette so much better than if the grape is left whole to slip around in the dressing protected by its skin.

Pickled grapes are the perfect accompaniment to pâtés and terrines, and also tongue, either smoked or in brine. To pickle grapes, place them in sterilised jars (I like to leave the grapes in bunches, if possible) and pour in a spiced vinegar that has been brought to the boil – you can make your own or use a commercial one. Leave the grapes in the jar for 6 weeks to mature; they will last for up to 12 months. I prefer a large black grape for this, such as Black Prince. I also like to preserve grapes using verjuice, rather than water. This gives me not only lovely sweet– sour grapes, but every bit of the verjuice can be used in sauces or pot-roasting.

Grapes team well with offal such as duck livers or hearts, or even sweetbreads, as the freshness of the grapes cuts through the richness of the offal. Just cook the livers, hearts or sweetbreads as normal and, 30 seconds before serving, throw a handful of grapes picked from the stem into the pan. If you want to go to a little more trouble, you could present the grapes in a little pastry tart. I love to toss grapes in at the last moment when making a sauce for chicken, pigeon, quail, pheasant or guinea fowl. Or try grapes in a stuffing – add them to the traditional breadcrumbs with onions, fresh tarragon and an egg to bind. Pour verjuice over the skin of the chicken three-quarters of the way through the cooking (¼ cup for a large bird).

At vintage, I always try to use the grape in every way I can. We now even make our own non-alcoholic 'bubbles' – based on verjuice, Desert Pearls has a wonderfully fruity nose, with the mouthfeel of wine and a dry finish, for those times when you don't want to drink wine. And as much as I am proud of my quince, cabernet, fig and blood plum pastes to go with cheese, during vintage I'd rather serve a bunch of fresh grapes alongside.

At this time of year I also make a simple butter cake that includes fresh sultana grapes, which keep the cake so moist it lasts a week. For another sure-fire hit, coat fresh sultana grapes with a little honey and a squeeze of lemon juice and put them under the grill until caramelised. Serve with cream or mascarpone for an instant dessert.

SCHIACCIATA

Makes 2 loaves

One of the treats for me at this time of year is to add wine grapes to cakes, desserts and festive breads. The Italians are fond of this combination too: the famous Tuscan bread *schiacciata con l'uova* sees a little sugar and olive oil added to a yeast dough studded with the region's sangiovese grapes. The bread is cooked until the edges are just burnt, so that it isn't oversweet and its surface appears dimpled.

20 g fresh yeast *or* 2 teaspoons dried yeast

180 ml warm water

25 g castor sugar

150 ml extra virgin olive oil

2 tablespoons finely chopped rosemary,
    plus small sprigs to scatter

2⅔ cups (400 g) strong flour
    (see Glossary)

pinch salt

1 kg ripe black grapes, washed and
    stems removed

Combine the yeast, warm water and 1 teaspoon castor sugar in a small bowl and set aside for 5–10 minutes until frothy. Gently warm the olive oil and chopped rosemary in a saucepan over low heat for 5 minutes, then leave to cool.

Place the flour and salt in a bowl, then make a well and add the yeast mixture and half of the rosemary-infused oil. Add 400 g of the grapes and mix vigorously, then turn the dough out onto a well-floured bench. Knead the grapes into the dough for 5 minutes (don't try using a dough hook as it will smash the grapes) – it will be very soft and sticky.

Return the dough to the cleaned and lightly oiled bowl and brush it with a little rosemary oil. Cover the bowl with plastic film and allow the dough to rise slowly in a draught-free place for 1½–2 hours, or until doubled in volume.

Turn out the dough and divide it into two portions (there is no need to knock it back). Generously brush 2 ovenproof frying pans or 24 cm springform cake tins with rosemary oil and, using your hands, flatten the dough over the base of each. Push the remaining grapes into the surface of the dough. Generously brush the dough with the remaining rosemary oil, then sprinkle over the rosemary sprigs and 1 tablespoon castor sugar. Leave to rise in a draught-free spot for about 30 minutes. Meanwhile, preheat the oven to 220°C.

Place the loaves on a baking tray, as the juices from the grapes will bubble up and may overflow. Bake for 20 minutes, then reduce the temperature to 180°C and bake for another 10 minutes. Slide out onto a wire rack and serve warm or at room temperature.

ALMOND AND GARLIC SOUP WITH GRAPES

Serves 4

At harvest time, as it would so often still be very hot, I loved to make this cold soup with seedless grapes for lunch. I first saw this recipe in the *Time Life Fruit Book*, but it is a well-known tradition of the Mediterranean. It is made a little like a mayonnaise, and if it is too thick it calls for iced water to be stirred in just before serving; I substitute chilled verjuice instead. It should be just like a gazpacho in thickness. The grapes are added at the last moment and they sink to the bottom very quickly – try to serve the soup straightaway, as the bobbing grapes add so much to the dish.

250 g bread, cut from a baguette

milk, for soaking

2 large cloves garlic, peeled

150 g almonds, roasted for flavour
  (I use skins and all)

2 tablespoons white-wine vinegar

½ cup (125 ml) extra virgin olive oil

sea salt flakes (optional)

iced water *or* ice blocks made of verjuice

200 g sultana grapes (I prefer them green;
  if they have turned yellow, they will be
  over-ripe for this dish)

Soak the bread in milk for 20 minutes. Gently squeeze the milk out of the bread, then put the bread in the blender with the garlic, almonds and vinegar. With the motor running, add the oil slowly until well blended. Add salt if required, then refrigerate. Just before serving, pour in iced water or add ice blocks of verjuice to suit desired taste and consistency. Add the grapes to the soup immediately prior to serving.

GRAPE GROWER'S CHICKEN   *Serves 4*

The cooking of poultry with grapes is well documented in French and Italian cookbooks. In particular, game birds such as pheasant, guinea fowl or partridge go with grapes or their juice in classic combinations: the fruit is either cooked with the bird (added at the last minute just to warm through) or a bunch of grapes is squeezed into the pan in the final moments of cooking. If you grow your own grapes, freeze some to use this way later in the year. Verjuice gives the same flavour and adds a desirable piquancy. If you wish to make this dish when grapes are out of season, take ½ cup raisins and soak them overnight in some verjuice. Add these to the sauce in the last 5 minutes of cooking. This recipe can also be made with pheasant.

180 ml verjuice *or* 1 kg unripe sultana
  grapes, to yield 180 ml verjuice

walnut oil, for cooking

1 tablespoon butter

sea salt flakes and freshly ground
  black pepper

4 large chicken marylands, thighs and
  drumsticks separated

¾ cup (180 ml) reduced Golden Chicken
  Stock (see page 57)

100 g unsalted butter, cubed and chilled
  (optional)

1 cup sultana grapes, to add to the sauce

If making your own verjuice, pick the green grapes off the stem, discarding any that are spoiled, and blend and strain the grapes to yield 180 ml juice. Heat enough walnut oil and butter to just cover the bottom of a heavy-based saucepan, season the chicken pieces and gently seal them over low–medium heat until golden brown. Add the verjuice and stock and gently braise the chicken, covered, over low heat. Be careful not to let the skin stick or the verjuice caramelise – if this starts to happen, add a touch more stock or water. Cook for about 20 minutes, or until tender and cooked through, and then remove the chicken pieces from the pan and set aside on a separate dish to rest, covered, for about 10 minutes.

Reduce the juices over high heat. Whisk in the chilled butter to 'velvet' the sauce while it is boiling rapidly (the butter is optional in these health-conscious days). Throw in the grapes in the last few seconds and serve the chicken with the sauce, along with a salad and boiled waxy potatoes in their jackets.

SHERI'S ROTEGRÜTZE   *Serves 4*

Rotegrütze is a local Barossa dessert made with leftover mataro or shiraz grapes at the end of vintage. It is such a simple dessert, using only the cooked grape, which is puréed and then simmered with sago. It's taken so seriously that there is a rotegrütze competition at the Tanunda Show each year. This dish is particularly significant because the Silesian immigrants brought the tradition of rotegrütze with them, but rather than making it with the berries traditionally used in their homeland, they adapted the dish to use the grapes they grew. A base of 550 ml grape juice and 2 tablespoons sago will serve 4.

very ripe black grapes (preferably shiraz)   **sago**

To extract the juice from the grapes, either use the finest setting on a food mill or purée the grapes in a food processor, and then strain through a sieve, pushing down on the solids to extract as much juice as possible. If a large amount of juice is required, gently heat whole bunches of grapes in a large saucepan until the grapes are soft enough that their stems can be pulled away easily. This mixture can then be strained and the skins and seeds discarded. This juice will be thicker than the juice made using a food mill.

Measure the juice into a stainless steel saucepan and bring it gently to a simmer over low heat. For every 550 ml juice gradually stir in 2 tablespoons sago. Simmer gently, stirring occasionally, for 45–50 minutes or until the sago is clear.

Pour the rotegrütze into a serving dish and leave it to cool, then chill in the refrigerator and leave it to set slightly. Serve with rich, runny cream.

GUINEA FOWL

GUINEA FOWL MAKE GREAT WATCHDOGS. I DEFY ANYONE TO sneak into a property that has guinea fowl in the yard. I'm sure some country people choose to have them for just this reason, and the bonus is that they are delicious to eat, and a nice change from mutton or chook.

In my experience, the French prefer guinea fowl to pheasant, and although this was a debate I once preferred to stay out of given that my restaurant was called the Pheasant Farm, we often bred our own guinea fowl for the menu. It wasn't until I spent time in both France and Italy – where my husband Colin and I enjoyed many holidays with friends, and we would cook the local guinea fowl, which was so plump and luscious – that I understood why it is so revered in these countries. We would rent a villa so that we could experience the joy of shopping at the local markets and cooking; we did this so enthusiastically we had to draw up a roster for who would have the privilege of cooking each day.

The guinea fowl we found in these markets, even though exactly the same genus as those found at home, were vastly superior, as the Australian stocks have had no new bloodlines introduced. This is for good reason, though – our authorities have tried to protect Australia from Newcastle's disease (a highly contagious virus that affects poultry and game) by not allowing the importation of poultry, with a blanket ban that lasted over 50 years. Although some poultry importation is now allowed, only the large poultry industries can afford the huge costs involved. This means that guinea fowl, pheasants and other game birds are not likely ever to be as good here as their counterparts in Europe. Having said that, they still have a wonderful flavour and I'd compare them to wild rabbit, in that they are both delicious but are trickier to cook than guinea fowl from Europe, which, along with farmed rabbit, are luscious enough even when overcooked, as can often unwittingly happen in the hands of the less experienced cook.

When cooked with care, guinea fowl is sweet, moist and delicious and marries particularly well with orange, lemon, thyme, rosemary or bay leaves, walnuts, liver and pancetta or bacon. It can be pot-roasted or baked, but not grilled as it doesn't have enough fat to remain moist.

It is easy to confuse raw guinea fowl and pheasant as their skin colour and leg meat are similar. Guinea fowl can be identified by the dark black spots on the skin of the upper breast and under the wings. Its breast is whiter, and the meat more delicate in taste, texture and structure than the pheasant's.

When buying guinea fowl, it is very important that you are aware of its age. At 12 to 14 weeks it is perfect to oven roast – any older and it will require pot-roasting. Farmers who keep only a few birds often let their flocks run together, which makes the birds' ages hard to gauge. It is also unusually difficult to determine the sex of guinea fowl, as males and females are identical to the untrained eye (and even to some very experienced eyes). This makes keeping breeding stock rather haphazard. Recently though I saw a program on British TV, *The View From River Cottage* (Channel 4), where a farmer was shown holding a young chicken, whose sex at that stage was unknown. The farmer placed a piece of white paper under the neck feathers in much the same way as a hairdresser would select one section of hair at a time and, when just a layer of feathers was accented by the paper, the rounded feathers showed the chicken was a hen (as pointy feathers would show it was a cockerel). I suspect this might well be the case with all poultry.

In Australia, a guinea fowl usually weighs 600 g to 1 kg. You really need a bird of at least 750 g to feed two people. Although some farms breed 450 g birds for single serves, I personally wouldn't bother, as these immature birds lack flavour. Incidentally, it is best to steer clear of frozen guinea fowl: although many types of game freeze fairly well, the guinea fowl has much less meat on its bones than, say, a pheasant or a duck, and so does not freeze successfully. Don't forget guinea fowl eggs – scrambled or pickled, they are a great treat. They are larger than quail eggs, yet smaller than chook eggs, and very creamy.

Very few cookbooks contain recipes for guinea fowl. Most chicken or pheasant recipes can be interchanged with guinea fowl, but as they have less flesh and little fat, guinea fowl will need a shorter cooking time or a lower temperature. Brush with a marinade of extra virgin olive oil and orange juice, lemon juice or verjuice and salt. This is both for flavour and to caramelise the skin. If you wish, marinate the bird first and add herbs or spices of your choice. My favourite additions are rosemary, thyme and citrus rind.

LIVER CROSTINI
Serves 4

200 g guinea fowl *or* chicken livers,
   cleaned and cut into quarters

8 sage leaves, finely chopped

150 g butter

1 tablespoon red-wine vinegar

1 tablespoon capers, drained

2 anchovy fillets, finely chopped

1 tablespoon flat-leaf parsley, chopped

4 slices of baguette

Preheat the oven to 220°C. Melt 75 g of the butter and brush one side of each bread slice with melted butter, then bake on a baking tray until golden.

Fry the livers and sage in a frying pan over high heat in the remaining butter until just pink (a bit over a minute on each side), then set aside to rest for 3–4 minutes. Add the vinegar, capers, anchovies and parsley. Serve on top of the baked croutons.

GUINEA FOWL IN ONION, GARLIC AND PROSCIUTTO SOFREGIT
Serves 4

Here I have borrowed the principle of a sofregit (usually based on olive oil, onion and tomato) from Colman Andrews' *Catalan Cuisine* and adapted it to cooking with game birds.

2 × 900 g guinea fowl

extra virgin olive oil, for cooking

6 sprigs thyme, leaves picked

1 lemon, thinly sliced

4 onions, finely chopped

3 heads garlic, separated into cloves
   and peeled

juice of ½ lemon

1 cup (250 ml) verjuice

1½ cups (375 ml) Golden Chicken Stock
   (see page 57)

4 fresh bay leaves

100 g prosciutto, cut into 5 cm-long strips

sea salt flakes and freshly ground
   black pepper

freshly chopped flat-leaf parsley, to serve

Rub the guinea fowl with olive oil, thyme leaves and sliced lemon, then cover and set aside in the fridge for 2 hours.

Pour about 1 cm olive oil into the base of a heavy-based cast-iron or enamelled casserole, then sweat onion and garlic cloves gently over low heat until softened and golden brown. Remove and set aside.

Cook the guinea fowl over low–medium heat in the casserole for 8–10 minutes, or until browned all over, adding olive oil as needed. Add the lemon juice, verjuice and stock to the pan and reduce by half over high heat, then add the bay leaves, a quarter of the prosciutto, and the onion and garlic mixture. Season with salt and pepper if needed. Simmer, covered, over low heat for about 10 minutes. Turn the guinea fowl over and simmer for another 10 minutes, then check for 'doneness' – they are cooked when the thighs pull away from the breast easily, and the thickest part of the breast feels springy to the touch. If the guinea fowl

Guinea fowl in onion, garlic and prosciutto sofregit

are not cooked, turn them back over to the other side and cook for another 5 minutes. Remove guinea fowl and set aside, covered. Reduce the sauce over high heat for 10 minutes or until it reaches a sticky consistency. Add the remaining prosciutto and check seasoning.

Cut the guinea fowl in half, then carve the breasts and legs off the frames and serve with the reduced sauce and lots of chopped flat-leaf parsley.

STUFFED GUINEA FOWL WITH RED-WINE SAUCE   *Serves 4*

The very first guinea fowl we ever sold in the early days of our farm was to some French customers who were kind enough to pass on their method of cooking it. They made a stuffing of onions, walnuts, juniper berries and the livers of the guinea fowl. This is a dish I have reproduced many times and I love the combination of flavours. Using such a stuffing, I might then serve the bird with a red-wine sauce.

If you prefer not to stuff the bird you could serve a Liver Crostini (see page 240) with the bird and the sauce.

2 × 900 g guinea fowl

STUFFING
1 large onion, finely chopped
1 sprig rosemary
butter, for cooking
200 g guinea fowl livers *or* chicken livers,
    cleaned and roughly chopped
3 juniper berries, crushed
sea salt flakes and freshly ground
    black pepper
½ cup (50 g) walnuts, roasted and
    skins rubbed off
100 g coarse, roasted breadcrumbs

SAUCE
200 ml red wine
50 ml port
1 tablespoon redcurrant jelly
1 tablespoon Dijon mustard
juice of ½ lemon
1 cup (250 ml) well-reduced game stock
butter (optional), for cooking

Preheat the oven to 180°C. For the stuffing, sauté the onion and rosemary in a frying pan in a generous amount of butter. Quickly toss in the livers for about 30 seconds on each side to seal, then set aside to rest. Add the crushed juniper berries, salt and pepper, then add the walnuts and breadcrumbs. Stuff the guinea fowl and sprinkle with salt.

Roast the birds in a roasting pan on one side first for 10 minutes, then turn onto the other side and roast for another 10 minutes. Sit the birds breast-side up and cook for another 6–10 minutes. They are cooked when the thighs pull away from the breast easily and the thickest part of the breast feels springy to the touch. At the end of the cooking period I like to turn the birds upside-down in the roasting pan, covered loosely with foil, and leave them for about 20 minutes before carving them.

To make the sauce, reduce the red wine and port by three-quarters in a saucepan over high heat, then whisk in the redcurrant jelly, mustard, lemon juice and stock. Bring to a rapid boil and reduce a little more. If you wish to 'velvet' the sauce, whisk in some butter.

GUINEA FOWL WITH CÈPE BUTTER AND GOLDEN SHALLOTS

Serves 6

finely chopped rind and juice of 2 oranges

2 tablespoons extra virgin olive oil

6 fresh bay leaves

12 sprigs thyme

2 teaspoons crushed juniper berries

3 × 800 g *or* 2 × 1.3 kg guinea fowl

1 kg golden shallots, peeled

sea salt flakes and freshly ground
    black pepper

1 litre reduced Golden Chicken Stock
    (see page 57)

½ cup (125 ml) verjuice, plus extra
    for deglazing

CÈPE BUTTER

50 g dried cèpes

verjuice, for soaking

200 g softened unsalted butter, chopped

2 tablespoons extra virgin olive oil

sea salt flakes and freshly ground
    black pepper

3 sprigs thyme, leaves picked

For the cèpe butter, cover the dried cèpes with verjuice and leave overnight to reconstitute.

Put the orange rind, orange juice, olive oil, bay leaves, thyme sprigs and juniper berries in a bowl and stir to combine. Place the birds in a glass or ceramic dish and pour over the marinade, then leave to marinate for at least 2 hours.

To make the cèpe butter, strain the cèpes, reserving the verjuice, then roughly chop. Sauté the cèpes in a frying pan in a little of the butter and the olive oil over medium heat, season with salt and pepper then deglaze the pan with the reserved verjuice. Cook for another 2 minutes or until the verjuice becomes syrupy. Place the cèpes (including any pan juices) and butter in a food processor and blend, then add the thyme leaves and blend again.

Remove the guinea fowl from the marinade and loosen the skin from the breasts and thighs. Ease the cèpe butter carefully under the skin of each breast and finish with a final rub all over the outside of the skin. Place the guinea fowl in a roasting pan and return to the refrigerator for 1 hour to let the butter firm.

Preheat the oven to 180°C. Add the shallots to the roasting pan. Season the birds and roast them on one side first for 10 minutes, then turn onto the other side and roast for another 10 minutes. Sit the birds breast-side up and roast for a further 6–10 minutes. They are cooked when the thighs pull away from the breast easily and the thickest part of the breast feels springy to the touch. »

Transfer the birds and shallots from the roasting pan to another dish, placing the birds breast-side down. Pour in ¼ cup of the stock (warmed) and ¼ cup verjuice, cover loosely with foil and rest for 20 minutes. To make the sauce, heat the roasting pan over high heat, deglaze with remaining ¼ cup verjuice, add the balance of the stock and reduce by half, then add the resting juices. Carve the birds by separating the legs from the breasts, then the thighs from the drumsticks. Carve the breasts from the frames and serve with thigh meat, sauce, shallots and Vino Cotto-glazed Radicchio (see page 382).

If not serving immediately, you can leave the guinea fowl to cool completely. Carve off the bone, leaving the guinea fowl breasts cut-side down in a little of the jus in the base of the pan. Save the bones to make stock. Before serving, place in a 180°C oven to warm with just a little of the sauce for a few minutes, then serve with the remaining reduced sauce.

HARE

'VIGNERON'S REVENGE' IS AN INTERNATIONALLY RECOGNISED tradition in the wine industry. At the 1996 Melbourne Food and Wine Festival, Italian winemaker Paolo di Marchi from the Isole e Olena winery in Chianti talked of the satisfaction he got from eating wild boar, which regularly decimate his vines. James Halliday talks of wine-maker Bailey Carrodus traditionally serving an end-of-vintage pie full of the starlings and blackbirds that plague his crop in the Yarra Valley. For us in the Barossa, the hare is our curse. Hares and, of course, rabbits, nibble the young vines and over the years have caused us a great number of setbacks. I love eating hare – but not only because of its love of tender new shoots.

When we had the Pheasant Farm Restaurant I put the word out that I would buy any hare (usually only shot for dog meat) brought to the kitchen door. The parameters were clear: only head shots were paid the premium price and no pellet shot was allowed. I always became very tense when deliveries would arrive at the restaurant during the busy lunch service, but the one exception I made was for a vigneron with a hare. Mind you, the many requests for a wine-makers' dinner of saddle of hare always left me anxious to the last that I would have enough. These days one can order wild hare (in small quantities only) through a game supplier or top-class butcher.

I prefer to hang hare skin on and with guts intact for a week in cool-room conditions. In the restaurant I gave enthusiastic would-be cooks something of a test by asking them to stand by my side while I gutted a hare: if they were not squeamish, I felt they deserved a chance (remember, mine was a game restaurant!). Many of the locals who ate hare at home at the time soaked it first in milk or vinegar and water to make the meat paler and rid it of strong game flavours. Not me – I think the flavour of a rare-roasted saddle of hare, where the meat is ruby-red, is one of the greatest game experiences of one's life.

Renowned chef Cheong Liew has been a great source of inspiration over the years and his depth of knowledge never ceases to amaze me. During a class on game I conducted with him years ago when he taught at Regency Park College of TAFE in Adelaide, he told me about the Chinese tradition of curing hare, skin intact but gutted, hanging between hams as they smoked. I sent my very next hare delivered in the skin to Schulz's, the Barossa's wonderful butcher and smallgoods manufacturer. I didn't put it in brine first and merely had it cold-smoked for three days. The resulting meat from the saddle had the most amazing texture – almost like butter. Not everyone shared my enthusiasm for it, finding it over-rich, but I'm not sure those words were in my vocabulary then, although they are now. I can still taste the hare as I sit here writing and can imagine it being served with a spiced plum sauce.

Jugged hare, that speciality of the English, is jointed hare marinated (jugged) in wine and herbs before being cooked very slowly with vegetables. However, recipes often omit the main ingredient required for authenticity: the blood of the hare. If the hare has

already been gutted – or paunched, as they say in more polite circles – then it must be quite fresh if any blood is to be collected from behind the 'lights' (lungs). Once the blood has been drained, half a teaspoon of vinegar is added to keep it fresh while the hare is hanging.

The first time I served jugged hare was at the request of a graduating class of commercial cooks, inspired by Trish Vietch, a member of the class and an outstanding student who had worked with both Phillip Searle and Cheong Liew. How I wish every class would ask for such a menu: it was entirely local, in season, balanced and adventurous. Beginning with salsify (a type of root vegetable) teamed with South Australian oysters and oyster mushrooms, it moved on to jugged hare with noodles and baby beetroot and was followed by game consommé as a palate cleanser. Pears poached in sherry with ginger finished the meal.

In many books hare and rabbit are used interchangeably. Although they have much the same body configuration, and are both at their best when the legs are cooked separately from the body (or saddle), there is actually a huge difference in flavour. Rabbit is pale, sweet and moist, whereas hare is dark, robust and gamy, and has a dense texture.

A very young (and therefore small) hare is quite wonderful baked whole. However, as young hare is not always available, I find the best method is to separate the legs from the saddle, and cook the front legs together as a confit, and the back legs long and slowly in a crockpot. Alternatively, if you wish to take the trouble to separate the muscles from each back leg and remove the sinew, you can then slice the meat and pan-fry it. This works best with hare that has been hung for a while. The saddle, as mentioned earlier, can be roasted rare.

If cooking the saddle of hare on the bone, it is essential that you first remove the sinew that protects the meat. This can be quite tricky but gets easier with practice, and is not unlike taking the sinew off a fillet of beef or skinning a fish. It is best undertaken with a long, thin, flexible knife – ideally either a fish or boning knife. There are two layers of sinew, and the trick is to get the knife under both layers and strip them off together. The meat should then be moistened with extra virgin olive oil and black pepper or bruised juniper berries and left to sit a while before roasting; it can, in fact, be left in the refrigerator for anything from a few hours to a few days. The fillets can be taken off the bone of the saddle (they are often referred to as backstraps). Once stripped of their sinew, hare fillets only take minutes to pan-fry in nut-brown butter. However, cooking the saddle whole then carving it off the bone after resting is the ultimate way to go.

Hare marries well with strong flavours such as port, red wine, sherry, balsamic or red-wine vinegar, bacon and mustard. Try cooking sliced golden shallots slowly in a little extra virgin olive oil and butter until almost caramelised. Scatter the sinew-free hare fillets with some chopped herbs, then season and seal them in the pan with the shallots over high heat. Turn the heat down to medium and turn the fillets over – depending on the thickness of the fillets, the cooking will only take 4–6 minutes in total. Remove the meat from the pan and leave it to rest for the same length of time it took to cook, then deglaze the pan with a good sherry or balsamic vinegar. Serve the hare fillets and the pan juices with fresh noodles.

Dare I write about the Hare Pies (see page 250) I made that didn't work? I was cooking a baroque banquet in the Octavius cellar at Yalumba, for 120 guests who were to see Purcell's opera *Indian Queen* as part of the 1995 Barossa Music Festival. And it was meant to be my last-ever big function (that still hasn't quite happened!). There were no kitchen facilities other than a barbecue, so the hare pies and sides of saltbush mutton had to be ferried from various ovens several kilometres away. We couldn't even tip any water down the drains for fear of interrupting the normal workings of the winery, so had to transport the dirty dishes back to the main Yalumba kitchen.

I planned to use Stephanie Alexander's wonderful lard pastry to encase sweet–sour hare and its incredibly rich stock. But I had forgotten to check whether the pastry could be made with a food processor: it tasted sublime but it fell apart! Not quite the ornately decorated pies I'd envisaged: we had to spoon the hare onto plates and balance the delicious but crumbling pastry on top. I felt every bit as bad as the pastry looked.

The real highlight of the night for me was the pure theatre going on 'behind the scenes' in the cellar, as the opera proceeded in the adjoining room. All the guests had to walk through the Octavius cellar on their way to the opera, and as only half of them had booked for the banquet, I wanted them all to experience the grandeur of the room (built in 1895, it has a soaring roof and rows of barrels lining each side, leaving only a narrow central aisle), whilst still keeping an element of surprise for those who were coming to dinner. As the guests walked through, candelabras stood sentinel along the length of the room, and the slow carriage of these people walking through, two or three abreast and filling the length of the room, with the heady aroma of maturing wine in the air, was a spectacle in itself.

Once the opera had begun, all our work 'backstage' in the cellar had to be undertaken in silence. We only had an hour and a quarter to transform the empty walkway into one long table draped with white linen and set for a banquet. The tables, handmade by Yalumba carpenters to fit exactly between the pillars that run down the central aisle, had to be installed using muffled wooden mallets. The staff, led by Colin, all garbed in academic gowns and jabots (the closest thing to period costume we could devise) noiselessly recovered the cutlery, glasses and linen from behind the barrels where they'd been hidden from view and put them all in place without a word spoken and with lots of pointing. Everyone hurried silently in the dim light of the candles. The dirt floor was dampened regularly so that no dust would be seen on the glasses, and noisier tasks such as putting bottles into ice barrels were timed to coincide with the crescendos of the orchestra. Suffice to say we were keyed up to fever pitch by the time the opera finished. Hare pies aside, it was a night to remember and would have been a wonderful way to bow out.

HARE COOKED IN DUCK FAT   *Serves 8*

This very rich meat is good with pasta, gnocchi, spätzle or polenta. Any leftover meat can be steeped in the duck fat and kept refrigerated for up to several months.

2 × 2 kg hares	2 small sprigs rosemary
extra virgin olive oil, for cooking	sea salt flakes
freshly ground black pepper	2 cups (500 ml) reduced Golden Chicken
2 litres duck fat	Stock (see page 57)
1 clove garlic, crushed	10 pickled walnuts in brine, including a little
2 teaspoons bruised juniper berries	pickling liquid (see page 347)

Joint the hares, separating the front and back legs from each saddle. Trim the sinew from the saddle, then rub the meat with olive oil and pepper and set it aside to be cooked separately. Melt the duck fat in an enamelled casserole, camp oven or crockpot on the stove. Add the garlic to the duck fat with the front and back hare legs, juniper berries and rosemary, then season. Cook for 2–4 hours over low heat until the hare almost comes off the bone. (As wild game is of an indeterminate age it is only by feel that you will know when each leg is tender.)

When ready to serve, preheat the oven to 230°C. Make sure the saddles are well oiled, then seal them in a heavy-based roasting pan on the stove. Transfer the dish to the oven and roast the saddles for 5 minutes. Remove the dish from the oven – if the meat is still not 'set' (it should be firm to the touch), turn the saddles over and return them to the oven for another 3 minutes. Rest the meat for 10 minutes before serving.

While the saddles are resting, reduce the oven temperature to 200°C. Warm the hare legs in the oven for about 5 minutes only, on an enamelled plate or similar to allow any excess duck fat to melt away. Reduce the stock with just a little of the walnut pickling liquid by half over high heat. Pull the muscles of the legs apart and reject any that are sinewy (the larger muscle is always so). Put the legs and saddles on a serving dish and pour over the reduced stock. Garnish with sliced pickled walnuts to taste and serve with mashed potato, parsnip or celeriac and a salad of bitter greens.

HARE WITH PINE NUTS, LEMON AND SULTANAS *Serves 4*

This is one of my favourite dishes using hare and is the result of combining two recipes – one from Elizabeth David's *Italian Food* (I have borrowed the title of her recipe) and the other from Ada Boni's *Italian Regional Cooking* (hare in sweet-and-sour sauce). The addition of chocolate will give another dimension of flavour to the dish rather than make it taste of chocolate.

1 × 2 kg hare (including heart, lungs and liver)
extra virgin olive oil, for cooking
1½ tablespoons sugar
½ cup (125 ml) red-wine vinegar
2 tablespoons pine nuts
2 tablespoons sultanas
30 g bitter chocolate
freshly ground black pepper

MARINADE FOR HARE
2 onions, roughly chopped
3 sticks celery, roughly chopped
3 sprigs rosemary
3 stalks flat-leaf parsley
600 ml red wine

MARINADE FOR OFFAL
rind of 1 lemon, chopped
150 ml red wine
1 tablespoon pine nuts
1 tablespoon sultanas
½ teaspoon sugar
pinch ground cinnamon
4 cloves

Joint the hare, separating the front and back legs from the saddle. Trim the sinew from the saddle. To make the marinade for the hare, combine the onion, celery, rosemary, parsley and red wine with the hare. To make the marinade for the offal, combine the marinade ingredients. Dice the heart, lungs and liver (if no gall bladder is attached) and add to this marinade. Marinate both the hare and the offal in the refrigerator overnight.

Drain and dry the hare, reserving the marinade. In a large enamelled heavy-based casserole, gently brown the hare legs in 125 ml olive oil over low–medium heat, then turn up the heat, add the vegetables from the marinade and cook at a high temperature until burnished, then add the marinade. Add the offal and its marinade and cook very, very slowly on the stove top over the lowest heat possible (use a simmer pad if you have one), turning the hare several times, for 2–4 hours. (As wild game is of an indeterminate age it is only by feel that you will know when each leg is tender.)

Preheat the oven to 250°C. In a small enamelled or stainless steel saucepan, slowly dissolve the sugar in the vinegar over low heat, then add the pine nuts and sultanas. Strain the liquid from the cooked hare legs into another saucepan and bring it to a rolling boil over high heat to reduce it if necessary – it should be thick enough to coat the meat. (Alternatively, the vegetables and cooking liquid can be put through a food mill and returned to the pan to warm through.) Stir the vinegar syrup into the cooking juices, then check for balance and add the chocolate.

Rub olive oil, salt and pepper into the saddle, then seal it over high heat in a heavy-based roasting pan on the stove. Transfer the dish to the oven and roast the saddle for 5 minutes. Remove the dish from the oven – if the meat is still 'unset' (it should be firm to the touch), turn the saddle over and return it to the oven for another 3 minutes. Rest the meat for 10 minutes before serving. Carve the saddle and add it to the leg meat, then pour over the sauce. This dish is great served with parsnips.

HARE PIE
Serves 4

The famous hare pie. Stephanie Alexander's pastry is like a traditional one from the north of England: it has a flaky tender crust and is somewhat biscuit-like. Don't, whatever you do, repeat my mistake of trying to make it in a food processor – by hand only!

1 × 2 kg hare

extra virgin olive oil, for cooking

250 g large flat mushrooms

2 sprigs thyme, leaves picked and chopped

sea salt flakes and freshly ground
   black pepper

125 g sugar-cured bacon, rind removed
   and meat cut into 2.5 cm cubes

12 golden shallots, peeled

1 tablespoon redcurrant jelly

butter, for cooking

1 tablespoon plain flour

1 egg, beaten with a little milk

SAUCE

1 large onion, roughly chopped

1 large carrot, roughly chopped

1 stick celery, roughly chopped

4 juniper berries, bruised

extra virgin olive oil, for cooking

150 ml red wine

50 ml port

2 cups (500 ml) reduced veal stock

STEPHANIE'S LARD PASTRY

200 g plain flour

200 g self-raising flour

pinch salt

200 g lard, at room temperature

180 ml cold water

To make the pastry, sift the flours together with the salt onto a work surface, then quickly rub in the lard. Make a well in the centre and work in the cold water, then knead the mixture for 2–3 minutes until you have a fairly soft, springy and elastic dough. Form the dough into a ball, then wrap it in plastic film and chill for 20 minutes before rolling.

Joint the hare, separating the front and back legs from the saddle. Using a sharp knife, follow the contours of the backbone and take the fillet off the saddle in a single piece, then remove the two layers of sinew. Smother the fillet with a little olive oil to keep it moist and set it aside. Dissect the back legs into their three main muscles. Trim away the sinew, then slice the meat across the grain, drizzle it with olive oil and put aside with the fillet. Chop the saddle, front legs and bones from the back legs into 5 cm pieces.

Preheat the oven to 220°C. To make the sauce, combine the onion, carrot, celery, bruised juniper berries and chopped hare bones in a roasting pan and drizzle with olive oil. Roast for 30–40 minutes until well caramelised. Deglaze the pan with the wine and port and reduce over high heat to a syrup. Add the reduced veal stock to the pan and boil vigorously until thick and luscious, then strain the sauce and leave it to cool.

Toss the mushrooms with the thyme and season. Render the bacon in a dry frying pan over high heat, then set aside the bacon and caramelise the shallots in the fat. Stir in the redcurrant jelly and leave it to melt, then set aside.

Thickly slice the hare fillet and seal it in a little olive oil and butter in another frying pan. Put the fillet aside, then seal the leg meat and set it aside too. Sprinkle the flour into the hot pan, then add the bacon, the shallot mixture and the mushrooms. Immediately remove the pan from the heat and stir in the strained sauce. Let the mixture cool, then carefully combine it with the meat and transfer it to an ovenproof pie dish.

Preheat the oven to 200°C. Roll out the chilled pastry and cut a lid to fit the pie dish. Brush the edge of the dish with the egg wash made by beating the egg with a little milk, then carefully place the pastry lid over the pie dish. Press the edges firmly and brush the surface with the egg wash. Bake the pie for 15 minutes, then lower the temperature to 180°C and bake for another 15 minutes. The filling needs only to be heated up in this process, so as soon as the pastry is cooked the pie is ready to eat.

MUSHROOMS

WILD FOOD – FORAGING FOR IT AND THEN COOKING THE BOUNTY – is one of my great loves. I remember well our first local mushroom sortie. It was a long weekend in the Barossa, and streams of people were walking through the trails of the forest yet, to my surprise, we were the only ones gathering mushrooms. What a different experience it was from walking in the woods of Umbria, on our first holiday there in 1995, where the hunt was intense. On a seemingly deserted mountainside the silence would suddenly be broken by the put-putting of small motorised bikes with baskets on the back to carry the spoils. Some gatherers were so secretive that, as we walked past, they stopped searching and pretended to be just contemplating the sky. Others proudly displayed their finds and pointed out where they had come from.

While autumn is generally believed to be the optimum season for mushrooms, all that is needed for a new flush of heads to peek provocatively from the ground is the right amount of rain and a burst of warmish sunshine.

I think foraging for food is an undervalued activity. So much goes to waste in the forest and it seems a great shame. We always go mushrooming on a weekday and we are often the only people around. It is wonderfully eerie to walk into the woods through the long straight rows of trees. The pine needles are so thick on the ground that they cushion your feet and it is so silent that you feel you are walking on air, as if you are floating. The pine trees are so tall they tend to block out the sun but every now and then powerful shafts of sunlight push through and add to the ethereal atmosphere.

You will definitely need some advice about what to pick and what to leave behind and it is important that you either gather scientific information from a book and study it carefully, or find a friend who already has the mushrooming bug and has become what English gastronome and opera critic Paul Levy calls a 'fungi bore'.

For over 30 years, my mushroom adviser has been my great friend Peter Wall, now retired from Yalumba. He has, all his Barossa life at least, been a gourmet of note, and an

Smoked mushrooms with rosemary and thyme (see page 257)

avid cook with an encyclopaedic mind and a passion for mushrooms, so what better person to learn from? When our families went mushrooming I felt very safe. Times are changing, though, and if foraging for mushrooms appeals to you, you should first find out what sprays are being used in the pine forests where you usually find mushrooms. Some of the spots where we used to mushroom are now sprayed by light aircraft and I wouldn't be eating the mushrooms until I'd had them tested.

Years ago now, when I was already, I thought, a confident forager, I couldn't resist a class being offered at the Melbourne Hyatt by George Biron, then of Sunnybrae Restaurant in Victoria. I was stunned by the breadth of his knowledge and for the first time realised there were many varieties of the familiar field mushroom that were just as dangerous as some of the poisonous exotics. A sobering thought. Not only did George show us specimens he'd been hunting for days, both edible and poisonous, he cooked a selection and tantalised us with some bread he'd baked to accompany them, brushed with truffle oil as it came from the oven – its perfume so overpowering. Like all foods found in the wild, mushrooms can be over-harvested, so make sure you leave some of the spore-generating bodies intact, simply by leaving behind some of the less-perfect specimens.

FIRSTLY, WHAT NOT TO PICK

Amanita verna Commonly called Destroying Angel. This is a pure white, stately, often large species. The best way to describe these fungi is that they grow out of a cup which becomes visible when you brush away the grass from the stem. This egg-shaped cup, called the 'volva', holds the mushroom in place. Other *Amanita* species (all of which are poisonous), including the beautiful Fly Agaric (*A. muscaria*) with its large, bright-red cap with white spots, can also be found in Australia, so caution is necessary.

Puffballs Some are edible, some are not. Without an expert in tow, it is best to leave these alone.

WHAT YOU CAN PICK

What you can pick and enjoy includes far more than the common field mushroom.

Suillus (**or** *Boletus*) *granulatas* This mushroom grows in pine forests and has a reddish-brown cap with a yellow stalk and spores. The upper part of the stalk is distinguished by granules. Its texture is quite chewy or rubbery. It is great sliced into salads or pickled.

Suillus (**or** *Boletus*) *luteus* Commonly known as slippery jack. The cap is slimy and pine needles easily stick to it. It is a dark, dull, reddish-brown when young. The tubes are yellow and there is a ring of a purplish-brown colour on the stalk. Wipe the slime from the cap and remove the tubes before cooking. These slippery treasures are the cousin of the famous cèpe of France or porcini of Italy, and in their fresh state are considered the poor side of the family and rejected by many, yet I love the delicate earthy flavour they have when the small firm heads are picked.

As my cooking is driven by what is available locally, it is the slippery jack that has become a staple. As delicious as they are fried and tossed with freshly cooked pasta and extra virgin olive oil, used in soups and risotto, or brushed with a mixture of walnut oil and verjuice and then barbecued, they also have an amazing affinity with yabbies, marron or Murray cod. Larger mushrooms, if not too wet and spongy, are great for drying. You can be creative by either stringing them up to dry naturally – scrub out an incubator if you happen to have one or invest in an electric dehydrator that sits on the kitchen bench through the season – or simply resort to the oven and dry them overnight with the pilot light on.

Coprinus comartus Known as the ink cap mushroom, this is one of the best-flavoured mushrooms and is also the one most commonly left behind. It is often thought to be a toadstool, since it looks like a parasol with a shaggy white coat. As it grows older, the cap dissolves into an inky mass. This mushroom must be picked really young. It is so prevalent in the Barossa that I find specimens in the most unlikely places, such as in the grass around the export kitchen and at home, where they are so strong that they actually push up some of the large terrace tiles (which measure about 12 × 12 cm, so that's no mean feat). Sadly, by the time I see the tiles raised, the mushrooms are too mature to eat. When picked young, before they become truly inky, they have a great flavour.

Agaricus campestris **and** *Agaricus robinsonii* These are the common or garden, wonderfully tasty, field mushrooms that poke through the ground from as early as April, when the soil is still warm and the first rains occur. These are still most people's favourites as they are easy to recognise and don't require specialist knowledge in order to identify them. *A. campestris* has a white cap, and *A. robinsonii* a brownish cap, and is not as intensely flavoured. Peter Wall cooks these with butter, a fresh bay leaf and a splash of champagne. **A word of caution**: There is a robust mushroom (Yellow Stainer: *A. xanthoderma*) often seen in urban lawns, which, although a white-capped, pink-gilled *Agaricus*, can cause severe gastro-intestinal reactions in some people. This mushroom has squarish immature caps, and cut or bruised surfaces stain bright yellow. It should *not* be eaten.

There are also many native fungi but they are a mystery to all but traditional Aboriginal wisdom, plus botanists and scientists. I'd love to think that we might have something as special as the flavour of the *Boletus edulis*, which is commonly known by its French name, cèpe, or Italian name, porcini. There are also native morels (*Morchella* species), but although technically edible, they are disappointingly bland compared to their European relative, the Yellow Morel (*Morchella esculenta*).

I've often delighted in cooking my local *Boletus granulatas* or *Boletus luteus* picked in selected pine forests, and have dried bucket after bucket of the more mature specimens to great effect. I suspect these are even better than most imported dried cèpes/porcinis, which vary greatly in quality. In Australia I've rarely tasted dried cèpes/porcinis of the quality I've experienced in Europe. I have such a lingering 'flavour memory' of walking down a steep cobbled street – was it in southwest France or in Tuscany? My memory of the place eludes me but it was a market town at breakfast time, and in one of the ancient buildings someone was pan-frying these mushrooms in nut-brown butter; the smell of them cooking on the street as we passed was the most beautiful mushroom smell I've ever experienced. I can smell it now as I write – quite wonderful.

And then there are those wild mushrooms I'm unable to name. During Tasting Australia in 1995 we had a riotous night in the Valley when Antonio Carluccio, the well-known television presenter and mushroom expert, came to stay. It happened to be a Wednesday night, which is the night of my singing group. So before we ate, singing took place and Antonio good-naturedly joined in, and then sat whittling a walking stick for me out of one of the saplings by the dam. There was so much activity that night and, as I had to prepare dinner for twelve after the singing was finished, there wasn't much talk of mushrooms until the next morning. Antonio had been out walking and came back with samples of tiny mushrooms that he said were very edible, which grow in what we've always called 'fairy circles'. One was quite dried out and full of aroma and the others still quite young, so after each rain now I'll wait until they have come into full circle and pick them. For inspiration in cooking wild mushrooms I can recommend Antonio's book *A Passion for Mushrooms*. In his London shop he sells the perfect tool for mushrooming fanatics – it is a knife at one end and a brush at the other, to dust away any debris.

I really must emphasise, though: *always* check with an expert before you eat a wild mushroom, and if remotely unsure it's better not to experiment.

Mushrooms have so much flavour that they can be cooked very simply. A special breakfast can be made by simply pan-frying mushrooms in butter with freshly ground black pepper and serving them on toast. Elizabeth David suggests that if in spring or summer you yearn for field mushrooms, you can bake cultivated mushrooms in vine leaves and olive oil to give a wonderful earthy flavour. It really works!

To make sautéed wild mushrooms on toast, wipe or peel (depending on the condition of the skin) the tops of a basket of boletus mushrooms. Slice them about 8 mm thick. Preheat the oven to 220°C. Cut thick slices of bread such as a baguette, then brush with extra virgin olive oil and rub with garlic. Toast the sliced bread on a baking tray in the oven until golden on both sides. Using a light frying pan, so that heat penetrates quickly (a non-stick one works well), add 2 tablespoons butter and heat until nut-brown, adding a dash of olive oil to stop it from burning. Working in batches, toss the mushrooms through quickly, just sealing each side and adding only enough at one time so the mushrooms are seared to golden brown. Liberally season each batch with salt and freshly ground black pepper and set aside. Take the juices that accumulate in the pan, reduce over high heat and add to the mushrooms with some roughly chopped flat-leaf parsley. Pile atop the croutons and serve.

Smoked mushrooms have a wonderfully intense flavour, and are delicious served as a light appetiser with rosemary and thyme. An easy way to smoke your own mushrooms is using a large wok lined with foil. Soak a few handfuls of vine cuttings or bought wood chips in water for half an hour, then place them in the bottom of the wok, and position a small 'cooling' rack over them. Heat the wok over high heat on the stove until the cuttings or chips begin to smoke (this should take about 10 minutes), then place your mushrooms on the rack, cover the wok with a lid and smoke for about 2 minutes (the mushrooms won't be cooked all the way through).

TRUFFLES

There are certainly indigenous Australian truffles but, as far as I know, no native versions with the scent and flavour of the imported ones. However, there is now a whole industry of truffle growing, which started in Tasmania and has grown to include south west Western Australia. While still in its infancy, it certainly has great potential if the flavour of the truffles matches those of France and Italy.

Just being able to grow truffles, however, is not enough. While in France in 2005 and cooking at La Combe, a beautifully restored farmhouse run by my colleagues Wendeley Harvey and Robert Cave-Rogers, I heard stories at the local markets from the truffle farmers about how beautifully formed Chinese truffles are being imported into France. They have so little aroma, which in truffles equates to flavour, that the importers take out the centres of the Chinese truffles and replace them with wonderfully perfumed French truffle. As truffle permeates everything around it, the French truffle scents the Chinese one; the unsuspecting buyer, sniffing the truffle, will be delighted – at the time of purchase, at least. When they get home and find that the pervasive aroma of the French truffle has faded, they will undoubtedly be most disappointed and, I suspect, very angry.

GERARD MADANI'S MUSHROOM SOUP   *Serves 6*

This recipe comes from Gerard Madani, an exciting chef I worked with at the Hotel Intercontinental in Sydney when I was a guest chef there eons ago. Gerard uses button mushrooms, which can be obtained all year round, for this tasty soup.

1 small onion, chopped
1 kg cultivated button mushrooms,
    roughly sliced
30 g butter
300 ml white wine
bouquet garni (2 stalks flat-leaf parsley,
    2 sprigs thyme, 1 bay leaf, ¼ stick celery,
    ¼ leek)

200 ml veal stock
200 ml Golden Chicken Stock (see page 57)
1 litre cream
6 teaspoons gewürztraminer wine

Sweat the onion and mushrooms in butter, without browning them, in a large saucepan over low heat. Add the white wine and bouquet garni, then increase the heat to high and reduce the liquid by two-thirds. Add the veal and chicken stock and bring to the boil. Add the cream and bring back to the boil, then simmer over low heat for 2 hours. Pass the soup through a fine strainer and season. Pour some of the strained mushroom soup into each warmed soup bowl, along with a teaspoon of the wine, then serve immediately.

PIGEON AND FIELD MUSHROOM PIE   *Serves 6*

6 pigeons
12 golden shallots, peeled
butter, for cooking
350 g field mushrooms, thickly sliced
200 g sugar-cured bacon, cut into strips
½ cup (125 ml) red wine
fresh herbs (whatever is available – I like to
    use thyme, marjoram or oregano)

1 litre reduced Golden Chicken Stock
    (see page 57)
1 × quantity Rough Puff Pastry
    (see page 100)
1 egg, beaten with a little milk
salt

In a frying pan, salt and gently brown the pigeons with the shallots in a little butter over low–medium heat and transfer to a heavy-based cast-iron casserole or saucepan, or use a pressure cooker and follow the manufacturer's instructions (the cooking time will vary enormously, depending on the method of cooking). You could also use a crockpot, an electric casserole-style appliance that cooks very slowly and can be left on low for long periods.

In the same frying pan, quickly toss the mushrooms in a little butter over high heat and transfer to the casserole, then brown the bacon and add to the casserole. Deglaze the frying pan with the red wine, reduce quickly over high heat and add the wine to the casserole, then cover the pigeons with fresh herbs and stock. The six birds may each have different cooking times as most pigeons we buy are wild and of varying ages.

If you are using a pressure cooker, cook using the lowest pressure possible and check every 30 minutes. If there is a lot of liquid remaining at the end of cooking, reduce to the desired consistency, either over high heat on the stove or in the pressure cooker with the lid off. A crockpot could safely be left on low overnight. A pot-roast on top of the stove would have to be checked during the cooking period and perhaps more stock added to the pan; the cooking time could vary from 30 minutes to 3 hours. The pigeons are cooked when the meat easily comes away from the bone in large pieces. Remove from the heat and leave to cool.

Make and chill the pastry as instructed, then preheat the oven to 220°C. When the pigeons have cooled, take the meat off the bones and place in the bottom of a pie dish and spoon over the mushrooms, bacon and juices. Roll out the puff pastry, then cut into a circle slightly larger than the diameter of the pie dish and let it rest in the refrigerator for 20 minutes before putting it over the pie dish and brushing with an egg wash. Bake for about 20 minutes or until the pastry is golden.

RISOTTO WITH MUSHROOMS   *Serves 4*

Years ago now, I greatly enjoyed *Risotto*, by Constance del Nero – a book devoted entirely to this subject. Now that making risottos is so much a part of daily life, many variations are possible.

1.5 litres Golden Chicken Stock
(see page 57) *or* vegetable stock
12 large mushrooms, stalks removed
and reserved, caps sliced
160 g butter, chopped
1 onion, finely chopped

2 cups (400 g) Arborio rice (see Glossary)
190 ml dry white wine
60 g freshly grated Parmigiano Reggiano
2 tablespoons freshly chopped
flat-leaf parsley

Place the stock and mushroom stalks in a large heavy-based saucepan and bring to the boil over high heat, then simmer over low heat for 30 minutes. Keep the stock hot over low heat while making the risotto.

Melt 120 g of the butter in a large cast-iron or enamelled saucepan over low heat. Add the onion and cook gently, stirring, until translucent. Increase the heat to medium, add the rice and stir well to coat with the butter. When the rice glistens, pour in the wine. When the alcohol has evaporated, stir in a ladleful of the hot stock, stirring until it is absorbed. Continue to add ladlefuls of hot stock, one by one and stirring until each has been absorbed, for another 10 minutes. Fold the sliced mushrooms into the risotto. Continue adding stock and stirring for another 10 minutes. The rice should be al dente and there should still be a little liquid left. Remove the pan from the heat and stir in the cheese, parsley and remaining butter.

Serve with a green salad and a dry white wine.

OLIVES

OF THE FEW BOOKS THAT SURVIVED MY FAMILY'S UPHEAVAL WHEN I was a teenager and my parents lost their business were works by Aldous Huxley and Rudyard Kipling. Every now and then I dip into them, glad to have something of my father's that survived. I love the lines in Aldous Huxley's *The Olive Tree*: 'If I could paint and had the necessary time, I should devote myself for a few years to making pictures only of olive trees. What a wealth of variations upon a single theme.'

It is much more accepted these days to be as passionate as I am about olives and, of course, extra virgin olive oil. I love everything about the olive, from the tree to the fruit to the oil, but it took me many years to convince my husband, Colin, of the beauty of the trees. He agreed to plant an olive grove for practical agricultural reasons but, as much as I wanted to have our own olive oil, I would have planted them just for the wonderful landscape they provide. We now have two groves of about 1000 trees for our oil, as well as 40 kalamata trees just for pickling; as it happens, they also make a good oil, but as good pickled olives are quite hard to find I prefer to use them for that.

As a cook and a grower, my greatest passion is reserved for extra virgin olive oil, but I would never want to be without olives for the table. Groves of olives are now a common sight in many areas of Australia and, while wild olive trees remain, they have been declared a noxious weed. Some council areas take this very seriously, while others are happy to leave them in the landscape. Whether used for oil or pickling, the small wild olives have amazing flavour, since most of these trees have the advantage of age, which seems to add flavour, just as an aged vine does to wine. There is certainly much competition in the Greek and Italian communities in Adelaide for these olives, including those from the trees in the Adelaide parklands.

For those lucky enough to have wild olive trees nearby, I urge you to give the fruit a try – no matter how small the olives, you'll find their flavour headily intense. It's a help, too, to get in before the birds start spreading the stones. In South Australia, there was a

Baked olives (see page 265)

very real danger of wild olive trees overtaking our native bush in some areas, and so we watched sadly while councils cut them down, as no one was prepared to accept the responsibility of pruning and picking these trees – I had even tried (unsuccessfully) to gather a group to look after some solitary roadside specimens that bore particularly well. The sad thing was not only to see age-old trees cut down, but to witness the beautiful wood turned into chips or burnt.

If foraging for food is not your style, then a trip to your local market between May and July should yield boxes of fresh olives of many different varieties for pickling. I've never

actually seen them for sale with their varieties named, though kalamatas, which grow particularly well in South Australia, are a great pickling olive and are easily identified by their pointy end. There are lots of olives that I can assure you aren't worth pickling, so it's a good idea to get to know your varieties. All olives start out 'olive green' and turn to green tinged with violet, then purple, then black as they ripen. Each stage has a different taste: the green olive is bitter and tart, with firmer flesh than the riper black olive.

You wouldn't think pickling olives would be difficult – it has been going on for centuries after all. However, the ancient process of pickling with just salt, or salt and water, introduces more pitfalls than you could imagine. It is essential that you use basic but thorough hygiene, sterilise your jars and throw away any olives that develop mould or blisters on them at any stage of the pickling process.

I've been pickling olives on and off for over twenty years now and have had good years and bad. In the early days of the restaurant we'd have quiet times mid-week, so we'd close the doors early afternoon in winter and all go out picking wild olives. This meant I then had buckets and buckets to pickle, so we'd set up the 'service yard' of the restaurant to tackle the forty-day process Stephanie Alexander first talked about in her book *Menus for Food Lovers*.

It was a laborious and messy job but worth it for the result, though I learnt that some olives take a lot longer to pickle than others. The difference in time needed lies in the level of ripeness when you pick the olives – many wild olive trees might have one side full of really black but unripe fruit and super-ripe fruit on the other side (if the tree is not in full sun, the fruit will not be nearly as ripe). Some olives take months to lose their bitterness, so just keep trying them – don't be reckless and throw away all your good work just because some of the olives are bitter.

Having wondered in the past why one bucket might spoil and others not, I was anxious before starting on this year's olives to find out as much as I could, but little has been written about the process. One occasional problem I have had has been the formation of a gas pocket, apparently the most common defect of table olives. Nothing can be done, and you must throw them out. If you were producing on a semi-commercial scale, this would certainly be cause for concern as it is an indication of bacteria being present.

None of this should stop you from following your neighbours' favourite recipe, particularly if they are Italian or Greek, but it's worth trying to pickle a small batch first. If luck is with you, the olives will be delicious and you'll eat them so quickly that 'keeping qualities' won't be an issue.

For several years I've used the dry-salt method of pickling for wild olives, layering 10-litre cream buckets, with holes in the bottom, alternately with olives first, then salt, until the bucket is about two-thirds full. The olives then need to be weighted down and the buckets covered and left for at least a month. This method leaves the olives very crinkled and dry and very salty, but their flavour intensifies amazingly – though I still don't have the secret for getting it right every time.

In 2000 we picked our own kalamatas for the first time; 40 trees gave us 80 kg, not a huge quantity but enough to trial salt-curing. They were sweeter and nuttier than any other olives I have tasted. I'm sure the success was due to a combination of variety, climate and terroir (soil), but perhaps most of all because we picked and cured the olives immediately.

If you're considering a semi-commercial operation, I urge you to get a copy of a fairly new paper, 'Processing Technology of the Table Olive', by Suzanne Colmagro, Graham Collins and Margaret Sedgley from the University of Adelaide. Suzanne chased every lead she had, researching and talking to everyone she could find with practical experience of pickling olives. The paper has an academic tone, as you would expect, and it gives more information on what not to do rather than including the perfect recipe but, as there is such potential in this burgeoning olive industry of ours, it's important to spread the word of any research that assists in maximising both flavour and quality.

With thousands of olive trees being planted across Australia, another essential read for olive lovers is Patrice Newell's *The Olive Grove*. This wonderful book gives a great account of the practicalities of starting out. It may take the romance out of the idea of growing olives for some, but this is farming after all.

The commercial pickling process uses a lye solution (potassium hydroxide), instead of water and salt. This, for me, has huge disadvantages: the olives lose flavour and texture, the lye masks the natural colour and then the lye has to be disposed of after processing, which can cause environmental problems. Lye-treated olives can be readily identified, as they are uniformly deep black.

Commercially prepared olives also differ in quality, depending on how they are pickled. Kalamatas are the most consistently high-quality black olive, though be wary of cheaper imports. Treating olives with water and salt is a longer and more expensive process, but the flavour is far more 'olivey', with a desirable edge of bitterness and some loss of colour.

Only a tiny proportion of the kalamatas consumed in Australia is grown here. Look out for the superb Coriole Kalamatas from South Australia, sold in cryovac packs. Kalamatas picked ripe go well with orange, thyme and rosemary or oregano; or orange, garlic and bay leaves; or thyme leaves, chopped flat-leaf parsley and tiny dice of preserved lemon; or honey and quince; or even toasted cumin seeds and tiny dice of raw fennel, finely chopped chilli and garlic and a fresh bay leaf.

Olives are best of all when bought from local groves, where they are sold in cryovac packs without any additives or extra flavourings. Some small producers, both local and international, present their olives in wine vinegar and olive oil, and these are worth seeking out. Avoid those pre-sliced black olives often used in commercial pasta dishes and pizzas – they taste like rubber. I also abhor the olives that are sold in supermarkets with stale dried herbs or chillies and poor-quality oil.

To marinate your own, start with good olives as a base and toss in your best extra virgin olive oil with some rosemary or thyme and, particularly if using kalamatas, some orange rind. In some gourmet shops you'll find Ligurian or Taggiasche olives from Italy. These are tiny wild olives with a large stone and not a great deal of flesh but an incredible intensity of flavour.

I keep an earthenware crock on the kitchen bench filled with olives immersed in brine or a mix of olive oil and wine vinegar. A harmless mould may form on the surface and can be removed – not with your fingers, which will introduce bacteria, but with an olive spoon (a wooden ladle with holes). There is no need to refrigerate them unless you've added flavourings that may perish, such as citrus or garlic cloves. If you do so, bring them to room temperature before use.

To cook with olives, bear in mind that they taste better when cooked with the stones in (but warn your guests) and that heating makes the flavour more intense. To bake olives, just cover the base of a baking dish with olives, olive oil, fresh chillies (if so inclined), cloves of garlic and rosemary, and bake in a 180°C oven until the olives are wrinkly and the garlic is cooked through. Add to pizzas, breads or polenta or toss through pasta with a roasted tomato sauce. Or add olives to pot-roasting lamb, kid, duck or veal, but only during the last part of the cooking or the dish will be too salty. Make a sauce from puréed pitted olives, fresh oregano, some chicken stock and a touch of cream to serve with poultry or rabbit.

You can make dips with olives; better still, make a classic tapenade where they are minced with extra virgin olive oil, capers and anchovies; try adding a splash of Cognac to the batch, and then serve with freshly toasted bread. You can also add olives to salads (not the pre-pitted pitch-black ones though), such as a classic Niçoise.

I've come to love green olives but finding really good ones is difficult. Large green olives are too large to pit with an olive or cherry pipping tool, but you can buy good-quality pitted green olives called Conserviera. Plump and fleshy, they are good for stuffing, especially with an anchovy. Or try deep-frying olives filled with meat or cheese.

I've given up trying to pickle green olives myself – I suspect they require quite different varieties to those we grow. One day I'll put together the cracked green olives with orange blossom tossed in extra virgin olive oil that I've heard so much about but never tried.

BAKED OLIVES
Serves 6–8

2 cups pickled olives

2 cloves garlic, finely chopped

rind of 1 orange, thinly sliced

4 bay leaves

⅓ cup (80 ml) extra virgin olive oil

2 tablespoons verjuice *or* lemon juice

2 teaspoons chopped rosemary

Preheat the oven to 180°C. Toss the olives with garlic, orange rind, bay leaves, olive oil and verjuice or lemon juice. Place in a baking dish and bake for 5–10 minutes. Leave to cool just a little before serving. If all the moisture is absorbed, add extra olive oil and verjuice or lemon juice along with the chopped rosemary, then serve with drinks.

GREEN OLIVE GNOCCHI WITH GREEN OLIVE SAUCE
Serves 4

This is one of my family's favourite comfort foods. My younger daughter Elli in particular will always ask for green olive gnocchi – and don't forget the sauce, Mum!

750 g desiree potatoes

125 g plain flour

freshly grated nutmeg, to taste

sea salt flakes and freshly ground
　black pepper

20 large green olives, pitted and
　finely chopped

2 egg yolks

butter, for pan-frying

SAUCE

3 cloves garlic, finely chopped

1 large onion, finely chopped

1 tablespoon extra virgin olive oil

100 ml Golden Chicken Stock
　(see page 57)

100 ml cream

200 g green olives, pitted and chopped

lemon juice, to taste

Steam the potatoes until cooked right through and mash while still warm. Allow to cool a little and then add flour, nutmeg, salt, pepper and chopped olives. Mix in the egg yolks to make a fairly firm dough. Knead it gently for a few minutes, then divide it into quarters and leave to rest on the bench for 20 minutes.

Bring a large saucepan of salted water to the boil. Roll each dough quarter into logs, 1 cm in diameter. Cut logs into 1 cm lengths and cover with a damp tea towel while you wait for the water to boil. Gently place the gnocchi into boiling water, and as they come to the surface, cook them for 1 minute. Remove with a slotted spoon and set aside.

To make the sauce, sweat the garlic and onion in olive oil in a saucepan over medium heat until softened. Add the chicken stock and cream and bring to the boil. Add the olives and adjust the flavour with lemon juice if necessary. Leave to cool a little before puréeing in a blender, and then return to the clean pan to gently reheat.

Just before serving, pan-fry the gnocchi in a frying pan in some nut-brown butter for a minute or two until they are golden brown. Serve with the warmed sauce.

AILEEN'S OLIVE BREAD   *Makes 2 loaves*

Aileen Proudfoot, such an important member of our restaurant and pâté-making team for so many years, was incredibly talented at everything she put her hand to, whether it was making fabulous bread, arranging flowers, or creating wonderful gardens from scratch.

2 tablespoons rosemary, finely chopped	15 g dried yeast
2 tablespoons extra virgin olive oil	⅔ cup pitted black *or* green olives
5⅓ cups (850 g) strong flour (see Glossary), plus extra for flouring	about 2 cups (500 ml) warm water (the exact amount used varies every time, depending
large pinch salt	on the weather, humidity and flour)

Fry the rosemary in the olive oil in a small frying pan until fragrant, then set aside. In a large bowl, mix the flour, salt, yeast and the rosemary oil mixture. Make a well in the centre, then add the pitted olives and begin to pour in the warm water to make the dough.

When the mixture reaches the desired consistency of a soft dough, remove to a floured bench and knead until smooth and satiny to the touch – this will take at least 15 minutes by hand. Smear the bowl with a little olive oil and return the dough to the bowl, then leave covered with a wet tea towel or plastic film for 1½ hours or until the dough doubles in size. Knock back the dough and shape it into rolls or loaves as required. Put on trays or in 2 greased loaf tins and leave to rise again for another 20 minutes, covered with a damp tea towel. Meanwhile, preheat the oven to 220°C.

Bake bread for 15–20 minutes, then turn upside-down and bake for another 5 minutes. Turn out onto a wire rack to cool. Eat with unsalted butter.

PARTRIDGE

 PARTRIDGE ARE LITTLE KNOWN IN AUSTRALIA, BUT WHEN WE had them on our menu at the Pheasant Farm Restaurant their delicate flavour was always commented on, and for many customers it reawakened wonderful memories of eating partridge in Europe, particularly England.

Rather than the grey and red-legged partridge known in Europe, the chukhar breed is farmed in Australia (the French are now crossing the chukhar and red-legged partridge, although the latter breed still dominates there). The meat of the chukhar is not as dark as that of the grey and red-legged partridge, but once you have mastered the cooking technique it is full of flavour. The birds range in size from 350 to 500 g, making them a perfect main course for one person.

Farming partridge commercially is frustrating, as my husband Colin and I know only too well. It is almost impossible to sex the birds, which is problematic since the hen is tenderer than the cockerel. All partridge, young or old, look identical and don't become scrawny with age as a pheasant does. As there is such a difference in how a young and an old bird of any species should be cooked, mistaking old for young and vice versa can be disastrous for the cook. A gate left open between runs caused much confusion in our first breeding season. Another year, my daughter Saskia came running in to say she had found a partridge walking down the track to the farm (the whole breeding stock, it transpired, had wandered off through an open gate).

In 1993 we finally had our first real season's breeding, of just a few hundred birds. It coincided with a huge dinner that Marjorie Coates, of Vintners Restaurant, and I put on at Seppeltsfield for the Barossa Vintage Festival. We based the main course on a 'partridge in a pear tree' theme, and I roasted the birds at home and then ferried them up the road to Seppeltsfield while the meat was resting. Working on low trestle tables in a makeshift kitchen set up in a huge tent, we cooked pears and caramelised garlic and pancetta while the birds were carved. As that dinner took almost the whole year's supply, I only had a few partridges with which to experiment before the restaurant closed later that year. After all those years of trying and almost giving up on the breeding, I now find it sad not to have more opportunities to cook and serve this bird.

The demand for our partridges fluctuated almost as much as the number we were able to successfully produce each year. One year we'd breed a large number, and nobody would be interested, then the next we'd have a bad hatching and only produce a few birds, and

demand would be sky-high. Colin had all but decided to give it up, when one year both Stephanie Alexander and Sydney chef Kylie Kwong decided they loved the birds. Stephanie and I cooked her delicious partridge pies together for special dinners at her Richmond Hill Cafe and Larder. After a weekend retreat in the Barossa with us, Kylie came up with a wonderful recipe for partridges using Chinese master stock, so very different to the way either Stephanie or I had cooked them before. However, this flutter of popularity would be short-lived, and again partridges would be off the menu. While Colin no longer breeds partridges in any great numbers, there are a few other small producers, including Ian Milburn of Glenloth Game in Victoria, and Game Farm in New South Wales.

If you can get your hands on partridge they make a very special dinner, but be warned, the legs and breast need different cooking methods, unless you use a recipe like Stephanie's Partridge Pies (see page 273). I can tell you that the lard pastry, which encases these pies, is truly magnificent – perfectly flaky and tender.

The breast of the partridge is the prime part of the bird. No matter how hard you try, if you cook the bird whole, the legs will always be on the chewy side. Even though I think we are a little too fixated on everything needing to melt in the mouth (I would much prefer to have flavour than melt-in-the-mouth blandness), the trick to avoiding chewy legs is to separate the breast from the legs, keeping the breast on the frame and both legs connected in one piece. The only time I deviate from this is if I am grilling partridge. In this case, I 'spatchcock' the bird by cutting it down the spine and, with the cut-side down on the bench, squash it as flat as I can with the palm of my hand.

When cooking spatchcocked partridge, you must be sure you have a young bird with a certain amount of fat. I make a marinade of walnut oil, verjuice, fresh thyme and freshly ground black pepper and turn the bird in this mixture for several hours. The marinated, salted partridge can be cooked on a chargrill plate, where it should be turned frequently to prevent it charring too much, or it can be brushed with the marinade and roasted at 250°C. Either way, the bird will take 10–15 minutes to cook, with about 10 minutes resting time away from the heat. If you've roasted the partridge, deglaze the roasting pan with a good dash of verjuice and a few tablespoons of reduced chicken stock to make a delicious jus. Surprisingly, a warm Anchovy Vinaigrette (see page 343) is a wonderful accompaniment, too.

Partridges, grapes and vine leaves or pancetta are a heady combination and, while cooking poultry on the bone always produces more flavour, there are times when it is handy to do the boning in advance. To stuff boned partridges, sweat a finely chopped onion and a couple of garlic cloves in extra virgin olive oil until softened, then combine with breadcrumbs made from day-old bread, sage leaves crisped in butter and seedless green grapes. Pack the stuffing into the boned partridges so that the birds regain their shape, then wrap them in either pancetta or fresh vine leaves poached in verjuice and brush them with walnut oil and more verjuice. Grill the birds if you have a good griller, otherwise roast them at 230°C for 10–15 minutes in a shallow roasting pan turning over halfway through the cooking (so that they get a good blast of heat all over), with 10 minutes resting time. To caramelise the skin, seal the salted birds first in nut-brown butter on the stove. Serve the partridge with a vinaigrette of 125 ml walnut oil, 2 tablespoons verjuice, ½ teaspoon champagne vinegar (or a good squeeze of lemon juice), a small handful of seedless green grapes and 30 g roasted and skinned walnuts.

If you need further inspiration for using partridge, you will find it in Spanish cookbooks. I love roasted or grilled partridge with pomegranate sauce. More of a vinaigrette than a sauce, almond oil is combined with pomegranate juice, then pomegranate seeds are added at the last moment before the lot is poured over the cooked bird. Wonderful! The classic Catalan paste of ground almonds, garlic and sherry that I use with pheasant (see page 193) is equally good with partridge.

Escabeche, the Spanish technique of steeping cooked fish or poultry in a hot marinade and then leaving it to cool for 24 hours, is great when partridge breast meat and legs, herbs and garlic are used. It was acclaimed Australian chef Cheong Liew who first taught me how to do this, years ago when we were exploring ways of using every possible part of the pheasant. When I first tried it I cooked the birds three-quarters of the way through, knowing that the hot marinade would continue the cooking. However, I also know that dealing with partially cooked poultry is like playing with fire, so I now recommend simmering spatchcocked birds for about 25 minutes in 2 parts red-wine vinegar to 1 part mild extra virgin olive oil and 1 part water, with lots of peeled garlic cloves, fresh bay leaves, black peppercorns and sprigs of thyme – make sure the birds are completely covered. After cooking, remove the pan from the stove and leave to cool to room temperature. The birds can be refrigerated in their cooking juices for 24 hours. Escabeche is served at room temperature, making it perfect for eating outdoors in our glorious autumn weather.

PARTRIDGE 'PUDDINGS' WITH SULTANAS AND VERJUICE   *Serves 4*

In 1994, Peter and Margaret Lehmann, winemakers and friends of ours, asked me to do a series of dinners in Melbourne and Sydney to launch their Stonewall shiraz. As our restaurant was no longer running by then, this seemed the perfect opportunity to showcase these birds, in a dish that was the essence of the Barossa. The Grand Hyatt in Melbourne and the Regent in Sydney allowed me to cook with their teams on the night, and we put on a true Barossa show in the big smoke.

1½ tablespoons sultanas

verjuice, for soaking

2 partridge

¼ cup (60 ml) walnut oil

2 tablespoons verjuice

2 sprigs thyme, leaves picked

freshly ground black pepper

1 carrot, roughly chopped

1 stick celery, roughly chopped

1 onion, roughly chopped

extra virgin olive oil, for cooking

¼ cup (60 ml) white wine

butter, for greasing

6 rashers very thinly cut streaky bacon,
    rind removed

Soak the sultanas overnight in enough verjuice to just cover them.

Next day, remove the breast meat from each partridge. Gently flatten each breast between sheets of baking paper with a wooden mallet until even, then cut into 2 cm pieces. In a bowl, mix the walnut oil, 2 tablespoons verjuice, thyme leaves and pepper and marinate the breast meat in this while you make the stock.

Preheat the oven to 220°C. Toss the carrot, celery, onion, partridge carcasses and legs in a roasting pan with a little olive oil and roast for 30–40 minutes or until caramelised. Over high heat on the stove, deglaze the pan with the wine and tip the contents into a stockpot. Barely cover the vegetables and bones with water, then simmer over low heat for 2 hours to make a flavoursome stock. Remove the stockpot from the heat, strain the stock into a bowl, then chill it and remove any excess fat when cold.

Pour 250 ml of the stock into a clean saucepan with 125 ml verjuice and reduce by two-thirds over medium heat, then remove from the heat. As it cools, the stock will become quite jellied.

Preheat the oven to 180°C. Smear the base and sides of 4 soufflé dishes or dariole moulds with butter and then line them with the bacon, reserving enough to cover the dishes later on. Remove the soaked sultanas and discard the verjuice. Layer the marinated meat, sultanas and jellied stock in the bacon-lined dishes until each has been filled. Top with the remaining bacon and cover with baking paper.

Stand the dishes in a roasting pan filled with boiling water, making sure the water comes two-thirds of the way up the sides of the dishes, then bake for 20 minutes. Carefully remove the pan from the oven, then the dishes from the pan. Leave them to cool a little before gently inverting them onto serving plates. Heat the leftover jellied stock and spoon it over the warm 'puddings' before serving with lamb's lettuce (mâche) or other delicate green salad.

PARTRIDGE WITH SAVOY CABBAGE, PANCETTA, WALNUTS AND VERJUICE

Serves 4

Partridge with cabbage has to be the most traditional of combinations and was the one I rejected for the longest. I'm now sorry I did, as Savoy cabbage, properly cooked, is the perfect foil to the richness and density of partridge breast. If you don't have a really large casserole it may be better to split the following ingredients between two dishes.

24 shelled walnuts

8 thin slices pancetta

4 partridge

juice of 1 lemon

sea salt flakes and freshly ground
   black pepper

¼ cup duck fat

1 large sprig rosemary, leaves picked
   and chopped

1 Savoy cabbage, trimmed, cored
   and shredded

1 cup (250 ml) verjuice

butter, for cooking

Preheat the oven to 220°C. Dry-roast the walnuts on a baking tray for 6 minutes, then rub off the skins with a clean tea towel and put the nuts aside. At the same time, place the pancetta on a baking tray and crisp in the oven, then put on kitchen paper to drain.

Separate the legs from the breast of each partridge, keeping both legs attached and in one piece and the breast on the frame. Squeeze lemon juice into the cavity of each bird and season. Melt the duck fat with half the rosemary over low–medium heat in a large heavy-based enamelled casserole dish with a tight-fitting lid. Brown the partridge pieces very slowly on all sides over low heat until almost cooked through. Don't crowd the pan or the skin will poach rather than caramelise – do it in batches if necessary. Remove the partridge from the casserole and set aside, reserving the duck fat in the pan.

Toss the cabbage in the reserved duck fat in the casserole over medium heat and season it very well, then return the partridge to the pan. Pour in the verjuice and cover with the lid. Increase the heat to high so that the verjuice reduces, the cabbage cooks in about 3–5 minutes and the cooking of the partridge is complete. The breasts may be ready before the legs. If the breasts feel firm, take them out and keep them warm and covered (the legs may only need a few more minutes – check by piercing a leg at its thickest point to see if the juices run clear).

In a frying pan, heat a knob of butter with the remaining rosemary until nut-brown, then toss in the walnuts. Discard the rosemary and tip the walnuts and butter into the cabbage, along with the crisp pancetta. Serve immediately.

KYLIE KWONG'S CHINESE-STYLE PARTRIDGE WITH
POMEGRANATE-CARAMEL SAUCE

Serves 6

3 partridge

CHINESE MASTER STOCK

3 litres cold water

1½ cups (375 ml) Shao Hsing rice wine
   or dry sherry

1 cup (250 ml) dark soy sauce

½ cup (125 ml) light soy sauce

1 cup (220 g) brown sugar

6 cloves garlic, crushed with back of knife

½ cup unpeeled ginger slices

4 spring onions, trimmed and
   halved lengthways

½ teaspoon sesame oil

5 star anise

2 cinnamon sticks

3 strips orange rind

POMEGRANATE-CARAMEL SAUCE

¼ cup (55 g) brown sugar

2½ tablespoons fish sauce

2 tablespoons lime juice

2 pomegranates, seeds removed and
   juice reserved

**SICHUAN SALT AND PEPPER
(OPTIONAL)**

1 tablespoon Sichuan pepper

¼ cup sea salt flakes

For the Chinese master stock, place all the ingredients in a large stockpot and bring to the boil over high heat. Reduce heat to low and simmer gently for 40 minutes to allow the flavours to infuse. Meanwhile, rinse the partridge under cold water. Trim away any excess fat from inside and outside the cavities, but keep the necks, parson's noses and winglets intact.

Lower partridges, breast-side down, into the simmering stock, ensuring they are fully submerged. Poach birds over low heat for exactly 9 minutes. There should be no more than an occasional ripple breaking the surface; adjust the temperature, if necessary, to ensure that stock does not reach simmering point again. Remove stockpot immediately from the stove and allow birds to steep in the stock for 2 hours at room temperature to complete the cooking process.

Using tongs, gently remove birds from the stock, being careful not to tear the breast skin. Place them on a tray or a plate and leave to cool.

For the sauce, melt sugar and fish sauce in a heavy-based saucepan over medium heat, stirring until sugar dissolves to create a caramel. Add lime juice and pomegranate seeds and juice. The texture should be thick, runny and caramel-like, and the flavour should be intense – salty, sour and sweet all at once. Remove from heat and set aside.

For the Sichuan salt and pepper, dry-roast pepper and salt in a heavy-based saucepan over medium–high heat. When the pepper begins to 'pop' and become aromatic, remove from the heat. Leave to cool, then grind using a spice grinder or a mortar and pestle.

Carve partridge as required and smother them in the sauce before serving. Sprinkle with Sichuan pepper and salt, if using.

STEPHANIE'S PARTRIDGE PIES
Makes 8 muffin-sized pies

Stephanie Alexander has been a part of my food life ever since we met at the first Symposium of Gastronomy in Adelaide over twenty years ago. Through the intervening years we've travelled together many times and I'm always in awe of her knowledge of any food matter that we're presented with. Ever since our holiday in Italy in the early 1990s, which led to the Tuscan cooking school we held, we've had so many food adventures together, along with my husband Colin and a group of close friends, across many countries. We are always armed with Stephanie's research about not-to-be-missed food experiences, and we have a lot of fun together. Here is Stephanie's melt-in-the-mouth partridge pie recipe, utilising Colin's partridges.

1 × quantity Stephanie's Lard Pastry
(see page 250)
120 g fat pork belly
120 g partridge leg meat, plus heart and liver
1 clove garlic, chopped
120 g minced chicken
20 g foie gras *or* rich liver pâté,
finely chopped

salt
pinch Quatre-Épices (see page 358)
2 teaspoons Armagnac
1 egg
dash milk

Make and chill the pastry following the instructions.

Preheat the oven to 200°C. Mince the pork in a food processor, then add the partridge and garlic and mince again. Mix well with the minced chicken, then add the foie gras and combine. Season with salt and quatre-épices, then add the Armagnac.

Roll out pastry to 5 mm thick, then cut out 16 pastry rounds slightly larger than the diameter of the holes of a 12-hole muffin tin. Line 8 of the holes with pastry rounds and spoon in the filling. Cover with remaining pastry rounds and seal well. Beat the egg with a dash of milk and brush the pastry with this egg wash, then bake for 5 minutes. Lower oven temperature to 180°C and cook for another 30 minutes or until golden.

PEARS

WHEN WE FIRST BOUGHT OUR PROPERTY IN 1987, THERE WERE three pear trees in the garden that were each more than a hundred years old. They still bore prolifically, but over the years we lost two to white ants and wind damage (though we rescued the pear wood from one of the trees and it's still 'curing', ready to be made into furniture). The remaining tree at the bottom of the garden is by the side of the dam with the well at its feet.

Every year this wonderful pear tree blossoms on the first weekend in October, which happens to be during our Barossa Music Festival. In the years when it coincides with the dam being full, it is the most beautiful place on earth to us. After a couple of weeks in full bloom the petals start to fall at the first strong wind. That's when I love to be home, having friends for a drink under the pear tree with the blossoms falling gently upon us.

The year before last we had our biggest winter rains in ten years and the pears were better than ever. Contrast that with this year, our worst drought ever, and the pears are dropping before maturity from lack of water. Considering how old our tree is, except in times of drought it crops amazingly well, and each year my husband Colin and our friend Peter Wall talk about making pear wine. They have it all worked out, but somehow neither of them ever has the time – there is always next year! In the meantime the fruit is not wasted, as we stack green pears into wooden boxes and store them in the cellar to use in the winter, the perfume lingering long after the last one has been eaten.

Living in the Barossa has given me such a sentimental attachment to pear trees. It is said that the Silesian settlers planted pear trees here even before building their houses, to make the well water sweet. Many grand old specimens are still standing, but as I look down from my attic window, our magnificent pear tree, older and taller than the cottage itself, is to me the most beautiful of all those I've seen.

Sentimentality aside, I do have a practical streak too. As soon as we realised we would lose two of the original three trees, we resolved to carry on the tradition, and planted five

Glazed pears (see page 282)

of the best eating varieties available to us. Those beautiful old trees were so tall that you could almost touch the blossom from the attic windows – the new trees won't reach such heights in our lifetime, but planting trees for our grandchildren and their grandchildren to enjoy is what we do.

Our first choice was the doyenné du comice, as I'd read so much about this being the *crème de la crème* of pears. They fruited for the first time this year; I picked the pears green and firm and ripened them in darkness (as you should with all pears to achieve maximum flavour), but 4 weeks have passed and I'm still waiting to see the telltale yellow flesh that indicates ripeness. My pear expert from the Barossa Farmers' Market, Margaret Ellis, tells me I should have put them in a brown paper bag to hasten the ripening (along with a banana, the ethylene in which speeds the process up even more). Over the years I've had lots of experience of leaving pears on the tree too long so that they become brown around

the core, so perhaps I moved a little too early this time, even though they came off the tree into my hand easily, which is one of the signs to look for. Maybe next time I will wait until the blush of pink on the skins is a little more intense.

We planted two trees that bear the tiny bella face pears, which are the perfect size for pickling whole. They grow particularly upright in stance, which makes them wonderfully easy trees to pick from and great to espalier against a wall.

Then we planted a Bartlett, also known as Williams or Duchess, which, contrary to widely held opinion, produces fabulous eating pears. When they are perfectly ripe and the skin has turned from green to pale yellow, and as long as they are not bruised, the pears are so juicy and delectable that every bit can be eaten, even the core, which seems to almost disappear into the flesh.

The last tree we planted was the brown beurre bosc, with its elegantly shaped fruit; so good to eat raw and wonderful to cook with. Sadly, this year the tree produced just one pear, with almost none of its usual russet colour (Margaret Ellis says this is because of the drought). I love beurre boscs peeled and poached in red wine with a stick of cinnamon, a vanilla bean or a piece of fresh ginger, or roasted or grilled to serve in a salad or as an accompaniment to game.

Whilst there are other varieties I'd like to plant or graft onto existing trees, like the winter cole and of course the corella (that beautifully rosy pear that began its life here in the Barossa), I'm not so tempted to grow the Packham triumph, a larger, knobbly pear that's probably the most widely available, as one of my guiding principles is to grow lesser-known varieties of fruit and vegetables that have great flavour.

As you'll rarely find pears in the greengrocer's in perfect condition for eating (if they were truly ripe they would be instantly bruised), buy your pears green and ripen them at home in a brown paper bag with a banana inside (don't keep them in the fridge).

Other than eating a ripe pear and experiencing the joy of having the juice dribble down your arm, what else can you do with this fruit? Eat pears dried or pickled, or make wine or liqueur with them. Pears and cheese are a traditional coupling: a firm, but not unripe, green pear, a slab of Parmigiano Reggiano and some new season's extra virgin olive oil is top of my list. A pear that is to be served with a blue cheese should be riper, as should a pear that is to be sliced and served on a bed of bitter greens with chunks of goat's cheese or blue cheese, roasted walnuts and a vinaigrette of walnut oil and lemon juice.

I love using pears in salad, either raw with rocket and Parmigiano Reggiano, or grilled or pan-fried in butter and then, whilst still warm, tossed together with fennel, watercress, prosciutto and a few dollops of gorgonzola. Such a simple combination, but what great flavours it produces.

I like a soup so intense that you need nothing else but a salad of bitter greens and crusty bread to complete the meal. Stilton soup, a rich number, is taken to another dimension if a pear purée is spooned on top just before serving. Roasted and ground walnuts cooked with a good reduced chicken stock then puréed can be finished with the same pear purée and served with a watercress salad.

Pears are an all-time dessert favourite. Perhaps my favourite way of preparing them is to make a compote of pears with quince and a vanilla bean and serve it with a vanilla Crème Anglaise (see page 225). Or sprinkle pears with a little sugar, dot them with knobs of butter and squeeze over a little lemon juice, then bake at 180°C for about 20 minutes before turning the oven up to 230°C or so for another 10 minutes to caramelise them – these are fantastic served with mascarpone or vanilla ice cream. Either fresh or dried pears can be poached in sugar syrup with verjuice or lemon juice added to give bite, then topped with a large dollop of cream. The combination of pear and chocolate works every time, especially when it comes to hot baked pears served with a richer-than-rich chocolate custard and super-cold slices of pear (skin on), or pear crumble with chocolate buttons mixed through the crumble mix.

SUN-DRIED PEARS, FARM FOLLIES STYLE

Peel and core firm, ripe pears. Place them in salted water as you go, then leave them for 15 minutes. This stops them going brown and also aids the drying. Lay the pears on wire racks in the hot sun, turning them as they dry. The exterior should form a skin, leaving the flesh moist inside. Store the dried pears in sealed airtight jars with sachets of silica gel (available from chemists).

Pan-fried pears with fennel, prosciutto, watercress and gorgonzola (see page 277)

DRIED PEARS POACHED IN VERJUICE   *Serves 4*

This is a savoury dish which can be used to make a perfect cool-weather salad, with rocket and radicchio, if in season, and slices of prosciutto. Add walnuts that have been roasted then rubbed of their skins, then toss the salad with a little extra virgin olive oil and slivers of blue cheese, bocconcini or goat's curd.

200 g dried pears	2 fresh bay leaves
1½ cups (375 ml) verjuice	6 black peppercorns
rind of 1 lemon	

Place all the ingredients in a heavy-based saucepan. Slowly bring to the boil over medium heat, then immediately reduce the heat to low and simmer for 8 minutes or until the dried pears are soft. Set aside, leaving pears to cool in the poaching liquid.

When the pears are cool, take out of the liquid and pat dry; this liquid can be used again for poaching or in the next vinaigrette you make.

POACHED PEARS ON FILO PASTRY WITH MASCARPONE   *Serves 6*

The same amount of dried peaches or nectarines could be used instead of pears.

1 cup (250 ml) verjuice	6 sheets filo pastry
½ cup (110 g) castor sugar	unsalted butter, melted, for brushing
200 g dried pears (about 12 pears)	200 ml mascarpone *or* thick double cream

To make the syrup, bring verjuice and sugar to the boil in a stainless steel saucepan over high heat, stirring until sugar has dissolved. Boil for 5 minutes or until syrupy. Add dried pears, then cover and poach gently over low heat for 20 minutes. Remove pears and set aside to cool. Increase heat to high and reduce syrup by half then set aside.

Preheat the oven to 200°C. Using a saucer as a template, cut 3 even circles into each sheet of filo pastry. Brush each circle with melted butter, then layer 3 filo circles on top of each other to make a total of 6 rounds. Place filo rounds on a baking tray lined with baking paper, then put the cooled dried pears atop the filo rounds, brushing the pears with the reduced syrup.

Bake for 8 minutes or until filo is crisp. Serve drizzled with extra syrup and a good dollop of mascarpone or double cream.

A TRIFLE OF PEARS, PRUNES AND SAUTERNES CUSTARD   *Serves 12*

I was tremendously fortunate to have the staff I did at the Pheasant Farm Restaurant, particularly in our last year, when Alex Herbert joined us; a driven person with so much talent and dedication, she always strove for perfection. I was very lucky to have her, along with my talented apprentice Natalie Paull and the always wonderful Steve Flamsteed. These three were the core of a group that made the last four months of the restaurant's life seem like one huge, exhausting party. It was the most exciting cooking time of my life. I knew that all those who came to my restaurant in those last weeks truly trusted me and, for the first time ever, I was able to throw caution to the wind. Nat called it organised chaos. All the team did an amazing job but Alex, Nat and Steve live in the history books of our family.

Alex and her husband have since moved to Sydney, where they became partners in their own restaurant, Bird Cow Fish, originally in Balmain and now in Surry Hills. This dessert of Alex's is for a special occasion – it's extravagant but marvellous. When I make it, the verjuice, pears, walnuts, lemons and eggs all come from our farm. I have always meant to make my own prunes, and am a step closer now that I have my own d'Agen prune plum tree. I should also put Sauternes production on the must-do list, but that's more of a pipe-dream!

This trifle can be moulded in a bowl and turned out after 24 hours, or it can be served from a traditional glass trifle bowl just a few hours after it has been made. Although it seems complicated, if done in two stages over two days, it is quite simple.

75 g shelled walnuts
375 g prunes, pitted
1½ cups (375 ml) Sauternes
½ vanilla bean
1 stick cinnamon
rind of 1 lemon, in large strips
8 beurre bosc pears
1½ cups (375 ml) verjuice
¼ cup (55 g) castor sugar
8 good-quality Italian macaroons

SYLLABUB
finely grated rind and juice of 1 lemon
2 tablespoons brandy
2 tablespoons castor sugar
300 ml thick cream
freshly grated nutmeg, to taste

GÉNOISE SPONGE
6 free-range eggs, separated
200 g castor sugar
135 g plain flour
100 ml melted clarified butter

CUSTARD
3 cups (750 ml) Sauternes
16 egg yolks
250 g castor sugar
1 litre 35 per cent fat cream
    (see Glossary)

Make the syllabub a day in advance. Put the lemon rind and juice into a bowl with the brandy and let steep for 12 hours. Next day, strain the brandy and lemon mixture into a large, deep bowl, then add the castor sugar and stir until it has dissolved. Pour in the cream slowly, stirring all the time. Grate in a little nutmeg, then whisk the mixture until it thickens and holds a soft peak on the whisk. Refrigerate until needed.

For the génoise sponge, preheat the oven to 190°C. Grease and line a round 26 cm cake tin. Beat the egg whites until soft peaks form, then beat in the castor sugar a tablespoon at a time until the mixture is stiff and all the sugar has been absorbed. Spoon a quarter of the egg white mixture into the yolks, fold it in then pour the lot back over the remaining egg white mixture and fold through. Sift the flour on top and then carefully fold it in. Fold in the cooled clarified butter to make a batter.

Pour the batter into the prepared tin and bake for 25 minutes or until the cake begins to come away from the sides of the tin and feels springy. Cool on a wire rack.

For the custard, heat the Sauternes in a saucepan over high heat and reduce it by half (you need 375 ml). In a bowl, whisk the egg yolks, then beat in the castor sugar until it has dissolved. In a saucepan, heat the cream until almost at boiling point, then add the reduced Sauternes and bring back to almost a boil over high heat, then add this to the egg mixture, whisking thoroughly and continuously. Pour the custard into the top of a double boiler over simmering water and cook it slowly until it coats the back of a spoon, then quickly strain it through a sieve into a clean bowl standing in iced water. If you don't have a double boiler, use a heatproof bowl that fits snugly over a pan of boiling water.

Preheat the oven to 220°C. Dry-roast the walnuts on a baking tray for 6–8 minutes, then rub off their skins with a clean tea towel. Soak the prunes in the Sauternes with the vanilla bean, cinnamon stick and lemon rind for 30 minutes. Peel and core the pears, then cut them into eighths and poach them gently over low heat in a saucepan with the verjuice and castor sugar for about 8–10 minutes or until softened.

Cut away the bottom of the génoise and set it aside – this will become the 'lid' of the trifle – then cut away and reserve the outer crust. Cut widthways across the trimmed cake to achieve thin, wide slices. Choose a bowl about the same diameter as the cake and line it generously with plastic film if you plan to turn out the trifle. Line the sides and base of the bowl with the slices of cake, then brush the cake with the juice from the pears and prunes to moisten and flavour it. Crush the macaroons and moisten them with these juices as well, then mould the macaroon mixture over the cake to form an inner shell.

Thinly slice the pear, then overlap the slices over the macaroon mixture to create another layer. Follow this with a layer of prunes. The bowl will be filling up by now and you will have created a strong outer structure. Spoon Sauternes custard over the pudding to moisten it, but don't make it too wet. »

Chop the roasted walnuts and, using a food processor, reduce the reserved outer crust of the cake to crumbs, then mix both into the syllabub. Smooth the syllabub mixture into the centre of the trifle, then top with the reserved base of the cake. Cover the trifle with plastic film and place a weighted plate on top, then refrigerate overnight.

If you are turning out the trifle, simply hold a plate over the top and invert the bowl, then carefully remove the plastic film. Rather than spooning out the dessert, as you would if it were still in the bowl, cut slices of trifle to show off its wonderful layers.

GLAZED PEARS WITH MASCARPONE   *Serves 4*

1 vanilla bean, halved lengthways
200 g unsalted butter, chopped
150 g castor sugar
rind of 1 lemon and 1 tablespoon juice
2 teaspoons verjuice
4 medium-sized pears, peeled
   (be careful to leave the stalks intact)

MASCARPONE
finely chopped rind and juice of 1 lemon
160 g mascarpone

Scrape out the vanilla seeds from the bean and set aside. Melt the butter in a heavy-based frying pan over low heat and add the sugar, lemon juice and verjuice. When the sugar has dissolved add the peeled pears, lemon rind, vanilla bean and scraped seeds. Cook over low heat for approximately 1 hour or until the pears are an even golden colour. If you have chosen ripe ones, this will take less time, but be careful not to overcook them while colouring. The final colour is important, so it's best not to use overly ripe pears or they will fall apart by the time you get the colour on them.

Check that the pears are done by inserting a thin-bladed knife or skewer into the centre and if there is no resistance when you pull it out, then they are ready. The cooking liquid should be a light caramel colour and can be used to give the pears a wonderful 'glistening' appearance on serving.

Gently fold the lemon rind and juice into the mascarpone; do not beat it as the mascarpone will become too runny.

Place a pear on each serving plate and pour over some caramel. Serve a dollop of the mascarpone next to the pear; its acidic creaminess will blend perfectly with the fruity, vanilla aroma of the poached pear.

PERSIMMONS

 SOME TIME AGO, WHILE BEING INTERVIEWED ABOUT MY book *Maggie's Orchard*, I was asked to name the fruit I would most like to be (or was it that I was most like?). My immediate response was 'a persimmon'. 'Why?' asked the journalist. 'Because of its rounded shape and luscious colour, and because when it is ready to eat it is squashy and mushy and sensuous,' I replied. (I could also have said that if it is not ripe, it is as astringent as hell and full of tannin!)

As it is, I love not only the fruit but the entire tree, particularly when it grows tall against a building (a stone one, for the best effect), lightly espaliered and climbing the wall in search of the sun. Planted this way, the tree shoots straight up and then branches thickly from the top. Should there be another building nearby, the branches arch out towards it, particularly if the tree is of one of the weeping varieties.

The large leaves are very decorative and become beautifully tinted with rich autumn colours before they fall, exposing the glowing reddish-orange fruit that remains on the bare branches. At every stage this tree is a study in the perfection of nature – even when its fruit has been picked, the wood of the tree is lovely to look at. If the tree is of the older astringent variety, I've found the fruit is best when left to totally ripen on the tree.

The big decision for anyone with room in the garden is whether to plant the astringent or non-astringent variety of persimmon. For the most part, the persimmons you buy at the market are non-astringent and can be eaten firm, though they too can be left until soft before eating, and I have learnt to appreciate them more this way.

Commercially, the non-astringent persimmon makes a lot of sense: it travels well and can be displayed in markets much more easily; it can be sliced to reveal its very attractive cross-section of seeds; and it can be eaten when quite hard. Firm, non-astringent persimmons make a crisp addition to a rocket or watercress salad dressed with a fresh lemon vinaigrette and can partner a wide range of other salad ingredients, from goat's cheese to smoked tongue.

However, while I now have many persimmon trees – some the newer non-astringent variety – nothing is quite as special as the astringent ones. I have to say that their jelly-like, sweet, unctuous fruit, left on the tree until almost diaphanous, is like nothing else. Unless you net your trees, you have to pick daily to beat the birds, so I had to resort to picking them before they reached this stage. This way we had just-ripe persimmons to finish off every meal for weeks on end. As the skin is so edible when the persimmons are ripe, amongst friends we would eat them as one luscious lump rather than serve them formally. For first-time eaters, though, I slice off the top and offer a spoon to scoop out the flesh, and serve them with a dish of clotted cream and cat's tongue biscuits alongside.

I now net my trees to protect them from the birds, and I can tell you it is worth it, as I can let my persimmons ripen on the tree. Remember, the fruit is never better than when totally ripe upon picking – the calyx is easily plucked out and you can eat the fruit just like that, skin and all. Persimmons are so much about texture – to describe them you could say they are a little like a very ripe apricot. When eating the firm, non-astringent variety, take advantage of that star-like pattern in the cross-section of the fruit, which looks so attractive in either salads or fruit salad or dessert.

If you have lots of persimmons, there are many different ways to cook them. When our friends Margaret and Peter Lehmann returned from a trip to the United States some years ago, they brought with them recipes for Persimmon Bread (see page 287) and puddings. My perennial favourite, a Sour-cream Pastry (see page 424) tart case thickly spread with mascarpone (while still a little warm from the oven) and topped with fruit, is wonderful made with ripe non-astringent persimmons still firm enough to cut widthways, skin, seeds and all. A dusting of castor sugar and a quick grill or blast with a kitchen blowtorch, if you have one, caramelises the flesh – the vibrant colour alone is worth the trouble.

A faded note in my file suggests drying persimmons and grinding them to make a powder. Then take a green mango, slice it and dust the flesh with the persimmon powder and salt; the resulting flavour is savoury, sweet and salty. At the time I had dried persimmons in the hydrator or the oven and found that those that were unripe dried without any chalkiness. A footnote reads: 'Next year, dry lots!' I'll just have to make sure that I'm not away next May.

Harold McGee, in his second book on food science and lore of the kitchen, *The Curious Cook*, has a chapter called 'Persimmons Unpuckered', which I recommend as serious reading for persimmon lovers and others interested in tannins; persimmons are astringent because of the huge amounts of tannin they contain. McGee tells us that an atmosphere rich in carbon dioxide can bring about a reduction in astringency long before the fruit softens, and gives examples of simple methods to achieve this. It certainly makes fascinating reading and explains the steps that led to this discovery, with tales of boys in Chinese villages burying persimmons in the ground, smothering them in covered earthenware jars along with a stick of incense, or sealing them in airtight, empty Japanese sake barrels, all in an attempt to deprive the persimmon of air. The astringency can be reduced by freezing the fruit but in large packed volumes this takes 10–90 days and the fruit is mushy as a result.

McGee also tells us that the Portuguese love to dry persimmons, the Chinese preserve them with sugar, and that the fruit is a member of the ebony family and its wood is much sought after for making golf clubs, shoe lasts and weavers' shuttles. The persimmon is grown widely in Japan, where they also make a traditional dessert from a persimmon paste which is teamed with yuzu, a citrus fruit.

Melbourne cook, writer and teacher Penny Smith once teamed some of my smoked kangaroo with persimmon for a special Australian dinner she served to some visiting African dignitaries. She told me it was a startling success.

To finish, here is a small piece out of a book I love, *Please to the Table: The Russian Cookbook* by Anya von Bremzen and John Welchman: 'To me one of the simplest and most delightful conclusions to a meal with a Mediterranean accent is a plate of lusciously ripe persimmons, peeled, sliced and garnished with mint sprigs.'

SEARED TUNA WITH PERSIMMON AND FENNEL SALAD   *Serves 4*

1 teaspoon fennel seeds
1 teaspoon coriander seeds
1 fennel bulb, trimmed and thinly sliced, fronds reserved
sea salt flakes and freshly ground black pepper
150 ml extra virgin olive oil

4 × 200 g bluefin *or* yellowfin tuna steaks
2 meyer lemons
2 non-astringent persimmons, thinly sliced widthways
¼ cup chopped mint
juice of 1 lemon
¼ cup (60 ml) walnut oil

Toast the fennel and coriander seeds in a dry frying pan, then cool and grind using a mortar and pestle. Chop the reserved fennel fronds finely and, in a small bowl, combine with the ground spices, then season with salt and pepper. Add about 100 ml of the olive oil and stir in, then rub this mixture on both sides of the tuna steaks. Set aside for 20–30 minutes.

Meanwhile, cut the lemons widthways into 4–6 slices, depending on their size. Drizzle with 1 tablespoon olive oil. Grill lemon slices under a hot griller until caramelised on both sides, then set aside.

Sear the tuna on a hot chargrill plate for 1½ minutes, then turn over and cook for another minute. Remove from the heat, transfer to a plate and top with the lemon slices, drizzle with the remaining olive oil and leave to rest for a few minutes.

Place the persimmon, fennel, mint, lemon juice and walnut oil in a bowl and toss together. Season to taste with a little salt and pepper, then serve with the seared tuna.

MARGARET'S PERSIMMON BREAD

Makes 2 loaves

This is Marg Lehmann's recipe for persimmon bread. I love to serve it with a ripe blue cheese, a fresh persimmon and walnuts.

2 free-range eggs	1 teaspoon ground cloves
1 cup (220 g) sugar	½ cup (125 ml) milk
2 tablespoons melted butter	1½ cups persimmon pulp
2 cups (300 g) plain flour	(about 4 persimmons)
2 teaspoons bicarbonate of soda	1 teaspoon vanilla extract
2 teaspoons ground cinnamon	1 cup (170 g) raisins
1 teaspoon freshly grated nutmeg	1 cup (140 g) walnuts *or* pecans

Preheat the oven to 180°C. Mix the eggs, sugar and melted butter in a large bowl. Sift the flour, soda and spices into the bowl, then stir in all the remaining ingredients. Divide the mixture between two greased loaf tins, then stand these in a roasting pan filled with warm water. The water should come about halfway up the sides of the loaf tins.

Bake for 1¼ hours, then turn the loaves out of their tins onto a wire rack to cool.

PERSIMMON AND AMARETTO

Serves 1

1 very ripe, non-astringent persimmon	50 g mascarpone
1½ teaspoons Amaretto	honey, to serve

Place the persimmon in the freezer for 24 hours, then remove it 2 hours before serving (it should be just soft to the touch). This gives the fruit a lovely sorbet-like consistency.

Cut the persimmon in half and drizzle ½ teaspoon Amaretto over each cut side. Fold the remaining Amaretto into the mascarpone.

Spoon the mascarpone over the persimmon, then spoon over a little honey and serve.

JANE'S PERSIMMON PUDDING

Serves 6

Marg Lehmann gave me this recipe from a friend of hers in the United States. Marg says it is a taste sensation and, as persimmon is in season at Christmas over there, it is often served flamed with brandy and surrounded by holly.

This recipe is a classic example of one that has been passed on to friends and added to and tweaked along the way – I love all the options given to turn it out successfully. Opinion is divided as to whether the addition of nuts and fruit overpower the persimmon – my version uses them, but you can omit them if you like.

½ cup (50 g) walnuts

1 cup (220 g) sugar, plus extra for dusting

125 g butter, melted

2 free-range eggs

1 cup (150 g) plain flour

¼ teaspoon salt

1 teaspoon ground cinnamon

1 cup persimmon pulp (about 3 persimmons)

2 teaspoons bicarbonate of soda dissolved
   in 2 tablespoons warm water

dash brandy

1 teaspoon vanilla extract

1 cup dried currants *or* chopped raisins

Preheat the oven to 220°C. Dry-roast the walnuts on a baking tray for 6–8 minutes, then rub off their skins with a clean tea towel.

Mix together the walnuts, sugar, butter and eggs. Stir in the flour, salt and cinnamon. Add the persimmon pulp, bicarbonate of soda and water mixture, brandy, vanilla extract and currants or raisins.

Take a 2-litre-capacity pudding mould with a lid and grease it thoroughly, then coat with the extra sugar. Fill two-thirds full with the batter. (Or substitute with a clean 1 kg coffee tin, using a doubled piece of aluminium foil as a lid.) Using a saucepan or stockpot large enough to hold the mould, create a rack on the bottom with jar lids. Place the covered mould on this rack and add water until it reaches halfway up the side of the mould, then cover the saucepan with a lid. Bring to the boil over high heat, then reduce heat to low and steam the pudding for 2½–3 hours (longer cooking won't harm it – the finished pudding should be dark, springy and may pull away slightly from the mould).

To unmould, turn the mould upside-down on a plate. If the pudding does not drop right out, shake and pound the sides of the mould vigorously, right-side up, then invert it again. The next alternative is to leave the pudding inverted on a plate to drop out once it is cool. The last resort is to loosen the pudding with a flat knife; if it breaks, it can usually be reassembled.

Serve the pudding warm with Crème Anglaise (see page 225), runny cream or ice cream.

SANDOR PALMAI'S PERSIMMON TARTS *Serves 6*

This tart is etched in my memory. It was made by a gifted young Barossa chef, Sandor Palmai, when he and his then wife had a tiny restaurant in Bethany called Landhaus. The tart truly showcased this fruit, bringing out the best of both astringent and non-astringent varieties.

The thin slices of the firm fruit created a counterbalance to the squelchy old-fashioned pulp of the astringent variety, and the addition of the lime sorbet was such a refreshing finish after the richness of the persimmon. Sandor Palmai suggests serving a lime sorbet adapted from *Jane Grigson's Fruit Book* with this dish. I find my Sour-cream Pastry (see page 424) also works well for this.

1 × quantity Sour-cream Pastry
   (see page 424)
½ cup (125 ml) crème fraîche
2 very ripe astringent persimmons
2 ripe non-astringent persimmons

SORBET
250 g sugar
3 limes, rind removed and very
   finely chopped

To make the sorbet, stir 1 litre of water and the sugar in a large saucepan over low heat until the sugar dissolves, then increase the heat to high and boil for 2–3 minutes. Place lime rind in a saucepan of cold water, then bring to the boil, strain in a sieve (reserving liquid) and cool under cold running water. Simmer the blanched rind in 150 ml of the reserved liquid for about 15 minutes or until tender, stirring occasionally; watch that it doesn't burn. Squeeze the limes, mix the juice with the remaining liquid, rind and cooking syrup, then taste and add extra sugar or lime juice if necessary. Churn in an ice cream machine following manufacturer's instructions.

Make and chill the pastry as instructed. Roll out to a 5 mm thickness, then cut into 6 circles and use to line six 12 cm individual tart tins with removable bases. Line pastry with foil pressed well into the edges and fill with pastry weights. Chill pastry for 20 minutes.

Meanwhile, preheat the oven to 200°C. Blind bake the pastry cases for 15 minutes, then remove the pastry weights and foil and bake for another 5 minutes. Cool to room temperature.

Add 1 tablespoon crème fraîche to each tart case. Remove the calyx from the astringent persimmons and spoon out the pulp, discarding the seeds, if any. Divide the pulp equally among the tarts. Remove the calyxes from the non-astringent variety and cut the fruit widthways into thin slices, then arrange these over the pulp in each tart case.

Serve the persimmon tarts with scoops of lime sorbet.

PHEASANT

IN THE LATE 1970s, WHEN WE OPENED THE PHEASANT FARM Restaurant, one rarely saw pheasant on a restaurant menu, let alone in the kitchen of a private house. Even now it is still not common. Yet pheasant is much more interesting to eat than chicken – it is sweet, moist and delicious, and not as strongly flavoured as duck or pigeon.

Is the pheasant fresh or hung? When someone asks this question it usually indicates that they are from Europe. Most game in Europe is wild and therefore of indeterminate age, and so it must be cooked with care to avoid the meat being tough. Hanging helps to tenderise the meat and gives the bird its 'high' gamy flavour. Many Europeans consider pheasant not worth eating unless it is hung until it is so high that it 'walks away' and the skin is actually green.

I would have to say that a hung bird would always be my preference, though ideally with someone else to cook it for me (as the pheasant is hung with its skin on and guts intact, the strong smell tends to permeate the cook's clothing and skin).

Late autumn is the time for pheasant, and of course it can be hung outside at this time in the northern hemisphere. In the United Kingdom it used to be illegal to serve pheasant in a restaurant outside of a twelve-week period each year, starting from 1 October, to ensure the birds were fresh. This is changing now, but there certainly were large fines for flouting this law, and restaurants could not serve birds that were caught in the season and frozen for later.

In Australia the general public finds the idea of hanging pheasant repugnant, due largely to our weather. An Australian autumn can be like an Indian summer, and game would go off very quickly in these conditions. So here we enjoy our birds fresh in season, and frozen at other times of the year.

Ultimately, the success of the Pheasant Farm Restaurant was a result of the direct link between farmer and cook. As the cook, I was able to tell my husband Colin how I wanted

the birds presented, at what age and size they were the most succulent, and even how I wanted them processed. In short, Colin raised our pheasants to suit my requirements for the restaurant. You could hardly have a more direct link than that!

Not that I would suggest every primary producer go that far, but what worked for us is that we were passionate about our product, and we learnt all we could about it by immersing ourselves in every bit of information available, as well as getting direct feedback from the public. Also, we loved to eat pheasant. I have heard many farmers say that they don't even like their product; how then can they truly believe in it, improve on and market it?

Pheasants are expensive – one reason for this is that they take a minimum of sixteen weeks to reach maturity. The birds are not given antibiotics to accelerate growth; they are free-ranged and given as much green feed as possible. Their vegetarian diet is of vital importance. Pheasants are particularly prone to misadventure, which, combined with low hatchability and a long growth period, sometimes made us wonder why we ever started breeding them.

Colin's dream of raising wild game dated back to his days in New Zealand when he took his commercial pilot's licence. He was based on the South Island, where game was plentiful, and it just seemed like a good idea to him as a country boy. In 1977 he was awarded a Churchill Fellowship to tour Europe and America to study the rearing of game birds, and on his return began breeding pheasants in earnest.

As much as I love pheasants, just sometimes I wondered how it would be to have called the restaurant 'The Guinea Fowl Farm' for a change of pace! In those days I cooked all sorts of game, but about 65 per cent of our customers insisted on pheasant. I was always seeking new ideas for using the birds that we raised and utilising every part, from the liver for pâté to the giblet and heart for confit and the head and feet for stock. I smoked the breeder birds and even had people collect feathers for fly fishing and jewellery.

Pheasant is very simple to cook when you know how to treat it. Cooking is all about enjoying yourself in the kitchen, so forget all you've read in European cookery books about larding (threading the fat through the meat with a larding needle) and barding (wrapping the meat in fat), or roasting the bird for anywhere from 40 minutes to 1½ hours. No wonder people think pheasant is dry!

The trick to cooking pheasant is to pot-roast it to a just-cooked state and then leave it to rest in its own juices. Alternatively you can roast it quickly in a very hot oven (although this can be tricky and may take some practice to get right). Easier for the home cook is to start it off at a high temperature to caramelise the skin, then cook it for longer at a lower temperature, or to gently seal the skin first in nut-brown butter before roasting.

The easiest way to prepare pheasant for roasting is to 'spatchcock' it. To do this, cut the spine out with kitchen scissors, making an incision either side of the vent, then flatten the bird with the heel of your hand. Brush generously with a marinade of olive oil, orange or lemon juice, fresh thyme and/or juniper berries, and leave it to sit in those juices in a dish in the refrigerator for several hours to allow all the flavours to penetrate.

If roasting at high temperature, say 220°C, brush the skin with orange juice and extra virgin olive oil and add salt just before cooking to aid caramelisation. Choose the shallowest roasting pan you have as the bird cooks for such a short time that the heat must penetrate the flesh with as few barriers as possible. Don't attempt to cook more than two birds at a time in a normal household oven, and position the shelves as far apart as possible. Make sure the oven has reached its peak heat before sliding the birds in; and be as quick as you can to minimise heat loss. Most ovens will need all the help they can get to obtain and sustain the heat required to caramelise the skin to perfection and ensure the fast cooking that produces moistness.

The cooking time depends on the size of the bird, the efficiency of the oven, and the thickness of the material from which the roasting pan is made. It will take anything from 12–20 minutes to cook a 900 g bird: it is ready when the thigh pulls away easily, the thickest part of the breast is springy to the touch, and the skin is golden brown. Remove the pan from the oven, then turn the bird upside-down and leave it to rest for another 20 minutes before carving it from the bone. Delicious.

MY WAY OF COOKING PHEASANT   *Serves 2*

In the restaurant days I always used the high-temperature method and always separated the legs from the breast, which I left on the frame. As so many people would order pheasant, I had to be able to cook it quickly so as to turn orders around in reasonable time. Since then, my experience has shown that a less fraught way for the home cook, given that ovens vary so much, is to cook it at a lower temperature than I used in the restaurant, as I've done here.

Renowned chef Cheong Liew gave me this recipe for his favourite marinade. It helps to give the skin a wonderful caramelised texture without having to seal the bird before cooking when roasting at a high temperature, but it is more foolproof to take the time to seal the skin first.

1 × 1.2 kg pheasant	extra virgin olive oil, for cooking
finely chopped rind and juice of 1 orange	sea salt flakes
6 juniper berries, crushed	verjuice (optional), for cooking
2 sprigs thyme	125 ml Golden Chicken Stock (optional)
gin (optional), for marinade	(see page 57), for cooking

To prepare the pheasant, cut the tips off the wings with a sharp knife and take the flesh off the wing joint to show bare bone. Because of the lack of fat in many pheasants (although not ours, which are especially raised on vegetarian grains), the wing is not a succulent part, and if the flesh is left on this part of the wing it inhibits the cooking of the breast. As a pheasant this size is perfect for two, to save the trouble of carving, keep the bird intact while cooking, then when ready to serve, simply cut it in half with a sharp cook's knife or kitchen scissors.

Place the pheasant in a dish with the orange rind and juice, crushed juniper berries and thyme. (If cooking more than one pheasant, use this quantity for each pheasant.) If you are feeling extravagant, slosh in a little good gin as well. Leave to marinate in the fridge for 3 hours.

Preheat the oven to 180°C. Remove the pheasant from the marinade and place in a large heavy-based frying pan. Mix the marinade with some olive oil and brush this on the skin of the bird.

Season the pheasant with salt and gently pan-fry over low–medium heat until the skin is a golden colour. Lay the bird on one side in a shallow roasting pan, then generously brush the oil and marinade over the skin once more.

Bake the pheasant for 10 minutes on one side, then turn the bird over and bake for another 10 minutes on the other side. Now turn the pheasant breast-side down, and bake for a further 10 minutes. By this stage the bird should be almost cooked through; check by pulling a leg away from the breast, making sure there are no signs of rawness anywhere. If unsure, insert a skewer into the thickest part of the breast – if any pink juices show, then it requires a little more cooking.

To rest, turn the bird so the breast is facing down in the roasting pan. Cover with foil and leave for 20 minutes. At this stage, if you wish to use the pan juices to make a sauce, splash the hot pheasant with verjuice, then add 125 ml warm, good-quality chicken stock to the pan while the bird rests.

The easiest way to serve the bird is to cut it in half, place each half on a plate, then spoon over the pan juices. Serve with roasted parsnips and a green salad.

WARM SALAD OF SMOKED PHEASANT   *Serves 6*

I have a special recipe for the older birds we fatten and smoke. They are so juicy that you would never guess they would otherwise have ended up in the stockpot. The first time I made this dish was at the Australian Symposium of Gastronomy in Adelaide, where they organised a huge 'Market to Table Fair' in Gouger Street. The whole street was blocked off and trestle tables stretched its length. About 25 restaurants participated, many of them cooking in the street. There was a queue from the minute we set up, and I prepared about 800 serves of this dish. The queue was so long my daughters kept offering tastings of our pâté to stop people from becoming restless. It was an exhausting, exciting day, cooking right there in the street with my customers talking to me as they waited – a great bit of street theatre.

1 cos lettuce, leaves separated and cut
   into large pieces
6 witlof (3 red and 3 white), bases trimmed
   and leaves separated
1 bunch rocket
½ cup (125 ml) extra virgin olive oil,
   plus extra for cooking
1½ tablespoons balsamic vinegar *or*
   vino cotto (see Glossary)

60 g butter
250 g Portobello mushrooms,
   trimmed and sliced
sea salt flakes and freshly ground
   black pepper
1 smoked pheasant *or* large smoked chicken,
   boned and thinly sliced
18 pieces Mustard Apricots (see page 15)

Wash and dry the salad leaves. Make a vinaigrette with the oil and vinegar. Heat the butter in a frying pan until nut-brown, then add a dash of olive oil to stop it burning. Add the mushrooms, season with salt and pepper and sauté until cooked, then add the pheasant and mustard apricots to warm them through. Toss in a little vinaigrette to just coat the ingredients.

Arrange the leaves on serving plates and dress with the vinaigrette. Divide the pheasant, mushroom and apricot mixture among the plates and serve.

PHEASANT WITH SULTANA GRAPES AND VERJUICE   *Serves 6*

3 × 800 g young hen pheasants
juice of 1 lemon
extra virgin olive oil, for cooking
½ cup (125 ml) verjuice
9 sprigs thyme
sea salt flakes

60 g unsalted butter, plus 100 g unsalted
   butter, cubed and chilled, extra (optional)
1 cup (250 ml) reduced Golden Chicken
   Stock (see page 57)
2 cups sultana grapes, removed from
   the stems

Preheat the oven to 180°C. With a sharp knife, cut the tips off the wings and take the flesh off the wing joint to show bare bone. Squeeze a little lemon juice into the cavity of each bird, then moisten the birds with a little olive oil and 2 teaspoons of the verjuice. Sprinkle over the thyme and season with salt.

Heat the 60 g butter in a large saucepan until nut-brown, adding a dash of olive oil to stop it burning. Brown the birds gently on all sides over low–medium heat until they are a golden colour. Place them on their sides in a shallow roasting pan.

Bake the pheasants in the oven for 10 minutes, then turn them onto the other side and bake for another 10 minutes; at this stage the skin should be golden all over and the birds cooked through. Check by pulling a leg away from the breast, making sure there are no signs of rawness anywhere. If unsure, insert a skewer into the thickest part of the breast – if any pink juices show, then it requires a little more cooking.

Remove the birds from the oven and transfer to another dish, each breast-side down, and rest, covered with foil, for 20 minutes. »

To make the sauce, deglaze the roasting pan with the rest of the verjuice, then add the stock and reduce by half over high heat. When ready to serve, cut the pheasants in half with a sharp cook's knife or kitchen scissors. Bring the sauce back to the boil then, if you wish, whisk in the extra butter to finish. About 40 seconds before serving, toss in the grapes, then pour over the sauce.

PHEASANT PIE   *Serves 8*

We now serve this pie regularly at the Farmshop, accompanied by a simple rocket and preserved lemon salad. This is also the game pie we once tried to launch on the Sydney market. It seemed the perfect product: we had pheasants to spare after the restaurant closed and we had lemons from our small grove at the Riverland vineyard. We even planted 36 thyme plants outside the pâté room but never managed to produce enough for the weekly pie orders. We made the mixture in our kitchen, then flew it up to Sue Patchett of Patchett's Pies in Sydney who made the pastry, cooked the pies and delivered them to David Jones. The pies were wonderful, if I do say so myself, but their shelf-life was so short and the ingredients so expensive that we were unable to sustain production.

If you can't get game birds for this pie, really good free-range chicken can be used instead. You need a total of 750 g meat off the bone – about 450 g breast meat and 300 g leg meat.

2 × 1 kg pheasants
250 g minced veal
250 g minced pork
250 g minced pork fat
125 g sugar-cured bacon, rind removed
   and finely chopped
2 cloves garlic, very finely chopped
finely chopped rind of 4 lemons
½ teaspoon juniper berries, bruised
sea salt flakes and freshly ground
   black pepper

150 g poultry livers, trimmed
   and finely chopped
butter, for cooking
500 g button mushrooms, chopped
1½ tablespoons thyme leaves
extra virgin olive oil, for cooking
1 × quantity Sour-cream Pastry
   (see page 424)
cream, for brushing

Remove the thigh meat from the pheasants and cut into small dice, then mix it with the minced veal and pork, pork fat and bacon. Add the garlic, lemon rind, juniper berries, 3 teaspoons salt and 1 teaspoon pepper, and mix well.

Toss the livers in a frying pan with a knob of butter over high heat until sealed, then season with salt and pepper and tip onto a plate to cool. In the same pan, toss the mushrooms and thyme with another knob of butter over medium–high heat until softened, then remove to a plate to cool. Reduce the juices in the pan over high heat to a glaze, then cool.

Cut the breast meat of the pheasant into 1 cm dice and sprinkle with a little olive oil. In a large bowl, combine the meat mixture, liver, mushrooms, glaze and, lastly, the breast meat. Cover and leave in the refrigerator overnight for the flavours to infuse.

Next day, make and chill the pastry as instructed. Cut out 8 pieces to fit 8 individual pie moulds, and another 8 for the lids. Line the pie moulds with the chilled pastry and spoon the filling into the pastry case. Top with the lids, pinching the edges to create a good seal. Brush the pies with cream and chill in the refrigerator for 20 minutes.

Preheat the oven to 230°C and cook the pies for 10 minutes, then lower the temperature to 210°C and cook for another 10 minutes. Rest the pies for 10 minutes before serving. They are fabulous eaten at room temperature and are great cold too.

POMEGRANATES

POMEGRANATES ARE FREQUENTLY OVERLOOKED BECAUSE people don't know how to eat them, and they are often only grown for the ornamental beauty of the trees when laden with fruit in autumn. However, I love the crunch of the brilliant red seeds and the tartness their juice provides as much as the beauty of their waxy skins, which blush from gold to deep rosy-pink, and are topped with a crown-like calyx.

Pomegranate trees are really tough. During a heatwave in January 1999 we were away and weren't able to water our trees and plants. On our return we found only a few plants had survived, and the only one to continue to thrive was the pomegranate – and it was growing against a garden wall, which would have exacerbated the already scorching temperatures.

Heartened by this, I planted forty more pomegranate trees the next month, to make a hedge against a couple of walls at the farm – one in full sun and the other shaded by gum trees. A year later, the plants in the sunny position were 1.5 metres tall and full of fruit, while the shaded trees had a lot less fruit and were a little more spindly, but they made up for this as their leaves were lush enough to hide a very pedestrian fence, and their fruit found many uses. I found I had ordered about ten more plants than were needed at the farm, so I put them in at home to hedge a new deck. I kept them in pots for months before planting them out, and within two years they had reached the height of the decking (1 metre), spreading to become a hedge with fruit.

Pomegranates have long been grown in the Riverland of South Australia and Victoria and are finally becoming of more interest to commercial growers. They will grow in almost all climates, although the perfect choice is a sunny, dry one (Mediterranean, in fact). There are many varieties, including some truly ordinary in flavour, so do your homework before going to a nursery and only buy those that are known.

The larger fruit is the most popular and is often bought for floral art and religious ceremonies. My grower in the Riverland has a hundred trees of ten varieties. He thinks the brilliantly crimson Wonderful is the best all-rounder, but he also has a paler variety with softer seeds that is very popular, as the seeds can be swallowed whole rather than spat out. I find these bland, with virtually no flavour – I'd prefer to put up with the inconvenience of the seeds to be sure of getting that wonderful tartness. I've since found a grower in Western Australia (www.fixedstars.com.au) who specialises in pomegranates and sends me cuttings by post. He selects for flavour and colour, and I eagerly await the first fruit.

It is hard to tell a ripe pomegranate by colour alone, since different varieties colour in different ways. If you have a pomegranate plant in your garden, you're perfectly placed to observe the hairline crack that appears in the waxy skin when the fruit is ripe. If relying on your greengrocer, buy one pomegranate first and cut into it to test for ripeness before planning a special pomegranate feast, as they are disappointing when under-ripe. Never buy fruit with mould in the crack as these pomegranates are already spoilt.

The pomegranate originated in Persia, and whereas it mostly featured in Persian, Russian or Greek cookbooks in the past, there are now many great Australian cooks who use and write about this intriguing fruit.

You can imagine people buying whole pomegranates just for show, as cut in half they reveal a wonderful display of red, crystal-like seeds. These can be used in many different ways, but first need to be separated from their yellowish membranes, which harbour the astringency or tannin that can make a dish unpalatable. The seeds can be used simply as a dessert fruit – perhaps on a plate of autumn fruits with persimmon and tamarillo. Or savour the crunch the seeds add when tossed into late autumn and early winter salads, such as one of ripe figs, prosciutto and goat's cheese. I love the crunchy texture of the brilliant red seeds in a dish, although some people may find them difficult as they are similar to the pips of the grape. If serving hummus, top with a little extra virgin olive oil and some pomegranate seeds.

To juice a pomegranate, simply cut in half, then squeeze in a citrus juicer. If not ripe, a great deal of tannin can be released when squeezing, so the juice needs to be tasted as it may be too astringent (often a little sugar syrup needs to be added, made by boiling equal parts sugar and water for 20 minutes). A large ripe pomegranate yields about 250 ml juice.

Pomegranate juice would make a very grown-up soft drink if you could get enough of it. But if you've only a little freshly squeezed juice, try it with gin – you won't need too much for that. For a cocktail, add a shot of Cointreau to a cocktail glass of pomegranate juice and finish with a few pomegranate seeds. For a non-alcoholic version, sweeten the pomegranate juice with a little sugar syrup, dilute with mineral water and top with a sprig of mint.

Like lemon juice, pomegranate juice contributes a significant sharpness to sauces, but it is more rounded, with a bittersweet characteristic that cuts the richness of game, pork, lamb or good poultry. Pomegranate juice and seeds lose colour when heated, so even though they give a brilliant lift of flavour to a sauce, it is worth holding back some of the seeds to add to the dish just before serving. I choose the ripest pomegranates in my pile and separate a tablespoon or so of seeds per person to add to the sauce at the very last moment so that it has crunch and colour.

I also make a warm vinaigrette to serve with partridge. I mix almond or walnut oil with pomegranate juice and seeds and chopped herbs (particularly mint), then pour this over the hot birds as they rest.

In the Middle East, a traditional soup combines spinach, leeks, rice or lentils, coriander, flat-leaf parsley and lots of pomegranate juice, with a final addition of fresh mint. Sugar is stirred in at the last moment, if required.

The first time I tasted pomegranate flesh I took one bite, spat it out and didn't try it again for years. Now I eagerly await the season to team the fruit with duck, pheasant or guinea fowl. I don't usually belong to the 'fruit with meat' school of thought, but there are exceptions! Certainly, lemon and orange are ideal with game, and the old-fashioned yet exotic pomegranate has a tartness that complements rich dishes extremely well.

Grenadine syrup was originally made from pomegranates, though sadly now it is chemically manufactured as 'nature identical' (as they say in the food-manufacturing trade to describe an ingredient made in a laboratory to mimic the natural product). Very popular in France with fruit salad or served with grapefruit instead of sugar, grenadine syrup is also used to make cordials, ices and jellies.

Pomegranate molasses is another by-product of this vibrant fruit. Available from Middle Eastern grocers, it can be used instead of fresh pomegranates when they are not in season; use it sparingly, adding water or verjuice to thin it down if necessary. It goes particularly well with poultry, lamb or game, so try adding it to a game or poultry sauce, or brushing it with extra virgin olive oil onto a rack of lamb before roasting.

POMEGRANATE SAUCE (SAVOURY) *Serves 4*

This is a simple sauce we created in the restaurant to team with roasted mallard duck. It has a Persian influence and can also be used with quail, chicken, pheasant or guinea fowl.

1 onion, finely chopped	pinch sugar
1 pomegranate, seeded carefully to avoid yellow membrane	dash red-wine vinegar
	juice of 1 lemon
pinch ground cardamom	100 ml Golden Chicken Stock
pinch ground turmeric	(see page 57)
freshly ground black pepper	sea salt flakes

Sweat the onion and pomegranate seeds until translucent in a saucepan with olive oil over low–medium heat. Add spices and continue to stir. Add sugar and vinegar to taste, then stir until caramelised. When almost catching, add lemon juice and reduce. Finally, add chicken stock and reduce again to desired consistency. Season to taste with a little salt before serving.

WALNUT AND POMEGRANATE SALAD *Serves 4*

1 pomegranate

2 slices walnut bread

2 teaspoons walnut oil, plus extra
　for brushing

2 punnets lamb's lettuce (mâche)

½ cup mint leaves

½ cup flat-leaf parsley leaves

2 tablespoons snipped chives

2 tablespoons walnuts

130 g fromage blanc *or* fresh ricotta

½ teaspoon rosewater

2 teaspoons extra virgin olive oil

sea salt flakes and freshly ground
　black pepper

Cut the pomegranate in half, then hold over a bowl, cut-side down, and tap each half with a wooden spoon to release the seeds into the bowl. Remove any bits of yellow membrane that have fallen into the bowl with the seeds.

Preheat the oven to 200°C. Brush the walnut bread with walnut oil, then tear into bite-sized pieces. Toast the walnut bread on a baking tray in the oven until golden, then set aside.

Assemble the lamb's lettuce, herbs, walnuts, fromage blanc and pomegranate seeds in a salad bowl. Mix the rosewater, olive oil and the 2 teaspoons of walnut oil together to make a vinaigrette, then pour over the salad. Top with the croutons, then season with salt and pepper and serve.

POMEGRANATE SAUCE (SWEET) *Makes 250 ml*

3 pomegranates

juice of ½ good-sized lemon

100 g sugar

Cut one of the pomegranates in half, then hold over a bowl, cut-side down, and tap each half with a wooden spoon to release the seeds into the bowl. Remove any bits of yellow membrane that have fallen into the bowl, and reserve the seeds.

Cut the remaining pomegranates in half and squeeze them in a citrus juicer. Boil the resulting juice, along with the lemon juice and sugar, in an enamelled or stainless steel saucepan over high heat for 2 minutes or more to reduce a little.

Cool and add reserved seeds. Serve with desserts such as a rich chocolate cake.

PUMPKIN

 MY MOTHER INTRODUCED ME TO OUR LOCAL GREENGROCER when I was very young. The reason was to teach me how to choose a perfect pumpkin. It was something to be taken very seriously and we would only buy one if we were sure of getting a good thing.

In those days the only pumpkin variety we knew was the Queensland Blue. Once cut, the deep-ochre centre was revealed, but I knew not to be dazzled by it as I had been told to look out for a bluey-green tinge on the edge of the flesh that promised good flavour.

We relied on the greengrocer to have a large blade strong enough to cut through the massive pumpkin – there were no dried-out bits of packaged pumpkin then. The knife was like a cane cutter's blade: long and curved and ever-ready. We didn't have today's array of sophisticated stainless steel knives and, like most families, had only a carving knife to perform all tasks. Years later, when I lived in Europe, my requests for pumpkin were met with contempt, as there it was only considered for the animals.

There are pumpkins and then there are pumpkins, so it is well worth taking the time to find the best. A great Queensland Blue is still amazing, but harder to find in perfect condition than it used to be. Reject pale-fleshed specimens – these often turn out to be watery and tasteless. Woodiness, easily evident in pre-cut pumpkins, is also to be avoided at all costs. Butternuts are always good. But also look for new varieties, among them the Kent or jap, a boldly striped green pumpkin, or the Crown prince, which has smooth grey skin. Both are full of flavour and easy to peel.

I have three pumpkin vines this year – luckily garden space is not an issue for me. One of them has yielded lots and lots of male flowers and looks lustrous, but has only one pumpkin to show for itself. I really don't mind as the others are laden. And pumpkin flowers, though a little larger than zucchini flowers, can be stuffed and deep-fried as a starter or as part of an antipasto platter (as they are in Italy; turn to a good Italian cookbook for a batter recipe or stuffing suggestions). I tend to use one flower per person and stuff it generously, making sure that any cheese used is either soft goat's curd or cut quite small to ensure it melts in the short time it takes to deep-fry the battered flower in hot olive oil. Make sure you are ready to serve the moment they are golden – crisp is the word here.

Early in March 2006 we were filming an episode of the ABC TV series *The Cook and The Chef* when pumpkins were at the peak of their season. This coincided with the Tanunda Agricultural Show, and I was asked to be a judge for the best pumpkin at the show. I felt

so incredibly proud of the Barossa, with the different entries in the show hall and various stewards and judges taking their assessment of produce so seriously.

With the cameras rolling, I talked with some of the characters of the show – indeed, characters of the Barossa. It was hard to confine the filming just to pumpkins as the show was probably the best I'd seen in the thirty-three years we've lived in the Valley. This was partly because 2006 was a good year – we had great winter rains in 2005 that continued into spring, and this showed in the bountiful produce – but also because of the energies of that year's committee.

I left the show with half of the winning Queensland Blue under my arm. Filming a few days later, we had the wood fire going, and while my co-presenter Simon Bryant cooked a Beggar's Chicken, I made a huge Pumpkin Risotto (see page 308) out in the courtyard.

Baked pumpkin with the weekly roast was a childhood favourite of mine (always cooked with the skin on, by the way). Over the years I've learnt that pumpkin is also great par-cooked and finished on the barbecue grill plate, brushed with olive oil. For soup, I love to slow-roast chunks of pumpkin in the oven, just moistened with oil, to heighten their flavour. This technique is also good when making pumpkin pie.

During my long pumpkin-less European sojourn, I should have discovered the delights of Italy's pumpkin-filled pasta, which comes from the Modena region in particular. There, freshly baked pumpkin is mixed with crushed amaretti biscuits, egg and breadcrumbs to fill tortelli. Little pillows are made by cutting rounds from a sheet of pasta, then putting some of the pumpkin mixture in the middle before moistening the edges. The pasta is folded over the stuffing to make half-moon shapes and the edges are pressed together to ensure a tight seal. The tortelli are poached in water for a few minutes only and then served with nut-brown butter and freshly grated Parmigiano Reggiano. Another favourite from Italy is pumpkin-filled ravioli served with mustard fruits, burnt butter and sage – a wonderful marriage of flavours. My first experience of this dish was prepared by Sydney chef Franca Manfredi at Bel Mondo and has never been equalled. The pasta, made fresh daily, had an incredible silky texture and we ate it in spectacular surroundings overlooking the harbour – magical.

CHICKPEA AND ROASTED PUMPKIN SALAD   *Serves 4*

4 baby beetroot

sea salt flakes

400 g pumpkin, seeded and cut into wedges
(skin on)

2 red onions, quartered

extra virgin olive oil, for cooking

freshly ground black pepper

2 heads Treviso radicchio, washed and dried

1 avocado, peeled and cut into chunks

lemon juice, for drizzling

1 × 140 g can chickpeas, rinsed and drained

freshly chopped flat-leaf parsley, to serve

VINAIGRETTE

¼ cup (60 ml) extra virgin olive oil,
or to taste

1 tablespoon red-wine vinegar, or to taste

Preheat the oven to 180°C. Place the beetroot in a saucepan of cold water and bring to the boil. Add a little salt then simmer over low–medium heat for 30 minutes or until almost cooked. Drain, cool, then peel and cut in half.

Meanwhile, place pumpkin and onions on a baking tray lined with baking paper, drizzle with olive oil and season with salt and pepper. Roast for about 30 minutes or until cooked through and caramelised. Toss the halved beetroot with olive oil, then place on another baking paper-lined baking tray and roast for 15 minutes.

Heat a chargrill pan over high heat. Slice the radicchio into quarters, removing as much of the core as possible while keeping the quarters intact. Toss with olive oil and chargrill on both sides for about 2 minutes each, or until caramelised. Remove from heat and set aside.

Drizzle the avocado chunks with lemon juice. Combine all the ingredients in a large bowl. For the vinaigrette, mix olive oil and vinegar together to taste, and add to the salad.

PUMPKIN PICNIC LOAF   *Serves 6*

I love picnics no matter what time of the year, and am constantly thinking of ways to make them as simple as possible. Nothing spoils a picnic more than having to carry a lot with you, particularly when you choose spots you can only access by climbing through fences or over rocks – and aren't the best spots always just a little inaccessible?

The other thing I have become a lot smarter about is the packing away and cleaning up once you are home. There is something about picnics that induces such relaxation, which can quickly dissipate if the chores upon return require any more effort than throwing the leftovers to the chooks.

This pumpkin loaf makes great autumn picnic fare and would work with many variations of loaf shape – it is the quality of the bread that is important. Optional extras include pitted olives, anchovies or capers.

3 medium-sized very ripe red capsicums,
trimmed, seeded and quartered

¾ cup (180 ml) extra virgin olive oil

500 g good-quality pumpkin like Queensland
Blue *or* jap, seeded, peeled and cut into
large chunks

1 sprig rosemary, leaves stripped

sea salt flakes and freshly ground
black pepper

100 ml verjuice

3 medium-sized zucchini, cut into
1.5 cm chunks

1 × 16 cm-diameter round loaf
wood-fired bread

¼ cup flat-leaf parsley, coarsely chopped

175 g Gruyère, thinly sliced

6 slices prosciutto

Preheat the oven to 220°C. Rub the capsicum skins with a little of the olive oil and place on a baking tray or enamel plate (I have a collection of such plates bought from a hardware store that I use continually for such jobs). Roast for 20 minutes or until skins blacken; alternatively, blacken over a naked flame. Let the capsicums cool for just a few minutes, then place in a plastic bag to sweat.

Meanwhile, blanch the pumpkin in a saucepan of boiling water for 5 minutes. Drain, then drizzle with a little of the olive oil, scatter with rosemary and season with salt and pepper. Bake in a shallow roasting pan for 10 minutes or until cooked through and caramelised. Pour 70 ml of the verjuice over the pumpkin, then return it to the oven and cook for another 2–3 minutes.

Halfway through cooking the pumpkin, place the zucchini in another shallow roasting pan and drizzle with a little olive oil. Bake the zucchini for 5–10 minutes or until cooked but still firm and green. Pour the remaining verjuice over the zucchini, then return to the oven for another 2 minutes.

Peel the capsicum and keep them moist in a dish with their juices. Cut the loaf in half widthways and take out sufficient bread from both the base and the lid to allow the vegetables and other ingredients to be generously housed. Crisp the hollowed-out bread in the oven. Add the parsley to the cooling zucchini and check if it needs seasoning.

Fill the base of the loaf with the roast pumpkin, then top with the sliced Gruyère. Lay prosciutto slices over that. Layer the capsicum and then the zucchini in the hollowed-out loaf top. Put the two halves together, then bake for 15 minutes to melt the cheese. Remove from the oven, then weigh down using cans from the pantry, and leave at room temperature to cool for 15 minutes before wrapping for a picnic.

Pumpkin picnic loaf (see page 305)

PUMPKIN PIZZA WITH OLIVES AND BOCCONCINI *Makes 6 individual pizzas*

For another great version of this pizza, lightly fry some sage leaves in nut-brown butter and olive oil and scatter them over the cooked pizza in place of the olives.

¼ Queensland Blue pumpkin, peeled, seeded
    and cut into 1 cm cubes
½ cup (125 ml) extra virgin olive oil
sea salt flakes and freshly ground
    black pepper
¼ cup (60 ml) verjuice
about 1 cup (250 ml) tomato sugo *or* passata
    (see Glossary)
6 bocconcini, cut into quarters
75 g pitted kalamata olives, roughly chopped

DOUGH

15 g fresh yeast *or* 1½ teaspoons
    dried yeast
500 g strong flour (see Glossary)
1 teaspoon castor sugar
1–1½ cups (250–375 ml) warm water
2 teaspoons salt
1 tablespoon extra virgin olive oil,
    plus extra for greasing

To make the dough, combine the yeast, 1 teaspoon of the flour, castor sugar and warm water in a large bowl and whisk together. Stand this mixture in a warm place for 5–10 minutes or until the yeast activates and froths up. Slowly add the rest of the flour and salt and combine to make a stiff dough. Turn the dough out onto a floured surface and drizzle with olive oil. Knead the dough until it is shiny and bounces back to the touch. Place in a bowl, cover and set aside to rise for 30 minutes.

Meanwhile, preheat the oven to 200°C. Toss the pumpkin in olive oil and season with salt and pepper. Transfer to a baking tray and spread out so the pumpkin pieces have room around them. Roast for 10–15 minutes or until the pumpkin is cooked and golden brown. Drizzle the verjuice over the pumpkin, then return to the oven and cook for another 5 minutes. Remove from the oven and leave to cool.

Increase the oven temperature to 220°C. Turn the dough out onto a floured bench, divide into 6 even pieces, then roll each to a 5 mm thickness and place on a well-oiled heavy-based baking tray. You can top each with about 2 tablespoons of your favourite tomato sugo or passata if you are traditionally minded. Par-bake for 15 minutes or until pale golden.

Remove the pizzas from the oven, drizzle with a little extra virgin olive oil, then top with bocconcini, pumpkin and olives. Return to the oven for 5–10 minutes or until the cheese begins to melt.

PUMPKIN, VERJUICE AND EXTRA VIRGIN OLIVE OIL RISOTTO
Serves 4

It was my friend Stefano de Pieri who asked me why I didn't use verjuice in risottos, as he thought it perfect for them. As I have such a fondness and respect for Stefano I immediately acted upon his advice and have been using verjuice in my risottos ever since, particularly when making vegetable or seafood ones. I now wonder why it took so long for me to open my eyes to the idea.

I have a huge enamelled paella pan I use for risottos when I'm cooking for a crowd. It's perfect for cooking outdoors, and holds enough to feed twenty to thirty people, depending on whether the risotto (or paella) is an accompaniment or main dish. Pumpkin and verjuice are such a magical combination, and when you add them to risotto (the perfect vehicle for both) it's the easiest way I know to cook for a large group.

2 cups (500 ml) Golden Chicken Stock
    (see page 57)
2 tablespoons extra virgin olive oil
500 g jap pumpkin, peeled and cut into
    2 cm cubes
50 g unsalted butter
1 onion, finely chopped

1¼ cups (250 g) Arborio rice (see Glossary)
100 ml verjuice
sea salt flakes and freshly ground
    black pepper
60 g freshly grated Parmigiano Reggiano
freshly chopped flat-leaf parsley and
    extra virgin olive oil, to serve

Heat the stock in a saucepan, then keep warm. Heat the olive oil in a wok over high heat and sauté the pumpkin until tender.

Heat the butter in a shallow, wide-based, large saucepan, add the onion and sauté over low–medium heat until golden. When the onion is cooked, add the rice and stir to coat with the onion mixture. Cook for 1–2 minutes then increase the temperature to high. Make a well in the centre of the rice and add the verjuice, continuing to stir until the liquid evaporates. Season with salt and reduce heat to low, then add a ladle of hot stock and stir until absorbed.

Continue adding the stock, a ladleful at a time, stirring until each has been absorbed, until half of the stock has been used; it should take 10 minutes. Add the pumpkin and its juices, then add the remaining stock, a ladleful at a time, until the rice is cooked.

Remove the pan from the heat and stir in the Parmigiano Reggiano. Serve topped with flat-leaf parsley and drizzled with olive oil.

QUINCES

THIS WONDERFULLY EVOCATIVE FRUIT WAS MY FIRST LINK TO the land in a sense, as when we were looking for a place in the Barossa, more years ago than I care to remember, we looked at many farmhouses and, even at the most derelict of places, where the gardens and orchards had been left untended for years, there would be a surviving quince tree.

With the fervour of the city-turned-country-dweller, I quickly learned to love the quince tree in all its seasons, so much so that we planted our own quince orchard at a time when most people were throwing quinces away.

I started dreaming about planting the quince orchard after I read a piece written by Stephanie Alexander in which she talked about drinking quince wine on a frappé of ice in France. At the time I had Steve Flamsteed, a passionate young wine-making student, working with me, so I threw him the challenge of making a quince wine and he was happy to give it a try.

Finding the quinces for our trial wasn't a problem as, like most properties in the Barossa, we have a sprawling quince tree in the creekbed that runs through our vineyard. Totally untended, this tree is abundant with small quinces that are incredibly intense in flavour. Ever the optimist, I could see the quince wine becoming a huge success, and decided that planting my own orchard was the only way I could have control over availability.

Since then we've planted some 350 quince trees at the Pheasant Farm – the spring blossom makes a beautiful sight. Not surprisingly, we've had our mishaps. Although we ordered the Smyrna variety we actually ended up with about fifty pineapple quince trees, and it wasn't until after harvesting the first crop that we realised. The flavour of the much larger pineapple quince doesn't suit my requirements. The Smyrna is more 'quince' in flavour and, very importantly, does not break up in long cooking. (Once you've tried the Pot-roasted Quinces on page 318 you'll understand the significance of this: these quinces need to hold their shape during cooking.)

Pot-roasted quinces (see page 318)

We've had several vintages of quince wine now, and it's still looking 'interesting'. Remember that we were guided by a whim, never having tasted quince wine before – between us, Steve and I had decided that it should be an apéritif with some spirit. If we had been more 'structured' people, we would have done more research, for it is very difficult to extract juice from mashed-up quinces, and juice is what we needed. We ended up blanching the quinces, then mashing them in a large commercial food processor before putting them through a basket press. It was a performance, with lots of physical work, and left a dreadful mess to clean up!

Steve Flamsteed was one of a core of incredibly talented people who worked for me during the restaurant days, and who are still part of our extended family. Steve is a bit of a one-off, having first trained as a chef then studied wine-making at Roseworthy during the time he worked for us. He then learnt to become a cheese-maker in France, with a Queen's Fellowship. Having excelled in all three fields, he is back to wine-making now, although he still has a great interest in food, particularly cheese – a very special mix of talents in one very special person.

In 1995 we started to make quince paste on a commercial scale, having only made it in small quantities during the restaurant days. It was Steve who produced the first thousand wooden boxes of paste, making it in three 20-litre pots at a time, day after day. Once the paste reached the right consistency (which required up to five hours of careful stirring, with lots of burns and splatters to show for it) it then needed to be dried out. For this, we ended up sterilising our pheasant incubator (the season being over, I hasten to add) and using it to dry the paste overnight in moulds. We had a side project of quince jelly on the go too, and the perfume of the quinces used in both preparations permeated for weeks.

By 1996 we were making 5 tonnes of quince paste a year. Now, twelve years later, our own trees are in full production, as are those of three orchards that grow for us, and we probably make 75 tonnes per year. It is the one product we have been able to upscale and cook in large batches, the absolute opposite of every other product we make, and I can truly say it gets better and better.

Quince paste has since became one of my signatures, and while its main use is to serve with cheese, particularly a sharp crumbly cheddar or a creamy, slightly stinky, waxed rind, that is only the beginning. Roll half teaspoonfuls of quince paste in melted bitter couverture chocolate. Cut it into small squares and dust all over with a mixture of cinnamon and sugar, then serve with coffee. Use leftover pieces to melt over roasting legs of lamb or add a teaspoon to a sauce for duck, venison or leg of mutton.

Quince trees bear really well, and one tree will have you making quincey things for the whole neighbourhood by the time the tree is five years old. Here in the Barossa we pick our quinces in April, and even in the coolest places in Australia, May would be the latest time for harvesting. So the wide availability of quinces on greengrocers' shelves in winter is due to the quinces being stored in cool-rooms.

There is no end to the quince's versatility. While quince paste is our hero quince product, we also make the quince wine (some years), small amounts of quince jelly and pickled quinces, quince vino cotto, quince glaze for Christmas, quince paste and roasted almond ice cream, and our latest (but by no means our last) quince product, a bitter chocolate with quince and almond filling.

The tartness of quince when peeled, cored and sautéed in nut-brown butter is the best antidote to rich and fatty food. If you are ever lucky enough to have fresh foie gras, try pan-frying slices of it with quince and you'll understand the joys of one of the greatest food combinations ever. (You'll need to be in Europe or the United States to have access to fresh foie gras, so you could instead use slices of fresh livers of very well-brought-up chooks, geese or ducks. If all else fails, team with pork or duck meat for much the same effect – though these options lack the silkiness of the livers.)

Quince purée can be served with duck, quail, guinea fowl, partridge or pheasant, or even a great-tasting chook. Cook chopped and peeled quince in a little water in a covered saucepan until it is just soft enough to purée in a food processor or to put through a food mill. You may have to add a little sugar to the purée – but only a couple of table-spoons per kg of fruit. A certain tartness is desirable, but it shouldn't be so intense that it puckers your mouth. The purée will be a light-apricot colour (not the deep red of slow-cooked quince, a process which gives such complexity of flavour). This paler hue is, by the way, the colour of most European quince paste, which is not cooked as long as mine is. Cooking quince changes its colour due, I believe, to an enzymatic reaction. It begins at pale yellow and goes through stages of pale orange to pink when cooked for a short period. To obtain the deep-red colour, it takes hours and hours of cooking.

Puréed quince can also be used as a dessert by adding more sugar and a vanilla bean during cooking. As figs are in season at the same time as quinces, try serving pan-fried or oven-baked figs in a pastry case with warm quince purée and a scoop of vanilla ice cream alongside.

Pickled quince can be teamed with pickled pork, lamb chops or barbecued kangaroo, or added to a Smoked Duck Breast Salad (see page 317). The cuisines of Morocco and the Middle East feature quinces in savoury dishes, too, particularly with couscous and in tagines, where sweet is mixed with sour. In her book *Mediterranean Cooking*, Paula Wolfert writes about a fish couscous that includes quinces, raisins and baharat (a mixture of 2 parts ground cinnamon to 1 part ground dried rosebuds). How exotic!

You can bake small quinces fresh from the tree. Peel and core the quinces, then stuff them with walnuts, butter and brown sugar or honey and bake, covered, for 45–60 minutes at 220°C, with a little verjuice in the bottom of the baking dish to prevent the juices burning.

Bake quartered or sliced quinces brushed with butter in a 160°C oven with a little verjuice or water in the baking dish for a couple of hours. Try then baking this with pastry or brioche as you would your favourite apple pie. Make a flat quince tart in the same style as a traditional French apple tart. Follow the instructions for preparing the pastry for the Quince and Prune Tart on page 319. While the pastry is still warm, brush quince or loquat jelly over it. Peel and core quinces, then arrange super-thin slices on the pastry and brush

with more jelly. Bake the tart at 180°C for 15–20 minutes, being careful the quince doesn't burn.

Preserving fruit or vegetables is a most satisfying occupation. I often don't put the fruits of my labours away in cupboards or the pantry for ages as I love gloating over them – until I can't cook for the clutter on the benches and one of my tidying frenzies comes upon me. Even then, the top of my huge stainless steel fridge holds masses of bottles (it dates from circa 1950 and in its previous life held specimens in a university laboratory!). The soft late-afternoon sun catches the colours of the preserved quinces and they glow like jewels. The jars on show are the last of the year's harvest to be used, a constant reminder of how clever I have been – and that a new season's bounty is waiting in the cupboards!

Preserving quinces as a breakfast fruit was my first experiment in bottling without adding a sugar syrup. They are delicious, and I now see no reason to use sugar with any fruit when preserving.

Quinces are wonderful to make jelly from as they have such a high pectin content – and the highest amount of pectin is to be had from new-season, just-picked, slightly under-ripe fruit that hasn't been refrigerated. Rosemary goes particularly well with quinces: add a sprig of rosemary to the boiling syrup – this is great brushed over a leg of lamb or fillets of pork before baking. If the jelly is too sweet, add a touch of red-wine vinegar before brushing it over the meat. You can also add allspice berries or black peppercorns to the quince in its initial cooking if you want to use the jelly mainly with savoury dishes.

Quince jelly takes my husband Colin back to his childhood. He toasts doorstops of white bread and adds unsalted butter (a modern-day refinement) before dolloping on the jelly. If there's cream in the fridge, and I'm not looking, he smothers the jelly with it.

To store fragrant quinces, rub the down off them carefully and place them in a wide-necked jar. Pour honey over them. This form of storage produces a wonderful liquid with the taste of honey and quince. We have a friend who for several years kept his beehives on our land and this was a favourite way to use the honey he kindly left for us. The same can be done with brandy to make a quince liqueur.

Pick the last quinces off the tree and when you can neither cook nor give away any more, put them in a basket in the mustiest part of your house – a cellar, store cupboard, or a room with no ventilation – and the perfume of the quince will transform it.

QUINCE PASTE   *Makes one 28 × 22 cm scone tray*

This quince paste is made just like a jam. It follows a traditional method, with the addition of a little lemon juice so it is not too sweet. I actually use less sugar in my quince paste to allow the quince flavour to shine, but that is because I do not have much of a sweet tooth. You can vary the sugar according to your taste – my paste uses 30 per cent sugar and 70 per cent fruit. You will need to wear a fair amount of armour to stop yourself from being burnt. The end result is worth the effort – every time you serve a beautifully ripe and creamy brie, this paste will be testimony to your determination.

2 kg quinces

castor sugar, to equal the weight
   of the purée when cooked

juice of 2 lemons

Wash and quarter the quinces. Keep the cores, wrap them in some muslin and cook them with the quinces. In a large heavy-based saucepan, pour just enough water over the quinces to cover them, and bring to a boil, simmering over low heat for about 30 minutes or until they are tender enough to purée easily. Drain the quinces, discard the cores and purée the fruit in a food processor or using a food mill, then weigh the purée.

Place the purée and an equal weight of sugar in a very deep, heavy-based saucepan. Add the lemon juice and cook over low heat, stirring almost continuously, for up to 4 hours or until the mixture thickens. (At this stage it is advisable to wrap a tea towel around your arm to protect it, and to use as long a wooden spoon as possible. The mixture will explode and pop and turn a dark red, and only by constant stirring will you prevent it from burning.) Cook until you can hardly push the spoon through the paste.

Remove the paste to a scone tray lined with baking paper and spread it out to a 12 mm thickness. When it cools, wet your hands and flatten the surface as you would when shaping polenta. Place the tray in an oven on the lowest possible setting (in a gas oven, the pilot light would be sufficient) and leave to dry overnight. When it has set enough to be cut into squares with a hot knife, it is ready to be cooled and stored. Pack the quince paste between layers of baking paper and store in an airtight container for up to 1 year.

FLO BEER'S PICKLED QUINCES

Flo Beer, my very special mother-in-law, shared this recipe with me the first time Colin took me home to Mallala to meet his family, only three weeks before our wedding – 38 years ago now. That first meal we had together, Mum (as I used to call her as well as my own mother) served these pickled quinces with pickled pork, and they remain a sentimental favourite. As a lover of pickles, I never miss making a batch every year, and I think of her every time. They are wonderful with ham and terrines or grilled meats, particularly duck or game. Adding some of the juices to a beef or poultry sauce, which is then reduced to a glaze, also works brilliantly.

This recipe is written to work equally well for those who have bought a kilo of quinces from the greengrocer and those wondering what to do with boxes and boxes of the fruit. The volume of liquid required is enough to just cover the cut quinces. You can establish this at the beginning by covering the cut quinces with water, measuring the water used, and using this amount of vinegar.

quinces	**castor sugar**
lemon juice	**whole cloves**
white-wine vinegar (the better the quality,	**black peppercorns**
the better the final product)	

Wash, peel and core the quinces and cut into quarters or eighths, depending on the size, retaining the skins and cores. Put the cut quinces immediately into water to which lemon juice has been added, to prevent discolouration.

For each 600 ml vinegar, add 440 g sugar, 1 teaspoon cloves and 1 teaspoon peppercorns. Heat the vinegar in a large heavy-based saucepan, then pour in the sugar in a stream to dissolve. Bring to the boil, then add the cloves and peppercorns and boil rapidly to begin forming a syrup. Turn the heat down to low and cook for 15 minutes.

Place the reserved peels and cores in a muslin bag and add to the syrup; it will immediately take on a rosy glow. Add the sliced quinces and cook for about 15 minutes or until they have turned pink and are soft but not mushy.

Store in clean airtight jars with the quinces well-immersed in the liquid. The colour of the quinces will deepen in the jar. Leave for several weeks before opening.

QUINCE ALLIOLI   *Makes about 250 ml*

I found references to quince allioli in books about Spanish food, and as I'm always interested in anything to do with quince, I experimented with the idea. Then one year, a friend brought me a jar of quince allioli from Spain. I didn't think quickly enough to note the ingredients listed on the jar, but was delighted by the fresh flavour, so once again I started playing around with ingredients and quantities and this is the result.

100 g Maggie Beer Quince Paste

2 tablespoons verjuice

1 clove garlic

sea salt flakes

1 dessertspoon finely chopped rosemary

½ cup (125 ml) extra virgin olive oil

lemon juice (optional), to taste

Melt the quince paste slowly with the verjuice (I find a microwave set on defrost works well for this; otherwise use a pan over very low heat). Leave to cool. Crush the peeled garlic clove and a pinch of salt on a chopping board with the flat side of a knife to make a paste. Transfer the garlic paste, quince paste mixture and chopped rosemary to a food processor and blend. With the motor running, slowly add the olive oil, starting a drop at a time until the mixture emulsifies; after about one-third of the oil has been absorbed, you can start to pour it in a thin, steady stream. (As this is quite a small quantity for many food processors, you might need to scrape the sides of the processor bowl with a rubber spatula now and then to make sure all the ingredients are combined.) Taste and adjust seasoning, squeezing in a little lemon juice if necessary.

Serve with barbecued chicken or rack of lamb, or cold pickled pork.

SMOKED DUCK BREAST SALAD WITH PICKLED QUINCE AND VINO COTTO DRESSING

Serves 4

2 smoked duck breasts

1 tablespoon unsalted butter

50 g Pickled Quinces, including pickling liquid (see opposite)

1 head radicchio, leaves separated, washed and dried

2 witlof, bases trimmed and leaves separated

1 bunch rocket, washed and dried

1 tablespoon lemon juice

½ cup (125 ml) extra virgin olive oil

vino cotto (see Glossary), to taste

3 golden shallots, thinly sliced

1 tablespoon thinly sliced ginger

1 tablespoon flat-leaf parsley leaves

sea salt flakes and freshly ground black pepper

Heat a chargrill plate over high heat. Carefully cut the skin of the duck breasts (not the meat) in diagonal lines, then sear them skin-side down for a couple of minutes – the time will depend on the thickness of the meat – to render the fat and crisp the skin. Turn and seal the other side until just brown, then set aside to rest.

Melt the butter in a sauté pan over medium–high heat, then add the drained quince and brown.

Combine the salad leaves in a large bowl. Make a dressing with a little of the pickled quince liquid, lemon juice, olive oil and vino cotto to taste. Add the quince, shallots and ginger to the salad bowl, then toss with the dressing. Thinly slice the duck breast, then add to the salad, along with the parsley. Season to taste with salt and pepper and serve.

LAMB NECK WITH QUINCES
Serves 2–4

Lamb neck is delicious and full of flavour when cooked slowly. You'll need to ask your butcher to leave the neck whole, as when it is cut into sections it's much more likely to dry out during cooking.

I often cook this the day before I want to serve it, as the easiest way to separate the fat is to refrigerate the lamb overnight then skim the solidified fat from the surface.

1 tablespoon extra virgin olive oil

½ knob ginger (2 cm), peeled and
  roughly chopped

2 cloves garlic, roughly chopped

8 onions, roughly chopped

1 × 850 g–1 kg large lamb neck, whole

1 large quince, washed, peeled,
  cored and roughly sliced

1 tablespoon sherry vinegar

1 teaspoon coriander seeds, crushed

½ teaspoon ground turmeric

1 teaspoon ground cumin

1–2 cups reduced Golden Chicken Stock
  (see page 57)

1 tablespoon Quince Pickling Liquid
  (see page 316)

2 quarters Pickled Quince (see page 316),
  thinly sliced

⅓ cup coriander leaves, chopped

Preheat the oven to 120°C. Heat the oil over medium heat in a heavy-based enamelled casserole dish with a tight-fitting lid. Toss in the ginger, garlic and onions and fry until golden. Add the lamb neck and brown evenly, then add the fresh quince slices. Deglaze the pan with the sherry vinegar and add the spices. Pour in enough stock to half-cover the lamb neck, place the lid on and transfer the casserole to the oven to cook for approximately 3½ hours or until the lamb is very tender. Set aside to cool, then place in the fridge overnight.

On the day of serving, remove the lamb from the fridge and skim off the fat, then warm the lamb slowly in the casserole over low heat. Once heated through, remove the lamb neck from the pan and set it aside, wrapped in plastic film to keep it moist. Add the quince pickling liquid to the casserole, turn the heat to high and bring to the boil. Carefully remove the meat from the bone of the neck, then add this to the casserole along with the pickled quince slices. The sauce should glisten invitingly.

Scatter with the chopped coriander and serve with creamy polenta.

POT-ROASTED QUINCES
Serves 6

Dessert is my least favourite part of the meal, but this dish, passed on to me by Hazel Mader, the mother of my friend, Jenny Beckmann, is one of such simplicity that it's a favourite of mine at this time of year. The effect of the long cooking is that the quinces change from bright yellow to a deep ruby-red. They remain whole, but are so well cooked you can even eat the cores! These baked quinces can be cooked and kept frozen in their juices, to bring out in the middle of winter. If you are lucky enough to have picked the quinces yourself and left the stem on with a few leaves still attached, there is nothing more to do after cooking than to serve them unadorned to revel in their own majesty.

This recipe works for small–medium quinces that will not fall apart when cooked for a long time. Avoid super-large or pineapple variety quinces for this dish.

6 quinces, picked with stems and leaves intact, if possible	4 cups (880 g) sugar juice of 3 lemons

Rub the down off the quinces and wash them. Pack them tightly in a heavy-based saucepan with the sugar and 1.5 litres water. Boil at a reasonably high temperature until a jelly starts to form, then reduce heat to low and simmer for up to 5 hours (I often use a simmer pad to control the temperature). The quinces should be turned at least 4 times during the cooking process so that the deep-ruby colour goes right through to the core. Add lemon juice at the last stage of the cooking to remove any excessive sweetness.

Serve the quinces whole or sliced with a little of the jelly and fresh cream or Crème Anglaise (see page 225).

QUINCE AND PRUNE TART
Serves 6

150 g pitted prunes	juice of 1 lemon
150 ml verjuice, plus 1 tablespoon for cooking	1 × quantity Sour-cream Pastry (see page 424)
1 tablespoon finely chopped lemon rind	1 tablespoon quince paste
3 large quinces (to yield 450 g peeled, cored, sliced quinces)	1 egg, lightly beaten mascarpone *or* double cream, to serve

Soak prunes in the 150 ml verjuice overnight (or microwave prunes and verjuice on low for 5 minutes), then add the lemon rind and leave for 15 minutes; the prunes will plump and absorb the verjuice. Either mash, roughly chop or purée the prunes in a food processor and set aside.

Peel and core the quinces, then cut into slices, placing them in a bowl of water acidulated with lemon juice as you go, to prevent discolouration. Blanch the drained quince slices in a saucepan of boiling water for 7 minutes or until partially cooked, then drain and transfer to a baking tray to cool.

Make and chill the pastry following the instructions. Roll out to a 3 mm thick rectangle to fit a scone tray, reserving the excess pastry. Chill the pastry on a tray in the refrigerator for 20 minutes.

Preheat the oven to 200°C. Prick the pastry all over with a fork, then cover with foil and pastry weights and blind bake for 15 minutes. Remove foil and weights and bake for another 5 minutes. Leave the tart shell to cool.

Spread the puréed prunes evenly over the cooled pastry base. Overlap the quince slices like roof tiles over the prunes. Melt the quince paste with the extra verjuice in a small saucepan over low heat until it reaches a spreadable consistency, stirring to combine.

Reset oven to 180°C. Brush quince paste mixture over the quince slices and bake for 10 minutes. Meanwhile, roll the reserved pastry off-cuts, then cut into strips. Increase the oven temperature to 210°C, arrange pastry strips in a lattice pattern over the quince, brush pastry with beaten egg and bake for another 15 minutes or until the pastry is golden.

Serve warm slices of the tart with mascarpone or double cream.

QUINCES AND PEARS POACHED IN VERJUICE

Serves 6

3 quinces	3 cups (750 ml) verjuice
juice of 1 lemon	1 kg beurre bosc pears, peeled, cored
sugar, to taste (optional)	and quartered

Preheat the oven to 180°C. Peel and core the quinces, then cut each one into 8 wedges, putting the cut quince into a bowl of water acidulated with lemon juice as you go to prevent discolouration. If you are using sugar, simmer it with the verjuice on a medium heat for approximately 20 minutes to begin to form a syrup. Poach the quince and pears in the oven with the verjuice and sugar (if using), in a large, flat baking dish until cooked through. (The cooking time will depend on the variety and ripeness of the fruit.) The fruit should be soft to the touch but still intact and will not be the deep ruby-red of long-cooked quince. Once cooked, put the quince with the syrup into a pan and, over high heat, reduce the verjuice until both the fruit and verjuice caramelise – turn the slices of fruit over once the first side has caramelised. Serve with mascarpone or fresh cream, or with a delicate Italian lemon biscuit.

RHUBARB

 ALTHOUGH RHUBARB IS USED ALMOST ENTIRELY AS A FRUIT, botanically it is a vegetable. It is available all year round (spring is when it shoots forth), but the largest rhubarb grower in South Australia tells me that the best rhubarb is actually to be had from May to June, as it grows more slowly then and the stalks are a deeper red.

If you have the room, rhubarb is worth growing at home as it is not always the staple it should be on greengrocers' shelves, considering what an established food plant it is (it is now deemed old-fashioned, and has to compete with so many more 'fashionable' fruit and vegetables).

No matter what time of the year, you should only select young and slender pinky red stalks of rhubarb, unless they are of the green variety available now. Large green–pink rhubarb is older and will be tough, stringy and acidic. Those of you who grow rhubarb will know from experience that it needs to be picked regularly – if you don't, you need to be strong-willed enough to throw the oversized stalks on the compost and not be tempted to cook them. I know people who pick young rhubarb straight from the garden, breaking off the stalks and eating them raw, although most would dip them in sugar first. I am told fresh uncooked rhubarb tastes like very sharp sorrel, which doesn't surprise me, since it is related to that wonderful bitter herb. Remember never to eat rhubarb leaves, though, as they contain poisonous oxalic acid.

In the main, rhubarb needs little stringing and this should only be considered if the rhubarb is large and therefore more likely to be old. Keep in mind that stringiness equates to acidity, which can be countered by adding a little more sugar when cooking. I say only 'a little more' as my main complaint with rhubarb is that it tends to be served over-sugared and waterlogged. Little, if any, juice or water needs to be added to rhubarb, as it gives off so much moisture as it cooks, but the amount of sugar required is open to negotiation. I do not have a sweet tooth and like to taste the tartness of the rhubarb, so I tend to err on the side of adding very little sugar or honey. Start sparingly, adding extra sweetness if necessary. The amount of sugar needed will differ every time you cook it.

Remove any signs of browning from the base of the stalks and chop into 2.5–3 cm lengths. Cook in an enamelled, earthenware or stainless steel casserole with a tight-fitting lid (never cook rhubarb in aluminium as its acidity will react with the metal and give the fruit a metallic taint). The size of the container is important: it should be just large enough to accommodate the rhubarb snugly. If you're nervous that the rhubarb might burn add a tablespoon of verjuice or orange juice rather than water, or instead add 60 g butter for every 500 g trimmed rhubarb. Drizzle with a little honey or sprinkle brown sugar on top – try ¼ cup sugar to 500 g trimmed rhubarb – then put the lid in place. Cook the rhubarb for about 10 minutes at 200°C, then check it for sugar and doneness (the cooking time will depend on the pot you are using). Cooked this way, the rhubarb will collapse but not become a mush.

It was very rare for us to have dessert in our house as I grew up, but rhubarb from the garden was a favourite. For special occasions Mum would make a rice pudding flavoured with nutmeg and served with stewed rhubarb alongside. The rhubarb was also brought out for breakfast, when we had it chilled from the refrigerator on Weetbix with hot milk.

The piquancy of rhubarb is a perfect foil to rich meat such as liver, duck, pork or lamb and, surprisingly to some, fish (particularly oily fish like tommy ruffs). Try cutting fresh young rhubarb into tiny dice and adding it to calf's liver cooking in a pan of nut-brown butter just as you prepare to turn the liver. The liver takes only a couple of minutes a side to cook, and the rhubarb should still have a crunch. Drizzle a little top-grade balsamic vinegar over the dish at the last moment.

I once had a truly remarkable quince tart made by Jennifer Hillier, of the wonderful Uraidla Restaurant in the Adelaide Hills, for the 1984 Symposium of Gastronomy. She had used a brioche recipe from a book very dear to her, *The Auberge of the Flowering Hearth* by Roy Andries de Groot. It presented like a tarte tatin, and the fragrant juices were taken up by the brioche when the tart was inverted. This would work so well with rhubarb, tossed in butter with brown sugar and cinnamon over medium heat to just soften. There is no doubt that one idea can lead to another, and every recipe should be seen as just a starting point.

RHUBARB, STRAWBERRIES AND CRÈME FRAICHE   *Serves 4–6*

500 g ripe rhubarb stalks, trimmed,
   washed and cut into 2.5 cm lengths
finely chopped rind of 1 orange and
   3 tablespoons juice
½ cup brown sugar
1 cup ripe strawberries
balsamic vinegar *or* vino cotto
   (see Glossary), for drizzling
   (optional)
1 cup crème fraiche
3 tablespoons cream
pinch freshly grated nutmeg
lemon juice, to taste (optional)

Place the rhubarb, orange rind, orange juice and brown sugar in a small pan with a tight-fitting lid. Bring to a gentle simmer with the lid on, then remove the pan from the heat, take the lid off and stir. Depending on the age of the rhubarb, you may only need to stand it in the hot saucepan for a few minutes more to cook it through, but if it needs further cooking, heat over low heat with the lid off for another 3 minutes. Transfer to a bowl and refrigerate, covered, for several hours.

Hull strawberries and cut into thin vertical slices. If the strawberries are not as ripe as they could be, drizzle the tiniest bit of vino cotto or balsamic over them.

Fold the crème fraiche and the cream together in a bowl, and then fold in the rhubarb and the grated nutmeg. Chill, covered, for another hour. Fold strawberries in at the last moment. Adjust the flavour if necessary with a squeeze of lemon.

RICE PUDDING WITH POACHED RHUBARB AND ORANGE *Serves 6–8*

6 eggs

3 tablespoons castor sugar

5 cups full-cream milk

½ cup cream

pinch freshly grated nutmeg

½ cup (115 g) short-grain rice

3 tablespoons chopped candied orange peel

1 tablespoon butter

POACHED RHUBARB AND ORANGE

750 g ripe rhubarb stalks, trimmed,
     washed and cut into 2.5 cm lengths

finely chopped rind of 1 orange

¼ cup orange juice

¼ cup (110 g) brown sugar

For the pudding, preheat the oven to 160°C. Beat the eggs and castor sugar together in a bowl, then add the milk, cream and grated nutmeg and mix together. Stir in the rice and candied orange peel.

Butter a ceramic soufflé mould (I use one that is 19 × 9 cm), pour in the mixture and bake for 1¾–2 hours, depending on the height of the dish, until cooked with a brown crust on top.

Meanwhile, to make the rhubarb, take a small pan with a tight-fitting lid and add the rhubarb, orange rind, orange juice and brown sugar. Bring to a gentle simmer with the lid on, then remove the pan from the heat, take the lid off and stir. Depending on the age of the rhubarb, you may only need to stand it in the hot saucepan for a few minutes more to cook it through, but if it needs further cooking, heat over low heat with the lid off for another 3 minutes. Once cooked, remove the pan from the heat and set aside to cool for a few minutes, then transfer the rhubarb to the refrigerator to chill.

Allow the pudding to cool a little and spoon a good serving into a dish with the chilled rhubarb and perhaps some runny cream.

CHOCOLATE ORANGE BROWNIE PUDDING
WITH RHUBARB AND MASCARPONE

Serves 8–10

I decided I liked the idea of rhubarb and chocolate together, and as the marriage of rhubarb and orange works so well, I thought I'd combine the lot. Then I found a packet of my friend Noëlle Tolley's glacé cumquats and took it one step further. Virgin Hills, a company from the Riverland in South Australia, produces a first-class moist orange peel, if you prefer to use this as an alternative to the cumquat.

150 g dark chocolate, chopped
200 g butter
2 large eggs and 2 egg yolks, beaten
300 g brown sugar
120 g plain flour
40 g unsweetened cocoa (see Glossary)
1 teaspoons baking powder
¼ teaspoon salt
100 g glacé cumquat *or* orange peel
mascarpone, to serve

RHUBARB
1.5 kg ripe rhubarb stalks, trimmed,
    washed and cut into 4–5 cm pieces
finely chopped rind of 1 orange
½ cup orange juice
½ cup (110 g) brown sugar

Preheat the oven to 160°C. To prepare the rhubarb, spread it out over a baking dish, and add the orange rind, juice and brown sugar, then bake for about 15–20 minutes, or until collapsed and tender. Allow to cool, then refrigerate.

For the pudding, grease and line a flat 26 × 16 cm slice tray. Melt the chocolate and butter together in the microwave on medium heat for 40 seconds at a time, repeating this 3 times (be careful not to overcook) stirring until smooth. Alternatively, you can use a double boiler, or a heatproof bowl that fits snugly over a pan of boiling water.

Using an electric mixer, beat the eggs with the sugar until thick and pale. Fold in the remaining ingredients, except the mascarpone, with a wooden spoon, stirring until well combined.

Spread the batter into the prepared tray and bake for 35 minutes. The pudding should still be moist and springy in the centre. Allow to cool a little, in which time it will 'cook' a little further.

Serve the pudding whilst still warm, with the chilled rhubarb and mascarpone.

RHUBARB CRUMBLE

Serves 4

What could be more old-fashioned than rhubarb crumble? I leave the rhubarb a little tart – the sweetness of the crumble provides the balance. A variation is to add chopped almonds to the crumble topping.

For this recipe, you'll need a dish that is around 26 × 18 cm, and not too deep, or the crumble will become soggy.

1.5 kg ripe rhubarb stalks, trimmed, washed
    and cut into 4–5 cm lengths
½ cup orange juice
½ cup (110 g) castor sugar
finely chopped rind of 1 orange
2 tablespoons unsalted butter
double cream, to serve

CRUMBLE
1 teaspoon ground cinnamon
80 g dark-brown sugar
125 g plain flour
140 g unsalted butter, cut into cubes
    and chilled

Preheat the oven to 200°C. Spread the rhubarb on a baking tray, then sprinkle with castor sugar, dot with butter and bake for about 10 minutes or until rhubarb is just cooked.

To make the crumble, mix the cinnamon, dark-brown sugar and flour in a bowl. Work the butter into the flour mixture with your fingertips.

Place the cooked rhubarb in a buttered soufflé mould (or 4 individual ramekins), then sprinkle with orange rind and top with the crumble mixture. Bake for 15–20 minutes or until golden. Serve with rich double cream.

VERJUICE

IN THE FOURTEENTH AND FIFTEENTH CENTURIES VERJUICE WAS so familiar to Parisian cooks that, writing in *Winestate* in 1984, Barbara Santich suggested: 'the flask of verjuice was probably always within the cook's easy reach and as frequently used as soy sauce in a Chinese kitchen today'.

Verjuice (or verjus) is made from the juice of unripe grapes. Its flavour has the tartness of lemon and the acidity of vinegar without the harshness of either. It lends a subtle hint of grapes and is a marvellous addition to almost any dish.

In the Middle Ages verjuice was used with wild duck, chicken, capon, goose and roasted pork and was also an important ingredient in sauces. In the eighteenth century, the son of a Dijon master vinegar-maker instituted a small but revolutionary change when he substituted verjuice for vinegar in his mustard. The supremacy of Dijon mustards is still evident today, and mustard made with verjuice is particularly fine, being slightly less acidic and pungent than that made with vinegar.

Even though it is a staple of French cooking, verjuice is rarely seen for sale commercially in France. Households once made their own, as they did vinegar. Certainly restaurants in France still make verjuice, either when grapes are in season, freezing the grapes or juice for later use, or stabilising the verjuice with alcohol (although this method masks its true flavour).

It was while reading about verjuice in books on French provincial cooking that I was first encouraged, as a cook and grape grower, to try making it myself. My first attempt, with the assistance of friend Peter Wall, was in 1984. I believe we were the first in the world to make verjuice commercially available all year round by using modern wine-making techniques. It took years before the next commercial trial, mainly because the only people who knew about our verjuice were the restaurateurs we were selling it to, including Stephanie Alexander and Lew Kathreptis, then of the Adelaide restaurant Mezes. This was our first lesson in marketing, and it took ten more years to really get it off the ground – now I'm pleased to say that the best gourmet delis across Australia have a regular supply of not only my verjuice, but many others as well, and ours is so popular it's also available in supermarkets. We also export to Japan, the United States, the United Kingdom, Dubai and Hong Kong.

Having led the way in making verjuice commercially in a form suitable to be stored is something that I am enormously proud of, yet it's also important that others have followed, both legitimising verjuice as an important ingredient in the serious cook's pantry and making it relatively accessible.

Since our early days of production, verjuice has become not only indispensable to my own cooking, but also to that of many chefs and home cooks alike. This in turn prompted me to write a book totally dedicated to the subject, *Cooking With Verjuice*, in an attempt to share just how versatile this product is. I never stop discovering new ways with verjuice and try to continually add ideas to my website. I can see *More Cooking With Verjuice* emerging as my next project!

Every year the choice of wine grapes for my verjuice varies with the season, but when I was offered some sangiovese grapes in 2000 for making verjuice I was keen to have a go and decided to crush them. I was delighted that they resulted in a beautiful rose-coloured product with a sweet fruitiness, which was offset by the grapes' natural acidity; so now, each year we make a small amount with these. While the sangiovese verjuice can be used in any of the recipes featuring verjuice in this book, I've found that using it when poaching soft fruits like nectarines or peaches and then setting the syrup as a jelly with the fruit suspended in it gives a wonderful flavour, as well as a colour that truly sparkles. When making a sangiovese verjuice sabayon, once again, its pale-pink colour becomes the defining character of the dish.

We also now make a non-alcoholic drink based on verjuice called Desert Pearls. It started out as an idea for an adult soft drink, but as I progressed with the idea I found it had more potential than I could have imagined. At first I called it Sour Grapes, a name I was inordinately proud of, since to me it seemed a perfect name for a drink based on verjuice. However, I found that those who understood the verjuice connection saw the humour in it, but those who felt the use of 'sour' was negative dismissed it out of hand. For once in my life I listened to others' opinions and renamed it Desert Pearls, a name my friend Gayle Gray helped me come up with (when drinking it, the bubbles feel like pink pearls, and, as we make Desert Pearls from the cabernet grapes in our Riverland vineyard, the Riverland is a desert climate and a pearl begins with a grain of sand, it all fell into place). Particularly as our first export market was Dubai, a desert climate, and the name seemed perfect there – and we also export it to Japan, a country where pearls are much revered. I've since grown to love the name.

As to how it's made, I'm not going to give away any trade secrets here as it is a patented product. I was very proud to receive a worldwide patent, as I have used very different methods to come up with a wonderfully refreshing and fruity (yet not sweet) non-alcoholic drink that feels like you are drinking a glass of champagne. It is a very sophisticated drink, with the hues and bubbles of a rosé champagne, and is incredibly popular with those who

Verjuice vinaigrette with oysters (see page 331)

prefer not to drink alcohol, as they truly don't feel left out. All other non-alcoholic drinks I have tried are made from de-alcoholised wines, and are often very sweet and lack freshness.

In a culinary context, Desert Pearls can be used for making a sorbet or jelly. My good friend Simon Bryant, my co-presenter on the ABC TV program *The Cook and The Chef*, made a jelly of Desert Pearls and poached pear (with the addition of chilli – I suspect just to have a go at me as I'm the chilli wimp of all time), which made for a really zesty and refreshing dessert.

If you have difficulty finding verjuice and you grow your own grapes, it can be made at home. While it is traditional to use wine grapes, any grapes picked 'green' (meaning sour), before they swell to ripeness, can be used. It takes about 4 kg grapes to produce 1 litre verjuice. I've found that the most practical method for home cooks is to first wash the grapes well, then pluck them from their stems and purée them in a food processor. Strain or pick out the seeds, then freeze the resultant juice in ice blocks to add to recipes calling for verjuice.

A dash of verjuice added to vine-ripened tomatoes pan-fried in nut-brown butter and seasoned with sea salt flakes and freshly ground black pepper balances the sweetness of the tomatoes. Or brush wild mushrooms with walnut oil and grill them for a couple of minutes a side before drizzling them with verjuice (and maybe a little more walnut oil to balance the vinaigrette) and seasoning for a true celebration of the best of autumn. I like to cook the mushrooms on our open grill over vine cuttings from the winter prunings for the extra flavour they add.

Try roasting pumpkin wedges with some extra virgin olive oil, bay leaves or rosemary and salt in a 200°C oven until caramelised and cooked through. Deglaze the roasting pan with verjuice and return it to the oven for a few more minutes – it's just wonderful.

Walnut oil seems to have a particular affinity with verjuice, as do grapes, of course. A simple vinaigrette can be made by combining 3 parts walnut oil to 2 parts verjuice, then adding 1 teaspoon Dijon mustard and seasoning with sea salt flakes and freshly ground black pepper. Toss the dressing, along with some grapes, through salad greens.

Verjuice and seafood make the finest of marriages. Make a simple sauce by deglazing the pan in which seafood has been cooked with verjuice, or use reduced verjuice to make a beurre blanc instead of white wine or vinegar. Verjuice also makes a hollandaise sauce without peer (see page 550). While talking seafood, make a simple vinaigrette for freshly opened oysters by finely chopping golden shallots and pouring verjuice over, then adding some fresh chervil if you have it – a stunning accompaniment, with so little effort.

Then there is game, another autumn ingredient. Pheasant, rabbit, hare, quail, guinea fowl and partridge all benefit from being partnered with verjuice. Quail and partridge lend themselves to being wrapped in vine leaves and poached slowly in verjuice; reconstitute sultanas, raisins or dried currants in verjuice to add to the finished sauce.

Try pot-roasting chicken, first browned in goose fat (or just plain nut-brown butter), with heads of garlic, a sprig of rosemary and 125 ml each of verjuice and chicken stock, for 40–60 minutes. (Goose fat is available in tins from good delicatessens or, if you cook a goose, collect it from the pan afterwards.) Turn the chicken occasionally and add more verjuice or stock, as necessary – a syrupy glaze will develop around the chook.

In countries in which duck or goose foie gras is available, verjuice added to pan-fried foie gras provides the most marvellous balance to the richness of the liver. In Australia, fresh blond livers from mature free-range chooks will have to suffice. (The more fat in the liver, the paler they are, hence the term 'blond'.) Sweetbreads and verjuice are an exceptional combination. Pan-fry blanched pressed sweetbreads in nut-brown butter and deglaze the pan with verjuice.

Try grilling tender young veal very quickly on the barbecue, first moistened with olive oil to save it from sticking, and then drizzle with verjuice while it rests after cooking. A sauce Barbara Santich found in her research from the sixteenth and seventeenth centuries still stands today as a good one to serve with grilled meat: reduce equal quantities of verjuice and good strong stock with finely chopped golden shallots, then season the finished sauce with sea salt flakes and freshly ground black pepper.

I add verjuice to sauces, soups, and when braising vegetables (particularly fennel and globe artichokes). I also use it to reconstitute dried fruit or for poaching soft fruits. I soak summer-caught riverfish in verjuice to rid it of its 'muddy' flavour. Verjuice also becomes a preserving agent for tropical fruit – the pH is low enough to extend the fruit's shelf-life without overtaking the flavour.

If all these seem a little fancy for everyday occasions, the easiest and most startling way to use verjuice is probably with chicken breasts or cubed chicken thigh meat (skin on, of course!) pan-fried in nut-brown butter. Wait until the chicken is almost cooked, then pour off any excess butter and turn up the heat as you add a good glug of verjuice. Loosen any residue in the pan with a spatula and reduce the verjuice to a syrup; the chicken will caramelise a little as the sauce reduces (you can also extend the sauce with some stock, if you like). I can promise you that this is the best way I know to give a boost to the flavour of a supermarket chook.

SEARED RAZORFISH ON SPINACH WITH VERJUICE BUTTER SAUCE

Serves 8 as an entrée

The following recipe is another created by Urs Inauen, Tom Milligan, Cheong Liew and me for the Seppelts Menu of the Year competition in 1991. Razorfish is a wonderful local mollusc not well known except among fishermen. If you can't find it, substitute with scallops.

16 razorfish hearts *or* 24 raw scallops

50 g unsalted butter

250 g baby spinach leaves, stalks removed, washed and dried

sea salt flakes and freshly ground black pepper

freshly grated nutmeg, to taste

2 teaspoons extra virgin olive oil

finely chopped rind and juice of ½ lime

finely chopped lemon rind, to serve

SAUCE

4 golden shallots, thinly sliced

1 cup (250 ml) verjuice

sea salt flakes

2 tablespoons cream

250 g unsalted butter, chopped

juice of 1 lemon

freshly ground black pepper

First, make the sauce. Cook the golden shallots and verjuice with salt in a small saucepan over high heat until reduced and syrupy. To help stabilise the sauce add the cream, gently warm and then gradually whisk in the butter, maintaining a medium–high heat through the cooking, but do not bring to the boil. Finish the sauce with lemon juice and adjust the seasoning. Set aside in a warm place.

With a paring knife, clean the razorfish hearts of all skin and remaining shell pieces or trim the scallops. Heat 30 g of the butter in a saucepan until just brown. Add the spinach, season with salt, pepper and nutmeg and stir well. Take out the spinach and place on kitchen paper. Wipe out the pan, then heat the olive oil with the remaining butter. Season the fish or scallops with salt, lime rind and juice, then sear in the pan for a few seconds only on each side and place on kitchen paper.

Divide the spinach evenly between 8 warmed plates. Place 2 razorfish hearts or 3 scallops on top of the spinach in the middle of each plate, leaning one on the other. Garnish with lemon rind. Pour the sauce around the spinach and grind over some pepper.

OCEAN TROUT IN VERJUICE JELLY   *Serves 16 as a small entrée*

This entrée is beautiful – it sparkles on the plate and palate. I first made it for a dinner for 400 guests using Murray cod, as I wanted something very fresh to serve as an entrée with Rhine Riesling. While Murray cod worked wonderfully, it can be hard to obtain. Here I've used ocean trout fillets, but if they aren't available, try salmon fillets instead.

unsalted butter, for cooking
2 × 750 g ocean trout fillets, skin off
    and pin-boned
1 bulb fennel
sea salt flakes and freshly ground
    black pepper
20 sage leaves
extra virgin olive oil, for cooking
2 stalks lemongrass, finely chopped
½ bunch flat-leaf parsley, leaves picked
    and finely chopped

1 bunch chervil, leaves picked
    and finely chopped
½ bunch chervil, leaves picked, to garnish

VERJUICE JELLY
6 × 2 g leaves gelatine (see Glossary)
3 cups (750 ml) verjuice
2 teaspoons castor sugar

Preheat the oven to 180°C. Liberally grease two sheets of baking paper, each large enough to wrap one of the fish fillets. Top each sheet of baking paper with a piece of fish, then scatter some fennel fronds over each fillet and salt well. Dot the fillets with some more butter and fold over the edges to seal the parcels. Carefully transfer the parcels to a baking tray and bake for 10 minutes on one side, then turn the fillets over and bake for another 5–8 minutes, depending on the thickness of the fillet. The fish should be just set and will continue to cook while it cools. Once the fish has cooled, remove from the baking paper and carefully cut into bite-sized pieces.

Now, make the jelly. Soak the gelatine leaves in cold water for 5 minutes. Meanwhile, warm the verjuice and the sugar in a stainless steel saucepan to dissolve the sugar; don't allow the mixture to boil or it will become cloudy. Remove the softened gelatine sheets from the water and squeeze out any excess moisture before dropping them into the warm verjuice mixture. Stir gently over low heat until the gelatine dissolves. Set aside to cool a little.

Melt a knob of butter in a frying pan over high heat until nut-brown, then crisp the sage leaves in the butter and drain on kitchen paper. Wipe out the pan and add a little extra virgin olive oil. Finely chop the fennel bulb and sauté, along with the lemongrass, in the oil, then remove the pan from the heat and add the parsley and the chopped chervil (this preserves the colour and flavour of the herbs). Season with salt and pepper and set aside to cool.

Pour just enough gelatine mixture to coat the bottom of the mould (in the finished dish the jelly layer should be just a little deeper than the thickness of the fish). Cover the mould with plastic film and refrigerate for 30–45 minutes or until set. Keep the remainder of the gelatine mixture in a warm place until required. »

As soon as the first layer of jelly has set, arrange the pieces of fish in a layer over the jelly, then top with the fennel and herb mixture, distributing it evenly over the fish. Arrange the crisped sage leaves evenly over the top. Pour over the remaining gelatine mixture, then refrigerate until set as before.

To serve, dip the base of the mould in hot water and quickly invert the jelly onto a plate. To present the herb-side uppermost, carefully invert the jelly onto another plate. Cut into portions using a hot, dry knife. Serve immediately, drizzled with a fruity extra virgin olive oil, seasoned with salt and garnished with chervil leaves. This jelly is great served with Grilled Asparagus and Verjuice Hollandaise (see page 550) or a side salad of avocado, chervil and extra virgin olive oil.

KANGAROO CARPACCIO WITH CUMQUATS, GREEN PEPPERCORNS AND VERJUICE

Serves 4

I first made this dish for a masterclass in Melbourne in 1994 and have used it so often since, not only with kangaroo but also venison or beef. It would be fabulous made with fillet of wagyu beef. A friend from the Riverland, Noëlle Tolley, had provided me with the most wonderful dried cumquats. These days I dehydrate my own in a small dryer I bought in an organic food store. It sits on the kitchen bench and is one of the kitchen toys really worthy of its position. When I can get hold of fresh green peppercorns I preserve them in verjuice – they last for months. Otherwise they can be macerated, as here. If you can't do either, rinse green peppercorns preserved in brine and steep them in verjuice overnight, at least.

1 teaspoon fresh green peppercorns	⅓ cup (80 ml) extra virgin olive oil,
1 tablespoon verjuice,	plus extra for brushing
plus extra for soaking	lemon juice, to taste
⅓ cup dried cumquat slices	2 tablespoons coriander leaves
1 × 300 g kangaroo fillet	

Macerate the green peppercorns in a little verjuice overnight. Next day, reconstitute the dried cumquats in verjuice for 30 minutes.

If you have a double fillet of roo (the best cut), follow the sinew down the middle with a sharp knife and separate the 2 pieces. Trim off all sinew, brush the meat with a little olive oil to minimise oxidation, then wrap the meat in plastic film to form a 'log'. Freeze the meat for about 20 minutes until it has firmed up (this will aid slicing). Finely slice the meat, then gently flatten each slice between pieces of plastic film with a wooden mallet (until it is as thin as prosciutto) or roll between 2 sheets of plastic film with a rolling pin. Arrange the meat on serving plates, with each piece just touching the next.

Combine the olive oil, 1 tablespoon verjuice and a squeeze of lemon juice to make a vinaigrette, then toss in the drained cumquats and green peppercorns and add the coriander. Dress the kangaroo and serve immediately.

VERJUICE SABAYON WITH GRILLED FIGS   *Serves 6*

I like to serve this with olive oil brioche made with bitter orange peel instead of candied Seville orange peel. If you can't buy brioche, try accompanying this with toasted and buttered slices of panettone.

1½ cups (375 ml) sangiovese verjuice

1 × Olive Oil Brioche (see page 469)
    or bought brioche

100 g unsalted butter, melted

3 free-range egg yolks

50 g castor sugar

12 figs

Heat the verjuice in a small saucepan over high heat, then simmer until reduced to 150 ml. Leave to cool. Bring some water to a simmer in a medium-sized saucepan.

Preheat the oven to 200°C. Cut the brioche into 2 cm-thick slices, then brush with melted butter and toast on a baking tray in the oven until golden brown. Keep warm.

Combine the egg yolks and castor sugar in a heatproof bowl that will sit over the saucepan of simmering water without touching the water, or use a double boiler. Whisk the egg yolks and sugar over the simmering water, slowly adding the cooled reduced verjuice, a little at a time, until the mixture is cooked and thick enough to form ribbons when the whisk is lifted. Keep the sabayon warm while you prepare the figs.

Cut the figs in half and brush with melted butter, then grill under a hot griller. Serve with the warm sabayon poured over them and the toasted brioche alongside.

VINEGAR

WHEN YOU THINK ABOUT IT, THE VINEGAR THAT HAS LONG BEEN made here in South Australia is a natural adjunct to the wine-making for which the state is so famous. And good vinegar is something I urge all cooks to investigate.

As a cook you need a variety of vinegars for different purposes. The best vinegars to use for cooking and making vinaigrettes are red-wine and sherry vinegars, made by the traditional Orleans method (see page 339), or top-class balsamics, depending on the dish. Vino cotto is a traditional Italian seasoning made from the juice of grapes and it has a unique sweet and sour flavour, known as *agrodolce* in Italy. We now make our own version of this, finished with our red-wine vinegar so it's truly sweet and sour. It is a delicious alternative to balsamic vinegar and adds piquancy to both sweet and savoury dishes.

It is a little extravagant to use these vinegars for making sauces and chutneys when there are many good-quality vinegars and spiced vinegars available for this purpose. However, we use our traditional red-wine vinegar in all our sauces and chutneys, and the results speak for themselves. In the early days of the Pheasant Farm Restaurant we produced pickled quail eggs virtually by the tonne using Seppelt's spiced vinegar, and I was very proud of them.

Malt vinegars were the flavour of my childhood, and it is no wonder that I was never a fan of my mother's cucumber and onion salad. Made today with a red-wine vinegar, it is a different dish altogether! Malt vinegar simply lacks the flavour and aroma of traditionally made wine vinegars.

A good-quality balsamic is a wonderful vinegar, but unfortunately not all balsamics are made to a high standard. To be awarded the *aceto balsamico tradizionale* tag, the vinegar must be made according to a traditional process, which takes twelve years. It is made exclusively from the unfermented musts (juices) of crushed grapes that are boiled and concentrated in copper pots. No flavourings and additives are permitted. The musts go through a gradual fermentation and acetification process in a series of casks made from

chestnut, mulberry, oak, cherry, acacia, ash and sometimes juniper. The juice is slowly decanted from one barrel to the next, each one smaller than the last since evaporation concentrates the liquid. This syrupy, dark-amber to honey-coloured vinegar has an amazing sweet–sour note to the nose and palate.

Naturally, you pay dearly for true balsamic, and justifiably so, but it should be used sparingly – an eye dropper or two of aged vinegar (twenty years or so – the age of the vinegar will be declared on the bottle) is all you need. I've actually tasted a balsamic that was a century old. Like Para Port, the 100-year-old liqueur made by Seppelt's, it was incredibly intense – more like an essence. When balsamic vinegars first hit the markets in Australia and the United States they became instantly fashionable, causing a shortage of traditionally made vinegar (not surprising, given the number of years required to make it). Specialised suppliers and the best gourmet food shops do offer some excellent aged balsamics that haven't reached the age required for *tradizionale* vinegars, but there are also many on the market with none of the same complexities. I find it a shame that so many cooks take the 'easy fix' with ordinary, very sweet balsamic vinegars, and ignore wonderful Australian red-wine vinegar with its toasty, aged flavours that add dimension to dishes without overpowering them.

I believe that we should be taking our red-wine vinegars very seriously – I prefer them to any of the imported red-wine vinegars I have come across. I urge you to think Australian, particularly when we have products of such outstanding quality.

On my doorstep, red-wine and sherry vinegars are being made using the traditional Orleans method by Yalumba under the Hill Smith label, and we also have one under our own label. Further south, Coriole is using the same technique, as are a small number of wineries around Australia, all producing red-wine vinegar on a small scale (Coriole has also released small quantities of an aged sweet vinegar). This is a natural offshoot of the wine industry, and as the public becomes more aware of traditionally made vinegar, more wine companies will no doubt start to make their own.

In the Orleans method, the vinegar bacteria are grown in a half-filled barrel containing a 'mother', or culture. The base always begins with good-quality wine, and the process is long and slow. Wine vinegars made this way have great depth of flavour – in fact, they share the flavours of the wine from which they are made.

Red-wine vinegar ages like red wine, and the unstable pigments drop out of the solution, leaving the vinegar reddish brown. As with wine, vinegar softens over time if unopened, and once opened will slowly oxidise. If you have a bottle of red-wine vinegar with sediment in it, decant it – the clear vinegar left will be wonderful.

Some time ago I took part in a vinegar-tasting at Yalumba where twenty-four vinegars were put to the test. Only a handful were really worthy of mention. We tasted both young and aged South Australian red-wine and sherry vinegars (all of which were great), French and Spanish red-wine vinegars, and malt, balsamic (but no *tradizionale*), rice and even coconut vinegars. Those vinegars brought to the tasting already open, some for a long time, were positively horrid (although it must be said that some others freshly opened for the occasion were just as bad!). Vinegar oxidises at varying speeds according to the conditions it's kept in once opened. (The trick is to buy a small bottle, use it regularly and keep it stored in cool conditions.)

Red-wine vinegar can, of course, be made at home. It is the perfect fate for any leftover red wine, as long as it was a good bottle in the first place. Remember, life's too short to drink bad wine; and the older and better the wine, the better the vinegar. Most good red wines include natural vinegar bacteria as they have not been sterile-filtered, a process that is sometimes used to remove anything that could spoil the wine but also ends up taking out some of the flavour, among other things. Cask wines have been sterile-filtered and are also highly sulphured, so avoid these. Good wine is clarified through traditional methods of extended maturation and racking in barrels, so it does not require filtering.

You can purchase a stone jar with a loose-fitting lid from wine-making shops for making vinegar, but I prefer to use wood as it gives a more appealing colour, aroma and flavour to the vinegar. Geoff Linton, my expert tutor from Yalumba, also prefers to keep away from ceramics when making vinegar, purely because he can't be sure that all the glazes are lead-free. He also worries about storing very acidic products in enamelled containers. Glass, however, is fine.

There are several ways you can acquire a vinegar 'mother'. You can make your own from scratch by simply putting some premium wine into a wooden half-open barrel. Of course, you could also beg, borrow or steal a vinegar mother from someone already making vinegar. Or you could try starting your mother by crumbling several thick slices of stale sourdough bread (made without preservatives) into an open jar and then pouring in half a bottle of good aged red wine (note that if the bread develops mould you must throw out the lot and start again, as the mould produces a toxin). Whichever option you choose, cover the container with muslin to keep out the vinegar flies. You know you are on the way when a filmy growth appears on the surface of the wine and it starts to smell like vinegar – this film is acetic acid bacteria and, in time, it will become so heavy that the mass sinks to the bottom of the barrel: this is your mother. Remember that the greater the surface area the better, as the vinegar needs aerobic activity to operate.

I was lucky enough to be given a mother by a vinegar-maker, and I keep it in an old 20-litre Yalumba port barrel that was shaved out by the coopers. It sits on a wooden cradle right next to the stove (maintaining warmth is important when making vinegar). Three holes (about a centimetre in diameter) are drilled in a line across the top of the barrel, which I never have more than two-thirds full because the vinegar must be open to the air to convert the alcohol in the wine to vinegar. The top is loosely covered with muslin. The barrel has a tap just up from its base from which to pour the vinegar – it is important that there is sufficient vinegar for the mother to swim in and that the tap is above the level of sediment so that it doesn't pour off when the vinegar is extracted.

Whichever way you start when making your own vinegar, enjoy the process, and make sure you smell, taste and look at it every month or so. Just draw off enough in a saucer to check what's happening. After three or four months it will have become quite vinegary, but it is probably best to leave it until it has been in the barrel for at least six months before you start to draw any off for everyday use – even longer is better, if you can be patient. (Starting with premium wine in a wooden barrel without an existing mother could require waiting twelve months before you can use it.) When your vinegar tastes strong, you can assume the microbiological changes have ceased and it is ready to use. In this case, you need to bottle some of the vinegar so that it isn't exposed to as much air – you don't want it to oxidise after waiting so patiently. Topping up the barrel with more wine will set the process in motion again.

Once your vinegar is well and truly established it is probably worth cleaning out the container and dividing your mother. A mature mother is a large rubbery mass, and if it gets too large it gets starved of oxygen and can become inactive. Pour off the vinegar and decant it into flagons, then flush out the barrel with hot water (no detergents). Divide the mother and return one portion to the barrel (give the other to a friend), along with the settled vinegar, and you're away again. The vinegar mother remains good for years and years.

If you had thought that a good vinegar was an imported one, please look again at the top-quality Australian red-wine vinegars now on the market and compare them with the plethora of imported ones. Obviously vinegar should be acidic but it should also have a

Vinaigrette of red-wine vinegar, extra virgin olive oil and lemon thyme

fruity nose (once you have gotten over the gasping effect if you have been too vigorous in your smell test!). Vinegar lovers, me included, will taste vinegar by the spoonful to ascertain its qualities. Years ago, in Tokyo, I was presented with elegant vinegar-tasting glasses – fragile, hand-blown, the size of a thimble on a long stem – and gingerly carried them back in my cabin luggage. A good red-wine vinegar is my first everyday option, but there are also incredibly complex vinegars made from sherry, champagne and, of course, vino cotto. Like my choice of oil, the choice of vinegar depends on what I'm preparing.

There is such a world of difference in quality. True artisan-made aged balsamic results in a vinegar so intense and syrupy it needs to be treated with great reverence. This vinegar, sold for exorbitant prices, is only added by the dropful at the last moment, perhaps to hot poached salmon, poultry or vegetables. Or try vino cotto or balsamic vinegar when deglazing roasted vegetables, particularly onion, or when pan-frying liver, duck or beef.

A good vinegar can be used in many ways: a salad of sliced sun-ripened tomato is enhanced further by a splash of red-wine vinegar. And a generous dash of good vinegar adds piquancy to a stew, soup or sauce in the same way as verjuice, but the result is much stronger.

I love adding vinegar to hare, venison or goat dishes. I was once sent a recipe for a Greek kid dish that required red wine vinegar. Whereas I usually cook very young kid extremely slowly, this recipe was for a larger animal and called for a kettle barbecue to be used to cook the leg or shoulder. The meat was rubbed with olive oil, dried oregano and freshly ground black pepper and studded with garlic cloves and then cooked on a rack over a bed of onions and tomatoes. (I recommend cooking the kid at a lower heat than you would a leg of lamb, and for half as long again.) The meat was basted regularly with red-wine vinegar, but it had to be watched carefully so that it didn't burn. I tried it myself – and it was wonderful!

Don't think that vinegar should only accompany savoury things. For example, not-quite-ripe strawberries sprinkled with aged balsamic vinegar or vino cotto are a surprisingly successful combination. And old-fashioned honeycomb made with sugar and bicarbonate of soda relies on a good vinegar for flavour.

During the pheasant season I would be allowed to use any blue-coloured eggs for cooking, as Colin knew they wouldn't hatch. A favourite way to cook them was to poach them with a touch of red-wine vinegar in the water. I'd render cubes of sugar-cured bacon (from Schulz's Butcher in the Barossa), then toss baby spinach leaves in the same pan; the eggs were served on the spinach and bacon with shavings of fresh Parmigiano Reggiano and a vinaigrette of extra virgin olive oil, my red-wine vinegar, sea salt flakes and freshly ground black pepper. Croutons were used to dip into the poached eggs (just like toast soldiers) – a wonderful Sunday night meal.

I am constantly amazed at how often I am asked how to make a good vinaigrette. No culinary question is more easily answered, and nothing is more special if you have the best-possible extra virgin olive oil and vinegar to hand, than to place them in glass cruets on the table with a dish of sea salt flakes and a good pepper grinder, and let people help themselves.

Then no one can say the dressing is too acidic or oily. A good vinaigrette will only ever be as good as its ingredients.

MORE TIPS FOR VINAIGRETTES

✦ For me, the first step in preparing a standard vinaigrette is to rub the bowl I am using with a clove of freshly cut garlic.

✦ Pour fresh (not rancid – check first) extra virgin olive oil into the base of the salad bowl (how much depends on the size of the bowl and the salad, but use an oil-to-vinegar ratio of 4:1). Vinegar is added next, then a few flakes of sea salt and freshly ground black pepper.

✦ Lettuce and herbs must be washed and well dried (use a salad spinner). Keep the salad leaves separate from the dressing until the very last moment.

✦ Be sparing with the amount of dressing. When ready, toss the leaves through the dressing, preferably using your fingers to check that the vinaigrette has just 'touched' the leaves.

✦ While many variations are possible, you might add mustard, sugar, cream, fresh herbs or preserved lemon, to name a few. Try making an anchovy vinaigrette by adding chopped anchovy fillets and flat-leaf parsley or torn basil to the vinegar and olive oil.

✦ If you have been using balsamic vinegar in your vinaigrettes, you might try vino cotto, or better still, a quality red-wine vinegar with a dash of vino cotto which, like balsamic, has to be used judiciously.

PETER WALL'S RASPBERRY VINEGAR   *Makes 500 ml*

Peter Wall, a great friend of mine, is a former wine-maker and fascinated by vinegar. His raspberry vinegar should be used with gusto – it is particularly good for deglazing, especially when cooking calf's liver. Be careful when buying the base vinegar for this: it must be at least 6 per cent acetic acid, which is stronger than many. A vinegar as strong as this will stop fermentation from occurring – and you can generally equate strength with quality.

200 g fresh *or* frozen raspberries   **400 ml red-wine vinegar (6 per cent)**

If you are using frozen raspberries, defrost them, then wash any remaining frost off and dry them well with kitchen paper. Blend the raspberries and vinegar in a food processor, then bottle and leave for 3 months. Pour the vinegar through a paper filter (like those used in a coffee machine) into a sterilised bottle (see Glossary) and discard any solids.

OLIVE TAPENADE WITH RED-WINE VINEGAR

Makes 300 ml

This recipe works brilliantly with either kalamatas or good-quality green olives, and it's the combination of olives and orange that I love so much.

You must use top-quality red-wine vinegar, though – the end result here is heavily dependent on the quality of the ingredients.

250 g pitted kalamata olives

1 clove garlic, chopped

1 tablespoon baby capers, rinsed

1 tablespoon chopped lemon thyme leaves

1 teaspoon chopped marjoram leaves

1 teaspoon chopped rosemary

1 tablespoon finely grated orange rind

2 tablespoons good-quality red-wine vinegar

80 ml extra virgin olive oil

Place all the ingredients in a food processor and pulse until roughly chopped and well combined, but not a smooth paste.

BABY BEETS IN VINO COTTO WITH ROCKET, WALNUTS AND GOAT'S CHEESE

Serves 4

1 bunch baby beets (around 12 baby beets)

1 teaspoon red-wine vinegar

¼ cup vino cotto (see Glossary)

½ cup extra virgin olive oil

sea salt flakes and freshly ground
   black pepper

100 g walnuts

1 bunch rocket

150 g firm goat's cheese, cut into pieces

Place the beets in a pan with enough cold, salted water to cover them, and bring to the boil, then turn the heat down and simmer with the lid on until the beets are cooked through (the cooking time will depend on the age of the beets). Remove the beets from the pan and set aside to cool, then peel them and cut them in half.

Preheat the oven to 200°C. In a small bowl, combine the red-wine vinegar, vino cotto and olive oil, and season with salt and pepper to taste. Toss the beets through the dressing, then transfer the mixture to a roasting pan and roast for 10 minutes.

Meantime, roast the walnuts on a baking tray for 10 minutes. Remove and, whilst still warm, rub their skins off with a clean tea towel then sieve away the skins.

Combine the walnuts, rocket and baby beets in a bowl. Mix through the pan juices from the roast beets, then top with goat's cheese and serve.

WALNUTS

IT DOESN'T SURPRISE ME THAT WALNUTS AREN'T AS POPULAR AS they deserve to be. It is simply because so few people have access to the new season's crop. A rancid walnut, as they so often are if stored badly, would make anyone think twice about eating them.

But there is nothing more delicious than picking, shelling and eating walnuts that are just about to drop (these nuts are described as being 'wet') – particularly if you're lunching under a walnut tree, as we used to many years ago at Kilikanoon, a restaurant in South Australia's Clare Valley, when Janet Jeffs and Susan Ditter owned it. The beauty of the tree and the delicacy of the just-fallen nuts, which we duly added to the cheese plate, encouraged me to plant my own grove.

My vision for my own walnut grove was inspired by a visit to a grove in the Napa Valley in California. Perched on the side of a hill, it was an extraordinary sight as the canopies of the mature trees touched to form a shaded sanctuary from the harsh sun. Here, however, very hot summers and years of drought, along with fierce gully winds, have meant that my walnut trees have struggled. As recently as 2005 I transplanted four of the surviving trees to better position them (I am still determined to have my mini-grove, even though the chestnuts I planted alongside them are obviously more suited to the conditions, as they are thriving). With so few trees, I'm not banking on a huge crop or turning it into a commercial enterprise, but the grove is in keeping with our philosophy that any tree we grow must produce food.

The most exciting prospect for me as a walnut grower is the multitude of uses to which I can put the bounty of this tree. The young fresh leaves can be used to make a wine, as they do in the south of France. Then comes the green walnuts, from which the French and Italians make a liqueur. Picked in late November or early December before the husks form, the nuts retain their wonderful colour and crisp texture, quite unlike blackened pickled walnuts that, interesting as they are, both fall apart and taste more of the vinegar than the nut.

My great friend Peter Wall taught me how to pickle green walnuts. Put the nuts, interspersed with fresh vine leaves, into a glass container, or even a large plastic bucket. Pack the container with extra vine leaves, then cover completely with white vinegar and leave for three weeks. Pour off the vinegar and discard the leaves, then re-fill the jar with the nuts and new vine leaves as before, cover with fresh vinegar and leave for another two weeks. Remove the vine leaves and pack the nuts back into the washed and dried jar. In a large stainless steel saucepan, combine 3 litres commercial wine vinegar with enough salt so that an egg will float in it. Add 30 g each of ground cloves, ground mace and ground allspice to the pan, then grate in two whole nutmegs. Simmer this mixture for a minute and immediately pour it over the nuts to cover. Seal the container and leave the walnuts to mature for three months before using them. The nuts remain green, although will turn more of an olive-green, and stay deliciously crisp. Pickled walnuts are a great partner to rillettes of pork, hare or rabbit, and are also good with rich duck or pork dishes or a really sharp cheddar.

Right through the season the leaves of the walnut tree can be used to wrap fish for cooking on the barbecue. The pungency of the cloudy, freshly pressed walnut oil I've tasted in France may well be too strong for the faint-hearted, but even when it needs toning down with a more neutral oil, it is still incredibly special. Compared with a standard walnut oil of indeterminate age purchased from the delicatessen, you may suspect the latter has been watered down, such is the difference in flavour. At present, you can only buy these top-class oils from really good providores, but I eagerly await the day when walnut oil of this quality is made by Australian growers.

Autumn is the time to be on the lookout for fresh nuts. A passionate farmer clears any debris from around the tree just before harvest and mows the grass so that the nuts can be picked up daily as they fall, just like eggs. Sadly, I know that this is hardly feasible on a commercial scale. Those growers large enough will machine-pick or trunk-shake harvest about ten days before the nuts are due to fall, taking the whole crop off at once. These nuts are then dried in ovens, as they turn black and rancid if stored without first being dried (traditionally they were dried in the sun).

As the walnut is full of oil, its potential for rancidity is high. It is not possible to detect a rancid nut by the colour of its skin – a dark skin does not automatically signify a rancid nut, as different varieties produce darker or lighter skins. The skins will also be lighter if the nuts have been harvested before maturity.

It is really only on tasting that you will know whether the nut is fresh or rancid. There should be some natural bitterness – this comes from the tannin that protects the nut from rancidity – but it should be in balance with the 'meat' of the walnut, and a rich nutty flavour should be left in the mouth. You can dry-roast walnuts back to life if they are old, even rancid, in a hot oven (220°C) for 6–8 minutes, before rubbing off the skins with a clean tea towel. This will take away the acute bitterness and produce a mellow-flavoured nut that is well worth using, but the flavour still won't touch the intensity of the fresh walnuts of the new season.

Proper storage is extremely important if rancidity is to be avoided. The best way is to store the nuts, dried in their shells, in the coolest possible place. Make sure there are no cracks in the shells and no mould present before storing. The next best thing is to keep shelled walnuts in an airtight container in the refrigerator, or even the freezer. Once opened, a bottle of walnut oil can be kept refrigerated for quite some time, and doesn't solidify as extra virgin olive oil does when chilled.

Walnuts have figured a great deal in my menus over the years, both in the restaurant and at home: rabbit with walnuts and pancetta; warm salad of pheasant confit, waxy potatoes and walnuts; guinea fowl stuffed with walnuts, liver and sugar-cured bacon; smoked rack of lamb with pickled walnuts; Duck Egg Pasta (see page 420) with Walnut and Parsley Pesto (see page 581); brains with a duxelle of walnuts and mushrooms; walnut cake with prunes in Sauternes with Sauternes custard; and the humble but wonderful combination of walnuts, slices of pear and Parmigiano Reggiano – all of these using fresh

walnuts or roasted ones with the skins rubbed off.

Walnuts make a great pasta sauce. In his book *The Fruit, Herbs and Vegetables of Italy*, Giacomo Castelvetro writes of an *agliata* sauce, made from pounding walnuts and garlic together using a mortar and pestle, that can also be used to thicken a sauce or stew or to make a hearty soup. Stale white bread which has been soaked in meat stock is then mixed in, along with some of the stock, which thins the sauce. Treated this way, a good game or Golden Chicken Stock (see page 57) would make an excellent soup; it would be a mushroom-pink colour and would only need a salad of bitter greens to make a meal.

I combine walnuts, bacon and herbs when making poultry stuffings, or prunes and walnuts if cooking goose. I love walnuts in salads, particularly with freshly cooked green beans in a creamy dressing. I add walnuts and grapes to a green salad, or stir them into a bath of walnut or olive oil in which a cooked, hot bird is rested to soak up the juices (grilled quail is superb this way).

Walnut bread is probably my first choice to serve with cheese, especially if a grainy flour is mixed with the bread flour. Or toss shelled walnuts and freshly picked rosemary in a little nut-brown butter, then add a little sea salt before serving warm with drinks. They're utterly addictive!

I only wish that a date stamp appeared on packaged walnuts so that everyone could enjoy the standard of walnut to which I have become accustomed. But just a use-by date wouldn't suffice: what I really want to know is when the walnuts were picked and shelled.

I believe that demand for walnuts would increase if everyone was able to taste the 'perfect' nut, and then people would be prepared to pay a premium for the new nuts of the season.

I bought the most wonderful walnut oil on a trip to France a few years ago. I had a week in Périgeux and spent it immersed (well, almost) in truffles, foie gras and walnut oil. It was one of the great privileges of my life. I am an inveterate note-taker and on this trip my notepad was so full that every page was used. Then that horror of horrors happened: I misplaced the notepad somewhere in Milan airport. Devastated though I was, as my camera is ever-present in my shoulder bag, at least I had the photographs from the trip so all was not lost.

Thumbing through these photographs now, I can almost smell the heady scent of walnuts crushing in the ancient mill at Moulin de la Tour, near Sarlat. Powered by a waterwheel (with a fair bit of human effort), the mill crushes hazelnuts and almonds as well as walnuts. The day I was there the small sales outlet was crammed with locals waiting for their walnuts to be crushed – it was a fascinating experience. Precious though luggage space always is, I managed to find room for a sample of each oil (sold in tins rather than bottles, fortunately).

While good nut oils are a thing of joy, those made with the passion and integrity demonstrated at the Moulin de la Tour are in a different league altogether. But all nut oils are incredibly susceptible to rancidity; once opened, they're generally best used within a week unless you refrigerate them. If you have an opened bottle of nut oil, make sure you smell it before using it again to make sure it's not rancid. Rancidity is easy to detect – just think of what butter left uncovered in the refrigerator smells like. Discard the oil if it is rancid.

The first time I tried walnut oil in France was with the simplest salad of green leaves, with a mound of soft goat's curd in the centre. The oil was drizzled over and a grind of black pepper finished off the dish. There was enough salt and acid in the cheese not to require anything else. What could be easier? If you have a really good walnut oil you must use it with discretion – you may even need to use another oil with it so you don't overpower the dish, but this will depend on your palate. The only way to find out is to try.

Walnut oil changes in character depending on the acidulant you use with it – be it wine vinegar, lemon juice or verjuice. A stronger acidulant should be used with stronger flavour bases. So, if you were using radicchio, watercress and walnuts (roasted and rubbed of their skins, if not from the current season), for example, you might use walnut oil and red-wine vinegar. If making a salad of cos lettuce hearts, avocado and grapes, you might use walnut oil and verjuice, then break down the intensity of the walnut oil with some grape-seed oil or mellow but still fresh extra virgin olive oil. And if you were combining rocket, witlof and fennel with roasted walnuts, you could use walnut oil, lemon juice and a little finely chopped lemon rind.

Walnut oil can add flavour to other dishes, too. If grilling chicken, rabbit or quail, make a sauce by slowly adding walnut oil to a large dollop of wholegrain mustard as if you were making a mayonnaise. Add a dash of walnut oil when making an *omelette aux fines herbes*, or toss mixed mushrooms with a touch of walnut oil before adding it to the eggs. Drizzle walnut oil over slices of stale but good bread before spooning rustic bean soup over the bread, then sprinkle with chopped flat-leaf parsley. And if you make a walnut cake, add a little walnut oil to the batter.

SASKIA'S WALNUT, MUSHROOM AND PROSCIUTTO TART   *Serves 8*

My daughter Saskia just loves to cook, and from a very young age would delight me by taking a dish I'd made at the restaurant, changing it around and making it hers, as with this dish.

1 × quantity Sour-cream Pastry (see page 424)	½ cup (125 ml) milk
100 g dried boletus mushrooms	10–12 slices prosciutto, thinly sliced
¼ cup (60 ml) verjuice	2 cloves garlic, finely chopped
2 cups (400 g) shelled walnuts	1 kg button mushrooms, chopped
2 slices white bread, with crusts on (about 75 g)	butter, for cooking
	sea salt flakes and freshly ground black pepper

Make and chill the pastry as instructed, then use to line a 20 cm tart tin with a removable base. Chill the pastry case for 20 minutes.

Reconstitute the dried boletus mushrooms in the verjuice for 30 minutes. Meanwhile, preheat the oven to 200°C. Line the pastry case with foil and pastry weights, then blind bake for 15 minutes. Remove the foil and weights and return the pastry case to the oven for another 5 minutes. Remove from the oven and reset the temperature to 220°C.

Dry-roast the walnuts on a baking tray for 6–8 minutes, then rub off their skins with a clean tea towel. Toast the bread in the oven until golden, cut it into cubes and soak in the milk until softened, then squeeze out the milk. Blend the soaked toast, prosciutto, garlic and walnuts in a food processor to make a paste, then set it aside.

Sauté the button mushrooms in a frying pan in a little butter over quite a high heat (do them in batches so that they don't stew), then season well and set aside. Toss the reconstituted boletus mushrooms in the pan in a little more melted butter, then season and purée them in a food processor.

To assemble the tart, spread the walnut and prosciutto paste in the bottom of the pastry case, then brush with the boletus purée and arrange the sautéed button mushrooms on top. Bake for about 20 minutes or until the edge of the pastry case is golden brown. Serve warm or at room temperature.

SALAD WITH WALNUT OIL VINAIGRETTE

Serves 4

Choose a mixture of sharp, peppery, crisp salad leaves and herbs.

12 shelled walnuts

2 handfuls mixed lettuce leaves and herbs, washed and dried

175 g seedless grapes

2 tablespoons top-quality walnut oil

2 tablespoons neutral vegetable oil (try grapeseed oil)

3 tablespoons verjuice

sea salt flakes and freshly ground black pepper

Preheat the oven to 220°C. Dry-roast the walnuts on a baking tray for 6–8 minutes, then rub off their skins with a clean tea towel.

Place the salad leaves and herbs in a salad bowl and add the grapes. Mix the remaining ingredients in a jar and pour over the salad leaves. Add the walnuts and toss thoroughly.

WALNUT FLATBREAD

Serves 6–8

I like to serve this flatbread with Pheasant Farm Pâté, as well as caramelised onions, warmed in a stainless steel saucepan to just above room temperature.

1 cup (250 ml) full-cream milk

7 g dried yeast (1 sachet)

½ cup (180 g) honey

1 cup (150 g) unbleached plain flour (see Glossary)

½ teaspoon ground ginger

1¼ cups (150 g) chopped walnuts

3 teaspoons sea salt

2 tablespoons extra virgin olive oil, plus extra for brushing

1⅔ cups (250 g) wholemeal flour (see Glossary)

finely chopped rind of 1 orange (optional)

Warm the milk in a microwave for 1 minute on high and then place in a large bowl. Whisk in the yeast, honey and 100 g of the unbleached flour. Let stand for 15 minutes, after which it should start to bubble.

Add the ginger, walnuts, salt, olive oil and orange rind (if using) to the yeast mixture and gradually incorporate most of the two flours. When the mixture becomes a bit stiff, remove it from the bowl and knead in the remaining flour on a bench; the dough should bounce back and be reasonably firm.

Roll the dough out to a 30 × 40 cm rectangle, approximately 5 mm thick, and brush with olive oil. Rest the dough for 1 hour, covered with plastic film to prevent dryness.

Preheat the oven to 180°C. Place the dough on a baking tray and bake for approximately 20 minutes or until golden. Remove bread from the oven and place on a wire rack to cool.

Cut the bread into 2 cm squares or triangles to serve. Leftover bread can be frozen and then warmed before next use.

CHOCOLATE SWEETMEATS   *Makes 25*

The prunes can be replaced with the same quantity of diced quince paste; in that case, soak in Cointreau rather than port. The chocolate mixture must be cool before the quince paste is added, otherwise the paste will melt.

150 g prunes, pitted and chopped
port, for soaking
1½ cups (150 g) shelled walnuts
400 g bittersweet couverture chocolate
    (see Glossary), chopped

200 ml cream (35 per cent fat)
    (see Glossary)
dutch-process cocoa (see Glossary),
    to serve

Soak the chopped prunes in port for several hours. Preheat the oven to 220°C. Roast the walnuts on a baking tray for 6–8 minutes, then rub off the skins with a clean tea towel and coarsely chop the nuts.

Heat the chocolate gently with the cream in the top of a double saucepan over boiling water. (If you don't have a double boiler, use a heatproof bowl that fits snugly over a pan of boiling water.) Remove from the heat before all the chocolate has melted. Stir continuously off the heat to finish melting the chocolate, then cool. Fold the drained soaked prunes and chopped nuts into the cooled chocolate mixture, then roll into balls and dust with cocoa.

WILD DUCK AND DUCK FAT

AUTUMN IS THE TIME FOR WILD GAME AND, AS THE WEATHER becomes cooler, slow-cooked dishes become more tantalising. The wild duck season usually runs from mid-February to mid-June in South Australia (unless it is cancelled altogether due to climatic conditions). Wild duck is a wonderful food but, as with most game, can be tricky to cook until you master the principles. It cannot be sold but, if shot with a licence, can certainly be shared with friends.

As with all wild game, it is hard to determine the age of a wild duck, so it is certainly safer to use slow-cooking methods. However, I have read, particularly in American books, of the practice of spit-roasting wild duck rare, in much the same way as I cook pheasant. Having tested this with young mallard (grown as a domestic duck), I can assure you it is effective if the bird is young. There are various tests you can use to determine the age of a wild duck, but some are quite hit and miss. So unless you are sure of the duck's age, I would suggest using slow-cooking methods – pot-roasting, pressure cooking (with a simmer mat under the pot to slow it down as much as possible), or roasting in an oven bag at a very low temperature.

The mallard is the most common wild duck in Europe and America, and most domestic ducks are descended from this breed. In Australia the mallard has caused a problem by breeding with native ducks and 'shandying' the breeds. In South Australia we have mainly black ducks, teals and wood ducks. The teal and black duck are considered the best for eating – the teal is small and succulent and the black duck is stronger and gamier. The duck's flavour is dependent on its breeding ground and, certainly in some parts of the world, can be 'fishy'. In such cases, the duck is precooked for a few minutes with onion in salty water to eliminate this. In Europe, particularly, they hang their wild duck, whereas in Australia most people do not bother.

One of the best food memories of my life was a wild duck dinner cooked by my friends the Walls, when Peter was still with Yalumba. Both Peter and Judith are great cooks and well understood the principle of slow pot-roasting for many hours. In this instance, they made a liver and sage *panade* (stuffing) for the duck, then wrapped it in bacon or back fat (I think – my memory is a bit hazy!), and kept it moist with stock and wine added as it cooked. It was the first time I had eaten wild duck and, washed down with some great Yalumba reds, it was magnificent.

It was the sort of experience that is hard to replicate – as with so many food memories, it is linked to the people the meal is shared with, the mood of the night and so on. I mention it because of the influence of a very special man, Alf Wark, who was Yalumba's company secretary from 1945 to 1971, and whom I was privileged to meet when we first came to live in the Barossa in 1973.

Alf Wark had a tremendous impact both in Yalumba and across Australia and he was passionate and knowledgeable about food. His influence on the Hill Smiths – founders of Yalumba and a very special family which has helped South Australia develop enormously – is evident. Alf was a keen hunter and fisherman and also a conservationist, as are his son and grandson today, who continue the tradition with their love of game. James, Alf's son, is a member of the South Australian Field & Game Association, whose members come from all walks of life. They are not only responsible hunters but are committed to conservation. One such member, at his own expense, has undertaken a rehabilitation program of wetland areas on his land that had been drained and dried out for farming. They now boast a flourishing and increasing population of many species of water birds.

In 1969, Alf wrote a tiny book, *Wine Cookery*, featuring recipes and ideas he had developed over the years through his long association with good food and wine. With the kind permission of his family, I give you his two recipes for wild duck on the following page.

I have cooked wild duck smothered in pork back fat and stuffed with olives and thyme, or simply stuffed with onion, apple and a few herbs, using about 12 mm of stock in the bottom of the baking dish, and a lid so that condensation helps to keep the bird moist. If pot-roasting duck in a roasting pan or heavy-based saucepan, I prefer to do it on top of the stove as I am reminded to check whether it needs more liquid, and the aroma of the food is so much greater than when enclosed in the oven – it creates a lovely atmosphere in the kitchen. If you don't have any stock to use as a braising medium, try water or sweet white wine and water combined with a little lemon juice.

Both orange and lemon marry very well with duck, as they do with most game. Tart jellies such as redcurrant, crabapple or native currant also go very well.

One last tip with duck is to remove the 'preen glands' (or oil glands) before cooking. In a wild duck they can impart a strong, musky flavour and in a domestic duck they can be bitter. They are located on either side of the duck's tail and are about the size of an elongated pea, with the consistency of kidney.

WILD DUCK POACHED IN WINE SAUCE

Serves 4

225 g butter

2 tablespoons Worcestershire sauce

300 ml burgundy (remembering that we used to call all red wine burgundy or claret when Alf wrote this book in 1969)

⅓ cup redcurrant jelly

finely chopped rind of 1 orange

4 teal duck breasts

¼ cup (60 ml) port

Melt the butter and add all ingredients, except the duck and port, and simmer. Add the duck breasts, then cover the pan and simmer over low heat as gently as possible for 20 minutes. (I would then take the breasts out of the pan.) Season to taste. Add the port and reduce the sauce to the desired consistency before serving.

BLACK DUCK AND ORANGE SAUCE

Serves 4

2 wild black ducks, with giblets intact

sea salt flakes and freshly ground black pepper

extra virgin olive oil, for cooking

2 medium-sized white onions, 1 roughly chopped, 1 quartered

2 sticks celery, 1 roughly chopped, 1 cut into 5 cm lengths

30 g butter

clarified butter, for cooking

⅓ cup (120 g) honey

4 oranges

½ cup (125 ml) port

Preheat the oven to 180°C. When cleaning the ducks, save the giblets, and make sure the cavity is well cleaned of blood from shot wounds. Rub salt and pepper inside and leave for some time before cooking. Over low–medium heat, simmer the giblets in a saucepan with just enough water to cover them, olive oil and the roughly chopped onion and celery pieces for stock. In the body cavity, place the quartered onion and long celery pieces. Add the butter to the cavity. Close the cavity with a skewer and smear the breast of each duck with clarified butter.

Pour 2 tablespoons of the honey (which has been diluted with some of the stock from the giblets) into a roasting pan, then add the duck and roast in the oven for 1½ hours or until cooked (soft to the touch). Baste with the pan juices a few times during the cooking, taking care that the juices do not dry out – add more stock or water if it looks like they are.

Squeeze the juice from 2 of the oranges and mix with port and the remaining honey. When the bird is nearly cooked, baste the breast frequently with this mixture to glaze it. Grate the orange rind from the other 2 oranges and cut the flesh into thin slices.

When the duck is cooked, place it on a hot plate and cover to keep warm. Add the remaining stock to the pan juices and boil until it reduces and thickens, then add the grated orange rind and pour over the duck. Garnish with the thin slices of orange and, with poultry scissors, cut the birds into 4 pieces and serve.

DUCK FAT

I first started using duck fat when I collected the excess from a bird I had cooked. Needing more for the restaurant, I bought it in 10 kg batches from Luv-a-Duck in Nhill, Victoria (through their South Australian distributors), and rendered it myself. These days they sell it in 1 kg tubs ready to use. It keeps for months and has myriad uses.

The easiest way of all to use duck fat is to bake it with potatoes (particularly waxy potatoes) that have first been boiled whole in their jackets and then sliced, with a little rosemary in a heavy-based roasting pan. Heat about 5 mm duck fat with the rosemary before adding the potato slices. They will take about 15 minutes in a hot oven, and the potato slices should be turned over as soon as the first side is golden brown. The moment the second side is golden, the potatoes should be slid out of the baking dish on to kitchen paper. If you wish to season them, sprinkle with sea salt flakes and freshly ground black pepper. Eat immediately! This is a more-ish snack and a great vegetable accompaniment to almost any dish. It cannot be done in advance and should be served crisp and straight out of the oven. There is absolutely no comparison in flavour to potatoes done similarly in oil or butter or a combination of the two – try it.

I first read about duck fat in Elizabeth David's books, but it was Paula Wolfert's *The Cooking of South West France* that converted me to using it as a cooking medium. I was so seduced by the flavour that it wasn't difficult for Paula also to convince me that it is healthier than other fats. She says that the US Department of Agriculture states that rendered poultry fat (goose, duck and chicken) contains 9 per cent cholesterol, lard contains 10 per cent, and butter contains 22 per cent. She continues, 'Since one needs less poultry fat, oil or lard than butter to sauté meat or vegetables, one will ingest far less saturated fat if these cooking media are used instead of butter. One needs less of these because butter breaks down and burns at high temperatures whereas poultry fat, lard and oil do not.'

As I have said, there is no doubt in my mind of the flavour benefits of cooking in duck fat, but that doesn't mean you have to serve fatty foods when you use it. The actual flavour component in the duck fat is water-soluble and can be separated from the fat itself, so the food can be served almost fat-free yet with all the advantages of the increased flavour.

Rillettes de canard (see page 359)

Braising meat at a very low temperature in duck fat to make confit is a foundation of the cuisine of southwest France, and is a technique I use with old game. I am very careful never to let the meat 'move' at anything more than a simmer, and always use the heaviest saucepan in my kitchen (with a tight-fitting lid). I often use a simmer mat between the pan and the flame to be sure there is virtually no movement. This method ensures that the food being cooked is totally immersed in the duck fat throughout.

When such low temperatures are used, the cooking fats mingle but do not incorporate with the wine or juices used in the cooking, and the 'fat' is therefore easy to remove by degreasing the dish after cooking. Where possible, I chill the dish overnight to allow the fat to settle in an easily removable slab – I have always found it difficult to totally degrease freshly cooked dishes. Flavours of slow-cooked dishes always improve by slowly reheating them the next day anyway.

If you want to render duck fat yourself, take a heavy-based stockpot or similar and place the duck fat and skin on the bottom. Some people cut up the skin into small pieces or even purée the fat and skin but, as time tends to be such a consideration now, unless you plan to use the skin for a salad, I suggest you simply add a few bay leaves and juniper berries and cover the fat with water. Cook slowly for about an hour until the fat turns clear, making sure that none of the skin sticks to the bottom and burns.

Strain while still hot, pour into a container and cool before refrigerating or freezing. If you wish to make the skin into crackling, slowly reheat the pieces of skin in another pot until they turn golden brown, stirring to avoid burning. Drain and sprinkle with sea salt flakes, then use in salads.

QUATRE-ÉPICES
Makes 1 tablespoon

This spice mixture is used for pâtés, rillettes and terrines. Although meant to be made of four spices, it can be modified to suit personal taste. Spices are much better freshly roasted and used straightaway than stored for a long period.

10 cloves
1 tablespoon white peppercorns
1 cinnamon stick

¾ teaspoon ground ginger
¾ teaspoon freshly grated nutmeg

Grind all ingredients to a fine powder in a spice mill.

RILLETTES DE CANARD
(COMPOTE OF SHREDDED DUCK)

Serves 6–8

I have adapted Paula Wolfert's recipe for duck rillettes, but you can also use rabbit, hare, pork or pigeon in exactly the same way. This recipe should be prepared one week in advance. It takes 30–45 minutes of active cooking time and unattended cooking time of 4–5 hours. Duck breast is not used, as it would dry out too much.

1½ cups duck fat, chilled

4 duck marylands (thigh and drumstick)
 or 6 pigeon legs *or* front and back legs
 of 2 large hares

340 g pork shoulder, cut into 2 cm cubes

duck carcass and wings (not breast),
 chopped

sea salt flakes and freshly ground
 black pepper

190 ml unsalted Golden Chicken Stock
 (see page 57)

190 ml dry white wine

1 bay leaf, crushed

1 teaspoon thyme leaves

1 large clove garlic, halved

2 golden shallots, peeled

½ teaspoon Quatre-Épices (see opposite),
 plus extra to taste

2 tablespoons Armagnac *or* brandy

Moisten the bottom of a crockpot, heavy-based cast-iron casserole or camp oven with a little of the duck fat, place the duck marylands in and cover with pork pieces. Add the chopped duck carcass and wings to the pan, then season with 1 teaspoon each of salt and pepper. Add the stock, wine, herbs, garlic, shallots and quatre-épices.

Cook over the lowest possible heat at barely a simmer, uncovered, until the meat falls off the bone (4–5 hours). Stir from time to time to prevent sticking – the liquid in the pan will evaporate.

Strain the pork and duck through a colander set over a deep bowl and set aside until it is cool enough to handle. Pick out all the bones and gristle, leaving aside the moist pieces of meat. Set aside ½ cup of the rendered fat.

Using a fork (not a food processor), shred the meat and add the remaining chilled duck fat, the cooked garlic and shallots and the Armagnac or brandy. Taste for seasoning, adding more salt, plenty of pepper, thyme and quatre-épices to taste. It should be very peppery.

Spoon the rillettes into clean stoneware or glass dishes, leaving about 1 cm at the top. Seal with the reserved fat from the cooking. Chill and keep refrigerated for a week for the flavours to develop.

Serve with rounds of crusty bread, cornichons (see Glossary), lots of black pepper and a glass of chilled Sauternes.

WINTER

CAVOLO NERO

MY FIRST SIGHTING OF CAVOLO NERO, ITALY'S 'BLACK CABBAGE', was at a stall in Florence's San Lorenzo market in 1997. The stall was the most expensive in the entire marketplace and the vendor was so charming to us during the first week of our visit because we bought so much from her.

By the second week we were a little savvier and would circle the market before returning to 'our' stallholder – and she became very bad-tempered when she saw how much we'd bought elsewhere. In fact, she was so cross we almost decided not to buy from her, only to find that she was the only one offering the purpley, greenish-black leaves of the first cavolo nero of the season.

A member of the *Brassica* family (a kale, actually), cavolo nero doesn't form a head but is instead made up of long, loose leaves growing from an upright stem that can be picked a little like silverbeet. Unlike a cabbage, it withstands long cooking, during which time the leaves become almost black, imparting a pleasantly bitter flavour – just right for lovers of savoury things.

I became such a convert to cavolo nero that when I returned home from Italy I brought packets of seeds with me (I declared them, of course), as I had never known the vegetable to be available here. I usually have great intentions of planting seeds and nurturing the seedlings and then in a flurry of chaotic activity forget to water them. Instead, this time I passed the seeds on to Mike Plane of Allsun Farm in New South Wales, who had chased me up after reading of the seeds in an article I wrote. In return, he sent a tray of seedlings with the heads just about to poke through the potting soil. Mike assured me the vegetable was easy to grow, the only problem being a few aphids on the outside leaves (these leaves went to the chooks).

Cavolo nero is now available in specialty greengrocers, though if you go to the trouble of growing it yourself, you can pick the young leaves for salad, before the leaves mature. They are such magnificent plants that they could almost be ornamental features in the garden.

Cavolo nero on bruschetta (see page 366)

Perhaps the best way to enjoy the distinctive flavour of cavolo nero is on bruschetta. This may not be the first dish that springs to mind – but it's a rustic dish for which I would travel miles. Wash and trim a couple of bunches of cavolo nero and chop into 5 cm pieces. Simmer the leaves in chicken stock until softened (this can take up to 30 minutes, depending on the age of the cavolo nero). Toast thick slices of crusty bread and rub these on one side with a clove of garlic. Dip the toast into the stock briefly to moisten, then put it on a plate and pile on the drained cavolo nero. Add sea salt, freshly ground black pepper and a really good dose of fruity extra virgin olive oil, particularly if you have access to the new season's. Amazing!

Recipes for hearty Ribollita soup (see page 368) usually appear with a note claiming that it is impossible to make it without cavolo nero ('ribollita' simply means re-boiled: the soup can be made one day and reheated the next). I'd made it with Savoy cabbage before our Italian sojourn, which I had thought a good substitute, but, as is so often the case, tradition wins out – it is fascinating to discover that one ingredient can make such a difference. In Italy I used cavolo nero with pork and when making a risotto. Now that I grow my own, I'll find many more applications, but it seems appropriate to include a recipe for a soup here, as this is what I had hoped to cook when scouring the San Lorenzo market for my first taste of cavolo nero.

CAVOLO NERO WITH GOLDEN SHALLOTS AND QUINCE   *Serves 4*

1 bunch cavolo nero, washed and chopped

50 g butter

extra virgin olive oil, for cooking

2 small golden shallots, thinly sliced

½ quince, peeled, cored and sliced

lemon juice, to taste

1 teaspoon chopped lemon thyme

Blanch cavolo nero by plunging it briefly in a saucepan of boiling water until just tender, if the leaves are young; if they are older you'll need to cook them a bit more at the end. Drain well and squeeze out any excess moisture. In a large frying pan, heat the butter over medium heat until nut-brown, then add a little olive oil to inhibit burning. Add the shallots and quince slices and cook until tender and golden. Add a good squeeze of lemon juice and the lemon thyme, then add the cavolo nero. If the leaves are older, cook until tender; otherwise, serve straight away.

BRAISED CAVOLO NERO

Serves 4

1 bunch cavolo nero, washed and
    roughly chopped
½ cup (125 ml) extra virgin olive oil

1 clove garlic
2 anchovy fillets

Blanch the chopped cavolo nero by plunging it briefly in a saucepan of boiling water until just tender, then drain immediately and set aside.

Heat the olive oil over low–medium heat, then sauté the garlic. Add the anchovy fillets and cavolo nero and season with a little salt and pepper. Sauté slowly for about 5 minutes, until the cavolo nero is tender on the tooth.

I like to serve this as an accompaniment, and it works especially well with Slow-roasted Oyster Blade with Onion Cream (see page 205).

MINESTRONE WITH CAVOLO NERO

Serves 8

Now that I grow cavolo nero in my own garden, I add it to my version of minestrone.

1⅓ cups (275 g) dried lima beans, soaked
    overnight in a deep bowl of water
125 ml extra virgin olive oil,
    plus extra for cooking
20 g butter
3 onions, roughly chopped
3 cloves garlic, roughly chopped
6 large sprigs thyme
2 carrots, roughly chopped
2 sticks celery, roughly chopped
3 rashers bacon, chopped
rind from a piece of Parmigiano Reggiano,
    if available

2 small fresh bay leaves
1 × 410 g can peeled and chopped
    roma tomatoes
2.5 litres Golden Chicken Stock
    (see page 57)
8–10 large cavolo nero leaves,
    stems removed and leaves shredded
2 zucchini, diced
100 g green beans, sliced
sea salt flakes and freshly ground
    black pepper

Drain the lima beans and set aside.

Heat 125 ml olive oil and the butter in a stockpot over medium heat until the butter is nut-brown, then gently sauté the onions and garlic until translucent. Tie the thyme sprigs together with kitchen string and add to the pan with the drained lima beans, carrots, celery, bacon, cheese rind and bay leaves, and toss to coat with the olive oil and butter.

Add the tomatoes and 2 litres of the chicken stock, then stir and bring to the boil over high heat. Turn heat down to low and gently simmer for 1½ hours. You may need to add a little more stock during cooking, so keep an eye on the pan. »

Heat a little olive oil in a saucepan, then add the shredded cavolo nero and toss until wilted. Add to the soup and simmer for another 10 minutes. Shortly before serving, add the zucchini and green beans to the soup and cook until just tender. Season with salt and pepper.

To serve, remove the cheese rind and bundle of thyme, then ladle the soup into warm, wide soup bowls and drizzle over a little extra virgin olive oil.

RIBOLLITA
Serves 4

Meaning 're-boiled', ribollita takes leftover minestrone made the day before and extends it with the addition of cavolo nero and extra stock, transforming it into a slightly different dish. I put cavolo nero in my minestrone anyway as I like it so much, but the ribollita still benefits from adding even more.

1 bunch cavolo nero, washed and
    chopped into 5 cm pieces
2 cups (500 ml) Golden Chicken Stock
    (see page 57)
4 large slices wood-fired bread

1 clove garlic
extra virgin olive oil, for drizzling
2 cups (500 ml) leftover Minestrone
    (see previous page)

Simmer the cavolo nero in the chicken stock over low–medium heat for 20–30 minutes or until tender; the time will depend on the age of the cavolo nero.

Grill the bread, then rub on both sides with the cut garlic. Place a slice of grilled bread in each soup bowl and drizzle with olive oil.

Remove the cavolo nero from the stock and set aside. Add the leftover minestrone to the stock and heat over high heat, stirring continuously. When the soup is hot, add the cooked cavolo nero and a good drizzle of olive oil. Serve poured over the grilled bread.

CELERIAC

WHAT A HUGE PREHISTORIC-LOOKING VEGETABLE THIS IS, AND yet how delicate its flavour. Celeriac is a versatile vegetable available from late autumn right through winter. It is as ancient a vegetable as celery, so its lack of popularity is hard to understand, although it has long been part of continental European cooking. Both celery and celeriac were cultivated from the original wild celery plant. I love the mild 'celery' flavour of the celeriac – cooked and puréed, it is a natural accompaniment to game.

While you might buy a bunch of celeriac with four bulbs from a wholesale fruit and vegetable supplier, it is most often sold individually, which is more appropriate for a small household (though if you have the chance to buy a bunch of younger, smaller bulbs, then take it!). As it has a rough surface, it is best to choose the smoothest you can find so that you don't lose too much of the vegetable in the trimming.

Celeriac discolours on cutting, so put it in a bowl of acidulated water (water with lemon juice or verjuice added) until you're ready to cook it. If you are going to eat it raw, just rub the exposed surface with a cut lemon as you would for an artichoke. Sliced finely, celeriac gives a lovely crunch to salads.

Celeriac cut thickly and roasted to a golden brown in extra virgin olive oil can be added to a dish of chicken or guinea fowl.

Going through old notebooks of visits to Paris, I found an account of my first ever Celeriac Rémoulade (see page 371), some years ago now. It was at one of those truly Parisian bistros – the type that is becoming harder to find these days – with a very limited lunch menu, checked tablecloths, wine only available in half or full carafes, and lots of tiny tables crammed together in a narrow room. The food was simply prepared with great flavour and served with speed and panache. Sometimes I can go a whole winter without remembering to make celeriac rémoulade, but when I do it immediately evokes the memory of this French bistro.

In the same notebook I found a description of a warm salad of quail with apple, celeriac, pine nuts, hazelnut oil, a little balsamic and the smallest touch of truffle oil (see page 131). Just reading through this list of ingredients transports me back to the occasion when I first tried it, and inspires me to make it again.

In this quail dish both the celeriac and apples were raw – peeled, shredded and tossed in lemon juice before being added to the salad. This brings me to the combination of apple and celeriac. It works whether they are raw, cooked together and puréed, or tossed in a pan with some chicken or duck livers. All of these become a real treat when a splash of verjuice is added, though a good squeeze of lemon juice would do.

Celeriac chips are really simple to make, and go beautifully with grilled fish, lamb chops or barbecued chicken. With a firm hand and a sharp knife, or using a mandolin or Japanese shredder, peel and cut the celeriac widthways into 2 cm-thick pieces, then soak in acidulated water for 10 minutes, drain and pat dry. Deep-fry in your favourite extra virgin olive oil until golden brown. Drain on kitchen paper and sprinkle with a little sea salt with grated lemon rind added.

CELERIAC RÉMOULADE

Serves 4

Celeriac rémoulade can be served with cold chicken, smoked potted tongue, a salad of radicchio, apples, walnuts and pancetta, or as Stephanie Alexander says in her culinary bible, *The Cook's Companion*, that I so often refer to, 'this delicious starter is very addictive with a bowl of fat olives and some good bread and maybe a platter of thinly sliced salami'. As it was Stephanie who first introduced me to this dish, I thought it absolutely fitting that I use her method.

1 large celeriac (reject if spongy
    in the centre after peeling)
1 lemon
½ cup (125 ml) mustard Mayonnaise
    (see page 400)

1 tablespoon freshly chopped
    flat-leaf parsley

Peel the celeriac and rub exposed surfaces with cut lemon. Cut into quarters and drop in a bowl of acidulated water. Shred celeriac using the shredding disc of your food processor or a mandolin slicer placed over a bowl containing the mayonnaise. Combine the celeriac and mayonnaise, stir to mix well, then add the parsley.

CELERIAC, APPLE AND WALNUT SALAD

Serves 4

2 small celeriac
juice of ½ lemon
2 small Granny Smith apples,
    cored and thinly sliced
80 g toasted walnuts
freshly chopped flat-leaf parsley, to serve

DRESSING
¼ cup (60 ml) sour cream
½ teaspoon Dijon mustard
¼ cup (60 ml) extra virgin olive oil
2½ tablespoons freshly grated horseradish
¼ cup (60 ml) walnut oil
1 tablespoon lemon juice (optional)
sea salt flakes and freshly ground
    black pepper (optional)

Trim the bases and tops from the celeriac, then cut down the sides to peel. Using a strong potato peeler, shave thick slices from the celeriac, dropping them into a bowl of water with the lemon juice added to stop them discolouring. Add the apple to the bowl.

To make the dressing, whisk the sour cream, Dijon mustard and olive oil until emulsified. Add the horseradish, then the walnut oil and stir to combine. Taste the dressing, and add lemon juice, salt or pepper if needed.

Toss the drained celeriac and apples with the dressing, then add the walnuts and some freshly chopped flat-leaf parsley. This salad is excellent served with slices of smoked salmon.

BRAISED CELERIAC   *Serves 4*

This dish is best of all when made using four small celeriac, which unfortunately I am yet to see in greengrocers. When made with young ones picked from your own garden, the flavour is extraordinary.

4 small *or* 1 large celeriac

lemon juice, to taste

1 cup (250 ml) Golden Chicken Stock
   (see page 57)

1 tablespoon butter

2 tablespoons freshly chopped
   flat-leaf parsley

sea salt flakes and freshly ground
   black pepper

Peel and cut the celeriac into slices. Squeeze with a little lemon juice and then simmer in a saucepan with the chicken stock and butter until tender – this will take up to 20 minutes depending on the size of the slices. Remove the cooked celeriac and drain, keeping it warm. Reduce the remaining stock to pour over the celeriac, then finish with the freshly chopped parsley, and salt and pepper to taste.

PURÉE OF CELERIAC TO ACCOMPANY GAME   *Serves 4*

This purée can also be made with either just potatoes or apples, depending on what you have to hand and what you are serving it with. Celeriac with apple goes well with pheasant, and celeriac with potatoes is wonderful alongside the best sausages you can buy.

1 medium potato, peeled and cut
   into thick slices

1 large celeriac, peeled and cut
   into thick slices

2 Granny Smith apples, peeled,
   cored and thickly sliced

50 g butter

150 ml cream

sea salt flakes and freshly ground
   black pepper

Boil the potato and celeriac in a large saucepan of salted water until tender, adding the apples after 5 minutes. Drain well and then purée in a mouli. Whisk in the butter and cream to make a fluffy purée. Season to taste.

VICTORIA'S CELERIAC AND CHESTNUT PIE   *Serves 6*

Victoria Blumenstein, formerly of Blumenstein's, came to work for me at the Farmshop in 2002 and stayed for three very eventful years. Victoria and I worked together on so many ideas, and so often it was a case of two heads being better than one. This is one of my favourite recipes from Victoria – a luscious dish for a cold winter's day.

1 × quantity Sour-cream Pastry
(see page 424)

juice of ½ lemon

1 celeriac (about 750 g)

100 g Swiss brown mushrooms,
trimmed and quartered

1 fennel bulb, trimmed and finely chopped

2 large onions, finely chopped

¼ cup extra virgin olive oil

sea salt flakes and freshly ground
black pepper

3 cloves garlic, finely chopped

125 ml verjuice

2 cups (500 ml) vegetable *or* Golden Chicken
Stock (see page 57)

2 sprigs rosemary

2 sprigs thyme

50 g chestnuts, peeled
(frozen, partly precooked chestnuts are
suitable if you can't get fresh ones)

50 g brancolete *or* other goat's cheese,
crumbled

1 egg, beaten with a little milk

Make and chill the pastry as instructed.

Add the lemon juice to a large bowl of water. Peel the celeriac and cut it into 1 cm pieces, then place it in the bowl of water. Place the mushrooms, fennel and onions in three separate bowls, drizzle each with olive oil and season to taste with salt and pepper. Add the garlic to the onions.

Heat a large frying pan over medium heat, then sauté the mushrooms until cooked, deglaze the pan with a dash of verjuice and transfer to a bowl. Repeat first with the fennel and then with the onion and garlic mixture, deglazing each time with verjuice.

Wipe the pan clean with kitchen paper, then add the stock, herbs and the remaining verjuice and bring to a simmer over medium heat. Add the chestnuts to the pan, reduce the heat to low and poach for 5 minutes or until tender but still whole, then remove chestnuts and set aside. Reduce the stock over high heat until syrupy, then add to the bowl with the sautéed onion mixture. Add all the vegetables and the chestnuts to the bowl, toss to combine, then leave to cool.

Meanwhile, preheat the oven to 200°C. Roll out the pastry and cut out a lid and base for a 24 cm pie mould. Distribute the vegetable mixture evenly over the pastry, then top with the cheese. Place the pastry lid on top, pinch edges to seal and brush with egg and milk mixture. Bake for 20 minutes or until golden brown. Serve with a rocket and shaved Parmigiano Reggiano salad.

CHESTNUTS

I ATE MY FIRST CHESTNUT, TOO MANY YEARS AGO TO WANT TO remember, on a street corner in Vienna during my first European winter. Vendors were roasting them over braziers and serving the hot chestnuts in a cone made from newspaper. It was such a surprise to bite into this smoky morsel and discover a flavour like that of a nutty sweet potato – the chestnuts warmed my hands as I held them and took some of the bitter chill away.

Thinking about this reminds me of when chefs Urs Inauen, Cheong Liew, Tom Milligan and I were in New York in the spring of 1992. The previous year we had won the Seppelt Australian Menu of the Year together, and our 'prize' was to cook a grand dinner for the American press at the Peninsula Hotel. It was unseasonably cold, and snow had brought the chestnut sellers out to ply their wares. The dinner was a mammoth effort, and we were lucky that Urs had arrived ahead of the rest of us in order to source ingredients, as we were beset by disasters (the most memorable of which saw our hare literally flying all over the country – turning up just in time at the last moment!). The night was a great success in the end, but when the dinner finished, the snow had stopped and the chestnut sellers had disappeared from the streets.

And now I have my own chestnut trees. These trees have flourished, even with years of drought and persistent gully winds that would blow a roof off at times. When I think of my long walks in the Umbrian mountains, where wild chestnuts abound without any tending, I guess their hardiness is not at all surprising. They even drop their crop when they are ready. Having said that, timing is everything, and as the chestnuts lose moisture quickly it doesn't pay to leave them on the ground. Pick them up and keep them refrigerated in plastic bags in the crisper section until you're ready to use them – the sooner the better.

Fresh chestnuts (not a nut, in fact, but a fruit) have become readily available in fruit and vegetable shops from late April through to July. The shinier and fuller the chestnut, the

fresher it is. If chestnuts are glossy, a deep mahogany-brown colour and heavy in the hand they will be very fresh. Don't be bothered with withered chestnuts or any that are mouldy. Fresh chestnuts should be cooked very soon after picking as they dry out very quickly, losing weight and flavour.

The area around Myrtleford in Victoria, with the influence of Italian immigrants, abounds with chestnut trees and chestnut festivals. Jane Casey of Cheznuts has a thriving business there, producing frozen, peeled chestnuts, as well as fresh ones, taking all the hard work out of getting your chestnut fix. They are delivered Australia-wide and Jane can be contacted through the website www.cheznuts.com.au. Closer to home for me is Nirvana, a truly beautiful property in the Adelaide Hills where Deb Cantrell and Quentin Jones farm chestnuts and redcurrants.

Because the Australian chestnut industry is so young, many new varieties are being introduced, so if you're looking for a tree for your own garden, check what works well in your area. A variety that performs well in South Australia may not do so in Victoria, and vice versa. The benefit of having such a young industry is that those involved realise the importance of commitment and progress, so much so that all growers pay a levy to fund research. The industry is also aware that the health benefits of chestnuts are a vital marketing aid: chestnuts contain no cholesterol, are very low in fat (less than 4 per cent), and are 50 per cent carbohydrate and 10 per cent protein (which is very similar to the amount of protein in an egg). You will certainly never get oil from a chestnut! There is tremendous potential for growth in this industry – at the moment the Australian population eats one chestnut per person each year, and although canned chestnuts and a small quantity of dried chestnuts are imported from elsewhere, the only country chestnuts can be imported from fresh is New Zealand.

Most exciting of all, however, is the fact that local chestnut growers are increasingly offering peeled, cooked and frozen chestnuts commercially. My first experience of this, some years ago now, was when I was sent a small hessian sack of fresh chestnuts still in their husks from Richard Moxham and Alison Saunders, who trade as Sassafras Nuts in Griffith, ACT. I was impressed by the fact that Richard had made sure I knew the chestnuts were coming so that I was ready to refrigerate them immediately on receipt, an important issue if their freshness is to be retained. (If you don't have a hessian bag to hand, a brown paper bag is the next best thing for storing chestnuts, in the crisper compartment of your refrigerator.)

The chestnuts came complete with a chestnut knife, the size of a paring knife but with the tiniest blade, which has a sharp protrusion to make cutting into the tough chestnuts much easier. Now, that's what I call clever marketing. In his letter, Richard explained that 'peelability' is the Australian chestnut industry's biggest problem and many growers, like themselves, were regrafting their trees to easier-peeling varieties – in their case to Sassafras Red, a good peeling variety that has a sweet, creamy flavour when roasted.

Chestnuts are notoriously difficult to peel. Collected after they fall from the tree, chestnuts are encased in a very prickly burr that makes the wearing of gloves essential. If you have your own tree you will need to remove the burr first, then slit the shiny shell beneath it to reveal the chestnut, which has a skin of its own that must be removed. If you buy direct from the farm in season or from a specialist greengrocer, the burr will already have been removed, leaving only the shell and the skin to be dealt with.

My favourite way of eating chestnuts is to slit the shells on the domed side and then roast them over a flame. My friend Steve Flamsteed gave me a chestnut-roasting pan when

he returned from his cheese-making *stage* (training) in France in 1994, though the black pan, with holes about 7 mm across drilled all over its base, hangs the whole year in the pot rack above my marble bench until the chestnut season. So many people are curious about what I could possibly cook in it, and even though it can go over a gas flame it only seems right over an open fire. The holes allow the flames to leap up and lick around the chestnuts. The secret when cooking chestnuts over a fire is to allow them to blacken and then to let them cool just a little (once burnt and crisp, they reach the desired flavour, but if allowed to become cold, the inner brown skin, or 'pellicle', is difficult to remove). One has to be careful not to scorch the chestnuts too much but the crispness this method produces is highly desirable, even if it means burnt fingertips as the skins of the chestnuts are gingerly pulled away.

Unless you have special equipment, the next best method to attain a smoky flavour is to slit the shells and then grill the chestnuts until they are charred, turning them after 15 minutes. They should take about 25 minutes in all to cook this way. Wrap the grilled chestnuts in a tea towel, where they will steam a little, making peeling easier.

If you have lots of chestnuts, they freeze particularly well once blanched and peeled. This is the method to follow if you plan to use the chestnuts in a dish rather than eat them roasted – this way most of the cooking is done in the final dish, so more flavour is taken up, and overcooking the chestnuts, which is quite easy to do and causes them to break up, is avoided. Slit the shiny brown shell with a very sharp knife and peel it away. Bring the chestnuts to the boil in a small saucepan of cold water – they are ready as soon as the water boils; left any longer they go grey, like canned chestnuts (however, should you wish to cook them completely this way, let them simmer for 15 minutes). Remove the pan from the heat then take out one chestnut at a time, and slip off the papery skin. If you are freezing the chestnuts, do so immediately. Thaw them just before they are required, to avoid discolouration.

At present, Australian chestnut growers do not see an immediate market for chestnut flour, although one or two grind their own supply. It is such a limited market, and competing with the small volumes already being imported into Australia would be prohibitive. I love to use chestnut flour to make flat, moist, flavoursome cakes to serve with coffee, as the Italians do (see page 383). The quality of some of the imported flour varies greatly, depending on freshness: one has no idea of the date of harvest and the flour can be full of weevils or rancid. As Australian growers' crops become larger and more viable, we should keep encouraging more of them to grind their own flour, so that those of us who want to use chestnut flour do not need to rely on imports.

Jane Casey of Cheznuts says that in the first four years of growing chestnuts she didn't even eat them. Now she understands that she needs to be passionate about them so she can advise, educate and enthuse her customers. Such a simple matter, and something I've tried to shout from as many rooftops as possible – just imagine what would happen if every producer adopted this philosophy.

Brussels sprouts hadn't been a vegetable Jane had liked at all until she tried steaming them with blanched and peeled chestnuts. They take exactly the same length of time (about 15–20 minutes) and the chestnuts have an inherent sweetness that complements the sprouts, and they also provide great texture. Or try pan-frying blanched chestnuts in nut-brown butter with fresh herbs for 5 minutes, then adding blanched Brussels sprouts that have been cut in half and cooking for another 5 minutes – delicious served with game.

Cooking chestnuts with rice adds another dimension to a stir-fry. Jane uses a rice cooker and merely adds a handful of peeled chestnuts with the usual volume of rice and leaves them to cook (the same result can be achieved if cooking rice by the absorption method). The chestnuts add crunch and their flavour permeates the rice.

Use whole blanched chestnuts in a traditional stuffing for turkey, goose or a really good chicken. Chestnuts, pancetta and rosemary are the perfect combination when cooking guinea fowl. Pot-roast a pheasant or guinea fowl with blanched chestnuts, baby onions, fresh bay leaves, orange rind and juniper berries in a little stock and some sage jelly – the dish will only take about half an hour to cook once you have your ingredients ready. Velvety, nutty chestnut soup (see page 380), a stock-based purée thinned with a little cream, is particularly good with the addition of a little pheasant, pigeon or quail meat tossed in a little oil or butter over heat with tiny onions and fresh herbs.

Take the time to make a chestnut purée as a base for desserts, although I admit it's a tedious job. Boil the chestnuts, reserve the water, and then peel and purée them in a food mill or food processor while still warm. Add some of the liquid to make it easier, if necessary. The purée is great mixed into ice cream or added to choux pastry that is then deep-fried like a doughnut. If you buy canned chestnut purée, check whether it is unsweetened or sweetened – I find the latter overly sweet and prefer to add the sweetness myself. You could use dried chestnuts to make your own purée: cover them with milk, bring to the boil, take off the heat and steep at room temperature overnight. Drain, purée and sweeten to taste.

Of course there is the classic Mont Blanc, a piped mass of sweetened chestnut purée topped with whipped cream; the purée can also be flavoured with a little liqueur and served with crème fraîche alongside.

Going through old notes and scraps of ideas, I came across a mention of a chocolate chestnut cake served with stewed mulberries. My tastebuds remembered it well, but there were no further notes to guide me. How I wish I'd documented all the dishes I've cooked! The problem was that I couldn't remember whether I used a canned unsweetened chestnut purée or chestnut flour; I've certainly made cakes with both. The purée would give a very moist pudding-like consistency, while the flour would produce a moist and nutty Italian-style cake. I would ice both versions with chocolate ganache. I think the purée probably wins out as my more likely choice.

Chestnut and chocolate make a good combination, particularly if you use a very bitter couverture chocolate. A great boon for chocoholics is Peter Wilson's Kennedy & Wilson Chocolates. A winemaker who worked for Bailey Carrodus of Yarra Yering Vineyards for ten years, Peter has made an art form out of this wonderful bitter chocolate, and though the company goes from strength to strength, Peter has now returned to wine-making. Peter was one of our favourite customers at the Pheasant Farm. He went to Roseworthy College to study oenology, and his group was so passionate about their food and wine that they celebrated all their special occasions in our restaurant. My husband Colin allowed them to bring wine in without corkage: they saved up for these dinners, always brought along the best wines they could muster and simply asked me to cook. This group was extraordinary, matched only by Steve Flamsteed's year. It was a delight to cook for them.

The point of all this is that chestnuts are extremely versatile, and this versatility is increased further by the forms in which they can now be bought: fresh, frozen (peeled and par-cooked), canned whole or puréed, dried pieces or ground as flour.

CHESTNUT SOUP

Serves 6

1 large onion, finely chopped	sea salt flakes
2 sticks celery, thinly sliced	1.5 litres Golden Chicken Stock
500 g blanched chestnuts	(see page 57)
2 fresh bay leaves	freshly ground black pepper
2 tablespoons extra virgin olive oil	½ cup (125 ml) cream

Sauté the onion, celery, chestnuts and bay leaves in the olive oil in a stockpot over medium–high heat until the onion is golden brown. Season with salt and add the stock, then simmer until the chestnuts are very soft, about 25–30 minutes. Remove the bay leaves and then purée the mixture in a food processor or blender. Season with pepper and check if more salt is needed, then add the cream. Reheat gently and serve immediately.

RAVIOLI WITH CHESTNUTS, MUSHROOMS AND MASCARPONE

Makes 18 ravioli

500 g peeled and blanched frozen chestnuts, defrosted

4 sprigs thyme

1½ cups (375 ml) Golden Chicken Stock (see page 57)

130 g unsalted butter

320 g Swiss brown mushrooms, sliced

⅓ cup chopped sage

sea salt flakes and freshly ground black pepper

125 g mascarpone

1 egg

dash milk

extra virgin olive oil, to serve

RAVIOLI

250 g plain flour

3 egg yolks

2 eggs

For the ravioli, tip the flour onto a bench and make a well in the centre. Whisk the egg yolks and eggs together and pour into the well. Incorporate them into the flour, and knead the pasta dough until it forms a shiny ball and is firm to the touch. Cover the dough with plastic film and rest it in the refrigerator for 30 minutes.

Meanwhile, place the chestnuts, thyme and chicken stock in a saucepan, then poach over very low heat for 10 minutes or until tender. Sauté the mushrooms in the butter over medium heat with the sage, 1 teaspoon salt, and pepper for 5 minutes or until cooked.

Drain the chestnuts, reserving the stock, and combine them with the mushrooms. Chop roughly or pulse once or twice in a food processor, adding 2 tablespoons of the reserved stock to pull the mixture together. Fold in the mascarpone, then chill in the refrigerator until firm. Season to taste with more salt and pepper.

Cut the dough into manageable portions. Using a pasta machine with rollers set at the widest setting, feed batches of the dough through the rollers. Reduce the settings on the rollers notch by notch, feeding the pasta dough through until you reach the second-last notch on the machine. It should be very thin, but not transparent (ravioli is often spoilt by pasta that's too thick). Cover each sheet with a damp tea towel to keep moist and continue to roll remaining pieces of dough. The sheets should be even in length – trim if they are not.

Lay the pasta sheets on a bench. Use a small ice-cream scoop or a generous tablespoon to mound spoonfuls of the chestnut filling in rows, 10 cm apart, on half of the pasta sheets. Combine the egg and milk, and brush the pasta sheets with egg wash around the filling and to the edges of the pasta. Lay another sheet of pasta over each of the chestnut-topped sheets, and, starting from the filling edge, press down to remove any air bubbles as you go. Cut into squares 10 × 10 cm, then chill in the refrigerator for at least 2 hours.

Poach the ravioli gently in batches, no more than four at a time, in a deep frying pan of simmering water. They should be cooked in about 5 minutes, but this will depend on the thickness of the pasta. Drizzle with extra virgin olive oil and serve.

SEARED DUCK BREASTS WITH CHESTNUTS, BACON AND VINO COTTO-GLAZED RADICCHIO

Serves 2

2 × 150 g duck breast fillets, skin on

sea salt flakes

1 cup frozen whole chestnuts, defrosted

milk, for cooking

freshly ground black pepper

2 rashers bacon, rind removed

60 g unsalted butter

2 small radicchio, trimmed and cut
   into wedges

1 tablespoon brown sugar

¼ cup (60 ml) vino cotto (see Glossary)

¼ cup freshly chopped flat-leaf parsley

Score the skin of each duck breast diagonally, then sprinkle with salt. If you have time, pour boiling water over the skin and place, uncovered, in the refrigerator overnight – this allows the pores to open and helps the fat under the skin to render beautifully during cooking. If you don't have that much time, even 10 minutes will help.

Simmer the defrosted chestnuts in just enough milk to cover them, for 20 minutes or until tender. Alternatively, if you are short of time, place the chestnuts in a microwave-proof container, add ¼ cup (60 ml) water, cover and cook on high for 2 minutes, then leave them to stand for 10 minutes. Drain and cut in half, then set aside.

Preheat the oven to 200°C. Heat a chargrill pan or heavy-based frying pan over high heat until very hot. Season the duck breasts with salt and pepper and place skin-side down in the pan to sear. Leave until well-browned, then turn over and sear the other side for 1 minute. Transfer to the oven and cook for another 4 minutes, then remove and leave to rest, skin-side down, in a warm place.

Add the bacon to the pan and cook until crisp, then cut into small pieces and set aside.

Meanwhile, heat half the butter in a frying pan over medium heat until nut-brown, then add the chestnuts and toss until light brown and crisp. Season to taste with salt and pepper, then remove and set aside.

For the vino cotto-glazed radicchio, add the remaining butter to the pan, and when nut-brown, add the radicchio. Cook until the radicchio just starts to wilt, then add the brown sugar and season to taste. When the sugar has melted, deglaze the pan with vino cotto and add the reserved bacon and chestnuts.

Carve each duck breast into slices on the diagonal, then fan them out a little. Divide the chestnuts, bacon and vino cotto-glazed radicchio between two plates and top each with a sliced duck breast. Drizzle with the resting juices from the duck, and serve.

CHESTNUT CAKE

Serves 6–8

In Italy, this flat, dense cake is served with coffee. Chestnut flour is available from Italian delis – the freshness of the flour will dramatically affect the flavour of the cake.

⅓ cup (50 g) dried currants

verjuice, for soaking

250 g chestnut flour

1½ cups (375 ml) cold water

¼ cup (60 ml) extra virgin olive oil

pinch salt

⅓ cup (50 g) pine nuts

2 teaspoons finely chopped rosemary

finely chopped rind of 1 orange

Strega (an Italian liqueur, optional) *or*

   mascarpone combined with grated

   orange rind (optional), to serve

Reconstitute the currants, in enough verjuice to cover them, for about 30 minutes. Preheat the oven to 200°C. Sift the chestnut flour into a bowl, then gradually stir in the cold water to make a thick paste (you may not need all of it). Make sure there are no lumps, then add the olive oil and salt.

Dry-roast the pine nuts on a baking tray for about 10 minutes until golden brown (watch them carefully as they burn easily). Reduce the oven temperature to 190°C.

Add the rosemary, orange rind, drained currants and pine nuts to the batter and stir vigorously until amalgamated. Grease a shallow 20 cm cake tin and pour in the batter to a depth of 2.5 cm, then bake for 30 minutes. Serve the cake warm, either moistened with Strega poured over it as soon as it comes out of the oven, or with mascarpone flavoured with grated orange rind alongside.

CHESTNUT AND CHOCOLATE POTS

Serves 8

This is a very rich dessert so I tend to serve it as a treat after supper in small demitasse coffee cups.

1 × 430 g tin unsweetened chestnut purée

120 ml pouring cream

80 g unsalted butter, chopped

30 ml Cognac

2 tablespoons Seville orange marmalade

GANACHE

150 g dark couverture chocolate buttons

   (see Glossary)

85 ml pouring cream

Place chestnut purée and cream in a saucepan and melt, stirring to combine, over low heat. If the purée is extremely thick and difficult to stir, add a little water. Add butter and continue stirring until it melts and combines. Add Cognac, then remove from the heat.

Using a hand-held blender or food processor, purée the chestnut mixture until smooth. Pour the purée evenly into 8 small demitasse coffee cups and refrigerate for about 20 minutes or until firm. »

Meanwhile, for the ganache, melt the chocolate and cream together in a small saucepan over low heat, stirring to combine.

Add 1 teaspoon marmalade to each cup, then cover with chocolate ganache and refrigerate until totally set.

CHOCOLATE AND CHESTNUT LOG   *Serves 12*

In fourteen years of cooking at the Pheasant Farm Restaurant I hardly wrote down any recipes, but fortunately this chocolate and chestnut log was recorded for posterity. I have no idea where the original recipe came from, as the card it is written on is now almost illegible, after fifteen years' worth of sticky fingers all over it. This dessert is unbelievably rich, so rather than offering cream with it, raspberries would be perfect, when in season, as would candied cumquats.

200 g unsalted butter
2 tablespoons castor sugar
1 large egg
1 tablespoon Cognac

450 g cooked, peeled and sieved fresh
chestnuts *or* canned unsweetened
chestnut purée
200 g dark couverture chocolate
(see Glossary), melted

Using a hand-held electric mixer, cream the butter, sugar, egg and Cognac until light and fluffy. If using fresh chestnuts, purée them until smooth. Add the chestnut purée to the butter mixture and mix thoroughly.

Transfer half the mixture into another bowl and mix in the melted chocolate thoroughly. Spread the chocolate mixture into a rectangle on a sheet of baking paper or foil, then top with the remaining chestnut mixture. Roll into a log and refrigerate until set.

To serve, cut the log with a sharp knife dipped in hot water.

CRABS

A TRIP AWAY SO OFTEN MAKES YOU REALISE JUST HOW wonderful things are at home. There are so many things I've become aware of following my trips overseas, such as the value for money we take for granted in Australia, and the quality of our produce. But we can't kid ourselves either – although superior-quality produce is available, you need to look for it. You have to search out the right seafood merchants, meat suppliers and greengrocers, or gain access to producers via farmers' markets, to be assured of quality. Importantly, you need to know the right questions to ask too, such as what variety it is, where the product was farmed and how, and whether it has been refrigerated.

When it comes to seafood, specialist shops in both the United States and the United Kingdom have over the past few years become exceptional, but I suspect our great advantage in Australia is that those of us who like to fish have access to a wide variety of bounty that would be hard to match anywhere.

For me, in South Australia, nothing stands out more than our blue swimmer crab. Years ago now I was part of a group that travelled to New York to cook a spectacular dinner at the Peninsula Hotel. Unable to bring in our own blue swimmers we had instead to use Dungeness crabs, the famous Californian variety, flown specially to New York. These crabs looked spectacular and were easy to shell, yet the flavour had none of the sweetness and intensity of our blue swimmers caught at Port Parham, on the Gulf of St Vincent near Adelaide, where recreational fishermen can spend an afternoon crabbing on the tidal beaches, then cook the catch in situ to enjoy one of the best meals of their lives. The flavour is wonderful – I prefer it to almost any seafood, as long as the crabs are fresher than fresh.

The crabs swim in as little as 30 cm of water in sandy or weed-covered areas and can be found at night by the light of a lantern, using nets or rakes to scoop them into a large tub of water – we use an old tin baby's bath. They can also be caught from a boat in deep water using drop nets.

Blue swimmer crabs will never taste as good away from the shore. Many years ago, when I first visited the 'beach' at Port Parham where my husband Colin's family has a shack, the flat, wide, desolate expanse of sand that is exposed when the tide is out came as a great shock to me. I had come from Sydney where, as a teenager, I'd travel from the western suburbs to the beach on weekends and was more used to rocky coves, headlands and the sea lapping on the shore. However, over the years I have learnt that, in perfect conditions, Parham can feel like the Greek Islands, and with a meal of crabs on the beach and a bottle of white wine, you can feel at peace with the world. 'Perfect conditions', by the way, means the tide being in at sunset, the water warm enough to wade in, the sun on your back and no one else around – it doesn't happen often but is such a delight when it does that it makes up for all the times you visit in the heat of summer and find there is nowhere to swim.

If you catch your own crabs, bring back some sea water to cook them in – have a bucket handy at the shore to remind you. We have a copper pot set up in the backyard of the shack and our first job is to get the fire started, to bring the sea water to a boil. While you are waiting for the water to boil, stun the crabs in the freezer for 20 minutes. The crabs are then thrown in the boiling water, about 25 at a time, and cooked for 3 minutes only. They are then scooped out and thrown onto an old wire mattress frame kept solely for the crabs to cool down on before eating. They are turned upside-down, with the white underside of the carapace showing, so that all the juices are retained. The crabs are allowed to cool just enough to be able to pick them up – for me, they are at their very best when warm. Any accompaniments you have prepared for them will be superfluous – the crabs are wonderful just as they are.

One of the food delights I experienced in New York was a visit to a fish market where, for the first time in my life, I saw soft-shell crabs for sale. I had read about these crabs for many years: they can be eaten in their entirety and are a great delicacy in America, particularly in Louisiana and in the crab restaurants of Chesapeake Bay. We arranged a detour to Chesapeake Bay just to eat in a crab house, but unfortunately we were a week shy of the fresh crab season and had to make do with frozen crab, which fell far short of our expectations.

Soft-shell crabs are, of course, available all over the world at the time when crabs shed their shells, which is different in every region. Colin likes to tell the story of having crabbed at Port Parham all his life, yet always throwing back these gelatinous specimens simply because he wasn't aware they could be eaten, let alone realising that they were a delicacy.

At Bribie Island in Queensland, exciting research is underway into large-scale commercial production of soft-shell crabs. There they have developed soft-shell varieties which 'moult' to order. As well as opening up huge export opportunities, these will be perfect for the restaurant table, if the sample I've had is anything to go by.

Crabs have to be treated very carefully to get the best out of them, so if you cannot catch and cook them live yourself, then buy them ready-cooked rather than 'green' at the market. Crabs begin to decompose the moment they die. If you are buying a whole cooked crab, make sure it has a fresh sweet smell and no hint of ammonia (a sign that the crab is either

old or has been badly handled), otherwise the crab will be unusable. Cooked crabs have a very short shelf-life and must be kept super-chilled. Freezing crab meat renders it stringy and dry, although it can be used for crab cakes. Cooked crab meat has to be handled with care so that it doesn't become tough.

Whether you pick the crab meat from the shells yourself or buy it ready done, you need only do very little to it for a really special treat if it's super-fresh. For example, cook and drain some dried pasta, then toss through room-temperature crab meat, extra virgin olive oil, loads of freshly chopped flat-leaf parsley or chervil, salt and freshly ground black pepper and serve immediately. Add a little freshly chopped red chilli with the olive oil too, if you like.

POTTED CRAB   *Serves 4*

I'm so incredibly spoilt to have ready access to Port Parham, one of the best crabbing beaches anywhere, that anything less than catching, cooking and eating the crabs within hours just doesn't quite match up. Having said that, after an experience many years ago when Colin and I cooked and picked fresh crabs by ourselves for an entrée for over 100 people, I resolved to investigate commercially picked fresh crab meat (there are times when even I have to be practical). This comes from crabs cooked immediately after catching and the meat is picked as soon as it has cooled, and I can tell you that I prefer this to buying green or cooked crabs from a fishmonger. Just remember that if you buy it vacuum packed, you must remove it from the bag half an hour before use to allow the plastic smell to dissipate.

Whilst potted crab might be thought of as a way of extending the shelf-life of crab, this version, with its thin layer of butter over the top, is meant to be eaten the day after making.

175 g unsalted butter	½ teaspoon sea salt flakes
¼ teaspoon ground mace	freshly ground black pepper
10–12 basil leaves (depending on size)	3 teaspoons verjuice
250 g freshly picked cooked crab meat	4 thick slices bread

In a shallow frying pan, heat 125 g of the butter with the mace and basil leaves until nut-brown. Remove from the heat and allow butter to cool for about 15 minutes, until the solids separate and the flavours are infused.

Shred crab meat using two forks, then mix in the salt and add pepper to taste. Add the verjuice and mix in well. Transfer crab meat to a large bowl, then pour in three-quarters of the clarified butter, being sure to leave the solids behind. Stir through and check seasoning, then pack the meat into 4 small ramekins or 1 large mould, smoothing the surface with the back of a spoon. Pour the remaining clarified butter over the top of each ramekin or the mould, forming a thin film.

Refrigerate until butter is set, then remove from the refrigerator 10 minutes before serving. Brush slices of bread with the remaining butter and bake in a preheated 220°C oven until crisp. Serve the potted crab with toast, some rocket leaves and a wedge of lemon.

PORT PARHAM CRAB SANDWICH

Makes 8 mini-loaves or 1 large loaf

Making mayonnaise by hand will always give a beautifully silky texture that cannot be matched by a machine. But the difference between homemade, even using a food processor, and shop-bought is so startling that you could start there and work your way up. Use the 'mustard' (innards) of the crab to enhance the mayonnaise.

80 g freshly picked blue swimmer crab meat per person (approximately 1 average-sized crab per person); reserve 1 whole crab claw per serve for garnish

MUSTARD BREAD
150 g burghul
125 ml tepid water
30 g fresh yeast *or* 15 g dried yeast
1 teaspoon sugar
380 ml warm water
2⅓ cups (350 g) wholemeal plain flour
1 cup (150 g) strong flour (see Glossary)
1 teaspoon sea salt
1 tablespoon extra virgin olive oil
⅓ cup (95 g) top-quality wholegrain mustard
1 tablespoon strong honey *or* maple syrup

MAYONNAISE
2 large egg yolks
¼ cup crab mustard (only if you can gather it from fresh crabs)
pinch salt
juice of 1 lemon
1½ cups (375 ml) mixture of extra virgin olive oil and a milder oil to suit your palette (I often use grapeseed oil or a good vegetable oil at half-and-half ratio so that it does not overpower the crab)
freshly ground black pepper

For the mustard bread, first preheat the oven to 200°C. Soak the burghul in the tepid water. If using fresh yeast, place it in a small bowl with the sugar and 80 ml of the water; when it froths, mix it with the flours and salt. If using dried yeast, mix the yeast and sugar with the flours and salt. Add the soaked burghul. In a small saucepan or frying pan, warm the olive oil, wholegrain mustard and honey or maple syrup. Gradually pour this mixture into the balance of the dry ingredients and mix with a wooden spoon. The consistency will resemble that of scone dough. Turn out and knead on a floured chopping board. Leave to rise for 2 hours and then separate the dough into 8 mini-loaves or shape into 1 large loaf. Leave to rise again for 30 minutes.

Bake the mustard bread in the oven for 25–35 minutes for mini-loaves, or 45 minutes for 1 large loaf. »

For the mayonnaise, place the egg yolks, crab mustard, pinch of salt and 1 tablespoon of the lemon juice in a bowl and whisk, or blend well in a food processor. Begin pouring the oil in as slowly as possible for the first 100 ml, then allow it to flow a little faster for the remainder, in a thin but steady stream. When all the oil is added and blended, adjust with as much lemon juice as you need and check for seasoning.

Make the sandwich by slicing each loaf of mustard bread diagonally in two, or cut thick slices if you have made a large loaf. Place the picked crab meat (being very careful that there are no pieces of shell) on one side and the crab mayonnaise on the other. Serve with a wedge of lemon, a crab claw and, for those who must have it, some chilli jam. I usually serve some peppery greens with this, such as mustard cress or rocket.

SALAD OF BLUE SWIMMER CRAB, FENNEL AND PINK GRAPEFRUIT

Serves 4

320 g freshly picked blue
    swimmer crab meat
sea salt flakes
1 large pink grapefruit, segments cut
    free of pith and juice retained
2 tablespoons extra virgin olive oil
½ large fennel bulb
1 bunch rocket
1 punnet baby mustard cress

VINAIGRETTE
2 tablespoons Champagne vinegar
1 golden shallot, very finely diced
½ teaspoon sea salt flakes
½ cup extra virgin olive oil
freshly ground black pepper

Spread the crab meat out on a plate and sprinkle with sea salt, a little of the pink grapefruit juice and some extra virgin olive oil, and set aside for 10 minutes to allow the flavours to mingle.

To make the vinaigrette, mix all the ingredients together in a small bowl.

Cut the fennel into very thin slices using a sharp knife or a mandolin. Toss together the sliced fennel, crab meat, rocket, cress and the vinaigrette (use only enough vinaigrette to just coat the salad leaves – you don't want to drench them). Divide the mixture evenly among 4 plates and arrange equal numbers of grapefruit segments on top of each to serve.

BLUE SWIMMER CRAB RISOTTO WITH VERJUICE

Serves 6

This is a family favourite, and a great way to serve a large number of guests. The risotto is full of flavour and works well as a warm buffet dish. If there is any left over, it can be rolled into balls and shallow-fried the next day.

500 g freshly picked blue
   swimmer crab meat
sea salt flakes and freshly ground
   black pepper
extra virgin olive oil (optional), for drizzling
squeeze of lemon juice (optional),
   for drizzling
1.25 litres jellied Fish Stock
   (see page 636) *or* crab stock

225 g unsalted butter
2 large onions, finely chopped
2½ cups (500 g) Arborio rice (see Glossary)
¾ cup (180 ml) verjuice
¼ cup coriander leaves
2 lemons, cut into wedges

If you have bought vacuum-packed crab meat, transfer it to a dish, season with salt and pepper and drizzle it with olive oil and lemon juice to get rid of any plastic taint.

Bring the stock to a simmer in a saucepan.

Heat 150 g of the butter in a heavy-based saucepan, then gently sweat the onions over low heat. Add the rice, stirring well until it is coated with butter. When the rice is glistening, turn up the heat to high, stir in the verjuice and let it evaporate. Season with salt.

Ladle in some hot stock and stir until it has been absorbed. Continue adding the stock a ladleful at a time, stirring frequently, until the rice is cooked but still firm – this will take about 20 minutes. A few minutes before the rice is cooked, check the seasoning and add salt if you wish, then add the remaining butter and gently fold in the crab meat, taking care not to break it up. Serve this lovely, rich risotto with a grind of black pepper and some coriander leaves, and wedges of lemon alongside.

EXTRA VIRGIN OLIVE OIL

THE ONLY OLIVE OIL I EVER USE IS EXTRA VIRGIN OLIVE OIL, and I suspect that hardly a day goes by when some part of a meal I have doesn't need it. I do at times use incredibly intense walnut, hazelnut or almond oils in small quantities, depending on the dish I'm serving (particularly as they all go so beautifully with verjuice), but it's extra virgin olive oil that is really my life's blood. All extra virgin olive oils are far from being equal, and while you often hear the comment that life is too short to drink bad wine or eat bad food, for me the rest of this adage is that life is too short to use bad oil.

There is a fascinating history to olive farming in Australia. The first groves were planted around 1805 in Parramatta, Sydney. While other states also had some early plantings in the early 1800s, South Australia took the lead in the 1830s, bringing in varieties from similar microclimates in the Mediterranean. To think that in 1851, a South Australian oil won an honourable mention at the London Exhibition, and in 1911 the Stonyfell Olive Oil Company of South Australia won gold medals for the oil they exported to Sicily! Yet the industry failed then, as our Anglo-Celtic settlers saw olive oil as medicinal rather than gastronomical. We have our Mediterranean immigrants to thank for the resurgence of extra virgin olive oil. For those interested in this history, Dr Michael Burr has a chronological account of the olive in Australia in his book, co-written with Karen Reichelt, *Extra Virgin: An Australian Companion to Olives and Olive Oil.*

We in the Australian olive industry have been on a steep learning curve over the past ten years, and although there is still much more to be learnt, I am truly proud of the top-quality extra virgin olive oils produced in Australia.

Dr Rod Mailer is a principal research scientist with the New South Wales Department of Primary Industries and is at the forefront of olive oil industry research. He has worked for many years to define the right harvest times and the best storage conditions to produce optimum-quality olive oil. He has worked closely with the industry to help growers understand oil quality and what they can do to produce the best oil. Currently he is working with Codex Australia and the Australian Olive Association to detect fraud in olive oil labelling, so we can be confident that if it says extra virgin olive oil on the label, then that is what it is. His laboratory does much of the testing for olive producers in Australia, as well as for the New Zealand Olive Association.

In Adelaide, we have Susan Sweeney, the Olive Horticultural Consultant within the

Waite Research Precinct, whose work with olives has led to an amazing wealth of practical knowledge. Her research into olive varieties, reported in the Autumn 2006 edition of *The Olive Press*, the Australian Olive Association's journal, is of great importance to anyone considering planting olives for oil.

Given its history and the remnants of the original groves which are still standing, I initially thought that South Australia would have a prime advantage as the leading state for oil production, yet it seems that our lack of water has led many of the bigger players across the border to overtake us.

On our own land, we have 1000 trees, mostly Tuscan varieties, the first of which we planted at the farm in 1995 and, soon after, the balance on our home block. Even though the trees are of much the same varieties, only 5 km apart, the fruit ripens differently – a huge logistical issue for me. The exterior colour of the olives gives only a rough indication of ripeness, and any individual tree will always have olives of varying degrees of ripeness on it.

The biggest challenge I face each year is deciding when to pick my olives. For my estate-bottled oil I always pick early in the season, when the olives are still half green and half ripe, yet not so early that their flavour hasn't developed, even though I know they will yield much less oil. No oil accumulation test in a laboratory will help me with this one. What I strive for in my oil is that perfect balance of fruitiness/bitterness and pungency. It's the oil I choose for that last flourish on a dish and for vinaigrettes and bruschetta, when I'm after a truly full flavour. Just a drizzle of great oil can turn the ordinary into the sublime.

I never fail to be excited by each year's harvest and after making the decision to pick I insist on following the whole process through, going down to Angle Vale for the milling of the olives each day. I wouldn't miss it, as seeing that green-gold liquid run into the tank is almost a sensual experience and the wonderful perfume of the crush permeates my very being. I go to the crusher prepared with a chunk of good wood-fired bread, some sea salt flakes, a pepper grinder and an enamel plate so I can dip the bread into that first cloudy oil with its strong peppery flavour; this is tasting extra virgin olive oil at its absolute best. To me it is nothing short of intoxicating.

OLIVE OILS

As a flavour-driven person who loves to cook, the only olive oil I use is extra virgin, as I've said before. But first let me attempt to explain the difference between the varying grades of olive oil.

EXTRA VIRGIN OLIVE OIL

Extra virgin olive oil is the oil or juice of fresh olives extracted purely by mechanical means. The crushed olives become a paste and the oil is extracted from this paste without the use of chemicals, and with only enough heat to naturally separate the oil, which is lighter than the water and solids of the paste.

Don't be misled by the term cold-pressed oil. This term has virtually no relevance in today's technological age, and the Australian Olive Association recommends that growers not use the term as it is no longer one that reflects modern-day practices. Therefore, if used, it is used incorrectly, and only because it is seen by marketers as being a statement of quality. In my opinion, it is not just a superfluous term that confuses the public but is also misleading in terms of the process alluded to.

To be considered as extra virgin olive oil, on testing the oil must be found to contain less than 0.8 per cent free fatty acids, measured as oleic acid. However, within this definition, there is a huge range of flavour profiles of extra virgin olive oils, from the fruity, aromatic, pungent and yet beautifully balanced, to the other end of the spectrum of mellow and even bland, and everything in between. Knowing that an olive oil is extra virgin should therefore only be the starting point to choosing a good-quality oil.

The level of free fatty acids in olive oil is a result of the degree of ripeness of the olives – oil from early season olives contains the least free fatty acids – and the care taken in handling the fruit between harvest and oil extraction. The quality of an extra virgin olive oil is the result of this, combined with the length of time between picking and crushing, the cleanliness of the olive crusher and the temperature at which the crushing process is carried out. The olive varieties used, as well as the terroir (that wonderful term that signifies the characteristics of the growing environment: the position, soil quality and prevailing weather conditions) also have an impact on flavour and quality. Many producers proudly display just how low a level of free fatty acids their oils contain, often so low as to hardly register – yet these oils, although they will have a longer shelf-life, can lack flavour if picked too early.

With our extra virgin olive oil, we are continually aiming to get the balance right between picking early for longevity, but with sufficient maturity to give flavour. Each year I learn enough to know how much more I need to know. The difference there is in the quality of the oil and its flavour when, having decided that our olives are perfect to pick, I can't get the picking organised until a week later, astounds me.

Although half-ripe fruit yields less oil, which is less economic for the grower, the resulting oil has greater quality, integrity and longevity. Riper fruit yields far more oil, but results in a rapid decline in quality a few months after harvest, whereas oil made from earlier picked fruit, assuming that it meets all the other necessary conditions for quality, is still fresh and sound a year after harvest.

All of this means that, although an oil could be termed 'extra virgin' because of its low level of free fatty acids, if it has flavour defects from processing such as being 'fusty', 'musty' or 'winey' (to name a few), this would deny the oil the extra virgin classification. Even if an oil makes the extra virgin classification because it contains under 0.8 per cent free fatty acids, but is a much riper oil, then it will not have the shelf-life of an earlier picked oil, so it will not necessarily retain its extra virgin status over time, particularly if stored badly. Rancidity, the most common fault in extra virgin olive oil, is usually a fault of bad storage and/or the age of the oil, and is so easy to detect once you've identified it – just think of the smell of sweaty socks, or butter left uncovered in the back of the refrigerator that has absorbed every 'off' odour around it.

Many people, when first beginning to learn about good olive oils, realise that they have only ever tasted what they are now able to identify as rancid oils. I always explain that I first smell any extra virgin olive oil I buy or that I'm offered to taste, just as you might an oyster to make sure it's not off before you slip it into your mouth. I cannot imagine, once you have smelled and tasted a good extra virgin olive oil, that you would ever use a rancid olive oil again.

VIRGIN OLIVE OIL

This is simply olive oil that didn't quite make the grade of extra virgin. Its free fatty acid measurement sits between 0.8 and 3 per cent, and it should be used soon after it is crushed. It will have less flavour and a much shorter shelf-life than extra virgin olive oil. In Europe, a little virgin olive oil is combined with 'pure' or refined olive oil to add some flavour.

OLIVE OIL

Still often referred to as 'pure' olive oil, it is almost at the bottom of the range in terms of quality, so this is really a misnomer. This olive oil is the result of industrial processing, deemed necessary because the oil has not met the above criteria for virgin or extra virgin olive oil. In this process, the olive oil is refined, using a chemical treatment in which peroxides and free fatty acids are removed to make it suitable for consumption. The oil may also be bleached and deodorised to remove any 'off' flavours but, at the same time, this removes many of the natural flavours and antioxidants that are characteristic of extra virgin olive oil. 'Pure' olive oil may be suitable for cooking where a less dominant flavour is required, as it still contains some of the fatty acids that make olive oil nutritionally attractive.

POMACE OIL

Pomace is the residue or olive waste left after the extra virgin olive oil has been mechanically removed from the olive paste. This solid waste product may contain 3–8 per cent oil, which is called pomace oil. The oil is recovered by washing the waste with an organic solvent such as hexane. The recovered oil is then heated to remove the solvent and the oil is subjected to the same refining processes described for olive oil. As with olive oil, bleaching and deodorising removes not just the unwanted odours but also the fruity characteristics of the olive. It strips any flavour, good or bad, out of the oil, and the resultant oil is fatty in the mouth and tastes of the industrial processes it has been subjected to, even though a small amount of virgin olive oil is generally added for flavour. I have no use for this oil, even for a marinade.

LIGHT OLIVE OIL

Light olive oil is a marketing term aimed at the weight-conscious. The only thing light about this oil is that it is light in character – or, to my mind, totally lacking in flavour, colour and aroma. It has exactly the same number of calories or kilojoules as extra virgin and other olive oils but, as it is refined, it lacks the health-giving antioxidants and polyphenols of extra virgin olive oil, as well as the flavour.

CHOOSING AND USING EXTRA VIRGIN OLIVE OIL

Extra virgin olive oil is never more vibrant than when first crushed. Unlike wine, it diminishes with age – although, as mentioned above, the earlier harvest extra virgin olive oils have a longer shelf-life. As a rule of thumb, only buy an extra virgin olive oil if it displays its year of harvest and you are buying within that year. This doesn't automatically mean the oil is no good if it's over a year from its harvest date, but it does mean that unless it has been picked early enough and has enough of that assertive character at the beginning, it will begin to lose its freshness and vitality after a year, and will become 'flat' and more prone to rancidity as it gets even older.

I keep two grades of extra virgin olive oil. The first is my own estate-bottled oil which comes from my own trees or those of other producers I respect – and there are many of those in Australia, I am delighted to say. This is the oil that makes all the difference to a dish when added as a last flourish; my own preference is for a robust, fruity oil for the majority of my food where the olive oil flavour dominates. I also use a less expensive Australian extra virgin olive oil from the supermarket that declares its year of harvest and, even though it is cheaper, it is still fresh and fruity. This is the oil I use when serving more delicate dishes (such as poached fish) or for cooking with, as high temperatures dissipate the flavour of extra virgin olive oil to some extent.

In summary, buy the finest extra virgin olive oil you can afford, and use it generously rather than keeping it for 'best'. I love to have a good extra virgin olive oil on the table at every meal, and either use it in a vinaigrette or simply drizzle it over piping hot vegetables to serve with grilled bruschetta. I also love to use it for dressing sliced raw tuna, moistening goat's cheese and lavishing over sliced tomatoes. With really good extra virgin olive oil you can turn a simple pasta, such as Spaghettini with Parmigiano Reggiano, Garlic, Capers and Flat-leaf Parsley (see page 402), into a spectacular dish. It is amazing how a splash of extra virgin olive oil over a hot bowl of soup or fresh cannellini beans adds a truly powerful dimension that lifts the flavour to another level.

I use my more mellow everyday extra virgin olive oil for sweating onions, coating foods for a marinade or grilling fish, chicken or meat. If I deep-fry (or probably more often, shallow-fry), once again I use this more mellow extra virgin olive oil. Even though it may sound extravagant, it imparts so much more crispness and flavour, as food fried in extra virgin olive oil gains a wonderfully crunchy coating that acts as a seal and prevents excess oil from penetrating further.

STORING EXTRA VIRGIN OLIVE OIL

It is very important to store oil properly to maintain its quality. It should be kept away from light – ideally in dark glass bottles, tins or bag-in-the-box 'bladders' to protect it from light, heat and oxygen. Whatever you do, don't sit the bottle by the heat of the stove or on your windowsill, no matter how jewel-like it may look in the sunshine!

Most importantly, once you open a bottle of extra virgin olive oil, never leave it without a stopper, as exposure to oxygen leads to rancidity. Better still, rather than save it for special occasions, use it frequently – even the smallest amount added to a dish can make such a difference to its flavour.

While I refrigerate my nut oils to control their rancidity, I never refrigerate my extra virgin olive oils as it changes their structure. Although this reverts to a certain extent if the oil is returned to room temperature, I find there is a loss of flavour and 'texture' – a funny word perhaps when talking of oil, but a relevant one nonetheless.

MAYONNAISE

Once you've made your first mayonnaise, you'll never want to buy it again. Homemade mayonnaise adds so much to a meal, with very little effort involved – its rich and velvety texture can make a really simple dish sing. Some people are anxious about making their own because they think it's difficult or they fear it will split, but the technique is really very simple (and even a split mayonnaise can be resurrected by starting again in a clean, dry bowl, with fresh egg yolks, before incorporating the split mixture drop by drop).

A basic mayonnaise consists of olive oil, egg yolks, some seasoning and an acidulant such as lemon juice, verjuice or vinegar. I use a mixture of half extra virgin olive oil and half a lighter vegetable or grapeseed oil (this is the one exception I make to my rule about only using extra virgin, as the flavour can be too sharp). The quality of the eggs will have a bearing on the final dish, so free-range eggs at room temperature are best. Mustard is often included but is optional, while salt, I think, is essential. Mayonnaise is at its silkiest when made by hand, but it can also be made successfully in a blender or food processor. Or, you could start using a machine and finish by hand to achieve that 'almost as good as handmade' effect.

Mayonnaise goes with almost every type of meat and fish (particularly when barbecued), not to mention vegetables and salads. Once you master a basic mayonnaise you can use your imagination to change the texture, flavour and colour. Depending on the dish with which the mayonnaise is to be served, you can experiment with verjuice or wine vinegar as the acidulant. Try adding herbs – lemon thyme mayonnaise is great with snapper, and give Sorrel Mayonnaise (see page 142) a go. Garlic mayonnaise (or Aïoli, see page 587) can be made by adding raw garlic, or puréed roasted garlic for a mellower, nuttier flavour. Rouille (see page 586), essentially an aïoli with puréed roasted capsicum, is wonderful added to a fish soup and is simple to make once you are confident with the technique. I serve roasted garlic and quince mayonnaise with kid pot-roasted with lemon, fresh herbs and garlic, so, as you can see, the combinations are endless.

2 large free-range egg yolks	½ cup (125 ml) extra virgin olive oil
(at room temperature)	½ cup (125 ml) vegetable *or* grapeseed oil
pinch sea salt flakes	freshly ground black pepper
1 tablespoon lemon juice	1 tablespoon boiling water (if necessary)
1 teaspoon Dijon mustard (optional)	

Rinse a bowl with hot water and dry thoroughly. Whisk the egg yolks in the bowl with a pinch of salt until thick, then add two-thirds of the lemon juice and the mustard, if using, and whisk until smooth. Continue to whisk whilst adding the oil slowly, drop by drop to begin with. Once the mixture begins to thicken you can add the remaining oil in a slow, steady stream, whisking continuously. When all the oil has been added, taste and add as much of the remaining lemon juice as needed. Season with pepper, and add more salt and lemon juice if needed. Only add the boiling water if the mayonnaise needs thinning and requires no more acidulant.

PEARS, PARMIGIANO REGGIANO AND GREEN EXTRA VIRGIN OLIVE OIL

Serves 6

When each ingredient is perfect, this makes an exceptional end to a meal.

3 pears, halved and cored

1 tablespoon lemon juice

300 g wedge Parmigiano Reggiano,
    cut into shards

1 bunch rocket, washed and dried

½–¾ cup (125–180 ml) extra virgin olive oil
    (ideally from an early season crush)

Slice the pear halves, then toss with lemon juice to prevent discolouration. Divide the sliced pear and shards of Parmigiano Reggiano among 6 plates, then add the rocket and drizzle a tablespoon or more of the fruity olive oil over each.

SALMON POACHED IN OLIVE OIL

Serves 4

This is a very special, even sensuous, dish. It works best when the salmon fillets are the same size and weight (ideally from the middle of the fish). The cooked salmon is quite pink inside and warm rather than hot, so make sure your guests don't belong to the 'if it's not piping hot or cooked well-done, it's just not right' school of thought.

about 1 cup (250 ml) mellow extra virgin
    olive oil (depending on size of saucepan or
    frying pan)

4 × 120 g trimmed salmon fillets,
    skin removed

sea salt flakes

juice and grated rind of 1 lemon

80 ml fresh extra virgin olive oil

fresh chervil, to serve

Choose a heavy-based saucepan or deep frying pan large enough to accommodate the fish in one layer; the smaller the pan, the less olive oil you will need to use. Pour the olive oil into the pan, then stand it over the lowest heat possible on your stove-top, bringing it to blood temperature only (briefly dip the blade of a knife in – it should feel warm to the touch, not hot). Salt the fish and rub in the lemon rind.

Slip the fillets into the oil – the fillets should lie just below the surface like submarines – and cook at this gentle temperature for 10–20 minutes (this will depend on how low you can keep the temperature on your stove – use a simmer mat if you have one). The fish should be more set than cooked. If white dots appear on the surface of the fish (these are beads of protein), the oil is too hot, so you'll need to reduce the temperature. Next time, you'll know to cook it less – I promise it's so delicious you'll want to.

Carefully take the fish out of the warm oil and drain. Reserve the oil to use again when cooking fish. Dress the salmon with the lemon juice, fresh extra virgin olive oil and sprigs of chervil and serve.

PIQUANT BREAD SALAD

Serves 4

This salad makes an ideal accompaniment for Salmon Poached in Olive Oil (see previous page). Or, served for lunch, it is so satisfying that it makes a complete meal in its own right.

2 slices wood-fired bread, crusts removed,
  cut into large pieces
⅓ cup (80 ml) extra virgin olive oil,
  plus 1 teaspoon for drizzling
½ small red onion, finely chopped
1 cup flat-leaf parsley leaves

1½ pieces preserved lemon, flesh removed
  and rind rinsed and cut into long,
  thin strips
1 tablespoon capers, rinsed and drained
6 green olives, pitted and quartered
freshly ground black pepper

Preheat the oven to 180°C. In a food processor, pulse the bread quickly into very coarse breadcrumbs, then place on a baking tray, drizzle with 1 teaspoon olive oil and toast in the oven for 10 minutes or until golden.

Toss all the ingredients together with enough olive oil to coat, then season with pepper (no salt is required).

SPAGHETTINI WITH PARMIGIANO REGGIANO, GARLIC, CAPERS AND FLAT-LEAF PARSLEY

Serves 4

sea salt flakes
500 g spaghettini
1 clove garlic
1 tablespoon capers, rinsed and drained
3½ tablespoons extra virgin olive oil,
  plus extra for drizzling

200 g grated Parmigiano Reggiano
freshly ground black pepper
½ cup freshly chopped flat-leaf parsley
juice of ½ lemon

Bring a large saucepan of water to the boil. Add a generous amount of salt and cook the spaghettini according to the directions on the packet.

Meanwhile, using the flat side of a large knife, crush the garlic with a little salt to make a paste. Fry capers in a small frying pan in 1½ tablespoons olive oil over medium heat, then remove from pan and dry on kitchen paper. Use the same oil to fry the garlic, being careful not to let it burn. Drain the spaghettini in a colander; do not refresh. Be ready with hot plates and all ingredients.

Add 2 tablespoons of oil to the drained spaghettini pan, then add the hot spaghettini, garlic and the cheese. Mix to combine, then add the capers. Season to taste, then add the parsley, lemon juice and a little more extra virgin olive oil to moisten. Pile onto 4 hot plates and serve immediately.

FLOUR

FLOUR IS SUCH AN ESSENTIAL PART OF SO MANY OF THE FOODS we eat every day, yet we tend to take it for granted. However, using the finest-quality flour (determined by the quality of the original grain, the method used to process it, and the amount of processing it undergoes), makes such a vast difference in the final outcome of a dish, both in taste and texture.

BREAD

What is it that makes really good bread? It's a question that deserves a lot of thought, since bread is the staff of life. While devotees beat a path to the handful of great bakeries scattered over this country, to buy bread with character made in wood-fired ovens, unfortunately the greater percentage seem happy to accept the mass-produced, often fairy-floss-like bread that's so readily available.

Wood-fired ovens aren't trendy – they've been in Australia since European settlement. Those that have survived modernisation are usually tended by passionate bakers, who use traditional methods to produce wonderful sourdoughs or crusty peasant loaves and the like. The Apex Bakery, on my doorstep at Tanunda, makes really good white loaves – bread that tastes of the wheat from which it is made.

In earlier times, just about every town had its own flour mill and each area produced a unique flour. This was certainly the case in South Australia – Loxton had a great reputation for the flour from which its bread was made, while the bakers in Mount Gambier would only use the local flour, which was particularly good for biscuits and soft cakes, as it was too expensive to buy in any other sort. But the spread of transport systems and the swallowing up of many of the mills by multinationals has meant the end of this regionalism to a large degree.

Those of us who live in the Barossa have been lucky to have Laucke Flour Mills as part of the Valley's history. I was introduced to Laucke's when I first moved to the Barossa. The business began in 1899, when flour was milled in Greenock – although the actual flour milling is now done at Laucke's in Strathalbyn, the quality remains the same. Mark Laucke, the grandson of the founder, tells of his early working days when the miller had no control over the wheat being delivered, thus requiring the baker to blend flours to ensure the best results. Mark remembers bakers combining three different bags of flour in the one bowl, each bag from a different mill! There must have been a lot of expertise in the baking industry then – today the tables have turned and the miller chooses the wheat to blend into grist before making the flour.

Small, passionate millers are treasured by those of us driven by flavour, including bakers and chefs targeting niche markets. Many bakers have to contend with the price pressures of supermarkets and are often forced to downgrade their products to service the demand for cheap bread. However, there are also a handful of specialist bakers (probably only one or two in each capital city), who stand out from the pack and are making extraordinary bread, in stark contrast to the mass-produced product. Supermarkets will continue to be a fact of life as more and more people depend on them for one-stop food shopping, but even with our much busier lives we would do well to demand and be prepared to pay for better bread, and champion the great bakeries, which will in turn use the small millers so that they too survive. Good bread, like all good food, should be available to everyone.

I've long realised how lucky I am to have access to top-quality, locally made bread, and need no convincing about the merits of bread made in wood-fired ovens. But to understand the rest of the equation – how good bread is actually made – I spent some time observing the process at the Apex Bakery. To give you just a glimpse of the wealth of tradition that abounds here, the patriarch, Keith Fechner (better known as 'Chiney'), started in the bakery as a lad in 1924, the first year of business. In 1948 he bought the bakery, and in 1982 he sold it to his three sons, Brian, David and Johnny. Until just a few years ago, Keith still started the ferment every night with Johnny, while the rest of the team began work at 3 a.m.

Keith has managed to keep a firm hold on the traditions of the bakery, although in truth this is probably more to do with the Barossa ethos that if you can't afford to pay cash then you can't afford a new piece of equipment. In the 1960s he successfully resisted his sons' idea to change over to gas-fired ovens as gas was cheaper than wood. Having had their attempts to modernise foiled, Keith's sons are now every bit as proud of the bakery's traditions – in fact, they still collect Mallee wood from Sedan, a 45-minute drive away, for the firing of the ovens.

I had arranged to visit one evening to observe the fermenting process, and luckily the night I was there was an uncharacteristically cool summer's night, so the crew didn't have to wait too long for the temperature to drop before mixing began. We were able to start as early as 10.30 p.m. – the previous night it had been much hotter and preparations couldn't begin until just before midnight (if the room is too hot, the dough will be too active and will over-prove).

The Fechners like a long, slow prove, so they measure the temperature of the flour and the water to ensure a mixed dough temperature of 76°F (24°C, although nothing is measured in Celsius). I expected rainwater to be used but was very wrong: the harder the water the better the bread, so Barossa tap water is perfect (it's the only good thing about it I can think of!). These days it is Johnny who draws four buckets of water and mixes the yeast and salt, and then the dough. It is not always possible to get the mix right the first time without adjustments – sometimes almost another half a bag of flour is added to the giant mixing bowl. This bowl rotates quite slowly and two huge claws come in from either side, simulating hands grabbing at the flour at the bottom, working the mixture into a moist

dough. It is a little like a volcano erupting – flour puffs up from the sides as it is pulled into the mixture. The machine works even more slowly than if you were mixing and kneading by hand, and the smell of the fresh yeast lingers. I found watching the bowl almost as mesmerising and soothing as kneading dough myself.

No timers are used, instead it is done by feel, and looking for the point when the dough starts to come away from the sides of the bowl. They showed me how to stretch a walnut-sized piece of dough and hold it up to the light – when it was quite transparent yet wouldn't break, it was deemed sufficiently kneaded. A proving ring was then placed on the rim of the bowl to give the dough plenty of room to grow, and a calico cover placed on top to keep out any draughts. The dough was left to rise to the very top, which usually takes four hours. (It was 11.30 p.m. at this stage, so I snuck away to catch some sleep, but Keith and Johnny still had a lot of work to do.)

As soon as the morning shift arrives at 3 a.m., the dough is knocked back and the table is floured. One of the boys pulls the dough out with his hands and then carries it to the table, where someone else cuts it with a dough knife (a blunt knife made especially for this purpose). The pieces of dough are then divided again into weights appropriate to the final loaves, then the ends are tucked under and the dough is rested for 5 minutes. These shapes are then put through a very old machine called a 'ribbon moulder'. A series of rollers, a little like those on an old washing-machine wringer, knocks the air out of the dough, which is then rolled into the rough shape of the final loaf on a small conveyor belt before being shaped by hand.

When I returned at 5.30 a.m. the giant mixing bowls were empty and the trolleys were full of moulds filled with dough – the same moulds that have been used since 1924. The fire in the Scotch oven, which seemed to have stalactites on its huge domed roof, takes a couple of hours to heat. It is an art to have the loaves proved and ready to go straight into the oven when it reaches the right temperature (450°F, according to the Fechners, or 232°C). As the loaves mustn't over-prove, or else they'll collapse and fail, timing is critical. When the fire is first lit, flames leap out from the right-hand side of the oven. This ceases when the wood in the firebox has been reduced to coals – and the oven is ready. The time this takes differs each day, depending on the density of the wood. While a gauge indicates the temperature now, it was broken for twenty years, so instead a handful of flour was thrown into the oven to test the temperature: if it ignited the oven was deemed too hot, and was allowed to cool with its door ajar.

When the decision is made that the oven is ready, the fire door is closed, the bottom of the oven and the flue are blocked off and the chimney is opened up. Again, no timers, no rigid instructions – just feel, rhythm and speed. The dough-filled moulds are put into the oven on long-handled paddles; the oven takes 500 loaves at a time.

I thought for a moment that empty moulds were being put into the oven, then I realised that to get square loaves the moulds were turned upside-down to keep the dough compressed. The oven was filled from the cooler back left-hand corner, where the bigger, high-top loaves that take longer to cook were baked. The day I was there the fire was hot and after 10 minutes the loaves were already golden brown – too soon! – so newspaper hats were placed over the bread to stop it scorching.

Sleepy as I was, the whole process was truly magical: the smell of the bread, the ferocity of the heat, the golden glow of the loaves, the skill of the Fechner boys, and the humour that abounded. I headed home for a bit more sleep with two warm loaves under my arm. But the temptation of the loaves was too great – and soon I was transported back to my childhood when I used to hollow out the warm bread that was delivered by horse and cart. I was embarrassed by how much I had eaten, so on my way home I trimmed the loaf with a bread knife to hide the evidence of my secret feast!

Good bread is truly the sum of all its parts. In the case of the Apex Bakery and others like it, it is all about craft and care: the hard flour full of the flavour of wheat, the dry heat of the wood-fired oven, the fresh yeast, the additive-free recipes that have remain unchanged since 1924, the gentle mixing of the dough, and the slow natural ferment.

Bruschetta is one of my favourite ways to eat bread, but it is only as good as the flour used to make the bread. We eat outside a lot, particularly on the weekend, frequently with our daughters, their partners and grandchildren and, more often than not, we have bruschetta. My husband Colin is the bruschetta-maker in our house and brooks no interference. But he isn't interested in making it unless the family is gathered around, or I'm busy on the other side of the kitchen window getting the rest of the dinner ready. In other words, he must have an audience. He has also become very pedantic, as one needs to be, about the quality of each ingredient used.

We all know bruschetta, but what makes a truly great one? Well, the bread has to be proper bread, with a good crust; if it's a wood-fired, chewy Italian-style loaf, all the better. It also has to be stale. Next is the extra virgin olive oil. Nothing is better than the first oil

of the season – greenish-tinged and peppery, but balanced, of course. A clove of garlic is vital, as is good sea salt and freshly ground black pepper.

The best bruschetta of all is grilled over a wood fire (although a gas barbecue does a pretty good job, too), hence our courtyard picnics. The bread is sliced quite thickly and grilled on each side until charred markings appear. As soon as each piece is done, it is rubbed on one side with a cut clove of garlic before being dipped into the oil (quickly or slowly, depending on your penchant for oil) seasoned with sea salt and freshly ground black pepper. It must be eaten immediately, and the oil running down your chin is part of the pleasure.

If that's all too basic for you, top your bruschetta with your favourite ingredients. Spread the toasted bread with tapenade, add sliced ripe tomatoes and round it off with anchovies, perhaps. Cut a chunk of Parmigiano Reggiano, or spread the bread liberally with goat's curd. Toss some mushrooms in a pan on the other side of the barbecue and top the bruschetta with them. Add a hint of truffle oil (if you can find the real thing), if you want to impress. Roast red capsicums on the fire as well and add the peeled, juicy flesh to the bruschetta. Or perhaps try slow-cooked beans when you need something more filling.

SOME SIMPLE TIPS TO ALLEVIATE THE MOST COMMON BREAD-MAKING PROBLEMS

+ To make bread by hand, give yourself plenty of space on a cleared workbench and, as for all recipes, have your quantities measured out and standing by. You will need a huge bowl the size of a wash basin, preferably an old ceramic one, although an inexpensive oversized stainless steel bowl from a commercial kitchenware shop will do, but remember a little warmth helps.

+ There is a huge variation in quality of flour, determined by the original grain, the amount of processing and the method of processing. High-quality bread mixes are readily available from Laucke's Flour Mills (www.laucke.com.au). They have a huge number of variations and you only need to add water and yeast. I also love the wonderful varieties of flour grown and milled by Gavin Dunn's company, Four Leaf Milling of Tarlee (www.fourleafmilling.com.au). It is biodynamic and stone-ground.

+ Next to the quality of the flour, the temperature of the water is most important, although in truth the more experienced you get, the more casual you can become about this. If the water is too hot, it will kill the yeast, and if too cold, it will not activate the yeast. When a recipe calls for tepid water, this means that your hand should feel comfortable in the water – not cold and not hot (about 34°C on a thermometer). To test this, leave your finger in the water for 10 seconds: if it becomes uncomfortably hot, you will need to add a little cold water. Your utensils and ingredients should be blood warm, even the flour.

✦ Remember, the amount of water needed will alter every time you make bread, depending on the flour and the temperature or humidity. Always begin with less water than a recipe states and add more as required.

✦ I prefer compressed fresh yeast in its block form to dried yeast. It gives a much better flavour to the bread, though dry yeast is easier to handle. Dry yeast is also more concentrated, so you need twice the quantity of compressed yeast.

✦ Not to make bread by hand is to deny yourself an addictive pleasure, but if you use a machine, be sure not to over-mix. When the mixing is finished, the dough should be at about 28°C.

✦ Bring the bread to the first rise on a bench away from any draughts. Cover it with a clean tea towel, with a piece of plastic film sprayed with oil separating the dough from the tea towel so it doesn't stick. In winter you could try putting it in tins in the oven with just the pilot light on, if it is gas, or at about 50°C in an electric oven.

✦ Fat gives a softer loaf and helps the bread last longer. Butter is possibly better than oil as the addition of liquid gives the dough a different structure. The butter should be soft and pliable, not melted.

✦ If you like crusty bread, cut down on the fat content (although this will reduce its keeping qualities) and bake at a lower temperature for longer, say 190°C for 40 minutes instead of the usual 220°C for 30 minutes. You could also try putting a bowl of water in the oven to make steam, but the first method seems to work better.

✦ A small amount of sugar gives a softer texture and adds colour to the crumb. It feeds the yeast, but bread can still be made without it.

✦ For me, salt is very important because it flavours the bread and controls the yeast activity. Too much salt will actually retard the yeast. Saltless bread is possible, but the dough has to be handled quickly or it will go mad.

✦ Freezing bread will dry it out a little, but if you do want to freeze bread, take the hot loaves from the oven and put them straight into bags and into the freezer. The condensation seems to make the bread fresher on thawing out. Splash the thawed loaf with a little water and put it in the oven to re-crisp. Make sure you add some fat to the dough of any bread you intend to freeze.

✦ I have never used natural bread improvers. They are made of vitamin C and modify the gluten so it is more extendable and gives a better crumb and height. The gas given off by the yeast is carbon dioxide – this blows up the gluten and forms bubbles in the dough. Using a bread improver allows a better 'bounce back' after retarding the bread in the refrigerator overnight. This is useful when you want to bake fresh bread in the morning but don't want to wake as early as the bakers.

SOPHIE'S FARMHOUSE LOAF

Makes 2 loaves

When I first worked with her, Sophie Zalokar was Sophie Harris, a young, wide-eyed Barossa girl with an enquiring mind and an ability to turn her hand to almost anything creative and practical. Sophie was a 'bread witch', as we say in the Valley – yeast and flour became magical in her hands. This innate skill, combined with her artistic abilities in painting and weaving, her proficiency in shooting and skinning rodents, and her talent for playing the piano (she would play in the restaurant after service had finished at night), makes her pretty much an all-rounder.

Sophie, like Natalie Paull, Alex Herbert and Steve Flamsteed, were the closest to us of all our Pheasant Farm Restaurant family, and are still part of our lives. After her four-year apprenticeship with me, Sophie travelled, then married, had a family and went to university; she now writes about food too. In 2002 I had the honour of launching her first book, *Picnic* – it is a beautiful book, but I would have expected nothing less.

Poolish is a French bread-making term to describe the 'pre-dough'. Other terms such as levain, biga, chef, sponge, mother and starter all mean the same thing.

POOLISH

½ cup (125 ml) warm water

½ teaspoon dried yeast

115 g strong flour (see Glossary)

FINAL DOUGH

1 kg strong flour (see Glossary),
    plus extra for kneading

2 teaspoons sea salt flakes

½ teaspoon dried yeast

600 ml warm water

1 teaspoon olive oil, plus extra for oiling

For the poolish, place the warm water and yeast in a small bowl and leave to sit for 1 minute, before stirring to dissolve. Stir the flour into this yeasted water until smooth and elastic. Cover with plastic film and leave in a draught-free place for 1 hour, or until mixture has doubled in size.

For the final dough, place the flour and salt in the bowl of an electric mixer. Stir the yeast and the poolish mixture into the warm water. Using a dough hook, slowly add this mixture to the bowl and knead until a soft, elastic dough forms. Generously flour the workbench, tip out the dough and knead it by hand for 5 minutes, using only enough flour to stop the dough from sticking to the bench. Brush the inside of a large bowl with the olive oil and roll the dough in the bowl to coat with oil. Cover the bowl with plastic film and leave in a warm place for about 1–2 hours, or until the dough has doubled in size. (If you want to slow down the rising process, say if the weather is warm, smear the dough with a little olive oil and then press plastic film closely over it before covering the bowl with a tea towel.)

Knead the dough again, then divide it in two (each piece should weigh about 900 g). Dust 2 proofing baskets or ceramic bowls with flour or oil two 1 kg bread tins, then place the dough pieces in them and shape to fit. Place each basket or tin in a plastic bag, seal and leave in a warm place to rise for 1–2 hours, or until the dough has doubled in size. »

Preheat the oven to 230°C. If using proofing baskets or ceramic bowls, gently invert the dough onto a greased and floured baking tray. Quickly slash the tops with a very sharp knife and gently place on the top rack in the oven, as close to the top of the oven as possible but still allowing room for the dough to rise. If using tins, slash the tops, then sprinkle with a little flour and place in the oven as instructed above.

Bake for 20 minutes, then turn the baking tray or tins around, reduce the temperature to 200°C and bake for another 25–30 minutes. Remove the loaves from the tray or tins and return them to the oven directly on the oven rack. Bake for another 5 minutes to crisp the bottom of the loaves. Remove from the oven and place on a wire rack to cool.

GRAPE AND WALNUT BREAD   *Makes 2 loaves*

125 g shelled walnuts	½ teaspoon salt
15 g fresh *or* 7 g dried yeast	2 tablespoons extra virgin olive oil,
1 teaspoon sugar (optional)	plus extra for oiling
1½ cups (375 ml) warm water	2 cups fresh red grapes *or* 1 cup
500 g unbleached strong flour (see Glossary)	dried muscatels

Preheat the oven to 200°C. Dry-roast the walnuts on a baking tray for 6–8 minutes, then rub off their skins with a clean tea towel. Using a sieve or colander, separate the skins from the nuts.

If you are using fresh yeast, mix it to a sludge with the sugar and 1 tablespoon of the warm water in a small container (a cup will do) and set it aside until it begins to froth (this will take about 10 minutes, depending on the weather).

Put the flour into a large bowl and make a well in the centre, then add the salt and olive oil. If you are using dried yeast, add it now (omit the sugar), otherwise tip the frothing yeast mixture into the bowl. Pour in half the warm water and start bringing the dough together with your hands. Add the walnuts and then whatever water you need to form a dough (you may find you need more than you've allowed). Scrape the mixture from the bowl and turn it out onto a floured workbench, then knead it gently for 10 minutes or until the dough is smooth and shiny.

Put the dough in a lightly oiled bowl, then cover the bowl with a loose piece of plastic film. (If you want to slow down the rising process, smear the dough with a little olive oil and press plastic film closely over it before covering the bowl with a tea towel.) Put the bowl in a draught-free spot and allow the dough to double in size; this will vary depending on the conditions of the day – allow about 1 hour, but be prepared to wait longer or retrieve it a little earlier. Remember, the slower the rise the better. Do not over-prove.

Knock back the dough, then tip it onto a floured bench and pat it into a large round. Push the grapes or muscatels into the dough, then fold the dough over them so as few grapes as possible poke through. Divide the dough in half and shape as required. Put the

Grape and walnut bread (left), and flatbread (right, see page 414)

loaves onto a lightly greased baking tray, then cover them with tea towels and allow to double in size again.

Meanwhile, preheat the oven to 220°C. Dust the tops of the loaves liberally with extra flour and bake for 10 minutes, then reduce the oven temperature to 180°C and bake for another 20 minutes.

FLATBREAD
Makes 6 rounds

This flatbread can take on all sorts of flavours or it can be served plain. It can be thick or thin, depending on your whim. Try adding slivers of garlic or rosemary leaves to the 'dimples' in the dough before the final rising. It can also be covered with slow-cooked onions and torn basil leaves before baking, and then drizzled with extra virgin olive oil and seasoned with salt and pepper while hot. Or toss a large handful of freshly chopped flat-leaf parsley with a vinaigrette of extra virgin olive oil and lemon juice and pour it over the just-baked flatbread.

15 g fresh *or* 7 g dried yeast
½ teaspoon sugar (optional)
1½ cups (375 ml) warm water
500 g unbleached strong flour (see Glossary)
2 tablespoons whole milk powder

1½ teaspoons salt
¼ cup (60 ml) extra virgin olive oil,
    plus extra for greasing
polenta (optional), for sprinkling

If you are using fresh yeast, mix it to a sludge with the sugar and 1 tablespoon of the warm water in a small container (a cup will do), and set it aside until it begins to froth (this will take about 10 minutes, depending on the weather).

Mix the flour, milk powder and salt in a large bowl, then make a well in the centre and add the 60 ml olive oil and the frothing yeast mixture (if you are using the dried yeast, add it now but omit the sugar). The milk powder gives richness without liquid, but you could use milk instead and then add less water. Pour in the remaining warm water and stir until well combined, then turn the dough out onto a floured workbench and knead for about 10 minutes until the soft dough is smooth and shiny. Put the dough in a lightly oiled bowl, then cover it with a tea towel and allow it to double in size in a draught-free spot (this will take about 1½ hours, depending on the weather).

Turn out the dough, knock it back and knead again for a few minutes, then divide it into 6 pieces. Roll each piece into a ball and leave these to rest under a tea towel for 15 minutes. Grease a baking tray with olive oil or sprinkle a baker's wheel with polenta. Spread each ball of dough into a round about 1 cm thick. Brush the rounds with oil, then 'dimple' the tops with your fingertips. Cover the dough with tea towels and allow to double in size again (45 minutes–1 hour).

Preheat the oven to 230°C with a pizza tile (or unglazed terracotta tile) in it, if you have one. If not, use a baking tray. Bake the flatbread for 10–15 minutes on the tile, or for a little longer on a baking tray.

CHICKPEA FLATBREAD

Makes 1 flatbread

This recipe is great for those who are being careful with their consumption of wheat. I just love the flavour of this bread.

Chickpea flour is made from ground chickpeas and is available from wholefood stores, Italian or Indian grocers. I buy it in small quantities as it tends to turn rancid quickly.

250 g chickpea flour	¼ cup (60 ml) extra virgin olive oil
4 sprigs rosemary	1 teaspoon salt

In a large bowl, mix the chickpea flour with about 500 ml water, whisking to avoid lumping (the dough should have the consistency of thick cream – add more or less water as needed). Add half the rosemary sprigs to steep. Leave overnight.

Next day, preheat the oven to 230°C. Remove any scum from the surface of the mixture, fish out the rosemary sprigs then add the olive oil and 1 teaspoon salt and stir to form a batter. Strip the rosemary leaves from the two remaining sprigs and add to the batter. Pour the batter onto a pizza tile or unglazed terracotta tile (or use a baking tray). Bake for about 10 minutes – it should resemble a very thin pizza-like flatbread.

BREAD AND BUTTER PUDDING

Serves 10

120 g dried apricots, diced	900 ml milk
½ cup (125 ml) verjuice *or* half white wine and half water	600 ml cream
	8 eggs
4 × 1 cm-thick slices good white bread	125 g castor sugar
60 g butter	1 vanilla bean, halved lengthways
220 g prunes, pitted and diced	

Reconstitute the apricots in the verjuice or wine and water overnight, or cheat and use the microwave on defrost for a few minutes. Meanwhile, remove the crusts from the bread, butter it and then grill on both sides until golden. Butter a 22 cm ovenproof dish (I use one that is 7.5 cm deep) and arrange the bread slices over the base. Drain the apricots and sprinkle them over the bread with the prunes.

Preheat the oven to 200°C. Bring the milk and cream to a simmer in a saucepan, then remove from heat. Beat the eggs and castor sugar in a large bowl, then scrape the seeds from the vanilla bean into the egg mixture. Stir the hot milk and cream into the egg mixture, then pour this carefully over the bread. Stand the dish in a larger baking dish and pour in hot water to come two-thirds of the way up the sides. Bake for about 30 minutes until set, then allow to cool a little before serving.

PIZZA

One of the great wood-fired-oven experiences is to be had at Russell Jeavons' fine establishment Russell's Pizza at Willunga, south of Adelaide. A few years ago, I was part of a contingent of more than sixty from the Slow Food Convivium that gathered at Russell's for an olive oil tasting, led by Zany Flannagan, a local with a good nose and palate. After the tasting was complete, a procession of food began, each 'course' served on a wooden board in the centre of the table. No knives, forks or plates were offered or needed, although serviettes were welcomed.

The food, all cooked in Russell's huge brick oven that sits in full sight, came out in waves. The first offering was wood-fired bread, baked that morning. It came with a dish of local extra virgin olive oil, Russell's dukkah, a green salad made with Island Pure kefalotiri and the last of that year's local olives, and a tray of smoked beef and prosciutto. This was all consumed literally within seconds.

But when the first wooden board of what Russell called 'bits' appeared, we all looked for more of the bread to mop up the sauces. Here was duck confit crisped in the oven on pizza trays with pheasant hearts and slow-cooked pork in a highly flavoured jus. A good dab of rosehip jelly (made by Russell, of course) sat in the middle of the board. A plate of Kangaroo Island haloumi came out next, the cheese sliced and caramelised in the oven with olive oil.

And then the pizzas! There were nine tables in the room, and Russell's staff fed us pizza after pizza. When I went into the kitchen to return a few plates (it's that sort of place), there were buckets of dough and several industrious young people rolling and preparing the bases. These bases – thin and tasty – were made of flour from Four Leaf Milling, the organic and biodynamic grain specialist from Tarlee. Each pizza took only five minutes to cook in the well-worked oven. The first pizza to appear used the duck confit again, this time separated into pieces and partnered with sliced par-boiled potato and rosemary and drizzled with extra virgin olive oil. Then came a tomato-based one with anchovies and next a chicken and chilli pizza. The last one was a triumph of seafood: tomato and fennel on the base, then a thick layer of squid caught off Port Willunga, all crowned with oysters in the shell. It was so generous it was almost impossible to cut.

Before dessert was served, Russell talked to us about his tiny place. He sees his brick oven as connecting the history of Willunga with that of the Welsh who first settled the area. And he sees the brick oven as the pivot, the centre of his cooking. Russell has had a more traditional career in the past, but rejected the norm of running a conventional restaurant. Instead, when he opened here in 1993, he decided not to open much at all. Up until recently he has only traded six hours a week, only opening on Friday nights, but since October 2005 he now also opens on Saturday nights much to the delight of his customers.

Russell makes pizzas to suit just about every taste, but the best way is to take pot luck and see what you get. I doubt whether you'll ever see a written menu at Russell's, and I also doubt you'll find a better pizza anywhere.

PIZZA WITH GOAT'S CHEESE, SEMI-DRIED TOMATOES AND BASIL *Makes 6 individual pizzas*

For years we played around with our wood-fired oven, but never enough to really get a handle on it. That is until Victoria Blumenstein came to work for me and, as a great cook and passionate advocate of wood-fired ovens, she took over the running of it and showed us just how it was done. Of the many occasions we used the oven, one night stays firmly in my mind as being just so incredibly special. I had agreed to hold a function at home as a favour to Adrian Geering, who had been my mentor on business matters and was someone I admired greatly. The dinner was for thirty of his colleagues, and knowing that, for them, business was more important than food, Victoria and I decided to turn the tables and get them very much involved, as we wanted to bring them firmly into our world for the night.

Our idea was to make lots of different pizzas and to chargrill some seafood on the coals from the wood-fired oven. On the day, the fire was lit in the early morning, and a 10 kg bucket of pizza dough was made in the large mixer at the Farmshop, then punched down with gay abandon every time it looked like over-proving. We pulled a solid wooden table from the shed to put in front of the fire, with all our ingredients laid out on it so we could work quickly and feed everyone at the same time.

We rolled out the dough on a granite bench to one side of the fire into beautifully thin ovals about the size of standard dinner plates, then set them aside with a damp tea towel over them to prevent them drying out. Victoria had made two sauces for the pizza bases, one of basil, preserved lemon and extra virgin olive oil, the other of fresh tomato, garlic and oregano. All the ingredients for the toppings were lined up on enamel camping plates on the table – raw tuna, olives, squid cooked quickly on the coals, four different cheeses, fresh figs, prosciutto and sopresso (a type of spicy Italian salami). There were also fresh scallops speared on rosemary skewers to grill, along with the necessary accompaniments of extra virgin olive oil, sea salt, pepper and vino cotto. We were ready for action.

The guests had simply been told we would be eating outside, but had no idea what they were in for. We made each pizza on the spot, adding ingredients as the mood took us. There is something about a fire that draws people in, and as each pizza came out of the oven – a new taste sensation – they devoured it with hungry delight. One after the other the pizzas came out: raw tuna and olives with just a hint of pepper on a basil base, grilled squid on a tomato base, fig and prosciutto with goat's cheese, the list went on and on. Then, as a finale to the night, we made a dessert pizza of figs soaked in my vino cotto, and a cheese-plate pizza of a mixture of cheeses topped with my cabernet paste, which became a luscious molten mass, giving that sweet–sour zing to finish the night. The buzz of the evening was amazing – everyone got involved in the food, both cooking and eating, and we were all carried away by the mesmerising aura of the fire.

Here's the recipe for my basic pizza base, with a delicious topping – but remember to experiment with different toppings each time you make it. You could use an unglazed terracotta tile or a pizza tile to cook the pizza on, or alternatively a flat oven tray will do the trick.

180 g goat's curd
180 g semi-dried tomatoes
extra virgin olive oil, for drizzling
freshly ground black pepper
basil leaves, to serve

PIZZA BASE

15 g fresh yeast *or* 1½ teaspoons dried yeast
½ teaspoon sugar (optional)
1½ cups (375 ml) warm water
500 g unbleached strong flour (see Glossary)
2 tablespoons whole milk powder
1½ teaspoons salt
¼ cup (60 ml) extra virgin olive oil,
      plus extra for greasing
¼ cup (40 g) polenta (optional), for dusting

Preheat the oven to 230°C or its highest possible temperature, and if using a pizza tile, place this in the oven to warm.

If using fresh yeast, combine it with the sugar and 1 tablespoon of the warm water in a small bowl, dissolve the yeast by mashing it with a fork, then set it aside for 5–10 minutes until frothy.

Mix the flour, milk powder and salt in a large bowl, then make a well in the centre and add the olive oil and the yeast mixture (if you are using dried yeast, add it now but omit the sugar). Pour in the remaining warm water and stir until well combined, then turn the dough out onto a floured bench and knead for about 10 minutes or until it is shiny and smooth. Return the dough to the lightly oiled bowl, then cover the bowl with plastic film and leave in a draught-free spot for about 60–90 minutes, or until the dough doubles in size.

Turn the dough out, knock it back and knead again for a few minutes, then divide into 6 pieces. Roll each piece into a ball and allow these to rest under a wet tea towel for 15 minutes. With a rolling pin, roll each ball of dough into a round about the thickness of your little finger.

Stretch the dough by resting it over your hands, clenched in fists with knuckles pressed together, then gently pull your hands apart, allowing the weight of the dough to stretch itself. This important step allows the air to stay in the dough so you get that lightness in your crust. Alternatively, you could try rolling the dough a little thinner to achieve a similar result. Lightly dust the pizza tile or baking tray with polenta or flour, then lay the dough on it.

Place the pizza in the base of your oven; it is important not to oil the dough at this stage. Pull it out when the dough has set (this should be after about 4 minutes, but will depend entirely upon the oven – you are looking for the dough to change from shiny to a soft, just under-baked look). Scatter dollops of goat's cheese and the semi-dried tomatoes over the base, drizzle with olive oil and season with pepper. Return the pizza to the oven for a few more minutes, then drizzle with more olive oil, scatter with basil leaves and serve.

PASTA

Nothing could be more fun than making pasta – all it takes is a little planning. Buy unbleached, 'strong' plain white flour and choose free-range eggs (for colour and flavour). You'll find strong flour in better supermarkets and good food stores.

If you don't have your own hand-cranked pasta machine, someone in your family or circle of friends might. In any case, they cost under $100 for a basic model, which usually comes with spaghetti and fettuccine cutters. Other implements needed include forks and a pastry scraper – a half-moon-shaped piece of plastic that is readily available and very cheap, and once you've developed a taste for homemade pasta, you'll need it again and again.

Making pasta by hand is like making cement: pouring egg into a 'dam' in the middle of the flour and mixing it bit by bit with the egg, making sure the dam walls don't collapse.

FRESH PASTA　　　　　　　　　　　　　　　　　　　　　　　　　　*Serves 4*

About 500 g fresh pasta will serve four adults as a main course. Great pasta doesn't need a sauce. Just drizzle olive oil over the hot pasta, then add some freshly shaved Parmigiano Reggiano, or make a simple, uncooked sauce with fresh tomatoes and basil.

The dough should be tight but malleable. If it becomes too loose, it will still be suitable for making ravioli.

500 g strong flour (see Glossary)	**4 × 61 g eggs**
1 teaspoon salt	**1–2 egg yolks (depending on the flour)**

Mix the flour with the salt, then spread it out into a circle 30 cm in diameter over a clean work surface. Hollow out the centre, leaving just a bank of flour around the edges. Break the eggs into the well, then add the yolks. Using one hand, whisk the eggs and yolks until they're amalgamated, and then, using a fork held in the other hand, scoop the flour a little at a time from the 'banks' into the egg mixture, still whisking with one hand. Keep doing this until the mixture becomes a paste.

Scrape up the dough, 'cutting' it until the mixture is well combined. This involves gathering the mass and smearing it across the bench with the pastry scraper until it all comes together. The dough should then be kneaded for 6–10 minutes, pushing the dough away from you with the heel of your hand, then turning it a quarter to the right, folding the dough over, pushing it away and so on.

Once the dough is shiny and silky, roll it into a ball and wrap it in plastic film. Rest it in the refrigerator for 30 minutes.

Set the pasta machine on a bench, screwing it down firmly. Cut the dough into 10 even pieces and cover with a tea towel. Working in batches, take one piece of dough and press it as flat as you can with the palm of your hand, then feed it through the rollers set on their widest aperture. Fold the rolled dough in thirds, and then pass the narrow end through the machine again. Repeat several times, preferably until you hear a sound that I can only describe as a 'plop' – this is the tension of the dough releasing as it goes through the rollers.

Adjust the machine to the next setting and pass the dough through. Repeat this with every setting until you get to the second to last. As the dough moves through each setting it will become finer and finer and the sheets will become longer and longer; you may need to cut the sheets to make them more manageable.

Unless I'm making ravioli, where I want the pasta to be almost diaphanous, I'll stop at the second to last setting, then adjust the machine, adding the cutters, and run the pasta through the cutters. If I'm making long pasta, I like to have someone help here. Hang the pasta ribbons over the back of a chair or a broom handle to dry.

When ready to cook, bring a large saucepan of water to the boil and add a generous amount of salt. Tip in the pasta and cook until done, testing a strand after 3 minutes. Have a large colander at the ready in the sink, strain the pasta and tip it back into the pan (you may also want to save a little of the cooking water, in case you need it to bind the sauce). Don't rinse the pasta or you'll lose the starch that helps the sauce or oil adhere. If you're not ready to use it immediately, spread out the pasta on a large tray to cool drizzled with extra virgin olive oil – I hate to admit it, but it reheats beautifully in the microwave.

DUCK EGG PASTA WITH SMOKED KANGAROO, SUN-DRIED TOMATOES AND PINE NUTS
Serves 6 as an entrée

I suspect that all cooks have one dish they are most proud of, and that's how I feel about this very simple dish, which starred on my restaurant menu for many years. It was the kind of dish where the total was greater than the sum of the parts. The key to it was the rich silkiness of the handmade duck egg pasta – made fresh every day – and the perfection of the ruby-red cold-smoked kangaroo fillet. I sometimes used roasted flaked almonds rather than pine nuts, to great effect. Of course, the pasta can be made with chook eggs too.

I can also proudly say that I have never had a better smoked kangaroo than the one I brined and cold-smoked at Schulz's Butchers in Angaston, and I regret that it is no longer possible to do this, due to changes in food laws. Rather than attempt this dish with a hot-smoked alternative, use raw kangaroo, venison or beef – freeze it first for 20 minutes to enable you to cut it paper-thin.

½ cup (125 ml) extra virgin olive oil

100 g sun-dried tomatoes (not those in
cotton seed oil), cut into strips

1 cup (155 g) pine nuts *or* flaked almonds

400 g kangaroo, venison *or* beef fillet, sliced
as thin as prosciutto

sea salt flakes and freshly ground
black pepper

shaved Parmigiano Reggiano, to serve

DUCK EGG PASTA (makes 500 g)

3⅓ cups (500 g) strong flour (see Glossary)

4–5 duck eggs, depending on their size

To make the pasta, tip the flour onto a bench and make a well in the centre. Whisk the eggs together and pour into the well, and gradually incorporate them into the flour, following the method described on page 419. Add an extra yolk if needed. Knead the pasta dough until it forms a shiny ball and is firm to the touch. Cover the dough with plastic film and rest it in the refrigerator for 30 minutes. Cut the pasta dough into about 8 equal portions.

Preheat the oven to 200°C. Roast the pine nuts on a baking tray for about 10 minutes or until golden brown.

Before beginning to roll the pasta, bring a large saucepan of salted water to the boil. Set the pasta machine on a bench, screwing it down firmly. Working in batches, take one piece of dough and press it as flat as you can with the palm of your hand, then feed it through the rollers set on their widest aperture. Fold the rolled dough in thirds, and then pass the narrow end through the machine again. Repeat several times, preferably until you hear a sound that I can only describe as a 'plop' – this is the tension of the dough releasing as it goes through the rollers.

Adjust the machine to the next setting and pass the dough through. Repeat this with every setting until you get to the second to last. As the dough moves through each setting it will become finer and finer and the sheets will become longer and longer; you may need to cut the sheets to make them more manageable. Adjust the machine, selecting the widest cutter, and run the pasta through to cut into strips. Hang the pasta ribbons over the back of a chair to dry.

Slide the pasta gently into the boiling water, then partially cover with a lid to bring back to a rapid boil. Stir the pasta gently to keep it well separated. Fresh pasta only needs to cook for 3 minutes or so. Drain the cooked pasta, reserving a little of the cooking water in case you need it to moisten the completed dish. Do not run the pasta under water or you will lose the precious starch that helps the sauce or oil adhere. Generously drizzle the pasta with olive oil immediately.

While the pasta is cooking, make the sauce. Heat half the olive oil in a small frying pan, then add the sun-dried tomatoes and pine nuts or almonds and heat over low heat. Toss the remaining olive oil through the slices of kangaroo.

To serve, pile the pasta on a serving dish or plates, top with the kangaroo, then spoon over the sun-dried tomato and pine nut sauce. Scatter over liberal amounts of shaved Parmigiano Reggiano and serve immediately.

PASTRY

Some years ago I witnessed Betsy Pie, then the organiser of the Brisbane Masterclasses, turn a calamity into a triumph when the star chef backed out only days beforehand. Expecting a dashing Frenchman to appear on stage, the students were instead greeted with a glass of French bubbly.

Betsy went on to tell the amazing story of how she had chased leads from one continent to another as she sought out a top-class presenter who could be lured to Australia on literally a few hours' notice. Clever Betsy managed to whisk Nancy Silverton from the Campanile Restaurant and La Brea Bakery in Los Angeles to fill in for the wayward Frenchman. Nancy was confident, unpretentious in her attitude to food, and had every one of us talking about all she had taught us over the weekend.

Nancy talked to us about pastry-making – very 'down home'. Gathering up the audience into her hands as confidently as she did her dough, Nancy shared her tricks, kept us engaged and, frankly, charmed us. As she demonstrated making dough for a tart, it was as if we were seeing the process for the first time. Nancy made the dough with a certain amount of irreverence – she tossed flour onto the bench with the carefree abandon of someone very sure of her craft. She used a food processor, adding the flour with the sugar sifted into it (at the same time telling us that, if making pastry by hand, you should use only the tips of your fingers). She then added very cold butter to the processor, pulsing it in, before adding egg yolks and cream (stirred together first) and stopped mixing just before the dough came together.

Then – and this was the bit we all loved – Nancy gathered the dough into a ball with her hands and bounced it on the bench! This apparently allows the proteins in the flour to relax so they don't shrink during cooking. As she uses a lot of butter, the pastry then went into the freezer to chill well (or to keep for later use) – this also helps prevent shrinkage. Nancy went on to bash the chilled dough heartily with a rolling pin to flatten it so that it wouldn't crack when rolled.

She urged us not to play with the dough by poking it into the corners and to always trim the pastry case by running a rolling pin over the top rather than using a knife. And, of course, she reiterated the need to chill the rolled-out case, to firm the pastry before baking.

My notebook was thick with scribbled tips. One I particularly liked was that, when blind baking, Nancy uses large paper coffee filters rather than foil to line the pastry before adding weights. The filters don't stick to the pastry and allow you to get the weights right into the corners. They also show you clearly whether the pastry is cooked – if it's not, the weights stick.

Another good idea (for me, anyhow) is to only use a plain flan ring when making a pastry case; I lose the detachable bases regularly and find myself with mismatched bases and rings. To do this Nancy uses a large metal baking tray without a lip, baking paper and an unfluted ring. This allows the cooked tart to slip straight onto a plate from the baking sheet; she then slides the band off gently.

As Nancy is as straightforward a writer as she is a teacher, her books are well worth tracking down. And if you are ever in LA, her restaurant Mozza is certainly worth a visit for the fabulous pizzas and antipasti.

SOUR-CREAM PASTRY
Makes enough to line a 20–24 cm tart tin

This recipe makes a very short, flaky pastry with a light, melt-in-the-mouth texture. It is a great all-rounder and can be used in a whole variety of dishes, both sweet and savoury. It's the pastry I make ninety-nine times out of a hundred because it's not only so good but so easy. I like to chill the pastry case in the freezer, as this ensures it is really well-chilled before it goes in the oven.

This pastry rises beautifully and is really light and flaky, which is great if you're making a tart or a pie, but if you want a flat pastry, like a thin pizza dough, a good trick is to 'inhibit' the pastry as it cooks. To do this, carefully open the oven halfway through the cooking (when the pastry is beginning to rise), take out the tray for a moment and press down on the pastry with a similar-sized tray or a clean tea towel, then return the tray to the oven. This will stop the pastry rising too much.

200 g chilled unsalted butter, chopped into small pieces

250 g plain flour
½ cup (125 ml) sour cream

Put the butter and flour into the bowl of a food processor, then pulse until the mixture resembles coarse breadcrumbs. Add the sour cream and pulse again until the dough just forms a ball. Use Nancy's trick of bouncing the pastry (see previous page) if shrinkage worries you. Carefully wrap the dough in plastic film and leave to rest in the refrigerator for 15–20 minutes.

Roll out the dough until it is 5 mm thick, then use it to line a 20 cm tart tin with a removable base. Chill the pastry case for 20 minutes.

To blind bake, preheat the oven to 200°C. Line the pastry case with foil, then cover with pastry weights. Blind bake the pastry case for 15 minutes, then remove the foil and pastry weights and bake for another 5 minutes.

CHOUX PASTRY-STYLE
GLUTEN-FREE PASTRY

Makes enough to line a 24 cm tart tin

As a friend who is a coeliac confided to me, the thing she most missed after being diagnosed was the lack of a luscious pastry. So, along with Victoria Blumenstein, my chef at the Farmshop at the time, I set about finding something to fit the bill.

This pastry browns beautifully, has a nice crispness and holds in moisture; it also has a lovely potato-ey undertone which is very pleasant. It is great for any type of pie and keeps well in the refrigerator for up to five days.

You could add 2 teaspoons of icing sugar to make a sweet pastry for fruit pies and other pastry-based desserts.

Xanthan gum is derived from corn sugar and acts as a binding agent in gluten-free pastry. It is available from most health food stores.

2 teaspoons salt

90 g unsalted butter

150 g gluten-free flour (I use a mix of
    potato flour, rice flour and maize flour),
    plus ½ cup extra for dusting

2 g xanthan gum

3 × 57 g eggs

In a heavy-based saucepan, combine the salt, butter and 250 ml water. Bring to a simmer over medium–high heat and add the flour and xanthan gum gradually, stirring with a wooden spoon. Reduce the temperature to low and continue to cook until the pastry is well combined and is coming away from the sides of the pan. Remove from heat and allow to cool to room temperature.

Whisk eggs to combine, then slowly add them bit by bit to the pastry mixture, incorporating fully before adding the next bit; you may not need all the egg mixture.

Turn the pastry out onto a bench that has been dusted with ½ cup gluten-free flour to assist rolling, then knead until shiny. Try to incorporate as little flour as possible so the pastry does not become too crumbly.

Chill the pastry for 20 minutes, then, using a rolling pin, roll the pastry between 2 pieces of baking paper which have been greased on both sides. Roll the pastry until it is 5 mm thick, then use it to line a 24 cm tart or pie tin.

To blind bake, preheat the oven to 200°C. Line the pastry case with foil, then cover with pastry weights. Blind bake the pastry case for 15 minutes, then remove the foil and pastry weights and bake for another 5 minutes.

CRISP GLUTEN-FREE PASTRY

Makes enough to line a 24 cm tart tin

This is a nice base for quiches and cheese tarts – it becomes very crisp when baked. Although this pastry does not need to be rested because it contains no gluten, it rolls more easily when chilled.

Xanthan gum is derived from corn sugar and acts as a binding agent in gluten-free pastry. It is available from most health food stores.

125 g cream cheese, cut into chunks

75 g cold unsalted butter, chopped

1 cup gluten-free flour, plus ¼ cup extra
   for dusting

2 g xanthan gum

2 teaspoons salt

In a food processor, pulse the cream cheese and butter to combine. Slowly add 1 cup of the flour, the xanthan gum and the salt and pulse just to combine. Turn the pastry out onto a bench which has been dusted with ¼ cup gluten-free flour and bring together with your hands, kneading for 5 minutes.

Chill the pastry for 20 minutes, then, using a rolling pin, roll the pastry between 2 pieces of baking paper which have been greased on both sides. Roll the pastry until it is 5 mm thick, then use it to line a 24 cm tart, pie or quiche tin.

To blind bake, preheat the oven to 200°C. Line the pastry case with foil, then cover with pastry weights. Blind bake the pastry case for 15 minutes, then remove the foil and pastry weights and bake for another 5 minutes.

KANGAROO

IT TOOK MANY YEARS FOR ALL THE AUSTRALIAN STATES TO come into line with uniform legislation about kangaroo meat. There are very strict quotas in place, which are necessary to protect the kangaroo population, and stringent requirements for the issuing of 'harvesting' licences. Kangaroo is probably still most widely available in South Australia, where it is readily accepted as a healthy, flavourful red meat. It is best of all when cooked on the barbecue, which certainly suits our way of life and our Mediterranean climate.

I first started serving kangaroo at the restaurant in the mid-1990s. It was much in demand as a uniquely Australian meat, and as such it was overseas visitors who were particularly keen to try it, as well as some interstaters who at the time were unable to eat it in their states and so thought it was somewhat daring. For me, flavour was the real motive, along with the knowledge that kangaroo fed on natural grasses in the wild. Also, as a native species, they are more suited to this fragile land of ours than cloven-hoofed sheep and cattle.

When roo first became available we used to buy a whole saddle and spend hours trimming and stripping sinew. Things are much simpler now and the meat is normally sold as fillets, although you can also buy the leg, tail or whole saddle. However, for home cooking, particularly barbecuing, the fillet is the most convenient cut.

I get quite nostalgic when I talk of or write about smoked kangaroo. In the Barossa I have a wealth of food tradition to draw upon, and smoking is one of the strongest. I was incredibly proud of the smoked kangaroo I used to produce at Schulz's Butchers in Angaston. Then, they were happy to let me brine the roo first, then string it up until I thought it was ready. When finished, it was ruby-red with a dense consistency, and I served it sliced paper-thin like prosciutto. As already mentioned, changes in food laws have placed greater restrictions on the smoking process, and it is no longer possible to have access to the local smokehouses.

I suggest that a barbecue or a ridged chargrill plate on a very hot stove is the best way to cook kangaroo fillets. Place them on a tray or plate with just enough olive oil to moisten them (they have absolutely no fat to speak of, so this is important), sprinkle with freshly ground black pepper, and set aside, covered, for about an hour. I don't use a red-wine (or any other) marinade for roo – it disturbs the natural flavour of the meat. Be sure not to buy more meat than required for your recipe – kangaroo meat oxidises on contact with air more readily than any other meat I know, and will spoil and turn grey quickly. It is usually sold vacuum-packed, so keep it tightly sealed until you are ready to cook and then add the olive oil to protect it.

Preheating the barbecue or pan is essential, as is brushing it with olive oil. Season the roo with sea salt flakes just seconds before cooking. After placing the first side down, leave it until properly sealed (at least 2 minutes); if you play with the meat with your tongs before

then, you will tear the fibres. Repeat on the other side for approximately the same time, and then the fillet will need to rest for at least 5–7 minutes before it is ready (depending on the thickness). The grain of the meat is looser than that of beef or lamb, and it is absolutely essential to cook kangaroo rare and never leave out the resting step. If overcooked, it will be like shoe leather.

A simple Anchovy and Olive Butter (see page 9) or horseradish or wasabi butter would add either a salty or hot component to the dish. Probably my two favourite accompaniments to kangaroo, either together or separately, are my Caramelised Onion Salad (see page 461) and a beetroot dish. Try beetroot either cooked, peeled and deglazed with vino cotto or balsamic, or raw, grated in a salad with extra virgin olive oil and orange rind (see page 559). In fact, even beetroot from a tin – heaven forbid – would be a great counterpoint to the richness of the roo.

If you want to make it more formal, try a rich red-wine and port glaze with some thinly sliced pickled quinces (and just a bit of the pickling liquor added) alongside creamy mashed potatoes or parsnips flavoured with extra virgin olive oil – combine this with perfectly rare and rested kangaroo and you are on to a winner!

For other ideas for kangaroo, look at recipes for venison in game cookbooks. Kangaroo also marries well with Asian flavours and you can happily substitute it for beef in many dishes.

SALAD OF SMOKED KANGAROO

Serves 6

This is such a refreshing dish. It can be made with commercially smoked kangaroo or venison, but would also work well with raw kangaroo that has been frozen for 20 minutes, then thinly sliced.

100 ml extra virgin olive oil

1 tablespoon red-wine vinegar

1 dessertspoon vino cotto (see Glossary)
    or balsamic vinegar

1 small clove garlic, very finely chopped

3 large witlof, bases trimmed and
    leaves separated

2 cos lettuce hearts, leaves separated

1 bunch rocket, leaves trimmed

300 g smoked kangaroo, thinly sliced

120 g salmon roe

Make a vinaigrette with the olive oil, red-wine vinegar, vino cotto and the garlic.

Wash and spin the lettuces dry. Divide the lettuce leaves among 6 plates and drape the kangaroo over the leaves. Dress each salad with the vinaigrette, then scatter with the salmon roe and serve immediately.

BARBECUED SUGAR-CURED KANGAROO

Serves 4

Select the thickest fillet you can find for this dish, as the denseness of the meat is important. Ask your butcher to trim off the sinew.

125 g cooking salt

125 g sugar

25 g black peppercorns, coarsely crushed

8 juniper berries, bruised

8 sprigs thyme

1 kg kangaroo fillet in one piece,
    sinews trimmed

extra virgin olive oil, for cooking

Mix the salt, sugar, peppercorns, juniper berries and thyme. Evenly spread the fillet with the mixture, place in a glass or ceramic dish and wrap to seal well with plastic film. Place a similar-sized dish on top, then place weights, such as cans from the pantry, on top of this, and leave in the refrigerator overnight.

Take the meat from the dish and wipe off any excess moisture. Brush with extra virgin olive oil and cook on a very hot barbecue grillplate. The cooking time will depend on the thickness of the meat and may be as little as 4 minutes, but no longer than 10 minutes – the meat needs to be rare. When cooked, it is essential to rest the meat for at least 15 minutes before serving.

Serve with horseradish cream and a salad of bitter lettuces such as witlof, radicchio and frisée.

KANGAROO TAIL PIE   *Serves 8*

The late Maurice de Rohan became a firm friend after he asked me to prepare a cocktail party for over 500 people in Paris in 2001. It was to be held at the Australian Embassy to commemorate the 200th anniversary of Nicolas Baudin's expedition to the southern Australian coast. Maurice gave me free reign to make this a totally South Australian gastronomic event, so with the help of the Ambassador's staff, I managed to fly in an amazing array of ingredients. I was determined that this was not going to be just standard 'cocktail food'. Based on the premise that if Matthew Flinders hadn't pipped Baudin at the post by just 5 nautical miles we might have been French, the concept was to feature the 'wild' food that Baudin might have found on his arrival.

Maurice immediately loved my idea of whole Murray cod baked in mud, as if they'd been cooked in coals by the side of the river, being opened in front of the guests by gloved chefs who pulled back the casing to reveal the succulent fish. We made damper to serve it as a sandwich (or 'schnitter', as we say in the Barossa) with Joseph Grilli's extra virgin olive oil and some dukkah. The guests crowded around, loving the theatre of it!

The assembled guests ate voraciously and loved it all. As noisily as they talked through the political speeches, they listened intently when I spoke about the food they were eating and the inspiration behind it. It was without a doubt the most exciting food event of my life. The support and cooperation of the then Ambassador, William Frazer, and his staff, particularly his chef Michael Walker, made the event a great success, but it was Maurice's vision that I was so happy to have made a reality.

I had to use artistic licence in sourcing my ingredients, as the logistics involved in transporting food from the other side of the world for such a large party were enormous. We used farmed Murray cod rather than fish straight from the Murray River, and the razorfish, a wonderful mollusc that is not fished commercially, had to be collected by a volunteer group in return for a 'donation' to their cause. The yabbies came from Western Australia because of technical issues with export licences in South Australia, but happily the oysters were from Coffin Bay, and the kangaroo tail was definitely South Australian!

We were to serve cocktail-sized kangaroo tail pies which, when the Parisian caterers and I trialled them, had turned out beautifully – succulent and delicious. As we were working from a kitchen not much larger than a normal household one, we decided to delegate the cooking of the pies on the night to the caterers, but something must have gone wrong and they turned out to be a disaster. So much so that, even though the guest numbers had increased by an extra 200, after a few tears of frustration I decided to throw most of the pies away because they were so dry. I was determined nothing was going to spoil the evening.

Whenever I've made this dish, whether as small individual pies or larger ones, the results have always been moist and more-ish – I urge you to give it a go.

1 large onion, roughly chopped

1 carrot, roughly chopped

1 clove garlic, roughly chopped

extra virgin olive oil, for cooking

1 cup plain flour

sea salt flakes and freshly ground
    black pepper

2 kangaroo tails, approximately 1.5 kg in
    total, cut into thirds

6 lemon myrtle leaves

500 ml jellied veal stock *or* reduced Golden
    Chicken Stock (see page 57)

375 ml red wine

8 golden shallots, finely diced

4 cloves garlic, finely diced

3 sticks celery, finely diced

PASTRY

1 packet Tandaco suet mix
    (believe me, it works and is terrific!)

2 cups flour

1 cup water

1½ teaspoons baking powder

freshly ground black pepper

1 egg, beaten

dash milk

Preheat oven to 140°C.

In a heavy-based casserole, seal the onion, carrot and garlic in olive oil on medium heat until softened, then remove from pan and set aside. Mix the plain flour with some salt and pepper, and dust the kangaroo pieces with the seasoned flour. Working in batches, gently seal them in olive oil on all sides over medium heat in the casserole. Add all the kangaroo back to the pan, placing the thickest tail pieces at the bottom, then add the vegetables and the lemon myrtle leaves. Turn the heat up to high and pour in the stock and red wine. Bring to a simmer, then cover the dish with a lid or two sheets of foil and transfer to the oven. Cook for 1½ hours, then turn the meat over and cook for a further 2 hours, or until all the tail pieces are cooked and the meat falls easily off the bone.

Once cooked, remove the casserole from the oven and set aside until the meat is cool enough to handle. Remove the meat from the tails and cut into dice, adding a little of the cooking juices to keep it moist. Strain the rest of the juices through a sieve and set aside.

In a heavy-based frying pan, sauté the shallots, garlic and celery in olive oil over medium heat until softened, then turn the heat to high, add the drained cooking juices and reduce for 10–15 minutes, until they begin to thicken. Season well, remove from the heat, and add the chopped tail meat. Transfer to the refrigerator to chill for several hours or overnight.

For the pastry, combine all the ingredients and knead on a floured workbench until the dough is smooth and uniform. Carefully wrap the dough in plastic film and leave to rest in the refrigerator for 20 minutes.

Roll out two pastry circles large enough to line the base and lid of a 28 cm pie dish. Line the dish with the base and fill with the chilled kangaroo mixture. Mix the egg with the milk and brush some of this around the pastry edge, then place the lid on and crimp the edges together with your fingers. Brush the lid with the rest of the egg wash, then chill the pie in the refrigerator for 20 minutes.

Preheat oven to 220°C. Cook the pie for 10 minutes, then turn the temperature down to 200°C and cook for another 10 minutes until the pastry is golden and the filling is hot.

LEEKS

LEEKS ARE NOT CALLED 'POOR MAN'S ASPARAGUS' BECAUSE THEY taste like asparagus but because the delicious thin ones can look similar. Personally, I have always aspired to Georges Blanc's dish *asperge du pauvre*, where the leeks are poached for 10 minutes, then refreshed under cold water and served with Beluga caviar. No longer for the poor man!

Why is it that when leeks are sold in a bunch they are not all the same size? I was trialling a dinner for 100 people for the Adelaide Symphony Orchestra and wanted to serve braised leeks. I had to figure out how many bunches I would need and how long they would take to prepare. In my first bunch I had three fat fresh leeks, one fat old leek and one very skinny young leek. Two of the leeks had lots and lots of dirt in them, while the others were clean. The grower probably put his bunches together according to a standard weight, but I objected heartily to the old leek being thrown in.

You may be thinking that this one example does not make for a definitive survey, but this has happened to me many times over, I can assure you. I would have been very happy if the leeks had all been of the thinner variety (called pencil leeks); in fact, I would have paid a premium for them. Even though you're left with something half the size once you've peeled the outside layers off, discarded the root end and trimmed away the darker leaves, these sweeter, more tender specimens provide twice the pleasure of their larger cousins.

Pencil leeks are now much more widely available in major city markets, but at the wrong time of year, they too can be woody in the centre. The leek is still one of the vegetables I give space to in my kitchen garden, as tender young leeks are so different from the fat, over-mature specimens shops often offer. Young leeks add an extra dimension to slow-cooked winter foods and give a fragrance that immediately excites. So many people try to escape cold winters, whereas I love them, if only to experience the joy of walking into a warm kitchen with a one-pot meal simmering away.

Washing leeks meticulously is essential, as the layers can harbour an extraordinary amount of dirt, and there is nothing worse than gritty cooked leeks. If you want to keep the shape of the whole leek, stand it root-end up in a large jug of water to soak out the grit. Another method is to cut through the leek at the point where the dark and light green meet – this way you'll cut away most of the dirt. Remove the tougher outer layers and make a cut about 5 cm into the top, then immerse the leek in a sink of cold water, shaking it to eliminate any remaining dirt. If you aren't cooking the leeks whole, cut them in half lengthways and rinse them thoroughly. It's a much simpler matter if the leeks are to be chopped up as you can reject or rewash any gritty pieces.

The leek is one of the few vegetables that must be a little 'overcooked' to ensure maximum flavour and texture. A simple, wonderful meal cooked this way by a French friend of mine, for Bastille Day years and years ago, showed me how special this vegetable can be. Choose three or four of the youngest leeks possible, of similar size, and wash them very carefully, keeping them whole but trimming away any dark-green leaves. In a frying pan, bring the leeks to a simmer in salted water, adding a dash of verjuice and a little butter or extra virgin olive oil, and simmer them until they change colour and no longer smell like onion – about 15 minutes. Drain the leeks, then refresh them under cold water and drain again, making sure no water remains. Make a small slit in each leek at the light-green end, so that they can be fanned out on the plate when served, then refrigerate them, covered, until really cold. Make a vinaigrette using 4 parts extra virgin olive oil to 1 part sherry vinegar and add a teaspoon of Dijon mustard, a good dash of cream and a little salt and freshly ground black pepper. Serve the dressed leeks with freshly chopped flat-leaf parsley and crusty bread.

Cooked well, leeks are deliciously sweet and they really do melt in the mouth. They are available all winter, and September is probably the last month to enjoy them before they become woody. The frustrating thing is that a fresh bunch gives no clear indication of that woodiness, so it is a case of buyer beware. (This might be the one time when the ever-increasing practice of selling trimmed vegetables on a polystyrene tray might work to your advantage!)

Try simmering the leeks as explained above, but instead of chilling them, arrange them over the base of a gratin dish. Cover the leeks with a layer of grated pecorino or Parmigiano Reggiano, then dot this with butter and add another layer of leeks, cheese and butter. Bake at 210°C for 10–12 minutes until the leeks are warm and the cheese melts.

Sweat off chopped leeks in a tiny bit of verjuice and butter. This makes a great side dish for pan-fried or poached chicken breast, or pan-fried fish (particularly a meaty one like tuna – try this with a rich, reduced red-wine sauce). Roasted whole leeks are also a great side dish for poultry or fish. I often roast pheasant breasts and bake leeks separately in butter, then arrange the leeks over the breast and glaze the whole with reduced pheasant stock.

Leek soup is a favourite on a winter's night. Slice lots of washed leeks into rings and sweat them in a little butter with peeled, chopped potato and onion until softened. Add chicken stock and a little chervil and simmer until the vegetables are cooked through, then purée the mixture and add a touch of cream and seasoning before serving. You could add some freshly shucked oysters to the soup with a spoon of crème fraîche to make it more of a meal.

There are lots of options for leek tarts. Try layering a warm pastry case with chopped and sweated leeks and topping this with pan-fried globe artichokes and crispy pancetta. You can also caramelise leeks in the same manner you do onions by cooking them slowly with butter and a touch of a quality vinegar. Anchovies can be added or the leeks can be studded with goat's cheese before the tart is heated in the oven.

LEEKS POACHED IN VERJUICE

Serves 4 as an accompaniment

6–8 small leeks, washed
½ cup (125 ml) verjuice
1 tablespoon butter
1 teaspoon salt
freshly ground black pepper
2 tablespoons pitted black olives

2 tablespoons soft cheese such as gruth
 (a soft, fresh quark)
1 tablespoon freshly chopped
 flat-leaf parsley
extra virgin olive oil

Trim the roots and tops from the leeks so that you are left with a firm, mostly white leek. Lay the leeks on a chopping board and cut horizontally through the first 4–5 cm of the tops of the leeks. Leave to soak in cold water to remove all remaining dirt.

Once perfectly clean, drain the leeks and place over very low heat in a frying pan just large enough to hold them. Pour in the verjuice and ½ a cup of water, add the butter, salt and pepper to taste, then simmer gently for about 1 hour or until the leeks are cooked all the way through. They should still hold their shape, but be soft to the touch. Add the pitted olives for the last few minutes of cooking.

Taste for seasoning and adjust if necessary, then place the leeks on a serving plate, spoon on the soft cheese and sprinkle with the flat-leaf parsley. Add a last flourish of olive oil, then serve.

LEEK AND PANCETTA TART

Serves 6–8

1 × quantity Sour-cream Pastry (see page 424)
12 tender young leeks, trimmed
butter, for cooking
sea salt flakes and freshly ground
 black pepper

4 eggs
½ cup (125 ml) cream
60 g thinly sliced mild pancetta, diced

Make and chill the pastry as instructed, then roll out the chilled dough and use to line a 20 cm loose-bottomed flan tin. Chill the pastry case for 20 minutes. »

Preheat the oven to 200°C. Line the chilled pastry case with foil and pastry weights, and blind bake for 15 minutes, then remove the foil and weights and return the pastry case to the oven for another 5 minutes. Remove the pastry case from the oven and reset the temperature to 220°C.

Discard the outer layers of each leek, then wash them well and slice them into rings. Cook the leek in a saucepan in a little butter over gentle heat for about 5 minutes or until softened, then season with salt and pepper. Purée the leek in a food processor, then add the eggs and cream and adjust the seasoning.

Scatter the diced pancetta over the pastry case, then add the leek mixture. Bake the filled pastry case for 20 minutes, watching that the pastry doesn't burn on the edges (cover it with foil if necessary). Allow the tart to cool a little before slicing and serving.

LEEK AND OYSTER PIES   *Makes 30*

Without a foil, the butteriness of a good pastry can be too much when combined with the butteriness of leeks. Here, the iron-like flavour of the oysters cuts into all that richness – although the champagne has a role to play, too, of course. This recipe is a favourite of mine to serve with pre-dinner drinks on those rare days when I have spare time.

I have a tray of tiny pie moulds I bought years ago from Chefs' Warehouse in Sydney that I use for these. It has 30 small indents that are about 3 cm wide and is just perfect.

1 × quantity Sour-cream Pastry
(see page 424)
butter, for cooking
12 young leeks, cleaned and cut into
5 mm slices
sea salt flakes and freshly ground
black pepper

½ cup (125 ml) champagne *or*
sparkling white wine
100 ml thin, runny cream
30 large Pacific oysters, shucked
1 egg, beaten with a little milk

Make and chill the pastry as instructed. Roll out the dough and use to line 30 small 3 cm-diameter pie moulds, then cut out 30 lids slightly larger than the moulds. Chill the pastry for 20 minutes.

Heat a little butter in a frying pan, then sweat the leeks over low heat until soft and season to taste with salt and pepper. Deglaze the pan with champagne, turn the heat up to medium–high and reduce the liquor by half. Add the cream and reduce a little more, then leave to cool.

Chop oysters in halves or thirds. Put a spoonful of leek mixture into each pie mould, then add 1 chopped oyster and cover with a little more leek mixture. Cover with pastry lids and seal carefully. Chill in the refrigerator for 20 minutes.

Meanwhile, preheat the oven to 220°C. Brush the egg wash over the pie lids. Bake pies until golden, about 15 minutes. Cool for 5 minutes in the tins before turning out and serving.

LEEK FRITTATA

Serves 4

6 tender young leeks

2 tablespoons butter

¼ cup (60 ml) extra virgin olive oil

sea salt flakes and freshly ground
    black pepper

1 sprig thyme, leaves stripped

6 eggs

Cut the tops from the leeks at the point where the light-green meets the dark-green, and discard them. Cut the light-green/white parts of the leeks in half lengthways and wash them well, then chop both parts into 1 cm slices.

Heat the butter and 2 tablespoons of the olive oil in a heavy-based enamelled saucepan until golden brown. Cook half the chopped leeks, and when they begin to collapse, quickly add the rest, then season with salt and pepper and add the thyme leaves. Cook the leeks for about 30 minutes or until soft and cooked through, then remove the pan from the heat and allow them to cool for at least 1 hour.

Beat the eggs in a large mixing bowl, then add the cooled leeks and any residue in the pan. Mix thoroughly.

Heat the remaining oil in a heavy-based frying pan, then carefully add the leek mixture and cook over medium heat. When the eggs have set and the frittata comes away from the bottom of the pan, put a plate over the pan and carefully invert the frittata onto it. Return the pan to the heat, then slip the frittata back into it and cook for just a minute more. Return the frittata to the plate using the same method and allow to cool a little – I prefer to serve frittata warm or at room temperature.

LEMONS AND LIMES

THE VERY CONVENIENCE OF HAVING A SUPPLY OF LEMONS ON a tree is absolutely wonderful: just to be able to walk into the garden when you need a squeeze of lemon for some fresh fish, to make a mayonnaise at the last moment, or if, like me, you sometimes have a squirt of lemon in very strong black coffee in the morning. To say nothing of the natural beauty of the tree laden with fruit and flowers – and don't forget the gin and tonic on a summer's afternoon!

Lemons are as indispensable to my cooking as garlic, verjuice, extra virgin olive oil and quality salt and pepper. I use lemon rind in my game pies; lemon juice squeezed into the cavity of all the game I cook; lemon juice to curdle the milk for banana cake; lemons in jam to increase the pectin content; lemon juice in mayonnaise, hollandaise and vinaigrettes; lemon with all kinds of seafood; lemon juice added to a pan of frying mushrooms; lemon juice added to water to stop vegetables oxidising; lemon juice to add balance and zip to a sauce; lemons squeezed on pancakes sprinkled with sugar and then rolled up tight; lemons in homemade lemonade; lemons for squeezing over grilled offal or a just-cooked risotto; lemons for adding to jugs of rainwater on the table; lemons for cleaning my hands after peeling beetroot; lemons for a burnt-butter sauce with capers and parsley to go with brains; and lemons for lemon curd or lemon meringue pie.

In the Riverland in South Australia, lemons begin their season in late July and continue through to November. The lemon tree in your home garden, however, can bear fruit for much of the year, particularly if it's a Lisbon variety; just thin out the main crop so that you are picking mature lemons alongside the forming baby lemons, and there will be flowers on the tree to keep the cycle going.

Lemons don't like clay, nor do they like wet feet. They need well-drained soil and consistent watering through the hot summer months and, though they shouldn't be overfed, if you see the leaves yellowing it means you need to fertilise. Overfeeding will give very large fruit and will make the skins too thick. Lemons can cope with the hottest spot in your

garden, against the northern side of a fence or shed, but only if you keep the ground moist. Their preference, though, is to have shelter. When the leaves turn yellow, it is often due to a lack of lime in the soil, so adding iron chelate can turn that problem around in a week.

While there are other varieties being trialled and grown, particularly in commercial groves where growers are looking for lemons to extend their production year, the other most common variety is the eureka. It is an upright tree like the Lisbon, and grows up to 5 metres tall. Its fruit is deliciously sour and is used for commercial juicing, as the fruit is large and easy to pick, with a thicker skin and barely any thorns. Lisbon lemons only have a thick skin when the tree is young and growing vigorously. As the tree gets older, the skins become thinner.

Then there is the meyer lemon, a lemon that adapts particularly well to pots and comes into fruit before the Lisbon. As I write this, I am looking out of the huge picture window of my piano room and can see five mature meyer lemon trees, which are so abundant with

almost-ripe fruit that they would make a beautiful still-life painting. I'm particularly partial to the meyer lemon, especially for desserts. It is deep yellow in colour, with the smoothest skin and a handsome round shape. Although sweeter than the conventional lemon, it still has a wonderful tang. Meyer lemons sliced super-fine and similarly thin slices of fennel, dressed with peppery, green extra virgin olive oil, salt and freshly ground black pepper, make a perfect salad to serve alongside grilled quail or barbecued lamb or kid.

I've just returned from a trip to California, where meyer lemons are very popular and are used in countless dishes. Whilst there I delighted in a meyer lemon *pot au crème*, as smooth as smooth yet with a delicious bite to it, and a meyer lemon semifreddo served with berries and meyer lemon curd. Consult Alice Waters' *Chez Panisse Menu Cookbook* for lots more ideas on how to use this wonderful variety.

A handy tip for extracting more juice from a lemon or lime is to pour boiling water over the whole fruit and leave for 5 minutes before squeezing it. Or if you have a microwave, heat the fruit on medium for 1 minute and leave to cool a little before squeezing. This is a particularly handy tip for limes (as they are often sold dark green and unripe and hence yield little juice) when you require enough juice for a refreshing summer drink of lemon, lime and bitters or, after a hard day, something more exotic such as a daiquiri or a margarita.

I find so many uses for lemon rind (the coloured part of the skin, not the white pith) that I try to be disciplined enough to peel any lemon before squeezing it. If not using the rind immediately, it can be kept in castor sugar until you are ready to use it, or it can be frozen in a plastic bag. I'm partial to dried rind and use it when making game sauces, stuffing chooks, preparing soup, or making risotto. And I add a few pieces to a bath of walnut oil into which I put grilled wild mushrooms. Drying lemon rind is easy – if you don't have a dehydrator, a low 120°C oven for a few hours will do the trick, as will the hot sun in summer.

Preserved lemons are also a regular part of my cooking. It's amazing how their salty–sour flavour enhances food. I find them incredibly versatile, quite apart from their use in traditional Moroccan fare: scrape out the pulp, quickly rinse and dry the rind, then chop it finely and toss it through a salad of peppery greens; or roast quarters with a whole chook; or bake chook thighs topped with slices of preserved lemon.

I seldom cook pork without using preserved lemon, as they cut through the richness of the fatty meat, but they also work well with chicken, lamb or fish. Make a salsa verde-style sauce to serve with chicken by adding preserved lemon – but go easy on the capers to balance out the salt.

You can add preserved lemon to a warm marinade to serve with fish: cook golden shallots in wine or verjuice and a little fish stock, then reduce and add finely chopped preserved lemon rind and fresh chervil at the end of the cooking. Off the heat, swirl in some extra virgin olive oil, then pour this over grilled or pan-fried fish. Try the same with a breast of chicken, pan-fried – and with the skin on of course – using chicken stock rather than fish stock.

Stuff a whole small fish with sliced preserved lemon and fresh dill or fennel before baking it. Or rub the skin of a whole fish with the oily juices from the preserving jar, along with a little olive oil, and grill on the barbecue. Turn the fish frequently to make sure you don't burn the skin.

If you ever make labna by draining yoghurt overnight so it can be worked into small balls, try rolling the balls in a mixture of finely chopped preserved lemon, finely sliced garlic and lots of chopped flat-leaf parsley to make a sort of gremolata ball. Serve these with slow-cooked or grilled lamb or kid, and couscous or polenta. Exceptional!

Make a warm lentil salad by adding diced preserved lemon, fennel, celery and carrot to freshly cooked lentils and then toss through masses of just-plucked coriander leaves. Dress this with a vinaigrette of extra virgin olive oil and lemon juice and serve with grilled quail.

The lemons I preserve have nothing more than salt and lemon juice added. While most dishes only call for the rind, I return the flesh of the lemon back to the jar for using when I'm slow-cooking lamb shanks or making a casserole. The pulp lasts forever in a jar in the refrigerator; just remember when you use it that you probably won't need to add any extra salt to the dish, but tasting the dish will tell you.

Whether lemons are squeezed, grated, zested or preserved, the uses for them are endless. I love them best of all simply sliced thickly, brushed with oil and grilled on the barbecue, to add a sweet zestiness to grilled meat.

PRESERVED LEMONS

I love the piquant yet mellow, sweet yet sour flavours of preserved lemons. Most people use only the rind, discarding the pulp before they rinse and finely slice or chop the rind. But it's all a matter of taste. The flesh can actually be kept aside in the jar (in the oily preserving liquid) and then be added to slow-cooked casseroles, particularly if you're using pork or lamb, or rubbed over a leg of lamb before baking. I tend to add it a fair way into the cooking, and don't add any other salt.

Use unwaxed lemons for preserving. If you can't buy them this way, scrub them well with hot water first.

8 lemons

150 g coarse kitchen salt

juice of up to 4 extra lemons

bay leaf *and/or* cinnamon stick (optional)

Make the lemons as juicy as possible by warming them in the microwave for 1 minute on medium, and leaving to cool a little. Cut each lemon in quarters, but not right through, stopping 1 cm from the bottom. Place 1 tablespoon of salt in the base of the preserving jar, then push the remainder of the salt inside the cut lemons, pushing each one back into shape afterwards. Place each lemon in the jar, pressing down as firmly as possible to release the lemon juice. Squeeze as many of the other lemons as you need to immerse the lemons completely in juice.

Leave in a cool, dry place for up to 6–8 weeks, depending on the weather, for them to mature (the warmer it is, the quicker they will mature). They will keep for years – the longer you keep them, the more intense the flavour. After opening, pour a layer of olive oil over the lemons and keep them in the fridge – they will last out of the fridge, but they will oxidise.

PRESERVED LEMON VINAIGRETTE

1 preserved lemon quarter, flesh removed, rind rinsed and finely diced

⅓ cup (80 ml) extra virgin olive oil

1 tablespoon good-quality red-wine vinegar

1 teaspoon vino cotto (see Glossary) *or* balsamic vinegar

1 tablespoon torn basil leaves

freshly ground black pepper

Toss all the ingredients together, then check for seasoning (the preserved lemon will add salt).

This vinaigrette is good simply served with peppery salad greens or with grilled fish or chicken.

SPINACH WITH LEMON AND CURRANTS   *Serves 4*

This is a wonderful accompaniment to grilled red meat, chicken and of course fish. The sweet sharpness of the reconstituted currants makes a delicious addition.

1 bunch spinach (about 200 g after cleaning
    and trimming off the first 2.5 cm of stem)
⅓ cup (80 ml) extra virgin olive oil
2 cloves garlic, bruised
½ cup currants, reconstituted in verjuice *or*
    water overnight

sea salt flakes and freshly ground
    black pepper
juice of ½ lemon

Reassemble the bunch of spinach, then cut into 6 pieces, including the stems. Toss quickly in a frying pan with the olive oil and the bruised garlic cloves over high heat until the spinach is just limp. Add the currants and season. Remove from the heat and toss until well incorporated, then add the lemon juice. The spinach should be only just cooked and should retain its colour.

MEYER LEMON RISOTTO WITH MASCARPONE AND SCAMPI   *Serves 8*

1–1.5 litres ginger-based Fish Stock
    (see page 636) *or* Golden Chicken Stock
    (see page 57)
40 g butter
1 red onion, finely chopped
400 g Arborio rice (see Glossary)
½ cup (125 ml) verjuice
2 meyer lemons *or* other thin-skinned
    variety, cut into thin slices, then each
    slice cut into quarters
125 g mascarpone
1½ cups firmly packed nasturtium leaves,
    sorrel *or* baby rocket

SCAMPI
8 raw scampi, halved lengthways and
    vein removed
½ teaspoon Ceylon tea (optional)
2 tablespoons extra virgin olive oil
2 teaspoons lemon juice
sea salt flakes and freshly ground
    black pepper

Bring the stock to the boil in a saucepan; keep warm over low heat. Melt the butter in a large, heavy-based saucepan over low heat, then add the onion and sauté until translucent. Add the rice, making sure there is enough butter to coat the grains.

Turn the heat up to high and add the verjuice. Reduce the heat to low and add one ladleful of heated stock at a time, stirring often until each is absorbed. Keep a close eye on the temperature, maintaining a simmer. After about 15–20 minutes, when the rice should

Lemon tart

be close to cooked and most of the stock has been absorbed, stir in the lemon pieces and cook for another 5 minutes.

Meanwhile, for the scampi, preheat the oven to 230°C or the highest temperature possible. Either grind a little Ceylon tea to a powder by simply rubbing it between your fingers, and sprinkle it over the scampi (I learned from Tetsuya Wakuda that this brings out the sweetness), or just brush the scampi with olive oil. Place on two baking trays and cook one tray of scampi at a time for about 3 minutes. The scampi are ready as soon as they feel hot to touch; they only need to be cooked about three-quarters through, until translucent. Make a vinaigrette with a little olive oil and lemon juice and toss the scampi through, then season.

Adjust the risotto seasoning and then fold in the mascarpone and nasturtium, sorrel or rocket leaves and serve with the roasted scampi.

LEMON TART   *Serves 8*

For freshness at the end of a meal, this tart, inspired by Sydney chef Tony Bilson's recipe, never fails to delight. I bake it in a deep-sided quiche tin. The texture should be that of a very ripe brie, which depends on the number of eggs used (you can add an extra yolk, if you'd prefer a firmer set). The tart is at its best cooked just before your guests arrive so that it settles to room temperature. It is pretty terrific with clotted cream.

1 × quantity Sour-cream Pastry (see page 424)	100 ml lemon juice
	grated rind of 1 lemon
150 g castor sugar	600 ml crème fraîche
8 egg yolks	icing sugar (optional), to serve

Make and chill the pastry as instructed. Roll out the chilled dough and use to line a 20 cm flan tin with a removable base. Chill the pastry case for 20 minutes.

Preheat the oven to 200°C. Line the chilled pastry case with foil and pastry weights and blind bake for 15 minutes. Remove the foil and weights and bake for another 5 minutes.

Reduce the oven temperature to 180°C. Meanwhile, beat the sugar, egg yolks, lemon juice and rind until smooth, then fold in the crème fraîche. Fill the warm pastry case with the lemon mixture, taking care not to overfill it. Bake until set, about 25 minutes.

Serve the lemon tart lukewarm, dusted with icing sugar, if desired.

LIMES

Limes have a very special flavour of their own. They fruit at the same time as lemons and are well worth a position in the garden or in a pot, although they do not do as well in Mediterranean climates as lemons. Although limes are most successful in tropical climates, they are still worth growing, even if only in pots. Limes are aromatic and have a strange coconut smell about them. They are interchangeable with lemons for most uses, bringing an extra tang to a dish as they are stronger in flavour.

Growers of Tahitian limes are struggling with the fact that the market demands green limes. However, a green Tahitian lime is simply under-ripe, while the lime picked ripe from the tree is yellow and has so much more aroma, flavour and juice. Whilst it's handy to know that you can get more juice from an under-ripe green lime by putting it in the micro-wave, it does make you wonder why they are not sold ripe. You need to ask for ripe yellow Tahitian limes – you'll delight yourself and make the growers very happy!

Mrs Beeton's Book of Household Management has a recipe for half lemon and half lime cordial where the juice and rind are reduced on the stove with sugar to taste and then kept cold in the fridge and diluted with a jug of iced water. For those of us who love lime cordial but don't have the time to make it, there is the truly South Australian institution of Bickford's Lime Juice Cordial, widely available throughout Australia. Bickford's have been produc-ing this top-class product since 1874. The base of lime concentrate actually has to come from the West Indies because no one in Australia can supply them with adequate quanti-ties of limes. The cordial is a golden brown colour because when it was originally transported from the West Indies a hundred years ago, the limes oxidised en route, and since then the public has become familiar with this colour. Bickford's managing director suggests that to change the colour now would be like making Coca-Cola clear!

LIME VINAIGRETTE   *Makes about 375 ml*

My daughter Saskia, Victoria Blumenstein and I made this incredibly simple vinaigrette for a cooking demonstration recently, and it was extraordinarily good served with freshly sliced raw kingfish. It is also great as an all-round salad dressing, or tossed through green beans with finely chopped almonds.

1 lime	1 tablespoon chervil leaves
1 clove garlic	½ cup (125 ml) verjuice
2 tablespoons flat-leaf parsley leaves	¾ cup (180 ml) extra virgin olive oil
5–6 mint leaves	

Remove the lime rind and chop finely, then, if the lime is under-ripe, microwave it on medium for 1 minute before juicing. Combine the lime rind and juice with the remaining ingredients in a food processor, then leave to stand for 1 hour before using, to allow the flavours to develop.

SCALLOPS WITH LIME RIND AND SEA URCHIN BUTTER *Makes 24 canapés*

When planning parties I want my offerings to delight and surprise. My favourite finger food of all – well, at the moment at least – is this delicious morsel on a shell. Of course you need to be organised and have a wine bucket, or similar, to collect shells as soon as the scallops have been eaten, but that's no more trouble than having a dish for olive pips or toothpicks, and much more interesting.

I use Port Lincoln scallops – they are so sweet and nutty (as long as they haven't been frozen) when barely cooked. Sea urchin roe is now being harvested in South Australia for the first time. It has long been a delicacy in Japan and France (and probably many more places I haven't yet travelled to), but here it is still considered anything from odd to incredibly adventurous.

For me, this recipe is one of the taste sensations of my life. I always leave the brilliant orange scallop roe on, both for colour and flavour: the sea urchin butter with its slightly metallic taste (like that of an oyster) and deep ochre colour gives such a perfect finish to the scallop that I'm always left wondering whether I should actually save any for my guests.

24 Port Lincoln scallops on the half-shell,
    roe intact
finely chopped rind of 1 lime
2 tablespoons extra virgin olive oil
sea salt flakes and freshly ground
    black pepper
120 g unsalted butter
100 ml verjuice
chopped chervil, to serve

SEA URCHIN BUTTER
75 g butter, softened
roe from 2 sea urchins *or* about 2 tablespoons
    harvested sea urchin roe
sea salt flakes and freshly ground
    black pepper
1 tablespoon lime juice

To make the sea urchin butter, combine all the ingredients and set aside.

Clean the scallops by pulling the meat away from the shells and cutting out the intestinal tract. Reserve the shells, then wash and dry them. Place the scallops, lime rind and a drizzle of olive oil in a bowl and season with salt and pepper.

In a frying pan, cook the butter a tablespoon or two at a time until nut-brown, adding a dash of olive oil to inhibit burning. Seal the scallops in several batches over high heat for about 30 seconds on each side, wiping the pan clean between each batch. Do not cook too many scallops at once as you want to sear, not poach, them. When they are all cooked, wipe out any butter from the pan, then return all the scallops to the pan with half the verjuice and deglaze over high heat for just a moment. Remove the scallops and set aside, then add the rest of the verjuice and reduce to a sauce.

Preheat the oven to 220°C or a griller to high. Place a scallop on each half-shell and dot with sea urchin butter. Place in the oven or under the hot grill for about 1 minute or just until the sea urchin butter begins to melt. Sprinkle with chervil and serve with the reduced sauce.

LIME POSSET WITH LIME CONFIT

Serves 6

550 ml cream

150 g castor sugar

finely chopped rind of 2 limes

½ cup (125 ml) lime juice, strained

LIME CONFIT

660 g castor sugar

4 ripe limes, scrubbed and thinly sliced

Either limes or meyer lemons are terrific for this posset. The confit is best made with really ripe limes whose skins have turned yellow.

Combine the cream, sugar and lime rind in a saucepan, then bring to the boil over high heat and boil, stirring, for 3 minutes. Transfer to a bowl and leave to cool.

Once the cream mixture is cool, whisk in the lime juice to aerate the mixture as much as possible. Continue whipping until the mixture begins to thicken. Pour into six 100 ml-capacity cups or moulds, then chill in the refrigerator for 4–5 hours or overnight.

Meanwhile, for the lime confit, preheat the oven to 150°C. Make a sugar syrup by combining the sugar and 750 ml water in a saucepan, then stirring over low heat until the sugar dissolves. Increase the heat and simmer for 5–10 minutes or until the liquid reduces to a syrupy consistency.

Lay the lime slices in a baking dish so they are just overlapping. Pour over the sugar syrup and cover with baking paper, then cover with foil. Bake for 1 hour. Remove the foil and baking paper and return to the oven until the syrup is reduced and the limes are caramelised; this will take another 30 minutes–1 hour. Cool and then refrigerate.

Serve the lime posset topped with a little of the lime confit. Any leftover lime confit will keep well in the refrigerator for up to 1 month.

OFFAL

 **I LOVE OFFAL SO MUCH THAT I CANNOT GO PAST IT WHEN** I see it on a menu, and have even been known to have three offal entrées instead of an entrée, main course and dessert. I share this passion with a group of like-minded offal fanatics, but whilst offal certainly gladdens the 'hearts' of many, it can also be particularly divisive at the dinner table.

As much as I love it, I'm aware that you have to choose your guests carefully when you serve it as it isn't everyone's cup of tea. Offal is far from revered in Australia, but for me it's an absolute favourite.

During the first Slow Food Convivium in the Barossa in 2004, my daughter Saskia and I prepared an offal brunch featuring six different offal dishes, all matched with magnificent wines from Seppelt's Winery. The dishes ranged from brains in a burnt-butter sauce, lemon and capers, to braised pig's ears stuffed with sweetbreads and mushrooms (a dish firmly embedded in my taste memory from the moment I first had it at Berowra Waters Inn what seems like a lifetime ago now, cooked by the incredible Janni Kyritsis).

This was such a success that we did it again for the March 2006 Barossa Slow feast, with the help of Richard Gunner of Coorong Angus Beef, who not only assisted, but supplied the offal. This time the six different offal-based dishes started with rabbit liver crostini with vino cotto and onion jam, progressing to lamb kidneys wrapped in *crépine* (caul fat), and then finishing with slow-braised intercostals (the rich meat between the ribs) in shiraz.

Generally I find the most adventurous eaters are offal lovers. In France, offal reigns supreme as a delicacy; the French word for it is *abat*, from 'abattoir'. The French are wonderfully resourceful in using every part of the animal. Because there is only a small amount of offal per animal and it is so highly prized, offal is quite expensive in France (and in Italy), whereas in Australia it is an amazing bargain for the cook.

Your attitude to offal as food will often depend on your upbringing – it was the very first food I learnt to cook. Many Australians shun it, however I have heard that some abattoir workers who understood the attraction of offal used to take home special 'treats' such as sweetbreads and calves' brains. These days, things are much more regulated, supposedly for our safety, and abattoirs must have special rooms if they want to keep the offal, otherwise they are forced to throw it away. (Although as the whole of the abattoir should be hygienic, I do not understand how offal dissected in a separate room makes it 'safer' for us.) As a result, offal is relatively scarce – for example, pig's ears are hard to find, but are still available if you organise yourself in advance; always try a Chinese butcher. A suckling pig served at a feast doesn't look the same minus the ears, so take the trouble to order your pig intact from a specialist source. Many years ago now, for our tenth anniversary party at the Pheasant Farm Restaurant, I had Schulz's Butchers of Angaston pickle a whole pig for me to serve as the centrepiece of the banquet. It was delivered *sans* ears not long before proceedings began, so some deftly draped grape leaves had to suffice for ears. It didn't spoil the taste, but often the visual effect is also important.

Our sensibilities seem to call for subtle euphemisms for the more confronting organ meats. We call lamb's liver 'lamb's fry' and bull's testicles 'prairie oysters', while the thymus gland and pancreas become 'sweetbreads'; at least an ear is an ear, when you can get it.

There are so many possibilities with offal that are such delicacies to the initiated. There is the heart, which you can stuff; the caul fat or *crépine* (the lining of a pig's stomach), which you can wrap delicate food in before baking or pan-frying; kidneys, which can be grilled or roasted, either encased in their own fat, or trimmed and sliced.

Pig's ears make the most wonderful eating, braised slowly in stock, cooled and then stuffed with sweetbreads or chicken, dipped in egg and breadcrumbs and baked dotted with butter. Pig's trotters are essential to my stock-making but I also love them slowly braised and served with lentils. I think my favourite offal is sweetbreads – I prefer calf's to sheep's, as the tiny lamb sweetbreads lack the nutty characteristics of the veal ones.

Then there is tongue, which was a firm favourite on my restaurant's menu. I often served it brined and smoked (from Schulz's Butchers), simmered gently with stock vegetables and light veal stock until soft to the touch. I simply let it cool a little, enough to be able to handle it, peeled and sliced it while still warm, then served it with pesto or a salsa verde. If you want to prepare it in advance, cut it into slices and cover with plastic film until you are ready to use it, then quickly toss it in a tiny bit of butter in a heavy-based pan over high heat. This caramelises the tongue, which is fabulous served with a salsa verde or pickled plums.

As a child I could never bear to even look at tripe in the traditional white sauce. Then years ago, in a session on rice at a Melbourne Masterclass, Stefano de Pieri cooked a tripe risotto. He had talked to me about it before and I suggested tripe might be too divisive, but he charged ahead and I had to eat my words. He used veal tripe, a delicacy in itself, and softened it further by making the risotto with milk (as often served to children in kindergartens in Italy). He braised the tripe with tomatoes for seven hours and then added this

Brains in caper butter (see page 452)

fragrant stew to the risotto. The two dishes could have been eaten separately, Stefano said, but he combined them as an alternative to the much-maligned tripe in white sauce. There must have been 150 people in the audience, and everyone seemed willing to give the tripe a go – so much for my prediction.

Lamb's brains are among the most accessible and delicious of all offal. The secret is to deal with a good butcher who will supply you with rosy-pink, fresh (or freshly frozen but not yet thawed) brains if you order well in advance. They must be cooked as soon as they thaw out if frozen, or within a day of buying them fresh from the butcher. But before they can be cooked, they must be soaked: soaking the brains in lightly salted water for a few hours gets rid of the blood.

BRAINS IN CAPER BUTTER

Serves 6 as an entrée

A trick to maintain the shape of the brains during poaching is to wrap each one in a small rectangle of foil, twisting each end like a Christmas bon-bon.

6 sets brains	sea salt flakes and freshly ground
1 dessertspoon lemon juice	black pepper
1 bay leaf	30 g capers
pinch black peppercorns	1 tablespoon freshly chopped
70 g butter	flat-leaf parsley

The brains should be very fresh – shiny and sweet smelling. Soak them in lightly salted water for several hours before use. Wrap each brain in foil so that they keep their shape while cooking.

Place the parcels in a saucepan of water with a little of the lemon juice added, the bay leaf and a few peppercorns. Start off the poaching in cold water then bring to a simmer over medium–high heat. The cooking time depends on how 'done' you like them (I like them only just set, which takes about 12 minutes). Take the brains out of the water and leave them to set overnight in the refrigerator before unwrapping, then cut in half lengthways. I usually find that by cooling and cutting them in half, then frying them cut-side down, the brains need absolutely no trimming.

Put the butter into a large frying pan and allow it to turn nut-brown over high heat with a touch of extra virgin olive oil to prevent burning. Seal the brains on their cut side. Be careful not to have too many in the pan at once or they will poach and turn soggy. As soon as they brown, turn them over. While the pan is still on the heat, season with salt and pepper. Add capers and parsley and deglaze with remaining lemon juice. Serve immediately.

TRIPE WITH SURPRISE PEAS, VERJUICE AND PANCETTA

Serves 6–8 (it's very rich)

When we decided to do a segment on tripe for the TV series *The Cook and The Chef* last winter, I wanted to cook a very different tripe dish to any I'd done before, to show that there was great potential in combining tripe with different flavours. It was suggested that we should set up a stall at the Barossa Farmer's Market one Saturday morning and offer the general public a taste of tripe, to see if anyone was game to try it.

It was one of those wonderful occasions when I suspect the producers expected people to be horrified or, at the least, put off by the idea of the dish, but they underestimated the people of the Valley and their interest in food. We set up a trestle table, handwrote a sign that said 'Tripe cooked in verjuice with peas and pancetta', and offered to give passers-by a taste. I was bowled over by the number of people who said, 'I've never been keen to taste tripe but I'll have a go.' We got a great reaction to it, and most people loved the dish, with

Tripe with Surprise peas, verjuice and pancetta

only a couple of exceptions. The most delightful thing of all, though, was the number of children who tasted it and loved it – you couldn't fake a child's reaction if you tried, and there for all to see were these youngsters hoeing in and coming back for more!

1 kg honeycomb tripe (ask your butcher for partially cooked tripe)
1 tablespoon butter
extra virgin olive oil, for cooking
8 small leeks, white part only, sliced into rings
1½ cups (375 ml) verjuice
2 tablespoons chopped lemon thyme
3 cups (750 ml) chicken stock
sea salt flakes and freshly ground black pepper
1 cup Surprise peas
12 thin slices pancetta

Soak the tripe in cold water for about 30 minutes before cooking. Drain and dry thoroughly, then cut into 2 cm × 3 cm strips. Heat butter in a large saucepan over medium–high heat until nut-brown, add a dash of olive oil to prevent burning, then add the tripe and seal on all sides until well-coloured. Remove the tripe and set it aside. Add the leeks and cook for about 10 minutes or until the leeks are just soft. Return the tripe to the pan. Deglaze the pan with verjuice over high heat, then add the lemon thyme and chicken stock and season to taste with salt and pepper.

Reduce the heat to low, then simmer gently, covered with a tight-fitting lid, for about 75 minutes. Add peas and cook over high heat for another 30 minutes or until the liquid has reduced and is syrupy. Adjust seasoning if desired.

Meanwhile, preheat the oven to 200°C. Lay pancetta on a baking tray and bake for about 10 minutes or until crisp.

Garnish tripe with the slices of crisp pancetta and serve.

TRIPE WITH TOMATOES AND OLIVES   *Serves 6*

This recipe is inspired by 'Tripe Prepared My Way' by Antonio Carluccio, in *An Invitation to Italian Cooking*. It was the dish that converted me! The slow-cooking in tomatoes and wine is light years away from the hated tripe and white sauce of my childhood.

1 kg honeycomb tripe, cut into 2 cm pieces
2 carrots, roughly chopped
3 celery stalks, roughly chopped
3 onions, roughly chopped
2 cloves garlic, thinly sliced
extra virgin olive oil, for cooking
2 sprigs oregano, chopped
2 sprigs rosemary, chopped
1 cup (250 ml) red wine
2 × 400 g cans chopped Italian tomatoes
100 ml Golden Chicken Stock (see page 57)
sea salt flakes and freshly ground black pepper
120 g kalamata olives, pitted
⅓ cup freshly chopped flat-leaf parsley

Most butchers sell tripe blanched and already partially cooked. If your tripe has not been prepared in this way, it needs to be boiled several times, in fresh water each time – giving the tripe about an hour's cooking time in total before proceeding with the recipe.

Toss the carrots, celery, onions and garlic with a little olive oil in a large frying pan over high heat until softened, then remove from the pan and set aside. In the same pan, toss the tripe with the oregano and rosemary in a little more oil. Add the wine and tomatoes and reduce rapidly.

Add the chicken stock and simmer, uncovered, over low heat for about 1 hour. Season with salt and pepper, then add the olives in the last few minutes. Serve with lots of chopped flat-leaf parsley.

GRILLED INTERCOSTALS

Serves 4–6

As mentioned, intercostals are the muscles which sit between the ribs and hold the lungs in place. The membrane on the inside of the intercostals needs to be trimmed off; the meat can then be chargrilled, stir-fried or braised. Their flavour is fairly rich and almost gamy.

6 intercostals

cornflour, for dusting

2 sprigs rosemary, leaves removed and
  finely chopped

6 bamboo skewers, soaked in cold water
  for 30 minutes

½ cup (125 ml) extra virgin olive oil

2 tablespoons red-wine vinegar

sea salt flakes and freshly ground
  black pepper

Trim away the inside membrane from the intercostals.

Preheat a chargrill plate over high heat until very hot. Combine the cornflour and rosemary, then dust the meat with the cornflour mixture. Thread the meat onto the skewers, then grill on each side for 3 minutes or until well-browned. Place in a dish with the olive oil and red-wine vinegar and leave to rest for 10 minutes. Season to taste with salt and pepper and serve.

ONIONS

OF ALL THE VEGETABLES WE EAT, ONIONS ARE PROBABLY THE most ubiquitous, and so we often forget that they, too, have their own season. Onions are at their best in autumn and winter, although, given the vastness of this country and the variations in climate, this season can be extended significantly.

For most of my cooking needs, I insist on clean, shiny, firm golden-brown onions, but I know that at certain times of the year, such as early spring when only the last of the season's onions are left, these are hard to come by. (Especially if you are a pâté producer, and use some 250 kg of onions each week – and even more now that we make caramelised onion commercially.) It is at this time that onions can start revealing the inner green shoot that signals they are past their best. These onions can still be eaten but can give a bitterness to dishes: the green is simply the leaf forming for the next planting (and a sprouting onion can in fact be planted) but its presence is a reminder of how we demand produce year-round without a thought for the seasons. For a food producer it means changing recipes to accommodate the difference in the onions or, as we do for our caramelised onion, stockpiling supplies for several months so we never have to use inferior onions. Not an easy logistical matter.

Shallots, golden shallots or eschallots (depending on which state you live in) are formed in small clusters a little like garlic and have a flavour that is reminiscent of both onion and garlic. They are naturally sweet and wonderful caramelised: cover the base of a tiny saucepan with peeled shallots, then dot them with butter and add a touch of sugar before covering them with a little water. Bring the pan to the boil with the lid off to reduce the liquid, tossing the shallots to make sure they all become glazed.

I like using raw red Spanish onions in a salsa. I love it even more if they are finely diced and cooked for just a few minutes in butter or extra virgin olive oil; I deglaze the pan with lemon juice, which turns the onion dice a brilliant crimson so that they look like sparkling jewels.

At home I store my onions in a string bag hanging on a nail in our garage. This not only keeps them in the dark, which slows deterioration, but also prevents their odour permeating the kitchen. Actually it is only when an onion is cut that its odour becomes truly penetrating. I refuse to leave a partially used onion anywhere in the house, even wrapped in plastic film in the refrigerator, much to my husband Colin's frustration.

I have peeled a lot of onions in my time and have been given masses of advice on how to make it a less distressing job: under running water, with goggles on, under the canopy of a strong exhaust fan (this last one really works too, as long as the stove isn't on at the same time) and so on. The variety used and time of year also have a bearing on how tear-provoking the onions will be, and some people are just more susceptible than others.

In the days when we made our pâté in a small room on the farm within sight of the restaurant, I found the best way to deal with the masses of onions needed was to do the job outside. The pâté-making girls, Esther and Rita, and I would sit on boxes and peel the onions together, unconsciously pitting ourselves against each other, and the fresh air and sunshine really helped. The trick is to use a very small and sharp serrated knife. If you have to cut the onion in half anyway, do so with the skin on, then it's simply a matter of prising off the skin and the outside layer of the onion at the same time. (Before my conscience pricks me, or my trusted pâté room lieutenants laugh heartily, I should declare that I don't do much peeling of onions these days, but I did my fair share back then.) Now that we have the state-of-the-art export kitchen in Tanunda we are actually not allowed to peel onions on the premises because of a possible mould under the skin, so we have to buy them in already peeled. Things continually change.

The aroma of onions frying immediately makes me feel hungry, no matter when I last ate. But the most luscious of all is slow-cooked onion: the transformation from crisp and sharp to caramelised and sweet is hard to credit. Use warm Caramelised Onion (see page 461) to line a just-baked pastry case (the Sour-cream Pastry on page 424 is good for this), then dot it with goat's cheese or gorgonzola and return it to a 180°C oven for 10 minutes to warm through and melt the cheese. Serve the tart (or individual tarts) with a salad of peppery greens and lunch is ready.

Caramelised onion makes an excellent base for a barbecued meal, too. Cook a kangaroo fillet, brushed with extra virgin olive oil and seasoned with freshly ground black pepper, for a couple of minutes a side on a hot barbecue. Allow the meat to rest for 5–10 minutes before serving it with caramelised onion and a dish of soft polenta or creamy mashed potato.

Sofregit, another slow-cooked onion preparation, has been part of Catalan cuisine since medieval times, and is something I have found invaluable in the cooking of game. There is nothing better than a camp oven for cooking sofregit. Pour extra virgin olive oil into the camp oven to a depth of about a centimetre, then add three finely chopped large onions and put the pot on the slowest possible burner. Stir the onion now and again – it may take an hour or more to colour. Tomatoes, garlic and leeks or lemon can also be added, but it is the slow cooking of the onion that makes the dish. I often add chopped garlic and grated lemon rind after the onions have collapsed and then use this mixture as a base in which to pot-roast older game, usually with the addition of fresh herbs and maybe stock, wine or verjuice.

Renowned Spanish cookery writer Néstor Luján, quoted in Colman Andrews' *Catalan Cuisine*, says that the onions in a sofregit 'should ideally reach the strange and mysterious colour that, in the School of Venice, the brushstrokes of the great master Titian obtained', which is a perfect description of the colour I look for.

Sofregit can become a topping for a flatbread, pissaladière or focaccia. Prepare the dough for the Flatbread (see page 414), then just before baking cover it liberally with sofregit. Add a tablespoon of torn basil leaves, then drizzle extra virgin olive oil over and sprinkle on some sea salt flakes. To make a pissaladière, arrange a pattern of anchovies and olives on top of the flatbread (on a traditional pissaladière the anchovies are criss-crossed to make a diamond pattern and the olives are centred in each diamond).

A caramelised onion or onion marmalade or jam can be made using much the same method as for sofregit. While thickly sliced onion is slowly cooking, add sugar, then stir in red-wine vinegar to counteract the sweetness. Caramelised onion or onion marmalade is a perfect accompaniment to duck confit or any grilled or barbecued meat. Peeled and sliced quince can be added, when in season, and will cook slowly with the onion and almost melt into a purée. This quince version is especially good with pork of any kind.

A rabbit dish I used to serve in the restaurant included tiny onions that had been caramelised in some verjuice and a little butter. The combination gave a delightful sweet–sour piquancy. The idea could be extended by adding muscatels and roasted pine nuts to the onions and serving the lot with a roasted chicken – or pot-roast the chicken with the same ingredients and some stock.

Try baking large red onions for 45 minutes to 1 hour at 180°C, then cut them in half and remove their centres. Purée the centres and mix with mustard mayonnaise, fresh bread-crumbs, lots of flat-leaf parsley and chopped anchovies. Pile the mixture back into the onion halves and serve them at room temperature as an entrée.

Baby onions roasted in vino cotto

CARAMELISED ONION SALAD

Serves 4 as an accompaniment

Although the onions for this dish need long, slow cooking, they can be prepared in advance and left at room temperature. This salad is wonderful with tongue or grilled steak or sausages. If you are using the caramelised onion in a tart, as suggested on page 458, you may want to exclude the dressing. You might need to warm the tart without the cheese first if the onion is at room temperature rather than hot.

5 large onions

2 sprigs rosemary, leaves stripped

100 ml extra virgin olive oil

1 clove garlic, finely chopped

2 teaspoons balsamic vinegar

2 tablespoons freshly chopped
flat-leaf parsley

sea salt flakes and freshly ground
black pepper

Preheat the oven to 150°C. Trim the ends of each onion, leaving the skins on, then cut the onions into 1 cm-thick slices. Mix the rosemary with 2 tablespoons of the olive oil.

Line a shallow, heavy-based roasting pan with baking paper, then brush this and both sides of the onion slices with the rosemary oil. Bake the onions for 30 minutes, then check whether they are starting to colour. When the onions are a deep caramel colour turn with a spatula and discard any burnt pieces. Remove the pan from the oven when all the onion has caramelised on both sides. This can take between 1 and 2 hours. Allow the onions to cool a little, then remove the skins and place the onions in a serving dish.

Mix the remaining olive oil with the garlic, vinegar, parsley, salt and pepper and pour over the onions while they are still warm. Serve at room temperature.

BABY ONIONS ROASTED IN VINO COTTO

Serves 4 as an accompaniment

500 g baby onions, outer skin removed

¼ cup (60 ml) extra virgin olive oil

½ cup (125 ml) vino cotto (see Glossary)

sea salt flakes and freshly ground
black pepper

sprigs of lemon thyme, to garnish

Preheat the oven to 120°C. Cut the onions in half. Line a roasting pan with a large piece of foil (enough to fold over the onions), then place the onions in the centre of the foil. Whisk together the oil and vino cotto and pour over the onions, then season. Fold the foil over the onions and seal to form a parcel, then roast for 2 hours or until the onions are soft.

Increase the oven temperature to 200°C. Open the foil parcel then return the pan to the oven for a further 10 minutes, to caramelise the onions. Garnish with lemon thyme and serve as an accompaniment to roasted or grilled meats or fish, or dot with goat's cheese and flat-leaf parsley and serve with crusty bread.

SQUID WITH ONION, PARSLEY AND ANCHOVY STUFFING *Serves 4*

4 × 300 g squid
4 onions, finely chopped
extra virgin olive oil, for cooking
10 g fresh white breadcrumbs
1 cup freshly chopped flat-leaf parsley
4–6 anchovy fillets, finely chopped
sea salt flakes and freshly ground
   black pepper

100 g thinly sliced mild pancetta
4 handfuls mixed baby lettuce leaves,
   washed and dried

VINAIGRETTE
60 ml extra virgin olive oil
1 tablespoon red-wine vinegar

Clean each squid by first removing the head and tentacles. Pull and twist the tentacles away from the body – you will find the guts will come away too. Chop off the tentacles and discard the head, guts and cartilage. Peel the skin from the body and tentacles under running water, then finely chop the tentacles.

Sauté the onions gently in a little olive oil in a frying pan over medium heat until softened and translucent. Drain off the oil and mix the onion with the chopped tentacles, bread-crumbs, parsley and anchovies, then season with salt and pepper. Stuff the squid tubes two-thirds full (the tubes will shrink during cooking) and close the ends with toothpicks. Pour the olive oil into a heavy-based enamelled casserole to a depth of 1 cm, then place the stuffed squid in the oil in one layer. Braise the squid, covered, over low heat for 5–10 minutes until the side in the oil is opaque, then turn the squid over and cook the second side for another 5–10 minutes. Remove the squid and allow to cool to room tempera-ture. Return the squid to the cooled oil to keep moist until required.

Preheat the oven to 220°C and crisp the pancetta on a baking tray (this can also be done in a dry frying pan over high heat). When you are ready to serve, arrange the lettuce leaves on serving plates and cut the squid into 1 cm slices. Add the squid and crisped pancetta to the lettuce, then dress with a vinaigrette made with the extra virgin olive oil and red-wine vinegar. Serve immediately.

ORANGES

THE FRAGRANCE OF ORANGES IS BEAUTIFULLY HEADY – FROM the once traditional orange blossoms at weddings, to the juicy, thirst-quenching orange of the sports field. Remember that squirt of juice cooling your overheated body, your nose buried sensuously in the flesh as you gulped every bit of juice, drained it and grabbed the next quarter? When I am in the kitchen zesting a juicy orange and the citrussy tang sprays in my face like champagne, I'm often reminded of 'quarter time' as a teenager playing hockey.

Although oranges are available throughout the year, they are at their best in winter from our local crops. Navels come on the market about the last week in May and are available until August. They have no pips and a thick skin that makes them easier to peel, and are sweeter than the Valencia, whose green-tinged skin is a characteristic of the variety, not an indicator of ripeness. The Valencia has pips and a thinner skin, and is the best orange for juicing (that is, unless you are lucky enough to have a surfeit of blood oranges), and the juice keeps well for days. The Valencia arrives in August and lasts right through until the following April. It's one of the great sights and smells to drive through the Riverland in South Australia when the groves are heavy with fruit; the trees in flower at the same time produce the most heavenly scent in the air.

Blood oranges, when dark red inside, are the sweetest of all oranges, but with a refreshing tang. Juiced, they are absolutely delicious. They are harder to grow to a size deemed acceptable for sale in supermarkets, and are also very climate-specific. They are therefore expensive and not widely available, and their colour and quality can be erratic.

There is no doubt that citrus fruit is better in some years than others, particularly when it comes to the colour of the blood orange. I have a blood orange tree grown in a pot that took several years to develop colour. I became convinced that its colour improved with age, and was looking forward to this year's crop as last year's was the best ever, but there's hardly a stain of red to be seen. So it seems the Barossa climate is a bit hit-and-miss for this wonderful fruit. Even without the ruby red colour, though, I love its flavour, sweet yet sharp.

It has taken years for blood oranges to become generally available, and I don't think I'll ever lose the excitement I feel when I see them. Nor will I ever tire of maltaise sauce, a hollandaise mixed with blood orange juice. The sharpness of the juice cuts the richness of the butter wonderfully. Make a maltaise mayonnaise by adding the finely grated rind and juice of two blood oranges to your homemade mayonnaise. Freeze the juice and grated rind so that you can try maltaise sauce with the first asparagus of the season, or the mayonnaise with cold poached chicken in spring. Or try a glass of blood orange juice, Campari and ice. It is one time I wish the seasons were reversed as it would so suit a hot summer's day. A jug of this heady mixture brought out as the sun sets really fits the bill.

One of the most successful, and indeed the most beautifully shaped, citrus trees in my orchard is the poor man's orange. The rind of this fruit is an amazing addition to my game pies all winter long. It deserves a place in any garden simply for its looks: its strong, bold trunk supports symmetrical leaves and large, thick-skinned, flat-topped, deep-orange fruit.

Arabs first planted the bitter orange in Seville in Spain during the seventh century. Today huge commercial groves there supply fruit for the English marmalade market. While the first Australian Seville oranges were listed as being grown in the Sydney Botanic Gardens as early as 1828, today very few are grown commercially, even though the trees withstand frost better than the more readily available oranges. The Seville is the most aromatic member of the citrus family.

Seville oranges are available in South Australia from July to the beginning of September. They are hard to find – and they are definitely not an orange to pluck heavy off the tree and eat fresh. But if you love your marmalade they are worth seeking out, or try growing your own if the climate in your area is suitable. They tend to be smaller and very deep-coloured, with more pips than you want to know about, but the intense bitter flavour makes the best marmalade ever (see page 471) – although cumquat marmalade runs a close second. Our Maggie Beer Seville Marmalade now has an amazing following and our orchardist is in planting mode.

Although Sevilles make a wonderfully bitter marmalade, it's a tricky preserve to make in anything but small to middling quantities, and as the citrus industry is as susceptible to changing fashions as any other, you may not find the marmalade readily available. If you are a real marmalade freak and can't track down one of the small handful of almost 'cottage' producers, then you will probably need to make your own. It is well worth doing – just 2 kg of fruit will give you a good supply.

I love all citrus. The length of time the fruit will hang on the tree until I need it makes it so accessible. Being loathe to waste a thing, if I haven't used all the fruit before it starts to get blousy with age, I'll have a cook-in and candy the rind, then squeeze the juice to freeze and use when cooking Muscovy duck or guinea fowl, which I love to serve with sauce bigarde.

To make sauce bigarde, heat some unsalted butter in a saucepan until nut-brown, then add an equal quantity of plain flour and cook, stirring, for several minutes until golden brown.

Add enough verjuice to make a smooth paste, then gradually stir in some chicken stock. Bring the sauce to the boil, simmer and reduce to whatever consistency you prefer. Peel a few Sevilles (or poor man's oranges, or a couple of small navels and a lemon) and cut the rind into fine strips. Put the rind into a saucepan and just cover with water, then boil until tender. Drain the rind, then add it to the sauce. Squeeze the oranges and add the strained juice to the sauce, then taste for seasoning and add another tablespoon of butter just before serving.

The thick, aromatic skin of the poor man's orange and Seville orange are superior for candying. If you have ever tried candied orange peel in Italy you'll know what I'm talking about – it is simply amazing, and you'll never be able to make do with commercial peel again.

To make candied Seville orange peel, cut young, sound fruit in half lengthways. Leaving the pith attached to the peel, remove the flesh. Put the peel into a heavy-based enamelled or stainless steel saucepan and cover it with water, then bring to the boil. Pour off the water and repeat this process twice to remove unwanted bitterness. Drain the peel well and weigh it, then return the peel to the saucepan with an equal weight of sugar. Starting over a low heat, dissolve the sugar and then simmer until the peel is translucent – this may take up to 1 hour. Drain the peel from the syrup and spread it on a cake rack to dry. Turn daily until dried, then store in an airtight container. With a quality dark chocolate, this peel is one of the great flavour combinations.

Orange rind contains a natural sunscreen, so when the rind is exposed to too much sun it will naturally turn green, while the fruit inside is mature and ripe to eat. This often causes problems when marketing the fruit, as consumers assume the green-tinged orange is not ripe. To counter this, as Lee Byrne from Australian Citrus Growers explained to me, both navels and Valencias are gassed with ethylene, a natural plant hormone that affects the growth, development and ripening of all plants. This gas changes the colour of the rind from green to an all-over orange, yet doesn't affect the maturity or taste of the fruit.

As with most foods, if you buy in the peak season, the fruit is at its best flavour and lowest price. There is some flavour variation in quality of crop from year to year, but the yield and size for the grower varies a lot, particularly with Sevilles.

Like the grape industry, the citrus industry has gone through peaks and troughs, but once again times are difficult for the grower. News abounds of tonnes of oranges being fed to cattle as the industry struggles to compete with foreign imports. We should be doing everything we can to protect our local industry by eating more oranges, as it will be our loss if the growers give up and opt for a more reliable crop. When buying orange juice, look for a label that says '100% Australian orange juice'. Labelling regulations now make it mandatory to clearly declare if juice has been reconstituted from imported frozen concentrate.

The vitality of orange makes it a very important ingredient in my cooking. It marries so well with guinea fowl and, of course, duck. I use orange juice in my everyday marinades for pheasant and put the rind into my game pies. I make pasta with orange rind, as well as salads, cakes and desserts. I add orange rind to the perfect scrambled eggs or when serving kalamata or green olives tossed in extra virgin olive oil.

CHICKEN WINGS WITH ORANGE PEEL

Serves 6–8

2 teaspoons Sichuan peppercorns

rind of 2 oranges, removed in strips
   with a potato peeler

2 cloves garlic, finely chopped

2 teaspoons minced fresh ginger

2 golden shallots, finely chopped

2 tablespoons soy sauce

¼ cup (60 ml) peanut oil

¼ cup (60 ml) sesame oil

2 kg (about 20–30) chicken wings

Preheat the oven to 220°C. Roast the peppercorns in a dry frying pan until fragrant, then crush using a mortar and pestle. Make a marinade by mixing together all the ingredients except the chicken wings. Place the chicken wings in a large bowl or ceramic dish, cover with the marinade and leave in the refrigerator to marinate for 4 hours.

Place the chicken wings and marinade in a baking dish, then roast for 12 minutes or until the chicken wings are golden and cooked, being careful they don't burn. Rest for 10 minutes before serving.

ROAST DUCK WITH SEVILLE ORANGE, APPLE, PRUNE AND PROSCIUTTO STUFFING

Serves 4

15 g butter

90 g duck *or* chicken livers, cleaned

100 ml extra virgin olive oil, plus extra
   (optional)

1 large onion, finely chopped

finely chopped rind and juice
   of 1 Seville orange

⅓ cup flat-leaf parsley, finely chopped

1 tablespoon finely chopped rosemary

1 tablespoon finely chopped thyme

1½ cups coarse breadcrumbs, toasted

65 g prosciutto, chopped

2 tablespoons pistachios

sea salt flakes and freshly ground
   black pepper

1 × 2.5 kg duck

1 tablespoon finely chopped rosemary

Preheat the oven to 150°C. Melt the butter in a frying pan over medium heat, then add the livers and seal until golden brown on the outside but still very pink in the middle. Remove the pan from the heat, transfer the livers to a large bowl and leave to rest for 5 minutes then, when cool, cut them into large pieces and return them to the bowl. Add 80 ml of the olive oil to the pan, then cook the onion over medium heat for 5 minutes or until golden. Deglaze the pan with most of the orange juice.

Add the orange rind, herbs, breadcrumbs, prosciutto, pistachios and onion to the bowl with the livers, then season with salt and pepper. Fill the cavity of the duck with the stuffing, then place on a trivet in a roasting pan (or you could make a bed of thick slices of potato to soak up the roasting juices). Prick the breast skin, then rub in rosemary, 1 tablespoon salt and the remaining olive oil.

Roast the duck for 1 hour, then reduce the oven temperature to 120°C and roast for another 1½–2 hours; the meat should be soft to the touch. Remove the pan from the oven, then drain the pan juices into a tall jar and place in the freezer for 20 minutes to solidify the fat.

Meanwhile, if the skin isn't caramelised, increase the oven temperature to 210°C. Brush the skin with some combined orange juice and olive oil and return to the oven for 10 minutes or until caramelised.

Remove the duck from the oven and leave to rest for 20 minutes, breast-side down, in the roasting pan. Meanwhile, remove the fat from the pan juices then place the juices in a saucepan and reduce over high heat until syrupy. Remove the stuffing from the cavity. Carve the breast from the bone and remove the legs. Serve a quarter of the duck per person with some stuffing and a little of the reduced pan juices.

OLIVE OIL BRIOCHE WITH CANDIED SEVILLE PEEL *Makes 2*

1 cup (250 ml) warm water

1½ teaspoons castor sugar

15 g fresh yeast *or* 1 teaspoon dried yeast

675 g unbleached strong flour (see Glossary)

3 × 55 g free-range eggs

¼ cup (60 ml) extra virgin olive oil

3 teaspoons salt

1 cup candied Seville peel (see page 467), roughly chopped

1 free-range egg yolk

1 tablespoon milk

In a bowl, combine the warm water, castor sugar, yeast and 2 tablespoons of the flour and whisk to combine. Set aside for 5–10 minutes or until frothy.

Whisk the eggs, then add the olive oil and stir to combine. Combine the remaining flour and the salt in a large bowl and make a well. Combine the yeast and egg mixtures and pour into the well. With your hands, gently fold in the flour until everything is combined and the dough starts to form a ball. Add the candied peel to the dough.

Turn the dough out onto a floured bench and knead for 10 minutes until soft and satiny, adding a little extra flour if it becomes too sticky. Return the dough to the bowl and cover tightly with plastic film, then refrigerate for 12 hours until doubled in volume.

Remove the dough from the refrigerator and let it return to room temperature (this will take about 1 hour). Knead the dough lightly for 1–2 minutes, then divide it into 2 portions and put into greased loaf tins or large brioche moulds. (This dough does not need to be knocked back – dough with a higher fat content struggles to rise again if knocked back.) Leave to rise in a draught-free spot for about 40 minutes or until it is 1½ times its original volume.

Preheat the oven to 220°C. Mix the egg yolk with the milk and brush this over the tops of the loaves. Bake for 10 minutes, then reduce the temperature to 180°C and bake for another 20 minutes. Turn the loaves out onto a wire rack and leave to cool.

ORANGE AND ALMOND TART

Serves 8

1 × quantity Sour-cream Pastry (see page 424)	50 g plain flour, sifted
150 g almonds	finely grated rind and juice of 1 orange
150 g castor sugar	2 tablespoons lemon juice
200 g butter	8 egg yolks
	mascarpone, to serve

Make and chill the pastry as instructed. Roll out the chilled dough and use to line a 25 cm tart tin with a removable base. Chill the pastry case for 20 minutes.

Preheat the oven to 200°C. Line the chilled pastry case with foil, then weight it with pastry weights and blind bake for 15 minutes. Remove the foil and weights and bake for another 5 minutes. Roast the almonds on a baking tray for 6–8 minutes, cool and grind them in a food processor.

Using an electric mixer, cream the castor sugar and butter until pale and then slowly, with the mixer on medium speed, add the ground almonds. Add the flour, orange rind and juice, then add the lemon juice and one egg yolk at a time, beating well after each addition. Pour the mixture into the pastry shell and bake for 30–45 minutes. The mixture should still be a little wobbly when taken out of the oven. Allow to cool a little and serve with mascarpone.

MARMALADE-À-LA-LIZZY

Makes 2 × 380 ml jars

Before I found my Seville orange grower, my favourite marmalade was a recipe given to me by an old friend by the name of Liz, with whom I've since lost contact. Another very special friend, Hilda Laurencis, who worked with me for years, always saw that my larder was well stocked with this marmalade. This is Hilda's version of Marmalade-à-la-Lizzy – a runny but wonderfully flavoured marmalade. It's the nicest way to start the day.

The whisky gives it that bitter edge (and a kick, of course) if you can't find Sevilles.

6 oranges, thinly sliced	900 g sugar
3 lemons, thinly sliced	1 cup (250 ml) whisky

Combine all the ingredients, except the whisky, in a large heavy-based saucepan or preserving pan, adding enough water to cover. Boil over high heat until the marmalade reaches setting point. Test by putting a spoonful of marmalade on a saucer in the refrigerator for a few minutes. If it wrinkles when you push it with your finger, the marmalade is ready. Cool a little, then add the whisky. Stir well and transfer to sterilised glass jars (see Glossary).

SEVILLE ORANGE MARMALADE

Makes 8 × 300 g jars

Marmalade is perhaps the most difficult preserve to make. Buy unwaxed fruit if you can, and do not refrigerate it. Although it is a fairly painstaking process, there is no substitute for hand-cutting the fruit to make a really great marmalade.

The trick is to cook the marmalade at as high a heat as possible; the quicker it reaches its setting point, the fresher the flavour will be. Marmalade is very susceptible to overcooking, leading to a caramelised quality that lacks the freshness of citrus.

Having said that, a marmalade should always be cooked until the rind of the oranges is soft to the touch but still intact. Adding lemon juice increases the natural pectin content, and as much of a problem as pips can be, these contain much-needed pectin too, so they are a necessary evil.

This is a marmalade that responds particularly well to being cooked in a pressure cooker, following the manufacturer's instructions carefully.

2 kg Seville oranges
1.4 kg sugar

juice of 1 lemon

Cut tops and bottoms off the oranges and discard. Slice fruit into thin rounds. Cover with 1 litre of water and leave to soak overnight, weighted down so all the fruit is immersed but only just covered. If you can, separate the pips as you cut, gather them together in a muslin bag and add to the soaking fruit; there will always be a pip or two that gets through!

The next day, transfer the oranges, soaking water and bag of pips to a heavy-based saucepan. Cook over high heat until the rind is just tender.

Heat the sugar in a preserving pan over low heat to dissolve, then add to cooked orange mixture, stirring and skimming off any scum as it comes to the surface. Add the lemon juice. Bring to a rapid boil until marmalade has reached setting point. Test by putting a spoonful of marmalade on a saucer in the refrigerator for a few minutes. If it wrinkles when you push it with your finger, the marmalade is ready.

Let the marmalade cool just a little before bottling in sterilised jars (see Glossary) – the fruit will float to the top if the marmalade is too hot.

PIGEON AND SQUAB

 THERE IS OFTEN CONFUSION ABOUT THE DIFFERENCE BETWEEN squab and pigeon. Squab is baby pigeon, killed before it leaves the nest. It is plump, as it hasn't flown, and very tender. Squab is reared by some farmers in Australia especially for the table; it is fairly expensive but really worthwhile for a special occasion. Pigeon, on the other hand, is caught wild and is of indeterminate age. It is inexpensive but erratic in its availability and quality. With wild pigeons you also need to consider whether they might have been feeding on sprayed crops.

Early in my food career in the Barossa I remember becoming excited by a phone call from Adelaide offering me hundreds, even thousands, of pigeons. I was delighted at such a find until it became clear to me that not only were the birds still alive, but I would also have to go and trap them myself. The call was from an enterprising member of the Adelaide City Council who thought it a perfect solution to both the council's problems and mine. I refused the kind offer.

I use squab and pigeon in totally different dishes and prefer not to compare them. Pigeon makes one of the best pies I have ever eaten and is also great in a ragoût or pasta sauce. Squab can be served elegantly with just a game jus, grapes and verjuice, or it can be barbecued and made into a warm salad. It can also be used in all the same ways as pigeon, although I find that a little too extravagant.

Squab is a truly exceptional bird. It is very easy to prepare – and it is always handy to know how to make a really spectacular dish with next to no effort. The squab available in Australia through Ian Milburn of Glenloth Game in Victoria or Game Farm in New South Wales is superb.

The differences in taste and texture between squab and pigeon are enormous. Tasting them side by side you could be forgiven for thinking they were entirely different species. Both require very specific cooking methods. Once you understand the principles, cooking them is simple.

The meat of the squab is thick and buttery and the breast should be served rare – though not 'blue', as it too often is. I insist on my squab being really pink, as I find that 'blue' has a more limited taste, whereas if overcooked, the meat is tough and 'livery'. Cooked rare, it is tender, moist and delicious. Squab is usually cooked very quickly at a high temperature followed by a long resting time. Pigeon, on the other hand, has to be cooked very slowly until the meat almost falls off the bone, otherwise the flesh can be dry. The flavour is strong and gutsy and the texture is fine when it has been cooked with loving attention. I prefer to use a crockpot or pressure cooker for pigeon, or the 'confit' method, where the bird is cooked in duck fat at barely a simmer for between 1–4 hours, depending on the age of the bird.

Pigeon should be cooked so slowly that each quarter seems just to 'lift off' the carcass. Even so, I am very careful, after having lifted the meat off the bone, to make sure that it is immersed skin-side down in some cooking liquor while it rests so it doesn't dry out. I then make a well-reduced pigeon glaze with the chopped bones of the carcass, chopped raw chicken bones, stock vegetables and veal stock.

Chestnuts are a wonderful accompaniment to pigeon. I used to buy dried chestnuts from Italian grocers and reconstitute them, but these days I'd opt for frozen cooked chestnuts, although fresh chestnuts in season would be the ultimate if you have the patience to

cook and peel them. The piquancy of pickled walnuts is also very good with pigeon. First cook the pigeon gently in some stock, with just a dash of pickled walnut juice, up to the stage of taking it off the bone and making the sauce. Reduce the pigeon stock, adjust it very carefully with some more pickled walnut juice, then cut the walnuts widthways and add to the sauce in the last few minutes with a little cream. (Commercially pickled walnuts will disintegrate very quickly.) Rosemary complements these flavours very well.

Another favourite recipe for good-sized pigeons is to stuff them with some sausage mince, perhaps studded with olives, to help keep them moist during cooking. Add some good-quality canned, peeled tomatoes, lots of herbs and some chicken stock and cook in a pressure cooker or crockpot. When the pigeons are cooked so that the meat is just coming away from the bone, transfer them to a plate to rest (upside-down to retain moisture) and cover to keep warm. Meanwhile, reduce the cooking liquid, then toss in some more olives at the last moment and serve with polenta.

Squab is a great restaurant dish and it is hard to resist on the menu of any serious chef. The most sensationally presented squab I ever had was when French chef Joël Robuchon was still running Jamin, in Paris. These are my notes from the night: 'Pigeon presented in flambé dish and then carved at the table using wooden board with deep ring around for juices. Fresh pepper ground. Hearts and livers spooned out on to a crouton. Finely cut, crisp game chips served with sauce "just a jus". MAGNIFICENT.'

WILD PIGEON   *Serves 4*

extra virgin olive oil, for cooking	1 teaspoon chopped thyme
2 tablespoons chopped rosemary	1 cup (250 ml) red wine
4 × 240 g wild pigeons	3 cups (750 ml) Golden Chicken Stock
80 g butter	(see page 57)
sea salt flakes and freshly ground	80 g bacon, rind removed, cut into
black pepper	2.5 cm strips
3 shallots, peeled and chopped	2 small bay leaves
200 g field mushrooms, cut into thick slices	flat-leaf parsley, to garnish

Mix a small amount of olive oil with 1 tablespoon chopped rosemary, and rub all over the pigeons. In a large heavy-based frying pan, melt about a third of the butter, then add the pigeons and a pinch of salt, and seal slowly and evenly over low heat. Once the birds have browned all over, remove them from the pan and set aside in a crockpot or pressure cooker.

In the same frying pan, brown the chopped shallots in oil and add to the crockpot. Add the rest of the butter to the pan and sauté the mushrooms and thyme for a few minutes. Season well and add to the crockpot or pressure cooker. Deglaze the pan with the red wine over high heat, reducing it a little. Add the chicken stock and reduce further for 5 minutes, then transfer to the cooking pot. Wipe the pan dry and render the bacon, then add to the pot, along with the bay leaves and 1 tablespoon rosemary. (If using a crockpot, cook on low for 5 hours or overnight. For a pressure cooker, cook on the lowest setting for 20 minutes before first checking. Take out any birds that are done, making sure to keep them moist with a little of the cooking juices, and continue to cook the rest, checking every 10 minutes.) The cooking time will depend on the age of the birds, and wild pigeons are of indeterminate age so cooking times will vary. The pigeon is done when it is tender to touch but still intact enough to pull away the breast and the legs from the carcass in one piece.

Strain the juices from the crockpot and reduce to the desired consistency in a saucepan. You can either serve the pigeon whole, or take the meat off the bone for your guests. Spoon over the reduced juices and serve topped with freshly chopped flat-leaf parsley.

SQUAB WITH FRESH FIGS AND GINGER
AND LEMON BUTTER

Serves 2

Squab is a bit of a luxury, and this is the sort of dish I would cook for a beautifully indulgent meal. For really tender, moist meat, it's important not to overcook the birds, and to rest them after cooking.

As a variation, instead of using fresh figs you could serve this with couscous dotted with verjuice-soaked currants and butter, and blanched spinach.

2 × 350 g squab

extra virgin olive oil, for cooking

½ cup reduced Golden Chicken Stock
    (see page 57), warmed

4 black figs, each cut into 3 slices

butter, for cooking

2 sprigs rosemary, leaves picked

sea salt flakes and freshly ground
    black pepper

GINGER AND LEMON BUTTER

2 tablespoons preserved ginger

¼ cinnamon stick, ground

80 g unsalted butter

grated rind and juice of 1 lemon

freshly ground black pepper

To make the ginger and lemon butter, mix the ginger, ground cinnamon, unsalted butter and grated lemon rind together using a food processor or mortar and pestle. Add lemon juice and freshly ground black pepper to taste. Chill the butter in the refrigerator until ready to use.

Preheat the oven to 230°C. Using kitchen scissors or a sharp knife, remove the heads and wing tips from the squab, then spatchcock the birds by cutting them down the spine and, with the cut-side down on the bench, squashing them as flat as you can with the palm of your hand. Cut the legs away a little from the breast frame so the bird is as flat as possible (this will ensure that the legs and breasts cook evenly). Ease your fingers between the skin and flesh of the breast and legs of each squab, then take just over a quarter of the prepared butter and push it under the skin of each bird, smoothing it gently over the flesh. Spread the remaining butter over the skin of the squabs, and sprinkle with sea salt.

In a large heavy-based frying pan, heat a little extra virgin olive oil over high heat and quickly seal the birds, skin-side up. Carefully turn them skin-side down, and seal them for 2–3 minutes, until the skin has caramelised. Transfer the birds, skin-side up, to a shallow roasting pan, and roast for 6–8 minutes. Remove the dish from the oven and turn the birds skin-side down again, pour over the warm chicken stock, and set aside to rest, covered, for 10 minutes.

Meanwhile, toss the figs in the same frying pan over medium heat with a little butter and the rosemary, and season.

Cut the birds in half and serve with the pan-fried figs alongside, drizzling over any juices from the roasting pan.

VIGNERON'S SQUAB

Serves 6

6 × 450 g squab, livers removed and reserved

sea salt flakes and freshly ground
  black pepper

juice of ½ lemon

1 tablespoon butter

2 onions, unpeeled, cut in half and
  roughly chopped

2 small carrots, roughly chopped

1 stick celery, roughly chopped

2 sprigs flat-leaf parsley

2 sprigs thyme

100 ml verjuice *or* white wine

2 cups (500 ml) reduced Golden Chicken
  Stock (see page 57)

1 bunch fresh, large, seedless green grapes
  (*or* muscatels dried on the stem
  if grapes are out of season)

CROUTONS (OPTIONAL)

80 g butter, softened

6 slices baguette

2 tablespoons sparkling white wine

sea salt flakes and freshly ground
  black pepper

Preheat the oven to 230°C or the maximum temperature for your oven. Season the cavity of the birds with salt and pepper and squeeze a little lemon juice inside. In a frying pan, seal the birds in nut-brown butter with a dash of oil over medium heat to a gentle golden brown, turning on all sides. Sit them in a roasting pan with the juices from the frying pan and roast for 8–12 minutes (depending on the heat of the oven). Check them after 8 minutes. Remove the squab from the oven and turn them upside-down to rest for a good 15 minutes before carving. After carving the meat off the carcasses, set the squab meat aside, cut-side down, on a baking tray with just enough of the cooking juices to keep it moist.

Meanwhile, skim the fat off the juices in the roasting pan and brown the onions, carrots, celery, parsley and thyme, drizzled with extra virgin olive oil, in the pan over high heat. While they are browning, roughly chop the carcasses and set aside. Once the vegetables are caramelised, add the carcasses back to the pan, then deglaze it with verjuice or white wine. Add the stock and cook vigorously over high heat for about 20 minutes or until the sauce is sufficiently reduced. Strain the sauce and keep it warm until ready to serve.

If you're making the croutons, melt half the butter in a heavy-based frying pan over medium heat, then fry the bread until golden brown on both sides. Drain on kitchen paper. Sauté the reserved livers in a little of the butter, then add the sparkling wine and deglaze. Mash the livers and the reduced pan juices with the rest of the soft butter and season. Spread on the croutons.

To serve, warm the carved meat in the oven for about 3 minutes, divide the squab meat among 6 plates, then spoon over a little of the sauce, place a crouton to the side and add the grapes at the last minute. Drink the rest of the sparkling wine!

PORK

 UNTIL A WONDERFUL HOLIDAY WITH EIGHT FRIENDS IN Umbria in 1995 I had little interest in eating pork, finding it dry and tasteless unless smoked to make bacon. Two simple meals on that holiday turned my lack of interest into a need to relive those sublime taste experiences when I returned home.

As friends, we were united by a love of food and, as the produce was so fabulous, there was a fair bit of competition to get to the stoves. We took turns in deciding what to eat, and shopping for food became a daily expedition. Our lives seemed to revolve entirely around who was cooking what. On market day Stephanie Alexander came home with pork to cook as brochettes. I was lukewarm about the prospect, but fortunately it was not my day to decide what we would eat. Grilled over an open fire with no extra attention, the meat was positively ambrosial.

Stephanie then led us to a simple trattoria, following notes her mother had made on a journey there many years before. Pig's kidneys were on the menu. The grilling took place in a large open fireplace, the heat of which must have been amazing for the cook – the aromas certainly were! The kidneys were as wonderful as the brochettes.

This trip was quite extraordinary, and not only because it reawakened my interest in pork. We were staying in a farmhouse on the side of a misty mountain with views so spectacular that each day was like waking up in a dream. The few buildings in view were nothing short of centuries old and the olive trees almost seemed abandoned, so steep were the slopes. Every weekend morning we were woken by the sounds of hunters calling, dogs barking and shots ringing through the air – wild boar were being hunted. The less aggressive locals appeared with baskets on the backs of motorised bikes (that struggled up the steep hill) in pursuit of fungi. (We also looked for mushrooms, but less successfully – obviously, local knowledge counts for a lot.) Wild chestnut trees, with branches weighed down by their hoary fruit, flanked each side of the steep track along which we walked each day to the monastery at the top of the mountain.

Roast pork belly with verjuice and Seville marmalade glaze (see page 488)

The huge fig tree at the side of the house seemed two storeys high because of the way the house was built into the slope. This meant we could pick the fruit by leaning over the terrace outside our bedroom, or by the kitchen door on the bottom floor where we breakfasted. The tree provided enough ripe figs for us each day, no matter how many ways we used them – for breakfast with yoghurt, lunch with prosciutto, or for dinner with cheese or in a dessert.

This trip gave us such a taste for Italy that we all returned to Australia declaring our need to visit again and again, and this led to the 'Stephanie and Maggie in Italy' cooking workshops, held in Siena in September 1997. This amazing experience – life-altering both for ourselves and some of our students – led to the publication of our *Tuscan Cookbook*.

When I returned, I asked myself why my experiences of pork in Italy were so very different from those at home. I now know it was a combination of many factors, and not just because I romanticised the memory. The pork we ate in Italy had been raised by small farmers who fed the pigs a varied diet (if only because the family's scraps became the pigs' food) and gave them room to move about, while also providing shelter. Perhaps most importantly, these pigs were of a breed that had not had the fat bred out of them.

In Australia, until recently, we have been intent on breeding the fat out of pigs. The emphasis has been on leanness before all else, driven by the market's fear of fat. Obviously the larger the animal grows in the shortest space of time, the better the profit for the farmer, whether it has 'boar taint' or not. (Boar taint is a flavour or odour that can spoil the meat – it's not present in female pigs but can manifest at any age in a male pig, and the risk of it developing increases significantly for pigs over 75 kg. Whilst a huge amount of work is being done in the industry to reduce boar taint, the risk is still higher for leaner, heavier pigs.) Fat is flavour, and the lack of fat is the major reason – though there are many – why I never eat mass-produced pork, as I find the meat deficient in flavour, juiciness and texture.

To turn the situation around, the industry needs to breed pigs with intramuscular fat – which gives meat tenderness and flavour – rather than a slab of fat encasing the meat. The great thing is that there are now some small-scale farmers producing beautifully flavoured pork that lives up to the memory of my Italian experience.

The pig has always been central to the Barossa tradition, given the German heritage of the Valley. When I first settled here in 1973, almost every farm was mixed and included a vineyard. It was normal practice to have a couple of hundred chooks, fifty turkeys and geese for the Christmas market, and a pig or two, complete with mud holes for wallowing.

Over the years I've seen that mixed farming tradition become rare, but some small traditional farmers have survived. Colin and Joy Leinert of Sheoak Log, who breed rare Berkshire pigs, are an important example, not only influencing Australian pig breeding but the progeny of Berkshires all over the world. Even though I live close by, it was only in 2006 that I first visited their stud 'Lynjoleen', and it was a real privilege to have an insight into the lives of this industrious couple.

Both of them have much to say about their history and their industry, and they are committed to providing a good life and a good death for the animals they raise. The issue of flavour, and the importance of the marbling of fat throughout the meat, is paramount to their business. How wonderful it is that the pendulum is swinging back, as more farmers, chefs and producers understand these issues. Even more remarkable is the fact that the Leinerts have never wavered in their convictions – they rode out the twenty years when they were ostracised for keeping Berkshire pigs when the trend was to raise hybrid pigs with the fat bred out of them. That's true passion! However, this is not easy farming, as they believe in controlling the whole cycle, which means that Colin and Joy grow and mix their own feed: the wheat, the barley and the peas (although they do buy in the lucerne).

Colin told me proudly that the Emperor of Japan will eat only Berkshire pork and that his stud's progeny has been an important part of the Berkshire pork world from Japan to the United Kingdom and United States. A single stud like the Leinerts' can't possibly supply a large market, and with retail outlets being so successful in selling their pork, as well as a burgeoning market from the smallgoods they produce (the best I have tasted), there are necessary plans for expansion in place. After my visit, I drove away so excited by their energy and enthusiasm that I completely lost my way home – in my own stamping ground!

We are lucky to have a small group of producers Australia-wide who are already aware of the need for better-tasting pork. Of special note is Bangalow Sweet Pork (www.sweetpork.com.au) of Ballina, New South Wales, the winner of a *Vogue Entertaining and Travel* magazine Produce Award in 2005. They have had an enormous impact on creating a discerning market for quality pork. Then there is Otway Pork (www.otwaypork.com.au), a larger concern breeding free-range pork in Victoria. There are also a handful of other producers of free-range pork from rare breeds in each state, driven by a passion for flavour.

All animals and poultry reflect the feed they are given, but none more so than a pig. If you can buy from farmers who allow their pigs to range in a field of fallen figs, apples or even onions, you'll taste the difference. The added advantage of buying from a small producer is that the animal is likely to have been slaughtered in a small abattoir and will not have been as stressed as an animal processed in a larger set-up. We dedicated meat-eaters have a responsibility to ensure that the animals we eat have been raised happily and slaughtered humanely. To make sure we take the best care of our land and animals we should understand the processes, and influence the marketplace accordingly. Too often we'd rather not know the gory details, but that's passing the buck.

If you want to seek out better pork and do not have access to a small producer, go to a Chinese or Vietnamese butcher. The Chinese and Vietnamese are very fussy about their

pork and are intolerant of boar taint – in fact, they insist on sows and are prepared to pay a premium for them, since the meat is sweeter than that of boars. Both cultures also value the role fat plays in providing flavour and texture, so carcasses with a good covering of fat are sought out.

There are pockets throughout Australia where the tradition of the home pig kill remains, and the long weekend in June sees rural Australia's pig population decimated. Italian and German families (many more of the former than the latter these days) take advantage of the cool weather and the three-day break to have their pigs slaughtered and to make sausages and pancetta.

On one such weekend some years ago, knowing I had changed my thinking about pork after my Italian sojourn, the Fanto family welcomed my participation. The selection of the pig is of great importance. The Fantos prefer the sweeter meat of the sow but like the breeder to reassure them that the animal has just come off heat, since they believe the keeping quality of the meat can otherwise be affected (most of their pork is used in dried sausages, pancetta and capocollo – the latter two being lean meat rolled and then brined before being smoked). The butcher came out to their property and killed the pigs in situ.

I wasn't a witness to the killing, so my first sight on arriving was of three pigs hanging from the rafters of the shed. The hair had been removed before the pigs were strung up and the skin was rubbed all over with salt and lemon to whiten and clean it. The pigs were then gutted and the blood collected and put aside to set. (I have a photograph on my office wall of a typical Barossa pig killing of probably a century ago – the pig is hanging from a tree and the ladies of the household are standing on one side with enamelled bowls ready to catch the blood, while the men stand on the other side with their large aprons, knives and steel. Some might think it a strange thing to photograph, but the picture reveals so much of our past and it is one I treasure.)

The Fanto family got straight to work once the pigs were gutted, as the sooner the intestines are cleaned the easier they are to manage. While this was being done, a large pan of water was boiled ready to take the blood, which cooks for about an hour and a half before being sliced and fried. I haven't yet organised myself enough to make my own blood sausage with apples or chestnuts, but after a short holiday in the Basque country of Spain, the image of fat blood sausage served with caramelised onion and apple spurs me on.

The tradition is to use every part of the animal, and as so much is set aside to preserve, the delicacies that are left – all those tidbits that others may reject from lack of knowledge – are for eating immediately. They are the rewards, and as a guest there to observe, take notes and learn, I was offered my choice of these treats, which were hanging on the Hills Hoist to dry a little. The caul fat (the 'veil') hung like lace curtains; the 'lights', or lungs, were light in weight but otherwise bulky. The table was set for lunch with pastas, salads and last year's sausages – all within easy reach of the huge logs burning not only to keep us warm but to grill the liver I had picked out. The liver was wrapped in caul fat and cooked quickly on the barbecue hotplate so that it was still rare. Delicious!

Late on the first day, when the meat was set, the carcasses were taken down and cut, ready for the mincer much later that night. The salt, crushed chillies and fennel seed gathered from the paddocks and roadsides were put on top of the meat until it was cold enough to mince, ready for the sausage-making the next day. (The meat wasn't refrigerated at all, as the Fantos feel it gets too cold and oxidises if refrigerated, changing colour when it is taken out of the fridge.)

On the second day, the cleaned casings were filled with the spiced minced pork and the sausages were hung in the smoking shed to dry for four or five days until the weather was right for smoking to begin.

On the Monday, the Fantos minced the pork lard and pressed it into the sides of a gas-fired stainless steel 'copper', then added the trotters, skin and bones and cooked the whole lot very slowly, so that the fat didn't burn, for eight hours or so (it can require up to ten

hours cooking) – the cooking pot had to be stirred constantly. About five hours into the cooking, salt was sprinkled onto the surface of the fat and left to penetrate before the stirring was resumed. Some of the children and adults couldn't wait for dinner and devoured the shoulder bones (these have the sweetest meat of all) straight from the pot.

At the end of cooking, the fat was drained away. (The family used to bottle the lard and cellar it for use during the year, but these days they throw most of it out, worried about their fat intake and the threat of contamination after long storage.)

The bones and other goodies were served for dinner – no knives and forks for this – with lots of salads and pickled vegetables heavy with vinegar to help cut the super-rich morsels. As the final treat, the remaining cooked blood was added to the scrapings in the copper and cooked for half an hour before being served with a fried egg. This reminded me of my father's favourite breakfast of fried eggs and black pudding, and my German heritage peeped through as I revelled in the feast.

My time with the Fantos was inspiring: while quite a constitution was needed, I found the weekend a fascinating tradition to observe. Such traditions must be encouraged, especially since those who partake in them insist that their pigs provide flavoursome meat, and that can only have a good effect on the market for the rest of us.

I might have eschewed pork meat in the past (until I discovered what it could taste like), but I have always been very interested in piggy bits. My parents always made Brawn with a pig's head at Christmas (see page 71) and, as an offal freak, I have always loved pig's liver and kidneys.

You can emulate the kidneys I enjoyed in Umbria using the oven instead of an open fire. Because it is almost impossible to purchase kidneys encased in their fat, buy caul fat from the butcher and wrap this around them instead. Allow one super-fresh kidney per person, then season it and wrap it in the caul fat (this will melt away during the cooking), placing a fresh bay leaf in the parcel. Strip sprigs of rosemary of their leaves and push one leaf into the middle of each kidney. Stand the parcels on a wire rack in a roasting pan and roast them at 230°C for 15–20 minutes in all, turning the kidneys over halfway through the cooking. Let the kidneys rest for 5 minutes before slicing and serving them with a very piquant mustard. The kidney is very rich – it would make a good first course served on a bed of gratinéed potato.

My first experience of stuffed pig's ears was at Berowra Waters Inn many years ago. It was such an amazing dish, and it gave me the courage to put pig's ears on our restaurant menu. I served them much as Janni Kyritsis had done, partnered by a rémoulade sauce, except that I used pheasant meat with mushrooms rather than chicken for the stuffing. Even though I was lucky to sell five serves a weekend, each time they were ordered they were loved, which gave me a great thrill.

As a child I was always attracted to the crackling and apple sauce that came with roast pork, long before the hysteria about breeding fat out of pigs, but even so, I left the meat, which my mother had overcooked for fear of infecting us all with tapeworm and other nasties. Trichinosis (*Trichinella spiralis*) was the main concern – but I'm advised by the Australian Pork Council that this does not exist in Australian pigs. The Council tells me my mother's fears were based on hearsay and that we should be cooking our pork only until it is no longer pink but still moist.

The way to ensure crisp crackling and moist meat is to first choose a roasting pan that is only a little larger than the pork itself, so that the juices don't burn in the cooking. Score the rind with a sharp knife, then moisten it with a little extra virgin olive oil and rub it thoroughly with salt. Stand the piece of pork on a wire rack in the roasting pan and roast at 210°C for 20 minutes (for a 1.2 kg piece of pork), then pour verjuice, wine or water into the baking dish – this creates steam and will help the meat remain moist. Reduce the oven temperature to 180°C and roast for another 50 minutes, then remove the pork and allow it to rest for 20 minutes. Pork needs to be just cooked: if you are unsure, insert a skewer in the thickest part of the meat to see if the juices run clear.

For a delicious change, rub fennel seeds into the meat with salt, or insert slivers of garlic into it. This is the base of the *porchetta* you see for sale in Italian marketplaces or fairs, where great slabs of pork are sandwiched between slices of crusty bread; you're even asked whether you want your pork from a leaner part, with fat, or a bit of both.

Try pan-frying pork fillet or chops and then deglazing the pan with verjuice. Serve the meat with slowly roasted heads of garlic and squeeze out the sweet, nutty cloves. The aniseed flavour of caramelised fennel is a great counterpoint to the richness of pork too.

Potatoes are wonderful with pork: crispy pan-fried potato, garlic and rosemary; perfect mashed potato, but go easy on the cream; or boiled waxy potatoes sprinkled with salt to counteract the richness of the meat.

STEVE'S SAUSAGES IN GRAPE MUST   *Serves 4–6*

Friend and former Pheasant Farm Restaurant chef Steve Flamsteed used to talk of cooking pork sausages in grape must for the first meal of each vintage when he worked in Bordeaux. Grape must is what remains once grapes have been pressed for their juice. Doing this at home, 1 kg of red wine grapes will give you the juice and must required – either put the grapes through a food mill or push them through a sieve.

This is how I've translated Steve's tales of the dish. Remember that this is traditionally a dish for vintage, and ideally you need wine grapes (preferably shiraz or mataro) rather than table grapes.

1 kg sweet Italian pork and fennel seed sausages (about 12)	2 cups (500 ml) red grape juice
1 tablespoon extra virgin olive oil	2 cups (500 ml) grape must

Gently seal the sausages over a moderate heat in a deep, heavy-based frying pan that has been brushed with the olive oil. Add ½ cup (125 ml) of the grape juice and cook for 10 minutes until reduced by half. Turn the sausages over, then add the grape must so that the sausages are smothered, then tip in the balance of the juice. Simmer for another 10 minutes, or a little longer if the sausages are thick (longer cooking will also enhance the flavour of the must). Serve the sausages on a bed of must with creamy mashed potatoes and finely sliced fennel drizzled with olive oil. (If you find the seeds in the must a problem, then just squeeze the juice from it over the sausages on serving.)

BRAISED PORK BELLY, COTECHINO AND GREEN LENTILS   *Serves 4*

What an amazing trio of talents Steve Flamsteed has – trained chef, wine-maker and cheese-maker – and, more than that, he is one of nature's gentle, beautiful people. Steve has the ability to bring calm and thoughtfulness to any situation. It therefore wasn't hard for him to talk me into being involved in a very special day for the Zonta Club of Toowoomba in August 2004 that his sister-in-law, Vicki Flamsteed, was helping to organise. It wasn't until after I arrived that I realised it was a far bigger occasion than I had envisaged.

Our responsibilities were to prepare lunch for the several hundred participants and do a cooking demonstration. Steve and I planned the menu from afar and, as we were aware that we would have to prepare all the ingredients in advance, this slow-cooked dish of pork belly was ideal. I arrived the day before assuming there would be lots to do, but in truth it was Steve who did all the work. Our cooking demonstration could have been a bit scary, as we were centre stage with a huge screen and bright lights, as if in a TV studio. But although Steve and I hadn't cooked together for eight years, we just slipped straight back into our familiar pattern – that's what happens with teamwork when it comes from intuition and not instruction. We were just a small part of a day that was a great success, raising huge amounts of money for a selection of children's and youth charities in Queensland and South Australia.

Now Steve, who is so obviously passionately interested in flavour when you look at the combination of skills he has amassed, is pulling all those threads together into one tapestry in his role as wine-maker/manager for Giant Steps Winery in the Yarra Valley. The winery is diversifying to provide all the ingredients necessary for living a good life: firstly, there is the wine; secondly, they have a sourdough bakery baking bread for sale at the cellar door; they also have their own coffee roaster from Germany; and lastly, although they no longer make cheese, Steve buys young cheeses and ages them to sell once they mature.

sea salt flakes and freshly ground
   black pepper
2 fresh bay leaves
8 sprigs thyme
600 g pork belly
1 × 500 g piece cotechino
extra virgin olive oil, for cooking
12 golden shallots, chopped
6 cloves garlic, chopped
1 × 400 g can tomatoes, strained,
   reserving ½ cup juice
⅓ cup (80 ml) verjuice
1 litre reduced Golden Chicken Stock
   (see page 57)

½ cup (125 ml) chardonnay
5 baby carrots, cut into large pieces
2 small sticks celery, chopped
Salsa Agresto (see page 22), to serve

LENTILS
250 g Australian green lentils, rinsed and
   soaked in water for 30 minutes
2 cloves garlic, peeled
1 tablespoon chopped preserved lemon rind
½ cup freshly chopped flat-leaf parsley
100 ml extra virgin olive oil

Start preparing the pork the night before. Sprinkle a baking tray with salt and pepper, the bay leaves and 4 thyme sprigs. Lay the pork belly in one or two pieces on the tray and massage in the salt, pepper and herbs. Keep it covered in the refrigerator overnight.

The next day, wash the cotechino, then place in a saucepan of cold water and slowly bring to the boil over medium–high heat. Simmer for 15 minutes, then remove and set aside.

Lightly rinse the seasoning off the pork belly, reserving the herbs, then pat the meat dry. Heat a little olive oil in a large heavy-based cast-iron casserole over low–medium heat, then gently seal the meat. Remove from the pan and set aside. Add the shallots, garlic, reserved bay leaves and thyme to the pan and sauté for 5–10 minutes or until the shallots are golden and soft. Deglaze the pan with most of the verjuice, then return the meat to the pan along with the cotechino. Pour in the tomatoes and ½ cup of their juice, the stock and wine, then increase the heat to high and bring to simmering point. Reduce heat to as low as possible and simmer, covered, for 3 hours or until the meat starts to soften; use a simmer mat if possible.

After the pork has been cooking for nearly 3 hours, heat a little olive oil in a heavy-based frying pan over low–medium heat and sauté the carrots, celery and remaining thyme for

6–8 minutes or until golden. Deglaze the pan with a little verjuice. Transfer the vegetables and verjuice to the casserole, then season to taste with salt and pepper.

Meanwhile, place the drained lentils and garlic in a medium-sized saucepan and cover generously with water. Cook over medium heat for 20 minutes or until soft and most of the liquid has evaporated; the lentils should retain a little of the cooking liquid. Remove the garlic cloves.

Just before serving, gently stir the preserved lemon, parsley and olive oil into the lentils. Slice the cotechino and pork belly into large pieces. Place a ladleful of the lentils in the centre of 4 warm large, shallow bowls, then top with a piece of cotechino and a piece of pork and a few of the vegetables. Serve with a dollop of salsa agresto (I might well add another cup of basil and a little more olive oil to the salsa when I make it to accompany this dish), a side dish of boiled waxy potatoes and a salad of bitter green leaves.

ROAST PORK BELLY WITH VERJUICE AND SEVILLE MARMALADE GLAZE

Serves 12

1 large clove garlic, chopped	2 tablespoons verjuice
sea salt flakes	2 tablespoons extra virgin olive oil
1 tablespoon minced ginger	2 kg pork belly, skin removed
⅓ cup (115 g) Seville marmalade	1 tablespoon freshly ground black pepper

Using the flat of a large knife blade, crush the garlic and 1 teaspoon salt to form a paste. Combine the garlic paste, ginger, marmalade, verjuice and olive oil in a bowl to make the glaze.

Place the pork belly in a roasting pan and season with the pepper and salt. Pour the glaze over the pork and let stand for 10 minutes. Meanwhile, preheat the oven to 120°C.

Roast for 3 hours, or until tender and well-glazed and serve with rapini (a peppery green vegetable that tastes somewhere between turnip and broccoli) or any other robustly flavoured green vegetable.

RABBIT

 **RABBIT, BOTH WILD AND FARMED, IS A FAVOURITE** ingredient of mine. In the Pheasant Farm Restaurant days I often had wild rabbit on the menu – a tricky beast to prepare until you learn to cook each part separately with great care.

Since the arrival of the calicivirus in the mid-1990s, which significantly reduced the numbers of wild rabbits in Australia, a previously thriving export market of wild rabbit (vermin to some, but big business to others) has come to a standstill. This is such a shame, to my mind – I saw it as a delicious irony that we exported our vermin back to the countries from which they were originally introduced to Australia. However, the calicivirus will move through a district, but soon rabbits are breeding again, so it has not really solved the problem – and even if you too like the flavour of wild rabbit, it is now much harder to find as the businesses that used to sell it went broke when the virus was introduced.

The wild rabbit's decimation of the countryside is a pretty emotive issue. This year we have noticed a profusion of young rabbits sharpening their teeth on our orchard trees, and have lost some mature trees as a result. So, until my supply of wild rabbits was curtailed by this virus, I always thought I was doing my bit by cooking rabbit as often as I could. Certainly people who grew up in the country loved to eat the food of their childhood (does anyone cook quite like mother – even if her dishes were sometimes overcooked to blazes?) and rabbit was the food of the Depression. My husband's grandfather was a butcher, and during the Depression he became a rabbit trapper at Mannum in order to earn a few shillings to feed his family. My mother-in-law often talked of grilling rabbit livers over hot coals, and remembers her father grilling rabbit kittens – a great delicacy then – over an open fire after the coals had died down. Even though she ate rabbit every day for many years as a child, she still loved me to cook it for her. And I was always surprised by how popular it was at the Pheasant Farm Restaurant.

Fortunately, there is a growing industry in farmed rabbits, which differ quite markedly from their wild cousins. Reared in hutches, they do not roam the countryside, and they are much more forgiving of the cooking process as they are larger, fatter, and therefore juicier, than their wild counterparts.

I have to admit it took me a long time to switch from wild rabbit to farmed, as I always followed the mantra of 'eat a rabbit, save the land' – and, when well chosen and cooked with great care, wild rabbit remains special to me, as long as it is in good nick and hasn't been grazing on onion weed. But if I'm being honest, I'd have to say that the plump young flesh of the farmed rabbit, as well as being a lot more succulent, is a lot easier to cook, as any part can be grilled, pan-fried or baked.

I try to buy the largest farmed rabbit I can, which is around the 1.7 kg range; a rabbit this size will serve three adults, and given enough notice, your butcher should be able to order one in for you. The more common weight of the farmed rabbit seems to be around 1.5 kg. Specify if you want the kidneys and liver too. Rabbit livers are a treat in themselves when seared and deglazed, then eaten immediately. All those scared of fat can skip the next suggestion: when cooking the saddle separately, make sure you keep the kidneys enclosed in the fat of the underbelly – nothing could be more succulent.

To cook a rabbit perfectly, it is actually best to treat the front legs, back legs and saddle as different cuts, all requiring different cooking times and methods. (The exception to this is the rabbit kitten, which is best barbecued whole.) If the thought of dissecting a rabbit is too off-putting, you can buy specific portions from butchers and specialist suppliers. Otherwise, dissect the rabbit with a sharp knife by first cutting off its front legs and then the back legs. The remaining piece is the saddle, which has a silvery sinew covering it that will drastically interfere with the cooking if not removed.

There are three ways of removing the sinew. Firstly, you can run a sharp knife along the spine and around the ribs to free a fillet from each side of the spine – a thin, flexible fish-filleting knife is best for this job. The fillets will still have sinew on the outside and should be trimmed in the same manner as a fillet of beef. The fillets can then be sealed in foamy golden butter and literally just turned over before turning off the gas and letting the residual heat in the pan finish off the cooking. The second way to handle the sinew is to seal and bake the saddle as is, and then carve off the fillets and trim the sinew after cooking. The third and, to my mind, most successful way is to remove the whole sinew with a filleting knife before you cook the saddle. This way you can prevent any shrinkage during cooking, and the meat will not be tough. The saddle can then be served on the bone, cut through the middle, accompanied with a sauce.

I used to discard rabbit bones as I was always told they can turn a stock bitter, but as long as they are only cooked for a short time (a little like fish stock), they make a really good stock.

I cook the saddle of rabbit by browning it on both sides, taking care that the butter stays golden by adding a dash of oil, and then placing it in a small baking dish in the oven for 5 minutes at around 220°C; a wild rabbit will take 5 minutes and a farmed one 8–10 minutes,

Pot-roasted rabbit with garlic, rosemary, preserved lemon and bay leaves (see page 492)

depending on its size. Then remove it from the oven and let it rest, covered, for 10 minutes before carving the meat off the bone. If you want to make pasta or risotto using rabbit, you could cook it in this fashion and then carve off the meat, but only add the meat at the last moment, otherwise it will overcook.

One of the simplest ways to serve the saddle is to make a sauce of reduced verjuice, chicken stock and cream with some basil leaves thrown in for flavour.

The front legs have the sweetest meat of all. I often pot-roast them in a heavy-based saucepan on top of the stove with some stock, garlic, rosemary, preserved lemon and bay leaves. I cook them very slowly and turn them several times during cooking until the meat readily comes away from the bone. This meat is also perfect in sandwiches and for rillettes as it is very moist and sweet.

The back legs I either braise gently at a low temperature or cook in a pressure cooker or crockpot with carrots, celery, onions or leeks and some chicken stock. When the meat

is cooked so that it comes away easily from the bone, I use it in a casserole or make a small pie of rabbit pieces and prunes by reducing the cooking liquid and then adding pitted prunes and rendered bacon to taste.

I recently barbecued a farmed rabbit for the first time ever, and was surprised but really delighted by how good it was. I separated the front and back legs, leaving the saddle, in one piece, with the kidneys encased in fat. (I took the sinew off the saddle so it wouldn't become tough, but then had to be incredibly careful to make sure it didn't overcook on the barbecue.) Before cooking it, I sat the meat in a dish of extra virgin olive oil, rosemary and thyme and a good dash of verjuice for an hour.

I cooked the saddle and legs together over two burners of our six-burner barbecue, taking care to turn the legs to cook them evenly, and making sure the saddle wasn't on the hottest part of the plate so it didn't burn. The total cooking time was just under 20 minutes. I then put all the pieces in a resting marinade of a little more extra virgin olive oil, some verjuice (just enough to moisten them well) and more fresh herbs for 15 minutes. The meat was really succulent, and I wished I'd made a prune mustard or aïoli to serve with it. I also thought it might have been a good idea to wrap the saddle in some pancetta or bacon as extra insurance that it wouldn't dry out.

Rabbit is marvellous when marinated in extra virgin olive oil, lemon juice and marjoram before cooking. It also has a good affinity with mushrooms. Farmed rabbit, even though it has a delicate taste, can be teamed with all kinds of bold flavours. Think of olives (either black or green), pancetta, anchovies, capers, globe artichokes, roasted garlic, prunes, figs, rosemary, thyme, bay or basil – all are winners. Remember not to overcook it and, as with all meats and poultry, leave it to rest. A ladleful of warm chicken stock, verjuice or a marinade, added as soon as the heat of the oven or flame is turned off, helps to keep rabbit meat moist.

RABBIT RILLETTES
Makes 2 kg

I like to serve rabbit rillettes with cornichons (see Glossary) together with crusty bread and lots of salt and freshly ground black pepper. Prunes soaked in tea or brandy, whichever is your tipple, and then puréed to a thick paste with a little wholegrain mustard also go down well, especially in concert with the crispness of the cornichons.

1 kg pork belly (with the rind and
    bones removed)
500 g pork fat
sea salt flakes
2 kg rabbit legs, front and back
    (if you have a choice, use all front legs
    as they are the sweetest – leave the
    saddle for other dishes as it overcooks
    easily and is wasted in rillettes)

1 clove garlic, crushed
4 sprigs thyme
2 sprigs rosemary, leaves stripped
    and finely chopped
freshly ground black pepper
⅓ cup (80 ml) stock *or* water
1 cup duck fat, melted (optional)

Rub the pork and fat well with salt and stand at room temperature overnight in winter (or in the refrigerator in summer or if you live in the hotter parts of Australia). Cut the pork into thick strips along the grooves where the bones were, and then again into small strips shorter than a match and about twice as thick. Cut the pork fat into small pieces.

Preheat the oven to 120°C. Leave the rabbit on the bone and put it into a heavy-based ovenproof dish with a lid, together with the pork strips and pork fat. Bury the crushed garlic, thyme and rosemary in the centre, season with pepper and add the stock or water. Cover the pan and cook in the oven for about 4 hours if you are using wild rabbit, and perhaps half the time if you are using farmed. The rabbit meat should be soft and falling off the bone. Taste to see if more salt and pepper are needed – rillettes can be insipid if not seasoned properly.

Turn the contents out of the pan into a wire sieve set over a large bowl so that the fat seeps through. When well drained, remove the rabbit bones. Using two forks, pull the rabbit and pork meat into fine shreds. Put the meat into a large jar, then pour the fat from the bowl into the jar, or use melted duck fat if you prefer. Rillettes will last for ages in the refrigerator if they are sealed properly.

RABBIT TERRINE

Serves 10–12

I like to serve this terrine with pickled figs, cornichons (see Glossary), wholegrain mustard and good crusty bread.

6 rabbit legs	¼ cup (60 ml) verjuice
250 g pork fat, diced	100 g white bread
1 tablespoon sea salt	milk, for soaking
1 tablespoon Quatre-Épices (see page 358)	2 egg yolks
1 tablespoon freshly ground black pepper	4 fresh bay leaves
2 tablespoons fresh thyme leaves	250 g thinly sliced smoked pork belly
¼ cup finely chopped lemon rind	*or* rindless bacon
butter, for cooking	80 g pitted prunes
250 g chicken livers	

Bone the rabbit legs and cut the meat into dice – you should have about 525 g. Combine the leg meat with the pork fat. Combine the salt, quatre-épices, pepper, thyme leaves and the lemon rind then grind in a spice grinder or using a mortar and pestle. Toss this spice mixture into the meat mixture and refrigerate for 1 hour.

Heat a little butter in a frying pan, then quickly sear the livers to just seal on both sides. Deglaze the pan with verjuice. Remove the livers while still quite rare and allow to cool.

Soak the bread in a little milk, then squeeze it out and combine it with the meat mixture. Pass the mixture through a meat mincer, choosing the largest plate so that the meat is coarsely minced. Place the mince and egg yolks in a large bowl and mix together, working the mixture to help release the proteins and bind it together. Return it to the refrigerator.

Line a terrine mould with baking paper and place the bay leaves on the bottom; this provides a nice presentation once the terrine is turned out. Line the terrine with the pork belly or bacon slices, leaving enough hanging over the edge of the mould to fold over the top of the terrine later.

Preheat the oven to 110°C. Add half the rabbit mixture to the mould and then layer in the prunes and livers. Add the remaining mixture then fold the pork belly or bacon slices over the top.

Wrap the terrine in foil and place in a water bath (a roasting pan half-filled with hot water). Place this in the oven and cook for approximately 3 hours, checking after 2 hours to see if the terrine is coming away from the sides. When the terrine is cooked, a meat thermometer inserted into the centre should read 65°C. If you don't have a thermometer, insert a skewer into the middle of the terrine and check that the juices that escape are clear rather than pink. Turn the oven off and let the terrine stand in the oven for another hour.

Remove the terrine from the oven and place on a tray or plate. Weight the top of the terrine down with cans and leave overnight in the refrigerator (this is essential to develop the flavours). The terrine will keep in the refrigerator for up to 1 week.

To serve, invert the terrine onto a plate, remove the mould, then slice and serve.

RABBIT WITH ROASTED GARLIC AND ANCHOVIES *Serves 6*

3 heads garlic

2 × 1.7 kg farmed rabbits
(including livers and kidneys)

extra virgin olive oil, for cooking

freshly ground black pepper

3 sprigs thyme, leaves stripped

2 sprigs rosemary, leaves stripped

6 fresh bay leaves

sea salt flakes

½ cup (125 ml) Golden Chicken Stock
(see page 57)

⅓ cup (80 ml) verjuice

1 × 45 g tin anchovies, freshly opened
and drained

½ cup roughly chopped flat-leaf parsley,
to serve

CROUTONS

30 g butter

extra virgin olive oil, for cooking

reserved rabbit livers *or* 120 g chicken livers

3 teaspoons red-wine vinegar

1 tablespoon tiny capers

sea salt flakes and freshly ground
black pepper

6 thick slices baguette

1 clove garlic, halved

2 tablespoons freshly chopped
flat-leaf parsley

Separate the garlic cloves, then blanch them in a saucepan of boiling water for 3 minutes to begin cooking and allow for easier peeling. Let cool a little, then peel and set aside.

Remove the legs from the rabbits and set aside. Reserve the livers, leaving the kidneys intact. Slip the top sinew off the saddles of rabbit (see page 490). Rub all the pieces of rabbit, including the livers and kidneys, with a generous amount of olive oil, then season with a little pepper and the thyme, rosemary and bay leaves. Toss together, then transfer to a tray and leave for 1 hour at room temperature.

Preheat the oven to 220°C. Select a roasting pan with shallow sides that will hold the meat in a single layer without crowding (or cook in two pans). Salt each piece of rabbit just before cooking. First add the hind legs, then the whole saddles, and then the garlic. Roast for 10 minutes, then turn the pieces over and add the front legs, seasoning them first with salt. Make sure the garlic isn't burning – remove it if it is – and cook the rabbit for another 8 minutes. Turn the front legs over and cook for another 6–8 minutes before testing for doneness.

Heat the chicken stock in a small saucepan and keep warm. Remove the rabbit from the oven and add the verjuice, up to 60 ml olive oil, and 80 ml of the warm chicken stock to the pan. Add the anchovies and lots of freshly chopped flat-leaf parsley and leave to rest for at least 10 minutes.

Meanwhile, to make the croutons, heat the butter and a little olive oil in a frying pan over high heat and quickly seal the livers on both sides. Deglaze the pan with the vinegar, then add capers and season with salt and pepper. Leave to cool a little, then chop the livers into pieces. Reheat when ready to serve, reducing any liquid. Meanwhile, brush the bread slices with a little olive oil and bake until golden, then rub with the cut clove of garlic while still warm. Add the chopped parsley to the liver mixture and pile onto the toasted bread slices.

Just before serving, using a cleaver or heavy knife, chop each saddle into three and place on a platter with the rabbit legs, drizzled with the juices from the roasting pan. Serve immediately with the warm croutons.

RABBIT RISOTTO
Serves 6

4 farmed rabbit saddles

¼ cup (60 ml) extra virgin olive oil

3 cloves garlic, finely chopped

3 sprigs lemon thyme, leaves stripped

freshly ground black pepper

3 oranges

3 fresh bay leaves

3 medium onions, finely chopped

80 g butter

1.75 litres Golden Chicken Stock
   (see page 57)

425 g Arborio rice (see Glossary)

¼ cup (40 g) pine nuts

extra virgin olive oil, for cooking

sea salt flakes

¼ cup (30 g) green olives, pitted

Remove the sinew from the top of the saddles (see page 490) and carve the meat off the bones. Cut the rabbit into 4 cm × 5 mm strips. Toss in a bowl with the olive oil, garlic, plenty of thyme and pepper. Shave the rind from one of the oranges, making a few long curls, and finely chop the rind of the remaining two oranges, then squeeze the juice from all three. Add all the orange rind and bay leaves to the bowl and stir to combine with the other ingredients. Cover and leave in the refrigerator for at least 1 hour.

Half an hour before you plan to serve the risotto, soften the onion in a saucepan in 60 g of the butter. Bring the stock to simmering point in a separate saucepan. Stir the rice into the softened onion, making sure the rice is coated with the butter mixture. Add the orange juice and cook over high heat, stirring regularly, until the rice absorbs most of the juice. Reduce the heat to low and add a generous ladleful of the hot stock, stirring until it is absorbed. Continue cooking gently, stirring occasionally and adding another ladleful of stock each time the previous one has been absorbed. After 15–20 minutes of cooking, the rice should be ready – creamy and tender with just a hint of bite at the centre of each grain.

While the risotto is cooking, lightly toast the pine nuts in a dry frying pan then set them aside. Heat the remaining butter in the frying pan and add a dash of olive oil. Remove the rabbit from its marinade, season with salt and sauté over medium heat for about 1 minute, shaking and stirring as necessary to cook the meat and lightly brown it. Only cook a small amount at a time so as not to poach the meat.

When the rice is almost cooked, tip the rabbit into the risotto. Use a spatula to ensure you scrape in every drop of the flavoursome rabbit juices. Add the pine nuts and olives. Mix well, check the seasoning and serve immediately with a crisp green salad.

ROAST SADDLE OF RABBIT *Serves 4*

2 × 1.7 kg farmed rabbits
   (including livers and kidneys)
⅓ cup (80 ml) extra virgin olive oil
2 bay leaves
1 sprig rosemary, leaves stripped
6 sprigs thyme, leaves stripped
sea salt flakes and freshly ground
   black pepper
50 g butter
½ cup (125 ml) reduced Golden Chicken
   Stock (see page 57)
100 ml verjuice

ANCHOVY BUTTER
1 × 45 g tin anchovy fillets
250 g unsalted butter, softened
juice of 1 lemon
freshly ground black pepper

To make the anchovy butter, mix the anchovy fillets with the butter and lemon juice and add pepper to taste. Form the mixture into a log the diameter of a 20 cent piece, then wrap it in baking paper and refrigerate.

Remove the legs from the rabbits and set aside for use in another dish. Reserve the livers, leaving the kidneys intact. Slip the top sinew off the saddles of rabbit (see page 490). Trim the saddles to form two compact rectangles, then marinate the meat in olive oil, bay leaves, rosemary, thyme and pepper for at least 1 hour or overnight.

Preheat the oven to 220°C. Salt and gently seal the saddles in 2 tablespoons of butter until they are a pale golden-brown colour. Place the saddles meat-side up in a large roasting pan and roast for 6 minutes, then turn over and roast for another 6 minutes. Check for doneness and return to the oven for another 4–6 minutes if required. Meanwhile, heat the stock in a small saucepan. Remove the pan from the oven, then pour over the verjuice and the warm stock, cover the dish, and leave it to rest in a warm spot for 20 minutes. This will create a beautiful jus to serve with the saddle.

In a separate pan, sauté the rabbit livers on both sides in the balance of the butter (2 minutes on one side, 1 minute on the other). Rest the cooked livers for 5 minutes.

To serve, top the saddles and liver with a slice of anchovy butter and briefly return them to the oven until the butter just starts to melt.

RIVERFISH

 **THE GREAT MURRAY RIVER IS NOT ONLY SOUTH AUSTRALIA'S** major water supply, it also nurtures grapes, citrus fruits, almonds, pistachios, olives and other crops important to the state. It is almost our lifeline, our umbilical cord – but, as ancient as the river system is, it is as fragile as a newborn baby. Only 45 minutes from the Barossa at its closest point, the Murray is another world, and is quite addictive if you've a passion for old wooden boats, riverfish and quiet times.

Riverfish are of immense value to recreational and commercial fishermen in South Australia, and are a well-managed resource. Each licensed fisherman is responsible for an area or 'reach' of the river, and for recording the daily catch; these records provide a long-term overview of the ebb and flow of both native and introduced fish.

But there is much that could be done to develop the river's full potential, and nothing more so than encouraging people to eat carp. European carp were introduced into lagoons in 1961, but when the Murray floods carp find their way into the river system, where they feed on the eggs of native fish and muddy the water, which in turn threatens aquatic vegetation. I call carp 'the rabbit of the river'.

Like the rabbit, carp is seen as a pest and so there is little encouragement for commercial fishermen to catch it since the returns are so low. But, when caught small (1–1.5 kg) from the deep running water of the river, and cooked with knowledge, carp can be highly desirable – in fact it is prized in China, Japan and Eastern Europe, places with strong food cultures in which every ingredient is maximised. It is a point of honour with me to find ways of cooking carp to satisfy a wide spectrum of tastes, from the adventurous to the conservative. We must stop seeing carp as vermin and market it as the viable and inexpensive food source it is, and then we will have a chance of eradicating it from our river systems. I would go so far as to say that, prepared by a good cook, using simple ingredients and eaten fresh, I'd prefer carp to redfin any day. I am determined to convert as many people as I can to carp – as the saying goes, 'eat a fish, save a river'.

Sweet-and-sour flavours are popular with carp in Asian and European countries, and the Mediterranean combination of olives, anchovies and capers also works well.

If you are camping by a river, try cooking carp on the campfire. Gut a 1 kg carp and stuff it with lemon and onion, season thoroughly with salt and freshly ground black pepper, then wrap it in about eight pages of wet newspaper and barbecue for 15 minutes a side or until the paper dries out. When you open the parcel, the skin will peel away, exposing the steamed flesh. Don't be worried about bones – use your fingers.

While the carp is the most reviled of our fish, the king of the river is the Murray cod. Fossils of fish identical to our modern Murray cod have been found in New South Wales, dating back 26 million years. It is thought possible that the species is as old as the Murray–Darling itself – some 50 to 60 million years. Prior to European settlement, Murray cod was not only a food source for Aboriginal people, but also central to their mythology, including their creation stories. It was the largest, most abundant and most beautiful of all our native fish.

Even though Murray cod is now listed as a 'vulnerable species', it can still be fished, but is subject to bag and size limits and closed seasons which vary from state to state. For South Australia the closed season is from 1 September–31 December.

Cod live to a grand old age and can wait out a bad drought in dried-up riverbeds until a flood brings food and scatters predators. However, there were very few floods in the 1980s and seven breeding years were lost. The pressure of excessive recreational fishing over centuries has been exacerbated by many other factors: the regulation of the river flow; the lack of spring flooding in so many years, which is essential to their breeding; the removal of the natural snags of red gum in the river, which are critical to their habitat; and degradation caused by stock grazing on the river bank.

I had heard of the delights of Murray cod for years, but my first taste surpassed my expectations. In March 2003, I had the privilege of sharing an amazing meal with two friends at the Grand Hotel in Mildura, during a weekend conference at which we discussed a national plan for growing olives in Australia. The chef was Stefano de Pieri and, from beginning to end, the meal was one of the 'greats' of my life.

Stefano takes seasonal local produce and cooks according to whim, offering his customers no choice. It's the perfect way to run a country restaurant – here was the food we had dreamed of finding in Italy in 1995 but which had often eluded us in restaurants.

We walked down to the hotel cellar, where Stefano had his 'cave'. The pristine white-clothed table was laid with nothing more than a bottle of Laudemio extra virgin olive oil that had a napkin around its neck, as one would do for a precious bottle of wine. It set the tone for the evening. Stefano cooked one course after another (small courses, I hasten to add), beginning with a slice of polenta and the finest salami and Parmigiano Reggiano, served with the olive oil. Then came a sublime pigeon broth with the breast, livers and croutons floating side by side; freshly grated Parmigiano Reggiano was to hand, as was the oil once more. A mushroom risotto, a quail ravioli and *bollito misto* with mustard fruits followed – and then came the Murray cod.

The fish was displayed on a bed of ice on the table in front of the kitchen, and fillets were cut from the side that wasn't on show. It was a true statement, and the flavour of the fish . . . ! It was sweet and dense, and mingled magnificently with the earthiness of the artichokes Stefano had included in the dish: a combination that was meant to be.

Murray cod is being farmed, although it's not easily available. Even though wild Murray cod have a superior flavour, I hope that the farmed version will succeed, so we can continue to have access to this fish.

The first time I handled a Murray cod myself was under the tutelage of Stefano, for the inaugural Barossa Slow Food Luncheon in 1996. The lunch marked the release of Michael Burr's Wild Olive Oils, so I served pickled wild olives, wild Murray cod and wild hare. Stefano and his wife, Donna, contributed the fish itself. This amazing fish, as long as a man's arm, was enough to feed fifty! I discovered it had a layer of fat, like chicken. So as not to waste anything, I braised the 'wings' in this fat and verjuice – much as I would for a confit. Although there was plenty of fish for all, it was the helpers in the St Hallett's winery kitchen who scored those prized morsels.

It was also Stefano who taught me about freshwater catfish. Another treat of the Murray River, catfish is in such short supply that the South Australian Government is considering legislation that will protect the wild population, while leaving those fish in dams for fishermen. However, at the time of writing, catfish can still be legally fished. Our catfish belongs to a different family from the fish of the same name that is farmed extensively in the United States. Bryan Pierce, one of Australia's most respected fisheries scientists, has eaten many 'catties' and says ours are superior in flavour and oil content. Certainly, under the sure hand of Stefano, catfish is a great delicacy. The flesh is sweet and slightly less dense than that of a rock lobster (catfish is sometimes called 'the crayfish of the poor'). The fish must

be skinned before it is cooked, since the skin is very fatty and has a bad smell – this is one fish from which Stefano doesn't make stock. But he loves to use catfish in a risotto, in which case he uses chicken stock. His favourite way of cooking catfish, however, is to fry floured fillets gently in nut-brown butter and then to deglaze the pan with verjuice. He serves these fillets with wild fennel – how often it is that the simplest way is the best.

What I call callop or yellow belly is now being marketed nationally as golden perch. Whatever the name, this fish is alive and well in the Murray River. I'm very partial to it and even love the jellied fat line that runs along its spine. I bake golden perch whole, gutted but not scaled, and stuff it with preserved lemons and wild fennel. I rub some of the salty, oily pulp from the preserved lemons into the skin, too, so that the flavour penetrates from both sides. I wrap the fish in foil and cook it at 210°C for 15 minutes and then turn the parcel over and cook it for another 15 minutes. Once removed from the oven, I let the fish rest for a while, then peel away the skin. If you have scaled the fish, open the foil for the last 5 minutes of cooking, and drizzle the skin with extra virgin olive oil to brown it.

Friends of ours from the Barossa have a tradition they enjoy every time they camp by the river: a sandwich of freshly caught, filleted and cooked golden perch. It absolutely must be served with white bread, butter, lemon, salt and freshly ground black pepper. Golden perch can also be cooked whole on a campfire, as described for carp on page 500.

Less successful, I find, are silver perch, which are in decline in the river system but are being farmed extensively, particularly in New South Wales. I find them a coarser fish than golden perch, with less oil and flavour. Similarly, while many fishermen claim the introduced redfin to be their favourite to barbecue, I find it a very bland fish. It has good texture, but for me it needs strong spices to make it interesting.

My first taste of bony bream, a freshwater herring, was a revelation. Henry Jones, a keen supporter of riverfish who fishes carp commercially at the mouth of the Murray near Clayton, gave me some bony bream to try. Unfortunately the excellent flesh is full of the tiniest bones imaginable, making eating them nigh on impossible, but they were so delicate, and the flesh whiter even than that of whiting, that I feel I simply must find a way around the bones. Henry Jones and Bryan Pierce were working on a solution to this problem, but I suspect it isn't high enough on a long list of priorities.

You'll often hear it said that riverfish are 'muddy' in flavour. In fact, this is caused not by mud but by algae living in the fat under the skin. This so-called 'muddiness' is not as obvious in winter, when all riverfish are at their best. If you really want to avoid this muddy flavour, you could always have your fish swim in clean water in the bath for a couple of days! An easier option is to remove the skin when cleaning the fish and then soak the fillets in verjuice, or a mixture of 1 part vinegar to 4 parts water, for 30 minutes. The advantage of using verjuice is that it won't mask the flavour of the fish as vinegar can.

It is worthwhile briefly mentioning the two types of crustaceans that inhabit the Murray River, as their respective numbers reflect the state of this waterway. Yabbies (see page 166) have good years and bad years, but are still very much part of the ecosystem – they are also now being farmed in most states. The same cannot be said of the Murray River crayfish, which is rarely seen now. Crays prefer clear, cool, running water, while yabbies thrive in poor-quality backwaters. Crays also need more oxygen than yabbies. As Bryan Pierce puts it, until the river habitat is improved, we can't expect Murray River crayfish to do well. But don't just blame the carp. The number of people who use the river, the eroding wash from speedboats, the overgrazing of river flats, the lack of tree regeneration, and the indiscriminate use of super-phosphates in the past have all contributed to the decline of the Murray, from its upper reaches in Victoria and New South Wales to where it meets the sea in South Australia. Things are improving in South Australia (farmers have to meet stringent criteria for new irrigation proposals and many are moving stock off riverbanks after floods to encourage regeneration, for example), but the three states that use the river must work in unison. We *must* look after our river!

PAN-FRIED CARP WITH ANCHOVY BUTTER *Serves 2*

1 small carp, filleted
plain flour, for dusting
sea salt flakes and freshly ground
   black pepper

butter, for cooking
generous dash of verjuice *or* lemon juice
Anchovy Butter (see page 497), to serve

Dust the carp fillets with flour seasoned generously with salt and pepper.

Heat a knob of butter in a frying pan until nut-brown, then pan-fry the fish for about 3 minutes over medium–high heat. Turn the fish over and cook for 2 minutes on the second side, then deglaze the pan with the verjuice or lemon juice.

Serve the fish with a slice of anchovy butter on top and a salad of peppery green leaves alongside.

THAI FISH BALLS

Makes 20

This is one of my favourite carp dishes. While it includes chilli, remember that I am not a fan, so it's not overly hot.

1 × 250 g carp fillet

1 × 2.5 cm piece ginger, peeled and grated

3–4 spring onions, finely chopped

½ cup firmly packed coriander leaves, roughly chopped

¼ cup basil leaves, roughly chopped

1 clove garlic, finely chopped

½ teaspoon chilli paste

2 teaspoons fish sauce

1 teaspoon soy sauce

2 teaspoons mirin

1 tablespoon coconut milk

vegetable *or* peanut oil, for shallow-frying

Make sure the fish is free of bones, then purée it in a food processor. Add the remaining ingredients, except the oil, to the fish and blend to a smooth paste. Scoop the mixture into little balls and shallow-fry in a frying pan in the hot oil until crisp. Serve with thinly sliced lemon as an appetiser with drinks.

CAMPFIRE MURRAY COD IN A SALT CRUST

Serves 10

It is important to coordinate the preparation of this dish so that you do not make the dough too far ahead. I like to accompany this with damper and some Joseph Foothills Extra Virgin Olive Oil, Russell Jeavons' dukkah, sea salt and native pepper, all of which can be bought from gourmet food stores. If Murray cod is unavailable, you could use snapper instead.

1 large fennel bulb, trimmed and shaved

1 lime, sliced

sea salt flakes

extra virgin olive oil, for cooking

1 × 1.4 kg farmed Murray cod

freshly ground black pepper

¼ cup (60 ml) verjuice

DOUGH

1 kg plain flour, plus extra for dusting

1 kg cooking salt

800 ml cold water

Toss the fennel and lime with sea salt and a little olive oil and set aside. Rub the fish with some olive oil, pepper and verjuice, and set aside to stand while dough is being made.

To make the dough, combine the flour, salt and cold water in a large bowl until a dough forms, then leave to rest for 10 minutes.

Sprinkle the fish with salt. Roll out dough on a piece of baking paper until it is about 6 mm thick. Stuff the fish cavity with the fennel and lime mixture until quite full so it holds its shape. Wrap the fish in the dough, folding the dough like a parcel and tucking the ends in – make sure the dough is not too thick or the crust will crack. Use off-cuts to decorate, brushing them with water to help them stick. Dust the parcel liberally with flour and rest it for 10 minutes in the refrigerator.

Meanwhile, preheat the oven to 180°C. Bake the fish parcel for 35 minutes only. Remove from the oven and rest for at least 35 minutes, preferably 1 hour. Carve the fish at the table, cutting into the dough and peeling it right back, taking the fish skin with it. The flesh will be very moist – use a fork and spoon to serve each portion.

STEFANO'S MURRAY COD   *Serves 6*

1 onion, chopped	¼ cup freshly chopped flat-leaf parsley
1 carrot, chopped	2 tablespoons white wine *or* verjuice
2 cloves garlic, chopped	2 cups (500 ml) Golden Chicken Stock
extra virgin olive oil, for cooking	(see page 57)
6 globe artichokes	100 g butter
1 lemon, halved	6 × 100 g Murray cod fillets
sea salt flakes	extra virgin olive oil, to serve

Gently sauté the onion, carrot and garlic in a little olive oil in a stainless steel or enamelled saucepan over low–medium heat until softened.

Meanwhile, trim the artichokes by cutting away the top third of the bulb, then squeeze the juice of the lemon over. Remove the outer leaves from the base and rub the cut surfaces with lemon. Halve the artichokes if they are large, then add them to the pan with the vegetables, along with salt and the parsley. Increase the heat to high and add the wine or verjuice and chicken stock, then cover the pan with a tight-fitting lid, reduce the heat to low and cook for about 30 minutes.

Preheat the oven to 220°C. Melt the butter in a roasting pan on the stove over low heat. Remove from the heat and slip in the fillets, then season with salt and add the vegetables and some of their cooking juices. Roast for about 7 minutes (depending on the thickness of the fillets), then remove from the oven and swirl the butter and juices to amalgamate. Put the fish on a warm serving plate and spoon over the juices and vegetables, then add a drizzle of your best extra virgin olive oil and serve immediately.

ROOT VEGETABLES

 ROOT VEGETABLES HAVE LONG BEEN FAVOURITES OF MINE, PERHAPS because of their special affinity with game. Their warm flavours and distinct earthiness complement so many dishes, and they are at their very best in winter, when there is a smaller variety of fresh vegetables available.

JERUSALEM ARTICHOKES

The Jerusalem and globe artichoke come from the same plant family, although they are very different species. The globe is part of the thistle genus and grows proudly above the ground, whereas the Jerusalem is a tuber and member of the sunflower genus. Yet this knobbly specimen does share a delicious earthy and nutty sweetness with the heart of the globe artichoke.

Jerusalem artichokes are prolific growers that require little attention and will spread like wildfire. Pristine white when they are first dug up, the tubers darken with age, but as long as they feel firm and crisp, they will be fine.

Most cookbooks won't overwhelm you with ideas for using Jerusalem artichokes. So when in doubt, turn to Stephanie Alexander's *The Cook's Companion*. I was aware that Jerusalem artichokes are particularly suitable for diabetics but it wasn't until I read this book that I learned why. Stephanie writes that these tubers 'contain no starch, so their carbohydrates are well tolerated by diabetics and hypoglycaemics. However, these same carbohydrates are of a type that cannot be broken down by any enzymes we possess. The undigested carbohydrates pass into the gut intact, where they produce great quantities of gas!' It seems these health benefits aren't without their side effects, and it pays never to accept a second helping, particularly in soup, as you'll really notice it.

Jerusalem artichokes have a unique flavour, particularly when they are baked until almost melting. To achieve this, roast halved artichokes (if left whole, they may explode in the oven)

Jerusalem artichoke and pink grapefruit salad with walnuts (see page 508)

at a high temperature (say 200°C) until the skin is golden on both sides and they are fully cooked. For a change, try roasting the artichokes in butter with fresh thyme, lemon rind or thinly sliced meyer lemon, sea salt and freshly ground black pepper.

Boiled artichokes, scrubbed but unpeeled, can be mashed and creamed with knobs of unsalted butter and a good dash of cream – the mash won't have the consistency of potato, so the cream and butter need to be added judiciously so that it doesn't become too runny. Boil or steam unpeeled Jerusalem artichokes and cut them in half as soon as they are cool enough to handle. Drizzle the artichokes with extra virgin olive oil and toss through a tiny bit of finely diced garlic, some flat-leaf parsley or chervil, lemon rind, sea salt and freshly ground black pepper, and serve warm with grilled meat or fish.

Simmer Jerusalem artichokes whole and then slice them thinly with a mandolin into a salad of spinach and pine nuts. As sweet as they are cooked, raw Jerusalem artichokes add a delightful crunch to salads (although some may find them difficult to digest). To peel or not to peel is very much a personal question, but if you do peel them, drop the peeled artichokes into acidulated water to prevent discolouration.

One of my great culinary discoveries was the affinity that Jerusalem artichokes have with seafood. I had two meals within weeks of each other that combined these ingredients. The first was at bel mondo restaurant in Sydney, when Steve Manfredi was chef, where silky tagliatelle overflowed with mussels and slightly crunchy Jerusalem artichokes – a great balance. A dish at the Landhaus restaurant at Bethany in the Barossa Valley (sadly no longer in existence) presented a tart of puréed Jerusalem artichokes topped with poached oysters. The pastry melted in the mouth and a sharp yet rich beurre blanc completed this magical marriage. The earth and sea combination just works so well – try Jerusalem artichokes with marron or scallops.

Jerusalem artichoke soup, perhaps the most familiar use for this vegetable, is simply a purée of the steamed, boiled or even baked vegetable that has been thinned with a little chicken or vegetable stock. To make the soup truly velvety, add a good slug of cream.

JERUSALEM ARTICHOKE AND
PINK GRAPEFRUIT SALAD WITH WALNUTS   *Serves 2*

This recipe could easily be made into a light meal with the addition of prosciutto or grilled pancetta.

2 tablespoons butter	40 g gorgonzola dolce
extra virgin olive oil, for cooking	(see Glossary), crumbled
3 Jerusalem artichokes, peeled and sliced	1 small bunch rocket
widthways (about 160 g)	1½ tablespoons walnut oil
1 small ruby grapefruit, peeled and sliced	1½ tablespoons verjuice
widthways, juice reserved	sea salt flakes and freshly ground
40 g walnuts, toasted	black pepper

Heat the butter with a dash of olive oil in a frying pan until nut-brown, then add Jerusalem artichokes and quickly toss until lightly coloured. Deglaze the pan with the reserved grapefruit juice, then transfer artichokes to a large bowl and leave to cool for a few minutes. Add the remaining ingredients and toss to combine, then serve.

PARSNIPS

Of all root vegetables, parsnips in particular speak to me of late autumn and winter, of warming food and crackling fires. Their rich, nutty, sweet butteriness is perfect with that ultimate cold-weather meal, the stew (or do we not have stews any more, just casseroles and pot-roasts?). I developed a love for parsnips after moving to South Australia over 33 years ago, as our neighbour grew them and always offered us their excess produce. I soon found parsnips to be wonderfully compatible with game, and so during the cooler months, parsnip was the vegetable of the day in our restaurant, coming to the table in many different guises.

Parsnips require a coldish winter to reach their peak. As with many other vegetables, frost plays a part in converting stored starch to sugar, giving that desirable rich, sweet flavour. Early-season parsnips cannot be passed up, however the flavours develop even further from July onwards, but watch out for woody end-of-season produce. When choosing parsnips, don't go for size but look for crisp flesh and pale skin, both of which indicate freshness. A parsnip that has travelled from afar and been displayed for a long time will darken and become limp, the most tell-tale sign of tiredness of all.

I rarely peel parsnips, but then I have access to the freshest specimens possible. I do peel them if making a purée, or the legendary Parsnip Puff (see page 511).

If mashing freshly dug parsnips, I simply give them a scrub and cut them into chunks then steam or boil them until just cooked, before mashing roughly with good extra virgin olive oil, freshly ground black pepper, sea salt and flat-leaf parsley. Leaving the skin on adds to the flavour and texture of the mash, however it's a good idea to peel the parsnips though if they are anything but young and fresh.

To make a purée to rival the creamiest of mashed potato, I peel and chop parsnips into rounds and then seal them in nut-brown butter in a frying pan. I then cook the parsnip until tender in a saucepan with just enough milk to cover, then drain it. I add a spoonful of butter and mash the parsnip, adding cream as I go, until the desired consistency is reached, then season it with salt and freshly ground black pepper.

A great way to use up large parsnips is to make parsnip chips. Peel and cut the tops off the parsnips and slice very thinly lengthways with a sharp knife and a steady hand (or use a mandolin if you have one). Soak the slices in cold water for 10 minutes, then drain and dry very well with a clean tea towel. Heat extra virgin olive oil to about 190°C and fry in small batches until crisp. Drain, salt and serve.

My favourite parsnip combination of all is roasted parsnips with hare – either the saddle, rare-roasted, or the legs, slowly cooked with red wine, bacon or mushrooms and fresh

Roast parsnips

herbs. Roasted parsnips are also great with beef or kangaroo cooked on the barbecue, or with slow-roasted mutton or grilled lamb chops. Whether I peel parsnips for roasting depends on their freshness. I cut them in half lengthways, par-boil them in a little salted water and drain them well. I melt a good amount of butter in a heavy-based roasting pan in a 220°C oven, then just before the butter turns nut-brown I add a little oil to stop it from burning. I put the par-cooked parsnips cut-side down in the melted butter, well spaced so they become crisp rather than soggy and butter-soaked, and then bake them for about 20–30 minutes until caramelised. Roast parsnips are addictive – I've even been known to eat them as a meal in themselves.

PARSNIP PUFF
Serves 4

In the early 1980s, before I knew her, Stephanie Alexander first visited my restaurant. I remember being delighted by her comment in the visitors' book, 'Parsnips were wonderful.' I suspect that it might have been a less-than-perfect day, particularly in those very early years of the restaurant, and finding something positive to say was her way of encouraging me.

That day I had served parsnip puff, a Beverley Sutherland Smith recipe, from her book *A Taste for All Seasons*. This is my adaptation of her recipe. I like the texture obtained from using the food processor but the trick is to start with good parsnips – they should be crisp, not wilted, and as smooth and creamy white as possible. I avoid really large parsnips and the woody ones found near the end of the season.

6 medium parsnips, 10–12 cm long
    and 3 cm wide, unpeeled
75 g butter, chopped
¼ cup (60 ml) cream
pinch freshly grated nutmeg
1 egg
sea salt flakes and freshly ground
    black pepper

TOPPING
1 tablespoon breadcrumbs made from
    stale bread
30 g melted butter

Preheat the oven to 180°C. Cook the parsnips in a saucepan of boiling salted water until tender. Drain well and purée in a food processor or put through a mouli while still warm. Add the butter, cream, nutmeg and egg to the parsnips and season with salt and pepper. Spoon into a buttered ovenproof dish.

Sprinkle the breadcrumbs over the top, then pour over the melted butter and bake in the oven for 20 minutes. This dish can be prepared in the morning and reheated at dinner time.

PARSNIP QUENELLES WITH WALNUTS

Serves 6

This dish combines two of winter's greatest offerings – parsnips and walnuts. It can be served with beef, lamb or kangaroo – warming fare on a chilly day. It will also stand on its own as an entrée, and makes a good luncheon dish with a leafy salad.

¼ cup freshly shelled walnuts

1 kg young parsnips

milk, for cooking

75 g unsalted butter

2 egg yolks

freshly grated nutmeg

sea salt flakes and freshly ground
    black pepper

plain flour, to combine

olive oil, for frying

Preheat the oven to 200°C. Roast the walnuts on a baking tray for 10 minutes or until coloured but not burnt. Rub the hot nuts in a clean tea towel to remove the bitter skin; if you are using local new season's nuts, you can skip this step.

If the parsnips are really small, just scrub them; if they are medium-sized, peel them. Cut the parsnips into even chunks, then put them into a smallish saucepan and cover with milk. Boil until tender, about 5–10 minutes. Drain well, then add butter and let it melt. Mix in the egg yolks, nutmeg, salt, pepper and roasted walnuts and add just enough flour to pull the mixture together.

Make quenelles using two dessertspoons: take a spoonful of the mixture, then use the other spoon to mould it into a smooth oval shape (this looks attractive, but is optional – any shape will do). Refrigerate the quenelles on a baking tray lined with baking paper for at least 20 minutes, or until ready to cook.

Pour olive oil into a heavy-based saucepan to a depth of 5 cm and heat until very hot. Fry the quenelles, a few at a time, until golden brown on both sides. Drain on kitchen paper and serve hot.

SALSIFY AND SCORZONERA

A vegetable that you have might only have seen in a book rather than a greengrocer's is salsify. To my knowledge, no one in South Australia is growing it in commercial quantities, though I sometimes hear of it on restaurant menus, which means it is being grown for specific markets. This is a vegetable we should all be demanding – it has a wonderful oyster-like flavour and is known by some as the oyster plant.

Scorzonera belongs to the same family as salsify but is a brownish-black colour, whereas salsify is whitish in appearance, like a fresh parsnip. Both have hairy roots that resemble those of ginseng.

Salsify grow in a similar way to carrots but take much longer to mature. To be honest, it's been years since I've grown salsify myself, having got out of the habit when a grower in Greenock supplied it to me in the Pheasant Farm Restaurant days.

Cut the tops off the salsify as you would a carrot and scrub the soil away under running water. Salsify can be peeled and tossed in acidulated water to keep them white, but I just leave them whole, with the skins on, and either steam or cook them in salted water. When tender, slip the skins off the salsify whilst they are still warm. I like to serve them on their own with a little butter and freshly ground black pepper. French and Italian dishes often team salsify with chicken, and it makes a terrific soup.

The flowers of the salsify are also edible. The buds taste a little like asparagus. They can be pickled: put alternate layers of the flowers in a jar with layers of sugar and pack down firmly. Cover with cider vinegar that has been boiled and cooled. Leave to mature for a week, then use in salads.

SALSIFY WITH COFFIN BAY OYSTERS AND OYSTER MUSHROOMS WITH A SPARKLING WINE SAUCE *Serves 6*

A simple yet very special dish is this one featuring a combination of oyster flavours.

juice of 2 lemons

12 salsify

sea salt flakes

18 medium–large oyster mushrooms

butter, for cooking

freshly ground black pepper

18 large Coffin Bay oysters (preferably
  unopened, with their juices)

SPARKLING WINE SAUCE

1 × 375 ml bottle Yalumba Brut de Brut *or*
  other dry sparkling white wine

1 cup (250 ml) rich double cream

80 g unsalted butter

Add the lemon juice to a large saucepan of water, then add the salsify and cook with a pinch of salt until tender. Drain and leave until cool enough to handle, then slip the skins off the salsify while still warm. Cut in half lengthways.

In a large frying pan over medium heat, toss the oyster mushrooms in butter until golden brown, then toss in the salsify to both warm and gently brown. Season to taste with a little pepper. Transfer mushrooms, salsify and any pan juices to a bowl, then set aside and keep warm.

Make the sparkling wine sauce by reducing the wine over high heat in a frying pan. At the last minute, open the oysters and drain the juices into the pan, along with any juices from the mushrooms bowl. Add the cream and reduce to the desired consistency.

Slip the oysters into the warm sauce and toss for just a few seconds. Remove the oysters and set aside with the mushrooms and salsify, then quickly whisk the cold cubed butter into the sauce.

To serve, spoon a little sauce into the centre of 6 plates, then stack the salsify on top. Arrange the oyster mushrooms on top, with the oysters cascading over.

SWEET POTATO, SWEDE AND TURNIP

Sweet potato is perfect simply par-boiled then baked, though it needs to be handled carefully so it is not oversweet – I like to add a little lemon juice for balance.

Swede is a vegetable that is often ignored but is delicious when dug fresh from the ground and simply boiled and mashed with a little butter and sprinkled with some freshly grated nutmeg and freshly ground black pepper. It makes a wonderful addition to any meal, from a piece of boiled silverside to a grilled lamb chop. In the restaurant I used to serve it with vegetable soup or lamb stew, and I found people either loved or hated its sweet earthiness.

Turnips are easy to grow. They are a little like radishes, in that they seem to mature very quickly – or perhaps it is just that I like them fairly small, as their sweetness is then at its peak, especially when they are pulled fresh from the ground. The bonus with turnips is that turnip greens have a lovely, sharp flavour which contrasts well with the sweetness of the vegetable. Turnips have a particular affinity with duck and, of all vegetables, they work best at the 'baby' stage. They look attractive whole, either caramelised or just boiled and tossed with butter and freshly ground black pepper.

CARAMELISED TURNIPS OR PARSNIPS   *Serves 4*

75 g butter

juice of 1 lemon

500 g turnips *or* parsnips, peeled
and cut into strips

1 tablespoon sugar

1 tablespoon red-wine vinegar

sea salt flakes and freshly ground
black pepper

Melt the butter in a frying pan or other shallow pan with a lid, add lemon juice and vegetables, then cover and simmer gently over low heat until just cooked (turnips will take about 5 minutes, parsnips a little longer).

In a saucepan, heat the sugar until it melts, then add the vinegar and simmer gently over low heat until the sugar caramelises. Add the vegetables and cooking juices to the caramel, season to taste, toss and serve.

GARDEN GREENS SOUP WITH PURÉE OF TURNIP   *Serves 4*

This soup was hastily created one Sunday in winter during the restaurant days, when I had run out of ingredients and, in desperation, turned to the greens growing in a very small vegetable patch. I made a soup of the fresh greens and spooned the puréed turnips into the centre instead of cream. I remember it as wonderful. Freshness is of paramount importance in this recipe, so don't try it if your turnips and greens aren't crisp.

450 g turnips, peeled

120 g unsalted butter

2 tablespoons cream

sea salt flakes and freshly ground
black pepper

1 bunch spring onions, chopped

2–3 cups turnip greens, washed and
finely chopped

3 sprigs flat-leaf parsley, leaves picked

10 leaves sorrel

3 cups (750 ml) Golden Chicken Stock
(see page 57) *or* vegetable stock

Cook the turnips in a saucepan of boiling salted water until tender, then purée in a food processor. Add 40 g of the butter, the cream and salt and pepper to taste. Keep warm.

Melt the remaining butter in a saucepan, add the spring onions and cook over low heat until translucent, then toss in the turnip greens and herbs and stir to combine. Add chicken stock and cook for a few minutes until tender. You could purée the greens and swirl through the turnip purée but I choose to serve it ladled into bowls with the greens just wilted, and spoon the purée into the centre.

SMOKED FOODS

 **SMOKED FOODS ARE THE BASIS OF THE BAROSSA CULINARY** tradition. The Silesians who settled the Valley and other parts of South Australia in the mid-1800s brought with them their sausage-making and smoking skills. Smokehouses were built as a matter of course, and many Barossa cottages and farms still boast them.

Our first Barossa home, across the river from the Pheasant Farm Restaurant, had one such smokehouse. In my enthusiasm for country life, soon after moving in I declared that we must raise, kill and smoke our own pigs. Step one was easy; steps two and three took some doing. We called upon Lachlan Marcus McKinnon, my husband Colin's uncle, and an old bushy who was an extraordinary man and the last of the packhorse bagmen. Uncle Lachie lived with us for six months, and the small challenge of killing and smoking a pig was easily within his grasp. Colin had organised the logistics – the bathtub in the paddock and other essentials – but on the morning of the 'occasion' he was nowhere to be seen. His uncle had to handle it all alone, and I suspect he never forgave Colin for disappearing when the deed was to be done.

Lachie's bad temper vanished, though, when he and I came to smoking the pig – we were so excited that the talk was of nothing else. We bought a brine pump especially for the occasion (the only time it was ever used), our neighbour, a saw-miller, supplied the sawdust, and we started the fire with eucalyptus twigs. Lachie kept the fire smouldering day and night, which interfered with his drinking, but he was a man with a mission. The pig smoked for days – the old smokehouse was so black from generations of use it was obvious it had produced successes in the past. The resulting bacon was the best I have ever eaten (Col thinks I got sawdust in my eyes); we fried it in great slabs every morning for breakfast and felt so indulgent and clever. There was no doubt it was very smoky bacon, but then I was looking for a smack-between-the-eyes experience – and I got it!

The smoking tradition is still alive and well in the Barossa. In each town the butcher smokes in his or her own distinctive style, and there is much discussion and debate about

who makes the best mettwurst, ham, pork hocks, sheep's or calf's tongue, lachschinken (a smoked fillet of pork sliced super-fine like prosciutto) and so on. Everyone has their favourites, often travelling to one butcher for a particular speciality, and on to a neighbouring town for another product. Until my daughter Saskia began making bacon and smallgoods from the Leinerts' Berkshire pigs, I relied on Schulz's Butchers of Angaston – Schulz's then made the best sugar-cured bacon but, as every butcher in the Valley smokes their bacon traditionally, it is really a matter of individual taste. In the Barossa hams are brined and then smoked a little before being cooked in a copper and given a final smoking. This technique imparts a wonderful flavour quite different from that of some commercial hams, which are often smoke-injected. The sugar-cured hams of the Barossa are sought after from far afield, as are the other products of traditional smokers committed to the smoking tradition Australia-wide. As in all food manufacture, you get what you pay for – the mass-produced market cannot afford the costs of traditional production.

Most products for smoking are brined first, whether they are to be cold- or hot-smoked. Cold-smoking is a long, slow process that preserves rather than cooks. Bacon, mettwurst, and lachschinken are cold-smoked for two to three days, depending on weather conditions. The temperatures at which the meat is smoked are carefully regulated. It is imperative, for example, that mettwurst is smoked at below 28°C for the first 24 hours; the next day it rises to 30–35°C. The art, of course, is maintaining the temperature when the smokehouse is unattended at night. Natural fermentation gives cold-smoked meat its acidic flavour, and a starter culture (which reduces pH levels to a level unattractive to bacteria) used in the commercial manufacture of mettwurst does the same.

As the term suggests, most hot-smoked food is smoked relatively quickly and at a higher temperature. This process effectively cooks the ingredient. While meat, poultry and game can all be hot-smoked successfully, the best results are to be had when a fat animal or bird is used, as the process can be very drying.

We used to brine and hot-smoke our breeders at the end of each pheasant season when they were at their fattest. They made a delicious salad with bitter greens, sautéed mushrooms and sweet-and-sour mustard apricots. As these birds were both old and fat, it was only the ample breasts that were tender enough for use in a salad; the smoked legs became such a great addition to our classic poultry stock that we always froze them for later use.

Although many of the Barossa smokehouses are still standing, lives have become so busy that many of us make special requests of our butchers, who, given enough notice, are happy to oblige. Smoked pork belly, tongues, pork fat, and legs or saddle of lamb can be ordered, and I have had Schulz's smoke a whole suckling pig for a banquet to great effect. I scored the skin and painted on a marinade of wholegrain mustard and brown sugar first and then borrowed my neighbour's blow torch to glaze it.

I was always indebted to Schulz's Butchers for allowing me to smoke my kangaroo saddle there for so many years. This smoked kangaroo was an integral part of our restaurant and epitomised my philosophy of using traditional Valley techniques and local (and in this case indigenous) produce. My Smoked Kangaroo and Duck Egg Pasta (see page 420) became the most famous of the Pheasant Farm Restaurant dishes, but was only one of the ways in which I used the roo.

What Colin misses most about the restaurant is the Sunday afternoons. After lunch service, our extended restaurant family would all eat leftovers and put the world right over good wine, basking in the glow of a successful day or blotting out a bad one. Whenever the cupboard was really bare, because we'd been incredibly cost-efficient and everything had sold, or we'd lingered on long past the afternoon and needed supper, we'd always be left with two ingredients: bread and a reserve supply of smoked kangaroo. Sometimes crusty bread, smoked roo, aïoli, squeezed cloves of slowly roasted garlic and slivers of pickled quince would come together with salad greens. On other occasions we'd feast on a salad of smoked kangaroo, sliced pear, rocket and Parmigiano Reggiano. Roasted capsicum, rocket and extra virgin olive oil were always favourites with the roo and bread too.

Chef and close friend Cheong Liew and I once spent a wonderful few days cooking and experimenting with my produce in my Barossa kitchen. He served smoked kangaroo on a bed of witlof and rocket with salmon roe and local fresh oysters alongside and a dressing of extra virgin olive oil, finely chopped garlic and balsamic vinegar. The sweet, sour and salty combination was great.

Chilled foods are fragile in nature, and it's important that the public is aware of this. I encourage everyone to carry an esky in the boot of their car, in order to ensure that any meat or smallgood on its way home from the butcher or being taken on a picnic is adequately chilled. After the tragic Garibaldi affair in 1995, when contaminated mettwurst resulted in the death of a child and the hospitalisation of several others, the South Australian Government moved quickly to upgrade all meat-processing as part of a quality-assurance program. The rest of the states followed suit, so that now every meat, pâté and smallgoods producer in Australia is regulated by heavily audited programs to ensure food safety. But some of the changes to food production have resulted in a change of flavour and texture in the interests of safety. As mentioned earlier, it is now mandatory to use a starter culture under controlled conditions when making mettwurst and salami commercially – natural fermentation no longer takes place. Mettwurst used to be made by allowing the seasoned minced meat to sit for a few days in a coolroom before it was put into skins to ferment naturally in the smokehouse. The wooden barrels in which the mixture was traditionally kept were replaced many years ago by plastic, at the request of health authorities – no one realised then that the wood had properties that helped with fermentation.

I understand the need for these changes in the mass-production of mettwurst and salami but I would dearly love to see the regulations revised to allow the operation of small producers bound by the highest standards of hygiene and the ability to maintain control via traditional methods (just like those cheese-makers who wish to make unpasteurised cheeses). These producers would stand apart as artisans. These changes represent a loss of our heritage and I think we should be able to strike a balance between maintaining safety and retaining flavour; traditional methods seem to offer us both. Food prepared by traditional methods meets the highest safety standards if these methods are followed properly.

GLAZED LEG OF HAM *Serves 12*

There is a world of difference between traditionally made and smoke-injected hams and it's worth seeking out specialist suppliers of the traditional product. I have been spoilt by having easy access to sugar-cured Barossa hams. Schulz's have always been my favourite, but all the Barossa butchers traditionally smoke theirs, as do smokehouses elsewhere. Although there are some in each state, the standout was probably the late Jonathon Gianfredo, of Jonathon's of Collingwood in Melbourne.

Traditionally cloves are often dotted over the glazed surface of a ham, but I find them too strong and use dried figs instead. The figs almost burn in the cooking, which gives their sweetness a slightly bitter edge.

1 × 7 kg leg ham
175 g brown sugar
½ cup (125 ml) Dijon mustard

1½ cups (375 ml) verjuice *or* white wine
400 g dried figs, halved

Preheat the oven to 220°C. Strip the skin off the ham but leave on the fat (you need 5 mm–1 cm). Score the fat quite deeply into a diamond pattern but be careful not to cut through to the meat.

Mix the sugar and mustard into a paste and pat it evenly over the top and sides of the ham. Pour half of the verjuice or wine into the base of a baking dish and bake the ham for 15 minutes. Reduce the temperature to 200°C.

Carefully fix the fig halves into the corners of the diamonds with toothpicks. Pour the remaining verjuice over the ham. Add a little water to the baking dish to prevent the juices from burning, if necessary. Bake the ham for another 10 minutes, then let cool before serving.

SMOKED LAMB'S TONGUE WITH RÉMOULADE SAUCE   *Serves 4*

The basis for this recipe for rémoulade sauce comes from Elizabeth David's *French Provincial Cooking*, although I've added to it over time. It was my friend Peter Wall who first made it with me – he added the cornichons – to serve with a brined and baked hand of pork for one of our picnic extravaganzas. After that, rémoulade became a favourite, especially with smoked food or offal. This is one instance where I might use a combination of grapeseed or vegetable oil and extra virgin olive oil, as the latter could be overpowering unless it was a ripe and mellow one.

You will need to order the smoked tongues in advance from your butcher. You could use a pressure cooker to speed up the cooking of the tongues – or a crockpot to make it very much slower. I find my crockpot handy for putting food on to cook in the morning to be ready that night.

12 smoked lamb's tongues,
    soaked overnight in cold water
1 onion, roughly chopped
1 carrot, roughly chopped
1 bay leaf
3 black peppercorns
butter, for cooking

RÉMOULADE SAUCE
2 hard-boiled egg yolks
red-wine vinegar, to taste
1 egg yolk
1 teaspoon Dijon mustard
sea salt flakes and freshly ground
    black pepper
150 ml extra virgin olive oil
2 cornichons (see Glossary), finely chopped
1 tablespoon tiny capers
1 tablespoon freshly chopped tarragon
1 tablespoon freshly chopped chives
squeeze of lemon juice (optional)

Place the drained tongues, onion, carrot, bay leaf and peppercorns into a stockpot. Cover with water and cook at a simmer for 1–2 hours or until the tongues yield to pressure when squeezed. Allow the tongues to cool in the cooking liquid.

To make the sauce, pound the hard-boiled egg yolks with a drop of vinegar using a mortar and pestle (or carefully and slowly in a food processor) to make a paste, then stir in the raw egg yolk and mustard and season with salt and pepper. Pour the olive oil in slowly in a thin stream, incorporating it into the sauce as you go (this is the same technique used for making mayonnaise). Once all the oil has been incorporated and the sauce is thick, fold the cornichons, capers and herbs into the sauce. If necessary, adjust the flavour with a little more vinegar (or a squeeze of lemon juice) – it should be piquant.

To serve, skin the tongues and then cut them in half lengthways. Heat a little butter in a frying pan over high heat until nut-brown, then seal the tongues on both sides for a minute or so. Serve the hot tongues with the rémoulade sauce and some peppery greens.

POLENTA WITH SMOKED KANGAROO
AND PARMIGIANO REGGIANO

Serves 4

This came from one of our Sunday nights with the restaurant family. I sometimes add goat's cheese to this dish as well.

150 g Parmigiano Reggiano

3 cups (750 ml) Golden Chicken Stock
   (see page 57)

185 g polenta

1½ teaspoons salt

butter, for cooking

⅓ cup (80 ml) extra virgin olive oil

200 g very thinly sliced smoked
   kangaroo *or* super-thinly sliced
   raw beef or venison fillet

2 handfuls rocket leaves

good-quality balsamic vinegar
   (optional), to serve

Preheat the oven to 150°C. Grate 100 g of the Parmigiano Reggiano and set it aside. Heat the stock in a deep, heavy-based saucepan until simmering, then pour in the polenta and salt, stirring constantly. Stir the polenta over very low heat for about 20 minutes or until it begins to come away from the sides of the pan, then add the grated Parmigiano Reggiano and stir through. Tip the polenta into an ovenproof bowl, then dot with a little butter and put it in the oven, covered, to keep warm.

When you are ready to serve, warm the olive oil gently in a frying pan over low–medium heat and toss the kangaroo in it quickly. The pan should not be too hot or the kangaroo will discolour and spoil. Turn the warm polenta out onto a serving platter and mound the roo and rocket around it, then shave the remaining Parmigiano Reggiano over the lot with a potato peeler. Add a drizzle of balsamic vinegar, if desired.

VENISON

WHEREAS VENISON WAS ONCE ONLY WITHIN THE AMBIT OF restaurateurs, who either bought a whole animal and butchered it themselves or imported specific cuts from New Zealand, it is now available from most specialty butchers and is usually sold off the bone and vacuum-packed. It is, admittedly, still expensive by the kilogram, but a piece of trimmed meat with no waste can be bought well within reason – and you only need about 150 g per person. Don't think, however, that you should only consider the prime cuts: shoulders or shins, surrounded by tendons, are full of flavour when slow-cooked and are a lot less expensive.

A promotional book called *Gold on Four Feet*, published in the late 1970s, encouraged dangerously high expectations for venison farming in this country, but the industry, although still small, is now settling in for the long haul. Fallow deer are the most common breed in South Australia, Victoria and New South Wales, while red deer are raised in Queensland and smaller numbers of rusa and chital deer are farmed in parts of northern Australia.

The red deer is my favourite, although the diet of the animal determines the meat's flavour – and those from the wild have a more distinctive flavour than those farmed. The fallow deer is less than half the size of the red deer; its meat is milder and finer in texture when young, and tends to be preferred by most Australian consumers. The rusa is closer to the red in flavour and texture and may even be a little stronger. The chital is proving not to be commercially viable, as it is a nervous animal; its meat is mild, pale and a little like veal.

In the Pheasant Farm Restaurant days, my venison supplier used to talk with regret of the 'old days', when he had a licence to shoot in the wild – although the powerful flavour imparted by the saltbush on which the deer had fed was too much for him and his customers of the time. I used to have access to such animals, shot in the field without stress and hung for weeks. I thought the flavour was superb, but I must admit I was in the minority.

Game and poultry producer Ian Milburn, of Glenloth Game in northwest Victoria, is now supplying wild field-shot venison. In truth it's the only venison I'm really excited about – I love the flavour of game and am not looking for the gaminess of an animal to be diluted, as some are. To me, the animals being shot in the field is the most humane way of killing them, and no stress for the animal means quality of meat.

The practice of harvesting farmed deer in their first year can result in the meat having a much less developed flavour than that of an older animal. To me it is like yearling beef – lacking in character – although this is a very personal opinion, as the venison I've tasted that has been shot in the wild has set a very high benchmark.

The industry has been pushing the notion that the flavour of today's venison is not as confronting as that of old or wild venison. This is not an issue for me: I love the gamy flavour of venison and like the carcass to be well hung to enhance that flavour and to tenderise the meat. When I had the restaurant I was able to make such demands of my suppliers, usually individual farmers, but I now let specific cuts age in their vacuum-packaging. (In fact, vacuum-packaging replaces the ageing and hanging process that so few butchers are able to undertake themselves because of lack of space.) If you choose to do this too, remember to

turn the package over every couple of days. The recommended shelf-life of vacuum-packed venison is three weeks; after four weeks the flavour of the meat is much gamier and more 'livery', encouraging some to keep the meat for up to six weeks. Just remember to keep it refrigerated throughout. When you come to use the meat, remove it from its packaging about an hour in advance to rid it of any plastic smell. Once out of its packaging, the meat needs to be used within a couple of days.

There is no shortage of ideas for cooking venison in European books but you'll have to keep in mind that farmed venison needs less cooking than meat from a wild animal. Overcooking venison (as with most game) ruins it, unless, of course, you are slow-cooking or braising the so-called lesser cuts. If you can't accept your meat rare, or medium–rare at the most, you'd be better off forgetting the prime cuts of venison from the saddle and the trimmed cuts from the leg muscles, as the meat will be tough, dry and mealy in texture. Because all venison is almost devoid of fat, if cooked beyond this it's important to protect it by marinating it in extra virgin olive oil before cooking, after it has been trimmed of all sinew. I like to add some bruised juniper berries, bay leaves and freshly ground black pepper to the olive oil.

When roasting or pan-frying venison, you need to cook the meat quickly at a high temperature and allow a long resting time. For pan-frying, the small eye fillet is the most tender cut, while hind cuts, trimmed from the leg or the saddle, are also suitable. Cut the meat across the grain to produce 1.5–2 cm-thick steaks, and cook them over high heat for about a minute a side in nut-brown butter with some fresh rosemary or sage leaves, then rest them for 5 minutes. A sharp jelly or Cumberland sauce added to the pan when the meat has been removed to rest is an easy way of making a sauce.

The saddle, on which the loin and fillet are joined, can be ordered on the bone (it comes as a rack with eight or ten chops) and is considered the best cut of all for roasting. Cooking on the bone retains moisture; the meat is tender and, I find, sweeter. A saddle of about 1 kg should be sealed before it is roasted at 230°C for 10–15 minutes, and then rested for about 15 minutes before it is carved.

Thicker pieces for roasting require more cooking and basting after the initial searing. For cuts off the bone, allow about 30 minutes per kilogram at 220°C. The resting time is a crucial part of the cooking process – rest the meat for the same length of time as it took to cook.

Pickled cumquats or pickled native currants have a piquancy that's attractive with venison. They can be added to the marinade before the venison is cooked, or rubbed into the meat with a little extra virgin olive oil and freshly ground black pepper before sealing and roasting it. Or throw some pickled cumquats or currants into the sauce in the final stages of cooking and add a little of the pickling liquid (but be judicious, as the liquid will be very vinegary).

Jane Casey's chestnuts and Brussels sprouts (see page 379) would be a perfect side dish for roasted or pan-fried venison, as would any form of root vegetable, such as roasted or puréed parsnips or swedes, or baked beetroot. Wide sheets of Duck Egg Pasta (see page 420) or spätzle (short German noodles that are made by forcing dough through the holes of a colander into a simmering sauce) provide a great contrast in textures.

Diced shoulder, blade, chuck or shin meat is great to use in braises – just seal small batches over high heat first. Braising venison slowly for a couple of hours at 180°C with lots of wine, juniper berries, bay leaves or rosemary, and orange rind or tamarind, produces wonderful results. Don't be afraid of adding strong flavours like field mushrooms and sugar-cured bacon or pancetta either, as venison can take them well.

Venison shoulder makes a great pie. I like to use mushrooms, as dark and old (but not slimy) as I can get them, lots of small onions or golden shallots, pancetta, rosemary, garlic and veal stock and perhaps some tomato paste. I then gently braise chunks of venison in these flavourings for about 2 hours. When the filling has cooked, I make a simple lid with Sour-cream Pastry (see page 424) and bake the pie for 20 minutes at 200°C.

In late 1996 I roasted five double saddles of venison on the bone at the Tokyo Park Hyatt for a dinner held to launch our pâté in Japan. The trimmed meat rested overnight smothered with olive oil and seasoned with lots of rosemary, bruised juniper berries and cracked black pepper. The next day we prepared a sauce along the lines of that served with stuffed loin (see page 530) – except that we started with 10 kg of venison bones and veal stock made by executive chef Rainer Becker, and we used 1991 Mountadam pinot noir to deglaze the baking dish! (In total we used two magnums of this wonderful wine, which also accompanied the dish.) More juniper, rosemary and pepper were added to the sauce as the meat was resting. The beautifully rare venison was then served with this fabulous

sauce, duck egg pasta (which took one patient cook the whole day to prepare) and Brussels sprouts and chestnuts caramelised with a touch of sugar, veal stock and wine. It was a huge hit.

Venison also saved the day in the restaurant on one memorable occasion. It was the longest Sunday lunch service I can remember: we had a power failure, and a full house. It was the middle of summer and no electricity meant no cooling, no ovens and no water, since we relied on pumps to supply bore or rainwater to the restaurant. Thankfully I noticed the lights flicker hesitantly, so we were able to fill stockpots with rainwater for making coffee and cooking vegetables, pasta and so on before we actually lost the power. (Later we formed a human chain to the dam to quickly fill huge plastic containers with water that was then heated over gas for washing the dishes.) The silence in the kitchen was amazing: no exhaust fan whizzing in our ears like an aeroplane about to take off and no whirr of the oven, just the hissing of the gas flames.

My menu was very oven-focused and most of the dishes were cooked to order and carved off the bone, particularly the pheasant. But suddenly, no ovens! I had just put a large haunch of venison into the oven at its usual high temperature minutes before the power failure and actually forgot about it in the drama (the clock had stopped too and, without the usual noise, the whole tempo of the kitchen had slowed). There was enough residual heat to cook the venison to perfection, yet it must have been in the oven for more than an hour and a half. The menu was hastily changed to include slow-cooked venison and, with my honour intact, I was relieved to learn that you can successfully cook a prime cut in a slow oven.

The use of venison meat is well documented, but as the Deer Association points out, there is also a market, particularly in Asia, for the tails, pizzles (penises), tongues, eyes, brains, blood and sinews of deer and, of course, the velvet from the antlers. While we're talking of things normally only whispered across the table, Jane Grigson gives a wonderful recipe for brawn in her book *Charcuterie and French Pork Cookery*. It's called *fromage de tête*, and I made it once using deer's penis and other parts of the animal, along with a pig's head. Suffice to say this was not a popular creation, and nearly caused a divorce in the family.

A quote that tickles my fancy comes from one of the few game books I respect, *Gourmet Game*, by Philippa Scott. (In many other game books I've come across the cooking times seem way off the mark, making me wonder if the authors actually cook.) Philippa explains that 'the edible entrails of a deer are known as umbles. These used to be made into a pie, usually a "below stairs" provision, which gave occasion to the expression "eating humble pie". The entrails were cooked with ginger, nutmeg, dates, raisins and currants, then baked in a pastry case in the oven.' Wonderful!

CARPACCIO OF VENISON WITH PARMIGIANO REGGIANO AND ROCKET *Serves 6*

Raw venison lends itself well to carpaccio. I've had it with fresh truffles shaved over it, and the earthiness of the truffles against the sweetness of the raw meat was sensational. Although truffles are very much a luxury, perhaps they will become more accessible and affordable in Australia as farmers in Tasmania and Victoria become more successful. In the meantime, truffles from Italy and France are imported by a handful of people, if you are willing to be extravagant.

1 clove garlic	1 × 300 g fillet of venison
1 small sprig rosemary, leaves stripped	2 handfuls rocket leaves
½ cup (125 ml) extra virgin olive oil	180 g Parmigiano Reggiano
freshly ground black pepper	sea salt flakes

Make a paste of the garlic, rosemary leaves and 1 tablespoon of the olive oil using a mortar and pestle, then add the pepper. Smear the paste over the venison, then wrap the meat in plastic film and put it in the freezer for 20 minutes.

Carve the chilled meat (it should not be frozen) into paper-thin slices. Arrange a layer of meat over the base of each serving plate and allow it to return to room temperature. Drizzle over the remaining olive oil, then add the rocket leaves and shavings of Parmigiano Reggiano. Season and serve immediately.

LOIN OF VENISON STUFFED WITH
MUSHROOMS AND HERBS

Serves 8–10

2 × 1 kg loins of venison (off the bone)

extra virgin olive oil, for cooking

2 tablespoons juniper berries, bruised

2 bay leaves

freshly ground black pepper

1 kg field mushrooms, finely chopped

2 bunches spring onions, finely chopped

2 sprigs thyme, chopped

10 stalks flat-leaf parsley, finely chopped

butter, for cooking

sea salt flakes

2 small carrots, roughly chopped

2 onions, roughly chopped

1 stick celery, roughly chopped

¼ cup (60 ml) brandy

1 litre reduced veal stock

Remove the venison from its packaging at least an hour in advance of cooking, then trim it of any sinews and even up its shape. Keep the trimmings for making a sauce later on. Put the meat in a bowl and smother it with olive oil, then add the juniper berries, bay leaves and lots of pepper.

Combine the chopped mushrooms, spring onions, thyme and parsley. Season generously, then cook small batches of this mixture at a time in a frying pan over medium heat, in a little butter until softened. Reduce any juices and add them to the mushroom mixture, which should be like a thick paste.

Preheat the oven to 230°C. In a roasting pan, toss the carrots, onions and celery with a little olive oil and the reserved meat trimmings and caramelise in the oven for 20 minutes. Meanwhile, cut a pocket the length of each piece of meat down the middle of the loin and stuff with the mushroom mixture, then tie up the meat with string if necessary. Season the meat and seal it on all sides on the stove in a heavy-based roasting pan, then transfer it to the oven and roast for 10 minutes. Turn the meat over and cook it for another 5–10 minutes. Remove from the oven and transfer the meat to a warm plate to rest for 20 minutes, loosely covered with foil.

While the meat is resting, tip the caramelised vegetables into the pan used to roast the meat and scrape every bit of goodness off the bottom with a spatula. Place the roasting pan over high heat and deglaze it with the brandy. Add the veal stock and reduce the resulting sauce to the desired consistency, then strain it into a hot jug for serving, discarding the vegetables. Don't forget to add the juices from the resting meat to the sauce at the last moment. Check the sauce for seasoning, then carve the meat and serve with the sauce.

WITLOF

I HAVE ALWAYS BEEN PARTICULARLY PARTIAL TO BITTER flavours. As Angelo Pellegrini writes in *The Food Lover's Garden*, 'my own fondness for chicory approaches addiction'. I love Pellegrini's writing and echo his sentiments here. What I know as witlof, a form of chicory, is called Belgian endive elsewhere. In case you are in any doubt, the vegetable I am referring to is shaped a little like an elongated tulip, with more tightly packed leaves. Witlof has been forced – that is, it is shielded from light in the latter stages of its growth by earth which is banked up around the roots and trimmed heads. Grown like this, its leaves remain tightly furled and white with just a flush of yellow or apple-green. The more green that is evident, the more bitter the witlof will be. Although by rights a winter vegetable, it is now available year-round.

Witlof is bitter and cleansing at the same time. In fact, it is so refreshing eaten raw that it can be used as a palate cleanser instead of a sorbet, since it acts as a balance to anything sweet. When cooked, it becomes bittersweet as it caramelises.

Witlof needs to be handled delicately or it turns brown on the edges. It is transported in a large tray, indented to give each individually wrapped 'bulb' maximum protection from bruising and light, which makes the leaves turn green and consequently more bitter. It has a fairly short shelf-life, becoming soft with age, but if you find yourself with witlof that is no longer crisp, bake them whole rather than waste them. However, fresh, crisp witlof is the most desirable of all and is absolutely essential for certain salads.

Fresh witlof is quite beautiful to look at. By pulling the leaves off one at a time you can make an extravagant-looking salad from just one bulb. Try combining witlof and rocket leaves: the mixture is as attractive as it is tasty. Witlof also goes really well with sliced fennel, blood orange and toasted walnuts. Dress the salad with a vinaigrette of walnut oil, garlic, Dijon mustard, red-wine vinegar and a little cream.

Witlof leaves, taken carefully from the bulb, make a natural cup for hors d'oeuvres. Swirl prosciutto-thin slices of smoked kangaroo brushed with some extra virgin olive oil onto witlof leaves and top with salmon roe. The combination of the bitterness of the witlof, the sweetness of the kangaroo and the saltiness of the roe is fantastic. Use the leaves, too, to encase rich pork, duck or Rabbit Rillettes (see page 493) and add a dab of quince chutney on top.

Fresh witlof leaves can become the base for a warm salad of pan-fried scallops (deglaze the pan with verjuice and use it as a dressing). Or try warm sweetbreads on a base of witlof, topped with salty, freshly shucked oysters.

Picking up a treasured cookbook is like visiting an old friend: memories come flooding back and ideas from past seasons are refreshed. It was the rereading of *Stephanie's Seasons*, in which Stephanie Alexander writes about, among many other things, a month spent at Patricia Wells' beloved Vaison-la-Romaine in Provence, which evoked the memory of a wonderful guinea fowl dish that Patricia had cooked for us the year before, in a tiny wood oven built into the stone wall of her courtyard. I re-created this dish at home and teamed it with braised witlof. Turning to Patricia's book *Simply French*, which presents the food of Joël Robuchon, I found a quote many will find relevant. Patricia prefaces the recipe for witlof with: 'I admit that until I began preparing it this way, I was not much of a fan of cooked witlof . . . even though I love this popular winter vegetable raw in salads.'

Patricia suggests cooking witlof in well-acidulated water with some sugar and salt for 20 minutes, then sprinkling it with a tablespoon of sugar and seasoning with salt and pepper, before setting it aside until cool enough to handle. She next squeezes the witlof firmly to extract any bitter liquid from the cooking water, then sautés it in butter until it caramelises. The witlof certainly caramelises quickly this way. My method for braising witlof (which is included in the recipe for Witlof Tart on page 535) differs only in that it is a one-step operation – but I should warn you that I use considerably more butter.

You needn't dose the witlof with butter and sugar as I've described. Instead, try baking witlof cut in half lengthways (the cut side brushed with extra virgin olive oil) with fresh thyme, garlic cloves and a little more olive oil at 220°C until well caramelised (about 25 minutes), turning the witlof halfway through. I expand this idea into a pasta dish on page 534.

Braised witlof makes a powerful side dish to roast duck, pheasant or other game. Many years ago, pheasant with a liver glaze and braised witlof appeared on the menu of a tiny restaurant run by Cedric Eu in the Adelaide Hills. Given my love of game and offal, there was never any doubt I would order it. The real surprise of the day was my first taste of bittersweet witlof. It married so well with the richness of the liver sauce and the flavour and texture of the pheasant.

Try adding a couple of tablespoons of freshly grated Parmigiano Reggiano and a handful of walnuts (roasted and rubbed free of their bitter skins) to six braised witlof. Or add strips of prosciutto, or you could crisp pancetta in the oven and bundle it on top.

The bitterness of witlof and the richness of smoked tongue are a great combination too, but be sure to go lightly on the sugar when braising the witlof as sugar is usually included in the brine for the tongue.

GRILLED ORANGE, ASPARAGUS AND WITLOF SALAD
WITH VINO COTTO DRESSING
Serves 2

1 large orange, cut into wedges
⅓ cup (80 ml) extra virgin olive oil
1 bunch asparagus, trimmed
1 tablespoon butter, melted

2 tablespoons vino cotto (see Glossary)
sea salt flakes and freshly ground
 black pepper
2 witlof, bases trimmed and leaves separated

Toss the orange wedges in a little of the olive oil. Heat a chargrill plate over high heat and grill the wedges on both sides until caramelised. Fill a sauté pan or deep frying pan with salted water, bring to the boil, then add the asparagus and poach until bright green and just tender. Drain and toss with melted butter.

Make a vinaigrette with the vino cotto and remaining olive oil, then season with salt and pepper. Toss the witlof, orange wedges and asparagus in a bowl with the vinaigrette and serve immediately.

PASTA WITH BAKED WITLOF AND RADICCHIO
Serves 4–6

6 cloves garlic
extra virgin olive oil, for cooking
3 plump witlof
2 heads radicchio
sea salt flakes and freshly ground
 black pepper
2 sprigs thyme
12 thin slices mild pancetta

2 teaspoons balsamic vinegar *or*
 vino cotto (see Glossary)
500 g penne
¼ cup flat-leaf parsley leaves
1 × 45 g tin anchovies, drained
squeeze of lemon juice
125 g freshly shaved Parmigiano Reggiano

Preheat the oven to 220°C. Caramelise the garlic slowly in a small saucepan over low heat with 1 tablespoon olive oil for about 20 minutes. Meanwhile, cut the witlof and the radicchio into quarters lengthways, then toss them in a bowl with 1 tablespoon olive oil, salt, pepper and the thyme. Crisp the pancetta slices on a baking tray in the oven, not too close together, for 10 minutes, then drain on kitchen paper.

Bake the witlof and radicchio, spread out on a shallow baking tray with the caramelised garlic and brushed with a little more olive oil if necessary, for 10 minutes. The cut surfaces of the vegetables will have begun to caramelise. Turn the vegetables, then cook for another 10–15 minutes or until cooked through. Sprinkle with the balsamic or vino cotto and return to the oven for 5 minutes.

To cook the pasta, bring plenty of salted water to the boil in a tall saucepan. Slide the pasta gently into the pan, then partially cover with a lid to bring it to a rapid boil. Take the lid off and cook the pasta following the instructions on the packet (the cooking times can differ), stirring to keep it well separated – a tablespoon of olive oil in the water can help this too. If using fresh pasta, it only needs to cook for about 3 minutes. Drain the pasta, reserving a little of the cooking water in case you want to moisten the completed dish. Do not run the pasta under water or you'll lose the precious starch that helps the sauce or oil adhere.

Toss the pasta with the hot vegetables, pancetta, parsley, anchovies, lemon juice and a sprinkling of extra virgin olive oil. Serve immediately with the shaved Parmigiano Reggiano.

WITLOF TART
Serves 6

This recipe includes my favourite way of braising witlof in butter.

1 × quantity Sour-cream Pastry (see page 424)	125 g butter
6 witlof	80 g Heidi Farm Gruyère, grated
1 teaspoon sugar	2 eggs
sea salt flakes and freshly ground black pepper	1 cup (250 ml) cream
	freshly grated nutmeg, to taste

Make and chill the pastry as instructed, then use to line a 20 cm loose-bottomed flan tin. Chill the pastry case for 20 minutes.

Preheat the oven to 200°C. Line the pastry case with foil and cover with pastry weights, then blind bake for 15 minutes. Remove the foil and weights and return the pastry case to the oven for another 5 minutes.

Pack the witlof tightly into a small enamelled or stainless steel roasting pan, then sprinkle on the sugar and season with salt and pepper. Melt the butter in a small saucepan and pour it over the witlof to cover them. Tightly cover the dish with foil and bake for 20 minutes, then turn the witlof over and bake for another 10 minutes. Remove the witlof from the butter and reset the oven to 180°C.

Mix the Gruyère, eggs and cream, then season with salt, pepper and nutmeg. Fan the witlof out over the warm pastry case and carefully pour in the egg mixture. Bake for about 20 minutes or until set, then serve at room temperature.

SPRING

ARTICHOKES

AS REVERED AS THEY ARE IN MEDITERRANEAN CUISINES, it continually surprises me how globe artichokes are so ignored here. Many would be familiar with the pickled varieties as a tasty addition to antipasto platters and pasta dishes, but it is the fresh artichoke I long for. Our family never tire of artichoke season, often eating them straight from the garden every second day when we've had a good year. We have ten to twelve plants and replace about half of them each year, as the artichoke bears less prolifically after the first few years.

We certainly have the right climate for growing them here in South Australia, as evidenced by the large number of wild artichokes that grow as noxious weeds in the countryside and need constant digging out or spraying. The artichoke can look quite forbidding, with the tough outer leaves tightly enclosing the globe, the bristly choke that protects the heart (although sometimes the choke is edible) and the thick stem, which needs to be peeled back to its inner core. There are two main varieties sold commercially in South Australia. One has a choke that is so insignificant you can eat the whole of it early in the season. The other is larger, with a hairier choke that needs to be scraped out. If all this sounds like a lot of work, rest assured that it's well worth the effort.

Like most vegetables, the most important thing is to buy artichokes at their very freshest. If you are lucky you may be able to find a grower, such as mine in Angle Vale, who will cut them for you while you wait. If you require a large amount, for pickling for example, you can let them know your requirements ahead of time. They can be ready for you in wet hessian bags and you can spend the rest of the day pickling – the fresher, the better. The difference in flavour of the just-picked artichoke, whether for eating fresh or pickling, is huge.

The sight of a huge bouquet of artichokes on the table is a delight and, as they are so easy to grow and look quite spectacular sharing a bed with roses, this is not difficult to organise if you have the space. While some varieties of globe artichoke are actually available as early as late May, the artichokes in our garden do not begin until mid-August, then

continue to produce until the first hot weather hits. We almost binge on fresh artichokes each spring.

The traditional way to prepare artichokes is to trim the first few centimetres from the top and rub the cut surface with lemon juice or verjuice to stop discolouration. Peel off the darker outer leaves and then rub any exposed surface with the acidulant, then soak them in acidulated water until you are ready to cook them. Boil the artichokes in salted water with a few fresh bay leaves and lemon slices added, until tender. They take about 20 minutes to cook, depending on their size. An enamelled or stainless steel saucepan is essential, as an aluminium pan will cause severe discolouration of both the artichokes and the pan.

Perhaps artichokes are something of an acquired taste and not the easiest vegetable to eat. They look so bold, so dramatic when spread out on a plate like a flower, yet few restaurateurs use them whole. Their argument is that not enough people have the confidence to tackle them and, to be sure, they do require a little knowledge to eat. It's worth it, though; not only do artichokes have a great flavour, they are a food to become involved in – with your fingers, which are a must in this case. The simplest way is to open the artichoke up and serve it with hot butter or your chosen sauce. Pick each leaf from the outside, dip it in sauce or butter and then suck on it, leaving the fibrous remains of the leaf. When you get to the choke you can discard the hairy part. But if the artichoke is young and fresh and of the right variety, and the choke is soft instead of thorny, you can eat the lot. It can be messy – be sure to have finger bowls and plenty of napkins on the table.

I love artichokes in all forms, though if treated with disrespect and overcooked they can taste like old tea leaves. They are delicious when they have been immersed in extra virgin olive oil and braised at a low temperature. Another alternative is to cut them in quarters, squeeze lemon juice or verjuice over them and sauté them quickly in olive oil or butter for about 10 minutes.

At the end of the season baby artichokes are available. They are the lateral buds pruned from the main plant. These are the ones we preserve for use during summer as the season finishes, sometime in November. If you are not inspired to pickle your own, there are plenty of commercial artichoke hearts in oil and vinegar available bottled and loose from delicatessens. However, they will only be as good as the quality of the oil and vinegar used (and I find many of them far too vinegary), so unless you seek out imported Italian ones from artisan producers who grow and pickle their own, nothing will ever taste as good as pickling your own just-picked artichokes. Pickled artichokes have myriad uses – such as on an antipasto plate with olives, pickled lemons and prosciutto. All of these foods can be sitting in the pantry or refrigerator, perfect for a 'spur of the moment' meal requiring virtually no effort.

Preserved artichoke hearts can be used as a bed for a dish of grilled chicken livers or can be tossed with a warm salad of quail. They can also be used for an artichoke risotto, with a brandade (purée of salt cod), or simply in a salad, but be mindful of the quality of the vinegar used so its flavour doesn't dominate.

I love preserved artichokes so much that a few years ago I tried, in conjunction with the artichoke industry, to come up with some specialist artichoke products using fresh and sweet tiny artichokes. After a few unsuccessful attempts, I finally came to the conclusion that processing the artichoke immediately after picking is the only way to retain its wonderful nutty sweetness. The best-quality artichoke products I've tasted come from the small artisan growers and producers themselves.

SANTIN FAMILY PRESERVED ARTICHOKES

The Santin family, who live on the Adelaide plains, used to grow their own artichokes and preserve them, and the secret to the flavour was the freshness of the artichoke. This recipe was given to me by them just as it is here, with no specific quantities included (but to give you an idea, I would use 2 cloves of garlic to every 10 tiny artichokes). To be sure of their keeping qualities it is important to use a sterilised jar and to store the preserved artichokes in the refrigerator. This is because raw garlic used in preserves kept at room temperature can spoil. Ordinarily I would resist using garlic when preserving, only adding it if it is part of a cooked recipe, such as tomato sauce for pasta.

I now like to use verjuice instead of vinegar, and combine it with extra virgin olive oil at a ratio of 1:1. The additional oil gives another dimension, but I wouldn't recommend doing this if you use vinegar.

tiny artichokes	**garlic, peeled**
lemon	**salt**
white-wine vinegar	**dash of extra virgin olive oil**
flat-leaf parsley, chopped	

Take as many tiny artichokes as available and clean them by taking off the outside leaves and cutting off the top third of the globe. Rub the cut surfaces with lemon.

Put the artichokes in a stainless steel or enamelled saucepan, cover with vinegar and bring to the boil for about 5 minutes or until just tender, being careful not to overcook. Remove and dry carefully with a tea towel, then discard vinegar mixture. In a large stainless steel bowl, mix the parsley, whole garlic cloves, salt and a little olive oil and toss in the cooked artichokes. The amounts will depend on your personal taste and the number of artichokes you have. Put into sterilised jars (see Glossary) and cover completely with vinegar. They are best kept refrigerated, where they will last for a few months.

JANNI'S BRAISED ARTICHOKES WITH ARTICHOKE PURÉE *Serves 8*

One of the most memorable artichoke dishes I ever had in a restaurant was cooked by Janni Kyritsis, chef of the much-missed Sydney restaurant MG Garage. For lunch I ate a braised artichoke sitting on a bed of beautiful pale-green artichoke purée that, in turn, sat atop a crouton. The two halves of the artichoke had been deep-fried first, then braised to perfection in extra virgin olive oil with slices of carrot, slivers of garlic and flat-leaf parsley.

When I rang Janni to ask if he would share the recipe with me he said that the very next day several more people 'in the trade' had been as glowing in their praise as I was, so he decided that he would sit down there in the restaurant to eat the whole dish himself, to see what all the fuss was about. Why not try my version of it yourself?

8 thin slices toasted focaccia

good extra virgin olive oil, to serve

gremolata (chopped flat-leaf parsley, crushed
    garlic and grated lemon rind), to serve

rind of ½ lemon, finely chopped

1 teaspoon each sea salt flakes and
    freshly ground black pepper

1 cup (250 ml) white wine

BRAISED ARTICHOKES

8 large globe artichokes

juice of 1 lemon

325 ml extra virgin olive oil

1 onion, finely chopped

2 tablespoons chopped thyme leaves

2 teaspoons chopped dill

½ cup chopped flat-leaf parsley

1 carrot, thinly sliced

8 cloves garlic, thinly sliced

ARTICHOKE PURÉE

½ cup (125 ml) extra virgin olive oil

½ onion, sliced

6 artichokes (about 250 g),
    trimmed and peeled

½ clove garlic, chopped

2 teaspoons lemon juice

sea salt flakes and freshly ground
    black pepper

To make the braised artichokes, trim the artichoke stems approximately 2 cm from the bases and remove tough outer leaves, then cut in half and remove the hairy chokes from the centres. Place the artichokes in a bowl of water acidulated with the lemon juice to stop discolouration. Heat 125 ml of the olive oil in a frying pan over medium–high heat and fry artichokes lightly, then discard oil. Fry the onion in the remaining 200 ml oil, then remove from heat and stir through the chopped herbs.

Stuff the artichoke cavities and between the leaves with the onion and herb mixture. Arrange the stuffed artichokes tightly, and standing upright, in a stainless steel saucepan. Add the remaining ingredients to the pan, then cover with a sheet of baking paper and a lid. Simmer over low heat for about 20–30 minutes or until soft. Cool artichokes in their cooking juices; they are best served the next day.

To make the artichoke purée, heat the olive oil in a stainless steel saucepan, then fry the onion over low heat until soft. Add the artichokes and fry lightly without browning.

Pour in 125 ml water, then cover with baking paper and a lid and simmer over low heat for 20 minutes or until tender.

Remove artichokes, place in a blender with garlic and lemon juice, then blend, slowly adding enough of the cooking juices to make a purée. Pass through a mouli, then season to taste.

Preheat the oven to 150°C and heat the braised artichokes in their juices. Spread the hot toasted focaccia with artichoke purée. Arrange 2 artichoke halves on each slice of focaccia, then serve with extra virgin olive oil, gremolata and sea salt.

ARTICHOKES AND MUSHROOMS BRAISED IN VERJUICE AND EXTRA VIRGIN OLIVE OIL

Serves 6

This is a dish I cooked for a group of friends once when we were in France together. To make a meal of the dish I added baby onions and small waxy potatoes to the artichokes and cooked them all together.

1½ cups (375 ml) verjuice	2 tablespoons unsalted butter
6 globe artichokes	100 g mushrooms
200 ml extra virgin olive oil	sea salt flakes and freshly ground
8 black peppercorns, cracked	black pepper
3 fresh bay leaves	½ cup chopped flat-leaf parsley

Place the verjuice in a glass or ceramic bowl. Trim the artichoke stems approximately 2 cm from the bases and remove tough outer leaves, then cut in half and remove the hairy chokes from the centres. Place the artichokes in the verjuice to stop discolouration.

In a large, wide, stainless steel frying pan, heat 70 ml of the olive oil over medium heat. Drain the artichokes, reserving the verjuice, then pat dry with kitchen paper and quickly seal them in the pan. Cover with the remaining olive oil and reserved verjuice then add the peppercorns and bay leaves. Place a sheet of baking paper closely over the top and cook over low heat on the stove. After 45 minutes, heat the butter in a frying pan over medium–high heat and sauté the mushrooms, then season with salt and pepper. Add the mushrooms to the artichokes for the final 15 minutes of cooking.

Transfer the vegetables to a serving dish, toss with parsley, then season to taste and add a little of the cooking juices.

RAGOÛT OF GLOBE AND JERUSALEM ARTICHOKES
WITH MUSHROOMS
Serves 6

This recipe marries globe artichokes with Jerusalem artichokes. They share a delicious earthy, nutty sweetness and overlap slightly in seasons.

6 Jerusalem artichokes
juice of 1 lemon
150 g butter
6 golden shallots, thinly sliced
300 g large mushrooms
   (preferably pine or cèpe) *or* large
   field mushrooms, thinly sliced
300 g shiitake mushrooms, stalks discarded
   and caps thinly sliced
6 sprigs thyme

sea salt flakes and freshly ground
   black pepper
6 small globe artichokes,
   outer leaves removed
1 lemon, halved
extra virgin olive oil, for cooking
3 teaspoons balsamic vinegar *or* vino cotto
   (see Glossary)
¼ cup chopped flat-leaf parsley

Slice the Jerusalem artichokes and place them in a bowl of water acidulated with the lemon juice to stop discolouration.

Heat 50 g of the butter in a frying pan over medium heat until nut-brown. Sauté the shallots until softened, then add the mushrooms and thyme, adding extra butter as required. Season to taste with salt and pepper, transfer to a bowl and set aside. Wipe out the pan.

Quarter the globe artichokes and remove and discard the chokes if necessary. Rub with lemon juice. Toss the globe artichokes in the clean frying pan with 50 g of the butter over medium heat until slightly golden. Transfer to the bowl with the mushrooms. Add the Jerusalem artichokes to the pan and sauté in the remaining butter with a dash of olive oil, to inhibit burning, until slightly golden. Return the mushroom and globe artichoke mixture to the pan and toss to combine. Sprinkle with balsamic vinegar or vino cotto and parsley and serve with crusty bread.

ASPARAGUS

I RECENTLY PULLED ONE OF MY MOST TREASURED BOOKS, *The Food Lover's Garden* by Angelo Pellegrini, from the shelves and re-read: '. . . when I use the word "gardening" my reference is invariably to the cultivation of those plants, such as asparagus, that are used as food; and those, such as rosemary, that are used to make food taste good. In other words, my approach to gardening is fundamentally utilitarian. I cultivate as much of the necessary herbs, vegetables, and fruit as time and place and space will allow, in order to enjoy a fine, even a distinguished, dinner every day.'

Pellegrini inspired me when we first moved to our cottage years ago. So much so that every tree or vine we planted on our 20 acres was food-bearing, and our orchard and vegetable garden became part of our lives, no matter how busy we were. Even though many of us have work or family commitments that preclude us from being able to enjoy fine dinners from the fruits of our own labour in our kitchen garden, we can, with a few well-chosen fruits and vegetables, supply ourselves with the 'special things' that can add that touch of extravagance and freshness to our table. This is particularly true if we choose those fruit and vegetables that are more difficult or expensive to obtain.

Asparagus comes immediately to mind. You really know spring has arrived when you see asparagus on sale. Although for the first week or two it is fairly pricey, that first taste of spring is worth the extra expense. In the Pheasant Farm Restaurant days we had a great thing going with the Fanto family, who would deliver asparagus spears, picked straight from their garden, two or three times a week. Rita Fanto, who delivered them, would be insistent that we put them in a vase of water, like flowers, as they had just been cut. We were so impressed with her that she became a full-time employee, working for many years as an integral part of the pâté-making team, then moving on to the export kitchen.

At the beginning of the season, little more than thin stems are available. These used to be my favourite, but now I tend to choose the plumpest – but only if they jump out at me in

a way that only a just-picked vegetable can, with tight buds and shiny stalks. You will soon know whether you've chosen good asparagus if the stem snaps when you break it off about a third of the way up from the end. The woody bits are rejected – I don't peel the ends, an arduous task that has more to do with tradition than necessity if you've bought well. If your asparagus fails the snap test, add a pinch of sugar to the cooking water with the salt.

Asparagus crowns (the part of the plant under the soil) usually need to be at least five years old before they will start to produce a really substantial crop. Most of the ones for sale are two years old, and you will usually need to go to a grower to get them, although some nurseries do sell them – New Gippsland Seeds and Bulbs (www.newgipps.com.au) have crowns in June and seeds at other times. Perversely, however, my new asparagus patch boasts twelve two-year-old crowns that have become rampant in the six months since I planted them. I was instructed to let them get firmly established by not picking any the first spring – the aim was to encourage thicker stalks next year. The trick to harvesting your own asparagus is remembering to pick them before they shoot away to just long thin strands.

Four plants will keep a family in asparagus right through until the hot weather hits – to the point where, as there are only two of us, Colin and I can get sick of it, though we never tire of the spears we eat raw straight from the garden, and our friends are happy to take the excess. We also have a patch of wild asparagus that grows on an incline down near the chook yard, but it's very thin and straggly and can be quite bitter.

Whilst nothing quite beats freshly poached asparagus with nut-brown butter or hollandaise, particularly if it's made with verjuice (see page 550), if you have your own patch you will need some more ideas. Try a salad of asparagus, caramelised garlic cloves and pitted olives, drizzled with an extra virgin olive oil and lemon juice vinaigrette and topped with grilled goat's cheese croutons. Medium to thin spears can be brushed with extra virgin olive oil then barbecued on a hot grillplate and served with a squeeze of lemon juice. And don't forget how well asparagus goes with a traditionally smoked leg of ham.

While talking traditional, how long has it been since you enjoyed fresh white bread – thinly sliced, crusts off – spread with good butter (salted, as asparagus needs salt) and wrapped around fat, just-cooked asparagus?

Old hat, I know, but you can't go past asparagus soup – a purée of the stalks (not any woody ends, though) with the tips kept as a garnish. All you need is vegie or chicken stock to cook the chopped asparagus in, then add seasoning and a little cream, and purée. Put the blanched tips in warmed soup bowls, then pour in the soup, add some chervil and you're done. And, rather than adding sultana grapes to Almond and Garlic Soup (see page 234), which is thickened with white bread and olive oil, you could try asparagus tips poached in verjuice.

Or perhaps poached asparagus could be added to an omelette, along with thin shavings of Taleggio cheese that melt as the omelette is turned.

When catering for a party, try poaching a mass of really fat asparagus. I don't own an asparagus cooker and find no need for one – I use a wide, flat stainless steel pan with sides 5 cm high. I bring water to the boil, add salt and simmer asparagus lying flat in the pan in a single layer. Cook till done (3–5 minutes, depending on size), then drain, arrange on a large platter and immediately brush with warm butter to gloss. Present with a huge bowl of thick, luscious verjuice hollandaise to dip into – great with drinks or on a buffet table. Using verjuice in the hollandaise will give you an astounding flavour. If making a hollandaise seems like too much trouble and you're going to eat the asparagus warm, then take a good dollop of butter and heat it to the nut-brown stage in a small frying pan. Just coat the warm asparagus with that, plus sea salt and freshly ground black pepper. It is polite to eat asparagus with your fingers, so have finger bowls on the table and remember to place any hollandaise or other sauce near the tips of the asparagus rather than the stems.

Don't forget a soft-poached egg served with asparagus and shaved Parmigiano Reggiano; let the asparagus stalks be the 'soldiers' to dip into the just-cooked yolk.

White asparagus has a much more delicate flavour than green asparagus. It is grown in a similar manner to celery, with earth mounded around it like a pyramid for the whole of its growing life, and the only part to gain any colour is the tip that breaks out of the ground. This is certainly something for the home gardener to consider.

Though my preference is for green, the white is revered by many and could be used in any of the recipes given here. The best white asparagus I've had was blanched for a few minutes in boiling salted water then gently pan-fried in nut-brown butter.

While staying with Patricia Wells in Vaison-la-Romaine in Provence, we bought a bunch of white asparagus at the wonderful food market there. Patricia peeled the asparagus, then steamed the spears before quickly refreshing them in iced water. She then lightly sautéed the asparagus in oil, and served it with a squeeze of lemon. Delicious!

GRILLED ASPARAGUS WITH VERJUICE HOLLANDAISE

Serves 4 as an entrée

I like to serve asparagus with hollandaise. When I do, I begin to make the hollandaise just as I put the water for cooking the asparagus on to boil.

1 tablespoon sea salt flakes	HOLLANDAISE
2 bunches fat asparagus	1½ cups (375 ml) verjuice
extra virgin olive oil, for brushing	1 bay leaf
freshly ground black pepper	6 black peppercorns
	250 g unsalted butter
	4 egg yolks

To make the hollandaise, combine the verjuice, bay leaf and peppercorns in a stainless steel saucepan, then bring to the boil and reduce over high heat to 2 tablespoons of liquid. Set aside. »

Grilled asparagus with verjuice hollandaise

Gently melt the butter in a small saucepan over very low heat, then leave it to cool. Once it's cool, skim off any white scum floating on top, then carefully pour the clear liquid that remains into another small saucepan, leaving behind as much of the milky-white sediment as possible. Keep the melted butter warm.

Bring a deep saucepan of water to the boil and add the salt. Break off the woody ends of the asparagus spears and discard them. Place a bowl of iced water by the stove, ready for refreshing the asparagus. Blanch the asparagus by plunging it momentarily into the boiling water, then quickly transfer the asparagus to the iced water, leave to cool, then drain.

Heat a chargrill plate over high heat, brush the asparagus with a little olive oil, season with pepper, then chargrill.

Combine the egg yolks and cooled verjuice mixture in the bowl of a food processor and pulse to emulsify. Make sure the butter is quite warm, then, with the motor running, add it very slowly to the egg mixture and continue processing until combined and thickened; the texture should be similar to that of mayonnaise. Season to taste.

Place the asparagus on a plate and serve with a large dollop of the hollandaise.

CHEONG LIEW'S SALT WATER DUCK ACCOMPANIED BY ASPARAGUS

Serves 4–6, depending on size of ducks

This salt water duck is served at room temperature with warm asparagus and a Japanese-style mayonnaise – together they make a great meal. As the duck requires curing for three days, and then needs to steep in the stock overnight, you will need to start this recipe at least four days before you wish to serve it. Dried mandarin peel, dried liquorice root and rice vinegar can be found in Asian supermarkets.

⅓ cup coarse salt

1 tablespoon Sichuan pepper

2 ducks

sea salt flakes

2 bunches asparagus

1 teaspoon cumin seeds

1 teaspoon Sichuan pepper

5 g dried liquorice root

2 cm piece ginger, bruised

2 spring onions

WHITE MASTER STOCK

2 cups (500 ml) boiling water

100 g sugar

1 star anise

1 cinnamon stick

3 pieces dried mandarin *or* tangerine peel
   (each the size of a 50 cent coin)

JAPANESE-STYLE MAYONNAISE

125 g sugar

2 teaspoons Keen's dry mustard

50 ml rice vinegar

2 egg yolks

2 cups (500 ml) extra virgin
   olive oil, warmed

In a small frying pan, dry-roast the coarse salt with the Sichuan pepper for a few minutes, until you can smell the perfume of the pepper coming off the pan. While still warm, rub the salt and pepper mix into the ducks, using 1 tablespoon of the mix for each kilogram of duck. Leave to cure for at least 3 days in the refrigerator.

To make the stock, combine all ingredients in a saucepan. Bring to the boil, then simmer over low heat for 30 minutes. Strain the stock through a sieve into a large stockpot.

Submerge the cured ducks in water and leave for 1 hour. Blanch each duck momentarily in a large saucepan of boiling water and refresh it in a bowl of iced water. Put the ducks into the master stock and poach for 20 minutes over medium heat. Leave the ducks to cool in the stock, then refrigerate overnight.

To make the mayonnaise, combine the sugar with 125 ml water in a small saucepan and slowly bring to the boil, then simmer to reduce by about a fifth. In a bowl, make the powdered mustard into a paste with 1 tablespoon of this sugar syrup and slowly mix in the vinegar, then add the remaining sugar syrup. Stir in the egg yolks. Slowly pour the warm oil into the mixture and mix as you would a mayonnaise. Taste and add more vinegar if necessary.

Bring some salted water to the boil in a shallow flameproof roasting or sauté pan. Snap the ends off the asparagus, then lay them in the pan and simmer over medium heat for about 3 minutes if they are thin, and 6 minutes if they are thick.

Carve the duck from the bone and serve with the warm asparagus and mayonnaise.

BEETROOT

OVER THE YEARS AT THE PHEASANT FARM RESTAURANT I DEVELOPED a keen sense of what my favourite customers liked. As they would sometimes drop in without warning when they had guests staying, it was a matter of some pride that I always managed to cater to their needs. Bob McLean (Big Bob), formerly of St Hallett winery and then a restaurateur himself for some time at barr-Vinum in Angaston, hates parsnip with a passion, and as I often teamed parsnips and game I always had to make sure I had potatoes on hand so I could give him mashed spud instead. And the pet hate of local artist Rod Schubert, whose work adorned the walls of the restaurant, was anything citrussy to end the meal, as the strong taste would all but ruin his favourite tipple to match with a dessert, one of Peter Lehmann's stickies.

But it was Peter's wife Marg's love of beetroot that led me to use this root vegetable in many different ways – she didn't mind how it was prepared, just as long as she could have beetroot. This was no hardship for me as I adore beetroot too. It has a natural affinity with game; in fact, the earthy sweetness of all root vegetables sits well with the richness of these meats. Looking through our old menus, I notice that as well as offering beetroot as a side vegetable, it was an integral part of many dishes that included guinea fowl, pheasant, rabbit, hare, pigeon and kangaroo. It also featured strongly with offal, especially smoked tongue (I tossed grated raw beetroot in butter over high heat and deglazed the pan with a good red-wine vinegar).

Beetroot is available all year but is at its very best in its natural season, from winter to late spring. Buying beetroot at its best means buying it with the leaves still attached. Nothing gives you a better indication of freshness than the vitality of the leaves – and you also get two vegetables for the price of one (in fact the leaves are a much better source of vitamins than the root). They are edible, as are the leaves of other root vegetables such as turnips, carrots and fennel. Beetroot is closely related to silverbeet, and the green or red leaves of the mature plant can be cooked in exactly the same way – quickly tossed over

Steak sandwich with beetroot and rocket mayonnaise (see page 556)

high heat with butter and freshly ground black pepper is pretty good, but only if the leaves are sparkling fresh.

I try never to waste the leaves from tender young plants. I might chop the smallest and brightest and add them to a salad of warm waxy potatoes, or blanch them quickly and toss them through freshly cooked pasta with flat-leaf parsley, extra virgin olive oil, freshly ground black pepper and some grated mature goat's cheese.

Beetroot is one of those vegetables we take for granted, but a steak sandwich or a hamburger just wouldn't be the same without it. My favourite steak sandwich includes freshly

cooked beetroot, lashings of caramelised onion, some peppery beetroot or rocket leaves and a good dollop of rocket mayonnaise. Much as I prefer home-cooked fresh beets, I'll admit to keeping a few tins just in case.

Like so many vegetables, beetroot reveals another dimension when it is used straight from the garden. I have just been out and harvested a huge bunch of beetroot that were all planted at the same time. Those plants that were showing perhaps a third of their beets above the ground are large and the skin is dry and marked. Those that were totally buried are the size of a large apricot and their skin, which hadn't seen the light of day until I pulled out the plants, is flawless.

Smaller beetroot like these are sweeter and less likely to be woody. However, unless the grower is satisfying a niche market for 'baby' vegetables, beetroot of different sizes are often bundled together to achieve an average weight per bunch. This is not always convenient for the cook – not only do different sizes require different cooking times, but it is also more attractive to have beetroot of a similar size in one dish.

I'll make a raw salad from the small ones to savour their sweetness. All that's needed is a good vinaigrette of 3–4 parts extra virgin olive oil to 1 part red-wine vinegar (the ideal ratio will depend on the intensity of your vinegar), some salt and freshly ground black pepper, a little Dijon mustard, a splash of orange juice and some chopped garlic. As the staining ability of beetroot is legendary, this is one time when those disposable gloves you see people behind deli counters wearing come in handy. Peel the beetroot and grate it on a stainless steel grater. Toss the vinaigrette through the salad and add fresh herbs – chives or salad burnet are particularly good.

Care needs to be taken when cleaning beetroot in preparation for cooking. If you tear the skin, disturb the fragile root or cut the leaves off too close to the root, the beetroot will 'bleed' and masses of colour and flavour will be lost. Presuming you have lovely fresh tops on your beetroot, cut them a couple of centimetres above the root and use them as soon as possible. A gentle wash will rid the root and leaves of any residual dirt.

The most common method of cooking beetroot is to boil it in salted water, which can take anything from half an hour to an hour and a half, depending on size. A dash of vinegar added to the cooking water rids the beetroot of the peculiar soapy taste it can develop when boiled if it's not super-fresh. Don't be tempted to pierce the beetroot with a skewer to check for doneness as this too will make it bleed. Instead, take a beetroot from the water and let it cool slightly before squeezing it: if it gives a little, it is cooked. Once all the beetroot are cool enough to handle, simply slip the skins off by rubbing them gently. I like to present small beetroot with about a centimetre of their tops in place, so I'm careful when doing this. (If you do stain your hands, it will come off with lemon juice, although whether every trace of pink vanishes immediately will depend on how many beetroot you've handled.)

I often bake rather than boil beetroot, as I find the flavour more intense. Pack the beetroot into an enamelled baking dish just large enough to hold them in a single layer and drizzle over extra virgin olive oil, then add a tablespoon of water and tuck in a sprig or two of thyme. Cover the dish with foil and cook the beetroot at 220°C for 40–60 minutes. These beetroot can be served in their skins or peeled as above. Beetroot can also be baked wrapped in foil and served with a dollop of sour cream and a sprinkling of chopped chives, just as you would a potato.

Garlicky aïoli or skordalia, a Mediterranean bread-based sauce, have to be among the most luscious accompaniments to beetroot. Try a salad of still-warm roasted beetroot, rocket and crisp pancetta served with grilled quail and a dish of aïoli. If going meatless, add melted goat's cheese to the rocket, along with some witlof, and finish off the salad with a wonderfully aromatic walnut oil vinaigrette and a few roasted walnuts. Or serve freshly cooked beetroot with skordalia made with roasted walnuts rather than the usual potato, and verjuice instead of water. Good crusty bread to go with it is mandatory.

Home-cooked beetroot need only a simple vinaigrette of good red-wine or balsamic vinegar, a little Dijon mustard, extra virgin olive oil and freshly ground black pepper to make a great salad. For a warm salad, try tossing diced baked beetroot with roasted garlic cloves, a freshly opened tin of anchovies, and a red-wine vinegar, orange juice and extra virgin olive oil vinaigrette.

Newer hybrid varieties such as golden or candy-striped beetroot look wonderful and provide an especially interesting effect when cooked and used in a salad. The variety called 'bull's blood' is an incredibly dark, purply black and the sweetest beetroot I've ever eaten, particularly when just picked. A word of caution, however. As much as I love raw beetroot – I often use the traditional purple beetroot grated raw in salads – I tried the same with a golden beetroot recently to disastrous effect. Colin and I tasted just a teaspoon of it and within minutes both our throats were burning so badly that we had to drink milk to try to ease the sensation. Even gargling with milk produced little result; it was a good 45 minutes before the burning subsided. I learn something new every day!

Toss beetroot with nut-brown butter and freshly ground black pepper for the simplest vegetable dish. Another option is to mash slightly softened unsalted butter with lots of freshly chopped herbs – try chives and basil or thyme – and a little garlic, a squeeze of lemon juice and some freshly ground black pepper then toss it with hot, peeled beetroot. Or use the Barossa combination of cream and red-wine vinegar, which is often added to a warm potato salad. Bring 75 ml cream to the boil and add 1 tablespoon red-wine vinegar and let it amalgamate, then pour the sauce over hot, peeled beetroot (this amount of dressing will do for about 500 g beetroot). For a change, halve the amount of red-wine vinegar and add some mustard.

Beetroot is well known as the main ingredient in borscht (see opposite), a Russian soup that can be served hot or cold. Although I love beetroot, I find this soup rather too intense unless served with lots of sour cream or crème fraîche. On the other hand, beetroot makes a delicious sauce or purée, and one in particular remains firmly in my mind. Gay Bilson, Janni Kyritsis and the staff at Berowra Waters Inn cooked a wonderful meal entirely on portable burners on a disused wharf in 1986 during the first Sydney Symposium of Gastronomy. The highlight was the hare, rare and juicy, served with a beetroot purée. From my notes (I always take notes at great meals), I see that it was made with beetroot, onion, tomato concasse, cream and balsamic vinegar.

HORSERADISH-FLAVOURED PICKLED BEETROOT   *Makes 500 ml*

Beetroot pickles well, particularly when strong flavours such as fresh horseradish or mustard are used. A handy relish to have on hand as a last-minute accompaniment, this goes well with barbecued kangaroo or lamb loin chops (the latter with the fatty bits left on and allowed to char).

750 g beetroot	freshly ground black pepper
sea salt flakes	1 tablespoon sugar
400 ml red-wine vinegar	4 cloves
1 clove garlic, thinly sliced	6 coriander seeds
¼ cup freshly grated horseradish	

Cut the tops off the beetroot, leaving at least 2 cm. You'll need to clean the beetroot thoroughly as some of the cooking liquid will be reserved for later use. If the beetroot is very dirty, soak it in water rather than scrubbing the skin. Boil the cleaned beetroot in a saucepan of water over low–medium heat with 1 teaspoon salt and a little of the vinegar added (depending on size and age, beetroot can take as long as 1½ hours to cook). Remove the cooked beetroot from the cooking liquid and allow to cool a little before peeling. Strain the cooking liquid through a fine-meshed sieve and set it aside.

Coarsely grate the beetroot. Mix the garlic and the grated horseradish into the grated beetroot and season with salt and pepper. Tip the beetroot mixture into a hot, sterilised (see Glossary) glass or earthenware jar. Boil the remaining vinegar with an equal amount of the reserved cooking liquid, and the sugar and spices, in a non-aluminium saucepan for 5 minutes. Pour this hot solution over the beetroot, making sure it is just covered (if more liquid is needed, boil equal amounts of water and vinegar and add to the jar to top up – these must be added in a 1:1 ratio to prevent the growth of harmful bacteria). Seal the jar and allow it to mature in the pantry for 2 weeks. Refrigerate after opening.

RAW BEETROOT SALAD WITH ORANGE RIND   *Serves 4*

This salad is an excellent accompaniment for barbecued kangaroo fillets.

1 bunch small red beetroot, trimmed,
   washed and peeled
rind of 1 small orange, cut into fine strips
¼ cup flat-leaf parsley leaves
1 tablespoon lemon juice

⅓ cup (80 ml) fruity green
   extra virgin olive oil
sea salt flakes and freshly ground
   black pepper

Grate the beetroot as finely as possible to yield 2 cups; the finer the beetroot, the more luscious the salad. Toss the grated beetroot, orange rind and parsley together. Whisk the lemon juice and olive oil together and dress the salad, then season with salt and pepper.

BORSCHT   *Serves 4*

I return to my desire for the simple by giving you my not-very-authentic version of borscht, a hearty soup that can be served hot or cold (I prefer it cold). When made from freshly dug beets, it can be exceptional. This soup is best not reheated as it tends to lose its colour.

butter, for cooking
extra virgin olive oil, for cooking
2 large onions, roughly chopped
6 beetroot (about 150 g each),
   peeled and cut into chunks
pale inner heart of 1 bunch celery, chopped

sea salt flakes and freshly ground
   black pepper
1.5 litres Golden Chicken Stock
   (see page 57) *or* vegetable stock
1 tablespoon red-wine vinegar
chopped dill, to serve
sour cream *or* crème fraîche, to serve

Heat some butter in a large saucepan with a little olive oil over medium heat until nut-brown, then sweat the onions until soft. Add the beetroot and celery heart and sauté for a few minutes, then season and cover with chicken or vegetable stock. Reduce heat to low and simmer for about 2 hours.

Purée in a food processor or blender and add the red-wine vinegar. Allow to cool and then chill soup in the refrigerator. Serve cold topped with fresh dill and a dollop of sour cream or crème fraîche.

BEETROOT SAUCE FOR KANGAROO, PIGEON OR HARE *Serves 4*

500 g beetroot

6 golden shallots, thinly sliced

1 sprig thyme

extra virgin olive oil, for cooking

1 teaspoon Dijon mustard

2 tablespoons cream

2 tablespoons reduced veal stock

sea salt flakes and freshly ground
black pepper

balsamic vinegar, to taste

Preheat the oven to 220°C. Cut the tops off the beetroot, leaving at least 2 cm. Wrap the beetroot in foil, then bake for 40–60 minutes. Remove the beetroot from the foil and allow to cool a little before peeling. Purée the beetroot in a food processor.

Sweat the shallots with the thyme in a little olive oil in a saucepan over low heat for 10–15 minutes until softened. Add the beetroot purée, mustard, cream and stock and check for seasoning, then add balsamic vinegar to taste. Serve immediately.

CUMQUATS

THE CUMQUAT, OR KUMQUAT, IS A VERY SPECIAL FRUIT TO THOSE who appreciate its many uses in cooking, as well as its ornamental beauty. There is nothing like the simple beauty of a cumquat tree in a large terracotta pot in a north-facing courtyard. Cumquats were grown commercially in South Australia many years ago, but found not to be profitable, and as far as I can tell don't appear to be grown on a commercial scale anywhere in Australia now other than at Tolley's Nurseries in Renmark. As an eating fruit, they are really an acquired taste, and unfortunately it's not financially viable to grow them just for jam-making. It comes back to the age-old dilemma of what should be developed first – a market or an orchard?

Commercial purposes aside, Ian Tolley, the well-known, now-retired Renmark nurseryman, says the important factors in growing cumquat trees, either in the ground or in pots, are reasonable drainage and consistent watering. In his many years of working with citrus fruit, the problem he was most often asked about concerned splitting fruit. The fruit splits when trees are allowed to dry out, then are over-watered, then allowed to dry out again. The cumquat is not strictly a citrus but is grafted to a dwarf citrus rootstock to limit its size to half that of an orange tree in an effort to improve the quality of the fruit. As a small tree it is often grown in pots, making the problem of drying out particularly relevant. All citrus trees do better with good drainage, although there are special rootstocks available for marginal drainage situations. The main thing is not to allow them to dry out.

Fertilising is important and two reasonable applications per year are recommended. It is better to use slow-release blood-and-bone, or Complete D, rather than inorganic fertilisers. It isn't necessary to put it through a dripper system, which is expensive and difficult. Simply spread it around the tree, scratch it in, and water with a sprinkling hose.

Ian describes the cumquat as a 'precocious bearer' because it yields some fruit in the second or third year, and a reasonable crop in six to eight years. In Renmark, the season runs from the end of August until the end of November.

Cumquats in sugar syrup (see page 564)

One of the reasons that the cumquat has not succeeded commercially in the past was that it was deemed suitable only for jam or glacé fruit, and the larger glacé manufacturers weren't interested, probably because of the cumquat's small size, as well as the number of seeds. Work to reduce the number of seeds in cumquats is slowly progressing. This is happening mainly through growers identifying trees that produce fruit with fewer seeds and letting nurseries grow stock from them. Talking with Ian about one of my favourite topics – cooks working directly with growers – I became quite excited about the possibilities, until he told me that the development of seed-free cumquats would mean reduced crop and fruit sizes. Sometimes it simply makes more sense to quit while you're ahead!

Even though commercial glacé manufacturers had spurned the cumquat, I persuaded Ian's wife, Noëlle Tolley, that there was a market for her homemade glacéd cumquats. I had the pleasure of taste-testing all her trials and her product was nothing short of sensational. One kilogram of glacéd cumquats went a long way, and I featured the fruit on the restaurant's dessert menus as often as I could. They added a great dimension to a silky buttermilk panna cotta or crème brûlée, and their glaze starred in an Almond and Cumquat Tart (see page 568) – what a winner. I also find that this glaze makes a wonderful basting liquid for slow-cooking ducks.

The two varieties of cumquat Noëlle and I worked with were the marumi, which has a sweet rind, and the nagami. The marumi is delicious eaten fresh, picked straight from the tree, and I prefer it glacéd for desserts, but the nagami, when prepared with less sugar, is an ideal accompaniment for game. Noëlle once sent me some cumquat slices that had been dried, using no sugar at all, in a dehydrator rather than in the sun. I found the flavour wonderful for stocks with poultry or venison. It is truly exciting to see products of such quality.

And now the Tolleys, even though retired, are planting more cumquat trees and are selling their dried and candied cumquats under the brand name Kumquaterie. They also produce a cumquat glaze and a mince 'krumble', as Noëlle calls it, from imperfect cumquat halves.

More than any other fruit, cumquats are offered to me by non-cooking gardeners at a loss as to what to do with their crop, feeling that they have neither the time nor the skill to make jam. I take advantage of such windfalls and am compelled to try as many options as possible to show that there's more to cumquats than just jam.

Having said that, cumquat marmalade is a joy – possibly even better than my much-loved Seville marmalade, and it's a cinch to make. Quarter the fruit and leave it to soak overnight just covered with water. The next day, measure the fruit with a cup into a heavy-based saucepan, then cover the fruit with the soaking water and cook until it is tender but still intact. Add the same number of cups of sugar as you did fruit, then boil rapidly until the mixture is set. To test this, place a spoonful onto a saucer and put in the fridge for a few minutes. Then test the marmalade by pushing it with your finger – if it wrinkles it is set. To make a smoother, less chunky marmalade, cook the cumquats whole and then cut them in half and remove their pips. Purée the cooked pulp in a blender, then simmer it with sugar until it reaches setting point.

Cumquat butter is wonderful to use when cooking poultry or rabbit. Chop cumquats finely, removing the pips, then work the fruit into softened unsalted butter with chopped herbs. The choice of herbs will depend on what you are cooking and what you have to hand: rosemary or thyme are particularly good. Stuff the mixture under the skin of a chicken or duck breast (a Muscovy duck, which doesn't have a great deal of fat, works well) – the butter bastes the meat as it cooks, keeping it moist and leaving the skin golden and crisp.

Whole or peeled cumquats (if you have time on your hands and don't like the bitter skin as much as I do) cooked slowly in a sugar syrup can be added to a moist, pudding-style cake. Serve this with a spoonful or two of clotted cream alongside. Allow a flourless chocolate cake to cool and then cut it in half carefully (it will be flat and dense). Halve the syrupy cumquats, remove pips, then dot the cut surface of the cake with them. Put the top back on the cake, then coat it with chocolate ganache. Cumquat marries with chocolate even better than orange does.

Or try pricking ripe cumquats once or twice with a needle, placing them in a sterilised glass jar (see Glossary), adding a little sugar if you have a sweet tooth, and then covering them with brandy. Leave them for a year – if you are strong enough to resist.

I was interested to learn that in the Philippines there are few lemons available and people actually prefer to use sliced green cumquats in drinks. The greener and more bitter the fruit, the more they enjoy it. They also squeeze ripe cumquats for juice in the same way as we squeeze oranges, and use the juice of green cumquats on noodles, where we might use lemon. They also combine soy sauce with cumquat juice (in roughly equal quantities, to get that balance of salt and sour) to serve alongside fried fish or chicken. And they use cumquats for medicinal purposes – the lukewarm juice of grilled cumquats is a remedy for an itchy throat after persistent coughing.

CHICKEN AND TARRAGON SAUSAGES WITH CUMQUATS *Serves 4*

I can't emphasise enough the importance of using good-quality sausages. I am lucky to be able to use my daughter Saskia's chicken sausages, which are made entirely from chicken meat and skin and the fat of the chicken when bred to maturity.

30 g unsalted butter	1 tablespoon chopped French tarragon
12 thin or 8 thick chicken and	*or* chervil sprigs
tarragon sausages	sea salt flakes and freshly ground
8 cumquats, sliced into 3 or 4 widthways	black pepper
and pips removed	
½ cup (125 ml) Golden Chicken Stock (see	
page 57), or more depending on pan size	

In a heavy-based frying pan large enough to hold all the sausages in one layer, melt the butter, then gently seal the sausages and cumquats over medium heat until the sausages are just browned, without pricking the skins. Add stock, then bring to a simmer, cover and cook gently for 5–7 minutes or until sausages are cooked through. Remove the sausages and set aside in a warm place, then quickly reduce the pan juices over high heat to a sauce consistency. Add the herbs and season to taste, then serve immediately.

SASKIA'S WEDDING CAKE   *Serves 50*

This is such a special recipe from a very special ex-staff member, Natalie Paull, one of the 'extended family' of talented youngsters who came through the Pheasant Farm Restaurant kitchens, and whose lives I have been fortunate enough to stay connected with as they go on to do great things of their own. Nat had an unshakeable path in life, and while still at school in Sydney, wrote me a beautifully penned letter to ask if she could come over and do work experience with me. It was one of those requests I couldn't refuse, especially from one so young. There was no doubt that Nat had talent right from the start, and her time working with me was such a vital period in the life of the restaurant.

I've already written about the highs of the last four months of the restaurant, after we had announced that we were closing down, and what an incredibly exciting time it was coping with the huge numbers of people who wanted to come one last time. Our elder daughter Saskia had planned her wedding for a week after we closed, so that we would have time to recover from the closing 'wake', which was one continuous party on 28 November 1993, finishing at five o'clock the next morning, which also was our younger daughter Elli's eighteenth birthday. This gave us time to cook for the wedding free of restaurant commitments, and the gang of three, Nat, Alex Herbert and Steve Flamsteed, stayed around so they could help and be part of the festivities.

Nat cooked this truly wonderful cake for Saskia's wedding. How I wish I'd recorded all the food of the event as it was a great feast, only some of which I remember. Then, going through boxes of memorabilia recently I found Nat's handwritten notes for this recipe – yet another gift from her. She now has her own dessert business called Little Bertha in Richmond, Melbourne, where she makes the most delectable treats, including the stunning Le Marjolaine, a dessert we used to make in the restaurant days. Even though I profess to have no sweet tooth, I did used to find myself in the coolroom suspiciously often – just checking!

According to Nat's notes, this recipe makes one large 28 cm and one medium 22 cm round cake, each of which stands about 5 cm high. It serves about 50 people as a celebratory treat. I recommend that all the ingredients be at room temperature for the best possible results. The method and amounts for the fruit layer can be adapted for any kind of dried fruit; you could use raisins and dried figs instead of the cumquats and infuse the butter cream with vanilla instead of orange-blossom water, as this would be amazing too. The cake would be just as wonderful to eat with a cream-cheese icing or even a ganache, which would go well with the cumquats.

This cake keeps well for up to three days.

580 g butter, softened

580 g castor sugar

12 × 55 g eggs, at room temperature

1 teaspoon vanilla extract

460 g plain flour

200 g self-raising flour

pinch salt

CUMQUATS

375 g dried cumquats

185 ml boiling water

200 ml dessert wine

BUTTER CREAM

9–10 egg yolks (180 g)

finely grated rind of 2 oranges

225 g castor sugar

1 cup (250 ml) light corn syrup

675 g butter, softened

1 tablespoon orange-blossom water

2 tablespoons Cointreau *or* other
  orange-flavoured liqueur

Soak the dried cumquats in a bowl of just-boiled water overnight, covered with plastic film. The next day, add the dessert wine and cook uncovered in the microwave on high for two 6-minute bursts, stirring between each. Leave to cool completely.

Preheat the oven to 150°C. Lightly grease a 28 cm and a 22 cm round cake tin with melted butter, then line the bases and sides with baking paper and set aside.

Cream the butter and sugar in an electric mixer on medium speed until pale and fluffy. Add the eggs slowly, about 2 at a time, beating between each addition, until all the eggs are incorporated, then add the vanilla extract. The mixture may start to curdle a little at the end of this process, which is why it is important to start with room-temperature ingredients.

Transfer the batter to a large bowl. Combine the flours and salt in another bowl. Sift the dry ingredients over the top of the batter, then gently fold the flour in thoroughly. Weigh out 1 kg of the batter and transfer it to the prepared 28 cm cake tin, then weigh and transfer 500 g of the batter into the smaller cake tin, reserving the rest. Spread the batter out, making it a little higher at the sides of the tins. Scatter two-thirds of the cumquat mixture over the batter in the large tin and the remaining cumquats over the batter in the smaller tin. Spread the remaining cake batter over the cumquats in both tins.

Bake the cakes for 75 minutes, then cool them in the tins, before turning out onto wire racks to cool completely.

Meanwhile, for the butter cream, whisk the egg yolks and orange rind together in an electric mixer. Place the sugar and corn syrup in a saucepan and bring to the boil over high heat. As soon as the syrup boils, transfer it to a heatproof jug; if you have a sugar thermometer, the syrup should be at 116°C or the soft boil stage. Working in 3 batches, immediately pour one-third of the syrup into the egg yolk mixture, then beat on high speed for 30 seconds. Turn the mixer off before adding the next batch of syrup as the beaters will spray the mix around the sides of the bowl and it will not incorporate properly. Mix in the last 2 batches, beating in between, then beat the mixture on high speed until cool. Add the butter in 6 batches and allow each batch to be taken into the mixture before adding the next. Stir in the orange-blossom water and Cointreau. This butter cream can be made in

advance and freezes beautifully. When ready to use, defrost it fully in the fridge, then soften to spreading consistency in a microwave; take care not to overheat or the mixture will separate.

Spread a thin layer of butter cream over each cake and refrigerate for 1 hour (this is called a crumb coat and hides any uneven surfaces or dark patches on the cake). Then spread enough icing over the crumb coat to fully cover the cakes. The cakes are sturdy enough to tier, if you wish, without the aid of a high-tech support structure.

Store and serve at room temperature as the butter cream is best when not refrigerated.

ALMOND AND CUMQUAT TART   *Serves 8*

Noëlle Tolley sells her cumquat glaze through specialty outlets in South Australia and Victoria, but it is not widely distributed and it's difficult to make unless you have lots of cumquat trees, so substitute with a strong honey such as leatherwood or mallee, or even imported chestnut honey.

6 cups (960 g) almonds	GLAZE
1 × quantity Sour-cream Pastry	175 g bitter chocolate
(see page 424)	¼ cup (60 ml) rich double cream
1 teaspoon ground cinnamon	1½ tablespoons cumquat glaze *or* honey
1 tablespoon finely grated cumquat rind	1 tablespoon brandy
½ cup (125 ml) brandy	60 g unsalted butter
1½ cups (375 ml) cumquat glaze *or* honey	
125 g unsalted butter, softened	
mascarpone mixed with a little grated	
cumquat rind and juice, to serve	

Preheat the oven to 200°C. Roast the almonds on a baking tray in the oven to release their flavour, leave them to cool, then grind in a food processor. Reset the oven temperature to 175°C. Make the pastry as instructed, then roll out to line a 22 cm tart tin. Refrigerate until required.

Mix the ground almonds with the cinnamon and cumquat rind. Stir in the brandy, cumquat glaze or honey and butter. Pat this mixture into the tart shell and dot with butter. Bake for about 30 minutes or until the crust is golden. Leave to cool at room temperature.

To make the glaze, heat the chocolate, cream, cumquat glaze or honey and 1 tablespoon water in the top of a double boiler until the chocolate has melted. (If you don't have a double boiler, use a heatproof bowl that fits snugly over a pan of boiling water.) Remove from heat and stir in the brandy and butter. Smooth the glaze over the tart with a spatula. Do not refrigerate.

Serve with mascarpone with a little finely grated cumquat rind and a dash of juice stirred through it – be careful not to make the mascarpone too runny.

BUTTERMILK PANNA COTTA WITH CUMQUAT SAUCE   *Serves 6*

4 × 2 g gelatine leaves (see Glossary)

400 ml cream

150 g castor sugar

1 cup (250 ml) buttermilk

CUMQUAT SAUCE

600 g cumquats, halved and seeded

400 g castor sugar

1 cinnamon stick

Soak the gelatine leaves in cold water to soften. Combine the cream and sugar in a sauce-pan over medium heat and bring almost to the boil. Squeeze the excess moisture out of the gelatine and whisk into the cream mixture, then add the buttermilk. Turn the heat to low, otherwise the buttermilk may split. Divide among six 125 ml moulds and place in the refrigerator to set overnight.

To make the cumquat sauce, combine all ingredients in a saucepan with enough water to cover the fruit (about 500 ml). Bring to the boil, then reduce heat to low and simmer for 1 hour, adding more water if necessary. Set aside to cool. Remove cinnamon stick before using.

Serve the panna cotta topped with a spoonful of cumquat sauce.

EGGS

ALTHOUGH EGGS ARE A SIMPLE FOOD, THEY ARE FULL OF SOUL.
When we ran the restaurant we had a goose that made a nest in the same spot
every year on a little strip of earth in front of the restaurant (in full view of
table three). She would lay her egg at around lunchtime every day, which is much later
than normal. I was convinced that she did it because she liked the attention of the customers, who were obviously enchanted by her. She was never successful with her 'sitting', as
she liked to put on a show by going for a swim in the middle of lunch, leaving the nest for
a lot longer than a good mum should. Once she had a nest full, she sat there for the whole
of spring in the vain hope that the eggs would hatch – usually the smell of rotten eggs
would remind us that it was time to take over from nature and chase her away.

Now that we have gone full circle – starting with opening the Farmshop way back in
1979, then running the restaurant for nearly fifteen years, now back running the Farmshop
again on the old restaurant site – instead of a goose, it is one of the wild peacocks who
takes up that position most days. Not because *he* is laying an egg, but because it is obviously a very desirable spot for a bird that craves attention.

It became obvious to me what a difference a good egg makes when Stephanie Alexander
and I held our cooking school in Tuscany. We were encouraging a group of students to
make pasta by hand. It was about 35°C and the humidity was high. The villa kitchen was
too hot for pasta-making, so we moved upstairs to make the dough in an ancient marble
sink, not just for its coolness but to contain the mess created by a dozen enthusiastic cooks.
The yolks of our eggs were the colour of gold, and the silky pasta we had kneaded long and
hard was now a shiny ball, in spite of the heat. Everyone was marvelling at how clever they
were – until I reminded them that the ingredients they had been working with probably
had something to do with their success, too.

The cry that 'eggs don't taste like they used to when we had our own chooks' has been
familiar to me ever since I moved to the Barossa some twenty years ago. In fact, chook

eggs didn't rate at the Pheasant Farm Restaurant. Instead, it was duck, goose, pheasant, guinea fowl or quail eggs. The yolks of these exotic eggs were so rich it was as if they had been injected with a creamy mayonnaise.

Until my time in Italy, I hadn't thought much about this, as we always had my friend Hilda's eggs when our daughters were young and used our farm eggs for the restaurant, so we seldom resorted to commercial chook eggs. But after Italy I was determined to have our own chooks on our home property. This is when I discovered that it's not enough to

give them a proprietary feed. What you feed them, and the greens they have access to, will have a huge impact on flavour and colour. If you have your own chooks, you will be struck by the difference between these and mass-produced eggs. Now, thankfully, free-range eggs with their deep-gold yolks and good flavour, which result from a combination of the grain they are fed and their ability to pick grass and insects, are available to all. However, they will still only be as good as the food the chook eats. If any hen's diet is supplemented by fish meal, that's how the eggs will taste. We need eggs to taste like eggs, not fish. I react so badly to commercially produced fried eggs when breakfasting away from home that I often wonder whether they are off, until I recall this.

Eggs are certainly one of the more versatile foods we have. They are marvellous on their own (think of a soft-boiled egg perched in an egg cup with toast soldiers or brown bread to dunk – still the food I crave when overtired, even for dinner), and they can be cooked in a variety of ways: soft-boiled, hard-boiled, poached or fried. Eggs combine well with other ingredients, either using the richness of the egg yolk with olive oil or butter to make Mayonnaise (see page 400), my Aïoli (see page 587), Hollandaise (see page 550) or béarnaise; or whole eggs, which are integral to custards, quiches, soufflés, omelettes, frittatas, and pasta and cake dough.

Every restaurant faces the question of leftover egg whites – how many meringues can you make? We used to put egg whites into dated and numbered containers in the fridge, hoping for an excuse to use them. I sometimes wonder if the Brownies or Scouts, instead of having a 'bottle round', could collect egg whites and make confectionery to sell.

Eggs are easier to beat in a copper bowl with a whisk than having to take out the electric mixer and then wash it all up afterwards. You are less likely to overbeat the eggs this way, and the copper bowl gives the whites a creamier, yellowish foam. The same eggs beaten in a mixer or stainless steel bowl will be snowy white and drier.

A meringue can be both over- and under-beaten. Soft meringues should be baked at 180–190°C for 15 minutes. This crisps the surface and leaves the interior moist and chewy.

Hard meringues are baked at 100°C for up to 2 hours, or left overnight after being placed in a hot oven, which is then turned off just as you put them in. If they leak syrup or collapse, it is because they are undercooked. If they have beads of syrup on the surface, they have been cooked at too high a temperature.

It is not just egg whites that are whipped. Whipped yolks are added to various breads and cakes to contribute to the yolky flavour or to help reinforce a foam. Sabayon is a warm, frothy, rich mixture of yolks, sugar and Marsala (or you can use verjuice, as on page 335).

Tips for peeling hard-boiled eggs would have saved me hours of anguish in the first few years of our business, when in the evening I would sit and peel bucket after bucket of quail eggs. My daughters Saskia and Elli were only four and two years old when we began farming quails, a year before we started the Farmshop. I used to sit with a bucket between my legs and the girls either side of me. We had a book propped on a chair and I would read to them, my hands in the bucket as they turned the pages. They used to love to eat the yolks if I tore the egg white, but they don't often eat eggs now – I wonder why! Looking back, I don't know how I managed this for so many evenings over so many years. After four years we contracted the job out and life started to improve.

The most important tip for hard-boiled eggs is that they should not be too fresh for boiling, because the fresher they are, the harder they are to peel. Preferably they should be one week old. For pickling, boil quail eggs for 6 minutes – you need to use a wooden spoon to move the eggs around in the water so that at their 'setting point' the yolks will be in the centre of the egg. The skins of quail eggs are much tougher than those of chook eggs. They are difficult to peel and if the yolk is too close to one end of the egg, the skin will be torn and the egg useless. The moment the eggs come out of the boiling water they should be thrown into iced water to cool, and be kept in this until you are ready to peel them. To peel, pick up the egg and crush the pointy end against the table so that the whole shell crazes in your hand. The skin should slip off in one piece.

Soaking the eggs overnight in vinegar dissolves the outer membrane of the egg shell and makes it very easy to peel. This is only useful if you are going to pickle the eggs rather than have them fresh, as the vinegar flavour is so strong. It is also expensive and plays havoc with your hands.

Freshly boiled quail eggs (boiled for only 2–3 minutes), cut in half lengthways and topped with caviar, make wonderful hors d'oeuvres.

I have often wondered why quail or chook eggs sometimes have a greenish-grey discolouration on the surface of the yolk. It happens mostly with less-than-fresh eggs (I noticed it with the quail eggs, of course, because I was using them not so fresh for ease of peeling). I then discovered, while reading Harold McGee's book *On Food and Cooking,* that the colour is caused by a harmless compound of iron and sulphur – ferrous sulfide – which is formed only when the egg is heated. Minimising the amount of hydrogen sulfide that reaches the yolk will reduce the discolouration: cook the eggs only as long as necessary to set the yolk and then plunge the eggs immediately into cold water and peel them promptly.

SCRAMBLED EGGS AND CAVIAR

Serves 3–4 for breakfast

Cooking scrambled eggs may be an art form, but serving them with smoked salmon and salmon roe, or with caviar as I've done here, elevates them to the luxury class. Then there are sea urchins: since rediscovering my taste for sea urchin roe after eating a sea urchin custard in Paris a few years ago now (which scored an 'ultimate experience' rating), I like to simplify the combination of eggs and sea urchin by adding the roe to scrambled eggs. When I do this, I press the roe of four sea urchins through a fine strainer, then whisk it into the egg mixture and season to taste, or simply drape the 'tongues' of roe over the just-cooked scrambled egg. After cooking, I divide the eggs among the cleaned sea urchin shells, then top with a little salmon roe and serve with rye toast and unsalted butter. This recipe is also good served with thick slices of smoked salmon.

The classic combination of eggs and caviar or sea urchin roe can also be served in little tartlets as a canapé or entrée, but be sure to use good buttery flaky pastry.

6 free-range eggs	30 g unsalted butter
¼ cup (60 ml) rich double cream	as generous an amount of caviar as you can
sea salt flakes and freshly ground	afford *or* the finely grated rind of
black pepper	1 orange

Whisk the eggs and cream together, and season with salt and pepper. In a heavy-based frying pan, melt the butter and as it heats pour in the egg mixture and lower the temperature. Scrambled eggs must be only just cooked, so keep on a low temperature and avoid stirring too much until they begin to set, then use a plastic scraper to gently pull the cooked edges into the centre. Remove the pan from the heat when the eggs are about three-quarters done, then stir very gently so that just the residual heat of the pan finishes the cooking. They must be moist and creamy. Serve immediately, piled high with the caviar or scattered with orange rind.

CRÈME CARAMEL

Serves 4

In the very early days of the Pheasant Farm Restaurant, the menu was *table d'hôte* – in other words, our guests had no choice at all. Whilst this may not have suited everyone, no one was ever disappointed with dessert. Although it changed according to the fruits in season, our 'never-fail' standard was a large crème caramel, served as individual slices with extra caramel on top. We used our own eggs, and always cooked the caramel to a bitter counterpoint to offset the custard's richness. We found making it the day before was important for it to properly set; we would then turn it out on to a large plate and slice it into wedges as if it were a cake.

These days we make individual serves in our export kitchen. Getting the caramel right every time is a tricky procedure, as even though we make our desserts and pâtés in much greater numbers now, I use exactly the same principles as I did in the restaurant kitchen. So the caramel is still made in one small saucepan after another, as it is the only way to get the quality I insist upon.

CARAMEL
½ cup (110 g) sugar
125 ml water

CUSTARD
4 large eggs
145 g castor sugar
1½ cups (375 ml) milk
190 ml cream
1 vanilla bean, halved lengthways

To make the caramel, use a small heavy-based saucepan to dissolve the sugar in the water over low–medium heat. Leave it until the mixture turns a very deep amber colour (just one step before burning) and pour into four 120 ml-capacity individual soufflé moulds or ramekins, turning them so the caramel coats the sides.

To make the custard, lightly beat together the eggs and sugar and cover with a cartouche (see Glossary) until needed.

Preheat the oven to 180°C. Heat the milk and cream in a saucepan with the scraped vanilla bean seeds and the bean itself, then bring to scalding point. Cool slightly. Gradually pour this over the egg mixture, stirring carefully. Strain the combined mixture through a fine sieve into another bowl to remove any large strands of egg. Carefully pour the custard into the dishes, over the caramel.

Place the dishes in a roasting pan two-thirds filled with hot water and bake for 25 minutes or until set. Allow the crème caramels to cool in the water bath, then remove from the pan, cover with plastic film and refrigerate.

Serve the following day, turned out onto plates. If you want to make extra caramel to pour over the crème caramels to serve, simply make another batch of the caramel, using the quantities and instructions from the start of the recipe.

PICKLED QUAIL EGGS

36 quail eggs, at least 1 week old
1½ cups (375 ml) white-wine vinegar
50 g sugar

1 level teaspoon black peppercorns
1 level teaspoon allspice berries
1 fresh bay leaf

Place the quail eggs in a saucepan and cover with cold water. Stir them gently with a wooden spoon until they come to the boil. Boil the eggs for 5–6 minutes and tip them straight into iced water to cool. This not only inhibits further cooking, but makes the job of peeling much easier. Tap the pointy end of the egg on the bench and gently crush the shell with your fingers; that way, once you have taken off the first bit of shell, the rest falls away. »

Place the peeled eggs in a large sterilised jar (see Glossary). Boil the other ingredients together in a saucepan for about 5 minutes, until the sugar has dissolved and all the ingredients are combined, and then pour them over the peeled eggs. The vinegar has such a low pH level that the eggs will keep for months at room temperature.

These eggs are delicious tossed in a salad, or cut in half and served with some salmon roe sprinkled on top.

GOOSE EGG CUSTARD TO SERVE WITH MULBERRIES *Serves 4*

If you have a mulberry tree, preserve some of the surplus fruit to try with this dish, as the combination of flavours is wonderful.

2 goose eggs	1 vanilla bean, halved lengthways
2 tablespoons castor sugar	butter, for greasing
1 cup (250 ml) milk	preserved mulberries (optional), to serve
1 cup (250 ml) cream	freshly grated nutmeg, to taste

Preheat the oven to 120°C. Lightly beat together the eggs and sugar and cover with a cartouche (see Glossary).

Heat the milk and cream in a saucepan with the scraped vanilla bean seeds and the bean itself, then bring to scalding point. Cool slightly. Gradually pour this over the egg mixture, stirring carefully. Strain the combined mixture through a fine sieve into a baking dish lightly greased with butter.

Put the dish in a roasting pan and pour in hot water to reach halfway up the sides of the dish. Bake for 1–1½ hours. Remove from the oven and allow to cool in the pan. Serve with preserved mulberries, if using, and garnish with freshly grated nutmeg.

FLAT-LEAF PARSLEY

AFTER YEARS OF ABUSE, PARSLEY ALMOST BECAME A DIRTY word in kitchen parlance. It was the token garnish of a sprig of curly parsley with the tired slice of orange found on almost every plate in the 1970s that made me reject this herb in any form for many years. It wasn't until we bought our farmhouse in 1987, and discovered a garden well established with a parsley very like the flat-leaf variety you can buy now, that I started to look on parsley more kindly. My opinion is so changed that when my daughter Saskia, who is a caterer, and her husband were planning their herb garden, I urged them to plant parsley, parsley and parsley!

The flavour of flat-leaf parsley is sweeter and nuttier than the curly variety and it's the only one I consider growing or using. In fact, I would say it's the herb I use most often. However, I know this is a very personal stance, as curly parsley has a very distinctive flavour that many love.

A few culinary tips for parsley. When you pick or buy a bunch of parsley, put it in water as you would flowers. Parsley quickly goes limp otherwise and its flavour will be inferior. When instructed to chop parsley, normally you just use the leaves and reserve the stalks for stock, although if they are very young I often use them chopped really finely. Wash the parsley well and dry it in a salad spinner or tea towel before chopping, and only chop it just before you need it. *Never* keep leftover chopped parsley for use the next day – it will taste like lawn clippings! And I'd never chop parsley leaves super-fine. If you don't feel confident with a knife, try just plucking the individual leaves, particularly if you're adding the parsley to pasta.

The traditional bouquet garni used in stocks and stews is a bundle of fresh parsley, thyme and a bay leaf; the proportions change according to the desired flavour of the end dish. A bouquet garni can also include basil, celery, chervil, tarragon, salad burnet, rosemary or savoury. The herbs, tied together with string, are lowered into the simmering pan and removed before serving.

If you are making a sauce such as a hot vinaigrette to serve with fish or chicken, throw in some parsley at the last moment. The same goes for parsley added to a hearty winter soup or rustic stew. And don't under-rate the simple practice of sprinkling chopped parsley over pot-roasted meat or a bowl of soup topped with just a drizzle of your favourite extra virgin olive oil.

Parsley fried in nut-brown butter is a great accompaniment to offal. It can also be deep-fried: immerse the parsley in bubbling clarified butter for just a few minutes – the flavour is wonderful.

If you have parsley in the garden, you'll never be caught short. Make a vinaigrette to serve with hot or cold barbecued chicken or seafood by mixing equal quantities of chopped parsley and extra virgin olive oil with enough red-wine vinegar to provide balance, then add salt and lots of freshly ground black pepper. Anchovies or capers can be added as well. Steep grilled chicken breasts or steamed broccoli fresh from the garden in the vinaigrette before serving. Braised leeks and this vinaigrette make a good pair, too.

Gremolata – chopped parsley, crushed garlic and lemon rind – sprinkled over dishes such as osso buco or lamb shanks adds a wonderful zing, and is also good with boiled meats. Try a French classic by making a *persillade*, a mixture of chopped parsley, golden shallots and breadcrumbs, and pressing it over a roasting shoulder of lamb in the last 10 minutes of cooking. *Jambon persillade* is a traditional French dish I have always admired; the version I make is simply cubes of ham captured in a glistening jelly of verjuice set with gelatine leaves, with loads of fresh parsley – it is a wonderful warm weather dish.

To continue the French influence, parsley and garlic butter is, of course, served with snails. Try mixing 75 g softened low-salt butter, 2 tablespoons chopped parsley, 2 crushed garlic cloves, a little lemon juice, salt and freshly ground black pepper. As butter picks up refrigerator odours and quickly becomes rancid, freeze the parsley butter (without the garlic) in small quantities rather than refrigerating it. (Chopped raw garlic becomes unpleasant once frozen and will alter the flavour of the compound butter – add it to the butter after defrosting.)

A really green butter can be made by mixing finely chopped parsley, sorrel and the green parts of spring onions with butter, a dash of lemon juice and a grind of black pepper. Let a slice of this butter melt over veal scaloppine, brains, chicken, fish or potatoes baked in their jackets.

I love tossing fresh vegetables with parsley and extra virgin olive oil, especially small zucchini that have been cooked whole. I let the zucchini cool a little, then slice them lengthways and dress them with small freshly plucked parsley leaves, a drizzle of extra virgin olive oil and a grind of black pepper. Freshly dug baby waxy potatoes boiled and tossed with butter, a squeeze of lemon juice, salt, freshly ground black pepper and lots of just-chopped parsley is another great favourite.

You can make parsley essence by putting a bunch through your electric juicer: add this to thick, homemade mayonnaise for a refreshing accompaniment to cold seafood.

Parsley has a natural affinity with tomatoes and eggs. Dress slices of ripe tomato and just-hard-boiled free-range eggs with the parsley vinaigrette mentioned opposite. Toss vine-ripened sliced tomato with equal quantities of chopped parsley and basil. Or make tabbouleh by mixing lots of chopped parsley and mint with diced tomato, burghul, lemon juice and diced onion.

When I get home late and find nothing much in the cupboard for dinner, I sauté onion in extra virgin olive oil in a frying pan until it is translucent and then toss in wedges of ripe tomato for a few minutes before seasoning the lot well. I slip eggs into the centre of the pan to cook and then serve this wonderfully satisfying concoction with lots of chopped parsley and salt and freshly ground black pepper.

The only dishes I can remember hating in my childhood were white sauce and parsley with tripe or corned silverside, and parsley added to scrambled eggs. I've never quite recovered from the white sauce/parsley combination, but I now love perfect scrambled eggs with chopped flat-leaf parsley folded in at the last moment in the same way I do an omelette with parsley, chives and tarragon. (I also now adore tripe, especially cooked in the Italian way with loads of onions, tomatoes and parsley.)

Onions and parsley are perfect partners. Try a variation on Squid with Onion, Parsley and Anchovy Stuffing (see page 462): use 1 rather than 4 onions, then add 3 finely chopped garlic cloves, an egg and 125 g freshly grated pecorino to masses of parsley and the bread-crumbs. Instead of braising the stuffed squid in oil on the stove, you can bake them, well oiled, at 180°C for 35–45 minutes. Serve the squid either hot, warm, at room temperature or cold – skip the salad, and simply sprinkle over chopped parsley, extra virgin olive oil and a drizzle of red-wine vinegar.

PARSLEY, PRESERVED LEMON AND CAPERBERRY SALAD *Serves 4*

12 caperberries

1 cup flat-leaf parsley leaves

1 tablespoon thinly sliced preserved
    lemon rind

⅓ cup (80 ml) extra virgin olive oil,
    plus extra for shallow-frying

2 thick slices wood-fired bread, torn into
    bite-sized pieces

1 tablespoon red-wine vinegar

Slice 6 of the caperberries in half and put into a glass salad bowl, then add the parsley leaves and preserved lemon. Heat enough olive oil for shallow-frying in a frying pan over high heat, then add the bread and fry until golden. Remove with a slotted spoon, then

add to the bowl, along with the olive oil, vinegar and remaining whole caperberries. Toss together so that the dressing soaks into the croutons, then serve.

WALNUT AND PARSLEY PESTO   *Serves 4*

If your garden is overflowing with parsley, try this variation of pesto, using parsley and walnuts ground with garlic and extra virgin olive oil, to serve with pasta and shaved Parmigiano Reggiano. This pesto is also delicious with smoked tongue.

2 cups (200 g) shelled walnuts

2 cloves garlic

1 cup firmly packed flat-leaf parsley leaves

100 ml extra virgin olive oil

2 teaspoons sea salt flakes

freshly ground black pepper

Preheat the oven to 220°C. Dry-roast the walnuts on a baking tray for 6–8 minutes, then rub off the skins with a tea towel and sieve away any remaining bitter skin. Allow to cool, then grind all the ingredients using a mortar and pestle or by pulsing in a food processor. The pesto will keep for a few days, covered with a film of oil, in a jar in the refrigerator. For longer keeping, see my notes on page 21 for preparing pesto for freezing.

SALSA VERDE   *Serves 4*

Salsa verde, an Italian green sauce, is often served with boiled meat (it is the traditional accompaniment to *bollito misto),* poached chicken breasts, fish or offal, and is especially good with tongue or brains.

1 boiled potato, peeled and chopped

1 cup firmly packed flat-leaf parsley leaves

3 anchovy fillets

1 clove garlic

2 tiny cornichons (see Glossary)

extra virgin olive oil

1 tablespoon red-wine vinegar

sea salt flakes and freshly ground
    black pepper

Combine the potato, parsley, anchovies, garlic and cornichons in a food processor. With the motor running, add enough olive oil, a little at a time, to make a thick sauce, then blend in the vinegar, salt and pepper. This sauce is best served on the day it is made.

GARLIC

WHEN YOU THINK OF THE IMPORTANCE OF GARLIC IN FOOD, IT IS no wonder it is celebrated. It is hard to think of a cuisine that doesn't embrace garlic. A garlic festival has been held in Tours in France on St Anne's day, 28 July, each year since 1838. More recently there has also been a garlic festival held each August in Gilroy, California. In her *Chez Panisse Café Cookbook*, Alice Waters talks at length about a garlic dinner she prepared for this festival. It is amazing to think of a whole menu using garlic. There were vegetables with garlic, Chinese garlic cakes, tortellini with garlic, fish with dried chillies and garlic, quail stuffed with whole garlic baked in grape leaves, and a Moroccan eggplant salad with garlic. Even the dessert was wine-spiced garlic sherbets. One might think that such a dessert was a novelty, devised to justify the inclusion of garlic, but Alice Waters' notes on the menu said that, 'The most memorable aspect of this meal for me was the garlic sherbets, which were made with red fruits macerated with red wine and garlic cloves, and with white fruits macerated with white wine and garlic cloves, to create a very fruity beginning flavour to the sherbet with a lovely garlic aftertaste.'

The whole issue of finding good garlic has become more and more difficult over the years in Australia. There has been so much importing, or should I say dumping, of garlic into our markets, that many Australian commercial growers have simply given up on the crop as they cannot compete with the cheap imported product. It seems the public did not appreciate the difference between imported garlic bleached white to kill bacteria and mould, and the fresh garlic from our own soils.

The one bright light here is that the organic movement has 'sprouted' interest in fresh, locally grown garlic. Often pink-striped, it appears in the marketplace around November and December. The flavour of this garlic is superb and makes a huge difference to a dish. So look for Australian garlic rather than the uniformly white imported garlic – the improvement in flavour is phenomenal, and Australian growers need to be encouraged.

Commercial producers who use chemicals to combat weeds plant garlic in February, while organic farmers plant in April or May. As a result, our garlic season is extended a little. Green garlic makes its way onto the market in early spring – this is an attempt on the part of the farmers to make production more economically viable. These shoots look similar to leeks, as the bulb is yet to form and separate into garlic cloves, while the flavour has the familiar pungency of dried garlic. Green garlic is handy to use before the local, better-keeping dried garlic becomes available from late spring – the shoots are deliciously sweet when roasted whole and can also be added to salads.

Garlic is really easy to grow, and once pulled from the garden it can be hung to dry in your shed; it will then be available for months and months, if kept dry and cool.

In the Barossa, we have a fantastic Saturday-morning farmers' market. Here, two young lads, the Marschall boys (as they are referred to at the markets, and who were only in years ten and twelve at school at the time), sold their crop of 1200 garlic plants in the first two weeks of December, and they have plans to double their crop next year. The boys had been lucky enough to have Michael Voumard, a great chef and organic gardener of note, as a mentor. Michael's garden is more like a wonderland, and he uses its bounty in his cooking at Rockford Wines for the dining room of the Stonewall Club.

To prepare garlic, take the clove – pulled away from the bulb – and press down on it on a chopping board with the flat side of a large-bladed knife. This will pop the skin off, which you can then remove. Add a sprinkle of salt, continue applying pressure with the knife, and the garlic will become 'creamed' and ready for use, without any trace of bitterness. If you do not want to add salt, use a sharp knife to cut the clove into fine pieces. (Raw garlic is very powerful and the finer it is chopped or sliced, the stronger it will be.) Using a garlic press to crush garlic will make it bitter. Be careful when sautéing garlic as it burns easily and will then become bitter too.

What would bruschetta be without a cut clove of garlic rubbed over warm, toasted bread before the tomato, basil and a drizzle of extra virgin olive oil are added? The same goes for a salad, where rubbing the inside of the bowl with garlic before tossing the lettuce in leaves a subtle note. And raw garlic mixed with lemon rind and flat-leaf parsley is delicious with boiled meats.

I love roasting the whole garlic bulb, whether fresh or dried, and using it in many different ways. I don't know why slowly roasted heads of garlic have gone out of fashion. When Alice Waters wrote of them in her *Chez Panisse Menu Cookbook* in 1982, many kitchens across the land offered roasted garlic with goat's cheese, a crouton and olive oil – a classic combination. Roasted garlic, easily squeezed from its papery shell onto a crouton, is wonderfully sweet and nutty. Or the roasted head of garlic can be served whole, or cut in half horizontally.

When garlic is cooked it becomes rich, sweet and buttery and marries well with foods as diverse as lamb, kid, beef, quail, chicken, goat's cheese and eggplant. Either rub the whole bulb with some extra virgin olive oil and roast it in a 180°C oven with a little thyme, or try cooking it slowly in the smallest container possible, either in the oven or on top of the stove, totally immersed in olive oil or stock with sprigs of thyme, bay or rosemary. Remember, in both cases, to prick the bulb beforehand to prevent it exploding.

Green-striped garlic heads just pulled from the ground and roasted whole are incredibly sweet. Although fresh jumbo garlic can be very bitter, growers are beginning to select their largest corms for their planting stock rather than selling them to eat, which seems to be making a difference.

Slow-cooking suits garlic perfectly. If pot-roasting, add unpeeled cloves with the meat or poultry. Once the dish is cooked, squeeze the garlic from its skin into the juices – if there are enough cloves, they can become a purée to flavour and thicken the sauce.

While not all Italians use garlic and Italian food is not just about pasta, the partnership seems natural. Spaghetti with garlic, oil and chilli is comfort food for many. In winter, try combining chopped garlic with toasted walnuts, cream and Parmigiano Reggiano in a sauce to toss through fusilli. I cook masses of peeled garlic cloves slowly in olive oil for about 20 minutes until they're golden, then toss these through wide pasta ribbons with caramelised fennel, preserved lemon and a generous amount of flat-leaf parsley and freshly ground black pepper. Shavings of Parmigiano Reggiano and a drizzle of extra virgin olive oil finish off this delicious combination of flavours.

Patricia Wells, in her book *At Home in Provence*, also combines garlic with preserved lemon, but this time in a dish with rabbit. Whole heads of garlic with the top third cut away are cooked cut-side down, and the preserved lemon melts into the cooking juices. Patricia also writes about garlic soup, where a head of garlic combines with leeks, onions, golden shallots, bouquet garni, potatoes and herbs. Elsewhere she describes cooking fresh white beans with garlic, fresh bay leaves and thyme, and suggests simmering a head of garlic in cream and adding the resulting purée to mashed potato.

The French are keen on using garlic in sauces. If a strong flavour appeals to you but you're trying to stay away from eggs, make an Authentic Aïoli (see page 587). Or make garlic butter by mixing roasted garlic together with unsalted butter cut into small portions, and keep it in the freezer (this prevents rancidity) to add richness to a sauce at the last minute.

I once wrote on garlic in a weekly column in *The Advertiser*, when I first started writing about food, and I received letters from readers asking what to do about garlic preserved in olive oil turning blue. I contacted the CSIRO and they told me the following about the dangers of holding garlic or similar products in oil.

The main cause of the problem is the level of acidity. The outer leaves of garlic, and to some extent the bulbs themselves, may contain anthocyanin pigments, which are colourless at the normal pH of garlic but turn blue or even pink under acid conditions. Most garlic cloves do not contain sufficient quantities of this pigment for the discolouration to pose a problem. Test each batch of garlic by adding vinegar to a small sample of garlic and warm it. If it discolours, seek out another supply of garlic.

At the same time the CSIRO made me aware of incidents of botulism in the United States involving garlic in oil products. Oil has no antimicrobial preservative action – its only function in preserving is to prevent oxidisation which can lead to discolouration of some foods. By excluding oxygen from the surface of vegetables, one is establishing anaerobic conditions, which actually favour the growth of some types of bacteria, one of which is *Clostridium botulinum*, the organism which causes botulism.

It is therefore essential that sufficient acid, usually in the form of vinegar, be added to the vegetable before oil is poured on, so that these bacteria cannot grow. This means that the pH level must be reduced to below 4.6. Mass-produced vinegars usually contain about 4 per cent acetic acid. Any mixture should therefore have a vegetable to vinegar ratio by weight not greater than 3 to 1, which would give 1 per cent acetic acid, ensuring that the final pH is below 4.6.

ROUILLE
Makes 400 g

A pungent and particularly more-ish way of using garlic is to make this paste to serve with a fish soup, stew, braised oxtail, lamb shanks or with a crudité of fresh vegetables. For those who like spicy heat, it can be adjusted by including a chilli with the red capsicum. *Rouille* is French for 'rust' – and this should be the colour of your sauce.

1 large, very red capsicum	4 cloves garlic
200 ml extra virgin olive oil, plus extra for roasting	50 ml red-wine vinegar
	a few saffron threads (optional)
2 slices bread, crusts removed	3 free-range egg yolks
milk, for soaking	sea salt flakes and freshly ground
½ teaspoon cayenne pepper	black pepper

Preheat the oven to 200°C. Cut the top off the capsicum and remove the seeds. Rub with some olive oil and roast in the oven until it collapses and seems to be burnt – usually about 20 minutes. Take the capsicum from the oven and let it rest for a few minutes before putting it in a plastic bag to sweat. When it is cool enough to handle, peel, removing all traces of blackened skin.

Soak the bread in a little milk for 10 minutes, then squeeze it thoroughly.

Place the capsicum, cayenne pepper, garlic, bread, vinegar, saffron threads, if using, and egg yolks in the bowl of a food processor and purée well. Season, then with the motor running, slowly pour in the olive oil in a stream as you would for mayonnaise, processing until emulsified.

AUTHENTIC AÏOLI

Aïoli is a garlic mayonnaise – a garlic lover's dream. It is a very important dish in Mediterranean cooking and a great accompaniment to something like octopus which has been marinated in extra virgin olive oil and lemon juice and then thrown on the barbecue.

A young man with a Catalan background once spent a few weeks in my kitchen, and from him I learnt that original aïoli in its purest form contains no eggs, is white and shiny, and very strongly flavoured with garlic. It is also said to be impossible to make a true aïoli in a food processor as the oil and garlic become too homogenised. So, for a truly authentic aïoli, take out your mortar and pestle.

6 cloves garlic, green shoots discarded, finely chopped	½ teaspoon salt
	1 cup (250 ml) extra virgin olive oil

The ingredients should be at room temperature. Mash the garlic using a mortar and pestle, mixing in the salt until it is a thick paste. Add the olive oil very slowly, a few drops at a time, and always stir in the one direction with the pestle. Continue adding the oil slowly until an emulsion forms. Serve immediately.

MAGGIE'S AÏOLI

I am more at home with the way I have always made aïoli – with eggs. I have calmed down about the amount of garlic I use these days and would now only use 3 cloves to every 250 ml extra virgin olive oil, but those who really want to have that hit of raw garlic can use up to 6 cloves. At times I roast the garlic before adding it to the mayonnaise, in which case it could be called roasted garlic aïoli. For this, I would use 6 or more cloves of garlic, as its flavour when roasted is sweet and nutty.

2–3 cloves garlic, or to taste	2 free-range egg yolks
½ teaspoon salt	1 cup (250 ml) extra virgin olive oil

Mash the garlic using a mortar and pestle, mixing in the salt until it forms a thick paste. Add the egg yolks, then proceed with adding the oil, remembering to proceed very slowly until at least one-third of the oil has been used. Continue adding the oil slowly until an emulsion forms. Serve immediately.

GOAT'S CHEESE

SPRING AND SUMMER MEAN LOTS OF GOAT'S MILK FOR MAKING cheese. As long as there is enough rain to provide green feed, goat's milk is at its most plentiful from October to March. During the winter months some dairies taper off production whilst others use frozen milk to maintain supplies.

Will Studd, a man who knows more about cheese than anyone else in Australia, tells me that goat's milk has smaller fat globules than cow's milk and so is more easily digested. He also says goat's cheese can be eaten late at night without the need for lots of red wine to break it down, as with other cheese – a theory many would relate to.

The person who first made us all take notice of Australian goat's cheese is the wonderful Gabrielle Kervella from Western Australia, who operates under the Kervella Fromage Fermier label. A farmer and cheese-maker, she is a passionate advocate for goat's cheese – and we have a lot to thank her for, since pioneering is never easy. Gabrielle has taken her passion one step further and has now become an organic producer, and year after year she manages to provide us with amazing cheese.

Many others Australia-wide have now joined Gabrielle in making high-quality goat's cheese. John Wignall of Tasmania's tiny but important Bothwell Dairy makes goat's cheese that is sold within the island state, as do one or two other small producers, such as Nick Haddow of Bruny Island Cheese, who is making some incredibly exciting cheeses and, small as their operation is, they are already exporting to great acclaim. South Australia is very proud of Woodside Cheese Wrights, whose Edith cheese was first established by the original makers, wine-maker Paula Jenkin and chef Simon Burr, bringing together technical ability and an innate understanding of flavours. The company, which produces a range of cheeses made from goat's and cow's milk, has gone from strength to strength and is now run by Kris Lloyd. Their Edith cheese is sold in an ashed round, as both Paula and Simon learnt to make it that way in France. In October, when the milk supply is plentiful again, Woodside makes Capricorn, a creamy goat's milk camembert. Like Gabrielle,

Paula and Simon also make a cabécou, which is great in all stages of its life, from fresh to so mature that it is covered with blue mould. Presented with some of this recently, I simply wiped off the mould and grated the cheese into pasta to great effect. Another South Australian contender making really good goat's cheese is Udder Delights – as small companies need to, they are always innovating. And Pino Marmorale at La Vera Mozzarella, a third-generation cheese-maker from Naples, makes a three-year-old matured goat's cheese that I marvel at.

Julie Cameron of Meredith Dairy in Victoria is another cheese-maker worthy of mention. As part of her range she makes fromage blanc and fromage frais, neither of which is salted, and so can be used in sweet as well as savoury dishes. She takes the top layer of the milk, where the cream settles, to make the blanc, a cheese that can be served individually and tends to be marinated (as I do with grappa on page 594) or used as a dessert dish. The fromage frais is the body of the milk drained of whey; it is used mainly on pizzas or in vegetable terrines. Also from Victoria, Laurie Jensen of Tarago River Cheese Co. makes Childers, a particularly wonderful goat's cheese camembert, as well as Strzelecki Blue.

Then there's Richard Thomas, who has been such a significant player in the industry since its beginnings, and whose influence on the development of cheese-making in this country has been immense. His past credits include stints at King Island, Kangaroo Island, Milawa, Meredith and Gippsland, and over the years he has developed some of Australia's finest cheese varieties. He started the Yarra Valley Dairy in 1996, and currently works with Paula Jenkin at Indigo making his beloved blue cheeses, as well as with De Bortoli Wines, where he buys cheeses from other cheese-makers to mature and sell. His aim is to sell cheeses at their perfect stage of ripeness, and to educate the public on how best to look after cheese once they get it home. The Yarra Valley itself is now becoming a wine and cheese mecca, with All Saints Estate and Giant Steps Winery also selling handmade cheese in addition to their wines. And a relative newcomer, Holy Goat Organic Cheese, east of Castlemaine, is making seriously good goat's cheese, from fromage frais to more mature varieties.

It is wonderful to be able to write that I cannot keep up with all the good producers who are appearing. As each region attracts passionate producers who are driven to maximise their potential, produce of all kinds just gets better and better.

The range of quality goat's cheeses today is quite extraordinary and it has indeed become a special part of our food life. It is such a versatile cheese and you have to do so little to present it as part of a meal – just remember to take the cheese out of the refrigerator well in advance so that it can come to room temperature first, otherwise its flavour won't be fully developed.

One of the great advantages of goat's cheese is that it makes a great entrée or luncheon dish, whether simply melted on croutons as part of a salad, cubed and tossed with roasted pumpkin, walnuts and rocket, or stuffed in the centre of roasted and peeled red capsicums. As a main course, toss it through pasta with zucchini flowers and anchovies, adding crunchy roasted almonds for texture; or layer pasta sheets with goat's cheese, eggplant and roasted tomatoes. The list of possibilities is endless, as goat's cheese marries so well with Mediterranean flavours: slowly roasted garlic, olives, anchovies, capers, eggplants, ripe tomatoes, peppery salad greens, walnuts and walnut oil.

Serve fromage blanc (without added salt) alongside poached fruit, as I so often enjoyed while travelling through the French countryside and eating at small country restaurants. No sugar was added, yet the cheese was sweet but piquant. Fromage blanc also works well wrapped in vine leaves and grilled – the cheese oozes out and the leaves caramelise. All these parcels need is a drizzle of extra virgin olive oil and a sprinkling of salt and freshly ground black pepper – let them cool a little, then devour them with crusty bread.

A tip if you are cooking goat's cheese – do not leave it in the oven or under the griller once it has melted, as it will become grainy and separate with prolonged heating.

To prove my point about the versatility of goat's cheese, let's start with goat's curd, a younger, softer version of the mature cheese. Surround the curd with your best young salad leaves; make a hole in the centre of the soft curd and fill with your best walnut oil. Serve with crusty bread – walnut bread would be best of all – sea salt and freshly ground black pepper and you've got a meal.

Curd is great for ravioli fillings. Drain it if it seems too moist, then mix chopped semi-dried tomatoes, basil leaves, sea salt and freshly ground black pepper and make little parcels of fresh pasta. You could add a sauce of very ripe chopped tomatoes, a little season-ing and a fruity extra virgin olive oil, or simply drizzle with just enough extra virgin olive oil to moisten the ravioli once cooked. Or mix goat's cheese with finely chopped cooked eggplant or mushrooms, or poached asparagus or artichokes, and use to fill fresh ravioli.

For something more substantial, place thin slices of pancetta on a baking tray and crisp quickly in the oven as you heat goat's cheese on croutons. Serve the croutons with the pancetta and strips of baked or shallow-fried eggplant on top. The same applies to roasted red capsicums, cut into strips. Drape them over the croutons, with anchovies or olives, and add lots of chopped flat-leaf parsley and extra virgin olive oil.

Stuff zucchini flowers with tiny knobs of goat's cheese, kneaded with roasted pine nuts and drizzled with olive oil. Coat them in a tempura-style batter, shallow-fry quickly and serve immediately.

A good dried pasta cooked and served with roasted garlic cloves, cubes of goat's cheese to melt over the hot pasta, flat-leaf parsley and extra virgin olive oil makes a truly great meal without fuss. Add and subtract as you like with any of the season's flavours. Don't forget, the goat's cheese left at the back of the fridge that has become truly matured and hard as a rock can simply be grated over hot pasta in the same way as Parmigiano Reggiano.

Goat's cheese and pastry are another time-honoured combination. Try a savoury tart – start with a rectangle of baked Sour-cream Pastry (see page 424), spread generously with a soft goat's cheese and topped with Caramelised Onion (see page 461), then returned to a 180°C oven for about 10 minutes, before serving with a final flourish of extra virgin olive oil and lots of peppery salad greens.

In very late spring you may be able to pick the first of the figs in hotter climes: layer sliced ripe figs with goat's cheese and basil, seasoning as you go with extra virgin olive oil and freshly ground black pepper, then serve with crusty bread. Or make a simple 'sandwich', which Chris Manfield, originally from Adelaide but whose fame has now spread much further afield, made famous during her days at the Paramount Restaurant in Sydney: her simple layering of deep-fried eggplant rounds, strips of roasted capsicum, freshly made pesto and fresh goat's cheese is just a great combination.

Goat's cheese featured at 'the wake' held the day the Pheasant Farm Restaurant closed, 28 November 1993, a wonderful event stage-managed by our friend Rod Schubert. The invitation to attend was an amazing version of Lewis Carroll's classic 'The Walrus and the Carpenter' read by Kate Jordan-Moore, an old team member. The sun was beginning to hit the hills on the far side of the dam and we wanted everyone to experience the light of the early evening sky reflected in the water as we had drinks (a scene familiar to the Wednesday table and other Barossa lunch groups). At exactly 7.45 p.m. Bob McLean and Rod Schubert lit the candles in the large candelabra in a corner of the restaurant, then Bob, he of the loud voice, called everyone in. At 7.50 p.m. the light flooded into the room, as did all our guests.

Rod had positioned four life-sized figures around the room: plaster-of-Paris bodies with glass mannequin heads, as seen in shop windows many years ago. One was sentinel at the end of a huge table that groaned with food; two were at the front windows; and another, dressed in a Pheasant Farm Restaurant T-shirt and long white apron, was by the table with the cutlery and crockery at the back of the room. The perfect 'silent' waiter! Almost in the centre of the food, right next to the suckling pig surrounded by pickled figs, was an up-ended elegant plaster leg. All these figures were spot-lit as dark descended, lending an ethereal feel to the room. Huge arrangements of flowers abounded – Aileen, their creator, must have stripped her garden bare.

My favourite tipple at the time, Yalumba's 'D' sparkling wine, flowed and the staff, wearing newly made T-shirts, black as usual with the gold pheasant on the front but with 'Ain't going to work on Maggie's Farm no more' in gold on the back, passed around baskets of delights. Labna made from goat's milk yoghurt was rolled into bite-sized balls and arranged on vine leaves with preserved wild olives, asparagus spears, prosciutto and olive bread croutons. Another basket, again lined with vine leaves, boasted olive bread and dishes of caperberries, sliced pickled quinces and more wild olives, plus a huge bowl of goat's curd doused with extra virgin olive oil. A basket of yabbies shared the limelight with boletus mushrooms I had preserved in the autumn, accompanied by caramelised garlic cloves, a dish of extra virgin olive oil and wedges of lemon.

On the table were masses of just-out-of-the-oven loaves of bread that Nat and Alex, two of my 'extended family' of staff, had made using dried muscatels. Bowls of duck egg pasta with olive paste and herbs or smoked kangaroo and pine nuts sat alongside. Eggplants, baked quail and couscous, leek tarts, sorrel tarts, octopus, more yabbies, oysters, tongue with salsa verde, pheasant pies and lots of salads of bitter greens all fought for space.

The festivities had several stages: the drinks beside the dam, the feast itself, and then the party after most of the guests had left, well after midnight. The after-party celebration was twofold, as the date we closed the restaurant had been chosen very particularly. It was the day before Elli's eighteenth birthday and the week before Saskia's wedding, which gave us time to prepare for another feast. Closing the restaurant, which had been my obsession in life but had taken so much of my time during most of their lives, was my gift to the girls. So at midnight Elli's party and the staff party began. We'd had music to begin the night, but the tempo changed now as Steve Grant, another ex-staffer, played the acoustic guitar and sang his heart out as we danced. At 5 a.m. we called it a night, exhausted but happy.

You don't need a feast to have an excuse to make labna. It's perfect as a nibble, with salads or as an accompaniment to lamb, kid or poultry, particularly if you also add strips of preserved lemon. Labna is really just cheese made from goat's, sheep's or cow's milk yoghurt (choose a naturally made one as some of the commercial brands are too thin). It's important to buy a thick yoghurt, and then mix 1 kg yoghurt with 1 teaspoon salt, and pour this into a muslin or Chux-lined sieve or colander and let it drain over a bowl in the refrigerator overnight, or if you want it firm enough to shape into balls, make it two days before using it. (In the winter you can hang the muslin 'bag' over the tap in the kitchen sink.) Form the drained yoghurt into bite-sized balls, then roll these in chopped herbs and drizzle with extra virgin olive oil before serving, Alternatively, add chopped rosemary or oregano, preserved lemon and roasted garlic cloves to the labna and cover with olive oil until required.

MARINATED GOAT'S CHEESE
Serves 4–6

When I first read of the idea of marinating goat's cheese in grappa, in Michele Scicolone's book *The Antipasto Table*, I couldn't wait to try it. I found it absolute dynamite with garlic and parsley. As a drink, grappa, which can be bought in specialist Italian groceries, is something I think you have to be born to, but here its fruity aggressiveness is balanced by the creaminess and sweetness of the unsalted cheese. If the goat's cheese you are using is more acidic, try using something smoother than grappa, perhaps Cognac.

1 large clove garlic, finely sliced
2 tablespoons grappa
⅓ cup (80 ml) extra virgin olive oil
⅓ cup roughly chopped flat-leaf parsley

freshly ground black pepper
2 × 180 g tubs Kervella *or* Meredith
   Dairy Fromage Blanc

Combine the garlic, grappa, olive oil, parsley and a few coarse grinds of pepper. Pour a little of this marinade into a glass or ceramic dish, then gently add the cheeses and pour the remaining marinade over them. Cover the dish with plastic film and place in the refrigerator for 24 hours to marinate, turning the cheeses once or twice.

Serve the cheeses, removed from the marinade, at room temperature with rocket dressed with extra virgin olive oil and a good balsamic or aged red-wine vinegar. Slabs of bread, brushed with extra virgin olive oil and toasted in the oven, are a must.

CROUTONS WITH GABRIELLE'S GOAT'S CHEESE, SALSA AGRESTO AND ROCKET
Serves 6

To make this a little more substantial, you could also add roasted garlic cloves, walnuts and prosciutto to the peppery rocket salad.

1 baguette, sliced diagonally
extra virgin olive oil, for cooking
6 handfuls rocket leaves, trimmed,
   washed and dried

red-wine vinegar, for drizzling
250 g Kervella Fresh Goat's Curd
1 × quantity Salsa Agresto (see page 22)

Preheat the oven to 200°C. Brush one side of the baguette slices with olive oil and toast in the oven until golden. Dress the rocket with a little of the extra virgin olive oil and vinegar.

Pile the croutons with goat's cheese and top each one with a dollop of salsa agresto, then serve with the rocket salad.

PASTA WITH BROCCOLINI, PANCETTA, GOAT'S CURD AND TOASTED BREADCRUMBS

Serves 4

I like to serve this when the pasta is warm enough to melt the goat's cheese just a little.

1 cup (70 g) firmly packed breadcrumbs, made from stale wood-fired bread

extra virgin olive oil, for drizzling

2 tablespoons chopped flat-leaf parsley

finely chopped rind of 1 lemon

24 thin slices pancetta

1 bunch broccolini

500 g penne

180 g goat's cheese, cut into 1 cm pieces

sea salt flakes and freshly ground black pepper

2 tablespoons lemon juice

Preheat the oven to 200°C. Place breadcrumbs on a baking tray and drizzle over 2 tablespoons olive oil, then roast until golden brown. Mix with the parsley and lemon rind. Bake the pancetta on baking trays for about 5 minutes or until crisp, and set aside.

Cook broccolini in a shallow pan of boiling salted water for 3–5 minutes, then drain and drizzle with olive oil.

Cook pasta following the directions on the packet and then drain. In a large bowl, toss the hot pasta with the warm breadcrumbs, pancetta and broccolini and the room temperature goat's cheese. Season, then add lemon juice and olive oil to taste.

HONEY

ONE OF THE SPECIAL TREATS OF LIVING ON THE FARM AND having space around us was being able to wander down to the creek on a warm evening, with a glass of sparkling wine in hand, to visit the bee-hives. We baby-sat the hives of our friend Nigel Hopkins for a couple of years. After he reclaimed them, we missed them so much that I bought my husband Colin an antiquated beehive to restore (however, it is still sitting in the shed awaiting repair as daily life and the more urgent matters of the farm and business took over). Its restoration is still on our 'must do' list, as it was such a special thing to lie in front of a hive and be part of its hypnotic hum of activity. (Nigel tells me the hum is the sound of the bees, having had a full day of nectar-gathering, fanning their wings to evaporate any moisture.) The sweet-ness of the air combined with the humid perfume of the honey is truly one of the most magical smells in the world. It is such a soothing experience – I can truly recommend it to anyone who is at all stressed.

Honey is becoming a scarce commodity, as there are fewer areas in which apiarists are allowed to keep their hives. Honey is normally 'fined' to remove any of the sediment that occurs when it is collected – mind you, I love it as it comes, with bees' knees and all. Bottling the honey without warming it excessively is a very slow process. Warming the honey makes it easier to bottle, but some of the flavour is lost. It is almost impossible to bottle honey without warming it at all, but passionate beekeepers try to keep it to an abso-lute minimum. There is a huge difference between honey prepared this carefully and ordinary commercial honey.

Pure honey direct from the beekeeper is becoming rare. Being a natural product with nothing added, honey will crystallise at cooler temperatures. The crystallisation can be reversed by heating the jar on the lowest setting in a microwave or by placing it in a roast-ing pan half-filled with water in the oven for a few minutes. You can then pop the jar of honey in the fridge for a short time to thicken it up again if you like.

For some years now, local Barossa apiarists Mark and Gloria Rosenzweig of Moculta have provided the honey for the Farmshop from their static apiary, the only one of its kind in Australia. Their honey is very beautiful, although as customers will not buy honey if it's starting to crystallise, we have to avoid it in the winter. It has a fantastic consistency: well-rounded on the palate, with floral overtones from the Salvation Jane plants that the bees pollinate. The under-note is from the Mallee honey myrtle tree, and is almost butterscotch in flavour. It has a gentle sweetness yet is not oversweet, which suits my palate.

The individual hives are kept in a long, very narrow, L-shaped corrugated-iron shed; the shed is roofed and also closed to the weather on the outer edge. Boxes stand on planks suspended from beams by metal rods, each passing through a pot of sump oil to keep ants at bay. These boxes are quite different from the hives that open from the top that you see in stacks in the countryside. Instead, each box has a glass window in front that allows the

apiarist to check the activity inside; a door on the side gives access to the frames that carry the honeycomb, and the front has a landing platform for the bees.

My first visit to them years ago was on a very hot, windy afternoon, and the bees were angry. Mark is allergic to bees, so no one was taking any chances when it came to gathering the honey. We all donned beekeepers' outfits to keep rogue bees at bay and Mark was armed with a smoker. Bees sense fear and can turn on those emitting it. For some reason I have never been fearful of bees – not lying in front of our hives and not there in the shed.

Nothing modern interrupted the activity in the shed, yet the honey flowed perfectly: a turkey feather brushed away the groggy bees and a century-old, hand-forged knife with a curved blade was used to slice off the wax capping the cells. Gloria lifted a frame, and the gold of the honey dazzled us as she slipped it into the old separator (bought second-hand at auction in the early 1900s by Mark's grandfather for 2 shillings and sixpence!). It was during this first visit that I thought how much I'd like to have access to the Rosenzweigs' honey: their traditions are so intact and the hives, honey room and associated equipment make it a living museum well worth preserving.

Kangaroo Island is unique for many reasons, one of them being that it is the oldest bee sanctuary in the world. Ligurian bees were introduced there in 1884, the following year a sanctuary was declared and since then no other bees have been brought to the island. The Kangaroo Island Ligurian bee is disease-free, exceptionally quiet, easy to handle and produces good honey. The native bees on the island do not produce honey and do not interbreed with the Ligurian, which is checked continually to ensure that it is true to type.

There is still today a strong trade in Kangaroo Island queen bees. The bees can be tricked into making extra queens but it requires a great deal of effort on the part of the beekeeper. The queen bees are then sent to apiarists around the world in wooden boxes the size of a match box. Each queen bee is fed on the journey by eight worker bees (these are known as escorts!) from supplies of honey and icing sugar. (This is the one instance when the worker bee is on 'light duties', as she – all the males are drones – usually spends half of her six-week-long life cleaning out the frames and the other half gathering nectar.)

I believe Australian honey to be among the purest and tastiest in the world, with only honey from New Zealand and Canada coming close. Our native trees lend their own particular scents and characters to the honey, as do introduced strawberry clovers and citrus blossom; spring is the peak time for blossom. Buy different honeys to assess which ones you like best. Try pale, mild blue-gum or sugar-gum honey, or gutsy leatherwood honey and full-flavoured red-gum, mallee or bottlebrush honey. The leatherwood honeys of Tasmania are particularly distinctive – they are not for the faint-hearted but they're an absolute favourite of mine as, even though it may sound strange, some honeys are too sweet for me. And one of my other favourites is orange-blossom honey, but the aromatics fade so quickly I have to make the most of it when it's at its peak in December. Lavender also produces a sweetly scented honey.

The difference between honey direct from the apiaries and much of the honey found in supermarkets (although there are definite exceptions) is pronounced – I'd equate this supermarket honey with cask wine. It's the bottom of the range and made by big producers: blended from different varieties, the honey is heat-treated and filtered very finely to achieve the maximum degree of 'user-friendliness'. Most producers, big and small, heat honey to help them bottle it, but the good ones keep the heat low enough so that the flavour is less affected. Very fine filtering removes some of the pollens and, along with them, some of the flavour. Consumers tend not to cope with bees' knees, wings and pieces of wax in their honey, but this thick, luscious honey straight from the hive is my favourite.

There is honey that falls somewhere between generic honey, which is always runny and has plenty of sweetness but no finesse or character, and the honey that I prefer, which can threaten to bend a spoon but has masses of flavour. Some larger producers pay premium prices for high-quality honey from small beekeepers and keep the varieties separate, meeting the rigid standards of ISO 9002 accreditation yet keeping the honey as close as possible to the optimum. Look for those companies that make named honeys – those that declare the plant source. And look out for signs advertising honey for sale when travelling in the country – you may be lucky enough to find unfiltered, and may even be able to buy honeycomb.

Creamed honey is simply runny honey that has been beaten with a little naturally candied honey. Many small producers have ruined electric mixers aerating honey this way!

As much as I love good honey, I don't use it a great deal in my cooking. I much prefer to spread it on a piece of toast or crusty, fresh, still-warm white bread with loads of unsalted butter. This is when I use my leatherwood or any other strongly flavoured honey such as imported Italian chestnut honey; these are also great poured over fresh ricotta. Every night I have a cup of hot milk flavoured with honey to help me sleep, but in this case I'm more likely to use a mild sugar-gum honey.

You often see honey used in cakes or puddings – Mrs Beeton gives a recipe for steamed honey pudding, which includes lemon rind and ginger and makes a delightfully comforting winter's treat.

When they were younger, my daughters loved chicken breasts that had been marinated with honey. Drizzle the chicken sparingly with honey, as if it were extra virgin olive oil, then add lots of chopped herbs and a squeeze of lemon juice and allow it to marinate for a good 30 minutes before baking at 180°C for 10–15 minutes, or grill it on the barbecue. Be careful that the chicken doesn't burn during cooking – if barbecuing, turn the chicken every minute or so to prevent this.

When I lived in Scotland and visited particular friends I was always given breakfast in bed on a beautifully set tray. Half a grapefruit was followed by a bowl of steaming porridge topped with a huge spoonful of honey almost as brown as treacle, and a big knob of butter that melted and oozed over the honey. It was marvellous.

A great tip from my honey supplier is to spray a small ceramic dish with a thin film of neutral-flavoured oil before filling it with honey to take to the breakfast table. The unused honey will then slip straight back into the jar.

If you can manage to substitute honey for sugar in a cake recipe (and it can't always be done), the cake will stay beautifully moist – if it lasts long enough in your household!

RICOTTA, HONEY AND PEARS   *Serves 12*

A whole round of ricotta surrounded by pears and drizzled with honey makes for a truly dramatic dessert, a new take on a cheese platter, or it works equally well as part of a Sunday brunch. I serve this on a raised cake stand, although you could use any large, round platter.

You'll need to visit a specialist cheese shop for the ricotta, and a rich, gutsy honey (not too sweet) really makes this dish special – try mallee, Manuka or leatherwood honey if you can find them. Or, to be totally indulgent, use imported chestnut honey.

3 ripe pears
juice of ½ lemon

2 kg round pure whey handmade ricotta
(23 cm diameter)
400 ml honey

Slice the pears lengthways into thin slices and squeeze lemon juice over them so that they don't discolour, then arrange them around the ricotta. Drizzle the honey over the top, letting it run down the sides, and serve.

STEVE'S 'FROMAGE BLANC' WITH HONEYCOMB AND DESSERT WINE

Serves 4

This dish was served by Steve Flamsteed in his King River Café back in the late 1990s. It is a combination of an Alsatian dessert he used to eat during vintage in France, and one made by Steve Cumper, another friend and ex-employee of mine. The way it is eaten is as important as the dish itself. Steve Flamsteed writes, 'It's almost too many sensations but it works wonderfully!' Sometimes he reduces 750 ml of the dessert wine served with the dish to 100 ml, then stirs 2 tablespoons of this into the yoghurt 'cheese' instead of the honey.

Steve now combines his skills as wine-maker, chef and cheese-maker in his role at Giant Steps Winery in the Yarra Valley, where he is director of wine-making.

¼ cup (90 g) subtle honey (Salvation Jane or gum-blossom, for example)

500 g sheep's milk yoghurt

200 g honeycomb

8 almond biscotti

Australian dessert wine, to serve

Mix 1 tablespoon of the honey into the yoghurt, then tip this into a muslin-lined colander or sieve, place over a bowl and allow to drain overnight (you can do this on the kitchen bench if the weather is not too hot). The next morning the drained yoghurt or 'cheese' will be the consistency of mascarpone. Fold the remaining honey through the cheese and refrigerate it to enable you to form shapes for serving.

Using 2 dessertspoons, make quenelles by taking a spoonful of cheese, then using the other spoon to mould it into a smooth oval shape. Arrange 2 quenelles per person on serving plates alongside a square of fresh, dripping honeycomb and a couple of almond biscotti. Stand a macchiato glass of dessert wine on each plate.

To eat, dip the biscotti into the wine and then into the cheese. Any leftover cheese can be moved around the plate to soak up the honey that has dripped from the honeycomb. The final indulgence is to cleanse your palate by sucking any remaining honey from the honeycomb. Follow this with an espresso, which will melt any wax on your teeth!

STEPHANIE'S HONEY AND LAVENDER ICE CREAM

Makes 2 litres

My first taste of a lavender and honey ice cream was when renowned teacher and writer Madeleine Kamman visited Australia, a trip arranged by Di Holuigue of The French Kitchen, the iconic Melbourne cooking school. Madeleine added thyme and orange to hers, to great effect. This recipe comes from my friend Stephanie Alexander and is a great favourite. I like to serve it with an almond tart.

1 litre milk

1 cup lightly packed unsprayed lavender flowers

8 free-range egg yolks

330 ml honey

600 ml cream (45 per cent fat; see Glossary)

Bring the milk to the boil in a small saucepan, then pour it over the lavender in a bowl. Leave the lavender to infuse until the milk is cold.

Beat the egg yolks well, then beat in the honey. Strain the cold lavender milk into the honey mixture and beat gently to combine. Stir in the cream, then churn the mixture in an ice cream machine according to the manufacturer's instructions, and freeze.

KID

ONE OF THE REALLY IMPORTANT FOODS ON MY SPRING MENU in the restaurant days was kid. As with all game, kid (baby goat) is very healthy – low in fat and cholesterol. It is simple to prepare and quite delicious, and it is certainly encouraging to know that a wild resource is being used – feral goats are a pest in the Australian bush. Kid is now fairly widely available from Italian butchers, who often call it *capretto*.

With the exception of the Greek and Italian communities, kid is avoided by most Australians, yet this meat can be sweeter than lamb, with its own distinctive flavour, and is considered a delicacy in most Mediterranean countries.

In the restaurant days I had a local supplier, Rosemary Langley of Elm Tree Farm at Springton and, as I liked the meat so much myself, I had no difficulty getting people to try it. The goat was hung for a week in cold storage before cutting. It was basically cut in the same way as lamb, and as the animals were young (between 3 and 4 months) the shoulder, when braised whole, was my favourite cut.

Once again, our Saturday Barossa market is now my source for many things, amongst them kid – though, unless I ask, they tend to sell the older animals (more like 8–12 months). These are cooked quite differently, and the shoulder is best boned out and cubed for casseroles or curries, or stuffed and pot-roasted. The loins can be rubbed with preserved lemon pulp and lots of rosemary and bay leaves, then roasted. The legs can be roasted in exactly the same way, or in cooler weather, slow-roasted and basted with a mixture of port, extra virgin olive oil and chopped rosemary; otherwise, the boned meat can also be cubed for casseroles and curries.

The legs of the younger animal are marvellous pot-roasted slowly on a bed of ripe tomatoes and eggplant with loads of fresh herbs, or smeared with a paste of finely chopped mint, diced preserved lemon, extra virgin olive oil, sea salt flakes and freshly ground black pepper and wrapped in *crépine* (or caul fat, see Glossary).

It was Rosemary Langley who suggested to me that baking in an oven bag is an effective way to handle a leg of kid or goat. Her way was to rub it with extra virgin olive oil and garlic beforehand. Alternatively you could roast the leg at low temperature, basting it with a mixture of extra virgin olive oil, red wine, redcurrant jelly and honey, adding a tiny amount of water in the bottom of the roasting pan if it looked like burning.

Although I definitely prefer young kid, if it has had a good life an animal between 8 and 12 months old certainly has lots of flavour – and if well fed, it will also have some fat, so is perfect for roasting on a spit. Rosemary's son-in-law, Bronte Mawson, would often spit-roast such an animal and says that with salads and accompaniments, it could feed forty to fifty people. He would hire a spit oven rather like a large kettle barbecue. The advantage is that it has a lid and so, once stuffed, the animal does not need basting. The oven needs pre-heating for 30 minutes and then its even, slow heat will cook the kid in 2 hours. My addition to this would be to brush the skin with a mixture of either quince paste melted with a little lemon juice, or something as simple as a good bitter marmalade with sea salt flakes.

A more romantic version has the spit rigged over an open fire. This is more difficult to control because one needs to dig a pit and have sufficient coals for a 4-hour cooking period, and the spit has to be turned and the meat basted during this time. Baste with a mixture of verjuice and extra virgin olive oil – I would also add some garlic and rosemary.

I can imagine a baked whole kid served with native currant jelly. The first time I tried native currants, found in the Williamstown area in South Australia and a few other secret places, I was delighted by their sharp yet sweet flavour. (If they are picked under-ripe the tannin will dominate, so they should be avoided.)

While in Provence with Patricia Wells many years ago we visited her local butcher, Monsieur Henny, who delighted in showing us the food he was preparing for an evening party for friends. He took us upstairs via a steep spiral staircase to where there were cool-rooms and a kitchen with a huge oven that could accommodate an animal in one piece. That afternoon M. Henny had a baby kid cut into legs, shoulder and rack, which he marinated in a stainless steel roasting pan with olive oil, lemon rind, fine slices of lemon, finely chopped garlic and parsley; the head was also cut in half with the brain left in. M. Henny intended to roast the kid, let it rest in the roasting pan and then serve it with just the juices that accumulated around it.

I have braised all cuts of young kid, browned first with rosemary and then tossed into a saucepan with tomatoes (frozen from the summer crop at the peak of their flavour) and lots of onions and heads of garlic, turning frequently to ensure the juices don't burn. This takes 2–3 hours, even for such a young animal, because I cook it very slowly, using two simmer pads under the pot, sitting on the lowest possible flame. In the last 10 minutes of cooking, I throw in some black olives.

Another restaurant favourite was to pot-roast a cut of kid with a little vinegar, white wine, lemon, fresh bay leaves and oregano. During the slow-cooking the meat creates its own syrupy glaze – the trick is to have no more than 1 cm of liquid in the pan at any one time. Globe artichokes and eggplant are natural accompaniments.

Rub a leg of kid with coriander seeds (heat the seeds first in a dry frying pan and then pound them using a mortar and pestle to release their flavour) or chopped rosemary, extra virgin olive oil, salt and pepper. Brown the leg in a heavy-based roasting pan in a little more olive oil and then deglaze the pan with dry sherry. Chop up a base of onions, carrots and celery and place in the roasting pan; put the meat on top with some heads of garlic and a can of peeled tomatoes. Cook slowly in the oven at 160°C for 1½–2½ hours, until the meat is soft to the touch, and add more tomatoes if the liquid has evaporated. For the sauce, roast 4 heads of garlic in the oven and then squeeze out the garlic (the garlic will be wonderfully nutty and buttery, without the pungent taste of raw garlic). Pound a 45 g tin of anchovies, drained of oil, using a pestle and mortar, then add them to the garlic. Pour any pan juices from the kid into this mixture, stirring as if it were a mayonnaise.

Over the years, I have often either bought a single joint or a whole animal to cook on the spit or in our wood-fired oven. While not everyone is set up to cook a whole animal, it is not difficult to improvise a spit to cook a joint. A barbecue with a hood is another option, as is a kettle barbecue. If cooking a leg (although the preparation is much the same for a whole animal) in a kettle barbecue, first smother it with olive oil and your preferred herbs and flavourings – try oregano, freshly ground black pepper and slivers of garlic; fresh thyme and fennel seeds or rosemary and garlic; or lemon rind, slivers of garlic, fresh bay leaves and lots of chopped flat-leaf parsley. Cook the leg on a rack over a bed of chopped onion and ripe tomatoes at a lower temperature than you would, say, a leg of lamb, and only cook it for half as long. It's hard to give a precise cooking time, as so many variables apply, so cook until tender to the touch. The lower temperature is important no matter how small the animal is – goat dries out if exposed to high heat. As it is cooking, baste the kid with verjuice and red- or white-wine vinegar, with a little olive oil added if the leg seems to be drying out. Leave the meat to rest, covered, and away from the heat for a good 30 minutes after cooking, before carving.

If you don't have a kettle barbecue, a camp oven or cast-iron casserole with a tight-fitting lid placed on a simmer pad on the stovetop will do the trick beautifully. Cooked this way, the dish produces its own syrupy glaze – just make sure the tomato and onion are well moistened with olive oil.

Slow-cooking is perfect for late-night suppers or lazy lunches, especially when the days start to get a bit shorter and the air a bit nippier. So do give kid a try next time you pass an Italian butcher – you will be in for a treat.

ROAST SUCKLING KID

Serves 8–10

This recipe is an old favourite inspired by Theodora Fitzgibbon's 1963 book, *Game Cooking*.

juice and finely grated rind of 1 lemon	1 tablespoon ground ginger
1 suckling kid (about 5 kg)	sea salt flakes and freshly ground
500 g Granny Smith apples (about 3–4)	black pepper
3–4 rashers streaky bacon, rind removed	60 g butter
3 sprigs rosemary	extra virgin olive oil, for roasting
3 cloves garlic, peeled and sliced	285 ml cider

Preheat the oven to 180°C. Squeeze the lemon juice inside the kid and insert the lemon rind as well. Peel and core the apples and slice them thickly. Cut the bacon into 2.5 cm squares, render it in a dry pan, and then sauté the apple slices in the bacon fat with the rosemary. Make cuts in between the muscles of the leg and insert some of the apple slices, stuffing the rest into the cavity, using skewers where necessary to keep the slices in place.

Insert the garlic slices into the legs, mix together the ginger, salt, pepper and extra virgin olive oil, then rub this over the entire animal. Put into a roasting pan with the butter and some olive oil and roast for 20–30 minutes per kg (until tender to the touch), basting frequently. When it is cooked, remove the kid to a warm dish to rest for at least 30 minutes, pour off the surplus fat and add the cider to the pan juices. Boil rapidly over high heat on top of the stove until reduced by half, then pour over the kid before serving.

ELM TREE FARM'S STUFFING FOR SPIT-ROASTED KID

Makes enough stuffing for one 8–12-month-old kid

breadcrumbs made from 2 loaves stale
    wood-fired bread

1 large onion, chopped

2 rashers bacon, chopped

2–3 cans pitted Morello cherries,
    drained and used whole

250 g pine nuts

250 g slivered almonds

150 ml white wine

150 ml homemade Plum Sauce
    (see page 116)

2 handfuls fresh flat-leaf parsley and
    marjoram, chopped

1 tablespoon coarsely ground black pepper

Mix together all the ingredients. The stuffing must be moist but not sloppy. Use to stuff a kid prepared for spit-roasting – it may be helpful to use an apple to hold the stuffing in place and stop it escaping during cooking.

CAFÉ C GOAT CURRY

Serves 12

For several years Mardie Palmer owned a tiny restaurant in Springton in the Valley called Café C. The food was simple and the place full of style; many Barossa stalwarts were regulars, and they loved this goat curry.

peanut oil, for cooking

4 onions, sliced

8 small red chillies, chopped (optional)

60 g fresh ginger, grated

4 cloves garlic, chopped

⅔ cup (200 g) red curry paste

2 kg diced goat

4 × 400 ml tins coconut milk

1.2 litres rainwater *or* spring water

20 kaffir lime leaves

juice of 4 limes

⅔ cup desiccated coconut, toasted

light soy sauce, to taste

Heat a little peanut oil in a large heavy-based saucepan over medium heat, then sauté the onions, chillies, ginger and garlic until onion is transparent – do not brown. Add the curry paste and fry gently for 3 minutes. Add the diced goat and stir until coated by the paste mixture. Increase the heat to high, then add the coconut milk, water, kaffir lime leaves and lime juice. Reduce the heat to low and simmer until tender. Stir in the toasted coconut and cook for another 5 minutes. Adjust seasonings to taste before serving.

LOQUATS

LOQUATS CAN, IN THE RIGHT CIRCUMSTANCES, BE A VERY welcome fruit. They are not much known or revered but it is their timing that, to me, makes them special. Often arriving in November, which is an in-between time for fruit, they are, along with strawberries, the first hint that summer is to come. Oranges are past their peak, apples and pears are only from the cold store, so apart from the imported exotics, the loquat it is, at least until the first flush of raspberries starts to appear. The fruit has a distinctive flavour and is beautifully juicy.

The loquat is actually native to China and possibly the south of Japan, and I think it has a 'Japanese' look to it. The fruit is orange, oval, shiny and firm. There has not been much done to improve the genes of loquats in Australia and as far as I know they are only grown commercially in Japan and the Mediterranean, where they can easily grow to 5 cm long by 4 cm across. The Japanese have worked at improving the size, as the seeds of the loquat take up a large part of the fruit, and this seems to have been achieved without loss of flavour. I must confess I love the shiny, slippery feel of the seeds in my hand.

The South Australian climate certainly allows loquats to flourish, and many old-fashioned gardens contain huge specimens. The fruit marks easily yet the tree will respond to good care. What a delight it is to come across this evergreen tree with its wonderful large leaves, and boughs laden with fruit. My grandfather's garden in Sydney had a huge tree and as children we loved lying in its shade and eating the ripe fruit that had fallen to the ground, spitting out the shiny seeds as we ate.

Only two of the three loquat trees I planted survived, which is a real surprise, considering how hardy they are. The survivors are large lush trees and, together with a dozen macadamia trees, provide year-round green screening from the road on our home property. The trick with loquats is to allow them to ripen enough to enjoy their juicy sweet flavour and that feeling of those shiny seeds rolling around your mouth. The birds love them too and as they don't ripen off the tree, it is a race to see who gets to enjoy the loquats first.

My dream of enclosing the loquat trees within a walled garden with 'weeder' geese to control the weeds just did not work, as the trees were on the wrong side of the house, and plans change as you spend time on a property. I simply transferred the idea of the geese to the quince orchard at the farm, although the fox problem there is still ever-present and I do not know what the long-term success of this will be.

With large loquats, it is worthwhile going to the trouble of quartering them, removing the seeds and poaching the fruit. (I only bother to peel them if the skins are marked, and then only once the fruit has been cooked.) Sprinkle the quartered fruit with sugar and then stand the saucepan over a gentle heat so the sugar starts to dissolve. Add enough sparkling wine to stop the fruit sticking and cook until the fruit has softened. Let the loquats cool, then serve with a dollop of cream, crème fraîche or mascarpone (depending on whether you delight in the slightly sour, as I do, or prefer something rich and sweet). Cooked in light sugar syrup with the addition of lemon to highlight their flavour, loquats make a lovely poached fruit to serve cold with fresh cream. They have a distinctive bitter-almond or marzipan flavour when poached.

APRICOT TART WITH CRÈME PÂTISSIÈRE
AND LOQUAT JELLY
Serves 8

Most apricot tart recipes will call for apricot jam for this, but I find the loquat jelly more subtle. Bake this tart in your favourite tart tin.

1 × quantity Sour-cream Pastry
(see page 424)
2 tablespoons Loquat Jelly
(see following page)

POACHED APRICOTS
1 cup (220 g) castor sugar
1 cup (250 ml) water
1 cup (250 ml) verjuice
20 apricots, halved and stoned

CRÈME PÂTISSIÈRE
2 cups (500 ml) milk
1 vanilla bean, halved lengthways
6 free-range egg yolks
70 g castor sugar
30 g flour
butter (optional), for cooking

Make and chill the pastry as instructed, then line a 20 cm tart tin with it. Chill the pastry case for 20 minutes. Preheat the oven to 200°C. Line the pastry case with foil, then cover with pastry weights and blind bake for 15 minutes. Remove the foil and weights and return the pastry case to the oven for a further 5 minutes or until golden brown.

To make the poached apricots, first make a syrup of the sugar, water and verjuice by heating them together until the sugar has dissolved (about 10 minutes). Gently poach the apricots in two batches in this syrup for 5–10 minutes, depending on their ripeness. Remove apricots from the syrup, and, when cool enough to handle, slip off their skins. »

To make the crème pâtissière, bring the milk to the boil in a saucepan, add the vanilla bean, then remove from the heat and allow it to infuse for 10 minutes. Whisk the egg yolks with the sugar until pale and the mixture forms a light ribbon. Sift in the flour and whisk again, then pour into a heavy-based saucepan. Strain the milk into the egg mixture, stirring constantly so no lumps form. Cook over a low yet direct heat, whisking constantly. Allow the mixture to come to the boil and simmer for a good 2 minutes to cook the flour. Add a tiny bit of butter at the last minute if you wish. Transfer the custard to a bowl to cool and place a piece of plastic film on the surface of the custard to prevent a skin forming.

Heat the loquat jelly in a small saucepan with a little water to thin it.

To assemble the dessert, fill the cooked pastry case with the crème pâtissière, then cover generously with the poached apricot halves, placed cut-side down. Brush the hot glaze over the apricots.

CARAMELISED LOQUATS
Serves 10–12 as a dessert accompaniment

The colour of this syrup is important: cook it until it is almost burnt or it will be too sweet. If you're worried about burning it, have a little cold water ready to add at the desired stage of caramelisation – but be warned, the mixture will splutter violently.

We would serve this at the restaurant, together with the Olive Oil and Sauternes Cake from Alice Waters' first book, *Chez Panisse Café Cookbook*. It is a cake I keep on using as a dessert in one guise or another; it is so moist it is almost a pudding, and it has a lovely lemony flavour.

1 kg large loquats, quartered and seeded
750 g castor sugar

rind of 1 lemon, removed in one piece,
if possible

Dry the loquats well with kitchen paper. Heat the sugar and 750 ml water in a shallow heavy-based saucepan (I use one with sides 12 cm high) over medium heat until the sugar dissolves and the syrup begins to change colour.

Gently slide the loquats and lemon rind into the pan and cook for a few minutes or until the loquats are soft but not pulpy. Transfer the fruit to a bowl with a slotted spoon, then continue cooking the syrup over medium heat until it becomes a deep-caramel colour. Let the syrup cool, remove the lemon rind and pour the caramel over the fruit (peeled, if you like).

LOQUAT JELLY

Loquats make a superior jelly for using as a glaze on fruit flans or tarts in the summer. The flavour of the loquat blends beautifully with the fruit rather than overpowering it. Crushing the cooked loquats to extract the juice gives off the most wonderful aroma, just like that of bitter almonds.

This recipe is adapted from one I found in Stephanie Alexander's book *Stephanie's Menus for Food Lovers* – I use a little less sugar and add lemon juice.

ripe loquats, roughly cut in half   **lemon juice, to taste**
sugar

Place the loquats in a heavy-based saucepan and add enough water to just cover the fruit. Bring to the boil and cook until the fruit is soft, approximately 15–20 minutes. Strain through a fine strainer, squeezing down on the fruit pulp to extract the juice, and discard the solids.

Measure out ¾ cup sugar for each cup juice and combine in a preserving pan. Taste the mixture, and add lemon juice if you find it too sweet. Bring to the boil and simmer until the jelly reaches setting point, skimming any scum off the surface as you go. To test, put a spoonful of jelly onto a saucer and cool in the refrigerator for a few minutes. If it wrinkles when you push it with your finger, the jelly is ready.

PEAS

THE BEST POSSIBLE PEA COMES DIRECT FROM THE GARDEN in the warmth of the afternoon. The sugar content of the pea picked this way is enough to satisfy the sweetest tooth. I'm sure any mother could persuade a recalcitrant child to eat greens like this. Who needs to cook greens anyway? Raw green peas – pods and all, if they are young enough – are a delight when eaten straight from the garden.

As peas grow older and larger, their sugar is converted into starch and they are not nearly as tasty. Few people bother shelling young peas. If you cannot buy young, freshly harvested peas then I'll go so far as to say that, in most cases, the ubiquitous frozen pea might even taste better. The sweetness of the pea is retained on freezing, but it is still a long way from the just-picked experience. Many of us have left behind the meat-and-three-veg principle (those old enough to have been brought up with it, I hasten to add), but I guess most people still rely on the convenience of frozen peas from time to time. For a quick fix, a green pea purée made from frozen peas can be a great accompaniment to a lamb chop, grilled fish, sweetbreads or lamb's fry.

Shelling peas is definitely a job to be shared around the kitchen table. As a child, I remember putting more in my mouth than in the pot. This never seemed to worry my mother – I'm sure she was a lot smarter about these things than me.

I wasn't aware until recently of how many varieties of pea there are. A close friend talked of eating telephone peas from her sister's garden in Tasmania – she called it one of life's sensuous pleasures. We have all become familiar with the snow pea or mangetout, which is picked for eating pod and all, with the peas inside hardly formed. This is lovely and crisp to eat raw or throw in salads, or to blanch for just a second and serve as a vegetable. The snow pea, along with the sugar snap pea (whose name says it all), has transformed the market for fresh peas. While more expensive than traditional peas, they keep their sweetness so much more than the normal pea. I can count on the fingers of one hand the

times that peas from my own garden have ended up in the pot – they're almost always eaten as they're picked. The same thing happens to a little delight called the asparagus pea, which looks like a delicate baby okra with frilled edges. For eating raw they should be picked when no more than 2 cm long. Not a vegetable you're likely to see flooding the market, but a nice one to grow for yourself. It really does have the characteristics of asparagus, with the sweetness of the pea, and is great as a crudité: you could serve it with a dish

of extra virgin olive oil, sea salt and freshly ground black pepper, or a rich garlic mayonnaise.

I have come to the conclusion that unless you grow peas yourself or buy them direct from growers' markets, they aren't worth the considerable trouble of shelling. The time between picking and buying them from a normal greengrocer is usually such that the sugars in the pea have all but vanished.

I once had a chef in my kitchen from the north of England and to him peas were mushy and accompanied fish and chips – all homemade, of course. He used dried peas which were soaked in a solution of bicarbonate of soda for four days. The peas were then washed and simmered in fresh water for 6–8 hours. When the peas were cooked to a mush, he added freshly ground black pepper, lots of butter and nutmeg.

Convenience foods are not necessarily bad, but nothing can compare with fresh produce in perfect condition, and this depends on seasonality and the distances involved in transporting produce to market. Years ago, I would cook fresh peas in just enough chicken stock to cover them, in a very small saucepan with a tight-fitting lid, adding a touch of sugar to compensate for the peas not coming fresh from the garden. Little cubes of butter and fresh mint were added at the last moment. I remember feeling very daring. Now my favourite way of serving fresh peas (those that make it to the saucepan) is to simmer them in a good stock until half done, then to finish cooking them in a little butter, salt and freshly ground black pepper. Throw in some prosciutto – the fatty parts particularly – just before finishing.

Should you be looking for reasons to shell and cook your own fresh peas (and I'd encourage you to do so, just to taste the difference), you don't need to look much further than Italian traditions. Angel hair pasta with fresh peas is one classic that's worth a look: poach peas and chopped leek in butter or extra virgin olive oil, then add fresh chervil and toss this through the just-cooked pasta. Or sauté the peas with chopped golden shallots over low heat and, when cooked, add strips of prosciutto or grilled pancetta and toss through the pasta.

So, what other dishes make peas worth the effort to shell? Pea mash, where fresh peas are simmered with golden shallots and butter until all the juice evaporates and the flesh mashes together, makes a lovely bed for a piece of grilled fish or great sausages. Then there is pea risotto, a dish I confess to making with dried Surprise peas out of season, on the advice of a good Italian cook, as they have a more intense flavour and are less likely to break up than frozen peas. Cook the base for the risotto in the same way as you would the pea mash and use a very delicate chicken stock to finish off the dish.

A soup worth the effort if you have just-picked peas to hand is chilled pea soup with buttermilk and chervil. First make a stock using the empty pea pods (but only if they are very fresh). Put half a chopped lettuce (iceberg will do fine), spring onions, celery, watercress (if you have it to hand) and chervil into the saucepan and just cover with water. Cook for about 30 minutes, then purée the mixture and press it through a colander to get rid of any fibrous matter. Sauté the shelled peas with some chopped leek over low heat for 10–15 minutes or until softened. Add the cooked peas and leek to the stock and purée with some buttermilk and fresh chervil to taste. This delicate and sweet soup is especially good chilled (as spring days can bring unexpected heat, cold soups can be very inviting). If you want to serve it hot, try adding a little cream instead of the buttermilk before heating gently.

The posthumous publication *The Enjoyment of Food: The Best of Jane Grigson* has a great recipe for a chilled soufflé of snow peas which I could imagine serving with some prosciutto, crusty bread and a glass of white wine for lunch.

PEAS WITH GOLDEN SHALLOTS
Serves 4 as an accompaniment

When I first married I was given a book with a recipe for peas cooked 'the French way'. I used to think myself so clever when I had friends for dinner; the 1970s was definitely the dinner-party era when we all thought we had to show off. I remember how such a simple dish, given beautiful peas to start with, used to create such a stir, and I still love them today. This dish is based on that old recipe, with a couple of modern additions we would never have been able to get in the 1970s: golden shallots and sea salt flakes.

2 golden shallots, finely chopped	pinch sugar
3 tablespoons butter	pinch sea salt flakes
250 g fresh peas, shelled	¼ cup Golden Chicken Stock (see page 57)

In a heavy-based saucepan, sweat the golden shallots in the butter over gentle heat, then add the shelled peas and toss together. Season with the sugar and salt, and add enough stock to almost cover the mixture. Heat without bringing to the boil, then simmer, covered with a tight-fitting lid, over medium heat until the juices in the pan are all absorbed and the peas are cooked (this should take about 10 minutes for young peas, longer if they are older). This dish is a great accompaniment to lamb, chicken or fish.

FRESH PEA AND BUTTERMILK SOUP   *Serves 8*

The sweetness of the fresh peas contrasts beautifully with the sourness of the buttermilk in this dish.

2 onions, chopped	sea salt flakes
¼ cup extra virgin olive oil	1 litre vegetable stock
600 g fresh peas, shelled	1 cup buttermilk
½ bunch fresh chervil	white pepper, to taste

Soften the onion in the extra virgin olive oil until translucent. Add the peas and chervil, season with salt and pour in the vegetable stock. Bring to the boil over high heat, then turn heat down to medium and simmer, uncovered, for 8–10 minutes, until the peas are tender. Add buttermilk and bring back to a simmer. Transfer to a food processor, being careful not to overfill it or the heat will push the lid off, and purée until smooth. Season with white pepper, and serve warm with sprigs of fresh chervil.

SWEETBREADS WITH GREEN PEA PURÉE
AND GOLDEN SHALLOTS   *Serves 4*

1 kg oval-shaped sweetbreads	10 golden shallots, 4 thinly sliced
(thymus gland if possible)	and 6 peeled but left whole
juice of 2 lemons	butter, for cooking
1 fresh bay leaf	extra virgin olive oil, for cooking
1 kg fresh peas in pods	freshly ground black pepper
sugar, to taste	100 g prosciutto, cut into 4 cm × 2 cm pieces
sea salt flakes	

Soak the sweetbreads, replacing the water several times until no signs of blood remain. Place the sweetbreads in a saucepan with cold water, half the lemon juice and the bay leaf. Bring very slowly to a simmer, and remove the sweetbreads as they become opaque (about 3 minutes). Drain well and place on a flat dish with a similar-sized dish on top, then weight down with cans, or other weights, and leave in the fridge for 4 hours. Peel the sweetbreads of skin and gristle, keeping their shape intact.

Meanwhile, shell the peas, and blanch them twice in a saucepan of boiling water with a little sugar and salt added. (If you want the final purée to be very smooth, you may wish to blanch the peas for a third time.) In a saucepan over medium heat, sweat the chopped shallots in butter. Beginning with cold extra virgin olive oil in a cold frying pan (so they don't burn), caramelise the whole shallots over low heat until they are a gentle, golden brown and cooked all the way through. Purée the sliced shallots and peas while still warm, adding a little of the pea water, and season.

Slice the sweetbreads to desired size. Pan-fry them in nut-brown butter, with a dash of olive oil to prevent burning, until golden brown. Deglaze the pan with the remaining lemon juice, then toss in the prosciutto and add the caramelised shallots. Serve on a base of the green pea purée.

PASTA RAGS WITH SMALL GULF OR HARBOUR PRAWNS, FRESH PEAS AND CHERVIL
Serves 4

I often buy small prawns from my local market, where every second week a fisherman from the Spencer Gulf sells his catch. These prawns remind me of my childhood, when I would fish for prawns by lantern light in the shallows of Sydney Harbour at dusk. They are incredibly sweet and light years away from the larger prawn, often prized for its size rather than its flavour. What surprises me is that the quality of these prawns, as with those sold by Ferguson Fisheries in Adelaide, are such that even though they have already been cooked, I'm happy to peel them and toss them through the pasta right at the end, so the sweetness of the prawn and the pea are drawn together.

Pasta rags are square-shaped, and as such allow the sauce to adhere more readily.

1 × quantity Fresh Pasta (see page 419)	1 sprig chervil
2 tablespoons butter	¼ cup extra virgin olive oil
sea salt flakes	1 kg small gulf *or* harbour prawns
pinch sugar	fronds from 1 fennel bulb
125 g fresh peas, shelled	freshly ground black pepper

Make, chill, and roll the pasta as instructed, then cut it into rags (I tend to cut mine on the slant into 5 cm squares) and spread out on clean tea towels until required. This prevents the pasta rags from sticking together or drying out too fast. If it will be a while before you start cooking, dampen the tea towels (don't leave it longer than about an hour, though – the pasta is best cooked soon after making).

In a small saucepan, add around ½ cup water (or enough to cover the base to just over 1 cm), and add 1 tablespoon of the butter, a pinch of sea salt and a pinch of sugar. Bring to a simmer, then add the peas and a sprig of chervil and cover the pan with a tight-fitting lid. Cook for 10 minutes, or until the peas are tender. Strain off the juices, then add the other tablespoon of butter and stir through.

Cook the pasta rags in boiling salted water. This should take 2–4 minutes after the water has come to the boil, depending on how fine the pasta has been rolled.

Drain the pasta, reserving a tablespoon or two of cooking liquid in case you want to moisten the completed dish. Add the extra virgin olive oil, prawns and peas to the pasta and toss together to heat the prawns through. Check for seasoning and serve with fennel fronds scattered over.

POTATOES

I RESISTED SERVING POTATOES IN THE WHOLE LIFE OF THE Pheasant Farm Restaurant (with the exception of the times when one of my regulars, Bob McLean, an ardent potato fan, was dining), simply because my childhood had a surfeit of them and, I have to admit, they just didn't excite me. That is, until the arrival of the waxy potato – what a change that made to my cooking. When made with waxy potatoes, I finally grew to love the mashed potato that my husband Colin likes to cook (one in his small repertoire of dishes). Most feel that waxy potatoes are ideal for boiling but not mashing, however I love waxies mashed (or 'smashed') with lots of unsalted butter or extra virgin olive oil. I now only make my gnocchi with waxy potatoes – any variety, from desiree to pink-eyes – and have found they add a whole new dimension. At times I just boil waxy potatoes, let them cool a little, then cut them in half and toss them in extra virgin olive oil with some rinsed salted capers and lots of flat-leaf parsley. Potatoes are one ingredient that I have changed my mind about completely, and now I love to use the waxy varieties in many different ways.

I had been spoilt: in my early twenties I lived on the Isle of Skye in Scotland and experienced the joys of potatoes grown in the paddock between the house and the sea. Seaweed was pulled up over the patch as mulch, and we'd dig up the potatoes as we needed them. No potato available to me here has ever reached the heights of these Scottish 'tatties'. It was not unusual to have a meal just of potatoes boiled and literally smothered in locally made butter. I can still taste them as I write, so similar to the iron-like tang of a fresh oyster, and it reminds me what a simple life it was.

Whilst in Scotland, I even learnt to cut peat for the fire and to make haggis in the kitchen sink. On reflection, it was here that my interest in game began (to tell the truth, I suspect our game was come by more from poaching than via any toffs' estate shooting party). I quickly learnt of the abundance of wild produce: cockles collected from the shore; the salmon offered by a neighbour. Once, while fishing in a tiny row boat (only metres from the front paddock where we had spent the day stooking hay), my companion spent his whole time extracting the fish from my hooks and baiting them again. (I also have memories of rowing the boat to another island under a full moon in search of something that I can no longer recall – through lack of skill, our expeditions were often more fanciful than fruitful.) And when we were too tired to cook, it was back to potatoes again. It was

an idyllic life, and one I was almost tempted to make my own for a time.

The waxy potatoes now available are, I feel, as close as I'll ever come to the perfection I enjoyed on Skye. They have a dense texture and a pronounced flavour, even without butter or olive oil. There has been a veritable deluge of new varieties, and a significant amount of research on these has been undertaken within Australia in recent years. The revolution has begun!

My favourite waxy variety of all is the Tasmanian pink-eye from the shaly soil south of Hobart. Pink-eyes (often marketed as Southern Gold potatoes on the mainland) are first ready for market near Christmas time, when you can eat them just picked, so young that the skins rub off in your fingers before cooking; I love them with loads of unsalted butter, and a meal of these alone is a feast. Now while I admit that this waxy variety is considered too dry to mash by most, I love the flavour so much that I do it anyway (I just add lots of butter or good extra virgin olive oil to ensure a moist result, leaving out the cream), and the result is delicious.

After these, I probably prefer kipfler (best boiled or steamed, although they are also good slow-baked whole in casseroles) and pink fir apple potatoes. Next in line would be the Dutch varieties such as bintje, nicola and patrone, which are excellent boiled for use in salads. The first and most readily available waxy potato was the desiree, a Dutch potato with a dark-pink skin and yellow flesh; I love it both boiled and mashed. When small, desirees are good for potato salads or roasting. Spunta, another Dutch variety, has a creamy-white skin and yellow flesh and is great for chipping. I never make gnocchi without the best waxies I can find, nor do I make a potato salad, warm or chilled, with anything else. It's waxies for me every time.

The irony is that the really delicious pink-eye has been grown in small pockets across Tasmania since about the late 1800s, when it is thought to have been introduced from the Canary Islands. At first it was grown quite specifically in black sandy dunes laden with shell grit at Seacroft in the south, land that would seem inhospitable to anything else. Perhaps there is something in the flavour of these potatoes grown so close to the sea that brings back memories of those I enjoyed on Skye.

I have also heard wonderful stories about an enterprising potato farmer who took the pink-eye to the heavier soils in Tasmania's north-west, the traditional potato belt. Apparently he made a killing on the Melbourne market during the 1956 Olympics, as chefs paid him a king's ransom for what were possibly the first waxy potatoes ever eaten on the mainland.

Traditionalists feel that black sandy soils give the best flavour of all, but opinion is divided. To me, the point here is that true regional differences should be celebrated. Whatever these are, in both the north and south of Tasmania, the best of the pink-eyes are planted so as to be ready for Christmas Day, when the flesh is at its yellowest and waxiest. And the most delicious of these new season's pink-eyes are the chats, left behind by traditional farmers – tiny round potatoes little more than a couple of centimetres across, and sweeter than you can imagine.

Fresh pink-eyes react badly to the fluorescent lights used in supermarkets, so need to be sealed in very thick brown paper bags and sold quickly. Grown for generations at his family's property 'Seacroft' in South Arm, in the traditionally favoured black sandy soil, John Calvert's pink-eyes are sold this way by renowned providore Wursthaus in Hobart, with the history of the farm written on the bag.

With the right potatoes, a dish can go from average to exceptional. Sitting in glorious late-winter sunshine at Bistro Moncur in Sydney, where my friend Damien Pignolet – a great chef and teacher and an absolute perfectionist – continually inspires me, I ate a warm salad of waxy potatoes with sorrel, soft-boiled egg and oil (was it olive or walnut?). The combination of first-class ingredients and the skill of the kitchen made the dish quite perfect, yet it wouldn't have reached the same heights if the potatoes used hadn't been waxy. With some good crusty bread and a glass of bubbles, it was all I could want, and the perfect antidote to exhaustion.

If you don't have easy access to a good range of waxy potatoes, simply search out the variety you want, let them go to seed, then plant them. I arrange them in neat rows because it is only when the plant dies back that the potatoes are ready to 'bandicoot' for, and I need good markers so I don't rip up the whole garden in my frenzy to find the buried treasure.

Now that waxy potatoes are so available I seldom use anything else, but the most readily available non-waxy potatoes are the coliban, sebago, pontiac and kennebec. The round, red-skinned pontiac is an all-purpose potato that is good boiled, mashed or roasted. I used to prefer small pontiacs and almost never peeled them for roasting or boiling. The coliban, a purple-blushed white potato, is round with white flesh. It breaks up when boiled but is not bad for roasting and is quite good for chips. While deemed an all-rounder, the oval, white sebago, which has white flesh, is best mashed. Another all-rounder, the large, white-skinned, white-fleshed kennebec is excellent for chips. The best variety of all for chips is the russet burbank, but this is rarely available commercially, since McDonald's buy it almost exclusively.

As staple a vegetable as the potato is, you would think that we would have learnt how to store it properly. But the increased use of plastic bags and fluorescent lights has meant we're further away from getting it right than ever: plastic makes potatoes sweat and causes them to deteriorate quickly, while exposure to light makes them develop bitter green patches that, at worst, can cause illness when eaten. Your best bet is to buy loose, unwashed potatoes in a brown paper bag. Avoid those with green patches (although the green can be cut away), cuts, cracks, bruises, wet patches or a musty smell.

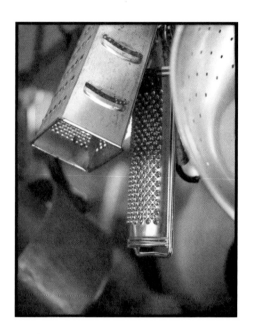

If you have succumbed to convenience and bought potatoes in a plastic bag, remove them from the bag as soon as you arrive home. Store the potatoes in a cool, dark place with good ventilation – do not refrigerate them. Do not scrub unwashed potatoes until ready to use them, as this will hasten deterioration (it is worth noting here that unwashed potatoes last longer than washed potatoes). I delight in finding potatoes just going to seed at the back of my cupboard: the starch of these old spuds has broken down and they are wonderfully sweet. I only throw them away if they're green. If you've found similar potatoes but think they're sprouting too much to eat, plant them so that you will have your own potatoes to dig on demand.

You need do very little to good-quality, flavoursome potatoes – but that doesn't mean they don't go well with exotic ingredients. Try something as indulgent as potatoes with caviar. Boil 500 g unpeeled waxy potatoes in salted water for 15–20 minutes or until cooked through (different varieties need different cooking times). While the potatoes are still hot, scoop out about half the flesh and either mash it or put it through a food mill or potato ricer. Allow a couple of knobs of butter to melt into the hot mashed potato, then stir in 150 ml crème fraîche and season with salt and freshly ground black pepper. Pile the mixture back into the potatoes and add a generous tablespoon of salmon roe or caviar to each. A small potato cake made from butter-fried mashed potato and topped with crème fraîche, fresh oysters and caviar is another way of combining these flavours. For me, it's important to bite into the oyster rather than just swallow it – it gives me that iron-like flavour I crave in the potato.

Another extravagant combination is to shave a fresh truffle over a salad of warm baby waxy potatoes drizzled with extra virgin olive oil and seasoned with sea salt flakes and freshly ground black pepper. This is all pretty powerful stuff, but the potato has the strength not to be drowned out.

Roast potato takes on a new meaning when you toss thickly sliced unpeeled potato with olive oil and intersperse it in a baking dish with thick slices of meyer lemon and sprigs of thyme. Drizzle over some extra virgin olive oil and season with salt and freshly ground black pepper, then bake at 200°C for about 45 minutes until the potato is soft, the lemon caramelised and the edges a little charred.

Potatoes are wonderful cooked in goose or duck fat left over from making confit. Cut 500 g potatoes into 5 mm-thick slices, then seal the slices on both sides in 125 ml fat in a 200°C oven. Turn the heat down to 180°C and allow the potato to cook through. A sprig of fresh rosemary or thyme is great added to the pan when sealing the potato slices.

Cook potato this way if you have freshly gathered young pine mushrooms, but use nut-brown butter with a dash of extra virgin olive oil rather than goose or duck fat. Seal the mushrooms the same way as you do the potato, but use a separate frying pan and only cook them for 3–5 minutes. I would use basil or thyme with the mushrooms, and might even add finely diced golden shallots. The mushrooms will give off lovely juices as they rest. As soon as the potato is done, toss it with the mushrooms, then season the dish and serve it as a meal on its own, or as a side dish to pan-fried veal chops; deglaze the veal pan with a little lemon juice to make a sauce.

Colin claims to make the best mashed spuds in the world, and I wouldn't dream of interfering, as I'm happy whenever he wants to cook anything for me. He almost always uses lashings of butter and cream (but not too much so it goes runny), and sometimes he uses the best extra virgin olive oil, lots of sea salt flakes and freshly ground black pepper. The ingredient that is always constant, though, is finely chopped onion – and he always uses only part of an onion, then wraps the rest and puts it carefully in the fridge, only to find the next time he looks that I have thrown it out, as I can't bear the odour of onion permeating the rest of the food in the fridge. Old habits die hard!

Both Saskia and Elli grew up in a household almost devoid of potatoes, due to my early prejudice against them, and unless their dad was showing off his mashed spuds, we almost never ate them. (Should I confess now that I hardly ever gave them a baked dinner either? They'd tell me they were deprived!) But times have changed. I have been known to get more excited about presenting a dish of freshly dug pink fir apple potatoes, some of them full-sized and some like tiny little nuggets, or at Christmastime a dish of pink-eyes from the markets, than a three- or four-course feast. Simply boiled and drained, then served with some very green extra virgin olive oil (although you could well use lots of butter instead), a good sprinkling of sea salt flakes and freshly ground black pepper, we devour them with gusto. When the mood is right, nothing else is needed for dinner.

BEST ROAST POTATOES WITH PRESERVED LEMON AND ROSEMARY
Serves 4–6

For this recipe I'd choose desirees or pontiacs if waxy potatoes are not available, as they are great when roasted.

2 kg best in-season potatoes
1 cup (250 ml) extra virgin olive oil
2 quarters preserved lemon, flesh removed, rind rinsed and cut into strips

sea salt flakes and freshly ground black pepper
2 sprigs rosemary

Preheat the oven to 180°C. Peel the potatoes or wash the skins, then cut into quarters. Place in a roasting pan and coat with the olive oil, lemon strips, salt and pepper. Roast the potatoes for 45 minutes, stirring occasionally to make sure they do not stick to the pan. Sprinkle on the rosemary and cook for another 10 minutes or until potatoes are crisp and cooked through, then serve immediately.

ROAST WAXY POTATOES WITH PANCETTA, CAPERS AND PRESERVED LEMON

Serves 4

250 g kipflers *or* other waxy potatoes, washed, dried and halved lengthways

½ preserved lemon, flesh removed, rind rinsed and thinly sliced

4 thin slices flat pancetta

50 ml extra virgin olive oil

freshly ground black pepper

2 teaspoons capers

1 tablespoon chopped flat-leaf parsley

sea salt flakes

Preheat the oven to 220°C. Toss the potatoes with the preserved lemon, pancetta, olive oil and some pepper in a large, shallow, heavy-based roasting pan. If the pan is too crowded, it is better to divide the ingredients between two pans so that the potatoes caramelise and the pancetta crisps, as they will stew rather than bake in a crowded pan.

Bake for 20–35 minutes or until golden; the exact time will depend on the variety of potato and oven used. Shake the pan to loosen the contents, then add capers and flat-leaf parsley, season to taste and serve immediately.

WARM SALAD OF WAXY POTATOES AND BEANS

Serves 6–8

2 cups (200 g) shelled walnuts

½ cup (125 ml) good quality walnut oil

2 tablespoons verjuice

generous squeeze of lemon juice

2 tablespoons cream

sea salt flakes and freshly ground black pepper

500 g baby green beans

500 g small waxy potatoes

Preheat the oven to 220°C. Dry-roast the walnuts on a baking tray for 6–8 minutes, then rub off the skins with a tea towel and sieve away any remaining bitter skin (new season's walnuts will not require this).

Make a vinaigrette by mixing the walnut oil, verjuice and lemon juice, then add the cream, season and set aside. Trim the beans if necessary. Put two saucepans of salted water on to boil.

Boil the potatoes in one pan for about 15 minutes until cooked, then drain immediately. Cook the beans in the other pan for 5 minutes so they are still a little al dente. Drain the beans and allow them to cool a little. Toss the potatoes with the vinaigrette, beans and walnuts and serve immediately.

GNOCCHI WITH CRISP SAGE LEAVES *Serves 6–8*

I love all things Italian, and gnocchi particularly. Success in making it always eluded me until I compared the results I got from using melted butter versus egg, and using kneaded versus un-kneaded dough. This recipe is now my preferred way of making gnocchi as it results in substantial, earthy, yet not heavy gnocchi, rather than the light-as-air variety. But this is a case of 'horses for courses', and if I was serving gnocchi with something delicate I'd probably do it differently to this. This dish is perfect as a first course or, without the sage leaves, makes an excellent side dish for a juicy braise.

1⅓ cups (200 g) plain flour	freshly ground black pepper
500 g waxy potatoes	handful sage leaves
salt	extra virgin olive oil, for cooking
175 g unsalted butter	Parmigiano Reggiano, to serve

Spread the flour out into a rectangle on your work surface. Peel the potatoes if you wish, then steam them for 15 minutes or until cooked through. While hot, pass each potato through a potato ricer and let it fall evenly over the flour on the bench. Sprinkle with salt.

Preheat the oven to 180°C. Melt 50 g of the butter and drizzle it evenly over the potato. Work the flour into the potato little by little using a pastry scraper until you have a firm dough. Knead the dough gently for a few minutes. Divide the dough into quarters and roll each piece to make a long thin sausage about 1 cm in diameter. Cut each sausage into 2.5 cm lengths. Put a buttered serving dish into the oven.

I find a large, heavy-based, 6 cm-deep roasting pan perfect for poaching gnocchi. Fill the tin with water, then salt it and bring it to the boil over medium heat. When the water is boiling, increase the heat to high and quickly slip in all the gnocchi at once (if the dish is large enough to take the gnocchi in a single layer), then reduce the heat to medium so the water isn't too turbulent. Allow the gnocchi to cook for 1 minute after they have risen to the surface, then skim them out, put them into the warm serving dish and season. Return the dish to the oven to keep warm while you crisp the sage.

Cook the sage leaves in a frying pan in the remaining butter and a dash of olive oil over medium heat until the butter is nut-brown and the sage crisp. It is important that the sage leaves become crisp without the butter burning. Pour the butter and sage over the hot gnocchi and serve immediately with shaved Parmigiano Reggiano on the table.

QUANDONGS

ABORIGINAL AUSTRALIANS TREASURED THE QUANDONG AND ATE the fruit raw or dried it for later use; it was a valuable source of vitamin C. In *Bush Food*, Jennifer Isaacs describes how Aborigines burnt the branches of the quandong tree and stood their children in the smoke in order to make them strong for long journeys. A tea was also made from quandong leaves and drunk as a purgative, and an infusion made from the roots of the tree was believed to help rheumatism sufferers. The bark was used for tanning leather and the wood was also of value, being closely related to sandalwood.

The first stanza of 'The Quandong Tree', a poem by Mary Flyn that appeared in the *Australian Women's Mirror* some forty years ago, reflects the ever-present nature of the tree in outback Australia:

> *In childhood books I read of these –*
> *Cherry and quince and walnut trees*
> *And many another old-world tree.*
> *Exotic and far they seemed to be,*
> *For all there was, my dears, for me,*
> *Was just one little quandong tree.*

The quandong evokes fond memories for people in the outback – childhood memories of gathering wild quandongs, eating quandong pies, and making necklaces out of the seeds.

The quandong tree will survive in the harshest of conditions and will cope with an amazingly high level of salinity, making quandongs a perfect desert-climate fruit. There are growers and CSIRO researchers working together on finding a way to propagate this fruit that is economically viable. Although there have been some successes, there is still a great deal to be done before the quandong can become more widely accessible.

While I have heard the taste of fresh quandongs described as somewhere between peach and rhubarb with a piquancy that makes your mouth pucker, I have not yet tried them myself. Once some were sent to me through the mail, but they did not survive the journey.

I really like the flavour of dried quandongs, although I've experienced huge variation in quality. It is a fruit that can be used for both savoury and sweet dishes. The only time I tasted a commercially made quandong pie, in the Flinders Ranges, I felt that too much sugar had been added and this masked the unique flavour. I have since been told by many people that it is better to use honey as a sweetener as this is less likely to mask the original flavour.

At the Pheasant Farm Restaurant, I used to team quandong with venison and kangaroo, finding the intense bittersweet flavour a great foil for the rich meat. In my quest to use local produce in as many ways as possible, I made a dessert of quandongs in a bread-and-butter pudding. As well as using quandongs in the pudding itself, I reconstituted some and served them in a caramel, making sure the caramel was almost bitter so that the natural sweet–sour flavour wasn't overpowered by too much sugar.

QUANDONG, MACADAMIA AND CHOCOLATE TART *Serves 10*

50 g dried quandongs

1 cup (250 ml) verjuice

1 × quantity Sour-cream Pastry
    (see page 424)

300 g sugar

250 g unsalted butter

250 g raw unsalted macadamias,
    roughly chopped

5 free-range eggs, at room
    temperature, beaten

80 g Haigh's bitter couverture chocolate
    (see Glossary)

Soak the quandongs in the verjuice overnight.

The next day, preheat the oven to 200°C. Make and chill the pastry as instructed, then roll it out and use to line a greased 26 cm tart tin. Trim the edges. Line the pastry case with foil, cover with pastry weights and blind bake for 15 minutes. Remove the foil and pastry weights and bake for another 5 minutes.

For the filling, dissolve 150 g of the sugar in 150 ml water in a saucepan, simmer for 5 minutes then gently poach the quandongs in this sugar syrup, along with any remaining verjuice, until tender. This should take approximately 20 minutes but will vary depending on how dried the quandongs were. Remove the fruit from the pan, then increase heat to high and boil the cooking liquid until it reduces to a syrup, then set aside. »

To make the macadamia filling, combine the butter and macadamias in a food processor, then slowly add the eggs and the remaining sugar with the motor running.

Arrange the cooked quandongs over the pastry base, grate over the chocolate, then spread with the macadamia mix. Return to the oven and bake for 20 minutes or until golden. While the tart is still warm, pour over the reduced syrup.

QUANDONG JAM
Makes about 1.5 litres

This recipe was inspired by one given to me by Jenny Treeby of CSIRO, using fresh quandongs. It is wonderful to see a researcher taking a real interest in the end product – the preserving of the fruit.

As dried quandongs are easier to find than fresh, I have adapted the recipe accordingly.

250 g dried quandongs
100 ml lemon juice

800 g sugar

Reconstitute the dried quandongs in 1 litre of water overnight. Place the soaked fruit and its soaking water, the lemon juice and 500 ml water in a large, heavy-based saucepan and simmer over medium–high heat for 20 minutes, then add the sugar. Turn the heat to low and simmer until jam reaches setting point (about 1½ hours). To test, put a spoonful of jam onto a saucer and cool in the refrigerator for a few minutes. If it wrinkles when you push it with your finger, the jam is ready. Transfer to sterilised glass jars (see Glossary).

SNAPPER

IT SEEMS I HAVE SPELT SNAPPER INCORRECTLY ALL MY LIFE.
I understood 'schnapper' to be the European spelling of the same fish, but
I now find that our snapper is actually a different fish from the European schnapper,
although they superficially resemble one another. The European schnapper is low-yielding
and relatively inexpensive, whereas our snapper is a lot fleshier, and is thought by many to
be the best-tasting snapper in the world.

The diet of the snapper includes crabs, squid, sea urchins and mussels. As many blue
swimmer crabs in South Australia moult and lose their shells between full moons in
November and December, it makes sense that spring is probably the peak time to eat local
snapper, making it the exception to the rule that fish are best in winter.

Over the years, my information about fish has come from such luminaries as John
Sussman, ex-Flying Squid Brothers, and Kim Rogers, formerly of International Oysters
of Adelaide, both of whom have been responsible for educating cooks and fishermen alike
throughout Australia for the last decade or more. In my lifetime the quality of Australian
fish has increased dramatically, from the way it is caught to the way it is brought to
market. People like John and Kim, who are concerned about quality and flavour, and the
various fisheries departments, which focus on research and development, are all vital
links in the chain.

Snapper is found along most of the southern coast of Australia, from inshore waters to
a depth of 100 metres. At times they can be seen in large schools of up to 30 tonnes in relatively shallow waters, where they tend to gather around natural or artificial reefs to spawn.
There is a tendency for snapper to move into deeper waters as they get older, where they
stay until they are twelve or thirteen years of age, before returning to inshore waters for
the remainder of their lives. Snapper reach legal size (38 cm) at six years of age, when
they weigh a bit less than a kilogram. These young snappers are known as 'ruggers' to
fishermen but are usually called 'baby snapper' in the market. They are the best prize of

all – the flesh is close, firm and at its sweetest. The bigger the fish, the bigger the flakes, making the flesh easier to separate. 'Nobbers' weighing around 10 kg can be up to thirty-five years old.

Snapper is definitely high on the list of my favourite fish, but then given the right conditions, flathead and King George whiting are truly exceptional, and the sashimi of southern bluefin tuna I have eaten in Japan is, at its best, nothing short of sensational. However, with any fish it is all about the quality that is available to you – and I think snapper is the best readily available fish you can buy. It is not cheap and, with such a large head (and gut cavity), snapper does not have a great deal of flesh, but it is still worth every cent. The heads make the best fish stock. Buying cutlets is the most economical way to purchase snapper, and a kilogram will feed five people exceptionally well for a main course.

There are lots of options for cooking snapper, but my favourites are the simplest. A well-seasoned fillet or cutlet (as my friend Michael Angelakis, South Australia's largest fish merchant, says, 'If it comes from the sea it needs salt!') seared in nut-brown butter for as little as 2–3 minutes a side, depending on its thickness, and finished with lots of freshly ground black pepper and a good splash of verjuice or a squeeze of lemon is all I need to be happy.

Snapper and oysters have a great affinity – it's that saltiness again, along with the combination of textures, that works so well. Reduce Fish Stock (see page 636) with a little champagne, then stir in some warm cream that has been infused with saffron threads and reduce the sauce further. Add the oysters and serve immediately with snapper that has been pan-fried or brushed with extra virgin olive oil and baked.

There is not a great deal of difference in the time it takes to bake whole snapper of varying weights: a fish that weighs 1 kg will take 20–25 minutes at 200°C, while a 3 kg fish might take 35–40 minutes. (A 1 kg snapper will feed two or three people, and a 3 kg fish will feed six to eight.) As overcooked fish is a travesty, don't compute minutes for kilograms, as you would for meat. However, as with meat and poultry, you should allow the fish to rest after it has been cooked to ensure moistness.

Snapper can withstand robust Mediterranean flavours in a stuffing, such as olives, capers, anchovies or preserved lemons with lots of flat-leaf parsley or basil. The main thing is to cook with ingredients to hand and not think you have to follow recipes slavishly. When Colin came home from the market with a whole snapper recently I mixed together chopped flat-leaf parsley, anchovies, olives and slices of meyer lemon (all of which I had in my pantry and garden), along with chunky roasted breadcrumbs, then seasoned the mixture and packed it into the fish before baking it. If you have snapper cutlets and want a quick and easy meal, butter a piece of foil or baking paper large enough to wrap a cutlet, then position the fish on it and pack on a layer of this lemon mixture. Close up the parcels and bake them at 200°C for about 7 minutes. Slide the fish and its 'stuffing' straight onto serving plates – the juices make a wonderful sauce – and drizzle with some more extra virgin olive oil.

SNAPPER WITH AVOCADO AND TOMATO SALSA   *Serves 6*

Whenever I serve raw fish I offer a vinaigrette in a separate jug for those who want it, as the lemon juice or other acidulant in the vinaigrette actually 'cooks' the raw fish – and I prefer my fish totally raw. Once, when I was in Sydney for a conference, I revelled in a dish of raw tuna at Neil Perry's Mars Bistro in Rushcutters Bay. Based on a salade niçoise, the dish had slices of just-cooked waxy potatoes at the base, stacked with a pile of cooked tiny green beans, quarters of peeled and seeded tomatoes, the smallest capers and green olives and a delicate vinaigrette. Right on top lay four large rosy-pink slices of raw tuna in perfect condition, overlapping like roof tiles and totally 'undressed'. It was as close to perfection as you could get!

But raw isn't everyone's bag, so if you prefer your fish cooked, then try the following. Save all your energy for finding a really good seafood merchant; the actual cooking of the fish is the easy part.

6 snapper fillets	SALSA
extra virgin olive oil, for cooking	1 large avocado, diced
6 quarters preserved lemon, flesh removed, rind rinsed and cut into strips	2 vine-ripened tomatoes, diced
	1 small red onion, diced
freshly ground black pepper	verjuice *or* lemon juice, to taste
butter, for cooking	sea salt flakes and freshly ground black pepper
sea salt flakes	
¼ cup (60 ml) verjuice	2 tablespoons flat-leaf parsley, roughly chopped
⅓ cup chopped flat-leaf parsley	extra virgin olive oil, for drizzling

Toss the fish with a little olive oil, the preserved lemon and some pepper. Set aside.

For the salsa, mix the avocado, tomato and onion, then add a dash of verjuice or a good squeeze of lemon juice to taste, season with salt and pepper and add the parsley and a little olive oil to combine.

In a large frying pan, melt 3 tablespoons butter and heat over medium–high heat until it turns nut-brown. Immediately add a dash of oil to save it from burning. Season the fillets with salt and cook the first side over medium–high heat with the preserved lemon, until the surface is sealed and lightly caramelised from the butter, then turn the fillets over and cook just until they become opaque, which takes minutes only.

Remove the cooked fish and lemon from the pan and reserve, then add the verjuice and reduce it quickly over high heat. Remove the pan from the heat and swirl in extra virgin olive oil to taste to make a warm vinaigrette, then add the parsley.

Serve the snapper fillets with the pan juices poured over, and some avocado and tomato salsa alongside.

SNAPPER IN A PARCEL
Serves 4

Serving fish *en papillote* is a breeze, and it means that you can create any number of different sauces by just adding a few flavourings to the parcel before cooking: a little butter, cream, extra virgin olive oil, wine, fresh herbs, slices of meyer lemon or a dash of lemon or lime juice, in whatever combination takes your fancy. Salmon fillets or cutlets are also delicious when treated this way.

extra virgin olive oil, for cooking

1 small fennel bulb, trimmed and sliced, fronds reserved

4 × 200 g snapper fillets of equal thickness, skin removed

1 meyer lemon, sliced

handful fresh chervil sprigs *or* bay leaves, optional

sea salt flakes and freshly ground black pepper

Heat a little extra virgin olive oil in a frying pan, then sauté the fennel over medium heat until cooked through.

Preheat the oven to 200°C. Liberally oil 4 sheets of baking paper or foil large enough to wrap the fish fillets. Arrange the cooked fennel and reserved fronds on the paper as a bed for the fish. Position the fillets on top, then add the lemon slices, followed by the chervil or bay leaves if using. Drizzle with extra virgin olive oil, then season and carefully fold in the edges to seal the parcel. Transfer the parcels to a baking tray (a scone tray is ideal for this) and bake for 8 minutes. Let the fish rest for another 5 minutes before serving.

When everyone opens their parcels they will be surrounded by a wonderful aroma as the juices spill onto the plate. Drizzle over a little more extra virgin olive oil, add a boiled waxy spud and a green vegie or salad and your meal is complete.

SNAPPER WITH SORREL AND PANCETTA
Serves 2–3

3 thick slices white bread, crusts removed and cut into large cubes

extra virgin olive oil, for cooking

1 very large onion, finely chopped

1 sprig thyme

8 thin slices mild pancetta, cut into strips

8 sorrel leaves

sea salt flakes and freshly ground black pepper

1 × 1 kg snapper

1 lemon

Preheat the oven to 200°C. Place the bread cubes on a baking tray, drizzle with a little of the olive oil and bake until golden brown. Allow the bread to cool, then process in a food processor – you will need ¾ cup breadcrumbs. Reset the oven temperature to 220°C.

Gently sweat the onion and thyme in a frying pan in a little olive oil until the onion is translucent. Add the pancetta and sorrel leaves to the pan, then stir in the breadcrumbs and season with salt and pepper. »

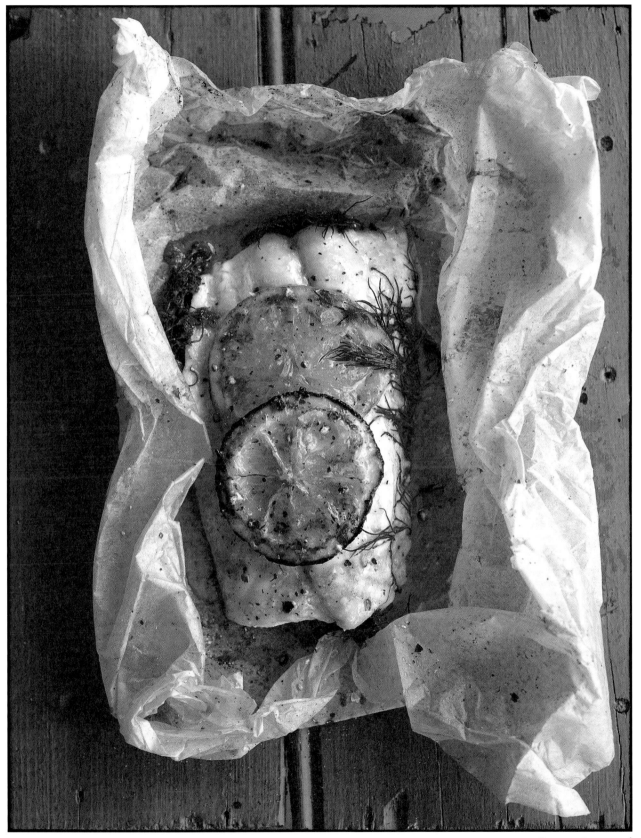

Snapper in a parcel

Put the fish on a baking tray and squeeze lemon juice into the cavity, then season and stuff it with the breadcrumb mixture. Brush both sides of the fish with olive oil, then squeeze over more lemon juice and season. Bake for 15 minutes, then carefully turn the fish over and cook it for another 10–15 minutes. Remove the fish from the oven and allow it to rest for 10 minutes before serving.

FISH STOCK

Makes 1.5 litres

As mentioned, snapper heads make the best fish stock, and if you have fish stock in the freezer you can make a simple soup or a rustic fish stew without a second thought. It also gives you a base for a sauce, or with the addition of the tiniest amount of gelatine (see Glossary) can become a quivering jelly – you could even serve it with poached seafood encased in it.

The addition of ginger to the stock gives an extra dimension to risottos (such as Meyer Lemon Risotto, see page 443). Just add 1 bruised knob of ginger to the stockpot before simmering. If I'm making a stock for a fish stew I use some fennel if it is in season (if it's not, I add a star anise). If the stock is to be used for a strongly flavoured dish you could use Pernod, and if you don't want to use wine at all you can add verjuice, which has a natural affinity with seafood. Just don't forget to label and date your stock before freezing it, and use it within three months.

1 kg snapper heads
1 large onion, finely chopped
1 leek, finely chopped
1 carrot, finely chopped
½ stick celery, finely chopped
¼ small fennel bulb (optional), finely chopped

2 tablespoons butter
½ cup (125 ml) dry white wine
1.5–2 litres cold water
10 stalks flat-leaf parsley
1 sprig thyme
½ fresh bay leaf

To clean the snapper heads, cut around the pointed underside of the head and the gills, then pull away the whole bottom part of the head and discard. Scrape out any trace of blood or innards, then rinse the head carefully and repeat with the remaining heads.

Put all the vegetables into an enamelled or stainless steel stockpot with the butter and sweat them over low heat for 2 minutes; the vegetables should not brown. Add the fish heads to the stockpot and sweat them for 1 minute more, then increase the heat to high, pour in the wine and boil vigorously for a few minutes. Pour in the cold water, then add the herbs and simmer gently over low heat for 20 minutes, without allowing the stock to boil at any stage – it will become cloudy if allowed to boil.

Strain through a fine sieve or muslin to give a good clear stock. Allow the strained stock to cool and then freeze or refrigerate it if you are not using it within the day. A good fish stock will set into a jelly after refrigeration.

SPRING GREENS

THOUGHTS OF PLANTING MY SPRING GREENS START TO enter my mind as soon as the cold weather hits. There is such a lot of planning to be done to be ready in time. I love winter, yet sometimes feel very lazy – a few stolen hours are more likely to be spent on the couch in front of the fire with a really good book than out in the garden – but this year, for the first time, I started to think about my spring greens in the dead of winter.

This was helped by the fact that I was yet again changing the garden around. Over the years, I've found that unless the vegetables are right in front of my nose every day I risk missing the opportunity to make the most of my harvest. We actually began this change in the soaring heat of January, making five raised garden beds in the spot where visitors used to park their cars too near the entrance to our house. I say 'the entrance' as though it's the front door, yet everyone always enters from the back veranda into the kitchen. In fact I don't know if I even have a key to the front door!

For a variety of reasons absolutely nothing happened with these beds until winter arrived, and that's when preparation really began. Organic loam and mushroom compost by the tonne was needed, as were more old red bricks. It wasn't until the new beds were finished and ready for planting that I suddenly realised the garden was now a little out of scale, because we had had to pull out a large old peach tree that was dying, hedged in against the wall of our huge farm shed, so the backdrop of the garden was suddenly missing. With the roses and shrubs dormant, winter gave me the chance to prune harshly, taking no prisoners, and to reposition many of the shrubs that suddenly seemed too tall in the middle of the garden, given the changes around them. I felt like I had a new landscape to work with and I spent more time than I had to spare poring over plant catalogues and gardening websites – whether for my kitchen garden or orchard, my choice of plants or trees is always guided by flavour. Invariably I seem to choose either a variety that is not readily available, or a plant that needs to be eaten just as it is picked.

I just love having a mixture of roses, vegetables and herbs planted together, but finding seeds for the vegetables I wanted to plant proved difficult, until I came across the website www.theitaliangardener.com.au. Just finding the seeds for these vegetables was a break-through. Then, much more importantly, given my frenetic life and haphazard approach to gardening, I found a very talented person who raised all the seeds to seedlings with such success that I was awash with the plants I had found impossible to buy from nurseries.

Having virgin beds to sow my greens in was such an exciting phase of the garden. I wanted to plant everything all at once so that spring would arrive with a bang, and that's exactly what we did. It's not quite spring as I write this (only August in fact), but the plants, the birds and the orchard are behaving as if spring is already here.

All of my greens have galloped. We've had more frost than normal this year and the cavolo nero is full of flavour. I probably put the celeriac in too late but it looks so healthy

that I'll persevere. I hate to think how many plants of rapini (*cima di rapa* or turnip greens) we put in, but with this early spring weather it's bolting like mad; it grows like a weed and is a little like a cross between a broccoli and a turnip. Picked in big bunches just before dinner each night, it's a green that's become the centre of our evening meals. Simply washed, chopped, blanched and tossed in extra virgin olive oil, it makes fantastic eat-ing – peppery and bitter yet somehow still sweet.

This year I also planted twelve one-year-old aspara-gus plants, as our older ones had been decimated by rabbits. While I'll have none ready to eat this year, it is so wonderful to see the promise of next year's crop in the form of a spear not much thicker than a matchstick poking through the mounded earth. Behind the aspara-gus I've planted asparagus peas but I'm still waiting for them to climb.

My chicory is ready to pick, while my garlic, perhaps planted a little late this year, hasn't yet formed to its full potential. Impatient as I am, though, I still picked a few tops and tossed them with a not-quite-formed bulb of Florence fennel while sautéing some baby squid I bought at the Barossa markets on Saturday, and they were delicious. I lost all of my sorrel to the snails, but now that I've learnt that coffee grounds repel them I'm about to ring my herb nursery and place my order.

I have the best position for growing spring lettuces – in a raised bed next to an old porcelain sink for washing the greens. It sits flush against a wall of glass that gets so hot in summer that I've yet to find a crop that survives the intense heat, but winter and spring plantings are protected. I picked my first borage flowers today. I love these delicate blue flowers with black trimmings that taste of cucumber, as they make such a beautiful show – although the plants are so large that I fear they'll crowd out the lettuce.

The big terracotta pots next to the wood-fired oven are lush with sweet marjoram, rosemary, thyme and more flat-leaf parsley. I'm picking great bunches of flat-leaf parsley and my rosemary is awash with pale blue flowers. The beautifully scented lemon thyme bush is abundant with its shiny leaves attached to delicate stems, partly because they are shaded by the borage – no stripping of woody stems is needed here. Then there is orange-peel thyme, so-called for its orange scent and the rough feel of the ground cover, similar to citrus skin. My tarragon plant is just poking its head up from the ground, and to me those first tarragon tips are the very taste of spring.

I got so carried away planting my Italian vegetables that I almost left out my staples, such as spinach and silverbeet. As readily available to buy as they are, my pleasure in the stalks, particularly of the silverbeet, only really comes to the fore when they've been picked fresh from my own garden. At least my local nurseryman has these as seedlings, so as soon as the cavolo nero finishes, there will be space to plant these, and with the warmth of spring, I'll be picking their young leaves within weeks

No two years are the same in our garden – there is just so much to learn.

SORREL

My first experience of sorrel was in 1985 in Sydney when I had my first meal at Claude's, then under the direction of that wonderful chef Damien Pignolet, now of Bistro Moncur. It was a Friday night, which meant it was bouillabaisse night: a rich and satisfying meal. Serving sorrel tart before the main course was a brilliant pairing. I went straight home to the Valley and planted this wonderful herb.

Seen growing wild throughout Europe, sorrel also sprouts like a weed in our conditions. It is nonetheless worthwhile having in the garden as it is quite difficult to find at the greengrocer's. Plant in the spring or autumn, water well in summer, and you will have a supply for years: if you cut the plants back at the base when the flower-stalks show, you won't have to replant. (If you aren't assiduous about this, just replant every year or two, unless the original plant has self-seeded.) Sorrel is greatly loved by snails, attracting them like no other herb, but sprinkling coffee grounds in the garden deters them, as it does the millipedes.

While some cookbooks describe sorrel as being similar to spinach, they are really just referring to its growing pattern; it is, rather, a cousin of the equally astringent rhubarb. Sorrel has a particularly piquant, lemony flavour and is a wonderful accompaniment to rich foods such as brains, sweetbreads, eggs, salmon or ocean trout, or oily fish such as herrings and sardines (try wrapping either of these in sorrel leaves and barbecuing them).

Sorrel can become quite strong and rank, so you must be vigilant about tossing over-grown leaves into the compost to ensure that young leaves come through all the time. This way you'll always have baby leaves to add to a salad (they may be a little sharp on their own but they add another dimension to mixed greens).

If you have an overabundance of young leaves, sweat them in a little extra virgin olive oil in a non-reactive frying pan (an aluminium pan will turn black and give the sorrel a metallic taste), until they break down to make their own purée. This mixture can be refrigerated, covered with a film of extra virgin olive oil, in a well-sealed jar for at least ten days. With the addition of onion, the purée can be diluted with chicken or fish stock and cream before being blended in a food processor and served as a simple sauce with any of the foods mentioned on the previous page. If you are not usually keen on cream sauces, bear in mind that the sorrel will cut the richness of the cream.

Sorrel soup can be made in a similar way, too. Cook a large, peeled potato with the sorrel, stock and onion, then put the potato through a potato ricer or food mill (a food processor will turn it into glue) and return it to the soup for reheating with cream stirred through.

Sorrel braised with tomato, lemon and capers is a great base for veal, tuna or chicken. Sweat a diced onion in a little butter and extra virgin olive oil until softened, then add 2 sliced lemons and turn up the heat so that both onion and lemon caramelise just a little.

Watch the pan carefully, though, and adjust the temperature if the mixture looks like burning. Add a handful of trimmed young sorrel leaves. Finely dice several peeled and seeded ripe tomatoes (or preserved or tinned ones, strained of juice) and add them to the sorrel mixture, then season it well and splash in a little more olive oil. The tomato only needs a minute or so over heat to warm through. Stir in a tablespoon each of capers and chopped flat-leaf parsley and let the mixture cool for the flavours to meld while you pan-fry a piece of veal, chicken or tuna. While the meat is resting, quickly reheat the sauce and then serve.

Sorrel Mayonnaise (see page 142) is a good counterpoint to a smoked tongue dish. It can also lift the flavour of a cooked rock lobster that has been refrigerated.

If you ever scramble duck eggs, rich as they are, do so with a good dollop of cream, a knob of butter, salt and freshly ground black pepper. When the eggs are just set, fold through shredded young sorrel leaves and serve.

Looking through old Pheasant Farm Restaurant menus, I now see how often I used to raid my bed of sorrel: smoked potted tongue and sorrel; kid pot-roasted with garlic and sorrel; scrambled guinea-fowl eggs with smoked ocean trout and sorrel; rabbit with a sorrel and mustard sauce; sausage of rabbit fillets, kidneys and livers wrapped in pastry and served with sorrel sauce; lamb with artichokes and sorrel; and fillet of hare with a brandy, peppercorn and sorrel sauce. What an indispensable herb!

OMELETTE WITH SORREL AND ANCHOVY

Serves 1

I have an omelette pan that is used for no other purpose: given that no metal implements go near the pan, my omelettes never stick. A pan like this is well worth having. Slow-roasted garlic cloves can also be added to the sorrel filling once it has been piled onto the omelette.

30 g unsalted butter	2 tablespoons verjuice
3 free-range eggs	good handful young sorrel leaves, trimmed
sea salt flakes and freshly ground	1 anchovy fillet, finely chopped
black pepper	squeeze of lemon juice (optional)
2 tablespoons cream	

Melt half the butter in an omelette pan and allow it to cool a little. Break the eggs into a bowl, then add the melted butter with a pinch of salt and a grind of pepper and beat lightly with a fork. Set aside.

Reduce the cream and verjuice by half in a small enamelled or stainless steel saucepan, then add the sorrel and anchovy. Check the seasoning, adding a squeeze of lemon juice if required. The sorrel will form its own purée in just a few minutes. Keep warm.

Melt the remaining butter in the omelette pan over medium heat, coating the base with the butter as it melts. When the butter is nut-brown, pour in the eggs, stirring quickly with a heat-resistant plastic spatula or wooden spoon. Lift the edge gently as it cooks to allow more uncooked egg to run underneath. The omelette must be shiny and very moist in the centre. When it is almost cooked, spoon the warm sorrel mixture into the centre, then turn the omelette onto itself as you slide it onto a warmed plate. Rub an extra bit of butter over the top – it melts in wonderfully. Serve immediately.

SORREL TART

Serves 6–8

Sorrel tart is one of my tried and true favourites. This is the tart I made from memory, helped by a recipe of Richard Olney's in his *Simple French Food*, after eating Damien Pignolet's memorable sorrel tart. I like to serve it as a first course, sometimes with crème fraîche (matching piquant with piquant). It also partners smoked salmon or gravlax well.

1 × quantity Sour-cream Pastry	6 large free-range eggs
(see page 424)	650 ml cream
600 g young sorrel leaves	sea salt flakes and freshly ground
2 onions, finely chopped	black pepper
butter, for cooking	

Make and chill the pastry as instructed, then roll out and use to line a 20 cm springform tin. Chill the pastry case for 20 minutes. »

Preheat the oven to 200°C. Line the pastry case with foil, then cover with pastry weights. Blind bake the pastry case for 15 minutes, then remove the foil and weights and bake for a further 5 minutes. Remove from the oven and reset the temperature to 190°C.

Strip the sorrel leaves from their stems, then wash the leaves carefully and drain well. Sweat the onions slowly in an enamelled or stainless steel saucepan over low heat with a knob of butter until softened, being careful not to let them colour. Add the sorrel leaves and cook with the onion for just a few minutes until a purée forms. Remove the pan from the heat and allow to cool a little. If you prefer a very fine purée, blend the onion and sorrel in a food processor.

Beat the eggs and add the cream, salt and pepper. Stir the sorrel purée into the egg mixture. Pour the filling into the still-warm pastry case and bake until set, 40–50 minutes for a deep tin (a shallower tin may only need 15–20 minutes). The tart will continue to set a little once it has been removed from the oven. Serve warm or at room temperature. Leftovers cold from the fridge are pretty good, too.

SPINACH AND SILVERBEET

As a child I always wondered about Popeye's love of spinach, my least favourite vegetable back then. In fact, I only knew of silverbeet, rather than true spinach, cooked to blazes, stalks and all, in an aluminium saucepan. The stalks were grey and lifeless and the leaves soggy and unappetising.

Thankfully, things have changed. Now I'm happy to eat spinach or silverbeet cooked to perfection – that is, quickly, so that the stalks still have a slight crunch and are almost sweet. I would quite happily eat a plate of silverbeet stalks on their own, drizzled with extra virgin olive oil and seasoned with sea salt and freshly ground black pepper, thank you very much. When I think back on the lost opportunities of my youth . . .

It did remind me, though, of how easily a vegetable can become overlooked, when I think of how I reacted to the availability of English spinach for the first time. I pushed silverbeet to the side completely until the time I ate it straight from a friend's garden, when I literally fought with my host for the stalks – English spinach stalks are not nearly so special.

Spinach and silverbeet have so many uses and are easy to grow in most areas, looking vibrantly healthy in the vegie garden for very little effort. They can even be beautiful. The lighter-coloured leaves of Swiss chard, milder in flavour than silverbeet, sit atop stalks of pink, red and the most vivid yellow (like my meyer lemons, I decided).

Another form of silverbeet, called perpetual spinach beet, is also worth considering planting; you simply pick the small leaves as you want them over months and the plant continues to grow.

Back to traditional English spinach. The young leaves are great raw in a salad, while mature leaves are better cooked. Wash the leaves well (no snails, please, or, for South Australians, millipedes), then chop them.

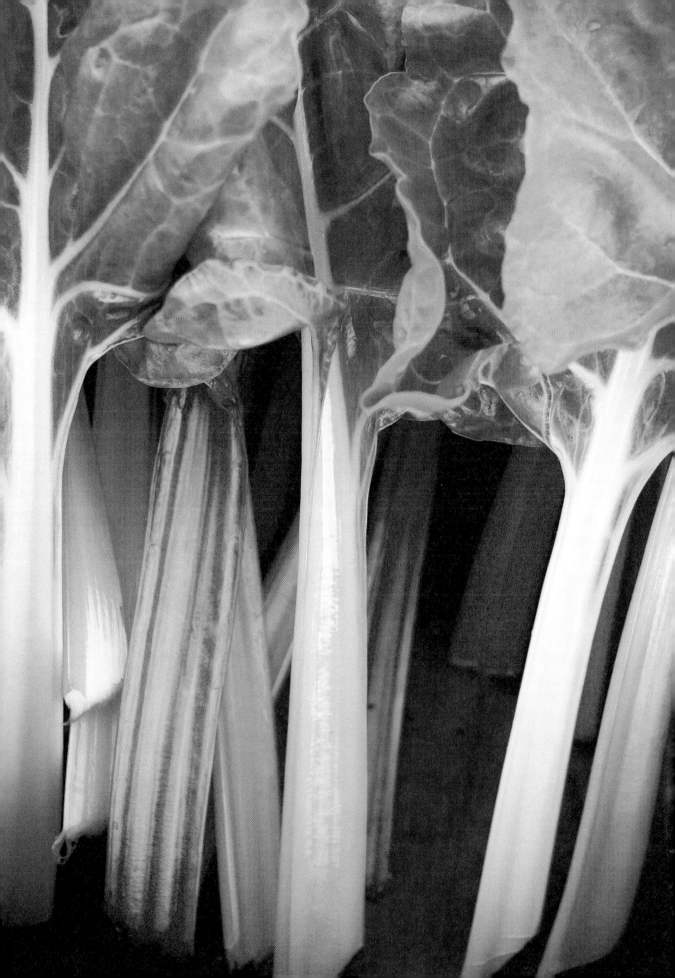

Cook the leaves in just the water that clings to them after you wash them, until they collapse. While I love to anoint my spinach with extra virgin olive oil, butter melted over the hot leaves is just as good – and, as spinach is so good for us, this addition is fine in my book.

If you have reluctant greens-eaters in your family, try starting them on raw young leaves prepared in any of the ways suggested below. Once they are hooked, then pounce with beautifully cooked and seasoned spinach. Well, that's the way I thought it would work

with two of my grandchildren, Zöe and Max. They used to love almost any food, from raw fish to anchovies, sweet cloves of caramelised garlic to mushrooms and offal – yet greens were 'enemy number one'.

Always keen to take on a challenge, my first offering was cooked spinach topped by a perfectly poached egg, all on a great slab of toast. The second was a salad of raw leaves with chopped freshly boiled egg, toasted pine nuts and currants soaked in a little verjuice to plump them up. No luck.

Rotolo, where a large sheet of pasta is used to roll up a filling of spinach, caramelised garlic, oregano and ricotta flavoured with just a hint of nutmeg, is an institution in my family (see below), so it seemed a sure winner. Zöe and Max helped make the pasta first, in a major morning's work, but it still didn't win them over. At least the grown-ups enjoyed the end result.

My quest continued. Spinach pasta never actually works for me – I find it tends to lack flavour – although spinach gnocchi does (as long as every last bit of water is wrung out of the cooked spinach), but not for Zöe and Max. My final attempt was a combination of some of the earlier efforts: a salad of young spinach leaves topped with caramelised garlic and a perfectly poached egg (with toast soldiers to dip into it), and anchovy mayonnaise on the side (see page 647). When a request was made for more soldiers I thought success was at hand, but they were used to mop up the last of the anchovy mayonnaise – the spinach languished on the plate.

Oh, well. With luck, as they all grow up, my grandchildren's tastes will change, just as mine did. In the meantime, I'll continue to eat spinach whenever I can.

ROTOLO DI SPINACI
Serves 8–10

This recipe is based on one in *The River Café Cookbook*, by Rose Gray and Ruth Rogers, and it also appeared in *Stephanie Alexander and Maggie Beer's Tuscan Cookbook*. It is a dish I have cooked so many times, both with students and when Stephanie and I were on tour launching the book, that making it has become second nature.

verjuice, for soaking

40 g dried porcini

1 tablespoon butter

1 red onion, finely chopped

1 tablespoon oregano leaves, chopped

800 g spinach, washed, blanched
    and chopped

finely chopped rind of 1 lemon

3 tablespoons extra virgin olive oil

2 cloves garlic, chopped

250 g field mushrooms *or* fresh porcini,
    roughly sliced

sea salt flakes and freshly ground
    black pepper

350 g ricotta

80 g freshly grated Parmigiano Reggiano,
    plus extra to serve

freshly grated nutmeg, to taste

PASTA DOUGH

3⅓ cups (500 g) unbleached strong flour
    (see Glossary)

½ teaspoon sea salt

1 large (55 g) free-range egg

6 large free-range egg yolks

semolina flour, for dusting

For the pasta dough, put the flour and salt into a food processor and add the egg and egg yolks. Pulse until the pasta begins to come together into a loose ball of dough. Knead the pasta dough on a workbench dusted with semolina flour for about 3 minutes or until it is smooth.

Divide the dough into quarters and roll each piece into a ball. Wrap the pieces of dough in plastic film and refrigerate for at least 20 minutes or up to 2 hours.

Meanwhile, for the filling, warm some verjuice in a saucepan, then use to reconstitute the dried porcini – this will take about 15–20 minutes.

Heat the butter in a frying pan and cook the onion until softened, then add the oregano, spinach and lemon rind. Stir to combine, then let cool.

Drain the porcini, reserving the strained soaking liquid. Wash the porcini to remove any grit. Heat the olive oil in a frying pan and gently cook the garlic for a few minutes over low heat. Add the field mushrooms or fresh porcini and cook, stirring, over high heat for 5 minutes. Add the soaked porcini and cook gently over low heat for 20 minutes, adding a little of the strained soaking liquid at a time to keep the mushrooms moist. Add the rest of the soaking liquid – you may need to turn up the heat to evaporate the remaining juices. Season and let cool. When cold, roughly chop.

Put the ricotta in a large bowl and break it up lightly with a fork, then add the spinach mixture, the Parmigiano Reggiano and a generous amount of nutmeg. Add salt and pepper, if necessary, and set aside.

Using a pasta machine, put a piece of pasta dough through the maximum setting, then repeat another 8–10 times until shiny and silky, each time folding one end into the centre and the other over this, then giving the dough a turn to the right before rolling it again. Once this has been done, put the dough through the other settings (going through 8–10 times on each setting) until you reach the second-last setting, then put it through twice. You should have a 30 × 10 cm pasta sheet. Repeat this process with the remaining 3 pieces

of dough. Join 2 sheets of pasta together at their longest edge, brushing the edges with water to seal, to make a sheet about 30 × 20 cm. Repeat with the remaining 2 sheets of pasta, then trim the edges to straighten them.

Working in two batches, transfer each joined sheet of pasta to a large, clean tea towel – choose one that is as smooth as possible as any texture will leave a pattern – and position it so the longer edge faces you. Spoon half the mushroom mixture in a 3 cm-wide line along the long edge of the pasta nearest you. Cover the rest of the pasta with half the spinach and ricotta mixture. Starting with the edge nearest you, gently roll up the pasta into a log 6 cm in diameter and 30 cm long, working away from you and using the tea towel to help guide you. Wrap the rotolo in the tea towel as tightly as possible, folding the edges in to secure the parcel, then tie it with kitchen string to hold it in shape during cooking. Repeat with the remaining pasta sheet and fillings.

Bring a fish kettle or large deep roasting pan of salted water to the boil. Carefully slip in a wrapped rotolo, making sure it is submerged, then cover and simmer over low heat for 18–20 minutes. Carefully remove the rotolo, turn it upside-down, and keep it warm while cooking the second.

Transfer the rotoli to a chopping board, carefully unwrap and cut into 3 cm-thick slices. Serve 2 slices per person and offer extra grated Parmigiano Reggiano at the table.

SALAD OF SPINACH WITH POACHED EGG AND ANCHOVY MAYONNAISE

Serves 4

When making the mayonnaise, simply mash in anchovies to taste as you blend the egg yolks before adding the oil.

1 × quantity Anchovy Mayonnaise
   (see page 9)
2 bunches baby spinach leaves
8 cloves garlic, peeled
⅓ cup (80 ml) extra virgin olive oil

4 slices crusty bread
1 tablespoon verjuice *or* vinegar
4 free-range eggs (use the freshest eggs
   possible for a perfect result)

Make the mayonnaise following the instructions and set aside.

Preheat the oven to 200°C. Pick through the spinach, rejecting any bruised or old leaves. Wash the leaves very well, then spin or pat dry. Blanch the garlic in a saucepan of boiling water for 4 minutes, then drain and infuse in the olive oil in a small frying pan over low heat until golden. Remove the garlic from the oil and set both aside.

Brush the bread with the garlicky oil and toast in the oven until golden, then cut into strips to make 'soldiers' for dipping.

Warm the plates, but only to just above room temperature, so that the mayonnaise doesn't melt. »

Two-thirds fill a deep stainless steel frying pan with water, then add a spoonful of verjuice or vinegar and bring the pan to a rolling boil over high heat. Crack the eggs onto a plate (or into 4 coffee cups), then slide them into the water as quickly as possible and turn the heat down to a simmer. Cook for 3 minutes, so that the white has just set but the yolk is runny. (If you don't have a helper in the kitchen, you can slip the eggs into a bowl of cold water to stop them cooking, although it's better to serve them immediately. Just remember to drain them on kitchen paper just before serving.)

Warm the garlic gently in the reserved oil, then toss the spinach through, just to warm it. Divide the spinach and garlic cloves between the plates, then add a poached egg and a good dollop of the mayonnaise and position the soldiers.

WATERCRESS

No one has ever offered me a watercress sandwich at an afternoon tea party. Perhaps it's because I never attend such events, or are they, like the sandwiches themselves, a thing of the past? There are, however, plenty of literary references to thinly sliced, white buttered-bread sandwiches with a watercress filling – somehow these are always 'dainty'. Only butter is used (never margarine), there is not a tea bag in sight, and fine china cups are de rigueur in the drawing rooms where these sandwiches are served.

While not a participant in afternoon tea parties, I have always loved watercress. In fact, I used to collect it in the spring from a nearby creek where it grew in such profusion that we'd pick buckets and buckets of it. Then one of my staff declared her concern that the grazing animals upstream might be polluting the water and that liver fluke could be present. As I'd been using the watercress for years, I was a little cavalier about the matter. But in the past two years we haven't had enough rain for the creek to run, so I've had to find another source anyway.

If you find watercress in the wild and are not sure of the water source, it is best to wash it thoroughly before cooking. Better still, if you have a pond in your garden you can transplant wild rooted watercress, but don't try planting it in your vegie garden – it just won't work, particularly with water restrictions.

Although I can imagine the sense of satisfaction at having such easy access to this delicious plant – and, as they say, it grows like a weed given the right environment – it is readily available from commercial herb growers.

Be selective, though, when choosing a bunch of watercress as it wilts quickly. Look for fresh, bright-looking leaves and stems, and refrigerate it after washing, either wrapped in kitchen paper inside a wet tea towel or in a jug of water covered with a plastic bag (remember to change the water daily).

Once you become addicted to the peppery hit watercress provides, you'll wonder how you ever lived without it. Watercress is a great foil to either very rich or quite bland flavours: try it with eggs, goat's cheese or ricotta. Add it to any other salad leaves, except rocket or nasturtium, which are peppery enough on their own. From bitter witlof to crispy iceberg, watercress provides a great contrast.

Toss watercress through a warm salad of waxy potatoes and hard-boiled eggs. Serve it with wedges of orange and sliced fennel with a dressing of good olive oil, orange juice and red-wine vinegar. Season with sea salt, but don't bother with pepper.

To make watercress mayonnaise, thoroughly wash a bunch of watercress, then strip away the leaves and dry them well. Mash the leaves to a paste with a little garlic and a good squeeze of lemon juice, then add to a homemade mayonnaise (make sure the emulsion is quite thick). Serve with grilled fish or poached chicken.

WATERCRESS AND BROAD BEAN SOUP *Serves 6*

Watercress soups are just about as well-documented as the infamous sandwiches. I've always found them too peppery for my liking and therefore have succumbed in the past to adding a lot of cream. So, faced with a huge bunch of watercress that was too limp to use in a salad after a very hot drive home from the market, I decided to make my own version of watercress soup. I rejected the very tired stems, then collected broad beans from the garden to add a touch of sweetness. The balance was perfect and I didn't need to add any cream – and the soup is just as good cold as hot, which makes it perfect for a warm spring day.

If you prefer, you can substitute peas for the broad beans. You'll find frozen peas useful to have on hand as sadly they're often in much better condition than the 'fresh' peas you buy to shell yourself, unless you're lucky.

60 g butter	sea salt flakes
1 tablespoon olive oil	1 litre Golden Chicken Stock
1 large onion, diced	(see page 57)
500 g shelled broad beans	plain yoghurt and freshly picked chervil,
(about 1 kg unshelled)	to serve
1 large bunch watercress	
(to yield 3 cups chopped leaves	
after washing and trimming)	

Melt the butter with the oil in a heavy-based stainless steel, enamelled or non-stick saucepan. Add the onion and cook for a few minutes, then stir in the broad beans, coating them with butter. Sauté gently over low heat for 5 minutes. Stir in the chopped watercress, then add the salt and stock. Simmer until the broad beans are tender (the exact time will depend on their age), but don't over-cook or you'll lose the brilliant green colour. Purée the mixture, then adjust the seasoning. Serve hot or cold with a dollop of yoghurt and a little fresh chervil.

SPRING LAMB

ONE OF THE MOST OBVIOUS SPRING DELIGHTS IS LAMB.
Spring lamb is the meat from lambs born in autumn and sold the following spring, so is usually from animals between four and six months old. The tender, juicy sweetness of the meat is a direct result of the nutritious diet the animals enjoy during their short lives. They are firstly suckled on mother's milk for a period (usually six to eight weeks, but sometimes longer), and then moved on to graze the verdant grasses of late winter/early spring.

I much prefer to eat breeds grown for their meat rather than their wool, and happily my two favourite breeds are both readily available to me. One is the 'pure Suffolk', a breed in which both sides of the gene pool come from meat stock. This would have to be described as the *crème de la crème* of lamb, and is grown south of Adelaide by Richard Gunner of Coorong Angus Beef. The other is the 'White Suffolk', a cross between a Suffolk and a Merino, cuts of which are available every Saturday from my local Barossa market, from Jan and John Angas of Hutton Vale.

It has taken a long time to have lamb for sale branded by breed and it is a practice that needs encouragement, since there is such a difference in the texture and flavour of the breeds mentioned above compared to the Merino, which is bred primarily for wool. As well as spring lamb from Suffolk and other meat breeds, another flavour treat is milk-fed lamb. It is a real delicacy – the meat is sweet, tender and buttery with such a special texture as well as a clean flavour. It lends itself wonderfully to slow-braising in extra virgin olive oil and verjuice with rosemary, or quick grilling on a barbecue then resting in a marinade. The meat also works beautifully with the Mediterranean tradition of spit-roasting whole, or being separated into shoulder and leg joints for slow-cooking and grilling, respectively. For centuries, Italians have headed for the hills at Easter to feast on platters of grilled milk-fed lamb (*abbacchio*). Two legs (each about 1 kg) will feed six, with an anchovy or garlic mayonnaise and a peppery salad to go with them.

While Australian producers may not have an ancient culinary tradition of their own to fall back on, they learn continually from countries with more entrenched food cultures that share a climate similar to ours. For example, in recent times we have enjoyed the marvellous milk-fed lamb of several producers Australia-wide, the first of which was from Illabo.

In 1994, Tony Lehmann of Illabo, in southern New South Wales, saw a niche and began to sell his milk-fed lambs to top-class restaurants and a few specialist retailers in Sydney, including Leichhardt's AC Butchery. His Border Leicester Merino Poll Dorset cross provides lambs varying in size from 8–12 kg, raised purely on their mother's milk for approximately eight weeks. Tony has been incredibly successful in his operation.

Once a niche market is established, other producers are tempted to join in. And now it's time for me to declare my hand. As an adjunct to her Barossa Farm Produce business, my elder daughter, Saskia, has set up a project to produce milk-fed lamb with the assistance of a very motivated and innovative group of farmers. She gave them her requirements for the product she wanted to cook, and together they have worked on a cross-breeding program to ensure flavour and texture. Saskia believes the differences in breeds, as well as the Barossa climate and pasture, will give their lamb a distinctive flavour.

Each chef who uses this lamb completes a 'trace-back' sheet so the farmer receives direct feedback. Collectively, these have formed a quality manual, useful not only at the farm gate but at the processors, where costs are high (only a niche market can support the cost of processing such a small animal) and where careful, humane handling is essential for the best results.

This is paddock-to-plate planning, and the outcome is stunning. The lamb is like the Italian *abbacchio*, which is so buttery and succulent; I was amazed by its delicate yet full-flavoured texture and the generous amount of meat. Its sweetness goes so well with all those Mediterranean flavours: olive oil, rosemary, golden shallots, preserved lemons, bay leaves, dill, garlic – and even my favourite, slow-roasted quinces.

Much of this milk-fed lamb is exported to Japan or sold direct to restaurants, but you can find it here at specialty retailers and farmers' markets such as ours in the Barossa, where at the right time of year Saskia sells her surplus, left over from the export market. Some of this finds its way to my kitchen for special occasions – often it's the shoulder (to my mind the sweetest cut of all) as her restaurant customers invariably want the legs or the saddle.

Most butchers are incredibly friendly, and certainly those of the old school know a great deal about their trade and are only too happy to help with advice. So many people buy on price only, not understanding the differences in quality. In these times of course it is important to receive value for money – yet you should still try to make an informed choice about the meat you are buying. I always want to know about the animal's life and if it has been respected in death, as this has so much to do with quality and sustainability.

I don't see as much evidence of it these days, but larger retailers used to package whole sides of lamb showcasing the leg at the top and advertise it for a ridiculously low price. To the person in a hurry it seemed to be a good buy, as a leg of lamb these days is many times the price of the rest of the carcass, but the use of 'lamb' as a descriptor was stretching it, and you got what you paid for – low-grade meat.

If it is still done then I guess it is clever marketing because under the leg would be the lesser cuts of meat, which are more likely to be wasted. These lesser cuts, if cooked correctly, can make good honest meals – say by pot-roasting the shoulder (though this would be better if sold in one piece and not as chops), or by making a stew or curry. My main complaint is the insistence of so many people who buy just on price to use these neck, shoulder or chump chops of inferior meat as barbecue chops. They are served up as leathery offerings and considered a proper meal. There is no food I dislike more, and it could fast make me a vegetarian!

In Australia, lamb is not classified by age, but instead on the eruption of teeth, so the moment the first baby tooth falls out is when lamb becomes hogget (usually at about twelve months old). Mutton is the meat from sheep over two years old. Many farmers prefer the taste of mutton to lamb and hogget, as it has a depth of flavour missing from the younger meat. I have to say my husband shows his Mallala upbringing in loving a rolled, seasoned mutton flap. His family never bothered with spring lamb, probably because it was that much more expensive than mutton or hogget.

If you get the chance to try saltbush mutton you'll be in for a treat. It has a superb flavour from the saltbush the lamb feeds on. Saltbush mutton can be bought from butchers in Quorn and further north in South Australia. It should definitely be slow-roasted – the ultimate 'baked dinner' in my opinion (see page 661). Try cooking it using the same method as that for a leg of kid (see page 606), pot-roasting very slowly with garlic and rosemary and adding just half a cup of stock at a time so that the juices become thick and caramelised.

So what should you look for in spring lamb? To start with, it should be stamped with a red vegetable-dye brand that validates it as coming from a young animal – the younger the animal, the pinker and more finely grained the meat (the lamb now available in spring is from animals about four months old).

While the quality of spring lamb is generally good, it's not always consistent, and this can be for several reasons. Regardless of the age of the animal, stress produces darker, tougher meat, so the issue of how the animal is handled becomes a factor. This concern has been recognised by the Australian Meat and Livestock Corporation and the sheep industry, with both determined to improve handling to give consistency to the Australian market first and then break into export markets.

Remember, let your butcher guide you. Ask about the differences in price, suggested cooking methods and final taste. A prime cut of spring lamb will be at least twice the price

of an inferior cut, but will taste ten times better. If cost is a limiting factor, then just serve a smaller, perfectly cooked portion as the highlight of the meal instead of the filler.

With improved farm management we have many more options than just spring lamb these days. However, there are questions you really must ask your butcher. Is it lamb, in fact, or mutton, or even hogget? All can be terrific, but the dishes you use them in and the cooking times required will differ significantly.

For lunch at the restaurant we used to make shoulder of baby lamb and pickled quince pies, and when we ran out of lamb, we used mutton – the cooking had to be varied markedly and the flavour was totally different, but the pies still made great eating. However, as soon as we offered a mutton and pickled quince pie on the menu, sales dropped off so dramatically we decided it wasn't worth it. Perhaps this made me understand a little more why truth in labelling is something butchers might feel is too hard to handle.

Cooking a leg of lamb on the bone gives maximum flavour and all the meat needs is a couple of bay leaves and a few sprigs of rosemary tucked into it. Always take the meat out of the refrigerator 2 hours before cooking to allow it to come to room temperature. Smear the skin with olive oil, stick slivers of garlic and bay leaves or sprigs of rosemary into little pockets cut with a sharp knife, then season with sea salt and freshly ground black pepper and roast.

If carving at the table puts you off cooking a roast leg of lamb, you can ask your butcher to butterfly the leg – that is, flatten it out so it's an even thickness and you can barbecue it in one piece – or have the butcher remove the thigh bone while retaining the shank, which keeps the joint intact. Called an easy-carve lamb leg, this really does make carving so much easier. Or you could ask for the leg to be tunnel-boned. You can then fill the cavity with a paste made from garlic and rosemary. Or you could use mushrooms chopped and sautéed with spring onion, or make an anchovy butter, adding some garlic and lemon juice. Let it sit for at least 30 minutes for the flavours to penetrate (or it can be left overnight in the refrigerator). A couple of lengths of cooking twine will keep the stuffing in place and maintain the shape of the joint. While this cut is a good idea, it does cook a little quicker than a normal leg of lamb – and remember that meat cooked on the bone always has the best flavour of all.

If you wish to bone and butterfly a leg of lamb yourself, turn a slightly larger leg on to its less fatty side. Using a sharp knife, cut right down the bone from the wide to the thin end of the leg. Carefully cut the bone out, slipping your knife under it and cutting it away from the sinew. Remove the bone, then open out the meat and pound it until it is about

2.5 cm thick all over, then stuff as described earlier, or marinate. For pink lamb, cook on the barbecue or under an efficient griller about 15 cm from the heat source for 15 minutes a side. If barbecuing, baste it with the marinade, if using, every 10 minutes. Throw some eggplant slices on the grill, then serve the lot with pesto.

For roasting, as a guide preheat the oven to 180°C, place the boned lamb leg in a roasting pan, then drizzle with olive oil and season to taste. Roast it for 15 minutes per 500 g, then rest it in a warm place for 20–30 minutes before carving.

It takes five minutes to prepare a leg of lamb; if the joint is around 2 kg it will take 60–80 minutes at around 200°C to cook, but it need only be attended to once – and that's only when you add the potatoes to the baking dish. What could be simpler? Well, possibly eschewing the usual roasted vegies and instead layering potato, onion and garlic (or perhaps eggplant, tomato and onion) in a baking dish and setting the leg of lamb straight on the rack above. Don't want to use the oven? Roast the lamb in a hooded barbecue: it will only take about an hour and you can sit it in a pan atop the potato or eggplant combinations above, if you want a great accompaniment – and no washing up!

But perhaps the easiest cut of all for roasting – or pan-frying or barbecuing – is a rack of lamb. A few tips are well worth noting, however, as not every butcher prepares a rack the same way. Ask the butcher to saw through the chine bone without removing it; the yellow membrane should be discarded. A properly trimmed rack should be free of any shoulder bone remnants. To do this, the butcher cuts off the fat and meat from the edge of the fillet to expose the bones, removing the outer membrane. Some might also trim excess fat, but remember that fat is flavour! The butcher then scrapes the exposed bones clean with a sharp knife, so each rib shows separately. You can rub a rack of lamb with garlic and rosemary paste before cooking or perhaps brush it with a quince or plum glaze. And the beauty of a rack is that it needs only about 20 minutes at 200°C with 15 minutes' resting time. If barbecuing a rack, the trick is to turn the meat frequently so it doesn't burn but caramelises instead.

While I now like to cook lamb racks with a quince glaze (see page 658), one of the classic dishes of provincial France is rack of lamb roasted with a mustard glaze. It combines beautifully with a sorrel sauce and boiled waxy potatoes, or roasted garlic and a salad of bitter greens. This marinade is inspired by one in *Mastering the Art of French Cooking, Volume One*, by Simone Beck, Louisette Bertholle and Julia Child. Blend mustard, soy sauce, a small clove of crushed garlic, some rosemary or thyme, and a pinch of ground ginger in a bowl. Gradually whisk in olive oil, drop by drop, to make a mayonnaise-like cream. Paint the lamb with the mixture – the meat will pick up more flavour if it is coated several hours before roasting.

For those in a hurry, spring lamb will cook very quickly and needs little preparation. The butcher can cut a leg of lamb into steaks for grilling or barbecuing. They can also section the leg into the silverside, topside and flank to make small roasts.

The under-fillet or tenderloin (the smaller part of a loin chop) provides the quickest fix of all: brush the meat with olive oil and sprinkle with oregano dried on the stalk, then pan-fry gently in the oil and squeeze on lemon juice to deglaze the pan. The meat will be ready before you have had time to cook the vegetables.

Lamb loin chops will grill in just 10 minutes. Don't be worried about the fat on the loin chops or saddle. Cook these cuts with the fat on – the flavour of the lamb is so much better this way – then by all means cut it off before eating if it worries you. You can barbecue double-cut loin chops until the outside is crisp and brown and the inside pink and moist. On such a chop, the normally rejected fat sizzles irresistibly on the barbecue and is almost my favourite morsel of the meat. You will need to visit a butcher for these chops rather than buying them pre-cut on a polystyrene tray.

And don't forget the beautifully sweet meat of the shoulder, which can be boned and stuffed with olives, walnuts and lemon rind or cut into cubes for a stir-fry or curry. This will need less cooking than the cheaper cuts that need long, slow cooking in a crockpot. If young it suits spit-roasting as the fat keeps the meat moist during cooking. I use the neck, another sweet cut, for slow-cooking, putting it in the oven in the morning at the lowest of temperatures – add preserved lemons or Pickled Quinces (see page 316).

Just remember to cook spring lamb quickly at a high temperature and then let it rest, or seal and then cook at a very low temperature. Lamb should be served pink (and by that I don't mean raw); resist the temptation to overcook it as you will miss out on the taste sensations I have been talking about. Again, ask your butcher for cooking tips.

ROAST LEG OF SUFFOLK LAMB   *Serves 6*

1 × 3 kg leg lamb
3 sprigs rosemary, leaves picked
   and finely chopped
¼ cup (60 ml) extra virgin olive oil

3 cloves garlic, sliced lengthways into 4
2 tablespoons sea salt flakes
½ cup (125 ml) verjuice

Remove the lamb from the refrigerator 2 hours before cooking to allow it to come to room temperature. Preheat the oven to 180°C. Combine the rosemary and olive oil and then rub all over the lamb skin. Make 12 incisions in the skin evenly over the surface of the lamb and insert garlic slices. Rub liberally with salt.

Place the lamb in a roasting pan and roast for 30 minutes. Turn the oven down to 160°C. Turn the lamb leg over and cook for another 20 minutes. Turn the lamb leg over again and cook for another 30 minutes. Turn the oven off and leave the lamb in the oven for 30 minutes with the door ajar.

Remove from the oven, pour off the pan juices into a tall jug and refrigerate the juices to solidify the fat so it can be skimmed from the surface. Leave the lamb to rest in a warm place for another 30 minutes. Remove the fat from the juices, then place the pan juices and verjuice in a saucepan and reduce over high heat to serve as a jus.

Serve with a green olive tapenade and labna.

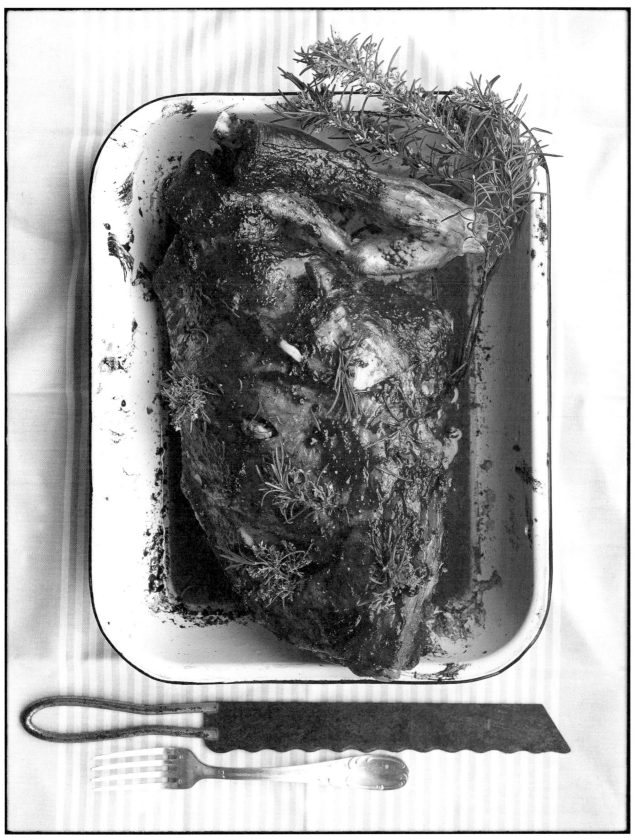

Roast leg of Suffolk lamb

LAMB SHOULDER POT-ROASTED WITH GARLIC
Serves 4

1.5 kg shoulder lamb

¼–⅓ cup (60–80 ml) extra virgin olive oil

3 sprigs rosemary

sea salt flakes and freshly ground
  black pepper

1 cup (250 ml) verjuice *or* white wine

4 heads garlic, separated into cloves
  but unpeeled

2 cups (500 ml) Golden Chicken Stock
  (see page 57)

chopped flat-leaf parsley, to serve

In a large heavy-based saucepan over low heat, brown the shoulder gently in the olive oil with the rosemary, and season. Pour off any excess oil and deglaze the pan with the verjuice or white wine with the heat turned up high. Add the garlic cloves and stock and bring to the boil. Cook, covered, on a very low heat for about 2 hours or until the meat is tender, turning occasionally. Be careful that the liquid doesn't evaporate, leaving the meat stuck to the bottom of the pan.

Remove the garlic cloves and cool before squeezing them out of their skins to serve alongside the lamb. Take the meat out of the pan and allow to rest, covered in foil, while you make the sauce. Skim the fat from the surface of the cooking liquid and heat, reducing a little. Garnish with chopped flat-leaf parsley and serve with mashed potatoes.

RACK OF LAMB WITH QUINCE GLAZE
Serves 2

2 × 4-rib racks of lamb

2 cloves garlic

½ teaspoon salt

3 sprigs rosemary, leaves picked

1 teaspoon quince paste

¼ cup (60 ml) verjuice

extra virgin olive oil, for cooking

Preheat the oven to 220°C. Ask the butcher to French-trim your racks of lamb, then wrap the exposed bones in foil to stop them burning. Using the flat side of a large knife, crush the garlic with a little salt to make a paste, then transfer it to a bowl. Add the rosemary, quince paste, 1 tablespoon of the verjuice and a little olive oil and stir to combine into a paste.

Massage the paste all over the lamb. Place the racks upright in a roasting pan and roast for 12–15 minutes for lamb still pink in the centre, or until cooked to desired doneness. If the verjuice and olive oil coat the entire surface of the meat, it should be sealed and caramelised in this time, but test by pushing a skewer into the fattest part of the meat. The skewer should feel warm to the touch and pink juices should be evident; if the skewer is still cool, then the meat is not cooked.

Remove lamb racks from the oven, turn them on their sides, then add another 2 tablespoons verjuice and a little more olive oil to the pan. Rest the lamb for 10 minutes before serving with garlicky mashed potatoes and pan juices.

PETER WALL'S LAMB, BARLEY AND CINNAMON CASSEROLE *Serves 4*

My friend Peter Wall has a special place in my life. He is the one who believed in my quest to make verjuice, and indeed made it possible. Peter loves to cook – I suspect as respite from a very cerebral life. Some thirty years ago it was Peter who taught me to make butter puff pastry and fondant, two things I'm sad to say I don't have the time to make these days. But our shared family meals continue, and it has become something of a tradition for Peter to cook for us that most welcome first meal after I return from business trips or holidays, as everyone knows that travel leaves you both tired and yearning for a home-cooked meal.

Peter served this absolutely melt-in-the-mouth dish of lamb and barley for one such meal after an exhausting trip to Dubai recently. We loved it so much that I cooked it for *The Cook and The Chef* program on the ABC.

This is a marriage of comfort food with fabulous flavour, and it is even better the second day, if you are strong-willed enough not to eat it all in one sitting.

extra virgin olive oil, for cooking

1 kg shoulder lamb, boned and cut into
    2.5 cm cubes (reserve the bones)

400 g pork belly, boned and cut into
    2 cm pieces

1 red onion, chopped

2 cloves garlic, crushed

100 ml red wine

2 tablespoons red-wine vinegar

1 × 410 g can tomatoes, chopped and
    juice reserved

2 cups (500 ml) Golden Chicken Stock
    (see page 57)

1 teaspoon black peppercorns

3 cm cinnamon stick

3–4 sprigs thyme

1 sprig rosemary

350 g pearl barley

salt

Preheat the oven to 125°C. Heat a little oil in a large frying pan over high heat, then add the lamb and seal on all sides. Transfer to a large flameproof casserole dish with a lid, along with the lamb bones. Add the pork to the frying pan and brown, then transfer to the casserole dish. Add a little more oil to the frying pan, then cook the onion and garlic over medium–high heat until browned and add to the meat.

Place the casserole over high heat, then deglaze the pan with the red wine and vinegar. Add the tomatoes and their juice, the chicken stock, spices and herbs. Place the covered casserole in the oven and cook for 3 hours, adjusting the heat if necessary to keep it simmering.

Meanwhile, cook the barley in a large saucepan of boiling salted water for 30–45 minutes or until tender, then drain. After the casserole has been in the oven for 3 hours, add the cooked barley, stir to combine, then cook for another hour. The barley will become almost like a risotto, taking up most of the juices in the dish.

Remove the cinnamon stick and serve.

BARBECUED LAMB CUTLETS

Serves 4

4 heads garlic

extra virgin olive oil, for cooking

4 double-cut lamb cutlets
   (2 bones in each cutlet)

1 clove garlic, thinly sliced

1 teaspoon finely chopped rosemary

sea salt flakes and freshly ground
   black pepper

Wrap the whole heads of garlic in foil, then cut in half widthways and brush the cut sides with olive oil. These will take about 20 minutes to cook on the barbecue, so you'll need to start them before the lamb.

Spike the lamb cutlets with slivers of garlic. Combine the rosemary with the barest trace of olive oil (so as not to flare the barbecue) then rub this mixture over the surface of the meat. Season with salt and pepper.

Place the cutlets on the barbecue, fat-edge down and seal well, then seal each side of the cutlet, turning often enough so the meat does not char. It will take about 12 minutes of cooking altogether. Rest the meat for 5–10 minutes before serving. Drizzle plenty of oil over the garlic head halves and serve alongside the meat.

ROAST SALTBUSH MUTTON

Serves 8–10

The fat content of mutton keeps the meat moist but makes it more susceptible to burning. It is important to watch that the juices do not burn in the bottom of the pan, as they will become bitter and taint the overall flavour. If this happens, you will need to change or clean the pan and return the meat to the oven for the balance of the cooking time.

1 cup (250 ml) port

1 × 3.5 kg leg saltbush mutton

extra virgin olive oil, for cooking

4 cloves garlic, thickly sliced

4 sprigs rosemary, leaves stripped

sea salt flakes and freshly ground
   black pepper

Preheat the oven to 180°C. Gently warm half the port in a small stainless steel saucepan over medium heat. Rinse the lamb under cold water, then dry it well and put it in a lightly oiled roasting pan. Cut tiny pockets into the meat, then poke garlic slices into them. Pour the warm port over the leg, scatter with the rosemary leaves, then season with salt and pepper.

Roast the leg for 2 hours, basting it with the pan juices every 30 minutes. Then warm the remaining port, pour it over the leg and return the meat to the oven for another 2½ hours.

Remove the meat from the oven and rest it, covered, for at least 20 minutes before carving.

LAMB RUMPS WITH FIG PASTE, ROCKET AND
PARMIGIANO REGGIANO SALAD

Serves 2–3

This is a dish that friend and former staff member Victoria Blumenstein liked to cook at the Farmshop, as much as anything to show off our fig paste.

3 quarters preserved lemon, flesh removed,
   rind rinsed and thinly sliced

⅓ cup (80 ml) verjuice

145 ml extra virgin olive oil

4 sprigs thyme

2 sprigs French tarragon

sea salt flakes and freshly ground
   black pepper

500 g milk-fed lamb rumps

200 g rocket

100 g fig paste, cut into 1 cm cubes

¼ cup (40 g) pine nuts

80 g Parmigiano Reggiano, shaved

Soak the preserved lemon in a mixture of 1 tablespoon verjuice and 1 tablespoon water for 30 minutes. To make the resting marinade, combine the remaining verjuice, ½ cup of the olive oil, thyme and tarragon in a glass or ceramic dish, and set aside.

Preheat the oven to 200°C. Season the lamb rumps with salt and pepper, then add the remaining olive oil to a frying pan and seal the rumps over low–medium heat. Transfer to a roasting pan and roast for 15–20 minutes or until cooked to your liking. Remove from the oven, transfer to the marinade and leave for 10–15 minutes.

Toss the rocket, fig paste, pine nuts, Parmigiano Reggiano and preserved lemon together in a bowl. Slice the lamb, then add to the rocket salad, along with a little of the resting juices. Toss gently to combine and serve immediately.

LAMB NECK WITH PRESERVED LEMON, GARLIC AND HERBS *Serves 4*

Although I have given the method for cooking this in a cast-iron casserole in the oven, when I cook this at home I often use a crockpot. For those who wish to do the same, preheat the crockpot on high while preparing the ingredients, then add the olive oil, onions, garlic and herbs and let them get a little colour if time allows. Add the lamb necks and quickly roll them in the onion mixture. Even though the lamb cooks well, the caramelisation of the skin is minimal, so the sealing of the meat with the herbs in a little olive oil before cooking adds greatly to the look and flavour of the dish. Add the preserved lemon, verjuice, stock and pepper, then turn the heat down to low and leave to cook. Eight hours later it's ready to eat. Separate the fat from the juices and then reduce to a sauce consistency; if desired, the olives can be added 10 minutes before the dish is ready to be served.

If you want to let this cook while you're out of the house, and think you may be away for as long as 12 hours, then simply leave out the first portion of cooking over high temperature. If you have any Pickled Quinces (see page 316), then two cored quarters of these added to the pot will go beautifully – the quince will disintegrate, but will add a great flavour.

I like to serve this with boiled waxy potatoes or pumpkin added to the juices. A pan of silverbeet (stalks and all) is a good balance for the rich sweetness of the dish.

⅓ cup (80 ml) extra virgin olive oil

4 onions, quartered

6 cloves garlic, peeled

2 sprigs rosemary

6 small fresh bay leaves

4 sprigs thyme

2 × 700 g lamb necks, each in one piece

2 quarters preserved lemon

100 ml verjuice

2 cups (500 ml) reduced Golden Chicken
 Stock (see page 57)

freshly ground black pepper

16 kalamata olives (optional), pitted

Preheat the oven to 180°C. Choose a cast-iron casserole with a tight-fitting lid that will just hold the lamb necks snugly. Heat the oil in the casserole, then add the onions, garlic and herbs and brown over high heat for a few minutes. Add the lamb necks and roll them to seal in the onion mixture. Add the preserved lemon, verjuice and stock and season with pepper.

Cook, covered, in the oven for 3–5 hours, depending on the quality of the lamb – older lamb will take longer. Skim the fat from the pan juices and reduce the sauce to the desired consistency. Add the olives, if using, then leave to rest for 10 minutes before serving.

BRAISED LAMB LEG WITH ROASTED ROOT VEGETABLES   *Serves 4*

2 cups (500 ml) verjuice

1 cup (250 ml) extra virgin olive oil,
     plus extra for drizzling

2 quarters preserved lemon,
     flesh removed, rind rinsed and diced

1 onion, roughly chopped

1 stick celery, roughly chopped

2 cloves garlic, roughly chopped

4 sprigs rosemary, leaves picked

4 fresh bay leaves

1 × 2.5 kg leg lamb with thigh bone removed

sea salt flakes and freshly ground
     black pepper

2 parsnips, peeled and halved

2 turnips, peeled and halved

1 celeriac, peeled and quartered

4 young carrots, peeled and halved

1 large fennel bulb, trimmed and quartered

1 cup (250 ml) lamb stock *or* Golden
     Chicken Stock (see page 57)

Make a marinade for the lamb by combining 250 ml of the verjuice, the olive oil, preserved lemon, onion, celery, garlic and herbs. Marinate the lamb in this mixture in the refrigerator overnight or for at least 8 hours.

Preheat the oven to 120°C. Place the lamb and marinade in a roasting pan and season. Slowly roast the lamb for 4 hours or until tender, occasionally basting with the marinade. Remove the lamb from the oven and rest it in a warm spot, then turn the oven up to 180°C.

Toss the remaining vegetables in olive oil and season to taste, then place in a shallow roasting pan and roast for about 20 minutes or until tender. Turn the oven temperature up to 200°C, then add the remaining verjuice to the vegetables and return to the oven for another 10 minutes, or until caramelised. Remove from the oven.

In a small saucepan, combine the stock with the juices from the lamb pan and reduce slightly over high heat to form a jus.

Serve the roast vegetables with the sliced lamb and a little jus.

MARINATED BUTTERFLIED LAMB LEG   *Serves 4*

I like to use milk-fed lamb for this recipe, as it is so tender and flavoursome. Ask your butcher to bone and butterfly your leg of lamb, so that it is a neat rectangular shape, or follow the instructions on page 654.

1 × 1.5 kg leg lamb, boned and butterflied

2 cloves garlic, sliced

¼ cup (60 ml) extra virgin olive oil

2 sprigs rosemary, leaves picked

freshly ground black pepper

verjuice, for sprinkling

4 fresh bay leaves

sea salt flakes

RESTING MARINADE

⅓ cup (80 ml) extra virgin olive oil

¼ cup (60 ml) verjuice

2 quarters preserved lemon, flesh removed,
     rind rinsed and finely chopped

3 golden shallots, finely sliced

¼ cup chopped flat-leaf parsley

freshly ground black pepper

Make incisions in the fat of the leg of lamb and insert slices of garlic. Combine the olive oil, rosemary and pepper and rub it well into the lamb in a flat ceramic dish. Sprinkle with verjuice and dot with bay leaves. Leave to marinate for several hours.

When you are ready to cook the meat, mix all the resting marinade ingredients together and pour into a dish large enough to hold the lamb. Set aside.

Preheat both the barbecue grill plate and flat plate to hot. Season the lamb with salt just before cooking. On the grill plate, seal the meat, skin-side down, until it caramelises. Depending on the heat of the grill, this may take a good 5 minutes. Reduce the heat of the flat plate to medium and seal the other side of the meat on the flat plate for 5 minutes. Continue turning the meat on the flat plate until it is cooked, being careful not to burn it; this will take 20–30 minutes, depending on the age of the lamb and how well done you like your meat. If the meat is cooking too fast, wrap it in foil after you have sealed both sides, and finish cooking it in a 180°C oven, if you prefer.

When the meat is cooked to your liking, slip it gently into the resting marinade (after removing the foil, if using) and leave it for a good 15 minutes, turning the meat once during this period.

Serve with sliced red onions grilled on the barbecue and tossed with a little vino cotto, extra virgin olive oil and chopped flat-leaf parsley.

STRAWBERRIES

I FIRST UNDERSTOOD HOW WONDERFUL STRAWBERRIES COULD be when I came across a grower, Bill Gray at Springton, who was so passionate about his produce that in the season he used to drive out to the Pheasant Farm Restaurant every second day to deliver his strawberries. I will never forget the perfume in my office, with 5 kg trays of the most beautiful ripe strawberries you could imagine sitting there. Left to ripen on the vine, then picked early in the morning and driven no more than 20 km, I was getting them at their best. Having them delivered so frequently meant that I never had to refrigerate them, and nothing masks their flavour more than being chilled and thereby picking up other 'fridge' smells; it also toughens their skins. Unfortunately, it got to the stage where people weren't prepared to pay the premium Bill needed to charge to cover the cost of picking the best fruit in perfect condition and, too far from interstate markets to benefit from them, he threw in the towel. The experience of Bill's strawberries has spoilt me forever, and I can no longer bring myself to buy strawberries in punnets of undeclared picking date, which have been refrigerated and come from who knows where.

Don't think big necessarily means sweet with strawberries (although it can). I am told the best strawberries in the world are the wild strawberries of Europe – the alpine strawberries, beach strawberries (actually found by the seashore in some parts of the continent) and forest strawberries (the French in particular are passionate about these *fraises des bois*). After 200 years of developing strawberry varieties, it is still these wild strawberries that are supreme in both taste and smell. They are very small and picked very ripe. Plants of alpine strawberries are available in Australia, in particular in South Australia and Victoria, but they have not proved viable for the fresh food market because the demand is for big, colourful fruit that will last.

Strawberry plants look so pretty in a garden, especially when planted along a path. When I had my own plants, I loved to pick a warm, ripe strawberry when arriving home

Moist buttermilk cake with strawberries (see page 669)

at night. The only trouble was that everyone in the family did the same thing, and we then had to buy strawberries from Bill to have enough to make a dessert. When we first moved to our cottage some years ago, all sorts of nooks and crannies were planted with strawberries. The fruit produced was not particularly large, I grant you, but the berries were always delicious, especially when picked and eaten straight from the garden. But then we were invaded by millipedes. After having too many mouthfuls of luscious strawberry spoiled by the skin-crawling crunch of a millipede, I gave up on my plants for many years. However, I have since found runners of smallish, intensely flavoured Japanese strawberries. They are so incredibly sweet it's almost sinful. I'm keen to try growing these, so have planted them in raised beds.

When buying strawberries, there are two things you must be on the lookout for. First, don't be seduced only by the size of the new season's fruit; second, develop a relationship with your greengrocer and find out on which days the strawberries are delivered. If you can get hold of strawberries that have been picked ripe and delivered without any chilling, you will be amazed by the difference in flavour.

How many times have you opened a punnet of strawberries that looked wonderful through the wrapping only to find mouldy berries at the base? The farmer is not trying to trick you; it's just that the fruit has been too long in the fridge. And that first act of chilling really dulls the flavour. However, leaving them out of the fridge also leads to mould.

Strawberries are not often marketed under varietal names, but the practice is increasing as the public becomes more discerning. With a little pressure it may well happen – especially now that more and more keen gardeners are checking out new varieties.

I am a keen but passive member of the Rare Fruit Society SA (www.rarefruit-sa.org.au) and always learn something from their newsletter. Mark Henley, the secretary, carried out trial plantings of six strawberry varieties all sourced through the Rare Fruit Society network. The trial was not without its problems – Mark had to play the 'guess-how-many-millipedes-can-get-into-one-strawberry' game, and had to deal with birds that could spot a strawberry within minutes of it ripening (or so it seemed).

The Aiberry, a bright-red (although not as deep-crimson as some), largish strawberry, won the trial hands down. Mark discovered he could pick this variety just before it was totally ripe and yet the berries were still full of flavour. Those that fully ripened were sweeter than any other he has tasted. Mental note – I must get him to taste my new plantings.

Next year, Mark plans to net the plants and tackle the millipedes whichever way he can. (Whilst I know that coffee grounds deter millipedes, I'm not sure what effect they have on beneficial insects.) He has also offered me runners to plant in May – perhaps one year I'll take the offer up.

Some years ago, a colleague, Di Holuigue, gave me a fascinating little book called *The Compleat Strawberry*, by Stafford Whiteaker. It gives the history of the strawberry and talks about how expensive a treat they were in days gone by. It also details their nutritional aspects. Apparently, strawberries contain large amounts of vitamin C and a high level of fructose, which is more easily assimilated by diabetics than any other type of sugar.

When you have strawberries in perfect condition there is nothing better than a big plateful with fresh cream – the definitive no-nonsense dessert. Another simple treat is to serve them unhulled on a dish with brown sugar and crème fraîche. An interesting accompaniment to strawberries is balsamic vinegar or vino cotto. This is particularly useful when the strawberries are less than perfectly ripe. To a 250 g punnet of strawberries, add 1–2 tablespoons balsamic vinegar or vino cotto to suit individual taste (balsamic vinegar varies in quality and age; the older it is, the more intense and syrupy it will be).

Strawberries can be used for so many desserts – strawberry shortcake, strawberry bread, strawberry tart, and as a filling for sponges. They can be used as a syrup, in a liqueur, as a sauce or a coulis, and to make jam or jellies. Strawberries can be teamed with other flavours such as rhubarb, oranges and raspberries. And pan-fried strawberries in nut-brown butter with freshly ground black pepper, a recipe my friend Ingo Schwartz taught me, really accentuates the strawberry flavour.

STRAWBERRY COULIS   *Makes 250 ml*

The amount of sugar should reflect the ripeness of the strawberries, so if you are using strawberries that are unripe, pour a little hot sugar syrup over them and leave for a few minutes before blending. To make sugar syrup, heat equal amounts of sugar and water until the sugar has dissolved – for 1 punnet of strawberries, ¼ cup of each should suffice. If you don't want to be bothered making such a small amount of syrup, 1 tablespoon of balsamic vinegar or vino cotto would also help bring out the flavour of the strawberries.

1 × 250 g punnet strawberries   **1 tablespoon castor sugar**

In a blender, purée strawberries and sugar together until liquid. Serve with ice cream or a fruit tart.

MOIST BUTTERMILK CAKE WITH STRAWBERRIES   *Serves 8*

This cake is very similar to one I made as a prize for a charity fund-raiser – a recipe written especially for the highest bidder. The concept was that the winner would choose the nature of the dish and at first I thought I'd bitten off more than I could chew, as the request was for a first birthday cake. How to make something so familiar different was more of a challenge for me, a person who hardly makes cakes at all, as I wanted it to be a cake that could possibly become a family tradition. I thought long and hard about it and, using my eldest granddaughter Zöe (who was seven at the time) as my critic, I cooked cake after cake for her approval. I sent the recipe on to the winner accompanied by a letter saying how I hoped that this was a cake that the child could make on their own, when they were old enough, and that it could grow as they grew, with different variations on a theme. »

The cake turned out to be such a hit with Zöe, who has a palate like mine and seldom eats cake, but I have altered it slightly to keep the exclusivity of the original recipe.

As, in my experience, everyone fights for the icing, I have been very generous with the quantity so it can be spread thickly over the cake.

butter, for greasing

vegetable oil spray, for greasing

1½ cups (225 g) self-raising flour

1½ teaspoons baking powder

¼ teaspoon salt

1 teaspoon pure vanilla extract

½ cup (125 ml) buttermilk,
   at room temperature

125 g unsalted butter, at room temperature

1¼ cups (275 g) sugar

2 large eggs, at room temperature

3 large egg yolks, at room temperature

finely grated rind of 2 lemons

⅓ cup (80 ml) extra virgin olive oil

really ripe strawberries, to serve

LEMON BUTTER ICING

100 g butter, softened

finely grated rind of 2 lemons

¼ cup (60 ml) lemon juice,
   plus extra to taste

2⅔ cups (430 g) icing sugar, sifted

Preheat the oven to 180°C. Grease an 18 cm cake tin with a little butter, then line with baking paper and lightly spray with vegetable oil.

Sift flour, baking powder and salt together into a bowl. In a separate bowl, add the vanilla extract to the buttermilk. Using an electric mixer, cream the butter on medium speed for 2–3 minutes or until pale, then, with the motor running, add the sugar in a steady stream. If the mixture is not well combined, scrape the sides of the bowl with a rubber spatula and mix for another 3 minutes.

Add the whole eggs, one at a time, and beat for 30 seconds after adding each one. Add the egg yolks, one at a time, and beat for 30 seconds after adding each one. Add the lemon rind, then pour in the oil and mix well with a rubber spatula. Fold in half of the flour mixture, then scrape the sides of the bowl and fold in half of the buttermilk mixture. Fold in the remaining flour, scraping the sides down well, then fold in the remaining buttermilk. Pour the batter into the prepared cake tin.

Bake for about 35 minutes or until the edges begin to come away from the sides of the tin. Cool in the tin for 15 minutes, then invert onto a cooling rack covered with baking paper. Peel the baking paper from the base of the cake, then turn, right-side up, onto another rack. Leave to cool before icing.

For the icing, add the lemon rind and juice and the icing sugar to the butter and stir to combine; add extra lemon juice to taste, as desired. Once the cake is cool, spread it thickly with the icing.

Alternatively, you can leave the cake un-iced and top with really ripe strawberries. It is wonderful sliced and served with a dollop of mascarpone.

DRIED STRAWBERRY BRIOCHE   *Serves 6*

When our daughter Saskia was in her late teens, we bought her a food dehydrator, as she was interested in pursuing her own food production business. Her first effort was dehydrated strawberries, and this marvellous recipe resulted from our wondering what on earth we were going to use them for. Saskia has now gone on to run her own food production business, as well as a catering business with our younger daughter Elli. I wonder if this dehydrator started it all?

1 cup dried strawberries	3 large free-range eggs, beaten
orange liqueur, for soaking	185 g unsalted butter
¼ cup (60 ml) lukewarm water	
7 g dried yeast (or 15 g fresh yeast)	GLAZE
3 teaspoons sugar	1 free-range egg
220 g plain flour	reserved strawberry soaking liquid
1 teaspoon salt	

Place the strawberries in a bowl and cover with orange liqueur to reconstitute.

Pour the lukewarm water into a small bowl and add the yeast and 1 teaspoon of the sugar. Set aside until the yeast dissolves.

Put the flour, remaining 2 teaspoons sugar and the salt into a large bowl and add the yeast mixture and the eggs. Mix by hand, squeezing and pulling the dough upwards, until it becomes elastic. This should take about 20 minutes.

Divide the butter into 6 even pieces and, again using your hands, incorporate the butter into the dough piece by piece. Each new piece should be added only when the last has been absorbed. The dough will be sticky but should retain its elasticity.

Place the dough in a clean bowl, cover with a tea towel and set aside in a draught-free area for about 4 hours to triple its bulk. This is a rich dough that does not need to be in a warm area in order to rise, so if the butter starts to melt and the dough looks oily, place it in the refrigerator from time to time.

Turn the dough onto a lightly floured work surface and shape it into a rectangle. Strain the excess liquid from the strawberries, reserving the liquid, and spread them over the dough. Fold the dough into three, as if you were making puff pastry, then press out again, and again fold it into three. Put the dough back into the bowl, cover, and leave it for about 1½ hours, until it has doubled in volume.

Shape the dough into a round and place it on a plate in the refrigerator for 30 minutes, to make the dough firm enough to shape.

Grease a loaf tin, shape the dough into a sausage and place it in the tin. Set it aside until the dough has doubled in volume (about 1½ hours).

Preheat the oven to 240°C. Make the glaze by beating the egg with the reserved strawberry soaking liquid, then brush over the top of the loaf. Bake for 15 minutes, then reduce the temperature to 200°C and bake for another 30 minutes. Cool on a wire rack.

VEAL

IN MY FIRST FORMAL ITALIAN LESSON, WHEN I ATTEMPTED IN vain to learn the language before my planned cooking school with Stephanie Alexander in Tuscany, the discussion was, of course, about food. 'Italians love to eat veal as they don't like strongly flavoured meat,' my teacher said, which took me aback. I certainly knew they loved veal but I also knew the Italians were just as passionate about game – and what could be stronger in flavour than that?

Don't think of veal as bland, though. It relies on its sweetness and moisture to be special, and can be married with strong Mediterranean flavours – just check your favourite Italian cookbooks for ideas.

In 1995, on my first long stint in Italy, I discovered that eating in local restaurants was not always the paradise I imagined it to be. I should have learnt to stop after the antipasto and pasta, which is fantastic even in the most modest establishments. For my taste, the following meat course was often a disappointment, as I found it overcooked. The exceptions were my beloved offal, and veal. After a while I learnt to play it safe and order a simple piece of pan-fried veal with lemon and sometimes rosemary.

There are several suppliers of milk-fed veal across Australia, but it's a very specialist product and not that easy to obtain, since most butchers sell yearling beef in place of true veal. There is a huge difference between the two, as milk-fed veal is moist, sweet and delicate; to me, yearling occupies a tasteless middle ground between this and the aged beef I like from a mature animal. 'Bobby veal', from unwanted dairy calves, makes a better and easily affordable alternative to yearling.

Milk-fed veal can be fed either mother's milk or formula, but the formula-fed calf takes longer to reach the desired weight than a calf fed by its mother. Age is not so much of an issue with veal as the beast does not have to be tiny for its meat to be tender. The best veal I have ever eaten was at Stephanie's Restaurant during the winter of 1996. I had an enormous veal chop that almost overflowed the plate and was at least a couple of centimetres thick. It was so sweet and succulent I could hardly believe it. I now know that the veal was supplied by Vince and Anne Garreffa's White Rocks Veal in Western Australia, which is still available through Mondo di Carne (www.mondo.net.au). Although White Rocks Veal is a year-round product, most of the choice cuts are pre-sold to a select number of top restaurants. This veal is of a truly amazing quality, so if you ever find yourself in a restaurant where it is on the menu, I recommend that you go for it!

It came as no surprise to me to hear that a young Italian butcher in Myrtleford in Victoria's Ovens Valley is providing veal almost the colour of rabbit (I presume it is milk-fed). There is such a strong Italian community around Myrtleford that many traditions have been kept alive. The Ovens Valley International Festival celebrates this cultural richness in October every second year – a showcase of regional food with a strong Italian influence, which is second to none in Australia to my knowledge.

If you want to give the real thing a go, the best value for money are the leg primals, the muscles that can be cut for quick pan-frying: rump, silverside, round and topside. Slice the meat thinly and give it a little slap with a wooden mallet to tenderise it, then pan-fry it in butter with rosemary, salt, freshly ground black pepper and a squeeze of lemon juice, for a taste of just how delicious veal can be (see page 676).

Veal should be cooked pink but, surprisingly, given the young age of the animal, larger pieces of meat need long, slow cooking to be tender, rather than the fast cooking you might associate with beef or lamb.

A great cut of veal and the most economical of all, other than the shanks, is the shoulder. Cooking on the bone is always best, as it provides sweetness, but there are times when the convenience of carving at the table takes over, and this is one of them. Boned shoulder rolled with a well-seasoned, very moist stuffing (there is so little fat content that you have to work at keeping the moisture in veal) is wonderful and very versatile. Try stuffing the meat with lots of onion sweated in extra virgin olive oil, chopped herbs, bread soaked in milk, and chopped anchovies before rolling and tying it up with string. Rub the shoulder with extra virgin olive oil, rosemary and freshly ground black pepper and wrap it in caul fat to be extra sure that the meat will remain moist. Add a little water to the roasting pan so the juices don't burn during cooking. Cook at 180°C for 20 minutes, then reduce the temperature to 160°C and cook for a further 1½–2 hours – the water and juices will produce a lovely syrupy glaze in the bottom of the pan.

You could add sorrel to the same stuffing, or instead of anchovies, try including a few pitted black olives that have been marinated in a little extra virgin olive oil with grated orange rind and chopped oregano in the stuffing, then rub the shoulder with oregano, olive oil and freshly ground black pepper before roasting.

A leg of veal can of course be prepared and cooked in much the same way. Make pockets to hold the stuffing and use a large piece of caul fat to wrap the leg and hold the stuffing in place. The cooking time will be shorter if you leave the bone in as it acts as a heat conductor – it could make as much as half an hour's difference if cooked at the same temperature as the shoulder.

I love pot-roasting veal shanks. Season and gently brown two shanks on top of the stove in extra virgin olive oil with oregano or rosemary in an enamelled cast-iron casserole and set them aside. Separate a head of garlic, then sauté the cloves in their skins in the same casserole, adding a little more olive oil if necessary. Add wedges of preserved lemon and cook until the garlic begins to soften a little. Deglaze the pan with white wine or verjuice, then add some veal or chicken stock. Return the meat to the casserole, then cover it with a tight-fitting lid and bake in the oven at 180°C for 30 minutes. Turn the shanks over and see if they need any more stock. Turn the oven down to 120°C and cook for another hour, then check the level of the stock and test whether the meat is nearly done – the shanks are ready when the meat begins to come away from the bone and a gelatinous syrup has formed. (Larger shanks may need another 30 minutes.) You could also add a handful of sorrel to the pan in the last 10 minutes of cooking – it will become a purée and add another dimension to the sauce.

The Pheasant Farm Restaurant menu often featured two rather extravagant veal 'sand-wiches'. For the first, I deep-fried long, thin slices of eggplant in extra virgin olive oil and then drained them and lightly dressed them with more of the oil, basil, balsamic vinegar, salt and freshly ground black pepper. I then made an aïoli, thick and luscious but with a good bit of lemon juice in it. Next I pan-fried several thin pieces of veal in nut-brown butter. The veal, eggplant (with dressing and basil) and aïoli were layered, finishing with veal and eggplant. A handful of rocket was served alongside, 'dressed' by the juices that oozed out over the plate. Sometimes we would spoon a little of this jus over the top of the sandwich so that it mingled with the dressing and the aïoli.

The second we served in autumn, when we would sauté fresh figs and slices of meyer lemon in lots of butter and freshly ground black pepper and pan-fry the veal with rosemary. Assembled the same way as the other 'sandwich', this dish was served with a lemon mayonnaise and rocket.

I remember the first time I made *vitello tonnato*. It was quite an occasion, since it used to be almost impossible to get proper veal, and this was also the first time I'd found good capers. For once in my life I followed a recipe to the letter and, thrilled with the outcome, I put the dish on the menu. There were no instructions for carving the veal in the Italian cookbook I was using, so I followed my instincts and preference for generosity. The result was a plate of quite hearty slices of succulent veal that I thought a triumph, blanketed as they were by the tuna mayonnaise. The first customer to try it was something of an Italophile, and condescendingly sent a message back to the kitchen saying the *vitello tonnato* was incorrect as the meat should have been thinly sliced. My confidence was bruised somewhat, but I heeded the advice and used thinly sliced veal from then on, with great success.

VITELLO TONNATO   *Serves 6*

I first came across this method for cooking *vitello tonnato* in Ada Boni's *Italian Regional Cooking*, and the following recipe is my adaptation of it. Poaching the veal the day before will really enhance the flavours. The trick to making the mayonnaise for this dish is to first make it super-thick by adding the oil very slowly, so that when you add the puréed mixture, it thins it to the right consistency.

While I've recommended using tinned Italian tuna here, I'm always hopeful that we'll soon see good-quality Australian tuna in olive oil on our supermarket shelves.

2 × 350 g pieces nut of veal

1 onion, finely chopped

2 × 95 g tins Italian tuna in olive oil, drained

2 fresh bay leaves

1 × 45 g tin of anchovies, drained

2 tablespoons capers

1 cup (250 ml) extra virgin olive oil

1½ cups (375 ml) verjuice *or* dry white wine

2 hard-boiled egg yolks

1 egg yolk

sea salt flakes and freshly ground
   black pepper

squeeze of lemon juice

1 lemon, thinly sliced

12 tiny cornichons (see Glossary)

Put the veal into a heavy-based saucepan or enamelled cast-iron casserole just large enough to take all the ingredients, so as to minimise the amount of liquid required. Cover the veal with the onion, tuna, bay leaves, 2 anchovy fillets and half of the capers. Tip in 75 ml of the olive oil, the verjuice or dry white wine and up to 375 ml water, adding just enough liquid to immerse the veal during cooking. Bring to a simmer, then cover, reduce the heat to low and cook at a gentle simmer for 1 hour (control the heat by using a simmer mat if necessary). Remove the pan from the heat and allow the meat to cool completely in its juices.

Once cooled, remove the meat and set aside, discarding the bay leaves. Strain the cooking liquid, reserving both the solids and liquid. Purée the solids with 250 ml of the strained cooking liquid using a sieve or food mill (or blend it in a food processor and then sieve it). Set aside. Reserve the remaining strained liquid to use as a light stock when making a risotto.

Using a mortar and pestle, smash the hard-boiled egg yolks to a paste with a dash of lemon juice, then add the raw egg yolk (this could also be done carefully in a food processor). Slowly add the remaining olive oil drop by drop, incorporating it into the mixture as you go, then add 250 ml of the sieved sauce. Check for seasoning and acidity, adding more lemon juice if required.

Slice the veal very thinly, making sure you cut across the grain, and overlap the slices on a platter like roof tiles. Cover the meat with the mayonnaise, then arrange the remaining anchovies, cut into strips, in a criss-cross pattern and place the remaining capers in the centre of each 'diamond'. Serve at room temperature with thinly sliced lemon and cornichons. If made the day before and refrigerated, then removed from the fridge to come to room temperature, the flavour of this dish will be enhanced.

VEAL PAN-FRIED WITH ROSEMARY AND LEMON *Serves 4*

8 thin slices veal, cut from the leg (about 500 g)	sea salt flakes and freshly ground black pepper
100 g butter	75 g (½ cup) plain flour
2 tablespoons rosemary leaves	1½ tablespoons lemon juice
extra virgin olive oil, for cooking	

Gently pat the veal with a wooden mallet. Heat half the butter in a frying pan with half the rosemary and cook gently over low heat until the butter is nut-brown, adding a splash of extra virgin olive oil to inhibit burning, then remove from the heat for a moment. Season the flour, then dust the veal with it and shake off the excess.

Adjust the heat to medium, return the pan to the heat and cook 2 slices of veal at a time so that the meat doesn't poach rather than fry. Gently seal for about a minute, then flip over and seal the other side. Remove the veal from the pan and keep it warm while you cook the next 2 slices of meat, then deglaze the pan with half the lemon juice and tip the

Vitello tonnato (see page 675)

juices over the resting meat. Cook the remaining rosemary with the balance of the butter until the butter is nut-brown, add some olive oil as previously, then pan-fry the next 2 batches of veal. Deglaze the pan with the last of the lemon juice and, using a spatula, add the contents of the pan to the resting veal. Serve the veal immediately, with the pan juices, a salad of bitter greens and a dish of steaming mashed potato.

CALF'S LIVER WITH SAGE

Serves 2

I'm such an offal freak that I can't bear not to include a liver dish here, even if this chapter is about veal. To my mind, veal or calf's liver is the best part of the animal. In the early days of the restaurant I was told that sweetbreads and calf's liver were either exported or taken home by the abattoir workers. Things have changed somewhat but it's still quite difficult to get fresh calf's liver: find a passionate butcher, order it in advance and make sure you cook it the day it comes in.

30 sage leaves
100 g butter
sea salt flakes and freshly ground
    black pepper

plain flour, for dusting
6 thin slices calf's liver (about 250 g)
dash good balsamic vinegar *or*
    vino cotto (see Glossary), optional

Cook the sage leaves and butter over low heat in a frying pan until the butter is nut-brown. Season the flour, then dust the liver with it. Gently cook 2 slices of liver at a time for about 1 minute, then flip them over and seal the other side. Keep the cooked liver warm while you seal the next batch. Make sure that the butter remains nut-brown and the sage leaves are crisp but not burnt – you may need to adjust the temperature. Pour off any excess butter and, if desired, deglaze the pan with a splash of balsamic vinegar or vino cotto. Serve the liver and sage leaves immediately, along with any pan juices.

VINE LEAVES

WHILE I NOW HAVE A BIT OF A THING FOR WRAPPING FOOD IN vine leaves, I regret the years of lost opportunity when I didn't use them for this purpose. I have had masses of vine leaves at my disposal since we moved to the Barossa in 1973 but my dislike of dolmades, with their tea-leaf flavour and rice filling, kept me away from them.

It was, in fact, my first trip to Bali in the mid-1980s that turned me around. There I delighted in fish wrapped in banana leaves with fragrant spices. I tried to grow a banana palm on my return home, against every law of nature considering our Mediterranean climate, but as it was just the leaf I was after I thought it worth taking a chance. It didn't work. I then became similarly intrigued by lotus leaves after an amazing meal cooked by Phillip Searle, then at Oasis Seros, at the fourth Symposium of Gastronomy in Sydney. He had stuffed boned quail with lots of bone marrow, pancetta and black rice flavoured with strangely piquant yet desirable fish sauce (it was so sticky and unctuous I can taste it now), then wrapped them in lotus leaves. He rolled out a piece of clay and made individual sarcophagi for the quail, which he then baked.

However, I finally gave in to the climate and gave up my ideas of the exotic. Vine leaves are now indispensable to me – and I can't understand my earlier rejection of them. Sometimes life can be so busy that you don't see or appreciate the wealth around you, even if you're food-obsessed like me. It was, for example, my friend Stephanie Alexander, who has taught me so much over the years through her writing, her cooking and, even better, her visits, who suggested I tried blanching vine tendrils early in the season to add an almost asparagus-like flavour to salads (pumpkin tendrils are also worthy of the same treatment, I've since discovered). I had never thought to use these before – yet, like vine leaves, they were quite literally on my doorstep. And I now know that it's all in the way you prepare them – the 'tea leaf' taste I hated so much about vine leaves can be easily avoided.

I use fresh young leaves in the spring just as they are. Most cookbooks suggest you blanch fresh vine leaves in water before use, but this isn't necessary if you have access to very young leaves (always assuming the vigneron isn't berating you for pinching too much of the canopy). Just wash them to remove any sprays and wrap them around the food as they are. Although I love the principle of putting produce aside to use in the winter, I have to admit that I never manage to preserve my own vine leaves for long-term storage. I keep a jar of vine leaves preserved in brine or vacuum-packed vine leaves as a backup, but these do require a fair bit of soaking to rid them of excess salt.

I thought of using wine for cooking older leaves in, then I extended the idea and cooked both the leaves and tendrils in verjuice. They were exquisite! My first experiment with vine leaves cooked in verjuice featured tiny yabbies from our dam. They were too small to make a significant dish – there had been a drought for several years and the yabbies had not grown to any size – so I cooked and peeled them, then wrapped each in a vine leaf and pan-fried them quickly in nut-brown butter. Served with a glass of four-year-old Barossa semillon, these were a heady combination.

Cooking vine leaves in verjuice is an easy way to preserve them for short-term storage. All you need do is bring verjuice to the boil and slip the leaves in, one at a time. Young leaves will take about a minute, while older leaves may take up to 3 minutes. Once they are poached, store them in a glass container and tip in fresh verjuice to cover them. The leaves lose their vibrant green colour but make up for it in flavour. The pH level of verjuice is not as low as that of vinegar but I have still found it suitable for keeping the vine leaves, refrigerated, for several months. The addition of a little salt, sprinkled between the leaves, would be an extra precaution. The verjuice-poached leaves, drained and dried, can be dotted with butter and baked at 220°C for 2 minutes to crisp up just like a sage leaf. I serve these alongside grilled quail.

I have now tackled dolmades again, and have come up with a simplified version that will probably make traditionalists tut-tut. I suggest you cook the rice the way you like it and then add your favourite flavourings. The Moorish influence found in Sicilian cooking suits me best of all: rice with lots of caramelised onion, currants, pine nuts, preserved lemon and fennel fronds or mint leaves. Wrap a little of the rice in each blanched vine leaf, then put the bundles into a dish, brush them with extra virgin olive oil and they're ready to eat – with none of the cooking that traditional dolmades require! As I prefer these 'dolmades' served warm, I put the dish into a 180°C oven for about 10 minutes.

Wrapping vine leaves around small game birds for grilling or baking is a very traditional practice in Italy and France, and is particularly successful with quail, partridge and baby chicken, as the leaves are just the right size to protect the breast. Small fish, such as red mullet or fresh sardines, are great done this way too. Brush the parcels with olive oil and squeeze some lemon juice over before grilling for just a few minutes for sardines, and up to 6 minutes for red mullet (if baking, do so at 230°C for a similar length of time). Grilling will render the leaves more brittle but the contents will still be protected and the leaves, though charred, will be edible. I love the smoky, grapey flavour the leaves impart.

You don't have to limit yourself to using small fish or fowl with vine leaves, however. You can also wrap a boned and stuffed chicken or a large fish. Arrange a 'sheet' of blanched vine leaves, overlapped like roof tiles, then carefully wrap it around the chicken or fish. If you are using fish and grapes are in season, try stuffing the cavity with seedless green grapes, breadcrumbs, lots of fresh herbs, and onion sweated until almost caramelised. A 3 kg fish may take 35 minutes to cook at 220°C, while a large boned fowl (say 2.5 kg) will take 45–55 minutes – both need to be turned halfway through the cooking.

CULTIVATED MUSHROOMS IN VINE LEAVES WITH VERJUICE *Serves 6*

The original inspiration for this dish was a recipe in Elizabeth David's *An Omelette and a Glass of Wine*. I served this dish in the restaurant as an accompaniment to rabbit in particular, when wild mushrooms were not in season and I wanted to add an earthiness to the dish that cultivated mushrooms couldn't provide. Vine leaves give a wonderful dimension to these mushrooms – it is as if you have picked your own from the paddock. My version uses vine leaves blanched in verjuice.

6 cloves garlic

150 ml extra virgin olive oil

200 ml verjuice

12 fresh young vine leaves

300 g (about 12) flat cultivated mushrooms

sea salt flakes and freshly ground
   black pepper

Preheat the oven to 200°C. In a small frying pan, slowly caramelise the garlic cloves in 1 tablespoon of the olive oil over low heat. Bring the verjuice to the boil in an enamelled or stainless steel saucepan, then blanch the vine leaves by immersing them one at a time into the hot liquid, then drain well. Reserve the verjuice.

Line a small ovenproof dish with 6 of the vine leaves. Drizzle with a little more of the olive oil, then arrange a layer of mushrooms, followed by the garlic, a pinch of salt and a turn of the pepper grinder, then another drizzle of the oil. Add another layer of mushrooms and repeat the procedure. Top with the remaining vine leaves and drizzle over the last of the olive oil. Bake for 25 minutes. While still hot, drizzle 2 tablespoons of the reserved verjuice over the dish to create a vinaigrette. Both the leaves and the mushrooms are eaten – and any leftovers are very good refrigerated for the next day.

VINE LEAVES FILLED WITH GOAT'S CHEESE AND WALNUTS   *Serves 4*

You can grill these on the barbecue or chargrill plate as an alternative to baking.

12 shelled walnuts

200 ml verjuice

12 fresh young vine leaves

2 tablespoons flat-leaf parsley leaves

300 g fresh goat's cheese

walnut oil, for brushing

sea salt flakes and freshly ground
   black pepper

Preheat the oven to 220°C. Dry-roast the walnuts on a baking tray for 6–8 minutes, then rub off their skins with a clean tea towel. Bring the verjuice to the boil in an enamelled or stainless steel saucepan, blanch the vine leaves by immersing them one at a time into the hot liquid, then drain well. Reserve the verjuice.

Roughly chop the walnuts and parsley and mix them into the goat's cheese. Form the cheese into a log (if too soft, refrigerate it to firm it up a bit). Cut the log into 12 even pieces and wrap each in a vine leaf. Brush each parcel with walnut oil, then season and bake for 4 minutes to warm the goat's cheese. Make a vinaigrette with walnut oil and some of the reserved verjuice and spoon it over the warmed parcels. Serve with crusty bread.

GLOSSARY

Wherever possible, I've explained any less familiar ingredients and techniques in the relevant recipes, but I've also included brief notes here on some ingredients and procedures that are used throughout the book.

Arborio rice

What distinguishes this pearly-white, short-grained rice is the amount of starch it releases during cooking, and it is this starch that makes a risotto creamy. Arborio rice should be cooked until it is *al dente*, which takes about 20 minutes, depending on the quality of the rice.

Blind baking

Baking a pastry case 'blind', or without its filling, helps to stop the filling from making the pastry soggy. Lining the pastry case with foil and holding it down with pastry weights prevents the pastry case from rising and losing its shape as it cooks. Special pastry weights are available at kitchenware shops, but dried beans work just as well.

Cartouche

This French term refers to a paper cover that is placed directly onto the contents of a pan or casserole to help retain moisture during or after cooking. To make a simple cartouche, take a square piece of baking paper slightly larger than your pan. Fold the square in half and in half again, then fold it diagonally to make a fan shape. Hold the pointed end of the fan to the centre of your pan, then tear or cut off any paper that extends beyond the outside edge of the pan. Open out the paper to reveal your cartouche – a disc of paper that will fit snugly over the contents of the pan.

Caul fat (*crépine*)

This is the lining of a pig's stomach, and can be used to wrap cuts of meat or delicate food such as kidneys before baking or pan-frying, to help retain moisture and add flavour.

You'll need to order caul fat in advance from your butcher.

Cheese

see Gorgonzola; Labna; Parmigiano Reggiano

Chocolate

The flavour of chocolate is determined by the amounts of chocolate liquor and cocoa solids it contains.

Bitter chocolate has the highest percentage of cocoa liquor and no added sugar, so it has a strong chocolate flavour, which adds depth to savoury dishes.

A good bittersweet chocolate may contain 65–70 per cent cocoa solids, and the best even more. Because it has sugar added, it is mostly used for sweet dishes – or eating.

Couverture chocolate is the name given to high-quality chocolate that melts well and dries to a glossy finish, making it perfect for covering cakes and for making fine desserts. It can also be used in any recipe calling for chocolate, since its high cocoa butter content gives it a fine flavour and texture.

Cocoa

There are two types of unsweetened cocoa powder: natural and Dutch-processed. The latter is treated with an alkali to neutralise its acids, giving it a gentler and more rounded flavour. It is available from delicatessens and specialty food shops.

Cornichons

Cornichons are tiny, crisp gherkins pickled in the French manner: picked when they are 3–8 cm long, and pickled in vinegar or brine. They are crunchy and salty, and are perfect to serve with rillettes, pâtés or terrines, to accompany a charcuterie plate, or as part of a ploughman's lunch.

Cream

In Australia, most cows are kept to produce milk rather than cream, so the fat content of their milk needs to be supplemented at various times of the year to bring it up to the 35 per cent fat content that is needed for pure cream. With nothing else added, this cream is good for enriching sauces.

Any cream labelled 'thickened cream' also has a thickener such as gelatine added. Because of the extra stability that the thickener provides, this is the best cream for whipping – just remember that reduced-fat thickened cream (with around 18 per cent fat) cannot be whipped successfully.

Double cream is very rich, with a fat content of 45–60 per cent. Some of the thicker ones are perfect for spooning alongside a dessert. Try to find farmhouse versions that have been separated from unhomogenised milk.

Flour

Strong flour, also known as bread flour or baker's flour, is my staple flour. What differentiates strong flour is its high gluten content, which allows dough to stretch rather than break during kneading and rolling, making it particularly suitable for making pasta and bread. The gluten in strong flour also helps to ensure an extensive and even rise in bread.

Flours are further classified according to the percentage of wheat grain present. Wholemeal flour contains the whole grain, and so has a wonderful nutty taste, while brown flour contains about 85 per cent of the grain and white flour between 75 and 80 per cent. The flour industry is moving to predominantly unbleached flour; bleached flour must be specially requested. I prefer unbleached flour as it contains slightly more nutrients; it also has a more robust texture, which works well in breads and pizza bases.

Self-raising flour is plain flour with baking powder and salt added during the milling process, in the proportions of about 1¼ teaspoons of baking powder and a pinch of salt for every cup of flour. It is used for making pancakes, cakes and muffins.

Gelatine

Gelatine leaves have a better flavour and texture than powdered gelatine. However, confusion can arise from the fact that the gelling strength of gelatine leaves is measured by their 'bloom' rather than their weight. All my recipes have been developed using Alba brand Gold-strength leaves, which weigh 2 g each and have a bloom of 190–220 g.

As gelatine will set more firmly over time, you may be able to use less gelatine if you can make the jelly the day before it is needed. A couple of other things to note: gelatine takes twice as long to dissolve in cream or milk as it does in water; and sugar can inhibit setting, so the higher the sugar content, the softer the set will be.

Gorgonzola

This Italian blue cheese comes in sweet (*dolce*) and spicy (*piccante*) versions. Gorgonzola dolce is soft and ripe, with a creamy, spreadable texture. Gorgonzola piccante is earthier in flavour, firmer, and has a more powerful aroma, having been washed repeatedly in brine during its year or more of cave-ageing.

Labna

Also referred to as yoghurt cheese, labna in its purest form is simply thick drained yoghurt. You can make it yourself by stirring 5 g salt into 500 ml plain yoghurt (the kind with no pectin, gums or other stabilisers) then placing it in a sieve lined with muslin or a clean Chux and leaving it to drain for at least 4 hours or overnight – the longer you leave it, the thicker it will get. Commercial labna is tart and tangy: some versions are thick enough to hold up a spoon, while others are more like soft sour cream.

Oils

As you will probably have gathered by now, I use extra virgin olive oil liberally in my cooking, and consider it vital to my food – and, indeed, my life. The only other oils I occasionally use are nut oils to flavour a salad dressing, and refined grape-seed oil in dishes where a more neutral-flavoured oil is desirable, such as in desserts, or to combine with extra virgin olive oil when making mayonnaise, to avoid a bitter after-taste.

Parmigiano Reggiano

Authentic aged parmesan cheese made in Italy according to specific traditional practices, Parmigiano Reggiano is my first choice for use in risottos, polenta, soups, and sauces such as pesto. I also love it as part of a cheese board or freshly shaved in salads. Grana Padano has a similar flavour to Parmigiano Reggiano, but has not been aged for as long, so can be a useful, less expensive alternative.

Pastry weights *see* Blind baking

Rice *see* Arborio rice

Sterilising jars and bottles

To sterilise jars that are to be used for storing or preserving food, wash the jars and lids in hot, soapy water, then rinse them in hot water and place them in a 120°C oven for approximately 15 minutes to dry out. This method also works for bottles.

Sugar syrup

Sugar syrup is a simple solution of 1 part sugar dissolved in 1–2 parts water (depending on its intended use) over low heat. It is great to have on hand if you are keen on whipping up your own cocktails at home!

Tomato sugo and passata

These dense, slow-cooked tomato sauces originate from Italy. They are usually made with just tomatoes, but herbs and spices may also be added. Sugo is coarser as it is made from chopped tomatoes, whereas the tomatoes for passata are sieved, making it more like a purée. Both can be used in soups, stews, sauces, or any other dish where a tomato flavour is desired, but without the texture or acidity of fresh tomatoes.

Vino cotto

Literally meaning 'cooked wine' in Italian, this traditional Italian preparation is made by simmering unfermented grape juice until it is reduced to a syrup. The one I produce is finished with traditional red-wine vinegar to make it truly *agrodolce* (sweet–sour). With a much softer flavour than vinegar, vino cotto can be used to make sauces for meat or salad dressings or even drizzled over strawberries. In fact, it can be used anywhere you would normally use balsamic vinegar.

Cooking

Palate   Pellegrini

Jane Grigson's Fruit Book   MICHAEL JOSEPH

stephanie alexander   Stephanie's Journal

MADELEINE KAMMAN   In Madeleine's Kitchen

ELIZABETH DAVID · SUMMER COOKING

THE GREAT WOMEN CHEFS OF

BEAUTI LEATH

PELLEGRINI   The Food Lover's GARDEN

BIBLIOGRAPHY

Alexander, Stephanie, *The Cook's Companion* (2nd edition), Lantern, Melbourne, 2004.

—— *Cooking and Travelling in South-West France*, Viking, Melbourne, 2002.

—— *Stephanie's Journal*, Viking, Melbourne, 1999.

—— *Stephanie's Seasons*, Allen & Unwin, Sydney, 1993.

—— *Stephanie's Australia*, Allen & Unwin, Sydney, 1991.

—— *Stephanie's Feasts and Stories*, Allen & Unwin, Sydney, 1988.

—— *Stephanie's Menus for Food Lovers*, Methuen Haynes, Sydney, 1985.

Alexander, Stephanie and Beer, Maggie, *Stephanie Alexander & Maggie Beer's Tuscan Cookbook*, Viking, Melbourne, 1998.

Anderson, Ronald, *Gold on Four Feet*, Ronald Anderson, Melbourne, 1978.

Andrews, Colman, *Catalan Cuisine*, Headline, London, 1989.

The Barossa Cookery Book, Soldiers' Memorial Institute, Tanunda, 1917.

Beck, Simone, *Simca's Cuisine*, Vintage Books, New York, 1976.

Beck, Simone, Bertholle, Louisette and Child, Julia, *Mastering the Art of French Cooking, Volume One*, Penguin, Harmondsworth, 1979.

Beer, Maggie, *Maggie's Table*, Lantern, Melbourne, 2005.

—— *Cooking with Verjuice*, Penguin, Melbourne, 2003.

—— *Maggie's Orchard*, Viking, Melbourne, 1997.

—— *Maggie's Farm*, Allen & Unwin, Sydney, 1993.

Beeton, Mrs, *Mrs Beeton's Book of Household Management*, Cassell, London, 2000.

—— *Family Cookery*, Ward Lock, London, 1963.

Bertolli, Paul with Waters, Alice, *Chez Panisse Cooking*, Random House, New York, 1988.

Bissell, Frances, *A Cook's Calendar: Seasonal Menus by Frances Bissell*, Chatto & Windus, London, 1985.

Boddy, Michael and Boddy, Janet, *Kitchen Talk Magazine* (vol. I, no's 1–13), The Bugle Press, via Binalong, NSW, 1989–92.

Boni, Ada, *Italian Regional Cooking*, Bonanza Books, New York, 1969.

von Bremzen, Anya and Welchman, John, *Please to the Table: The Russian Cookbook*, Workman, New York, 1990.

Bureau of Resource Sciences, *Marketing Names for Fish and Seafood in Australia*, Department of Primary Industries & Energy and the Fisheries Research & Development Corporation, Canberra, 1995.

Carluccio, Antonio, *A Passion for Mushrooms*, Pavilion Books, London, 1989.

—— *An Invitation to Italian Cooking*, Pavilion Books, London, 1986.

Castelvetro, Giacomo, *The Fruit, Herbs and Vegetables of Italy*, Viking, New York, 1990.

Colmagro, Suzanne, Collins, Graham and Sedgley, Margaret, 'Processing Technology of the Table Olive', University of Adelaide, in Jules Janick (ed.) *Horticultural Reviews* Vol. 25, John Wiley & Sons, 2000.

Cox, Nicola, *Game Cookery*, Victor Gollancz, London, 1989.

David, Elizabeth, *Italian Food*, Penguin, Harmondsworth, 1989.

—— *An Omelette and a Glass of Wine*, Penguin, Harmondsworth, 1986.

—— *English Bread and Yeast Cookery*, Penguin, Harmondsworth, 1979.

—— *French Provincial Cooking*, Penguin, Harmondsworth, 1970.

—— *Summer Cooking*, Penguin, Harmondsworth, 1965.

De Groot, Roy Andries, *The Auberge of the Flowering Hearth*, The Ecco Press, New Jersey, 1973.

Dolamore, Anne, *The Essential Olive Oil Companion*, Macmillan, Melbourne, 1988.

Ferguson, Jenny, *Cooking for You and Me*, Methuen Haynes, Sydney, 1987.

Field, Carol, *Celebrating Italy*, William Morrow, New York, 1990.

Fitzgibbon, Theodora, *Game Cooking*, Andre Deutsch, London, 1963.

Glowinski, Louis, *The Complete Book of Fruit Growing in Australia*, Lothian, Melbourne, 1991.

Gray, Patience, *Honey From a Weed*, Prospect Books, London, 1986.

Gray, Rose and Rogers, Ruth, *The River Cafe Cook Book*, Ebury Press, London, 1996.

Grigson, Jane and Fullick, Roy (eds), *The Enjoyment of Food: The Best of Jane Grigson*, Michael Joseph, London, 1992.

Grigson, Jane, *Jane Grigson's Fruit Book*, Michael Joseph, London, 1982.

—— *Jane Grigson's Vegetable Book*, Penguin, Harmondsworth, 1980.

—— *Good Things*, Penguin, Harmondsworth, 1973.

—— *Jane Grigson's Fish Book*, Penguin, Harmondsworth, 1973.

—— *Charcuterie and French Pork Cookery*, Penguin, Harmondsworth, 1970.

Halligan, Marion, *Eat My Words*, Angus & Robertson, Sydney, 1990.

Hazan, Marcella, *The Classic Italian Cookbook*, Macmillan, London (rev. ed.), 1987.

Hopkinson, Simon with Bareham, Lindsey, *Roast Chicken and Other Stories*, Ebury Press, London, 1994.

Huxley, Aldous, *The Olive Tree*, Ayer, USA, reprint of 1937 ed.

Isaacs, Jennifer, *Bush Food*, Weldon, Sydney, 1987.

Kamman, Madeleine, *In Madeleine's Kitchen*, Macmillan, New York, 1992.

—— *The Making of a Cook*, Atheneum, New York, 1978.

Lake, Max, *Scents and Sensuality*, Penguin, Melbourne, 1991.

Manfield, Christine, *Christine Manfield Originals*, Lantern, Melbourne, 2006.

McGee, Harold, *The Curious Cook*, Northpoint Press, San Francisco, 1990.

—— *On Food and Cooking*, Collier Books, New York, 1988.

Ministero Agricultura e Foreste. D.O.C. *Cheeses of Italy* (trans. Angela Zanotti), Milan, 1992.

Molyneux, Joyce, with Grigson, Sophie, *The Carved Angel Cookery Book*, Collins, 1990.

Newell, Patrice, *The Olive Grove*, Penguin, Melbourne, 2000.

del Nero, Constance and del Nero, Rosario, *Risotto*, Harper and Row, New York, 1989.

Olney, Richard, *Simple French Food*, Atheneum, New York, 1980.

Peck, Paula, *The Art of Fine Baking*, Simon & Schuster, New York, 1961.

Pellegrini, Angelo M., *The Food Lover's Garden*, Lyons & Burford, New York, 1970.

Pepin, Jacques, *La Technique*, Hamlyn Publishing Group, New York, 1978.

Perry, Neil, *The Food I Love*, Murdoch Books, Sydney, 2005.

Pignolet, Damien, *French*, Lantern, Melbourne, 2005.

Reichelt, Karen, with Burr, Michael, *Extra Virgin: An Australian Companion to Olives and Olive Oil*, Wakefield Press, Adelaide, 1997.

Ripe, Cherry, *Goodbye Culinary Cringe*, Allen & Unwin, Sydney, 1993.

Santich, Barbara, 'The Return of Verjuice', *Winestate*, June 1984.

Schauer, Amy, *The Schauer Australian Cookery Book* (14th ed.), W.R. Smith & Paterson, Brisbane, 1979.

Scicolone, Michele, *The Antipasto Table*, Morrow, New York, 1991.

Scott, Philippa, *Gourmet Game*, Simon & Schuster, New York, 1989.

Silverton, Nancy, *Nancy Silverton's Pastries from the La Brea Bakery*, Random House, New York, 2000.

Simeti, Mary Taylor, *Pomp and Sustenance*, Alfred A. Knopf, New York, 1989.

Stobart, Tom (ed.), *The Cook's Encyclopaedia*, Papermac, London, 1982.

Studd, Will, *Chalk and Cheese*, Purple Egg, Melbourne, 2004.

Sutherland Smith, Beverley, *A Taste for All Seasons*, Lansdowne, Sydney, 1975.

Sweeney, Susan, *The Olive Press*, The Australian Olive Association, Autumn 2006.

Symons, Michael, *One Continuous Picnic*, Duck Press, Adelaide, 1982.

Taruschio, Ann and Taruschio, Franco, *Leaves from the Walnut Tree*, Pavilion, London, 1993.

Time-Life Fruit Book, Time-Life, Amsterdam, 1983.

Wark, Alf, *Wine Cookery*, Rigby, Adelaide, 1969.

Waters, Alice, Curtan, Patricia and Labro, Martine, *Chez Panisse Pasta, Pizza and Calzone*, Random House, New York, 1984.

Waters, Alice, *Chez Panisse Café Cookbook*, Random House, New York, 1999.

—— *Chez Panisse Menu Cookbook*, Chatto & Windus, London, 1984.

Weir, Joanne, *You Say Tomato*, Broadway Books, New York, 1998.

Wells, Patricia, *At Home in Provence*, Scribner, New York, 1996.

Wells, Patricia and Robuchon, Joël, *Simply French*, William Morrow, New York, 1991.

Whiteaker, Stafford, *The Compleat Strawberry*, Century Publishing, London, 1985.

Wolfert, Paula, *The Cooking of the Eastern Mediterranean*, Harper Collins Publishers, New York, 1994.

—— *The Cooking of South-West France*, The Dial Press, New York, 1983.

—— *Mediterranean Cooking*, The Ecco Press, New York, 1977.

Zalokar, Sophie, *Picnic*, Fremantle Arts Centre Press, Perth, 2002.

LIST OF SOURCES

The author and publisher would like to thank the following people and companies for allowing us to reproduce their material in this book. In some cases we were not able to contact the copyright owners; we would appreciate hearing from any copyright holders not acknowledged here, so that we can properly acknowledge their contribution when this book is reprinted.

Extracts

Alexander, Stephanie, *Stephanie's Australia*, Allen & Unwin, Sydney, 1991; Alexander, Stephanie, *The Cook's Companion*, Lantern, Melbourne, 2004; Andrews, Colman, *Catalan Cuisine*, Headline, London, 1989; von Bremzen, Anya and Welchman, John, *Please to the Table: The Russian Cookbook*, copyright © 1990 by Anya von Bremzen and John Welchman, used by permission of Workman Publishing Co., Inc., New York, All Rights Reserved; Castelvetro, Giacomo (trans. Gillian Riley), *The Fruit, Herbs and Vegetables of Italy*, Viking, New York, 1990; Gray, Patience, *Honey From a Weed*, Prospect Books, London, 1986; Grigson, Jane, *Jane Grigson's Fruit Book*, Michael Joseph, London, 1982; Grigson, Jane, *Jane Grigson's Vegetable Book*, Penguin, Harmondsworth, 1980; Huxley, Aldous, *The Olive Tree*, Ayer, USA, reprint of 1937 edition; Lake, Max, *Scents and Sensuality*, Penguin, Melbourne, 1991; Pellegrini, Angelo M., *The Food Lover's Garden*, Lyons & Burford, New York, 1970; Pepin, Jacques, *La Technique*, Hamlyn Publishing Group, New York, 1978; Santich, Barbara, 'The Return of Verjuice', *Winestate*, June 1984; Scott, Philippa, *Gourmet Game*, Simon & Schuster, New York, 1989; Waters, Alice, *Chez Panisse Café Cookbook*, Random House, New York, 1999; Wells, Patricia and Robuchon, Joël, *Simply French*, William Morrow, New York, 1991, reprinted with permission of HarperCollins Publishers; Wolfert, Paula, *The Cooking of South-West France*, The Dial Press, New York, 1983, reprinted with permission of John Wiley & Sons, Inc.

Recipes

Black duck and orange sauce, Wild duck poached in wine sauce: Alf Wark; Cheong's figs, Cheong Liew's salt water duck accompanied by asparagus: Cheong Liew; Gooseberry pavlovas: Tina Duncan; Hare pie, Stephanie's honey and lavender ice cream, Stephanie's partridge pies: Stephanie Alexander; Janni's braised artichokes with artichoke purée: Janni Kyritsis; Kylie Kwong's Chinese-style partridge with pomegranate-caramel sauce: Kylie Kwong; Margaret's persimmon bread: Margaret Lehmann; Peter Wall's lamb, barley and cinnamon casserole, Peter Wall's raspberry vinegar: Peter Wall; Rose's pressed eggplants: Rose Fanto; Sandor Palmai's persimmon tart: Sandor Palmai; Skye Gyngell's torn bread salad with rocket, sour cherries, capers and verjuice: Skye Gyngell; Stefano's Murray cod: Stefano de Pieri; Upside-down apricot tarts: Ferguson, Jenny.

ACKNOWLEDGEMENTS

This book represents the culmination of a life's work to date, so how can I possibly conjure up all the people that have been instrumental in so many ways over the years?

Perhaps the best place to start is with my family. My husband, Colin, is my rock – a true partner in every sense of the word – and his wicked wit never fails to keep me, and the rest of the family, laughing. My daughters, Saskia and Elli, have grown into strong, independent women of real substance. Living so close, we share the cut and thrust of daily life and regular boisterous meals with their partners and our much-loved grandchildren, Zöe, Max, Lilly, Rory – and one more on the way.

Writing this book has been much more difficult than I expected. The indomitable Julie Gibbs ('Jewels' to those who love her), originally suggested an update of *Maggie's Farm* and *Maggie's Orchard*, an idea which developed over time into this tome. Believe me, it's been a long journey, but I always had faith in Julie's extraordinary ability to know just what will make a book special.

Photographer Mark Chew effortlessly captured the essence of the produce in the book – it feels so Barossan! He happily waded through all the old bits and pieces we accumulated around the house over the years to give the pictures real character and warmth. Deb Brash, Penguin's Art Director, helped on two of the photo shoots, bringing her repertoire of recordings to share with me – her rendition of 'Black Coffee' is quite something. Daniel New, the book's designer, who is originally from Gawler, raided his father's shed of 'wonderful junk' for the photography, and weaved his magic with the design. Marie Anne Pledger not only helped out on the shoots, but provided paraphernalia from her own kitchen and that of her friends for us to use.

There are so many in the team at Penguin I'd like to thank. I started the editing process with Kathleen Gandy, and I couldn't have had a more gentle soul to work with; her delight in the project gave me the courage to keep going. How frustrating it must have been for her to leave the project halfway through – albeit for a very good reason, to give birth to her second child. It's a scary thing changing editors mid-stream, and my enormous thanks go to Virginia Birch, who has seen me through thick and thin, and taken my very unstructured, undisciplined writing and brought it in check, while still allowing my voice to shine through. I'd also like to thank Nicole Brown for keeping us all on track, Anouska Jones for proofreading, and Jocelyn Hungerford and all at Penguin Surry Hills for eleventh-hour assistance.

Over the years I have had an incredible array of staff who have contributed so much to both my business and my life. First and foremost was the lovely Hilda Laurencis, who sadly died as I wrote the very last pages of this book. Right up to her death at the age of 78, Hilda was still helping Saskia around the house – so closely connected was she to our family. Everyone who knew her loved her.

From the Pheasant Farm Restaurant days, Sophie Zalokar, Steve Flamsteed, Nat Paull and Alex Herbert remain part of our extended family, and more recently Victoria Blumenstein and Gill Radford have both done much to ease my daily life. Each of them has had a hand in inspiring and creating some of the recipes in this book.

The friendly, hard-working team at the Farmshop are the public face of our business and help to keep the tradition of the farm alive. I have so much to thank them for. I am also indebted to those who work behind the scenes: in production, management, the tenacious driver of our financial ship, and our committed board members. The loyalty of all our staff, past and present, and their shared commitment to our vision, has enabled our business to grow without ever losing the essence of where we started. Our customers, from the early days of the Pheasant Farm Restaurant, to those who buy our products all over the world today, have believed in us and what we've done.

The ABC TV series *The Cook and The Chef* has given me a welcome platform to showcase seasonal produce to a wide audience. The unexpected bonus has been the sheer good fun of working with my co-presenter Simon Bryant. It was executive producer Margot Phillipson's vision that this partnership would be a successful one – a masterstroke on her part.

I would also like to thank the following people who have lent their expertise in specific areas: Louis Glowinski, for his invaluable advice on all things relating to growing fruit (how I wish I'd known of him years ago!); Geoff Linton of Yalumba, for sharing his passion and knowledge of vinegar with me over many years; Dr Rod Mailer, Principal Research Scientist at the NSW Department of Primary Industries (who I'm delighted to say works exclusively with the olive oil industry now), deserves a big vote of thanks for giving me chemistry lessons and for reviewing the text on olive oil; Brian Jeffries, Director of the Tuna Boat Owners Association of South Australia, for updating me on the current status of tuna; Dr John Conran of the School of Earth and Environmental Sciences at the University of Adelaide, for reading and checking the chapter on mushrooms; Ashleigh Nicole Lyons, a family friend who first borrowed my camera for her Year 12 project and is now a keen photographer, for taking the additional shots in 'Autumn'; and Richard Gunner of Coorong Angus Beef, for his passionate endeavours and wealth of knowledge on beef and lamb.

INDEX

Upside-down Apricot Tarts 17

LANTERN

Published by the Penguin Group
Penguin Group (Australia)
250 Camberwell Road, Camberwell, Victoria 3124, Australia
(a division of Pearson Australia Group Pty Ltd)
Penguin Group (USA) Inc.
375 Hudson Street, New York, New York 10014, USA
Penguin Group (Canada)
90 Eglinton Avenue East, Suite 700, Toronto, Canada ON M4P 2Y3
(a division of Pearson Penguin Canada Inc.)
Penguin Books Ltd
80 Strand, London WC2R 0RL England
Penguin Ireland
25 St Stephen's Green, Dublin 2, Ireland
(a division of Penguin Books Ltd)
Penguin Books India Pvt Ltd
11 Community Centre, Panchsheel Park, New Delhi – 110 017, India
Penguin Group (NZ)
67 Apollo Drive, Rosedale, North Shore 0632, New Zealand
(a division of Pearson New Zealand Ltd)
Penguin Books (South Africa) (Pty) Ltd
24 Sturdee Avenue, Rosebank, Johannesburg 2196, South Africa

Penguin Books Ltd, Registered Offices: 80 Strand, London, WC2R 0RL, England

First published by Penguin Group (Australia), 2007

3 5 7 9 10 8 6 4 2

Text copyright © Maggie Beer 2007
Photography copyright © Mark Chew 2007

Cover and text design by Daniel New © Penguin Group (Australia)
Typeset in Cochin by Post Pre-Press Group, Brisbane, Queensland
Colour reproduction by Splitting Image, Clayton, Victoria
Printed in China by 1010 Printing International Limited
Photographs on pages 32, 239, 268, 501 copyright © Photolibrary
Photographs on pages 230, 255 copyright © Ashleigh Nicole Lyons
Photograph on page 629 copyright © Belinda Hansen

National Library of Australia
Cataloguing-in-Publication data:

Beer, Maggie.
Maggie's harvest.

Bibliography.
Includes index.
ISBN 9781920989545 (hbk.).
1. Cookery, Australian. I. Chew, Mark. II. Title.
641.5

penguin.com.au